THE HYMNAL

THE HYMNAL

1940

With Supplements I and II

According to the use of
The Episcopal Church

The Church Hymnal Corporation, New York

CERTIFICATE

It was voted by both Houses of the General Convention, held in the year of our Lord one thousand nine hundred and forty:

That the Hymnal, as reported by the Joint Commission on the Revision of the Hymnal, be authorized and approved for use in this Church.

That the Commission be continued with authority to perfect the details of its work and to complete, for the benefit of the Church Pension Fund, choir and pew editions of the revised Hymnal.

That the publication of the Hymnal be committed to the Trustees of the Church Pension Fund for the benefit of that Fund.

Attest:

JOHN H. FITZGERALD
Secretary of the House of Bishops

FRANKLIN J. CLARK
Secretary of the House of Deputies

RUBRIC FROM THE BOOK OF COMMON PRAYER
HYMNS AND ANTHEMS

Hymns set forth and allowed by the authority of this Church, and Anthems in the words of Holy Scripture or of the Book of Common Prayer, may be sung before and after any Office in this Book, and also before and after Sermons.

CANON 24

It shall be the duty of every Minister to see that music is used in his congregation as an offering for the glory of God and as a help to the people in their worship in accordance with the Book of Common Prayer and as authorized by the Rubric or by the General Convention of this Church. To this end he shall be the final authority in the administration of matters pertaining to music with such assistance as he may see fit to employ from persons skilled in music. It shall be his duty to suppress all light and unseemly music and all irreverence in the rendition thereof.

COPYRIGHT, 1940, 1943, 1961
BY
THE CHURCH PENSION FUND
ISBN 0-89869-000-5 Red
002-1 Blue
001-3 Organ

PREFACE

THE HYMNS

A new hymnal was authorized by General Convention in 1937, and a Joint Commission was appointed to prepare it and report. The report of the Commission was accepted by General Convention in 1940, and the Commission was instructed to provide a music edition, perfect details, and arrange for its publication.

The Commission reports with sorrow and a deep consciousness of loss the death of the chairman, Bishop Henry Judah Mikell of Atlanta, and of the vice-chairman, Dean Philemon F. Sturges of St. Paul's Cathedral, Boston. Both rendered invaluable services in the preparation of the Hymnal, and also endeared themselves to their colleagues by their wisdom, humor, and personal charm.

The Commission began its work upon the principle "Prove all things; hold fast that which is good." Every hymn in the Hymnals of 1892 and of 1916 was read with care and criticized from the viewpoints of reality, religious feeling, literary worth, and usefulness, and those which met these tests were retained. Translations from the Greek, Latin, and German were assigned for study by subcommittees and by them compared with the originals, with a view to obtaining accuracy and idiomatic renderings.

During the past twenty-five years, which is the average lifetime of a hymnal, other Christian communions in the revision of their hymnals have included some new hymns of distinguished excellence. These and others were studied in subcommittees, with the result that our Hymnal has been enriched by the best hymns now in use in the English-speaking world and by a number of new translations of hymns in foreign languages, including some of the great German chorales. Especial efforts were made to secure new hymns suitable for children, and hymns which voice the social aspirations of our day. Some of the latter group express the hope of a new world founded upon justice and expressive of international brotherhood. The ecumenical movement, with its hope of Christian unity, has also received fitting recognition in the Hymnal.

To make room for these new hymns, certain lesser used and less useful hymns have been omitted, but the great body of hymns remains. It would be possible for a parish to continue to use almost the same hymns as in the past. It is hoped, however, that every parish will gradually add new hymns to enrich its worship and to deepen and ennoble its sympathies. It may be safely predicted that if this is done many of the new hymns will speedily become known and loved throughout the Church.

Some hymns can be properly used only at certain seasons of the Christian year or on specific occasions. Only such hymns are printed under special headings; but at the end of each section are listed additional hymns, often of equal appropriateness but of less restricted usefulness. It is frequently desirable to shorten a hymn. The Commission has indicated, by use of the asterisk, those stanzas in certain hymns which may properly be omitted without violating the sense. It has seemed proper to provide for the singing of the Amen at the conclusion of those hymns only which end with the note of praise or prayer.

Every member of the Commission has assumed his share of responsibility in the work of revision. Each has made his contribution. The meetings of the Commission have addressed themselves with a singleness of purpose to the provision of a hymnal adapted to the needs of a truly comprehensive Church. These needs are so diversified that some hymns will be less widely used than others, yet the use of the one book will manifest the essential unity of spirit within the Church. Like our use of the Book of Common Prayer the use of the one Hymnal is an expression of our sense of fellowship with one another.

The Commission acknowledges gratefully the help it has received in its work from advisory committees set up in the different dioceses, and from the generous co-operation it has received from publishers and holders of copyrights. The *Oxford University Press* in particular has rendered assistance of quite incalculable importance.

We send this book out with the prayer that God may bless it to his service, and that it may truly serve the needs of our people and help them to voice ever more fittingly their praise and adoration of him.

The Music of the Hymns

The music of the hymns has been prepared in response to a mandate of the Church for a book suitable for congregational singing. Thousands of private letters, many communications in the Church press, and resolutions both by Diocesan Music Commissions and by the Joint Commission on Church Music, made this clearly evident.

To provide such a Hymnal, the following steps have been taken:

All tunes except a few of very wide range have been placed at such a pitch as will enable both men and women to sing them without strain from congregational editions printed with the melody only. Two such editions have been prepared, matching the two sizes of the Book of Common Prayer.

Familiar and generally accepted tunes have been retained throughout, but have been printed with a more accurate, legible, and convenient notation than before. Many well-loved tunes have been restored from earlier versions of the Hymnal.

When two or even three tunes have been associated with a hymn in different parts of the country, they have been kept. When a tune new to our books has been judged preferable to the familiar one, both have been printed in most cases.

A considerable number of established hymn melodies has been added, because their use is already widespread, as evidenced in the recently revised hymnals of other Christian bodies. In some cases, great poems new to our Hymnal have brought with them their own great tunes. In others, fine hymns of unusual rhythmical patterns have caused a rewarding search for parallel settings of equal beauty. We have included many sacred folk melodies of American, English, Irish, Scandinavian, Dutch, German, and French origin. The survival of this music is evidence of its permanent popularity. It has an increasing place in the praise of God. The contemporary hymn composers of England are well represented by tunes, some of which are already widely known and loved in our Church.

We have also included forty-eight new tunes by American composers from every part of the country and from Canada. They were chosen from over four thousand manuscripts sent in anonymously to the Commission, which adjudged them with no knowledge of the composers' identity. These, with the large body of earlier American tunes either kept or added, make the Hymnal as representative of a noble and characteristic American tradition as it is of the great traditions of England and of continental Europe.

> In Christ there is no East or West,
> In him no South or North,
> But one great fellowship of love
> Throughout the whole wide earth.

The rich heritage of Christian hymnody in this book is of a like catholicity.

The printing of the hymns has the following distinctive features:

1 The pages are identified only by hymn numbers, page numbers being omitted. First, second, or third tunes are clearly marked after tune numbers.

2 In the choir edition two or more stanzas are printed between the staves of the music. Irregular hymns are so printed throughout. All stanzas are printed in larger and clearer type than in earlier editions of the Hymnal.

3 Distinctive notation has been used for different periods and styles: quarter notes for the main body of the music; half notes for the older chorales and psalm tunes, and for some recent melodies of a grave character; eighth notes for all plainsong.

4 Directions as to pace and style are given immediately under the names of the tunes.

5 Commas are used to indicate slight normal pauses for breath.

6 In the choir edition, all elided syllables are clearly marked.

7 Instead of the indeterminate and unsatisfactory hold sign, final notes of phrases are of the proper length, as they should actually be sung.

8 As in many recent hymnals, time signatures are wholly omitted. In tunes of free rhythm, now so common, they are confusing; and in perfectly regular measures, obviously needless.

9 The system of barring is that devised by the late Horatio Parker. A double bar almost invariably denotes the close of a musical phrase, rather than the end of a line of verse.

PREFACE

Both the choice and the presentation of the music of the hymns have been planned to bring a greater sense of reality into our praise. We must make the words the utterance of our own souls; the music the expression of our own personal worship, our own joy or sorrow or brave determination. Only so can we rightly use this richly varied treasure bequeathed us from every age of the Church.

THE SERVICE MUSIC

The Service music has been prepared with the co-operation of the Joint Commission on Church Music, which also acted in an advisory capacity in the selection of the hymn tunes.

The Choral Responses at Morning and Evening Prayer, both ferial and festal, have been provided.

The Invitatories have been printed for convenience on the page opposite *Venite, exultemus Domino.* As they give the special liturgical tone to the Psalms on the days for which they are appointed, they should always be used on those days.

A larger number of Anglican chants, both single and double, has been included, and a much clearer arrangement of Plainsong chants. The three Gospel Canticles are noted with accompaniments written out in full.

Five unison chants have been provided for *Te Deum laudamus*, in the hope that it may be generally restored to frequent use and to congregational singing.

Four complete Communion Services have been printed. Two of them are simple unison settings. The other two are richer festival settings, already widely in use in this Church and well suited to small choirs. The customary separate numbers for Holy Communion follow.

A list of hymns which may also be sung as choir anthems has been added to the indexes. Practically all of them have been so used by well-known choirs and choruses. With this in mind, it will be seen that the revised Hymnal fully equips any Church for every essential need of its musical worship.

Benjamin M. Washburn	Arthur W. Farlander	Holly W. Wells
†Henry J. Mikell	Charles L. Gomph	Ray F. Brown
James Craik Morris	Frederick C. Grant	Roland Diggle
†Herman Page	John Henry Hopkins	†H. R. Fairclough
Robert N. Spencer	Harvey B. Marks	Harold W. Gilbert
*Robert E. L. Strider	John W. Norris	Bradford B. Locke
Vedder Van Dyck	Howard C. Robbins	Joseph T. Ryerson
Frank Damrosch, Jr.	†Philemon F. Sturges	Leo Sowerby
Winfred Douglas	F. Bland Tucker	David McK. Williams

† Deceased   * Resigned

CONTENTS

THE HYMNS

SERVICE MUSIC

INDEXES

CONTENTS

THE HYMNS

SERVICE MUSIC

INDEXES

THE HYMNAL

THE CHRISTIAN YEAR

*At the end of each section are listed additional hymns
also appropriate for the season or the occasion.*

1

Advent

87. 87

STUTTGART

Majestically

Adapted from a melody by
CHRISTIAN FRIEDRICH WITT, Gotha, 1715

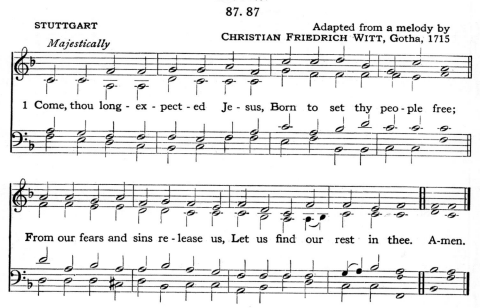

1 Come, thou long - ex - pect - ed Je - sus, Born to set thy peo - ple free;

From our fears and sins re - lease us, Let us find our rest in thee. A-men.

2 Israel's strength and consolation,
 Hope of all the earth thou art;
Dear desire of every nation,
 Joy of every longing heart.

3 Born thy people to deliver,
 Born a child, and yet a king,
Born to reign in us for ever,
 Now thy gracious kingdom bring.

4 By thine own eternal Spirit
 Rule in all our hearts alone:
By thine all-sufficient merit
 Raise us to thy glorious throne. Amen.

CHARLES WESLEY, 1744

2

Advent

88. 88. 88

VENI EMMANUEL

Melody adapted from plainsong, Mode I,
by THOMAS HELMORE, 1854

In unison, boldly

1 O come, O come, Em - man - u - el, And ran - som cap - tive
*2 O come, thou Wis - dom from on high, Who ord-'rest all things
3 O come, O come, thou Lord of might, Who to thy tribes on

Is - ra - el, That mourns in lone - ly ex - ile here
migh - ti - ly; To us the path of knowl-edge show,
Si - nai's height In an - cient times didst give the law,

Refrain

Un - til the Son of God ap - pear. Re - joice! Re - joice!
And teach us in her ways to go.
In cloud, and ma - jes - ty, and awe.

Advent

Em - man - u - el Shall come to thee, O Is - ra - el!

4 O come, thou Rod of Jesse's stem,
From every foe deliver them
That trust thy mighty power to save,
And give them vict'ry o'er the grave.
Rejoice! Rejoice! Emmanuel
Shall come to thee, O Israel!

5 O come, thou Key of David, come,
And open wide our heav'nly home;
Make safe the way that leads on high,
And close the path to misery.
Rejoice! Rejoice! Emmanuel
Shall come to thee, O Israel!

6 O come, thou Day-spring from on high,
And cheer us by thy drawing nigh;
Disperse the gloomy clouds of night,
And death's dark shadow put to flight.
Rejoice! Rejoice! Emmanuel
Shall come to thee, O Israel!

*7 O come, Desire of nations, bind
In one the hearts of all mankind;
Bid thou our sad divisions cease,
And be thyself our King of Peace.
Rejoice! Rejoice! Emmanuel
Shall come to thee, O Israel! Amen.

A-men.

Hymnal Version, based on Latin, c. 9th cent.; St. 1, 3, 4, 5, 6, pub. Cologne, 1710

3

Advent

898. 898. 664. 448

SLEEPERS, WAKE

Melody, PHILIP NICOLAI, 1599
arr. and harmonized J. S. BACH, 1731

Broad and solemn; may be sung in unison

1 Wake, a-wake, for night is fly-ing: The watch-men on the
2 Si-on hears the watch-men sing-ing, Her heart with deep de-

heights are cry-ing, A-wake, Je-ru-sa-lem, a-rise!
light is spring-ing, She wakes, she ris-es from her gloom:

Mid-night's sol-emn hour is toll-ing, His char-iot wheels are
Forth her Bride-groom comes, all glo-rious, In grace ar-rayed, by

near-er roll-ing, He comes; pre-pare, ye vir-gins wise.
truth vic-to-rious; Her star is ris'n, her light is come!

Advent

Rise up, with will - ing feet Go forth, the Bride - groom meet:
All hail, In - car - nate Lord, Our crown, and our re - ward!

Al - le - lu - ia! Bear through the night Your well-trimmed light,
Al - le - lu - ia! We haste a - long, In pomp of song,

Speed forth to join the mar - riage rite.
And glad - some join the mar - riage throng. A - men.

3 Lamb of God, the heav'ns adore thee,
And men and angels sing before thee,
   With harp and cymbal's clearest tone.
By the pearly gates in wonder
We stand, and swell the voice of thunder
   That echoes round thy dazzling throne.
No vision ever brought,
No ear hath ever caught
   Such rejoicing:
We raise the song, We swell the throng,
To praise thee ages all along.   Amen.

PHILIP NICOLAI, 1597; *Tr.* CATHERINE WINKWORTH, 1858, *alt.*

4

Advent

76. 76. D.

GREENLAND
Joyously

JOHANN MICHAEL HAYDN, 1819

1 Re - joice, re - joice, be - liev - ers! And let your lights ap - pear;
2 See that your lamps are burn - ing; Re - plen - ish them with oil;

The eve - ning is ad - vanc - ing, And dark - er night is near.
Look now for your sal - va - tion, The end of sin and toil.

The Bride-groom is a - ris - ing, And soon he will draw nigh;
The watch - ers on the moun - tain Pro - claim the Bride-groom near;

Up, watch in ex - pec - ta - tion! At mid-night comes the cry.
Go meet him as he com - eth, With al - le - lu - ias clear. A-men.

3 O wise and holy virgins,
　Now raise your voices higher,
Until in songs of triumph
　Ye meet the angel choir.
The marriage-feast is waiting,
　The gates wide open stand;
Rise up, ye heirs of glory!
　The Bridegroom is at hand.

4 Our hope and expectation,
　O Jesus, now appear;
Arise, thou Sun so longed for,
　O'er this benighted sphere!
With hearts and hands uplifted,
　We plead, O Lord, to see
The day of earth's redemption,
　And ever be with thee! Amen.

LAURENTIUS LAURENTI, 1700; *Tr.* SARAH B. FINDLATER, 1854, *alt.*

Advent

87. 87. 87

ST. THOMAS
Majestically

J. F. WADE'S *Cantus Diversi*, 1751

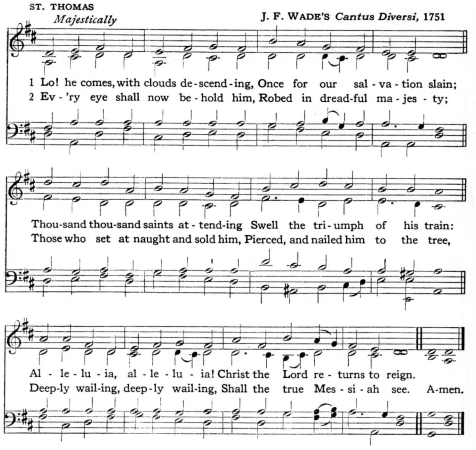

1 Lo! he comes, with clouds de-scend-ing, Once for our sal-va-tion slain;
2 Ev-'ry eye shall now be-hold him, Robed in dread-ful ma-jes-ty;

Thou-sand thou-sand saints at-tend-ing Swell the tri-umph of his train:
Those who set at naught and sold him, Pierced, and nailed him to the tree,

Al-le-lu-ia, al-le-lu-ia! Christ the Lord re-turns to reign.
Deep-ly wail-ing, deep-ly wail-ing, Shall the true Mes-si-ah see. A-men.

3 Those dear tokens of his passion
Still his dazzling body bears,
Cause of endless exultation
To his ransomed worshippers:
‖ With what rapture ‖
Gaze we on those glorious scars!

4 Yea, Amen! let all adore thee,
High on thine eternal throne;
Saviour, take the power and glory;
Claim the kingdom for thine own:
‖ Alleluia! ‖
Thou shalt reign, and thou alone. Amen.

CHARLES WESLEY, 1758, *alt.*

5 *Second Tune*   𝕬𝖉𝖛𝖊𝖓𝖙

87. 87. 12 7

HELMSLEY
Unison, in moderate time   *Select Hymns with Tunes Annext,* 1765

1 Lo!   he   comes,   with   clouds   de - scend - ing,
2 Ev - 'ry   eye   shall   now   be - hold   him,
3 Those   dear   to - kens   of   his   pas - sion
4 Yea,   A - men!   let   all   a - dore   thee,

Once   for   our   sal - va - tion   slain;
Robed   in   dread - ful   ma - jes - ty;
Still   his   dazz - ling   bo - dy   bears,
High   on   thine   e - ter - nal   throne;

Thou - sand   thou - sand   saints   at - tend - ing
Those   who   set   at   naught   and   sold   him,
Cause   of   end - less   ex - ul - ta - tion
Sa - viour,   take   the   power   and   glo - ry;

Advent

Swell the tri - umph of his train:
Pierced, and nailed him to the tree,
To his ran - somed wor - ship - pers:
Claim the king - dom for thine own:

Al - le - lu - ia, al - le - lu - ia, al - le -
Deep - ly wail - ing, deep - ly wail - ing, deep - ly
With what rap - ture, with what rap - ture, with what
Al - le - lu - ia, al - le - lu - ia, al - le -

lu - ia! Christ the Lord re - turns to reign.
wail - ing, Shall the true Mes - si - ah see.
rap - ture Gaze we on those glo - rious scars!
lu - ia! Thou shalt reign, and thou a - lone. A-men.

CHARLES WESLEY, 1758, *alt.*

6 *First Tune*

Advent

L. M.

CONDITOR ALME
Unison, not slow

Sarum Plainsong, Mode IV

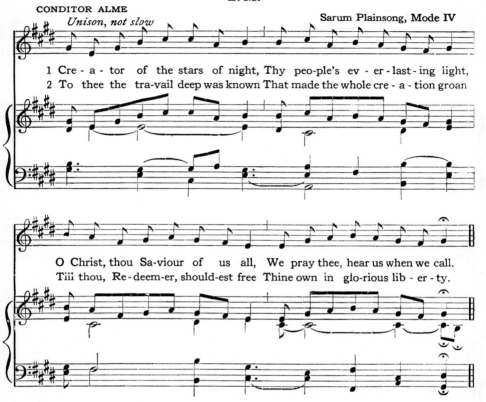

1 Cre - a - tor of the stars of night, Thy peo-ple's ev - er - last - ing light,
2 To thee the tra-vail deep was known That made the whole cre - a - tion groan

O Christ, thou Sa-viour of us all, We pray thee, hear us when we call.
Till thou, Re - deem-er, should-est free Thine own in glo-rious lib - er - ty.

3 When the old world drew on toward night,
Thou camest, not in splendor bright
As monarch, but the humble child
Of Mary, blameless mother mild.

4 At thy great name of Jesus, now
All knees must bend, all hearts must bow:
And things celestial thee shall own,
And things terrestrial, Lord alone.

5 Come in thy holy might, we pray;
Redeem us for eternal day
From every power of darkness, when
Thou judgest all the sons of men.

A - men.

6 To God the Father, God the Son,
And God the Spirit, Three in One,
Laud, honor, might, and glory be
From age to age eternally. Amen.

Latin, 9th cent.; Hymnal Version, 1940, *after* J. M. NEALE

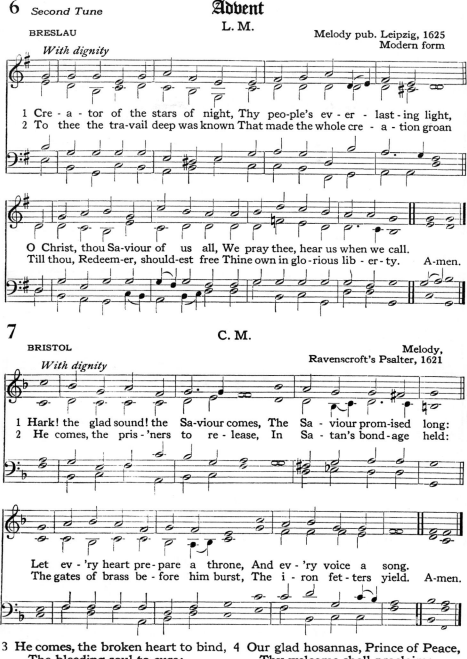

6 *Second Tune*

Advent

L. M.

BRESLAU

With dignity

Melody pub. Leipzig, 1625
Modern form

1 Cre - a - tor of the stars of night, Thy peo-ple's ev - er - last-ing light,
2 To thee the tra-vail deep was known That made the whole cre - a - tion groan

O Christ, thou Sa-viour of us all, We pray thee, hear us when we call.
Till thou, Redeem-er, should-est free Thine own in glo-rious lib - er - ty. A-men.

7

C. M.

BRISTOL

With dignity

Melody,
Ravenscroft's Psalter, 1621

1 Hark! the glad sound! the Sa-viour comes, The Sa - viour prom-ised long:
2 He comes, the pris-'ners to re - lease, In Sa - tan's bond-age held:

Let ev - 'ry heart pre - pare a throne, And ev - 'ry voice a song.
The gates of brass be - fore him burst, The i - ron fet - ters yield. A-men.

3 He comes, the broken heart to bind,
The bleeding soul to cure:
And with the treasures of his grace
To enrich the humble poor.

4 Our glad hosannas, Prince of Peace,
Thy welcome shall proclaim;
And heav'n's eternal arches ring
With thy belovèd Name. Amen.

PHILIP DODDRIDGE, 1735, *alt.*

Advent
L. M.

VERBUM SUPERNUM

Sarum Plainsong
Mode II tr.

Quick, flowing

1 O Word, that go-est forth on high From God's own depths e - ter-nal-ly,
2 Pour light up-on us from a - bove, And fire our hearts with ar-dent love,

And in these lat - ter days wast born For suc - cor to a world for-lorn;
That, as we hear thy truth to - day, All wrong de-sires may burn a - way;

3 And when, as judge, thou drawest nigh
The secrets of our hearts to try,
To recompense each hidden sin
And bid the saints their reign begin;

4 O let us not, weak sinful men,
Be driven from thy presence then,
But with thy saints for ever stand
In perfect love at thy right hand.

5 To God the Father, God the Son,
And God the Spirit, ever one,
Praise, honor, might, and glory be
From age to age eternally. Amen.

A - men.

Hymnal Version, Tr. from Latin, c. 7th cent.

8 *Second Tune*

Advent

REX GLORIOSE

L. M.

Melody
Andernach Gesangbuch, 1608

In moderate time

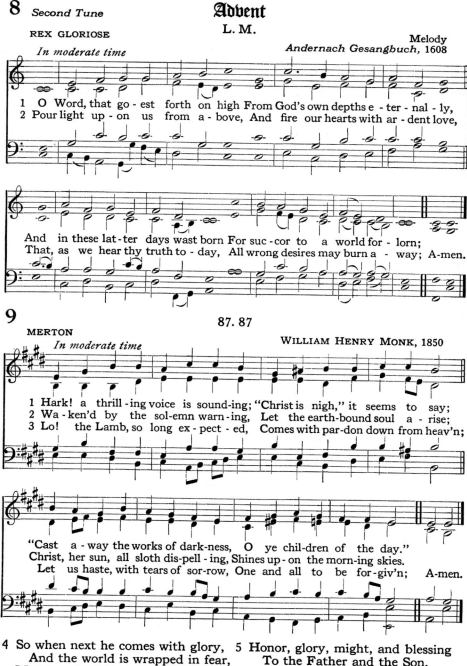

1 O Word, that go-est forth on high From God's own depths e-ter-nal-ly,
2 Pour light up-on us from a-bove, And fire our hearts with ar-dent love,

And in these lat-ter days wast born For suc-cor to a world for-lorn;
That, as we hear thy truth to-day, All wrong desires may burn a-way; A-men.

9

87. 87

MERTON

WILLIAM HENRY MONK, 1850

In moderate time

1 Hark! a thrill-ing voice is sound-ing; "Christ is nigh," it seems to say;
2 Wa-ken'd by the sol-emn warn-ing, Let the earth-bound soul a-rise;
3 Lo! the Lamb, so long ex-pect-ed, Comes with par-don down from heav'n;

"Cast a-way the works of dark-ness, O ye chil-dren of the day."
Christ, her sun, all sloth dis-pell-ing, Shines up-on the morn-ing skies.
Let us haste, with tears of sor-row, One and all to be for-giv'n; A-men.

4 So when next he comes with glory,
  And the world is wrapped in fear,
May he with his mercy shield us,
  And with words of love draw near.

5 Honor, glory, might, and blessing
   To the Father and the Son,
With the everlasting Spirit
   While unending ages run. Amen.

Latin, c. 6th cent.; Tr. EDWARD CASWALL, 1849, *alt.*

L. M.

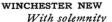

WINCHESTER NEW
With solemnity

Adapted from
Musikalisches Handbuch, Hamburg, 1690

1 On Jor-dan's bank the Bap-tist's cry An-noun-ces that the Lord is nigh;

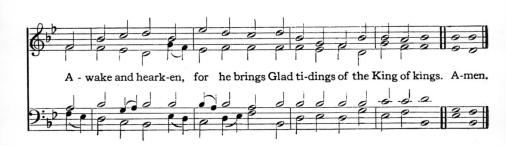

A - wake and heark-en, for he brings Glad ti-dings of the King of kings. A-men.

2 Then cleansed be every breast from sin;
Make straight the way of God within,
And let each heart prepare a home
Where such a mighty guest may come.

3 For thou art our salvation, Lord,
Our refuge, and our great reward;
Without thy grace we waste away
Like flowers that wither and decay.

4 To heal the sick stretch out thine hand,
And bid the fallen sinner stand;
Shine forth, and let thy light restore
Earth's own true loveliness once more.

5 All praise, eternal Son, to thee,
Whose advent doth thy people free;
Whom with the Father we adore
And Holy Ghost for evermore. Amen.

CHARLES COFFIN, 1736; *Tr.* JOHN CHANDLER, 1837, *alt.*

11   𝕬𝖉𝖛𝖊𝖓𝖙

C. M.

ST. STEPHEN   WILLIAM JONES, 1789

In moderate time

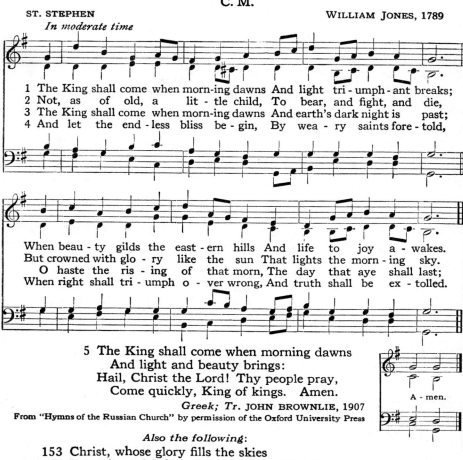

1 The King shall come when morn-ing dawns And light tri - umph - ant breaks;
2 Not, as of old, a lit - tle child, To bear, and fight, and die,
3 The King shall come when morn-ing dawns And earth's dark night is past;
4 And let the end - less bliss be - gin, By wea - ry saints fore - told,

When beau - ty gilds the east - ern hills And life to joy a - wakes.
But crowned with glo - ry like the sun That lights the morn - ing sky.
O haste the ris - ing of that morn, The day that aye shall last;
When right shall tri - umph o - ver wrong, And truth shall be ex - tolled.

5 The King shall come when morning dawns
   And light and beauty brings:
   Hail, Christ the Lord! Thy people pray,
   Come quickly, King of kings. Amen.

A - men.

Greek; Tr. JOHN BROWNLIE, 1907

From "Hymns of the Russian Church" by permission of the Oxford University Press

Also the following:

153 Christ, whose glory fills the skies
468 Day of wrath! O day of mourning, Part I
573 Go, labor on! spend and be spent
316 Hark! the voice eternal
473 High o'er the lonely hills
318 Hosanna to the living Lord (*For the First Sunday in Advent*)
484 Lift up your heads, ye mighty gates (*First Sunday*)
522 Lord Christ, when first thou cam'st to men
525 O Day of God, draw nigh
541 O North, with all thy vales of green
442 O very God of very God
312 The Lord will come and not be slow
595 The world is very evil
544 Thy kingdom come, O God
391 Thy kingdom come! on bended knee
440 Watchman, tell us of the night

Hymns 133, 134, 253, 398-403 *inclusive* (*For the Second Sunday, Holy Scriptures*)

12 Christmas

Irregular, with Refrain

ADESTE FIDELES

J. F. WADE'S
Cantus Diversi, 1751

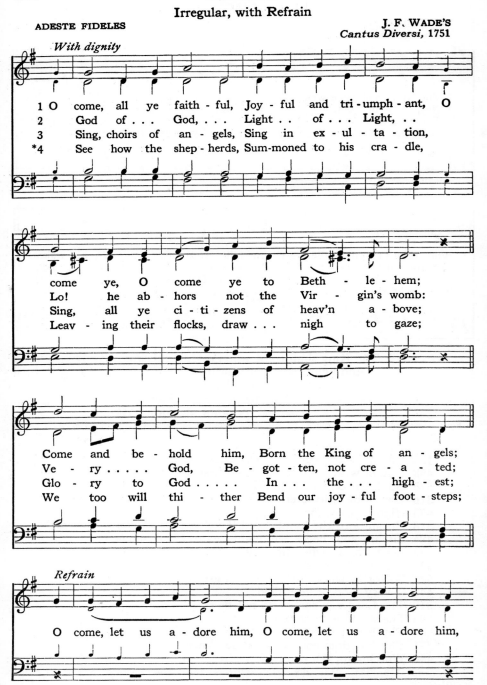

With dignity

1 O come, all ye faith - ful, Joy - ful and tri - umph - ant, O
2 God of . . . God, . . . Light . . of . . . Light, . .
3 Sing, choirs of an - gels, Sing in ex - ul - ta - tion,
*4 See how the shep - herds, Sum-moned to his cra - dle,

come ye, O come ye to Beth - le - hem;
Lo! he ab - hors not the Vir - gin's womb:
Sing, all ye ci - ti - zens of heav'n a - bove;
Leav - ing their flocks, draw . . . nigh to gaze;

Come and be - hold him, Born the King of an - gels;
Ve - ry . . . . . God, Be - got - ten, not cre - a - ted;
Glo - ry to God . . . . . In . . . the . . . high - est;
We too will thi - ther Bend our joy - ful foot - steps;

Refrain

O come, let us a - dore him, O come, let us a - dore him,

Christmas

O come, let us a-dore him, Christ the Lord. A-men.

*5 Child, for us sinners
   Poor and in the manger,
We would embrace thee, with love and awe;
   Who would not love thee,
   Loving us so dearly?
              Refrain

6 Yea, Lord, we greet thee,
   Born this happy morning;
Jesus, to thee be glory giv'n;
   Word of the Father,
   Now in flesh appearing;
              Refrain

Latin, 18th cent.; Tr. FREDERICK OAKELEY *and others*

13 *First Tune*   C. M.

WINCHESTER OLD

Melody from T. EST'S
Whole Book of Psalmes, 1592

In moderate time

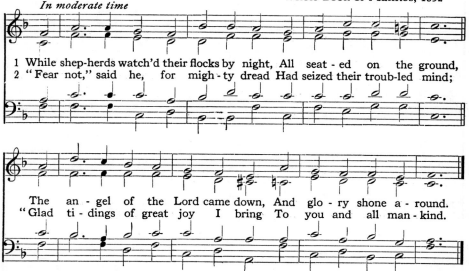

1 While shep-herds watch'd their flocks by night, All seat-ed on the ground,
2 "Fear not," said he, for migh-ty dread Had seized their troub-led mind;

The an-gel of the Lord came down, And glo-ry shone a-round.
"Glad ti-dings of great joy I bring To you and all man-kind.

3 "To you, in David's town, this day
   Is born of David's line
The Saviour, who is Christ the Lord;
   And this shall be the sign:

4 "The heav'nly Babe you there shall find
   To human view displayed,
All meanly wrapped in swathing bands,
   And in a manger laid."

5 Thus spake the seraph, and forthwith
   Appeared a shining throng
Of angels praising God, who thus
   Addressed their joyful song:

6 "All glory be to God on high
   And on the earth be peace;
Good will henceforth from heav'n to men
   Begin and never cease."

NAHUM TATE, 1700

13 *Second Tune* 𝕮𝖍𝖗𝖎𝖘𝖙𝖒𝖆𝖘
C. M. D.

CAROL
Brightly   RICHARD STORRS WILLIS, 1850

1 While shep-herds watch'd their flocks by night, All seat-ed on the ground,
2 "To you, in Da-vid's town, this day Is born of Da-vid's line
3 Thus spake the ser-aph, and forth-with Ap-peared a shin-ing throng

The an-gel of the Lord came down, And glo-ry shone a-round.
The Sa-viour, who is Christ the Lord; And this shall be the sign:
Of an-gels prais-ing God, who thus Ad-dressed their joy-ful song:

"Fear not," said he, for migh-ty dread Had seized their troub-led mind;
"The heav'n-ly Babe you there shall find To hu-man view dis-played,
"All glo-ry be to God on high And on the earth be peace;

"Glad ti-dings of great joy I bring To you and all man-kind.
All mean-ly wrapped in swath-ing bands, And in a man-ger laid."
Good will hence-forth from heav'n to men Be-gin and nev-er cease."

NAHUM TATE, 1700

Christmas

O come, let us a - dore him, Christ the Lord. A-men.

*5 Child, for us sinners
　Poor and in the manger,
We would embrace thee, with love and awe;
　Who would not love thee,
　Loving us so dearly?
　　　　　　Refrain

6 Yea, Lord, we greet thee,
　Born this happy morning;
Jesus, to thee be glory giv'n;
　Word of the Father,
　Now in flesh appearing;
　　　　　　Refrain

Latin, 18th cent.; Tr. FREDERICK OAKELEY and others

13 *First Tune*　　　　　C. M.

WINCHESTER OLD

Melody from T. EST'S
Whole Book of Psalmes, 1592

In moderate time

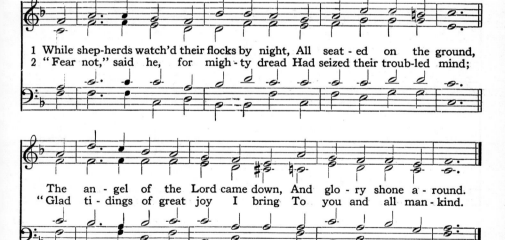

1 While shep-herds watch'd their flocks by night, All seat - ed on the ground,
2 "Fear not," said he, for migh - ty dread Had seized their troub-led mind;

The an - gel of the Lord came down, And glo - ry shone a - round.
"Glad ti - dings of great joy I bring To you and all man - kind.

3 "To you, in David's town, this day
　Is born of David's line
The Saviour, who is Christ the Lord;
　And this shall be the sign:

4 "The heav'nly Babe you there shall find
　To human view displayed,
All meanly wrapped in swathing bands,
　And in a manger laid."

5 Thus spake the seraph, and forthwith
　Appeared a shining throng
Of angels praising God, who thus
　Addressed their joyful song:

6 "All glory be to God on high
　And on the earth be peace;
Good will henceforth from heav'n to men
　Begin and never cease."

NAHUM TATE, 1700

13 *Second Tune*   **Christmas**
C. M. D.

CAROL
Brightly   RICHARD STORRS WILLIS, 1850

1 While shep-herds watch'd their flocks by night, All seat - ed on the ground,
2 "To you, in Da - vid's town, this day Is born of Da - vid's line
3 Thus spake the ser - aph, and forth-with Ap - peared a shin-ing throng

The an - gel of the Lord came down, And glo - ry shone a - round.
The Sa - viour, who is Christ the Lord; And this shall be the sign:
Of an - gels prais-ing God, who thus Ad-dressed their joy - ful song:

"Fear not," said he, for migh - ty dread Had seized their troub-led mind;
"The heav'n-ly Babe you there shall find To hu - man view dis - played,
"All glo - ry be to God on high And on the earth be peace;

"Glad ti - dings of great joy I bring To you and all man - kind.
All mean - ly wrapped in swath-ing bands, And in a man - ger laid."
Good will hence-forth from heav'n to men Be - gin and nev - er cease."

NAHUM TATE, 1700

14

Christmas
67. 67. 66. 66

DARMSTADT

AHASUERUS FRITSCH, 1679
arr. and har. by J. S. BACH

Slow

1 Now yield we thanks and praise To Christ en-throned in glo - ry,
2 What trib - ute shall we pay To him who came in weak - ness,

And on this day of days Tell out re - demp-tion's sto - ry,
And in a man - ger lay To teach his peo - ple meek - ness?

Who tru - ly have be - lieved That on this bless - ed morn,
Let ev - 'ry house be bright; Let prais' - es nev - er cease:

In ho - li - ness con - ceived, The Son of God was born.
With mer - cies in - fi - nite Our Christ hath brought us peace.

HOWARD CHANDLER ROBBINS, 1929

15   Christmas
11 11. 12 11, with Refrain

AVISON

Adapted from a melody by
CHARLES AVISON, c. 1710–1770

Gaily. *Refrain*

Shout the glad ti - dings, ex - ult - ing - ly sing, ... Je -

ru - sa - lem tri - umphs, Mes - si - ah is King!

Stanzas commence here

1 Si - on, the mar - vel - ous sto - ry be tell - ing, The Son of the

High - est, how low - ly his birth! The bright-est arch - an - gel in

Christmas

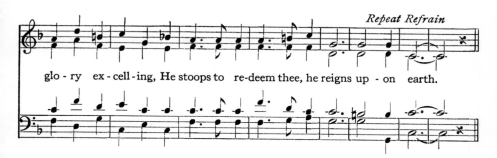

glo - ry ex - cell - ing, He stoops to re-deem thee, he reigns up - on earth.

2 Tell how he cometh; from nation to nation
   The heart-cheering news let the earth echo round:
   How free to the faithful he offers salvation,
   His people with joy everlasting are crowned.
                                      Refrain

3 Mortals, your homage be gratefully bringing,
   And sweet let the gladsome hosanna arise:
   Ye angels, the full alleluia be singing;
   One chorus resound through the earth and the skies.

Final Refrain

Shout the glad ti - dings, ex - ult - ing - ly sing, ... Je - ru - sa - lem

tri-umphs, Mes - si - ah is King, Mes - si - ah is King, Mes - si - ah is King!

WILLIAM AUGUSTUS MUHLENBERG, 1826

16

Christmas

10 10. 10 10. 10 10

YORKSHIRE

JOHN WAINWRIGHT, 1750

Joyously

1 Chris - tians, a - wake, sa - lute the hap - py morn, Where - on the
2 Then to the watch - ful shep - herds it was told, Who heard the an -

Sa - viour of the world was born; Rise to a - dore the
gel - ic her - ald's voice: "Be - hold, I bring good ti - dings

mys - ter - y of love, Which hosts of an - gels chant - ed
of a Sa - viour's birth To you and all the na - tions

from a - bove; With them the joy - ful ti - dings first be -
on the earth: This day hath God ful - filled his prom - ised

Christmas

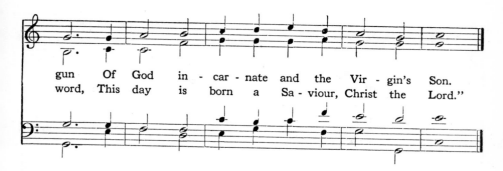

gun | Of | God | in - car - nate | and | the | Vir - gin's | Son.
word, | This | day | is | born | a | Sa - viour, | Christ | the | Lord."

* 3 He spake, and straightway the celestial choir
    In hymns of joy, unknown before, conspire;
    The praises of redeeming love they sang,
    And heav'n's whole orb with alleluias rang;
    God's highest glory was their anthem still,
    Peace on the earth, and unto men good will.

* 4 To Bethl'hem straight the happy shepherds ran,
    To see the wonder God had wrought for man;
    And found, with Joseph and the blessèd maid,
    Her Son, the Saviour, in a manger laid;
    Amazed, the wondrous story they proclaim,
    The earliest heralds of the Saviour's name.

  5 Let us, like these good shepherds, then employ
    Our grateful voices to proclaim the joy;
    Trace we the Babe, who hath retrieved our loss,
    From his poor manger to his bitter cross;
    Treading his steps, assisted by his grace,
    Till man's first heav'nly state again takes place.

  6 Then may we hope, the angelic thrones among,
    To sing, redeemed, a glad triumphal song;
    He that was born upon this joyful day
    Around us all his glory shall display;
    Saved by his love, incessant we shall sing
    Eternal praise to heav'n's Almighty King.

JOHN BYROM, 1749, alt.

17

76. 76. 676

ROSA MYSTICA

Traditional Melody, har. by
MICHAEL PRAETORIUS, 1609, *alt.*

Gently, but with movement

1 I know a rose-tree spring-ing Forth from an an-cient root,
2 This rose-tree, blos-som-la-den, Where-of I - sa-iah spake,
3 O Flower, whose fra-grance ten-der With sweet-ness fills the air,

As men of old were sing-ing. From Jes-se came the shoot
Is Ma-ry, spot-less maid-en, Who moth-ered, for our sake,
Dis-pel in glo-rious splen-dor The dark-ness ev-'ry-where;

That bore a blos-som bright A-mid the cold of
The lit-tle child, new-born By God's e-ter-nal
True man, yet ve-ry God, From sin and death now

win-ter, When half-spent was the night.
coun-sel On that first Christ-mas morn.
save us, And share our ev-'ry load. A-men.

Speier Gebetbuch, 1599; *Hymnal Version,* 1939

Christmas

76. 76. 676

ROSA MYSTICA

Unison, with movement

Traditional Melody, har. by
MICHAEL PRAETORIUS, 1609, *alt.*

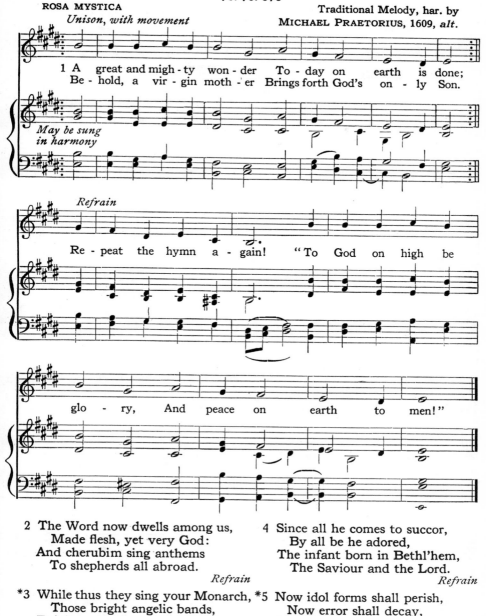

1 A great and migh-ty won-der To - day on earth is done;
Be - hold, a vir-gin moth-er Brings forth God's on - ly Son.

*May be sung
in harmony*

Refrain

Re - peat the hymn a - gain! "To God on high be

glo - ry, And peace on earth to men!"

2 The Word now dwells among us,
Made flesh, yet very God:
And cherubim sing anthems
To shepherds all abroad.
Refrain

*3 While thus they sing your Monarch,
Those bright angelic bands,
Rejoice, ye vales and mountains,
Ye oceans, clap your hands.
Refrain

4 Since all he comes to succor,
By all be he adored,
The infant born in Bethl'hem,
The Saviour and the Lord.
Refrain

*5 Now idol forms shall perish,
Now error shall decay,
And Christ shall wield his sceptre,
Our Lord and God for aye.
Refrain

ST. GERMANUS, 634–734; *Hymnal Version,* 1940, *after* J. M. NEALE

19 *First Tune* **Christmas**
C. M. D.

NOEL

English Melody, adapted by
ARTHUR SEYMOUR SULLIVAN, 1874

In moderate time

1 It came up-on the mid-night clear, That glo-rious song of old,
2 Still through the clo - ven skies they come With peace-ful wings un-furled,
*3 Yet with the woes of sin and strife The world has suf - fered long;

From an - gels bend - ing near the earth To touch their harps of gold:
And still their heav'n-ly mu - sic floats O'er all the wea - ry world;
Be - neath the heav'n-ly strain have rolled Two thou-sand years of wrong;

"Peace on the earth, good will to men, From heav'n's all - gra - cious King."
A - bove its sad and low - ly plains They bend on hov-'ring wing,
And man, at war with man, hears not The ti - dings which they bring;

The world in sol - emn still - ness lay To hear the an - gels sing.
And ev - er o'er its Ba - bel - sounds The bless - ed an - gels sing.
O hush the noise, ye men of strife, And hear the an - gels sing!

4 O ye, beneath life's crushing load,
 Whose forms are bending low,
Who toil along the climbing way
 With painful steps and slow,
Look now! for glad and golden hours
 Come swiftly on the wing;
O rest beside the weary road
 And hear the angels sing!

5 For lo! the days are hast'ning on,
 By prophets seen of old,
When with the ever-circling years
 Shall come the time foretold,
When peace shall over all the earth
 Its ancient splendors fling,
And the whole world give back the song
 Which now the angels sing.

EDMUND HAMILTON SEARS, 1846, *alt.*

Christmas
C. M. D.

CAROL

RICHARD STORRS WILLIS, 1850

Brightly

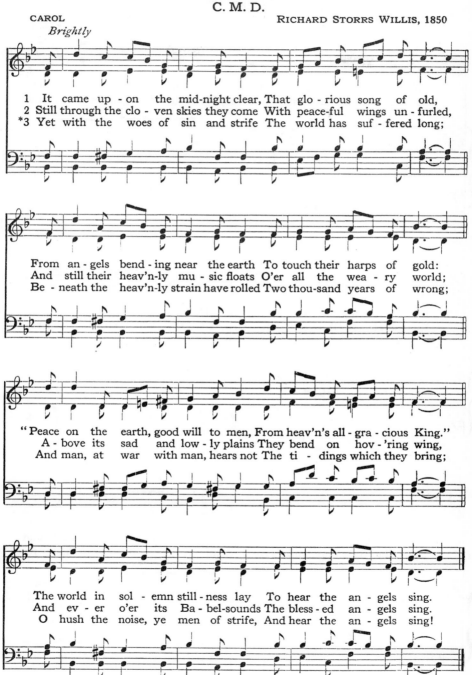

1 It came up-on the mid-night clear, That glo-rious song of old,
2 Still through the clo-ven skies they come With peace-ful wings un-furled,
*3 Yet with the woes of sin and strife The world has suf-fered long;

From an-gels bend-ing near the earth To touch their harps of gold:
And still their heav'n-ly mu-sic floats O'er all the wea-ry world;
Be-neath the heav'n-ly strain have rolled Two thou-sand years of wrong;

"Peace on the earth, good will to men, From heav'n's all-gra-cious King."
A-bove its sad and low-ly plains They bend on hov-'ring wing,
And man, at war with man, hears not The ti-dings which they bring;

The world in sol-emn still-ness lay To hear the an-gels sing.
And ev-er o'er its Ba-bel-sounds The bless-ed an-gels sing.
O hush the noise, ye men of strife, And hear the an-gels sing!

Christmas

87. 87. 877

DIVINUM MYSTERIUM

13th century Plainsong
Mode V

Flowing, not slow

1 Of the Fa-ther's love be - got - ten, Ere the worlds be - gan to be,
2 O that birth for ev - er bless - ed, When the Vir - gin, full of grace,

He is Al - pha and O - me - ga, He the source, the end - ing he,
By the Ho - ly Ghost con - ceiv - ing, Bare the Sa - viour of our race;

Of the things that are, that have . . . . been, And that
And the Babe, the world's Re - deem - - - er, First re -

Christmas

fu - ture years shall see,   Ev - er - more and   ev - er - more!
vealed his   sa - cred face,   Ev - er - more and   ev - er - more!

3 O ye heights of heav'n adore him;
    Angel hosts, his praises sing;
  Powers, dominions, bow before him,
    And extol our God and King;
  Let no tongue on earth be silent,
    Every voice in concert ring,
      Evermore and evermore!

*4 Thee let old men, thee let young men,
    Thee let boys in chorus sing;
  Matrons, virgins, little maidens,
    With glad voices answering:
  Let their guileless songs re-echo,
    And the heart its music bring,
      Evermore and evermore!

5 Christ, to thee with God the Father,
    And, O Holy Ghost, to thee,
  Hymn and chant and high thanksgiving,
    And unwearied praises be:
  Honor, glory, and dominion,
    And eternal victory,
      Evermore and evermore!   Amen.

AURELIUS CLEMENS PRUDENTIUS, 348-413;
Tr. J. M. NEALE, 1854, HENRY W. BAKER, 1859

21 *First Tune* 𝕮𝖍𝖗𝖎𝖘𝖙𝖒𝖆𝖘

FOREST GREEN

76. 86. D.

In moderate time

English Melody arr. by
R. VAUGHAN WILLIAMS, 1906

1 O lit - tle town of Beth - le - hem, How still we see thee lie!
2 For Christ is born of Ma - ry, And gath - ered all a - bove,
3 How si - lent - ly, how si - lent - ly, The won - drous gift is giv'n!

A - bove thy deep and dream-less sleep The si - lent stars go by;
While mor-tals sleep, the an - gels keep Their watch of won-d'ring love.
So God im-parts to hu - man hearts The bless - ings of his heav'n.

Yet in thy dark streets shin - eth The ev - er - last - ing Light;
O morn - ing stars, to - geth - er Pro - claim the ho - ly birth!
No ear may hear his com - ing, But in this world of sin,

The hopes and fears of all the years Are met in thee to - night.
And prais - es sing to God the King, And peace to men on earth.
Where meek souls will re - ceive him, still The dear Christ en-ters in.   A-men.

*4 Where children pure and happy
　Pray to the blessèd Child,
Where misery cries out to thee,
　Son of the mother mild;
Where charity stands watching
　And faith holds wide the door,
The dark night wakes, the glory breaks,
　And Christmas comes once more.

5 O holy Child of Bethlehem!
　Descend to us, we pray;
Cast out our sin and enter in,
　Be born in us to-day.
We hear the Christmas angels
　The great glad tidings tell;
O come to us, abide with us,
　Our Lord Emmanuel! Amen.

PHILLIPS BROOKS, 1867

21 *Second Tune* **Christmas**

ST. LOUIS   76. 86. D.
In moderate time   LEWIS H. REDNER, 1868

1 O lit - tle town of Beth - le - hem, How still we see thee lie!
2 For Christ is born of Ma - ry, And gath - ered all a - bove,
3 How si - lent - ly, how si - lent - ly, The won - drous gift is giv'n!

A - bove thy deep and dream-less sleep The si - lent stars go by;
While mor - tals sleep, the an - gels keep Their watch of won-d'ring love.
So God im-parts to hu - man hearts The bless - ings of his heav'n.

Yet in thy dark streets shin - eth The ev - er - last - ing Light;
O morn - ing stars, to - geth - er Pro - claim the ho - ly birth!
No ear may hear his com - ing, But in this world of sin,

The hopes and fears of all the years Are met in thee to-night.
And prais - es sing to God the King, And peace to men on earth.
Where meek souls will re - ceive him, still The dear Christ en - ters in. A-men.

*4 Where children pure and happy
   Pray to the blessèd Child,
 Where misery cries out to thee,
   Son of the mother mild;
 Where charity stands watching
   And faith holds wide the door,
 The dark night wakes, the glory breaks,
   And Christmas comes once more.

5 O holy Child of Bethlehem!
   Descend to us, we pray;
 Cast out our sin and enter in,
   Be born in us to-day.
 We hear the Christmas angels
   The great glad tidings tell;
 O come to us, abide with us,
   Our Lord Emmanuel! Amen.

PHILLIPS BROOKS, 1867

Christmas
L. M.

FROM HEAVEN HIGH

The Angel's Message

Melody pub. Leipzig, 1539
harmonized by W. D., 1940

In moderate time

1 "From hea - ven high I come to you, I bring you ti - dings
2 "For you a lit - tle child is born Of God's own cho - sen
3 "Lo, he is Christ, the Lord in - deed, Our God, to guide you

good and new, Good ti - dings of great joy I bring:
maid, this morn: A fair and ten - der ba - by bright,
in your need: And he will be your Sa - viour, strong

There - of will I both say and sing:
To be your joy and your de - light.
To cleanse you from all sin and wrong." A-men.

23 Part II of Hymn 22

Our Response

4 Now let us all right merry be,
And, with the shepherds, go to see
God's own dear Son, within the stall;
His gift, bestowed upon us all.

5 Mark well, my heart; look well, mine eyes;
Who is it in the manger lies:
What child is this, so young and fair?
It is my Jesus lieth there.

6 Ah, dearest Jesus, be my guest:
Soft be the bed where thou wilt rest,
A little shrine within my heart,
That thou and I may never part.

Christmas

After Part I or Part II

*7 Praise God above on his high throne,
Who giveth us his only Son.
The angel hosts rejoice in bliss
To chant a glad New Year like this. Amen.

MARTIN LUTHER, 1535; *Tr.* WINFRED DOUGLAS, 1939

24   **C. M.**

ST. AGNES
Quietly   JOHN B. DYKES, 1866

1 Calm on the lis - t'ning ear of night Come heav'n's mel-o-dious strains,
2 Ce - les - tial choirs from courts a - bove Shed sa - cred glo - ries there·
3 The answ'ring hills of Pal - es - tine Send back the glad re - ply;

Where wild Ju - de - a stretch - es far Her sil - ver - man - tled plains.
And an - gels, with their spark - ling lyres, Make mu - sic on the air.
And greet, from all their ho - ly heights, The Day-spring from on high.

4 O'er the blue depths of Galilee
 There comes a holier calm,
And Sharon waves, in solemn praise,
 Her silent groves of palm.

5 "Glory to God!" the sounding skies
 Loud with their anthems ring,
"Peace to the earth, good will to men,
 From heav'n's eternal King!"

6 Light on thy hills, Jerusalem!
 The Saviour now is born:
More bright on Bethl'hem's joyous plains
 Breaks the first Christmas morn.

EDMUND HAMILTON SEARS, 1834

SCHOP

Joyously; may be sung in unison

JOHANN SCHOP, 1641
har. J. S. BACH, 1734

Break forth, O beau-teous heav'n-ly light, And ush - er in the morn - ing; Ye shep - herds, shrink not with af - fright, But hear the an - gel's warn - ing. This child, this lit - tle help-less boy, Shall be our con - fi - dence and joy, The powers of hell o'er - throw - ing, At last our peace be - stow - ing.

JOHANN RIST, 1641; *Hymnal Version*, 1940

26

Christmas

77. 77. 77

ENGLAND'S LANE

Traditional English Melody,
adapted by GEOFFREY SHAW, 1919

With spirit; may be sung in unison

1 Sing, O sing, this bless-ed morn, Un-to us a child is born,
2 God of God, and Light of Light, Comes with mer-cies in-fi-nite,
3 God with us, Em-man-u-el, Deigns for ev-er now to dwell;

Un-to us a son is giv'n, God him-self comes down from heav'n;
Join-ing in a won-drous plan Heav'n to earth and God to man.
He on Ad-am's fall-en race Sheds the full-ness of his grace.

Refrain

Sing, O sing, this bless-ed morn, Je-sus Christ to-day is born. A-men.

4 God comes down that man may rise,
Lifted by him to the skies;
Christ is Son of Man that we
Sons of God in him may be.

Refrain

5 O renew us, Lord, we pray,
With thy Spirit day by day,
That we ever one may be
With the Father and with thee.

Refrain
Amen.

CHRISTOPHER WORDSWORTH, 1862

Alternative Tune, ST. ATHANASIUS, No. 270

Christmas

77. 77. 77. 77, with Refrain

MENDELSSOHN

Adapted from a chorus by
FELIX MENDELSSOHN, 1840

Vigorously

1 Hark! the her - ald an - gels sing Glo - ry to the new - born King!
2 Christ, by high - est heav'n a - dored; Christ, the ev - er - last - ing Lord;

Peace on earth and mer - cy mild, God and sin - ners re - con - ciled!
Late in time be - hold him come, Off - spring of the Vir - gin's womb.

Joy - ful, all ye na - tions, rise, Join the tri - umph of the skies;
Veiled in flesh the God-head see; Hail the in-car-nate De - i - ty,

With the an-gel - ic host pro - claim Christ is born in Beth - le - hem!
Pleased as man with man to dwell; Je - sus, our Em-man - u - el!

3 Mild he lays his glory by,
Born that man no more may die,
Born to raise the sons of earth,
Born to give them second birth.
Ris'n with healing in his wings,
Light and life to all he brings,
Hail, the Sun of Righteousness!
Hail, the heav'n-born Prince of Peace!

Christmas

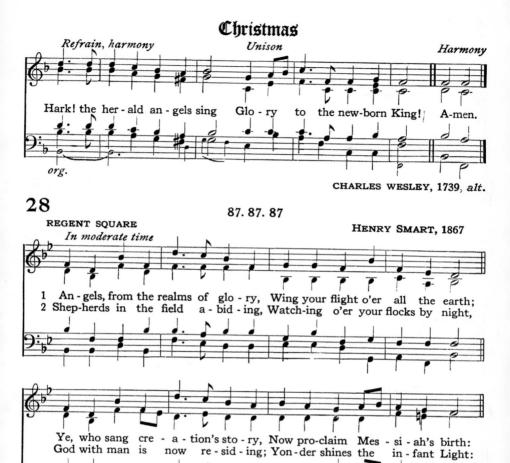

Refrain, harmony   *Unison*   *Harmony*

Hark! the her - ald an - gels sing   Glo - ry   to   the new-born King!   A-men.

org.

CHARLES WESLEY, 1739, alt.

28

87. 87. 87

REGENT SQUARE

HENRY SMART, 1867

In moderate time

1 An - gels, from the realms of glo - ry, Wing your flight o'er all the earth;
2 Shep-herds in the field a - bid - ing, Watch-ing o'er your flocks by night,

Ye, who sang cre - a - tion's sto - ry, Now pro-claim Mes - si - ah's birth:
God with man is now re - sid - ing; Yon-der shines the in - fant Light:

Refrain

Come and wor - ship, come and wor - ship, Wor - ship Christ, the new-born King.

3 Sages, leave your contemplations;
   Brighter visions beam afar:
Seek the great Desire of nations;
   Ye have seen his natal star:
        Refrain

4 Saints before the altar bending,
   Watching long in hope and fear,
Suddenly the Lord, descending,
   In his temple shall appear:
        Refrain

JAMES MONTGOMERY, 1816

29 *First Tune*

Christmas
Irregular

DIES EST LAETITIAE

Melody, Hohenfurth Ms., 1410
harmonized by W. D., 1940

1 Dost thou in a man-ger lie, Who hast all cre-a-ted,
2 "Pi-tying love for fall-en man Brought me down thus low; . . .

Stretch-ing in-fant hands on high, Sa-viour, long a-wait-ed?
For a race deep lost in sin, Came I in-to woe. . . .

If a mon-arch, where thy state? Where thy court on thee to wait?
By this low-ly birth of mine, Sin-ner, rich-es shall be thine,

Christmas

Roy - al pur - ple, where? Here no re - gal pomp we see;
Match - less gifts and free; Will - ing - ly this yoke I take,

Naught but need and pen - u - ry: Why thus cra - dled here?
And this sac - ri - fice I make, Heap-ing joys for thee." A - men.

3 Fervent praise would I to thee
    Evermore be raising;
For thy wondrous love to me
    Thee be ever praising.
Glory, glory be for ever
Unto that most bounteous Giver,
    And that loving Lord!
Better witness to thy worth,
Purer praise than ours on earth,
    Angels' songs afford.   Amen.

JEAN MAUBURN, 1494; *Tr.* ELIZABETH CHARLES

Christmas
Irregular

MAUBURN

In a flowing manner

T. TERTIUS NOBLE, 1918

1 Dost thou in a man - ger lie, Who hast all cre -
2 "Pi - tying love for fall - en man Brought me down thus

a - ted, Stretch - ing in - fant hands on high,
low; . . . . . For a race deep lost in sin,

Sa - viour, long a - wait - ed? If a mon - arch,
Came I in - to woe. . . . . . By this low - ly

where thy state? Where thy court on thee to wait?
birth of mine, Sin - ner, rich - es shall be thine,

Christmas

Poco rit.   *a tempo*

Roy - al pur - ple, where?   Here no re - gal pomp we see;
Match-less gifts and free;   Will-ing-ly this yoke I take,

Rall.   *Slower*

Naught but need and pen - u - ry: Why thus cra - dled here?
And this sac - ri - fice I make,   Heap - ing joys for thee." A-men.

3 Fervent praise would I to thee
   Evermore be raising;
For thy wondrous love to me
   Thee be ever praising.
Glory, glory be for ever
Unto that most bounteous Giver,
   And that loving Lord!
Better witness to thy worth,
Purer praise than ours on earth,
   Angels' songs afford.   Amen.

JEAN MAUBURN, 1494; *Tr.* ELIZABETH CHARLES, 1858

Also the following:

30

Christmas Carols
Irregular, with Refrain

THE FIRST NOWELL

Traditional Melody, pub. 1833

With spirit

1 The first Now - ell the an - gel did say
2 They look - ed up and saw a star

Was to cer - tain poor shep - herds in fields as they lay;
Shin - ing in the east be - yond them far,

In fields as they lay, keep - ing their sheep,
And to the earth it gave great light,

On a cold win - ter's night that was so deep.
And so it con - tin - ued both day and night.

Christmas Carols

Now - ell, Now - ell, Now - ell, Now - ell,

Born is the King of Is - ra - el. A - men.

3 And by the light of that same star
  Three wise men came from country far;
  To seek for a king was their intent,
  And to follow the star wherever it went.
Refrain

4 This star drew nigh to the northwest,
  O'er Bethlehem it took its rest,
  And there it did both stop and stay
  Right over the place where Jesus lay.
Refrain

5 Then entered in those wise men three
  Full rev'rently upon their knee,
  And offered there in his presence
  Their gold, and myrrh, and frankincense.
Refrain

6 Then let us all with one accord
  Sing praises to our heav'nly Lord;
  That hath made heav'n and earth of naught,
  And with his blood mankind hath bought.
Refrain

Old English Carol

Christmas Carols

31

66. 77. 78. 55

IN DULCI JUBILO

Fourteenth century Melody
harmonized by W. D., 1918

With marked rhythm

1 Good Chris-tian men, re - joice, With heart, and soul, and voice;
2 Good Chris-tian men, re - joice, With heart, and soul, and voice;

Give ye heed to what we say: Je - sus Christ is born to - day;
Now ye hear of end - less bliss: Je - sus Christ was born for this!

Ox and ass be - fore him bow, And he is in the man - ger now.
He hath oped the heav'n-ly door, And man is bless - ed ev - er - more.

Christ is born to - day! Christ is born to - day!
Christ was born for this! Christ was born for this!

3 Good Christian men, rejoice,
   With heart, and soul, and voice;
      Now ye need not fear the grave:
      Jesus Christ was born to save!
   Calls you one and calls you all
   To gain his everlasting hall.
      Christ was born to save!
      Christ was born to save!

JOHN MASON NEALE, 1853

Christmas Carols

83. 36. D.

EBELING

Melody, JOHANN GEORG EBELING, 1666

Not slow

1 All my heart this night re - joic - es As I hear, Far and near,
2 Hark! a voice from yon - der man - ger, Soft and sweet, Doth en - treat:
3 Come, then, let us hast - en yon - der! Here let all, Great and small,

Sweet-est an - gel voic - es. "Christ is born," their choirs are sing - ing,
"Flee from woe and dan - ger! Breth - ren, come! from all doth grieve you,
Kneel in awe and won - der! Love him who with love is yearn - ing!

Till the air Ev - 'ry - where Now with joy is ring - ing.
You are freed; All you need I will sure - ly give you."
Hail the star That from far Bright with hope is burn - ing!

4 Thee, dear Lord, with heed I'll cherish;
  Live to thee
  Faithfully:
Dying, never perish;
But abide in life eternal
  Where with thee
  I shall be
Filled with joy supernal.

PAULUS GERHARDT, 1656; *Tr.* CATHERINE WINKWORTH, 1858, *alt.*

33

Christmas Carols

Irregular

HOLY NIGHT

FRANZ GRUEBER, 1818,
harmonized by CARL REINECKE

Steadily, in moderate time

1 Si - lent night, ho - ly night, All is calm, all is bright
2 Si - lent night, ho - ly night, Shep-herds quake at the sight,
3 Si - lent night, ho - ly night, Son of God, love's pure light

Round yon vir - gin moth-er and child. Ho - ly in-fant so ten - der and mild,
Glo - ries stream from hea-ven a - far, Heav'n-ly hosts sing al - le - lu - ia;
Radiant beams from thy ho - ly face, With the dawn of re - deem - ing grace,

Sleep in hea - ven - ly peace, Sleep in hea - ven - ly peace.
Christ, the Sa-viour, is born! Christ, the Sa-viour, is born!
Je - sus, Lord, at thy birth, Je - sus, Lord, at thy birth. A - men.

JOSEPH MOHR, 1818

34

77. 77

PUER NOBIS NASCITUR

From *Piae Cantiones*, 1582,
arr. by GEOFFREY SHAW

Unison, moderately fast

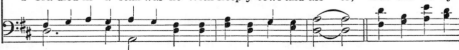

1 Un - to us a boy is born! The King of all cre - a - tion, Came he to a
2 Cra-dled in a stall was he With sleep-y cows and ass - es; But the ve - ry

Christmas Carols

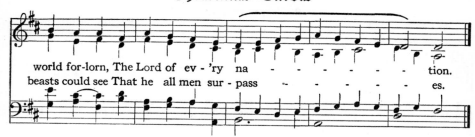

world for-lorn, The Lord of ev - 'ry na - - - - - - tion.
beasts could see That he all men sur - pass - - - - - es.

3 Herod then with fear was filled:
  "A prince," he said, "in Jewry!"
All the little boys he killed
At Bethl'hem in his fury.

4 Now may Mary's son, who came
So long ago to love us,
Lead us all with hearts aflame
Unto the joys above us.
Latin Carol, 15th cent.; Tr. O.B.C.

Music and words from Enlarged Songs of Praise, by permission of the Oxford University Press

35

888. 7

QUEM PASTORES

Joyously

Melody, Hohenfurth Ms., 1410

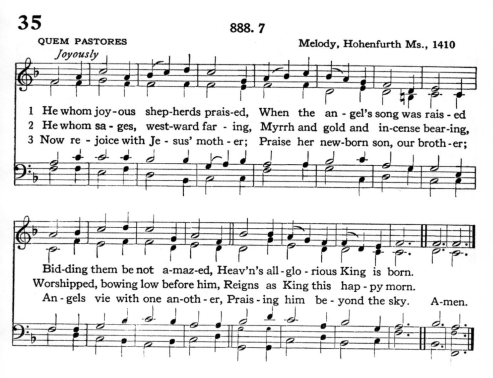

1 He whom joy-ous shep-herds prais-ed, When the an - gel's song was rais - ed
2 He whom sa - ges, west-ward far - ing, Myrrh and gold and in-cense bear-ing,
3 Now re - joice with Je - sus' moth - er; Praise her new-born son, our broth-er;

Bid-ding them be not a-maz-ed, Heav'n's all - glo - rious King is born.
Worshipped, bowing low before him, Reigns as King this hap - py morn.
An - gels vie with one an-oth - er, Prais - ing him be - yond the sky. A-men.

4 Sing to Christ, the King who reigneth,
Yet of Mary manhood gaineth,
Born our God; let us adore him:
Glory be to God on high. Amen.

Latin, 1410; *Tr.* WINFRED DOUGLAS, 1940

87. 87, with Refrain

GREENSLEEVES 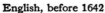 English, before 1642

In moderate time

1 What child is this, who, laid to rest, On Ma-ry's lap is sleep-ing?
2 Why lies he in such mean es-tate Where ox and ass are feed-ing?

Whom an-gels greet with an-thems sweet, While shepherds watch are keep-ing?
Good Christian, fear: for sin-ners here The si-lent Word is plead-ing.

Refrain

This, this is Christ the King, Whom shep-herds guard and an-gels sing:

Haste, haste to bring him laud, The babe, the son of Ma-ry.

3 So bring him incense, gold, and myrrh,
Come, peasant, king, to own him,
The King of kings salvation brings,
Let loving hearts enthrone him.

Refrain

WILLIAM CHATTERTON DIX, c. 1865

37   Christmas Carols

76. 76. D.

WEIMAR

Tenderly

Melody, MELCHIOR VULPIUS, 1609

1 Gen - tle Ma - ry laid her child Low - ly in a man - ger;
2 An - gels sang a - bout his birth; Wise men sought and found him;

There he lay, the un - de - filed, To the world a stran - ger.
Hea - ven's star shone bright-ly forth, Glo - ry all a - round him.

Such a babe in such a place, Can he be the Sa - viour?
Shep - herds saw the won-drous sight, Heard the an - gels sing - ing;

Ask the saved of all the race Who have found his fa - vor.
All the plains were lit that night, All the hills were ring - ing.

3 Gentle Mary laid her child
  Lowly in a manger;
He is still the undefiled,
  But no more a stranger.
Son of God, of humble birth,
  Beautiful the story;
Praise his Name in all the earth,
  Hail the King of glory!

By permission of Alta Lind Cook

JOSEPH SIMPSON COOK, 1919

87. 55. 56

GEVAERT

French Noel, 13th century

In unison, simply

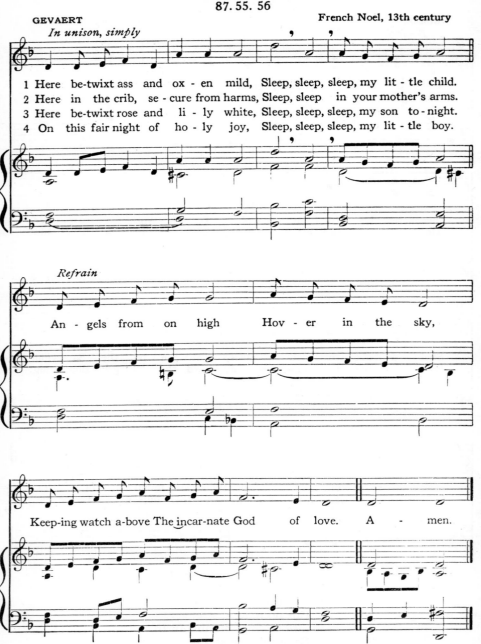

1 Here be-twixt ass and ox - en mild, Sleep, sleep, sleep, my lit - tle child.
2 Here in the crib, se - cure from harms, Sleep, sleep in your mother's arms.
3 Here be-twixt rose and li - ly white, Sleep, sleep, sleep, my son to - night.
4 On this fair night of ho - ly joy, Sleep, sleep, sleep, my lit - tle boy.

Refrain

An - gels from on high Hov - er in the sky,

Keep-ing watch a-bove The incar-nate God of love. A - men.

French, 13th cent.; Tr. WINFRED DOUGLAS, 1940

Irregular

CORNER

Traditional Melody pub. by
D. G. CORNER, Vienna, 1649

Simply

1 A babe lies in the cra - dle, A lit - tle babe so
2 The babe with - in the cra - dle Is Je - sus Christ our

dear, With no - ble light he shin - eth As shines a
Lord; To us all peace and am - i - ty At this good

mir - ror clear, This lit - tle babe so dear.
time af - ford, Thou Je - sus Christ our Lord!   A - men.

By permission of the Oxford University Press

3 Whoso would rock the cradle
   Where lies the gentle child,
   A lowly heart must lead him,
   By passions undefiled,
   As Mary pure and mild.

4 O Jesus, babe belovèd!
   O Jesus, babe divine!
   How mighty is thy wondrous love!
   Fill thou this heart of mine
   With that great love of thine!   Amen.

German Carol, pub. CORNER'S *Geistliche Nachtigal,* 1649; *Tr.* PAUL ENGLAND

Christmas Carols

76. 76. 76, with Refrain

GOD REST YOU MERRY

London Melody, 18th century,
harmonized by W. D., 1940

Fast

1 God rest you mer - ry, gen - tle - men, Let noth - ing you dis - may,
2 From God our heav'n - ly Fa - ther A bless - ed an - gel came;

Re - mem - ber Christ our Sa - viour Was born on Christ-mas Day;
And un - to cer - tain shep - herds Brought ti - dings of the same;

To save us all from Sa - tan's power When we were gone a - stray.
How that in Beth - le - hem was born The Son of God by name.

Christmas Carols

Refrain

O ti - dings of com - fort and joy, com - fort and joy; O ti - dings of com - fort and joy!

3 "Fear not, then," said the angel,
   "Let nothing you affright;
   This day is born a Saviour
   Of a pure virgin bright,
   To free all those who trust in him
   From Satan's power and might."
                                    Refrain

4 Now to the Lord sing praises,
   All you within this place,
   And with true love and brotherhood
   Each other now embrace;
   This holy tide of Christmas
   Doth bring redeeming grace.
                                    Refrain

London Carol, 18th cent.

Christmas Carols
Irregular, with Refrain

VENITE ADOREMUS

Traditional Melody
har. by LEO SOWERBY, 1941

In unison, cheerfully

1 The snow lay on the ground, The stars shone bright, When
2 'Twas Ma - ry, daugh-ter pure Of ho - ly Anne, That
3 Saint Jo - seph, too, was by To tend the child; To

Christ our Lord was born On Christ - mas night.
brought in - to this world The God made man.
guard him, and pro - tect His moth - er mild:

Ve - ni - te a - do - re - mus Do - mi - num; Ve -
She laid him in a stall At Beth - le - hem; The
The an - gels hov - ered round, And sung this song, Ve -

Christmas Carols

ni - te a - do - re - mus Do - mi - num.
ass and ox - en shared The roof with them.
ni - te a - do - re - mus Do - mi - num.

Refrain

Ve - ni - te a - do - re - mus Do - mi - num, Ve -

ni - te a - do - re - mus Do - mi - num. A - men.

4 And thus that manger poor
    Became a throne;
  For he whom Mary bore
    Was God the Son.
  O come, then, let us join
    The heav'nly host,
  To praise the Father, Son,
    And Holy Ghost.
           Refrain

Traditional Carol

Christmas Carols

77. 77, with Refrain

GLORIA

French Carol Melody
arr. by EDWARD SHIPPEN BARNES, 1937

In moderate time

1 An - gels we have heard on high, Sing - ing sweet - ly through the night,
2 Shep-herds, why this ju - bi - lee? Why these songs of hap - py cheer?
3 Come to Beth - le - hem and see Him whose birth the an - gels sing;
4 See him in a man - ger laid Whom the an - gels praise a - bove;

And the moun - tains in re - ply Ech - o - ing their brave de - light.
What great bright-ness did you see? What glad ti - dings did you hear?
Come, a - dore on bend - ed knee Christ, the Lord, the new - born King.
Ma - ry, Jo - seph, lend your aid, While we raise our hearts in love.

Refrain

Glo - - - - - - - - - - - - - ri - a

in ex - cel - sis De - o, Glo - - - - - - -

Christmas Carols

- - - - - - ri - a in ex - cel - sis De - o.

Traditional French Carol, alt. by EARL MARLATT, 1937

43

11 11. 11 11

CRADLE SONG

Melody, WILLIAM J. KIRKPATRICK, 1838–1921,
harmonized by R. VAUGHAN WILLIAMS, 1931

Unison, in moderate time

1 A - way in a man-ger, no crib for his bed, The lit - tle Lord
2 The cat - tle are low - ing, the ba - by a - wakes, But lit - tle Lord

Je - sus laid down his sweet head. The stars in the bright sky looked
Je - sus no cry - ing he makes. I love thee, Lord Je - sus! Look

down where he lay, The lit - tle Lord Je - sus a - sleep on the hay.
down from the sky, And stay by my side un - til morn-ing is nigh. A - men.

Traditional Carol

44   Christmas Carols

Irregular

CRANHAM   GUSTAV THEODORE HOLST, 1906

1   In the bleak mid - win - ter,   Fros - ty wind made moan,
2 Our God, heav'n can - not hold him,   Nor . . . earth sus - tain;
3   An - gels and arch - an - gels   May have gath - er'd there,
4   What . . can I give him,   Poor . . . as I am?

Earth stood hard as i - ron,   Wa - ter like a stone;
Heav'n and earth shall wel - come him   When he comes to reign:
Cher - u - bim and ser - a - phim   Throng-ed the . . . air;
If I were a shep - herd,   I would bring a lamb;

Snow had fall - en, snow on snow,   Snow . . on . . snow,
In the bleak mid - win - ter   A sta - ble-place suf - ficed   The
But his moth - er on - ly,   In her maid-en bliss,
If I were a wise . . man,   I would do my part;   Yet

In the bleak mid - win - ter,   Long a - go.
Lord . . God in - car - nate,   Je - sus Christ.
Wor - shipped the be - lov - ed   With a kiss.
what I can I give him —   Give my heart.

CHRISTINA GEORGINA ROSSETTI, c. 1872, alt.

45

Christmas Carols
Irregular, with Refrain

RESONET IN LAUDIBUS

German Carol Melody, 14th century,
har. by R. VAUGHAN WILLIAMS, 1906

Unison, in flowing style

1 (*Mary*) "Jo - seph dear - est, Jo - seph mine, Help me cra - dle the child di - vine;
2 (*Joseph*) "Glad - ly, dear one, la - dy mine, Help I cra - dle this child of thine;

God re - ward thee and all that's thine In par - a - dise," So
God's own light on us both shall shine In par - a - dise, As

Refrain

prays the moth-er Ma - ry. He came a - mong us at Christ-mas-tide, At
prays the moth-er Ma - ry."

Christ-mas-tide, In Beth - le - hem; Men shall bring him from far and wide Love's

di - a - dem: Je - sus, Je - sus, Lo, he comes, and loves, and saves, and frees us!

German Carol, c. 1500

MORNING STAR

JAMES P. HARDING, 1892

With movement

1 Bright-est and best of the sons of the morn-ing, Dawn on our
2 Cold on his cra-dle the dew-drops are shin-ing, Low lies his
3 Shall we then yield him, in cost-ly de-vo-tion, O-dors of

dark-ness, and lend us thine aid; Star of the east, the ho-
head with the beasts of the stall; An-gels a-dore him in
E-dom, and of-f'rings di-vine, Gems of the moun-tain, and

ri-zon a-dorn-ing, Guide where our in-fant Re-deem-er is laid.
slum-ber re-clin-ing, Ma-ker and Mon-arch and Sa-viour of all.
pearls of the o-cean, Myrrh from the for-est, and gold from the mine?

4 Vainly we offer each ample oblation,
   Vainly with gifts would his favor secure;
   Richer by far is the heart's adoration,
   Dearer to God are the prayers of the poor.

5 Brightest and best of the sons of the morning,
   Dawn on our darkness, and lend us thine aid;
   Star of the east, the horizon adorning,
   Guide where our infant Redeemer is laid.

REGINALD HEBER, 1811, *alt.*

STEWART   ALBERT J. STROHM, 1933

With vigor; may be sung in unison

1 Bright-est and best of the sons of the morn - ing, Dawn on our
2 Cold on his cra - dle the dew - drops are shin - ing, Low lies his
3 Shall we then yield him, in cost - ly de - vo - tion, O - dors of

dark - ness, and lend us thine aid; Star of the east, the ho -
head with the beasts of the stall; An - gels a - dore him in
E - dom, and of - f'rings di - vine, Gems of the moun-tain, and

ri - zon a - dorn - ing, Guide where our in - fant Re - deem - er is laid.
slum - ber re - clin - ing, Ma - ker and Mon-arch and Sa - viour of all.
pearls of the o - cean, Myrrh from the for - est, and gold from the mine?

4 Vainly we offer each ample oblation,
    Vainly with gifts would his favor secure;
    Richer by far is the heart's adoration,
       Dearer to God are the prayers of the poor.

‹ 5 Brightest and best of the sons of the morning,
    Dawn on our darkness, and lend us thine aid;
    Star of the east, the horizon adorning,
       Guide where our infant Redeemer is laid.

REGINALD HEBER, 1811, *alt.*

Epiphany
L. M.

PUER NOBIS

Unison, in flowing style

Adapted by MICHAEL PRAETORIUS, 1609,
har. by GEORGE R. WOODWARD, 1904

1 What star is this, with beams so bright, More beau - teous
2 True spake the pro - phet from a - far Who told the
3 The guid - ing star a - bove is bright; With - in them
*4 Their love can brook no dull de - lay, Though toil and

than the noon - day light? It shines to her - ald forth the
rise of Ja - cob's star; And east - ern sa - ges with a -
shines a clear - er light, And leads them on with power be -
dan - ger block the way; Home, kin - dred, fa - ther - land, and

King, And Gen - tiles to his crib to bring.
maze Up - on the won - drous to - ken gaze.
nign To seek the Giv - er of the sign.
all, They leave at their Cre - a - tor's call. A - men.

Epiphany

5 O Jesus, while the star of grace
Impels us on to seek thy face,
Let not our slothful hearts refuse
The guidance of thy light to use.

*6 To God the Father, heav'nly Light,
To Christ, revealed in earthly night,
To God the Holy Ghost we raise
Our equal and unceasing praise.   Amen.

CHARLES COFFIN, 1736; *Tr.* JOHN CHANDLER, 1837, **alt.**

48   87. 87

STUTTGART

Adapted from a melody by
C. F. WITT, Gotha, 1715

Majestically

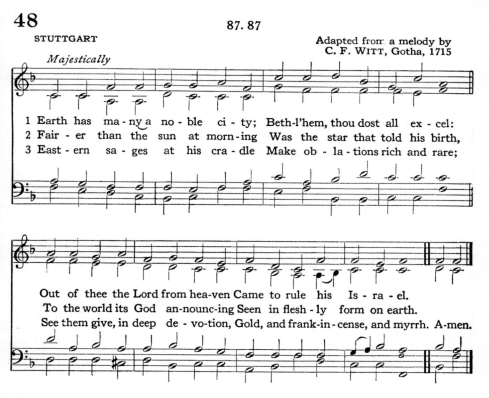

1 Earth has ma-ny a no-ble ci-ty; Beth-l'hem, thou dost all ex-cel:
2 Fair-er than the sun at morn-ing Was the star that told his birth,
3 East-ern sa-ges at his cra-dle Make ob-la-tions rich and rare;

Out of thee the Lord from hea-ven Came to rule his Is-ra-el.
To the world its God an-nounc-ing Seen in flesh-ly form on earth.
See them give, in deep de-vo-tion, Gold, and frank-in-cense, and myrrh. A-men.

4 Sacred gifts of mystic meaning:
Incense doth their God disclose,
Gold the King of kings proclaimeth,
Myrrh his sepulcher foreshows.

5 Jesus, whom the Gentiles worshipped
At thy glad epiphany,
Unto thee, with God the Father
And the Spirit, glory be.   Amen.

AURELIUS CLEMENS PRUDENTIUS, 348–413; *Tr.* EDWARD CASWALL, *alt.*

65. 65. D., with Refrain

VALOUR   ARTHUR HENRY MANN, 1889

With movement

1 From the east-ern moun-tains Press-ing on they come,
2 There their Lord and Sa - viour Meek and low-ly lay,

Wise men in their wis - dom To his hum - ble home;
Won-drous Light that led them On - ward on their way,

Stirred by deep de - vo - tion, Hast-ing from a - far,
Ev - er now to light - en Na - tions from a - far,

Ev - er jour-ney-ing on - ward, Guid - ed by a star.
As they jour - ney home - ward By that guid - ing star.

Epiphany

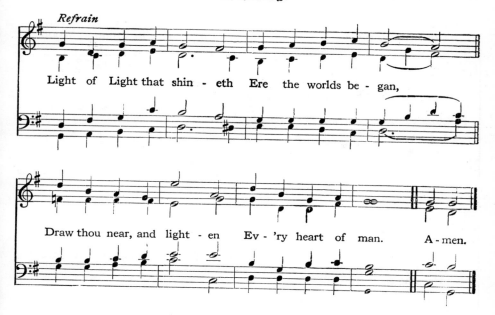

Light of Light that shin - eth Ere the worlds be - gan,

Draw thou near, and light - en Ev - 'ry heart of man. A - men.

3 Thou who in a manger
   Once hast lowly lain,
Who dost now in glory
   O'er all kingdoms reign,
Gather in the heathen,
   Who in lands afar
Ne'er have seen the brightness
   Of thy guiding star.
              Refrain

4 Gather in the outcasts,
   All who've gone astray,
Throw thy radiance o'er them,
   Guide them on their way,
Those who never knew thee,
   Those who've wandered far,
Lead them by the brightness
   Of thy guiding star.
              Refrain

5 Guide them through the darkness
   Of the lonely night,
Shining still before them
   With thy kindly light,
Until every nation,
   Whether bond or free,
'Neath thy starlit banner,
   Jesus, follows thee.
            Refrain

        Amen.

GODFREY THRING, 1873, *alt.*

50 *First Tune*

Epiphany
87. 87. D.

CHARTRES
In moderate time

15th century French Melody,
harmonized by CHARLES WOOD

1 Saw you nev - er, in the twi - light, When the sun had left the skies,
2 Heard you nev - er of the sto - ry How they crossed the des - ert wild,
3 Know ye not that low - ly ba - by Was the bright and morn-ing Star?

Up in heav'n the clear stars shin - ing Through the gloom, like sil - ver eyes?
Jour-ney'd on by plain and mountain, Till they found the ho - ly Child?
He who came to light the Gen - tiles, And the dark-en'd isles a - far?

So of old the wise men, watch-ing, Saw a lit - tle stran-ger star,
How they o - pen'd all their trea - sure, Kneel-ing to that in - fant King;
And we, too, may seek his cra - dle; There our hearts' best treasures bring;

And they knew the King was giv - en, And they fol - lowed it from far.
Gave the gold and fra-grant in - cense, Gave the myrrh in of - fer - ing?
Love, and faith, and true de - vo - tion For our Sa - viour, God, and King.

CECIL FRANCES ALEXANDER, 1853

Epiphany
87. 87. D.

THE WISE MEN

Quietly

BERTHOLD TOURS, 1881

1 Saw you nev - er, in the twi - light, When the sun had left the skies,
2 Heard you nev - er of the sto - ry How they crossed the des - ert wild,
3 Know ye not that low - ly ba - by Was the bright and morn - ing Star?

Up in heav'n the clear stars shin - ing Through the gloom, like sil - ver eyes?
Jour - ney'd on by plain and moun - tain, Till they found the ho - ly Child?
He who came to light the Gen - tiles, And the dark - en'd isles a - far?

So of old the wise men, watch - ing, Saw a lit - tle stran - ger star,
How they o - pen'd all their trea - sure, Kneel - ing to that in - fant King;
And we, too, may seek his cra - dle; There our hearts' best trea - sures bring;

And they knew the King was giv - en, And they fol - lowed it from far.
Gave the gold and fra - grant in - cense, Gave the myrrh in of - fer - ing?
Love, and faith, and true de - vo - tion For our Sa - viour, God, and King.

CECIL FRANCES ALEXANDER, 1853

Epiphany

88. 446, with Refrain

THREE KINGS OF ORIENT

JOHN HENRY HOPKINS, Jr., 1857

Joyously

Gaspard

1 We three kings of O - ri - ent are, Bear - ing gifts we trav - erse a -
5 Glo - rious now be - hold him a - rise, King, and God, and Sac - ri -

Melchior

1 We three kings of O - ri - ent are, Bear - ing gifts we trav - erse a -
5 Glo - rious now be - hold him a - rise, King, and God, and Sac - ri -

Balthazar

1 We three kings of O - ri - ent are, Bear - ing gifts we trav - erse a -
5 Glo - rious now be - hold him a - rise, King, and God, and Sac - ri -

far, Field and foun - tain, Moor and moun-tain, Fol-low - ing yon - der star.
fice, Heav'n sings Al - le - lu - ia: Al - le - lu - ia the earth re - plies.

far, Field and foun - tain, Moor and moun-tain, Fol-low - ing yon - der star.
fice, Heav'n sings Al - le - lu - ia: Al - le - lu - ia the earth re - plies.

far, Field and foun - tain, Moor and moun-tain, Fol-low - ing yon - der star.
fice, Heav'n sings Al - le - lu - ia: Al - le - lu - ia the earth re - plies.

Epiphany

Refrain after each stanza

O star of won-der, star of night, Star with roy-al beau-ty bright;

West-ward lead-ing, Still pro-ceed-ing, Guide us to thy per-fect light! A-men.

Interlude

Gasp. 2 Born a King on Beth-le-hem's plain, Gold I bring to crown him a-
Mel. 3 Frank-in-cense to of-fer have I, In-cense owns a De-i-ty
Bal. 4 Myrrh is mine; its bit-ter per-fume Breathes a life of gath-er-ing

gain, King for ev-er, Ceas-ing nev-er O-ver us all to reign.
nigh, Prayer and prais-ing, All men rais-ing, Worship him, God on high.
gloom; Sorrowing, sigh-ing, Bleed-ing, dy-ing, Sealed in the stone-cold tomb.

JOHN HENRY HOPKINS, Jr., 1857

Stanzas 2, 3, and 4 should be sung as solos, the accompaniment and refrain being unchanged. The refrain only should be sung by the congregation. Men's voices are preferable for the parts of the three kings.

Epiphany

77. 77. 77

CONRAD KOCHER, 1838, *alt.*

DIX

Joyfully

1 As with glad-ness men of old Did the guid-ing star be-hold;
2 As with joy-ful steps they sped To that low-ly man-ger-bed;
3 As they of-fer'd gifts most rare At that man-ger rude and bare;

As with joy they hailed its light, Lead-ing on-ward, beam-ing bright;
There to bend the knee be-fore Him whom heav'n and earth a-dore;
So may we with ho-ly joy, Pure and free from sin's al-loy,

So, most gra-cious Lord, may we Ev-er-more be led to thee.
So may we with will-ing feet Ev-er seek the mer-cy-seat.
All our cost-li-est treasures bring, Christ! to thee, our heav'n-ly King. A-men.

4 Holy Jesus! every day
Keep us in the narrow way;
And, when earthly things are past,
Bring our ransomed souls at last
Where they need no star to guide,
Where no clouds thy glory hide.

5 In the heav'nly country bright,
Need they no created light;
Thou its light, its joy, its crown,
Thou its sun which goes not down:
There for ever may we sing
Alleluias to our King. Amen.

WILLIAM CHATTERTON DIX, 1860

53

77. 77. D.

SALZBURG
With great dignity

Melody by JAKOB HINTZE, 1678, *alt.*,
harmonized by J. S. BACH, 1685–1750

1 Songs of thank-ful - ness and praise, Je - sus, Lord, to thee we raise,
2 Man - i - fest at Jor - dan's stream, Pro - phet, Priest, and King su - preme;

Man - i - fest - ed by the star To the sa - ges from a - far;
And at Ca - na, wed - ding-guest, In thy God-head man - i - fest;

Branch of roy - al Da - vid's stem In thy birth at Beth - le - hem;
Man - i - fest in power di - vine, Changing wa - ter in - to wine;

An-thems be to thee ad - drest, God in man made man - i - fest.
An-thems be to thee ad - drest, God in man made man - i - fest. A-men.

3 Manifest in making whole
Palsied limbs and fainting soul;
Manifest in valiant fight,
Quelling all the devil's might;
Manifest in gracious will,
Ever bringing good from ill;
Anthems be to thee addrest,
God in man made manifest.

4 Grant us grace to see thee, Lord,
Mirrored in thy holy word;
May we imitate thee now,
And be pure, as pure art thou;
That we like to thee may be
At thy great epiphany;
And may praise thee, ever blest,
God in man made manifest. Amen.

CHRISTOPHER WORDSWORTH, 1862

Epiphany

54 (*For the last Sunday after Epiphany*)

87. 87. 87

DULCE CARMEN   *An Essay on the Church Plain Chant*, 1782

With joyful dignity

1 Al - le - lu - ia, song of glad-ness, Voice of joy that can-not die;
2 Al - le - lu - ia thou re - sound-est, True Je - ru - sa - lem and free;
3 Al - le - lu - ia we de - serve not Here to chant for ev - er - more;
4 There-fore in our hymns we pray thee, Grant us, bless - ed Tri - ni - ty,

Al - le - lu - ia is the an-them Ev - er dear to choirs on high;
Al - le - lu - ia, joy - ful moth-er, All thy chil - dren sing with thee;
Al - le - lu - ia our trans-gres-sions Make us for a while give o'er;
At the last to keep thine Eas-ter In our home be - yond the sky;

In the house of God a - bid-ing Thus they sing e - ter - nal -ly.
But by Bab - y-lon's sad wa-ters Mourn-ing ex - iles now are we.
For the ho - ly time is com-ing Bid - ding us our sins de-plore.
There to thee for ev - er sing-ing Al - le - lu - ia joy - ful-ly. A-men.

Latin, 11th cent.; Tr. JOHN MASON NEALE, 1851, *alt.*

Pre-Lenten Season

Also the following:

55   Lent

HEINLEIN

77. 77

M. H., in
Nürnbergisches Gesangbuch, 1676

Solemnly

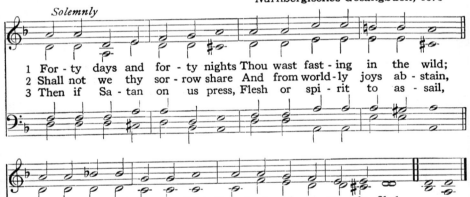

1 For-ty days and for-ty nights Thou wast fast-ing in the wild;
2 Shall not we thy sor-row share And from world-ly joys ab-stain,
3 Then if Sa-tan on us press, Flesh or spi-rit to as-sail,

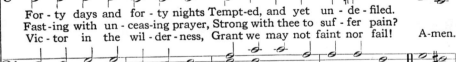

For-ty days and for-ty nights Tempt-ed, and yet un-de-filed.
Fast-ing with un-ceas-ing prayer, Strong with thee to suf-fer pain?
Vic-tor in the wil-der-ness, Grant we may not faint nor fail!   A-men.

4 So shall we have peace divine:
   Holier gladness ours shall be;
   Round us, too, shall angels shine,
   Such as ministered to thee.

5 Keep, O keep us, Saviour dear,
   Ever constant by thy side;
   That with thee we may appear
   At the eternal Eastertide.   Amen.

GEORGE HUNT SMYTTAN, 1856, *alt.*

56

𝕷ent

L. M.

JESU DULCIS MEMORIA

Melody pub. Andernach, 1608

Quietly

1 Kind Ma-ker of the world, O hear The fer-vent prayer, with
2 Each heart is man-i-fest to thee; Thou know-est our in-
3 Spare us, O Lord, who now con-fess Our sins and all our

ma-ny a tear Poured forth by all the pen-i-tent
fir-mi-ty; Now we re-pent, and seek thy face;
wick-ed-ness, And, for the glo-ry of thy Name,

Who keep this ho-ly fast of Lent!
Grant un-to us thy par-d'ning grace.
Our weak-en'd souls to health re-claim. A - men.

4 Give us the self-control that springs
From abstinence in outward things;
That from each stain and spot of sin,
Our souls may keep the fast within.

5 Grant, O thou blessèd Trinity;
Grant, O unchanging Unity;
That this our fast of forty days
May work our profit and thy praise! Amen.

ST. GREGORY THE GREAT, 540–604; *Hymnal Version*, 1941

57 *First Tune*

HOLY GHOST

Lent

777

Slow

Melody adapted by
JOHANN CRUEGER, 1640

1 Lord, in this thy mer - cy's day, Ere for us it
2 Lord, on us thy Spi - rit pour, Kneel - ing low - ly

pass a - way, On our knees we fall and pray.
at thy door, Ere it close for ev - er - more. A - men.

3 By thy night of agony,
By thy supplicating cry,
By thy willingness to die,

4 By thy tears of bitter woe
For Jerusalem below,
Let us not thy peace forego.

5 Judge and Saviour of our race,
Grant us, when we see thy face,
With thy ransomed ones a place.

6 On thy love we rest alone,
And that love shall then be known
By the pardoned, round thy throne. **Amen.**

ISAAC WILLIAMS, 1842, *alt.*

57 *Second Tune*

ST. PHILIP

777

WILLIAM H. MONK, 1861

In moderate time

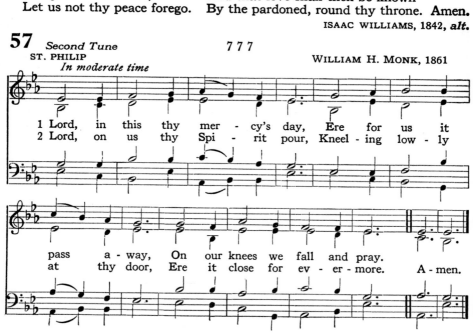

1 Lord, in this thy mer - cy's day, Ere for us it
2 Lord, on us thy Spi - rit pour, Kneel - ing low - ly

pass a - way, On our knees we fall and pray.
at thy door, Ere it close for ev - er - more. A - men.

Lent

10 10. 10 10

LANGRAN

JAMES LANGRAN, 1862

In moderate time

1 Wea - ry of earth, and la - den with my sin, I look at heav'n and
2 The while I fain would tread the heav'n-ly way E - vil is ev - er

long to en - ter in, But there no e - vil thing may find a home:
with me day by day; Yet on mine ears the gra - cious ti - dings fall:

And yet I hear a voice that bids me "Come."
"Re - pent, con - fess, thou shalt be loosed from all." A - men.

*3 It is the voice of Jesus that I hear;
His are the hands stretched out to draw me near,
And his the blood that can for all atone,
And set me faultless there before the throne.

*4 'Twas he who found me on the deathly wild,
And made me heir of heav'n, the Father's child,
And day by day, whereby my soul may live,
Gives me his grace of pardon, and will give.

Lent

5 O great Absolver, grant my soul may wear
The lowliest garb of penitence and prayer,
That in the Father's courts my glorious dress
May be the garment of thy righteousness.

6 Yea, thou wilt answer for me, righteous Lord;
Thine all the merits, mine the great reward;
Thine the sharp thorns, and mine the golden crown;
Mine the life won, and thine the life laid down.   Amen.

SAMUEL J. STONE, 1866

59   C. M.

ST. FLAVIAN   JOHN DAY'S *Psalter*, 1562
Moderately slow

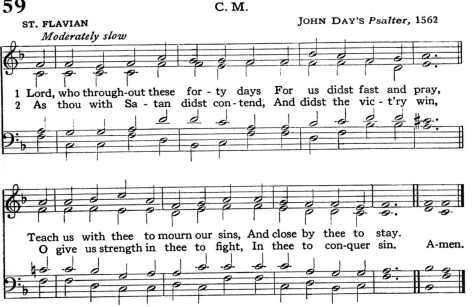

1 Lord, who through-out these for - ty days For us didst fast and pray,
2 As thou with Sa - tan didst con-tend, And didst the vic - t'ry win,

Teach us with thee to mourn our sins, And close by thee to stay.
O give us strength in thee to fight, In thee to con-quer sin.   A-men.

3 As thou didst hunger bear and thirst,
    So teach us, gracious Lord,
  To die to self, and chiefly live
    By thy most holy word.

4 And through these days of penitence,
    And through thy Passiontide,
  Yea, evermore, in life and death,
    Jesus! with us abide.

5 Abide with us, that so, this life
    Of suff'ring overpast,
  An Easter of unending joy
    We may attain at last!   Amen.

CLAUDIA F. HERNAMAN, 1873

Lent
L. M.

BABYLON'S STREAMS

Moderately slow

THOMAS CAMPIAN, 1613

1 With bro - ken heart and con - trite sigh, A trem-bling sin - ner,
2 I smite up - on my troub - led breast, With deep and con - scious
3 Far off I stand with tear - ful eyes, Nor dare up - lift them

Lord, I cry: Thy par - d'ning grace is rich and free:
guilt op - prest, Christ and his cross my on - ly plea:
to the skies; But thou dost all my an - guish see:

O God, be mer - ci - ful to me.
O God, be mer - ci - ful to me.
O God, be mer - ci - ful to me. A - men.

4 Nor alms, nor deeds that I have done,
Can for a single sin atone;
To Calvary alone I flee:
O God, be merciful to me.

5 And when, redeemed from sin and hell,
With all the ransomed throng I dwell,
My raptured song shall ever be,
God has been merciful to me. Amen.

CORNELIUS ELVEN, 1852

61

Lent

L. M.

SPIRES

J. KLUG'S *Geistliche Lieder,* 1543,
harmonized by J. S. BACH, 1685–1750

Slow and solemn, in unison

1 The glo - ry of these for - ty days We cel - e - brate with songs of praise; For Christ, by whom all things were made, Him - self has fast - ed and has prayed.

2 A - lone and fast - ing Mo - ses saw The lov - ing God who gave the law; And to E - li - jah, fast - ing, came The steeds and char - i - ots of flame.

3 So Dan - iel trained his mys - tic sight, De - liv - er'd from the li - ons' might; And John, the Bride-groom's friend, be - came The her - ald of Mes - si - ah's name.

4 Then grant us, Lord, like them to be Full oft in fast and prayer with thee; Our spi - rits strength-en with thy grace, And give us joy to see thy face. A-men.

5 O Father, Son, and Spirit blest,
To thee be every prayer addrest,
Who art in threefold Name adored,
From age to age, the only Lord. Amen.

Latin, 6th cent.; Tr. MAURICE F. BELL, 1906

Lent

Passiontide

62

Passiontide

For Palm Sunday
76. 76. D.

ST. THEODULPH   MELCHIOR TESCHNER, pub. 1615

Majestically; may be sung in unison

†*Refrain* All glo - ry, laud, and hon - or To thee, Re - deem - er, King!

To whom the lips of chil - dren Made sweet ho - san - nas ring. A - men.

Stanzas commence here

2 Thou art the King of Is - ra - el, Thou Da - vid's roy - al Son,
3 The com - pa - ny of an - gels Are prais - ing thee on high;
4 The peo - ple of the He - brews With palms be - fore thee went:

Repeat Refrain

Who in the Lord's Name com - est, The King and Bless - ed One.
And mor - tal men, and all things Cre - a - ted, make re - ply.
Our praise and prayers and an - thems Be - fore thee we pre - sent.

5 To thee before thy passion   6 Thou didst accept their praises;
   They sang their hymns of praise: Accept the prayers we bring,
To thee, now high exalted,   Who in all good delightest,
   Our melody we raise.   Thou good and gracious King.
      Refrain   *Refrain*

ST. THEODULPH, c. 820; *Tr.* JOHN MASON NEALE, 1854

†*The choir may sing the stanzas of this hymn alone, the congregation always joining at the Refrain.*

Passiontide
L. M.

VEXILLA REGIS

Sarum Plainsong, Mode I

In unison, with steady dignity

1 The roy - al ban - ners for - ward go, The cross shines forth
2 Ful - filled is all that Da - vid told In true pro - phet -
3 O tree of beau - ty, tree most fair, Ordained those ho -

in mys - tic glow Where he, as man, who gave man breath,
ic song of old; How God the na - tions' King should be,
ly limbs to bear; Gone is thy shame, each crim - son'd bough

Now bows . . . . . be - neath the yoke of death.
For God . . . . . is reign - ing from the tree.
Pro - claims . . . . the King of glo - ry now. A - men.

Passiontide

4 Blest tree, whose chosen branches bore
The wealth that did the world restore,
The price of humankind to pay,
And spoil the spoiler of his prey.

5 O cross, our one reliance, hail!
Still may thy power with us avail
More good for righteous souls to win,
And save the sinner from his sin.

6 To thee, eternal Three in One,
Let homage meet by all be done:
As by the cross thou dost restore,
So rule and guide us evermore.   Amen.

St. 1–4, VENANTIUS HONORIUS FORTUNATUS, 569; *Hymnal Version, 1940*

63 *Second Tune*   **L. M.**

PARKER

HORATIO PARKER, 1894

1 The roy - al ban - ners for - ward go, The cross shines forth in
2 Ful - filled is all that Da - vid told In true pro - phet - ic
3 O tree of beau - ty, tree most fair, Or - dained those ho - ly

mys - tic glow Where he, as man, who gave man breath, Now
song of old; How God the na - tions' King should be, For
limbs to bear; Gone is thy shame, each crim-son'd bough Pro -

bows be - neath the yoke of death.
God is reign - ing from the tree.
claims the King of glo - ry now.   A - men.

64 *First Tune*

Passiontide

For Palm Sunday

L. M.

THE KING'S MAJESTY

GRAHAM GEORGE, 1940

In unison, with dignity

1 Ride on! ride on in ma - - jes - ty! Hark! all the tribes ho - san - na cry; Thy hum - ble beast pur - sues his road With palms and scat - ter'd gar - ments strowed.

2 Ride on! ride on in ma - - jes - ty! In low - ly pomp ride on to die: O Christ, thy tri - umphs now be - gin O'er cap - tive death and con - quer'd sin.

3 Ride on! ride on in ma - - jes - ty! The an - gel ar - mies of the sky Look down with sad and won - d'ring eyes To see the ap - proach - ing sac - ri - fice. A - men.

Passiontide

4 Ride on! ride on in majesty!
Thy last and fiercest strife is nigh;
The Father on his sapphire throne
Expects his own anointed Son.

5 Ride on! ride on in majesty!
In lowly pomp ride on to die;
Bow thy meek head to mortal pain,
Then take, O God, thy power, and reign. Amen.

HENRY HART MILMAN, 1827, *alt.*

64 *Second Tune*   L. M.

WINCHESTER NEW

Adapted from
Musikalisches Handbuch, Hamburg, 1690

With solemnity

1 Ride on! ride on in ma - jes - ty! Hark! all the tribes ho -
2 Ride on! ride on in ma - jes - ty! In low - ly pomp ride
3 Ride on! ride on in ma - jes - ty! The an - gel ar - mies

san - na cry; Thy hum - ble beast pur - sues his road
on to die: O Christ, thy tri - umphs now be - gin
of the sky Look down with sad and won - d'ring eyes

With palms and scat - ter'd gar - ments strowed.
O'er cap - tive death and con - quer'd sin.
To see the ap - proach - ing sac - ri - fice. A - men.

Passiontide
L. M.

ST. DROSTANE

JOHN B. DYKES, 1862

With vigor

1 Ride on! ride on in ma - jes - ty! Hark! all the tribes ho -
2 Ride on! ride on in ma - jes - ty! In low - ly pomp ride

san - na cry; Thy hum - ble beast pur - sues his road With
on to die: O Christ, thy tri - umphs now be - gin O'er

palms and scat - ter'd gar - ments strowed.
cap - tive death and con - quer'd sin. A - men.

3 Ride on! ride on in majesty!
The angel armies of the sky
Look down with sad and wond'ring eyes
To see the approaching sacrifice.

4 Ride on! ride on in majesty!
Thy last and fiercest strife is nigh;
The Father on his sapphire throne
Expects his own anointed Son.

5 Ride on! ride on in majesty!
In lowly pomp ride on to die;
Bow thy meek head to mortal pain,
Then take, O God, thy power, and reign. Amen.

HENRY HART MILMAN, 1827, *alt.*

65 *First Tune*

Passiontide

C. M.

HORSLEY

WILLIAM HORSLEY, 1844

Simply

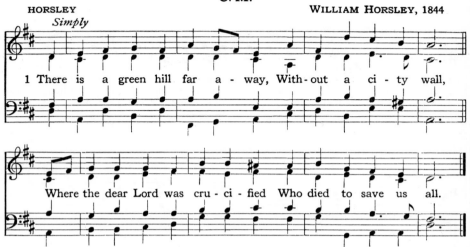

1 There is a green hill far a - way, With - out a ci - ty wall,

Where the dear Lord was cru - ci - fied Who died to save us all.

2 We may not know, we cannot tell,
What pains he had to bear,
But we believe it was for us
He hung and suffered there.

3 He died that we might be forgiv'n,
He died to make us good,
That we might go at last to heav'n,
Saved by his precious blood.

*4 There was no other good enough
To pay the price of sin,
He only could unlock the gate
Of heav'n, and let us in.

5 O dearly, dearly has he loved!
And we must love him too,
And trust in his redeeming blood,
And try his works to do.

CECIL FRANCES ALEXANDER, 1848

65 *Second Tune*

C. M.

MEDITATION

JOHN H. GOWER, 1890

Simply

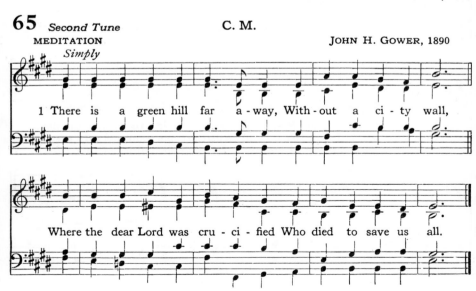

1 There is a green hill far a - way, With - out a ci - ty wall,

Where the dear Lord was cru - ci - fied Who died to save us all.

Passiontide

87. 87. 87

PANGE LINGUA

In unison, with movement

Sarum Plainsong,
Mode III, trans.

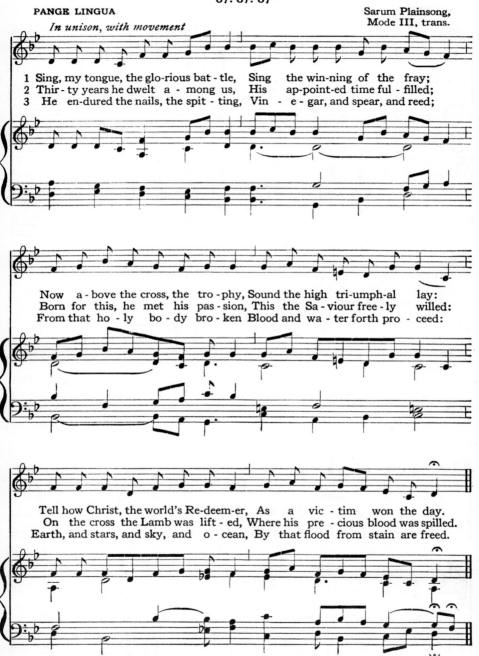

1 Sing, my tongue, the glo-rious bat - tle, Sing the win-ning of the fray;
2 Thir - ty years he dwelt a - mong us, His ap-point-ed time ful - filled;
3 He en-dured the nails, the spit - ting, Vin - e - gar, and spear, and reed;

Now a - bove the cross, the tro - phy, Sound the high tri-umph-al lay:
Born for this, he met his pas - sion, This the Sa - viour free - ly willed:
From that ho - ly bo - dy bro - ken Blood and wa - ter forth pro - ceed:

Tell how Christ, the world's Re-deem-er, As a vic - tim won the day.
On the cross the Lamb was lift - ed, Where his pre - cious blood was spilled.
Earth, and stars, and sky, and o - cean, By that flood from stain are freed.

Passiontide

4 Faithful cross! above all other,
    One and only noble tree!
  None in foliage, none in blossom,
    None in fruit thy peer may be:
  Sweetest wood, and sweetest iron!
    Sweetest weight is hung on thee.

5 Bend thy boughs, O tree of glory!
    Thy relaxing sinews bend;
  For awhile the ancient rigor
    That thy birth bestowed, suspend;
  And the King of heav'nly beauty
    On thy bosom gently tend!

6 To the Trinity be glory
    Everlasting, as is meet:
  Equal to the Father, equal
    To the Son, and Paraclete:
  God the Three in One, whose praises
    All created things repeat.   Amen.

A - men.

VENANTIUS HONORIUS FORTUNATUS, 569;
Hymnal Version, 1940, *after* J. M. NEALE

Alternative Tune, ORIEL, No. 326

67

77. 77

HALLE
Gravely

The Psalmist, 1830

1 See the des-tined day a - rise! See a will - ing sac - ri - fice!
2 Je - sus, who but 'thou had borne, Lift - ed on that tree of scorn,
3 Who but thou had dared to drain, Steeped in gall, the cup of pain,

Je - sus, to re - deem our loss, Hangs up - on the shame-ful cross.
Ev - 'ry pang and bit - ter throe, Fin - ish-ing thy life of woe?
And with ten - der bo - dy bear Thorns, and nails, and piercing spear?   A-men.

4 Thence the cleansing water flowed,
  Mingled from thy side with blood;
  Sign to all attesting eyes
  Of the finished sacrifice.

5 Holy Jesus, grant us grace
  In that sacrifice to place
  All our trust for life renewed,
  Pardoned sin, and promised good.
                        Amen.

VENANTIUS HONORIUS FORTUNATUS, 569;
Para., RICHARD MANT, 1837

Alternative Tune, ST. PRISCA, No. 79

68
Passiontide
C. M.

BANGOR
WILLIAM TANS'UR, 1734

Moderately slow

1 A - lone thou go - est forth, O Lord, In sac - ri - fice to die;
2 Our sins, not thine, thou bear - est, Lord, Make us thy sor - row feel,

Is this thy sor - row naught to us Who pass un - heed-ing by?
Till through our pi - ty and our shame Love an-swers love's ap - peal. A-men.

3 This is earth's darkest hour, but thou
  Dost light and life restore;
  Then let all praise be given thee
  Who livest evermore.

4 Give us compassion for thee, Lord,
  That, as we share this hour,
  Thy cross may bring us to thy joy
  And resurrection power. Amen.

PETER ABELARD, 1079–1142; *Tr.* F. BLAND TUCKER, 1938

69
10. 10

SONG 46
ORLANDO GIBBONS, 1623

Not fast

1 Drop, drop, slow tears, And bathe those beau - teous feet,
2 Cease not, wet eyes, His mer - cies to en - treat;
3 In your deep floods Drown all my faults and fears;

Which brought from heav'n The news and Prince of Peace.
To cry for venge - ance Sin doth nev - er cease.
Nor let his eye See sin, but through my tears. A-men.

PHINEAS FLETCHER, 1633

70

PETRA

RICHARD REDHEAD, 1853

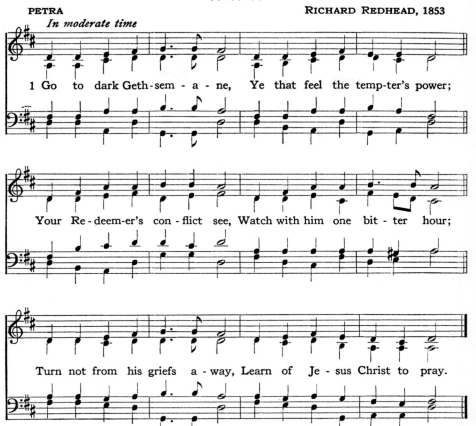

1 Go to dark Geth-sem-a-ne, Ye that feel the temp-ter's power;

Your Re-deem-er's con-flict see, Watch with him one bit-ter hour;

Turn not from his griefs a-way, Learn of Je-sus Christ to pray.

2 Follow to the judgment hall;
   View the Lord of life arraigned;
O the wormwood and the gall!
   O the pangs his soul sustained!
Shun not suff'ring, shame, or loss;
Learn of him to bear the cross.

3 Calvary's mournful mountain climb;
   There, adoring at his feet,
Mark the miracle of time,
   God's own sacrifice complete;
" It is finished! " hear him cry;
Learn of Jesus Christ to die.

JAMES MONTGOMERY, 1825

Passiontide

11 11. 11 5

HERZLIEBSTER JESU

JOHANN CRUEGER, 1640

Slow; may be sung in unison

1 Ah, ho - ly Je - sus, how hast thou of - fend - ed, That man to
2 Who was the guil - ty? Who brought this up - on thee? A - las, my
3 Lo, the Good Shep - herd for the sheep is of - fer'd; The slave hath

judge thee hath in hate pre - tend - ed? By foes de - rid - ed,
trea - son, Je - sus, hath un - done thee. 'Twas I, Lord Je - sus,
sin - ned, and the Son hath suf - fer'd; For man's a - tone - ment,

by thine own re - ject - ed, O most af - flict - ed.
I it was de - nied thee: I cru - ci - fied thee.
while he noth-ing heed - eth, God in - ter - ced - eth. A - men.

4 For me, kind Jesus, was thy incarnation,
Thy mortal sorrow, and thy life's oblation;
Thy death of anguish and thy bitter passion,
For my salvation.

5 Therefore, kind Jesus, since I cannot pay thee,
I do adore thee, and will ever pray thee,
Think on thy pity and thy love unswerving,
Not my deserving. Amen.

JOHANN HEERMANN, 1630; *Tr.* ROBERT BRIDGES, 1899

Passiontide

11 11. 11 5

ECCE JAM NOCTIS
With movement

Sarum Plainsong, Mode IV

1 Ah, ho - ly Je - sus, how hast thou of - fend - ed, That man to
2 Who was the guil - ty? Who brought this up - on thee? A - las, my
3 Lo, the Good Shep - herd for the sheep is of - fer'd; The slave hath

judge thee hath in hate pre - tend - ed? By foes de - rid - ed,
trea - son, Je - sus, hath un - done thee. 'Twas I, Lord Je - sus,
sin - ned, and the Son hath suf - fer'd; For man's a - tone - ment,

by thine own re - ject - ed, O most af - flict - ed.
I it was de - nied thee: I cru - ci - fied thee.
while he noth - ing heed - eth, God in - ter - ced - eth. A - men.

BATTY   Moravian Melody, 1745

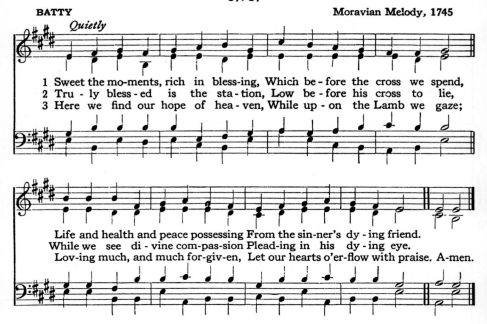

1 Sweet the mo-ments, rich in bless-ing, Which be-fore the cross we spend,
2 Tru-ly bless-ed is the sta-tion, Low be-fore his cross to lie,
3 Here we find our hope of hea-ven, While up-on the Lamb we gaze;

Life and health and peace possessing From the sin-ner's dy-ing friend.
While we see di-vine com-pas-sion Plead-ing in his dy-ing eye.
Lov-ing much, and much for-giv-en, Let our hearts o'er-flow with praise. A-men.

4 Lord, in loving contemplation
   Fix our hearts and eyes on thee,
Till we taste thy full salvation,
   And thine unveiled glories see.

5 For thy sorrows we adore thee,
   For the griefs that wrought our peace;
Gracious Saviour, we implore thee,
   In our hearts thy love increase.   Amen.

WALTER SHIRLEY, 1770, *from* JAMES ALLEN, 1757, *alt.*

73   C. M.

WETHERBY   SAMUEL SEBASTIAN WESLEY, 1872

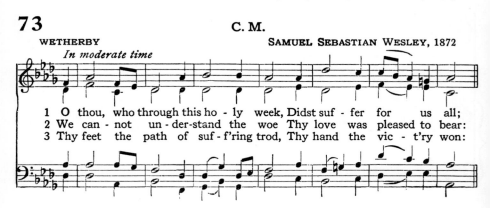

1 O thou, who through this ho-ly week, Didst suf-fer for us all;
2 We can-not un-der-stand the woe Thy love was pleased to bear:
3 Thy feet the path of suf-f'ring trod, Thy hand the vic-t'ry won:

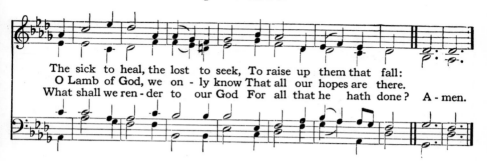

The sick to heal, the lost to seek, To raise up them that fall:
O Lamb of God, we on - ly know That all our hopes are there.
What shall we ren - der to our God For all that he hath done? A - men.

4 To God, the blessèd Three in One,
 All praise and glory be:
 Crown, Lord, thy servants who have won
 The victory through thee. Amen.

JOHN MASON NEALE

74

ST. CROSS

L. M.

JOHN B. DYKES, 1861

Moderately slow

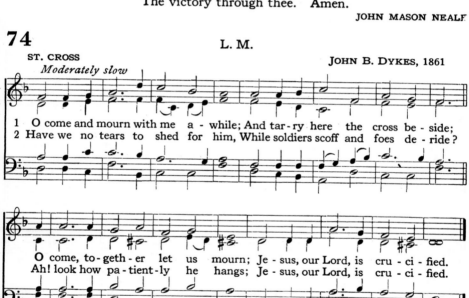

1 O come and mourn with me a - while; And tar - ry here the cross be - side;
2 Have we no tears to shed for him, While soldiers scoff and foes de - ride?

O come, to - geth - er let us mourn; Je - sus, our Lord, is cru - ci - fied.
Ah! look how pa - tient - ly he hangs; Je - sus, our Lord, is cru - ci - fied.

3 Sev'n times he spake, sev'n words of love;
 And all three hours his silence cried
For mercy on the souls of men;
 Jesus, our Lord, is crucified.

4 O love of God! O sin of man!
 In this dread act your strength is tried;
And victory remains with love;
 For thou our Lord, art crucified!

FREDERICK WILLIAM FABER, 1849, *alt.*

𝕻assiontide

76. 76. D.

PASSION CHORALE

HANS LEO HASSLER, 1601,
adapted and har. by J. S. BACH

Solemnly, but not too slow; may be sung in unison

1 O sa - cred head, sore wound - ed, De - filed and put to scorn;
2 Thy beau - ty, long - de - sir - ed, Hath van - ished from our sight;

O king - ly head, sur - round - ed With mock - ing crown of thorn:
Thy power is all ex - pir - ed, And quench'd the light of light.

What sor - row mars thy grand - eur? Can death thy bloom de - flower?
Ah me! for whom thou di - est, Hide not so far thy grace:

O coun-te-nance whose splen - dor The hosts of heav'n a-dore!
Show me, O Love most high - est, The bright-ness of thy face. A-men.

3 In thy most bitter passion
   My heart to share doth cry,
With thee for my salvation
   Upon the cross to die.
Ah, keep my heart thus movèd
   To stand thy cross beneath,
To mourn thee, well-belovèd,
   Yet thank thee for thy death.

*4 My days are few, O fail not,
   With thine immortal power,
To hold me that I quail not
   In death's most fearful hour:
That I may fight befriended,
   And see in my last strife
To me thine arms extended
   Upon the cross of life. Amen.

PAULUS GERHARDT, 1656; *Tr.* ROBERT BRIDGES, 1899

By permission of The Clarendon Press, Oxford

Passiontide

887

MAINZ

Adapted from Mainz *Gesangbuch*, 1661, harmonized by W. D., 1940

In unison, simply

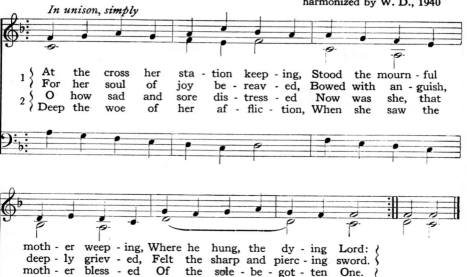

1 At the cross her sta - tion keep - ing, Stood the mourn - ful
  For her soul of joy be - reav - ed, Bowed with an - guish,
2 O how sad and sore dis - tress - ed Now was she, that
  Deep the woe of her af - flic - tion, When she saw the

moth - er weep - ing, Where he hung, the dy - ing Lord:
deep - ly griev - ed, Felt the sharp and pierc - ing sword.
moth - er bless - ed Of the sole - be - got - ten One.
cru - ci - fi - xion Of her ev - er - glo - rious Son.   A - men.

3 Who, on Christ's dear mother gazing,
  Pierced by anguish so amazing,
    Born of woman, would not weep?
  Who, on Christ's dear mother thinking,
  Such a cup of sorrow drinking,
    Would not share her sorrows deep?

4 For his people's sins chastisèd,
  She beheld her Son despisèd,
    Scourged, and crowned with thorns entwined;
  Saw him then from judgment taken,
  And in death by all forsaken,
    Till his spirit he resigned.

5 Jesus, may her deep devotion
  Stir in me the same emotion,
    Fount of love, Redeemer kind;
  That my heart fresh ardor gaining,
  And a purer love attaining,
    May with thee acceptance find.   Amen.

Latin, 13th century

Passiontide

887. 887

STABAT MATER

Mechlin Plainsong, Mode IV

In flowing style

1 At the cross her sta-tion keeping, Stood the mournful moth-er weep-ing,
2 O how sad and sore dis-tress-ed Now was she, that moth-er bless-ed
3 Who, on Christ's dear moth-er gaz-ing, Pierced by an-guish so a - maz - ing,
4 For his peo - ple's sins chas-tis-ed, She be-held her Son de - spis - ed,

Where he hung, the dy - ing Lord: For her soul of joy be - reav - ed,
Of the sole - be - got - ten One. Deep the woe of her af - flic - tion,
Born of wo - man, would not weep? Who, on Christ's dear mother think-ing,
Scourg'd, and crown'd with thorns entwined; Saw him then from judgment ta - ken,

Bowed with an-guish, deep-ly griev-ed, Felt the sharp and pierc - ing sword.
When she saw the cru - ci - fi - xion Of her ev - er - glo - rious Son.
Such a cup of sor-row drink-ing, Would not share her sor - rows deep?
And in death by all for - sa - ken, Till his spi - rit he re - signed.

Passiontide

5 Jesus, may her deep devotion
   Stir in me the same emotion,
      Fount of love, Redeemer kind;
   That my heart fresh ardor gaining,
   And a purer love attaining,
      May with thee acceptance find.   Amen.

Latin, 13th century

77

ISLEWORTH   88. 86   Samuel Howard, 1765

1 His are the thou-sand spark-ling rills That from a thou-sand foun-tains burst, And fill with mu-sic all the hills; And yet he saith, "I thirst."

2 All fier-y pangs on bat-tle-fields; On fe-ver beds where sick men toss, Are in that hu-man cry he yields To an-guish on the cross.   A-men.

3 But more than pains that racked him then,
      Was the deep longing thirst divine
   That thirsted for the souls of men:
      Dear Lord! and one was mine.

4 O Love most patient, give me grace;
      Make all my soul athirst for thee;
   That parched dry lip, that anguished face,
      That thirst, were all for me.   Amen.

CECIL FRANCES ALEXANDER, 1875, *alt.*

Alternative Tune, SAFFRON WALDEN, No. 409

78

Passiontide
78. 87. 87. 87

SEBASTIAN

Melody from
J. A. FREYLINGHAUSEN'S *Gesangbuch*, 1714

With dignity

1 It is fin-ished! Christ hath known All the life of men way-far-ing;
2 It is fin-ished! Christ is slain, On the al-tar of cre-a-tion,

Hu-man joys and sor-rows shar-ing, Ma-king hu-man needs his own.
Of-f'ring for a world's sal-va-tion Sac-ri-fice of love and pain.

Lord, in us thy life re-new-ing, Lead us where thy feet have trod,
Lord, thy love through pain re-veal-ing, Purge our pas-sions, scourge our vice,

Till, the way of truth pur-su-ing, Hu-man souls find rest in God.
Till, up-on the tree of heal-ing, Self is slain in sac-ri-fice. A-men.

GABRIEL GILLETT, 1906

79

𝔓𝔞𝔰𝔰𝔦𝔬𝔫𝔱𝔦𝔡𝔢
77. 77

ST. PRISCA
Solemnly

RICHARD REDHEAD, 1853

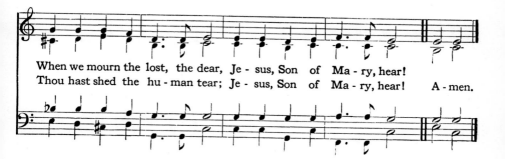

1 When our heads are bowed with woe, When our bit - ter tears o'er - flow,
2 Thou our throb-bing flesh hast worn, Thou our mor - tal griefs hast borne,

When we mourn the lost, the dear, Je - sus, Son of Ma - ry, hear!
Thou hast shed the hu - man tear; Je - sus, Son of Ma - ry, hear! A - men.

3 When the solemn death-bell tolls
For our own departing souls,
When our final doom is near,
Jesus, Son of Mary, hear!

4 Thou hast bowed the dying head,
Thou the blood of life hast shed,
Thou hast filled a mortal bier;
Jesus, Son of Mary, hear!

5 When the heart is sad within
With the thought of all its sin,
When the spirit shrinks with fear,
Jesus, Son of Mary, hear!

6 Thou the shame, the grief, hast known,
Though the sins were not thine own;
Thou hast deigned their load to bear;
Jesus, Son of Mary, hear! Amen.

HENRY HART MILMAN, 1827

80

Passiontide
Irregular

WERE YOU THERE

Negro Melody

With deep reverence

1 Were you there when they cru - ci - fied my Lord? Were you
2 Were you there when they nailed him to the tree? Were you
3 Were you there when they laid him in the tomb? Were you

there when they cru - ci - fied my Lord?
there when they nailed him to the tree? Oh! . . . .
there when they laid him in the tomb?

Some-times it caus - es me to trem - ble, trem - ble, trem - ble.

Were you there when they cru - ci - fied my Lord?
Were you there when they nailed him to the tree?
Were you there when they laid him in the tomb?

Negro Spiritual

81

Passiontide
L. M.

KEDRON

Southern Harmony, 1835,
harmonized by HILTON RUFTY, 1934

In unison, broad and solemn

1 Sun - set to sun - rise chang - es now, For
2 E'en though the sun with - holds its light, Lo!
3 Here in o'er - whelm - ing fi - nal strife The

God doth make his world a - new: On the Re - deem - er's
a more heav'n - ly lamp shines here, And from the cross on
Lord of life hath vic - to - ry; And sin is slain, and

thorn-crown'd brow The won - ders of that dawn we view.
Cal - vary's height Gleams of e - ter - ni - ty ap - pear.
death brings life, And sons of earth hold heav'n in fee.

Alternative Tune, PARKER, No. 63

ST. CLEMENT of Alexandria, c. 170–220;
Para. HOWARD CHANDLER ROBBINS

82 *First Tune*

Passiontide

The Words on the Cross
PART I

"Father, forgive them; for they know not what they do." St. Luke xxiii. 34

SWEDISH LITANY   Swedish Melody, 1697

77. 76

May be sung in unison

1 Je - sus, in thy dy - ing woes, E - ven while thy life - blood flows,
2 Sa - viour, for our par - don sue, When our sins thy pangs re - new,
3 O may we, who mer - cy need, Be like thee in heart and deed,

Crav - ing par - don for thy foes: Hear us, ho - ly Je - sus.
For we know not what we do: Hear us, ho - ly Je - sus.
When with wrong our spi - rits bleed: Hear us, ho - ly Je - sus. A - men.

82 *Second Tune*

77. 76

TON-MÂN   DAVID EVANS, 1912

1 Je - sus, in thy dy - ing woes, E - ven while thy life - blood flows,
2 Sa - viour, for our par - don sue, When our sins thy pangs re - new,
3 O may we, who mer - cy need, Be like thee in heart and deed,

Crav - ing par - don for thy foes: Hear us, ho - ly Je - sus.
For we know not what we do: Hear us, ho - ly Je - sus.
When with wrong our spi - rits bleed: Hear us, ho - ly Je - sus. A - men.

The tunes may be alternated if desired

Passiontide

PART II

"To-day shalt thou be with me in paradise."
ST. LUKE xxiii. 43

1 Jesus, pitying the sighs
Of the thief, who near thee dies,
Promising him paradise:
Hear us, holy Jesus.

2 May we, in our guilt and shame,
Still thy love and mercy claim,
Calling humbly on thy Name:
Hear us, holy Jesus.

3 O remember us who pine,
Looking from our cross to thine;
Cheer our souls with hope divine:
Hear us, holy Jesus.

PART III

" Woman, behold thy son!" " Behold thy mother!"
ST. JOHN xix. 26, 27

1 Jesus, loving to the end
Her whose heart thy sorrows rend,
And thy dearest human friend:
Hear us, holy Jesus.

2 May we in thy sorrows share,
And for thee all peril dare,
And enjoy thy tender care:
Hear us, holy Jesus.

3 May we all thy loved ones be,
All one holy family,
Loving for the love of thee:
Hear us, holy Jesus.

PART IV

" My God, my God, why hast thou forsaken me?"
ST. MATT. xxvii. 46

1 Jesus, whelmed in fears unknown,
With our evil left alone,
While no light from heav'n is shown:
Hear us, holy Jesus.

2 When we vainly seem to pray,
And our hope seems far away,
In the darkness be our stay:
Hear us, holy Jesus.

3 Though no Father seem to hear,
Though no light our spirits cheer,
Tell our faith that God is near:
Hear us, holy Jesus

PART V

" I thirst."
ST. JOHN xix. 28

1 Jesus, in thy thirst and pain,
While thy wounds thy life-blood drain,
Thirsting more our love to gain:
Hear us, holy Jesus.

2 Thirst for us in mercy still;
All thy holy work fulfil;
Satisfy thy loving will:
Hear us, holy Jesus.

3 May we thirst thy love to know;
Lead us in our sin and woe
Where the healing waters flow:
Hear us, holy Jesus.

PART VI

"It is finished."
ST. JOHN xix. 30

1 Jesus, all our ransom paid,
All thy Father's will obeyed,
By thy suff'rings perfect made:
Hear us, holy Jesus.

2 Save us in our soul's distress,
Be our help to cheer and bless,
While we grow in holiness:
Hear us, holy Jesus.

3 Brighten all our heav'nward way
With an ever holier ray,
Till we pass to perfect day:
Hear us, holy Jesus.

PART VII

" Father, into thy hands I commend my spirit."
ST. LUKE xxiii. 46

1 Jesus, all thy labor vast,
All thy woe and conflict past,
Yielding up thy soul at last:
Hear us, holy Jesus.

2 When the death shades round us lower,
Guard us from the tempter's power,
Keep us in that trial hour:
Hear us, holy Jesus.

3 May thy life and death supply
Grace to live and grace to die,
Grace to reach the home on high:
Hear us, holy Jesus. Amen.

THOMAS BENSON POLLOCK, 1870

83

O TRAURIGKEIT

Easter Even

447. 76

Würzburg, 1628

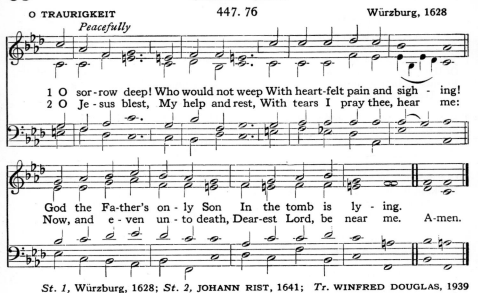

Peacefully

1 O sor-row deep! Who would not weep With heart-felt pain and sigh - ing!
2 O Je-sus blest, My help and rest, With tears I pray thee, hear me:

God the Fa-ther's on - ly Son In the tomb is ly - ing.
Now, and e - ven un - to death, Dear-est Lord, be near me. A-men.

St. 1, Würzburg, 1628; *St. 2*, JOHANN RIST, 1641; *Tr.* WINFRED DOUGLAS, 1939

84

Easter

NEW ENGLAND

C. M.

T. TERTIUS NOBLE, 1941

In moderate time

1 "O who shall roll a - way the stone," The faith - ful wo - men said;
2 But look-ing up, at dawn, they saw The great stone rolled a - way,
3 Look up, O doubt-ing soul, look up! Eyes fixed up - on the earth
4 Look up! and ev - er look - ing up, Thine eyes shall clear-ly see

"The hea - vy stone that seals the tomb, And shuts from us our dead?"
And from the emp - ty tomb a light More dazz-ling than the day.
Can nev - er see the life that finds In death its glo - rious birth.
The tombs of earth filled with the light Of im - mor - tal - i - ty.

MARION FRANKLIN HAM, 1936

EASTER HYMN

Stately

Altered, 1749, from
Lyra Davidica, 1708

1 Je - sus Christ is ris'n to - day,
2 Hymns of praise then let us sing, Al - le - lu - ia!
3 But the pains which he en - dured,

Our tri - umph-ant ho - ly day,
Un - to Christ, our heav'n - ly King, Al - le - lu - ia!
Our sal - va - tion have pro - cured;

Who did once up - on the cross,
Who en - dured the cross and grave, Al - le - lu - ia!
Now a - bove the sky he's King,

Suf - fer to re - deem our loss.
Sin - ners to re - deem and save. Al - le - lu - ia! A-men.
Where the an - gels ev - er sing.

4 Sing we to our God above, Alleluia!
Praise eternal as his love; Alleluia!
Praise him, all ye heav'nly host, Alleluia!
Father, Son, and Holy Ghost. Alleluia! Amen.

Latin, 14th cent.; Tr. TATE *and* BRADY, 1698;
St. 4, CHARLES WESLEY

Easter

Irregular, with Refrain

SALVE FESTA DIES

R. VAUGHAN WILLIAMS, 1906

In unison, with vigor

† *Refrain* Hail thee, fes-tiv - al day! blest day that art hallowed for ev - er;

Day whereon Christ a - rose, breaking the king-dom of death. death.

1st time | 2nd time

Women and boys

2 Lo, the fair beau-ty of earth, from the death of the win-ter a - ri - sing!
4 Dai - ly the love - li-ness grows, a - dorned with the glo-ry of blos - som;
6 God the All-Fa-ther, the Lord, who rul - est the earth and the hea - vens,
8 Spi - rit of life and of power, now flow in us, fount of our be - ing,

Music by permission of the Oxford University Press
† *The choir sings the Refrain first; then all repeat it*

Easter

Repeat Refrain

Ev - 'ry good gift of the year   now with its Mas-ter re-turns:
Hea - ven her gates un - bars,   fling-ing her in-crease of light:
Guard   us from harm with - out,   cleanse us from e - vil with-in:
Light   that dost light-en   all,   life that in all dost a-bide:

Men

3 He who was nailed to the cross is   Lord and the ru - ler of all men;
5 Rise from the grave now, O Lord, who art au-thor of life   and cre-a-tion.
7 Je - sus the health of the world, en-light-en our minds, thou Redeem-er,
9 Praise to the Giv-er of good! Thou Love who art au-thor of con-cord,

Repeat Refrain

All things cre - a - ted on earth   sing to the glo - ry of God:
Tread-ing the path-way of death,   life thou be-stow-est on man:
Son of the Fa-ther su-preme,   on - ly - be-got-ten of God:
Pour out thy balm on our souls,   or - der our ways in thy peace:

VENANTIUS HONORIUS FORTUNATUS, 530–609

From Enlarged Songs of Praise, by permission of the Oxford University Press. Translation altered by special arrangement with the Oxford University Press.

11 11. 11 11. 11

FORTUNATUS   ARTHUR SEYMOUR SULLIVAN, 1872

With animation

1 "Wel - come, hap - py morn - ing!" age to age shall say:
2 Earth her joy con - fess - es, cloth - ing her for spring,

Hell to - day is van-quished, heav'n is won to - day!
All fresh gifts re - turned with her re - turn - ing King:

Lo! the dead is liv - ing, God for ev - er - more!
Bloom in ev - 'ry mea - dow, leaves on ev - 'ry bough,

Him, their true Cre - a - tor, all his works a - dore!
Speak his sor - row end - ed, hail his tri - umph now.

Easter

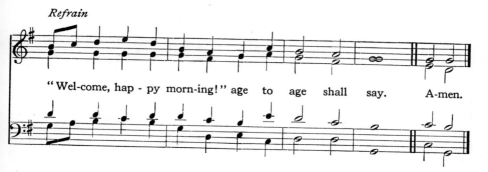

Refrain

"Wel-come, hap-py morn-ing!" age to age shall say. A-men.

3 Months in due succession, days of length'ning light,
Hours and passing moments praise thee in their flight.
Brightness of the morning, sky and fields and sea,
Vanquisher of darkness, bring their praise to thee.
"Welcome, happy morning!" age to age shall say.

4 Maker and Redeemer, life and health of all,
Thou from heav'n beholding human nature's fall,
Of the Father's Godhead true and only Son,
Manhood to deliver, manhood didst put on.
"Welcome, happy morning!" age to age shall say.

5 Thou, of life the author, death didst undergo,
Tread the path of darkness, saving strength to show;
Come then, true and faithful, now fulfil thy word,
'Tis thine own third morning! rise, O buried Lord!
"Welcome, happy morning!" age to age shall say.

6 Loose the souls long prisoned, bound with Satan's chain;
All that now is fallen raise to life again;
Show thy face in brightness, bid the nations see;
Bring again our daylight: day returns with thee!
"Welcome, happy morning!" age to age shall say. Amen.

VENANTIUS HONORIUS FORTUNATUS, 530–609;
Tr. JOHN ELLERTON, 1868

88 **Easter**

78. 78, with Alleluia

ST. ALBINUS
Joyously

HENRY J. GAUNTLETT, 1852

1 Je - sus lives! thy ter - rors now Can no long - er, death, ap -
2 Je - sus lives! hence-forth is death But the gate of life im -
3 Je - sus lives! for us he died; Then, a - lone to Je - sus

pall us; Je - sus lives! by this we know Thou, O
mor - tal; This shall calm our trem - bling breath, When we
liv - ing, Pure in heart may we a - bide, Glo - ry

grave, canst not en - thrall us. Al - le - lu - ia!
pass its gloom - y por - tal. Al - le - lu - ia!
to our Sa - viour giv - ing. Al - le - lu - ia!

4 Jesus lives! our hearts know well
  Naught from us his love shall sever;
Life, nor death, nor powers of hell
  Tear us from his keeping ever.
        Alleluia!

5 Jesus lives! to him the throne
  Over all the world is given:
May we go where he has gone,
  Rest and reign with him in heaven.
        Alleluia!

CHRISTIAN F. GELLERT, 1757;
Tr. FRANCES E. COX, 1841, *alt.*

89   **Easter**

77. 77. D.

SALZBURG   Melody by JAKOB HINTZE, 1678, *alt.*,
With great dignity   harmonized by J. S. BACH, 1685–1750

1   At the Lamb's high feast we sing Praise to our vic - to - rious King,
*2 Where the Pas - chal blood is poured, Death's dark an - gel sheathes his sword;

Who hath washed us in the tide Flow - ing from his pierc - ed side;
Is - rael's hosts tri - umph - ant go Through the wave that drowns the foe.

Praise we him, whose love di - vine Gives his sa - cred Blood for wine,
Praise we Christ, whose blood was shed, Pas - chal vic - tim, Pas - chal bread;

Gives his Bo - dy for the feast, Christ the vic - tim, Christ the priest.
With sin - cer - i - ty and love Eat we man - na from a - bove. A-men.

3 Mighty victim from the sky,
  Hell's fierce powers beneath thee lie;
  Thou hast conquered in the fight,
  Thou hast brought us life and light:
  Now no more can death appall,
  Now no more the grave enthrall;
  Thou hast opened paradise,
  And in thee thy saints shall rise.

4 Easter triumph, Easter joy,
  Sin alone can this destroy;
  From sin's power do thou set free
  Souls new-born, O Lord, in thee.
  Hymns of glory, songs of praise,
  Father, unto thee we raise:
  Risen Lord, all praise to thee
  With the Spirit ever be.   Amen.

Latin; Tr. ROBERT CAMPBELL. 1849, *alt.*

90   **Easter**

87. 87. 77

NEANDER   JOACHIM NEANDER, 1680
Stately

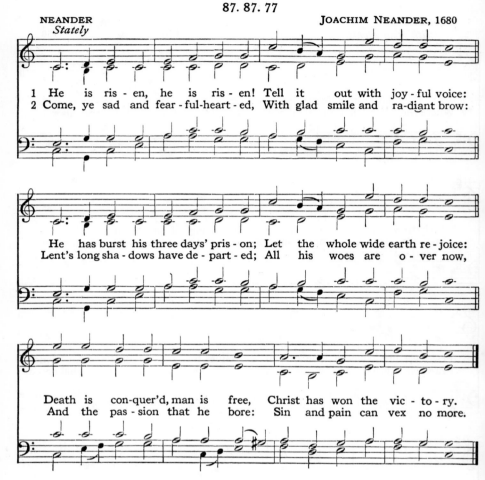

1 He   is   ris - en, he is ris - en! Tell it   out with joy - ful voice:
2 Come, ye sad and fear - ful-heart - ed, With glad smile and   ra-diant brow:

He   has burst his three days' pris - on; Let   the whole wide earth re - joice:
Lent's long sha - dows have de - part - ed; All   his woes are   o - ver now,

Death is   con-quer'd, man is   free, Christ has won the   vic - to - ry.
And the pas - sion that he   bore: Sin and pain can vex no more.

3 Come, with high and holy hymning,
   Chant our Lord's triumphant lay;
Not one darksome cloud is dimming
   Yonder glorious morning ray,
Breaking o'er the purple east,
Symbol of our Easter feast.

4 He is risen, he is risen!
   He hath opened heaven's gate:
We are free from sin's dark prison,
   Risen to a holier state;
And a brighter Easter beam
On our longing eyes shall stream.

CECIL FRANCES ALEXANDER, 1846, *alt.*

888, with Alleluias

VICTORY

G. P. SANTE DA PALESTRINA, 1588,
adapted with Alleluias by WILLIAM H. MONK, 1861

With dignity

Al - le - lu - ia! Al - le - lu - ia! Al - le - lu - ia!

Org. *p*

1 The strife is o'er, the bat - tle done, The vic - to -
2 The powers of death have done their worst, But Christ their
3 The three sad days are quick - ly sped, He ri - ses

ry of life is won; The song of tri - umph
le - gions hath dis - persed: Let shout of ho - ly
glo - rious from the dead: All glo - ry to our

has be - gun. Al - le - lu - ia!
joy out - burst. Al - le - lu - ia!
ris - en Head! Al - le - lu - ia! A - men.

4 He closed the yawning gates of hell,
The bars from heav'n's high portals fell;
Let hymns of praise his triumphs tell!
Alleluia!

5 Lord! by the stripes which wounded thee,
From death's dread sting thy servants free,
That we may live and sing to thee.
Alleluia! Amen.

Latin, pub. Cologne, 1695; Tr. FRANCIS POTT, 1861, *alt.*

Easter

87. 87. D.

LUX EOI

ARTHUR SEYMOUR SULLIVAN, 1874

Joyously

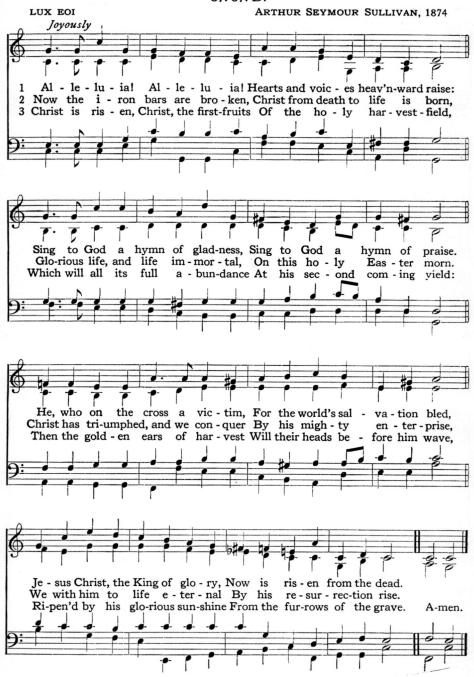

1 Al - le - lu - ia! Al - le - lu - ia! Hearts and voic - es heav'n-ward raise:
2 Now the i - ron bars are bro - ken, Christ from death to life is born,
3 Christ is ris - en, Christ, the first-fruits Of the ho - ly har - vest - field,

Sing to God a hymn of glad-ness, Sing to God a hymn of praise.
Glo-rious life, and life im - mor - tal, On this ho - ly Eas - ter morn.
Which will all its full a - bun-dance At his sec - ond com - ing yield:

He, who on the cross a vic - tim, For the world's sal - va - tion bled,
Christ has tri-umphed, and we con - quer By his migh - ty en - ter - prise,
Then the gold - en ears of har - vest Will their heads be - fore him wave,

Je - sus Christ, the King of glo - ry, Now is ris - en from the dead.
We with him to life e - ter - nal By his re - sur - rec-tion rise.
Ri-pen'd by his glo-rious sun-shine From the fur-rows of the grave. A-men.

Easter

4 Christ is risen, we are risen!
   Shed upon us heav'nly grace,
Rain and dew and gleams of glory
   From the brightness of thy face;
That, with hearts in heaven dwelling,
   We on earth may fruitful be,
And by angel hands be gathered,
   And be ever, Lord, with thee.

5 Alleluia! Alleluia!
   Glory be to God on high;
Alleluia to the Saviour
   Who has won the victory;
Alleluia to the Spirit,
   Fount of love and sanctity;
Alleluia! Alleluia!
   To the Triune Majesty.   Amen.

CHRISTOPHER WORDSWORTH, 1872

Alternative Tune, HYFRYDOL, No. 347

93

EISENACH

87. 87. 88

JOHANN HERMANN SCHEIN, 1629

With joyful dignity

1 Thou hal-lowed cho-sen morn of praise, That best and great-est shin-est:
2 Come, let us taste the vine's new fruit, For heav'n-ly joy pre-par-ing;

Fair Eas-ter, queen of all the days, Of sea-sons, best, di-vin-est!
To-day the branch-es with the root In re-sur-rec-tion shar-ing:

Christ rose from death; and we a-dore For ev-er and for ev-er-more.
Whom as true God our hymns a-dore For ev-er and for ev-er-more.

ST. JOHN of Damascus, *8th cent.; Tr.* J. M. NEALE, 1862, *alt.*

Easter
76. 76. D.

GAUDEAMUS PARITER
With vigor

J. HORNE, 1544

1 Come, ye faith-ful, raise the strain   Of   tri-umph-ant   glad - ness;
2 'Tis the spring of souls to - day;   Christ hath burst his   pris - on,

God hath brought his   Is - ra - el   In - to   joy from sad - ness;
And from three days' sleep in   death   As   a   sun hath ris - en;

Loosed from   Pha-raoh's bit - ter   yoke   Ja - cob's sons and daugh - ters;
All   the   win - ter of   our   sins, Long and dark, is   fly - ing

Led them with un-moisten'd foot Through the Red Sea   wa - ters.
From his light, to whom we give   Laud and praise un - dy - ing.   A - men.

3 Now the queen of seasons, bright
    With the day of splendor,
With the royal feast of feasts,
    Comes its joy to render;
Comes to glad Jerusalem,
    Who with true affection
Welcomes in unwearied strains
    Jesus' resurrection.

4 Neither might the gates of death,
    Nor the tomb's dark portal,
Nor the watchers, nor the seal
    Hold thee as a mortal:
But to-day amidst thine own
    Thou didst stand, bestowing
That thy peace which evermore
    Passeth human knowing.   Amen.

ST. JOHN of Damascus, *8th cent.*; *Tr.* J. M. NEALE, 1853

Easter

76. 76. D.

ST. KEVIN   ARTHUR SEYMOUR SULLIVAN, 1872

With animation

3 Now the queen of seasons, bright
   With the day of splendor,
With the royal feast of feasts,
   Comes its joy to render;
Comes to glad Jerusalem,
   Who with true affection
Welcomes in unwearied strains
   Jesus' resurrection.

4 Neither might the gates of death,
   Nor the tomb's dark portal,
Nor the watchers, nor the seal
   Hold thee as a mortal:
But to-day amidst thine own
   Thou didst stand, bestowing
That thy peace which evermore
   Passeth human knowing. Amen.

ST. JOHN of Damascus, *8th cent.; Tr.* J. M. NEALE, 1853

Easter

77. 77, with Alleluia

NASSAU

Dresden, 1694

With movement

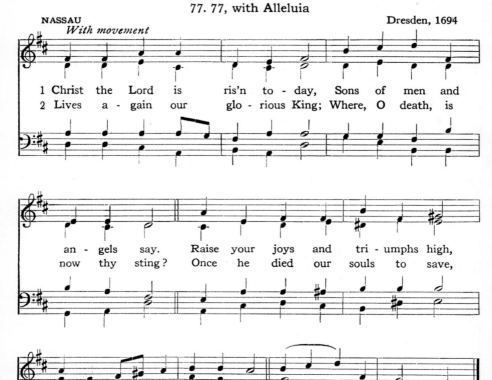

1 Christ the Lord is ris'n to - day, Sons of men and
2 Lives a - gain our glo - rious King; Where, O death, is

an - gels say. Raise your joys and tri - umphs high,
now thy sting? Once he died our souls to save,

Sing, ye heav'ns, and earth re - ply, Al - - le - lu - ia!
Where thy vic - to - ry, O grave? Al - - le - lu - ia!

3 Love's redeeming work is done,
  Fought the fight; the battle won.
  Death in vain forbids him rise;
  Christ has opened paradise.
          Alleluia!

4 Soar we now where Christ has led,
  Following our exalted Head;
  Made like him, like him we rise,
  Ours the cross, the grave, the skies.
          Alleluia!

CHARLES WESLEY, 1739, *alt.*

77. 77, with Alleluias

GWALCHMAI
With movement

JOSEPH DAVID JONES, 1868

1 Christ the Lord is ris'n to - day, Al - le - lu - ia!
2 Lives a - gain our glo - rious King; Al - le - lu - ia!
3 Love's re - deem - ing work is done, Al - le - lu - ia!

Sons of men and an - gels say. Al - le - lu - ia!
Where, O death, is now thy sting? Al - le - lu - ia!
Fought the fight, the bat - tle won. Al - le - lu - ia!

Raise your joys and tri - umphs high, Al - le - lu - ia!
Once he died our souls to save, Al - le - lu - ia!
Death in vain for - bids him rise; Al - le - lu - ia!

Sing, ye heav'ns, and earth re - ply, Al - le - lu - ia!
Where thy vic - to - ry, O grave? Al - le - lu - ia!
Christ has o - pen'd par - a - dise. Al - le - lu - ia!

4 Soar we now where Christ has led, Alleluia!
Following our exalted Head; Alleluia!
Made like him, like him we rise, Alleluia!
Ours the cross, the grave, the skies. Alleluia!

Easter

76. 76. D.

ELLACOMBE
Boldly

Wirtemberg, 1784

1 The day of re - sur - rec - tion! Earth, tell it out a - broad;
2 Our hearts be pure from e - vil, That we may see a - right

The Pass - o - ver of glad - ness, The Pass - o - ver of God.
The Lord in rays e - ter - nal Of re - sur - rec - tion light;

From death to life e - ter - nal, From earth un - to the sky,
And, list - 'ning to his ac - cents, May hear so calm and plain

Our Christ hath brought us o - ver With hymns of vic - to - ry.
His own "All hail!" and, hear - ing, May raise the vic - tor strain.

3 Now let the heav'ns be joyful,
    Let earth her song begin,
The round world keep high triumph,
    And all that is therein;
Let all things seen and unseen
    Their notes together blend,
For Christ the Lord is risen,
    Our joy that hath no end.

ST. JOHN of Damascus, *8th cent.; Tr.* JOHN MASON NEALE, 1853

Easter
76. 76. D.

ALL HALLOWS

GEORGE C. MARTIN, 1892

In unison, triumphantly

1 The day of re - sur - rec - tion! Earth, tell it out a - broad;
2 Our hearts be pure from e - vil, That we may see a - right

The Pass - o - ver of glad - ness, The Pass - o - ver of God.
The Lord in rays e - ter - nal Of re - sur - rec - tion light;

From death to life e - ter - nal, From earth un - to the sky,
And, list - 'ning to his ac - cents, May hear so calm and plain

In harmony

Our Christ hath brought us o - ver With hymns of vic - to - ry.
His own "All hail!" and, hear - ing, May raise the vic - tor strain.

Small notes, org.

Easter

Irregular

VICTIMAE PASCHALI
Lightly, with flowing rhythm

Plainsong Sequence, Mode I,
ascribed to WIPO, c. 1030

Full choir

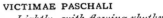

1 Chris-tians, to the Pas-chal vic-tim Of - fer your thankful prais - es!

Women and boys

2 A lamb the sheep re-deemeth: Christ, who on-ly is sin-less, Re-con-cil-eth

Full choir

sin-ners to the Fa-ther. 3 Death and life have contended In that combat stu-

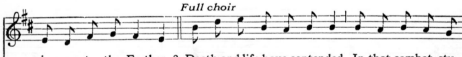

Easter

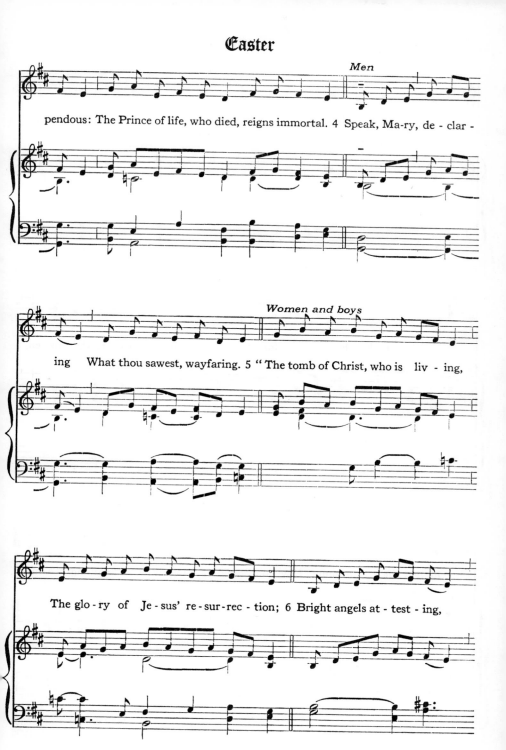

pendous: The Prince of life, who died, reigns immortal. 4 Speak, Ma-ry, de - clar -

ing What thou sawest, wayfaring. 5 "The tomb of Christ, who is liv - ing,

The glo - ry of Je - sus' re - sur - rec - tion; 6 Bright angels at - test - ing,

Easter

The shroud and nap-kin rest-ing. 7 Yea, Christ my hope is a - ris - en:

To Gal - i - lee he goes be - fore you." 8 Christ in-deed from death is ris - en,

Full Choir

Our new life ob-taining. Have mercy, vic-tor King, ev - er reign-ing! A-men.

rit.

Ascribed to WIPO, c. 1030;
Tr. from The English Hymnal, 1906

98 **Easter**

L. M.

PUER NOBIS
Unison, in flowing style

Adapted by MICHAEL PRAETORIUS, 1609,
har. by GEORGE R. WOODWARD, 1904

1 That Eas - ter Day with joy was bright, The sun shone
2 His ris - en flesh with ra - diance glowed; His wound - ed
3 O Je - sus, King of gen - tle - ness, Do thou thy -
4 O Lord of all, with us a - bide In this our
5 All praise, O ris - en Lord, we give To thee, who,

out with fair - er light, When, to their long - ing eyes re -
hands and feet he showed; Those scars their sol - emn wit - ness
self our hearts pos - sess That we may give thee all our
joy - ful Eas - ter - tide; From ev - 'ry wea - pon death can
dead, a - gain dost live; To God the Fa - ther e - qual

stored, The a - pos - tles saw their ris - en Lord.
gave That Christ was ris - en from the grave.
days The will - ing trib - ute of our praise.
wield Thine own re - deemed for ev - er shield.
praise, And God the Ho - ly Ghost, we raise. A - men.

Latin, 5th cent.; Hymnal Version, 1939

Easter

888, with Alleluia

O FILII ET FILIAE

French Melody, 15th cent.;
Solesmes Version, Mode II,
harmonized by W. D., 1918

Before the first stanza

Al - le - lu - ia! Al - le - lu - ia! Al - le - lu - ia!

In unison, with vigor

1 O sons and daugh - ters, let us sing! The King of heav'n, the
2 That Eas - ter morn, at break of day, The faith - ful wo - men
3 An an - gel clad in white they see, Who sat, and spake un -

glo - rious King, *O'er death to - day rose tri - umph - ing. Al - le - lu - ia!
went their way To seek the tomb where Je - sus lay. Al - le - lu - ia!
to the three, "Your Lord doth go to Gal - i - lee." Al - le - lu - ia!

*On the First Sunday after Easter and on the Feast of St. Thomas, read "O'er
death and hell rose triumphing."

Easter

After the last stanza

Al - le - lu - ia!   Al - le - lu - ia!   Al - le - lu - ia!

4 That night the apostles met in fear;
Amidst them came their Lord most dear,
And said, " My peace be on all here."
     Alleluia!

†5 When Thomas first the tidings heard,
How they had seen the risen Lord,
He doubted the disciples' word.
     Alleluia!

†6 " My piercèd side, O Thomas, see;
My hands, my feet, I show to thee;
Not faithless, but believing be."
     Alleluia!

†7 No longer Thomas then denied,
He saw the feet, the hands, the side;
" Thou art my Lord and God," he cried.
     Alleluia!

8 How blest are they who have not seen,
And yet whose faith has constant been,
For they eternal life shall win.
     Alleluia!

9 On this most holy day of days,
To God your hearts and voices raise,
In laud, and jubilee, and praise.
     Alleluia!

JEAN TISSERAND, *15th cent.;* Tr. JOHN MASON NEALE, 1852

†*Appropriate with stanza 1 for First Sunday after Easter*

Easter
S. M.

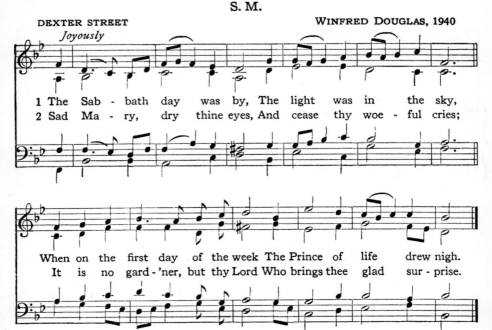

DEXTER STREET   WINFRED DOUGLAS, 1940

Joyously

1 The Sab-bath day was by, The light was in the sky,
2 Sad Ma-ry, dry thine eyes, And cease thy woe-ful cries;

When on the first day of the week The Prince of life drew nigh.
It is no gard-'ner, but thy Lord Who brings thee glad sur-prise.

3   Simon, thy Lord knows all;
        He doth forgive thy fall,
    And sends thee forth to feed the sheep
        That heed the Shepherd's call.

4   So did the Lord draw near
        To his disciples dear,
    When he came back from death and hell,
        And to them did appear.

5   Blest were the eyes of yore
        That saw their Friend once more,
    And blessèd we, who have not seen,
        But love him and adore.

HOWARD CHANDLER ROBBINS, 1929

By permission of the author

Also the following:

101 Rogation
C. M. D

KINGSFOLD

Traditional English Melody,
arr. by R. VAUGHAN WILLIAMS, 1906

With spirit

1 O Je-sus, crowned with all re-nown, Since thou the earth hast trod,
2 Lord, in their change, let frost and heat, And winds and dews be giv'n;
3 That we may feed the poor a-right, And, gath-'ring round thy throne,

Thou reign-est, and by thee come down Henceforth the gifts of God.
All fos-tering power, all in-fluence sweet, Breathe from the bounteous heav'n.
Here, in the ho-ly an-gels' sight, Re-pay thee of thine own:

Thine is the health and thine the wealth That in our halls a-bound,
At-tem-per fair with gen-tle air The sun-shine and the rain,
That we may praise thee all our days, And with the Fa-ther's Name,

And thine the beau-ty and the joy With which the years are crowned.
That kind-ly earth with time-ly birth May yield her fruits a-gain:
And with the Ho-ly Spi-rit's gifts, The Sa-viour's love pro-claim. A-men.

EDWARD WHITE BENSON, 1860, alt.

Also the following:
497 O God of Bethel, by whose hand
138 We plow the fields, and scatter

102 Ascension

Irregular, with Refrain

SALVE FESTA DIES

R. VAUGHAN WILLIAMS, 1906

In unison, with vigor

† *Refrain* Hail thee, fes-tiv - al day! blest day that art hallowed for ev - er;

1st time | 2nd time

Day when the Christ as-cends, high in the hea - vens to reign. reign.

Women and boys

2 He who was nailed to the cross is Lord and the rul - er of all men;
4 God the All - Fa-ther, the Lord, who rul - est the earth and the hea - vens,
6 Spi - rit of life and of power, now flow in us, fount of our be - ing,

† *The choir sings the Refrain first; then all repeat it*

Ascension

Repeat Refrain

All things cre - a - ted on earth sing to the glo - ry of God:
Guard us from harm with - out, cleanse us from e - vil with - in:
Light that dost light-en all, life that in all dost a - bide:

Men

3 Dai - ly the love - li - ness grows, a - dorned with the glo - ry of blos - som;
5 Je - sus the health of the world, en - light - en our minds, thou Re-deem - er,
7 Praise to the Giv - er of good! Thou Love who art au - thor of con - cord,

Repeat Refrain

Hea - ven her gates un - bars, fling - ing her in - crease of light:
Son of the Fa - ther su - preme, on - ly - be - got - ten of God:
Pour out thy balm on our souls, or - der our ways in thy peace:

VENANTIUS HONORIUS FORTUNATUS, 530–609

From Enlarged Songs of Praise, by permission of the Oxford University Press. Translation altered by special arrangement with the Oxford University Press.

103 *First Tune* 𝕬𝖘𝖈𝖊𝖓𝖘𝖎𝖔𝖓

87. 87. D.

IN BABILONE†

Traditional Dutch Melody
harmonized by W. D., 1918

With breadth

1 See the Conqu'ror mounts in triumph; See the King in roy - al state,
2 He who on the cross did suf - fer, He who from the grave a - rose,
3 Thou hast raised our hu - man na - ture On the clouds to God's right hand:

Rid - ing on the clouds, his char - iot, To his heav'n-ly pal - ace gate!
He has vanquished sin and Sa - tan; He by death has spoiled his foes.
There we sit in heav'n-ly pla - ces, There with thee in glo - ry stand.

Hark! the choirs of an - gel voic - es Joy - ful al - le - lu - ias sing,
While he lifts his hands in blessing, He is part-ed from his friends;
Je - sus reigns, a-dored by an-gels; Man with God is on the throne;

And the por-tals high are lift - ed To re - ceive their heav'n-ly King.
While their ea - ger eyes be - hold him, He up - on the clouds as-cends.
Migh-ty Lord, in thine as - cen-sion, We by faith be - hold our own. A-men.

CHRISTOPHER WORDSWORTH, 1862, *alt.*

†*Another harmonization, No. 357*

103 *Second Tune* 𝕬𝖘𝖈𝖊𝖓𝖘𝖎𝖔𝖓
87. 87. D.

REX GLORIAE

With movement

HENRY SMART, 1868

1 See the Con-qu'ror mounts in tri-umph; See the King in roy - al state,
2 He who on the cross did suf - fer, He who from the grave a - rose,
3 Thou hast raised our hu - man na - ture On the clouds to God's right hand:

Rid - ing on the clouds, his char - iot, To his heav'n-ly pal - ace gate!
He has vanquished sin and Sa - tan; He by death has spoiled his foes.
There we sit in heav'n-ly pla - ces, There with thee in glo - ry stand.

Hark! the choirs of an - gel voic - es Joy - ful al - le - lu - ias sing,
While he lifts his hands in bless - ing, He is part - ed from his friends;
Je - sus reigns, a - dored by an - gels; Man with God is on the throne;

And the por-tals high are lift - ed To re-ceive their heav'n-ly King.
While their ea - ger eyes be-hold him, He up - on the clouds as-cends.
Migh - ty Lord, in thine as - cen-sion, We by faith be-hold our own. A-men.

CHRISTOPHER WORDSWORTH, 1862, *alt.*

104 *First Tune*   𝕬𝖘𝖈𝖊𝖓𝖘𝖎𝖔𝖓

77. 77, with Alleluias

ASCENSION   WILLIAM HENRY MONK, 1861

Triumphantly

1 Hail the day that sees him rise,
2 There the glo - rious tri - umph waits; Al - le - lu - ia!
3 See! he lifts his hands a - bove;

Glo - rious to his na - tive skies;
Lift your heads, e - ter - nal gates! Al - le - lu - ia!
See! he shows the prints of love:

Christ, a - while to mor - tals giv'n,
Wide un - fold the ra - diant scene; Al - le - lu - ia!
Hark! his gra - cious lips be - stow,

En - ters now the high - est heav'n!
Take the King of glo - ry in! Al - le - lu - ia! A-men.
Bless - ings on his Church be - low.

4 Lord beyond our mortal sight, Alleluia!
   Raise our hearts to reach thy height, Alleluia!
   There thy face unclouded see, Alleluia!
   Find our heav'n of heav'ns in thee.   Alleluia!   Amen.

CHARLES WESLEY, 1739, *alt.*

Ascension

77. 77, with Alleluias

LLANFAIR

Triumphantly

Melody, ROBERT WILLIAMS, 1817,
har. by JOHN ROBERTS, 1837

1 Hail the day that sees him rise,
Glo-rious to his na-tive skies;
Christ, a-while to mor-tals giv'n,
En-ters now the high-est heav'n! Al - le - lu - ia! A-men.

2 There the glo-rious tri-umph waits; Al - le - lu - ia!
Lift your heads, e-ter-nal gates! Al - le - lu - ia!
Wide un-fold the ra-diant scene; Al - le - lu - ia!
Take the King of glo-ry in! Al - le - lu - ia!

3 See! he lifts his hands a-bove;
See! he shows the prints of love:
Hark! his gra-cious lips be-stow,
Bless-ings on his Church be-low.

In unison

4 Lord beyond our mortal sight, Alleluia!
Raise our hearts to reach thy height, Alleluia!
There thy face unclouded see, Alleluia!
Find our heav'n of heav'ns in thee. Alleluia! Amen.

CHARLES WESLEY, 1739, *alt.*

105

Ascension
87. 87. 47

CORONAE

WILLIAM H. MONK, 1871

With exultation

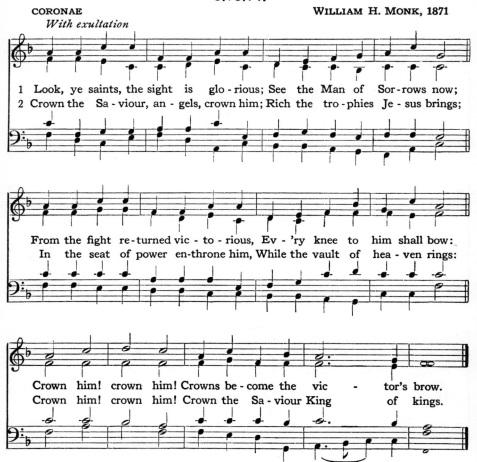

1 Look, ye saints, the sight is glo-rious; See the Man of Sor-rows now;
2 Crown the Sa-viour, an-gels, crown him; Rich the tro-phies Je-sus brings;

From the fight re-turned vic-to-rious, Ev-'ry knee to him shall bow:
In the seat of power en-throne him, While the vault of hea-ven rings:

Crown him! crown him! Crowns be-come the vic - tor's brow.
Crown him! crown him! Crown the Sa-viour King of kings.

3 Sinners in derision crowned him,
   Mocking thus Messiah's claim;
Saints and angels throng around him,
   Own his title, praise his Name:
      Crown him! crown him!
   Spread abroad the victor's fame!

4 Hark! those bursts of acclamation!
   Hark! those loud triumphant chords!
Jesus takes the highest station;
   O what joy the sight affords!
      Crown him! crown him
   King of kings, and Lord of lords.

THOMAS KELLY, 1809

Ascension
C. M.

ST. MAGNUS

JEREMIAH CLARK, 1709

In moderate time

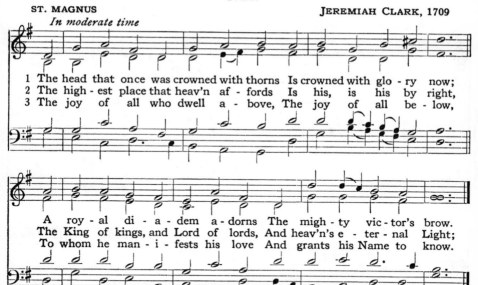

1 The head that once was crowned with thorns Is crowned with glo - ry now;
2 The high - est place that heav'n af - fords Is his, is his by right,
3 The joy of all who dwell a - bove, The joy of all be - low,

A roy - al di - a - dem a - dorns The migh - ty vic - tor's brow.
The King of kings, and Lord of lords, And heav'n's e - ter - nal Light;
To whom he man - i - fests his love And grants his Name to know.

4 To them the cross with all its shame,
    With all its grace is giv'n;
Their name, an everlasting name;
    Their joy, the joy of heav'n.

5 They suffer with their Lord below,
    They reign with him above,
Their profit and their joy to know
    The mystery of his love.

6 The cross he bore is life and health,
    Though shame and death to him:
His people's hope, his people's wealth,
    Their everlasting theme.

THOMAS KELLY, 1820

Also the following:

Whitsunday

Irregular, with Refrain

SALVE FESTA DIES

R. VAUGHAN WILLIAMS, 1906

In unison, with vigor

† *Refrain* Hail thee, fes-tiv - al day! blest day that art hallowed for ev - er;

Day where-on God from heav'n shone in the world with his grace. grace.

1st time | 2nd time

Women and boys

2 He who was nailed to the cross   is Lord and the rul - er of all   men;
4 God the All - Fa-ther, the Lord,   who rul - est the earth and the hea - vens,
6 Spi - rit of life and of power,   now flow in us, fount of our be - ing,

Music by permission of the Oxford University Press
† *The choir sings the Refrain first; then all repeat it*

Whitsunday

Repeat Refrain

All things cre - a - ted on earth sing to the glo - ry of God:
Guard us from harm with - out, cleanse us from e - vil with - in:
Light that dost light-en all, life that in all dost a - bide:

Men

3 Lo, in the like-ness of fire, on them that a - wait his ap-pear - ing,
5 Je - sus the health of the world, en - light - en our minds, thou Re-deem - er,
7 Praise to the Giv - er of good! Thou Love who art au - thor of con - cord,

Repeat Refrain

He, whom the Lord had fore-told, sud-den-ly, swift - ly, de - scends:
Son of the Fa - ther su-preme, on - ly - be - got - ten of God:
Pour out thy balm on our souls, or - der our ways in thy peace:

VENANTIUS HONORIUS FORTUNATUS, 530–609

From Enlarged Songs of Praise, by permission of the Oxford University Press. Translation altered by special arrangement with the Oxford University Press.

Whitsunday
L. M.

VENI CREATOR

Sarum Plainsong, Mode VIII

In unison, smoothly and fluently

1 O come, Cre - a - tor Spi - rit, come And make with - in our
2 O Gift of God, most high, thy name Is Com - fort - er; whom
3 The sev'n - fold gift of grace is thine, Thou fin - ger of the

souls thy home; Sup - ply thy grace and heav'n - ly aid
we ac - claim The fount of life, the fire of love,
hand di - vine; The Fa - ther's prom - ise true, to teach

To fill the hearts which thou hast made.
The soul's a - noint - ing from a - bove.
Our earth - ly tongues thy heav'n - ly speech. A - men.

Whitsunday

4 Thy light to every sense impart;
Pour forth thy love in every heart;
Our weakened flesh do thou restore
To strength and courage evermore.

5 Drive far away our spirit's foe,
Thine own abiding peace bestow;
If thou dost go before as guide,
No evil can our steps betide.

6 Through thee may we the Father learn,
And know the Son, and thee discern,
Who art of both; and thus adore
In perfect faith for evermore. Amen.

Latin, 9th cent.; Hymnal Version, 1939

108 *Second Tune*   L. M.

GRACE CHURCH

IGNAZ J. PLEYEL, 1815

With quiet dignity

1 O come, Cre - a - tor Spi - rit, come And make with - in our
2 O Gift of God, most high, thy name Is Com - fort - er; whom
3 The sev'n-fold gift of grace is thine, Thou fin - ger of the

souls thy home; Sup - ply thy grace and heav'n - ly aid
we ac - claim The fount of life, the fire of love,
hand di - vine; The Fa - ther's prom - ise true, to teach

To fill the hearts which thou hast made.
The soul's a - noint - ing from a - bove.
Our earth - ly tongues thy heav'n - ly speech. A - men.

109 *First Tune* 𝕎𝕙𝕚𝕥𝕤𝕦𝕟𝕕𝕒𝕪
77. 77. 77

THE GOLDEN SEQUENCE

Plainsong Sequence, Mode I,
11th century

In unison, lightly and quickly

† 1 Come, thou Ho - ly Spi - rit, come! And from thy ce - les - tial home
Come, thou Fa - ther of the poor! Come, thou source of all our store!

Shed a ray of light di - vine! 2 Thou, of com-fort - ers the best;
Come, with-in our bo - soms shine! In our la - bor, rest most sweet;

Thou, the soul's most wel - come guest; Sweet re - fresh-ment here be - low;
Grate-ful cool - ness in the heat; Sol - ace in the midst of woe.

† *The stanzas may be sung by alternating groups, changing at each repeat mark*

Whitsunday

3 O most bless - ed Light di - vine, Shine with - in these hearts of thine,
Where thou art not, man hath naught, Noth-ing good in deed or thought,

And our in-most be - ing fill! 4 Heal our wounds, our strength re-new;
Noth - ing free from taint of ill. Bend the stub - born heart and will;

On our dry - ness pour thy dew; Wash the stains of guilt a - way:
Melt the fro - zen, warm the chill; Guide the steps that go a - stray.

109 *First Tune, continued*

5 On the faith-ful, who a - dore And con - fess thee, ev - er - more
Give them vir - tue's sure re - ward; Give them thy sal - va - tion, Lord;

Full choir

In thy sev'n - fold gift de - scend;
Give them joys that nev - er end. A - men.

Latin, 12th cent.; Tr. EDWARD CASWALL, *alt.*

109 *Second Tune* 77. 77. 77

VENI SANCTE SPIRITUS SAMUEL WEBBE, 1782

With movement

1 Come, thou Ho - ly Spi - rit, come! And from thy ce - les - tial home
2 Thou, of com - fort - ers the best; Thou, the soul's most wel - come guest;

Whitsunday

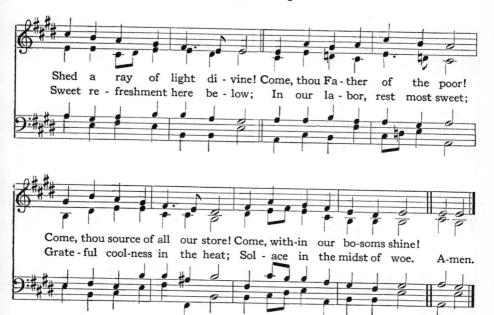

Shed a ray of light di-vine! Come, thou Fa-ther of the poor!
Sweet re-freshment here be-low; In our la-bor, rest most sweet;

Come, thou source of all our store! Come, with-in our bo-soms shine!
Grate-ful cool-ness in the heat; Sol-ace in the midst of woe. A-men.

3 O most blessèd Light divine,
   Shine within these hearts of thine,
      And our inmost being fill!
   Where thou art not, man hath naught,
   Nothing good in deed or thought,
      Nothing free from taint of ill.

4 Heal our wounds, our strength renew;
   On our dryness pour thy dew;
      Wash the stains of guilt away:
   Bend the stubborn heart and will;
   Melt the frozen, warm the chill;
      Guide the steps that go astray.

5 On the faithful, who adore
   And confess thee, evermore
      In thy sev'nfold gift descend;
   Give them virtue's sure reward;
   Give them thy salvation, Lord;
      Give them joys that never end.   Amen.

Latin, 12th cent.; Tr. EDWARD CASWALL, *alt.*

110

𝔚𝔥𝔦𝔱𝔰𝔲𝔫𝔡𝔞𝔶
88. 887

COWLEY

Majestically

WALTER S. VALE, 1935

1 Hail thee! Spi-rit, Lord e-ter-nal, Love om-ni-po-tent, su-
2 Hail, free Spi-rit, all tran-scend-ing, Yet to mor-tals con-de-
3 Gra-cious Spi-rit, light dif-fus-ing, Breath of life in man in-

per-nal; Hon-or meet to thee we ren-der, Ven-er-a-tion
scend-ing! At this fes-tal tide we laud thee, Praise and hom-age
fus-ing; Bless-ed are the souls that know thee, Joy and peace thy

Refrain

deep and ten-der:
we ac-cord thee: Hail, Lord God the Ho-ly Ghost! A-men.
chil-dren owe thee:

4 Truth eternal, wise Creator,
Fallen man's illuminator!
Light of reason, hope, ambition,
Fire of love and true contrition:
    Hail, Lord God the Holy Ghost!

5 Spirit, man for sin reproving,
Wayward hearts most gently moving;
When by sin we sorely grieve thee,
Naught but pleading love perceive we:
    Hail, Lord God the Holy Ghost!

Whitsunday

6 Purest Spirit, sanctifying
  Quickened souls, on grace relying;
  Cleanse, renew thy creatures lowly,
  Guide, inspire, and make us holy:
     Hail, Lord God the Holy Ghost!

7 Spirit, Comforter indwelling,
  Mightiest earthly aid excelling;
  Lord, who in thy Church abidest,
  There to us thyself confidest:
     Hail, Lord God the Holy Ghost!

8 Paraclete, anointing, sealing,
  Secret things of God revealing;
  Souls by inner light transforming,
  Heart and will to Christ conforming:
     Hail, Lord God the Holy Ghost!

9 Lord, to thee who all sustainest,
  God, with Father, Son, who reignest,
  Glory be from all creation,
  Worship, love, and adoration:
     Hail, Lord God the Holy Ghost! Amen.

SYDNEY JAMES WALLIS, 1934, alt.

111   L. M.

MELCOMBE   SAMUEL WEBBE, 1782
Deliberately

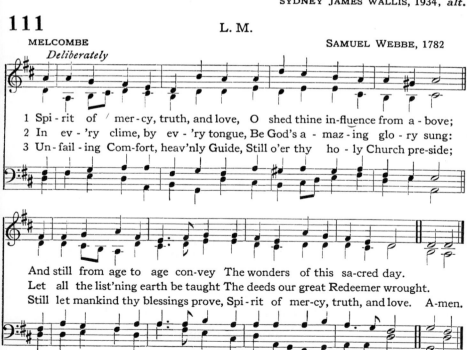

1 Spi-rit of mer-cy, truth, and love, O shed thine in-flu-ence from a-bove;
2 In ev-'ry clime, by ev-'ry tongue, Be God's a-maz-ing glo-ry sung:
3 Un-fail-ing Com-fort, heav'n-ly Guide, Still o'er thy ho-ly Church pre-side;

And still from age to age con-vey The wonders of this sa-cred day.
Let all the list'ning earth be taught The deeds our great Redeemer wrought.
Still let mankind thy blessings prove, Spi-rit of mer-cy, truth, and love. A-men.

Anonymous, pub. London, 1774, alt.

Whitsunday

376 Come down, O Love divine
378 Come, gracious Spirit, heavenly Dove
218 Come, Holy Ghost, Creator blest
217 Come, Holy Ghost, our souls inspire
369 Come, Holy Spirit, heavenly Dove
371 Creator Spirit, by whose aid
379 Gracious Spirit, Holy Ghost
377 Holy Spirit, Truth divine
372 O Holy Spirit, God
374 O King enthroned on high
256 O Spirit of the living God
368 Our blest Redeemer, ere he breathed
370 Spirit divine, attend our prayers

Trinity Sunday

274 Ancient of Days, who sittest throned in **glory**
271 Come, thou almighty King
267 Holy Father, great Creator
273 Holy God, we praise thy Name
270 Holy, Holy, Holy, Lord
266 Holy, Holy, Holy! Lord God Almighty
268 I bind unto myself to-day
567 Lead us, heavenly Father, lead us
269 Round the Lord in glory seated
272 Thou, whose almighty word

SAINTS' DAYS AND HOLY DAYS

*Additional hymns will be found under the headings
of Apostles, Evangelists, Martyrs, and All Saints.*

St. Andrew
November 30

566 Jesus calls us; o'er the tumult

St. Thomas
December 21

99 O sons and daughters, let us sing (Stanzas 1, 5, 6, 7, 8)
98 That Easter Day with joy was bright (Stanzas 1, 2, 3)

St. Stephen
December 26

549 The Son of God goes forth to war

St. John Evangelist
December 27

437 They cast their nets in Galilee

Saints' Days and Holy Days
The Holy Innocents
December 28
C. M.

HOLY INNOCENTS

Brightly

D. VINCENT GRAY, 1941

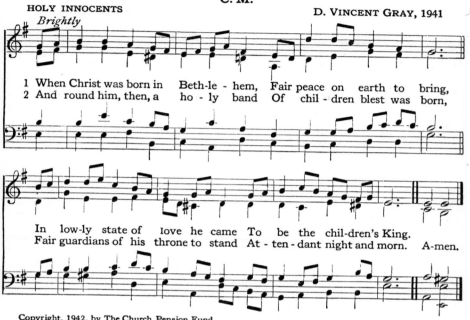

1 When Christ was born in Beth-le-hem, Fair peace on earth to bring,
2 And round him, then, a ho-ly band Of chil-dren blest was born,

In low-ly state of love he came To be the chil-dren's King.
Fair guardians of his throne to stand At-ten-dant night and morn. A-men.

Copyright, 1942, by The Church Pension Fund

3 And unto them this grace was giv'n
   A Saviour's name to own,
   And die for him who out of heav'n
   Had found on earth a throne.

4 O blessèd babes of Bethlehem,
   Who died to save our King,
   Ye share the martyrs' diadem,
   And in their anthem sing!

5 Your lips, on earth that never spake,
   Now sound the eternal word;
   And in the courts of love ye make
   Your children's voices heard.

6 Lord Jesus Christ, eternal Child,
   Make thou our childhood thine;
   That we with thee the meek and mild
   May share the love divine.   Amen.

By permission of the Oxford University Press

LAURENCE HOUSMAN, 1906

Also the following:
34 Unto us a boy is born

𝕿𝖍𝖊 𝕮𝖎𝖗𝖈𝖚𝖒𝖈𝖎𝖘𝖎𝖔𝖓

January 1

S. M.

ST. MICHAEL

With dignity

Melody by LOUIS BOURGEOIS, 1551,
adapted by WILLIAM CROTCH, 1836

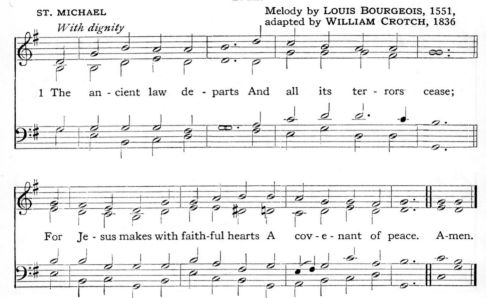

1 The an-cient law de-parts And all its ter-rors cease;

For Je-sus makes with faith-ful hearts A cov-e-nant of peace. A-men.

2 The Light of Light divine,
    True brightness undefiled,
He bears for us the shame of sin,
    A holy, spotless child.

3 To-day the Name is thine,
    At which we bend the knee;
They call thee Jesus, Child divine!
    Our Jesus deign to be. Amen.

SEBASTIEN BESNAULT, 1736;
Tr. Hymns Ancient and Modern, 1861

Also the following:

355 All hail the power of Jesus' Name
366 All praise to thee, for thou, O King divine
356 At the Name of Jesus
324 Conquering kings their titles take
  6 Creator of the stars of night (4 Stanzas)
342 Jesus, Name all names above (Stanza 1)
323 Jesus! Name of wondrous love
325 O for a thousand tongues to sing
349 O Saviour, precious Saviour
326 To the Name of our salvation

Conversion of St. Paul
January 25
76. 76. D.

MUNICH

In moderate time

Meiningen Gesangbuch, 1693

1 We sing the glo-rious con-quest Be-fore Da-mas-cus gate,
2 O glo-ry most ex-cel-ling That smote a-cross his path!

When Saul, the Church's spoil - er, Came breath-ing threats and hate;
O light that pierced and blind - ed The zea - lot in his wrath!

The rav-'ning wolf rushed for - ward Full ear - ly to the prey;
O voice that spake with - in him The calm, re-prov - ing word!

But lo! the Shep - herd met him, And bound him fast to - day.
O love that sought and held him The bond-man of his Lord! A-men.

3 O Wisdom ord'ring all things
   In order strong and sweet,
What nobler spoil was ever
   Cast at the Victor's feet?
What wiser master-builder
   E'er wrought at thine employ
Than he, till now so furious
   Thy building to destroy?

4 Lord, teach thy Church the lesson,
   Still in her darkest hour
Of weakness and of danger,
   To trust thy hidden power:
Thy grace by ways mysterious
   The wrath of man can bind,
And in thy boldest foeman
   Thy chosen saint can find.   Amen.

JOHN ELLERTON, 1871

115 $\mathfrak{Saints'}$ $\mathfrak{Days}$ $\mathfrak{and}$ $\mathfrak{Holy}$ $\mathfrak{Days}$

$\mathfrak{The}$ $\mathfrak{Purification}$

February 2

OLD HUNDRED TWENTIETH

Melody from THOMAS EST'S
Whole Book of Psalmes, 1592

66. 66. 66

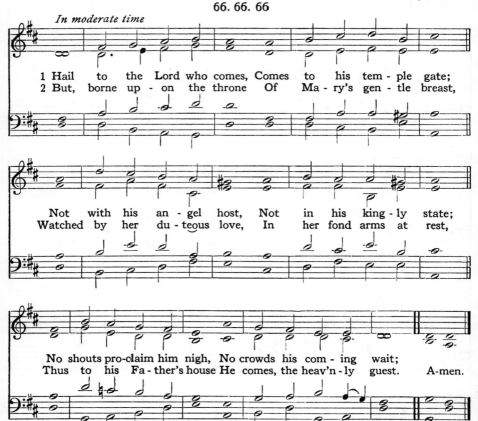

In moderate time

1 Hail to the Lord who comes, Comes to his tem-ple gate;
2 But, borne up-on the throne Of Ma-ry's gen-tle breast,

Not with his an-gel host, Not in his king-ly state;
Watched by her du-teous love, In her fond arms at rest,

No shouts pro-claim him nigh, No crowds his com-ing wait;
Thus to his Fa-ther's house He comes, the heav'n-ly guest. A-men.

3 There Joseph at her side
    In rev'rent wonder stands;
And, filled with holy joy,
    Old Simeon in his hands
Takes up the promised child,
    The glory of all lands.

4 O Light of all the earth,
    Thy children wait for thee!
Come to thy temples here,
    That we, from sin set free,
Before thy Father's face
    May all presented be! Amen.

JOHN ELLERTON, 1880, *alt*.

$\mathfrak{The}$ $\mathfrak{Purification}$

C. M.

BEDFORD
Moderately slow

WILLIAM WHEALL, 1723

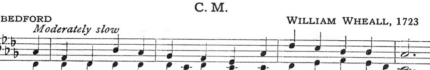
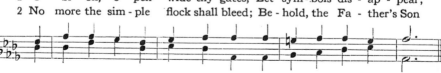

1 O Si - on, o - pen wide thy gates, Let sym - bols dis - ap - pear;
2 No more the sim - ple flock shall bleed; Be - hold, the Fa - ther's Son

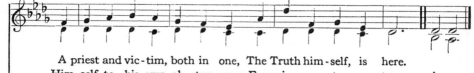

A priest and vic - tim, both in one, The Truth him - self, is here.
Him - self to his own al - tar comes For sin - ners to a - tone. A-men.

3 Conscious of hidden deity,
  The lowly virgin brings
Her new-born babe, with two young doves,
  Her humble offerings.

4 The aged Simeon sees at last
  His Lord, so long desired,
And Anna welcomes Israel's hope,
  With holy rapture fired.

5 But silent knelt the mother blest
  Of the yet silent Word,
And pond'ring all things in her heart,
  With speechless praise adored.

6 All glory to the Father be,
  All glory to the Son,
All glory, Holy Ghost, to thee,
  While endless ages run.   Amen.

JEAN BAPTISTE DE SANTEÜIL, 1680;
Tr. EDWARD CASWALL, 1849, *alt.*

$\mathfrak{St.}$ $\mathfrak{Matthias}$
February 24
136 Let us now our voices raise

Saints' Days and Holy Days
The Annunciation
March 25
87. 87. D.

PLEADING SAVIOUR
Somewhat slowly

Plymouth Collection,
New York, 1855

1 Sing of Ma - ry, pure and low - ly, Vir - gin - moth - er un - de - filed,
2 Sing of Je - sus, son of Ma - ry, In the home at Na - za - reth.

Sing of God's own Son most ho - ly, Who be - came her lit - tle child.
Toil and la - bor can - not wea - ry Love en - dur - ing un - to death.

Fair - est child of fair - est moth - er, God the Lord who came to earth,
Con - stant was the love he gave her, Though he went forth from her side,

Word made flesh, our ve - ry broth - er, Takes our na - ture by his birth.
Forth to preach, and heal, and suf - fer, Till on Cal - va - ry he died. A - men.

3 Glory be to God the Father;
   Glory be to God the Son;
   Glory be to God the Spirit;
   Glory to the Three in One.

From the heart of blessèd Mary,
   From all saints the song ascends,
And the Church the strain re-echoes
   Unto earth's remotest ends.   Amen.

From The Book of Common Praise

Anonymous, c. 1914

Saints' Days and Holy Days
The Annunciation

ST. GEORGE   S. M.   HENRY J. GAUNTLETT, 1848

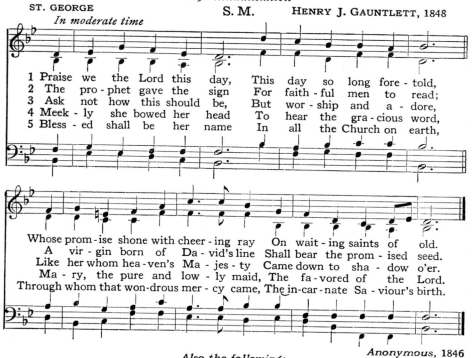

In moderate time

1 Praise we the Lord this day, This day so long fore-told,
2 The pro-phet gave the sign For faith-ful men to read;
3 Ask not how this should be, But wor-ship and a-dore,
4 Meek-ly she bowed her head To hear the gra-cious word,
5 Bless-ed shall be her name In all the Church on earth,

Whose prom-ise shone with cheer-ing ray On wait-ing saints of old.
A vir-gin born of Da-vid's line Shall bear the prom-ised seed.
Like her whom hea-ven's Ma-jes-ty Came down to sha-dow o'er.
Ma-ry, the pure and low-ly maid, The fa-vored of the Lord.
Through whom that won-drous mer-cy came, The in-car-nate Sa-viour's birth.

Anonymous, 1846

Also the following:

Saints' Days and Holy Days
St. James
July 25
132 The eternal gifts of Christ the King
The Transfiguration
August 6

119

L. M.

WAREHAM

WILLIAM KNAPP, 1738

In moderate time

1 O won - drous type! O vi - sion fair Of glo - ry
2 With Mo - ses and E - li - jah nigh The in - car - nate
3 With shin - ing face and bright ar - ray, Christ deigns to
4 And faith - ful hearts are raised on high By this great

that the Church may share, Which Christ up - on the moun - tain
Lord holds con - verse high; And from the cloud, the Ho - ly
man - i - fest to - day What glo - ry shall be theirs a -
vi - sion's mys - ter - y; For which in joy - ful strains we

shows, Where bright - er than the sun he glows!
One Bears rec - ord to the on - ly Son.
bove Who joy in God with per - fect love.
raise The voice of prayer, the hymn of praise. A - men.

5 O Father, with the eternal Son,
And Holy Spirit, ever One,
Vouchsafe to bring us by thy grace
To see thy glory face to face. Amen.

Latin, 15th cent.; Tr. J. M. NEALE, 1854, *alt.*

Also the following:

571 Not always on the mount may we
498 Where cross the crowded ways of life

Saints' Days and Holy Days

St. Bartholomew
August 24
135 Blessèd feasts of blessèd martyrs

St. Matthew
September 21
134 Come, pure hearts, in sweetest measure

St. Michael and All Angels
September 29

120   L. M.

ABENDS

Melody by
HERBERT S. OAKELEY, 1873

In flowing style

1 A-round the throne of God a band Of bright and glo-rious
2 Some wait a-round him rea-dy still To sing his praise and

an - gels stand; Sweet harps with - in their hands they hold,
do his will, And some, when he com - mands them, go

And on their heads are crowns of gold.
To guard his ser - vants here be - low. A - men.

3 Lord, give thine angels every day
Command to guard us on our way,
And bid them every evening keep
Their watch around us while we sleep.

4 So shall no wicked thing draw near
To do us harm or cause us fear;
And we shall dwell, when life is past,
With angels round thy throne at last. Amen.

JOHN MASON NEALE, 1842, *alt.*

St. Michael and All Angels

10 10. 10 10

TRISAGION   HENRY SMART, 1868

Brightly

1 Stars of the morn - ing, so glo - rious - ly bright, Filled with ce -
2 These are thy min - is - ters, these dost thou own, God of Sa -
3 These keep the guard a - mid Sa - lem's dear bowers, Thrones, prin - ci -

les - ti - al splen - dor and light, These that, where night nev - er
ba - oth, the near - est thy throne; These are thy mes - sen - gers,
pal - i - ties, vir - tues, and powers, Where, with the liv - ing ones,

fol - low - eth day, Raise the "Thrice Ho - ly" song ev - er and aye:
these dost thou send, Help of the help - less ones! man to de - fend.
mys - tic - al four, Cher - u - bim, ser - a - phim bow and a - dore.

*4 " Who like the Lord ? " thunders Michael the chief;
     Raphael, " the cure of God," comforteth grief;
     And, as at Nazareth, prophet of peace,
     Gabriel, " the light of God," bringeth release.

*5 Then, when the earth was first poised in mid space,
     Then, when the planets first sped on their race,
     Then, when were ended the six days' employ,
     Then all the sons of God shouted for joy.

6 Still let them succor us; still let them fight,
     Lord of angelic hosts, battling for right;
     Till, where their anthems they ceaselessly pour,
     We with the angels may bow and adore.

ST. JOSEPH the Hymnographer, *9th cent.; Tr.* J. M. NEALE, 1862, *alt.*

Saints' Days and Holy Days
St. Michael and All Angels
10 10. 10 10

SLANE

In unison, with movement

Traditional Irish Melody

1 An - gels and min - is - ters, spi - rits of grace, Friends of the
2 Mes - sen - gers clad in the swift-ness of light, Sub - tle as
3 Earth's myr - iad crea - tures live af - ter their kind, Dumb, in the
4 You do God's bid - ding, un - sha-ken and strong; We are dis -
5 We too shall join you as com-rades in grace, Here but a

chil - dren, be - hold-ing God's face, Mov - ing like thought to us
flame, and cre - a - tive in might, Helmed with the truth and with
life of the bo - dy con - fined; You are pure spi - rit, but
traught 'twixt the right and the wrong; Yet would we soar as the
lit - tle be - low you in place; Then, when we climb from our

through the be - yond, Mold - ed in beau - ty, and free from our bond!
cha - ri - ty shod, Wield - ing the wind of the pur-pose of God!
we here be - low, Linked in both or - ders, are tossed to and fro.
bird from the mesh, Freed from the weak-ness and won - der of flesh.
low - ness in worth, We too shall her - ald good will up - on earth.

By permission of the Oxford University Press

PERCY DEARMER, 1933

123 Saints' Days and Holy Days
St. Michael and All Angels

First Tune

11 11. 11 5

CHRISTE SANCTORUM

Sarum Plainsong, Mode I

With spirit

1 Christ, the fair glo - ry of the ho - ly an - gels, Ma - ker of all men, rul - er of all na - tions, Grant of thy mer - cy un - to us thy ser - vants Steps up to hea - ven.

2 Send thine arch - an - gel Mi-chael to our suc - cor: Peace-ma - ker bless - ed, may he ban - ish from us Striv - ing and ha - tred, so that for the peace - ful All things may pros - per.

3 Send thine arch - an - gel Ga - bri - el, the migh - ty; Her - ald of hea - ven, may he, from us mor - tals, Drive ev - 'ry e - vil, watch - ing o'er the tem - ples Where thou art wor-shipped.

4 Send from the hea - vens Ra-phael thine arch-an - gel, Health-bring-er bless - ed, aid-ing ev - 'ry suf - f'rer, That, in thy ser - vice, he may wise - ly guide us, Heal - ing and bless - ing.

5 May the blest moth - er of our Lord and Sa - viour, May the ce - les - tial com-pa - ny of an - gels, May the as - sem - bly of the saints in hea - ven, Help us to praise thee.

Saints' Days and Holy Days
St. Michael and All Angels

6 Father Almighty, Son, and Holy Spirit,
   God ever blessèd, hear our thankful praises;
   Thine is the glory which from all creation
   Ever ascendeth.   Amen.

ST. RABANUS MAURUS, 776–856; *Hymnal Version,* 1940

123 *Second Tune*

11 11. 11 5

COELITES PLAUDANT

Rouen Melody, 17th cent.

In unison, with dignity

1 Christ, the fair glo - ry of the ho - ly an - gels, Ma - ker of
2 Send thine arch - an - gel Mi - chael to our suc - cor: Peace - ma - ker
3 Send thine arch - an - gel Ga - bri - el, the migh - ty; Her - ald of
4 Send from the hea - vens Ra - phael thine arch - an - gel, Health-bring-er
5 May the blest moth - er of our Lord and Sa - viour, May the ce -

all men, rul - er of all na - tions, Grant of thy mer - cy
bless - ed, may he ban - ish from us Striv - ing and ha - tred,
hea - ven, may he, from us mor - tals, Drive ev - 'ry e - vil,
bless - ed, aid - ing ev - 'ry suf - f'rer, That, in thy ser - vice,
les - tial com - pa - ny of an - gels, May the as - sem - bly

un - to us thy ser - vants Steps up to hea - ven.
so that for the peace - ful All things may pros - per.
watch-ing o'er the tem - ples Where thou art wor - shipped.
he may wise - ly guide us, Heal - ing and bless - ing.
of the saints in hea - ven, Help us to praise thee. A-men.

Saints' Days and Holy Days

St. Michael and All Angels

Also the following:

472 Hark, hark my soul! angelic songs are swelling
197 Let all mortal flesh keep silence
600 Ye holy angels bright
599 Ye watchers and ye holy ones

St. Luke

October 18

516 Father, whose will is life and good
515 From thee all skill and science flow
360 Immortal Love, for ever full

St. Simon and St. Jude

October 28

124 For thy dear saints, O Lord

All Saints

November 1

124

S. M.

ST. GEORGE

HENRY J. GAUNTLETT, 1848

In moderate time

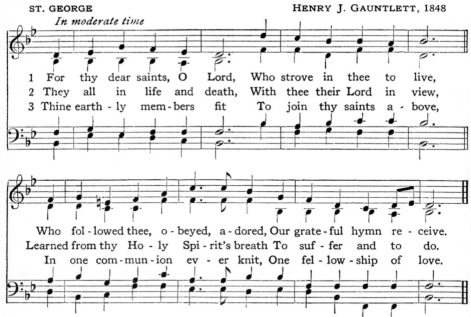

1 For thy dear saints, O Lord, Who strove in thee to live,
2 They all in life and death, With thee their Lord in view,
3 Thine earth-ly mem-bers fit To join thy saints a-bove,

Who fol-lowed thee, o-beyed, a-dored, Our grate-ful hymn re-ceive.
Learned from thy Ho-ly Spi-rit's breath To suf-fer and to do.
In one com-mun-ion ev-er knit, One fel-low-ship of love.

4 Jesus, thy Name we bless,
    And humbly pray that we
May follow them in holiness,
    Who lived and died for thee. Amen.

RICHARD MANT, 1837, *alt.*

A-men.

Saints' Days and Holy Days
All Saints
87. 87. D.

MOULTRIE

In moderate time

GERARD F. COBB, 1838–1904

1 Hark! the sound of ho - ly voic - es, Chant-ing at the crys - tal sea,
2 Pa - tri-arch, and ho - ly pro - phet, Who pre-pared the way for Christ,
3 March-ing with thy cross, their ban - ner, They have triumphed, fol - low - ing

Al - le - lu - ia, Al - le - lu - ia, Al - le - lu - ia, Lord, to thee!
King, a - pos - tle, saint, con-fes - sor, Mar - tyr and e - van - gel - ist,
Thee, the Cap - tain of sal - va - tion, Thee, their Sa - viour and their King.

Mul - ti - tude which none can num-ber Like the stars in glo - ry stands,
Saint - ly maid - en, god - ly ma - tron, Wi - dows who have watched to prayer,
Glad - ly, Lord, with thee they suf-fer'd; Glad - ly, Lord, with thee they died;

Clothed in white ap - par - el, hold-ing Palms of vic - t'ry in their hands.
Joined in ho - ly con - cert, sing - ing To the Lord of all, are there.
And by death to life im - mor - tal They were born and glo - ri - fied.

4 Now they reign in heav'nly glory,
Now they walk in golden light,
Now they drink, as from a river,
Holy bliss and infinite:

Love and peace they taste for ever,
And all truth and knowledge see
In the beatific vision
Of the blessèd Trinity.

CHRISTOPHER WORDSWORTH, 1862

126

First Tune

All Saints

10 10 10, with Alleluias

SINE NOMINE

R. VAUGHAN WILLIAMS, 1906

In moderate time, unison

1 For all the saints, who from their la - bors rest, Who
2 Thou wast their rock, their for - tress, and their might:
3 O may thy sol - diers, faith - ful, true, and bold,
*7 But lo! there breaks a yet more glo - rious day; The
8 From earth's wide bounds, from o - cean's far - thest coast, Through

thee . . . . by faith be - fore the world con - fessed,
Thou, Lord, their Cap - tain in the well-fought fight;
Fight as the saints who no - bly fought of old,
saints . . . . tri - umph - ant rise in bright ar - ray;
gates . . . . of pearl streams in the count - less host,

Thy Name, O Je - sus, be for ev - er blest.
Thou, in the dark - ness drear, the one true light.
And win, with them, the vic - tor's crown of gold.
The King of glo - ry pass - es on his way.
Sing - ing to Fa - ther, Son, and Ho - ly Ghost,

Saints' Days and Holy Days
All Saints

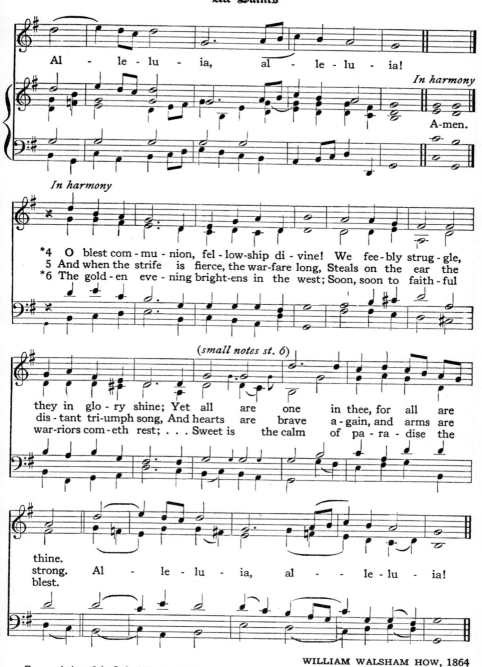

Al - le - lu - ia, al - le - lu - ia!

In harmony

A-men.

In harmony

*4 O blest com - mu - nion, fel - low-ship di - vine! We fee - bly strug - gle,
5 And when the strife is fierce, the war-fare long, Steals on the ear the
*6 The gold - en eve - ning bright-ens in the west; Soon, soon to faith - ful

(small notes st. 6)

they in glo - ry shine; Yet all are one in thee, for all are
dis - tant tri - umph song, And hearts are brave a - gain, and arms are
war-riors com - eth rest; . . . Sweet is the calm of pa - ra - dise the

thine.
strong. Al - le - lu - ia, al - le - lu - ia!
blest.

WILLIAM WALSHAM HOW, 1864

Second Tune All Saints

10 10 10, with Alleluias

SARUM JOSEPH BARNBY, 1868

With vigor

1 For all the saints, who from their la - bors rest, Who thee by
2 Thou wast their rock, their for - tress, and their might: Thou, Lord, their
3 O may thy sol - diers, faith - ful, true, and bold, Fight as the

faith be - fore the world con - fessed, Thy Name, O Je - sus,
Cap - tain in the well - fought fight; Thou, in the dark - ness
saints who no - bly fought of old, And win, with them, the

be for ev - er blest. Al - le - lu - ia, al - le - lu - ia! A - men.
drear, the one true light.
vic - tor's crown of gold.

*4 O blest communion, fellowship divine!
We feebly struggle, they in glory shine;
Yet all are one in thee, for all are thine.
Alleluia, alleluia!

5 And when the strife is fierce, the warfare long,
Steals on the ear the distant triumph song,
And hearts are brave again, and arms are strong.
Alleluia, alleluia!

*6 The golden evening brightens in the west;
Soon, soon to faithful warriors cometh rest;
Sweet is the calm of paradise the blest.
Alleluia, alleluia!

Saints' Days and Holy Days
All Saints

*7 But lo! there breaks a yet more glorious day;
   The saints triumphant rise in bright array;
   The King of glory passes on his way.
                    Alleluia, alleluia!

8 From earth's wide bounds, from ocean's farthest coast,
   Through gates of pearl streams in the countless host,
   Singing to Father, Son, and Holy Ghost,
                    Alleluia, alleluia!   Amen.

WILLIAM WALSHAM HOW, 1864

127

C. M.

BALLERMA

Melody by F. H. BARTHÉLÉMON,
adapted by ROBERT SIMPSON, pub. 1833

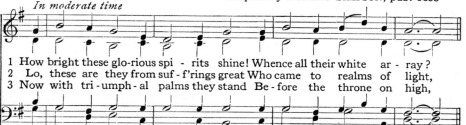

In moderate time

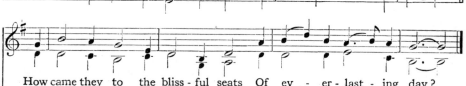

1 How bright these glo-rious spi - rits shine! Whence all their white ar - ray?
2 Lo, these are they from suf - f'rings great Who came to realms of light,
3 Now with tri - umph - al palms they stand Be - fore the throne on high,

How came they to the bliss - ful seats Of ev - er - last - ing day?
And by the grace of Christ have won Those robes that shine so bright.
And serve the God they love a - midst The glo - ries of the sky.

*4 Hunger and thirst are felt no more,
   Nor sun with scorching ray;
   God is their sun, whose cheering beams
   Diffuse eternal day.

5 The Lamb, which dwells amid the throne,
   Shall o'er them still preside,
   Feed them with nourishment divine,
   And all their footsteps guide.

6 In pastures green he'll lead his flock
   Where living streams appear;
   And God the Lord from every eye
   Shall wipe off every tear.

Scottish Version, 1781, after ISAAC WATTS, 1707

First Tune

JERVAULX ABBEY

French Psalter Melody, 1562
adapted by ALEXANDER GALLOWAY, 1912

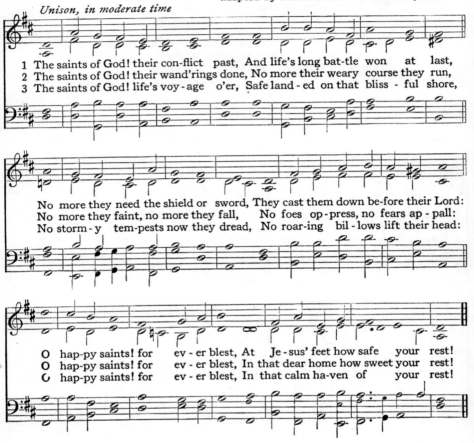

Unison, in moderate time

1 The saints of God! their con-flict past, And life's long bat-tle won at last,
2 The saints of God! their wand'rings done, No more their weary course they run,
3 The saints of God! life's voy-age o'er, Safe land-ed on that bliss-ful shore,

No more they need the shield or sword, They cast them down be-fore their Lord:
No more they faint, no more they fall, No foes op-press, no fears ap-pall:
No storm-y tem-pests now they dread, No roar-ing bil-lows lift their head:

O hap-py saints! for ev-er blest, At Je-sus' feet how safe your rest!
O hap-py saints! for ev-er blest, In that dear home how sweet your rest!
O hap-py saints! for ev-er blest, In that calm ha-ven of your rest!

4 The saints of God their vigil keep,
  While yet their mortal bodies sleep,
  Till from the dust they too shall rise
  And soar triumphant to the skies:
    O happy saints! rejoice and sing:
    He quickly comes, your Lord and King!

5 O God of saints! to thee we cry;
  O Saviour! plead for us on high;
  O Holy Ghost! our guide and friend,
  Grant us thy grace till life shall end;
    That with all saints our rest may be
    In that bright paradise with thee! Amen.

In harmony

A-men.

WILLIAM DALRYMPLE MACLAGAN, 1869

128 Saints' Days and Holy Days
All Saints

Second Tune

88. 88. 88

BEATI

In moderate time

JOHN STAINER, 1873

1 The saints of God! their con - flict past, And life's long bat - tle won at last, No more they need the shield or sword, They cast them down be - fore their Lord: O hap - py saints! for ev - er blest, At Je - sus' feet how safe your rest!

2 The saints of God! their wan-d'rings done, No more their wea - ry course they run, No more they faint, no more they fall, No foes op - press, no fears ap - pall: O hap - py saints! for ev - er blest, In that dear home how sweet your rest!

3 The saints of God! life's voy - age o'er, Safe land - ed on that bliss - ful shore, No storm - y tem - pests now they dread, No roar - ing bil - lows lift their head: O hap - py saints! for ev - er blest, In that calm ha - ven of your rest!

In unison

In harmony

A-men.

All Saints

87. 87. 77. 88

BOURGEOIS

In moderate time

Composed or adapted by
LOUIS BOURGEOIS, 1551

1 Joy and tri-umph ev-er-last-ing Hath the heav'n-ly Church on high;
*2 Here the world's per-pet-ual war-fare Holds from heav'n the soul a-part;
3 There the bo-dy hath no tor-ment, There the mind is free from care,

For that pure im-mor-tal glad-ness All our feast-days mourn and sigh:
Le-gioned foes in sha-dowy ter-ror Vex the Sab-bath of the heart.
There is ev-'ry voice re-joic-ing, Ev-'ry heart is lov-ing there.

Yet in death's dark des-ert wild Doth the moth-er aid her child;
O how hap-py that es-tate Where de-light doth not a-bate!
An-gels in that ci-ty dwell; Them their King de-light-eth well:

Guards ce-les-tial thence at-tend us, Stand in com-bat to de-fend us.
For that home the spi-rit yearn-eth, Where none lan-guish-eth nor mourneth.
Still they joy and wea-ry nev-er, More and more de-sir-ing ev-er.

4 There the seers and fathers holy,   There the saints, whose memories old
    There the prophets glorified,   We in faithful hymns uphold,
    All their doubts and darkness ended,   Have forgot their bitter story
    In the Light of Light abide.   In the joy of Jesus' glory.

ADAM of St. Victor, *12th cent.; Tr.* ROBERT BRIDGES, 1899

All Saints
87. 87. 77

ALL SAINTS
With dignity

Darmstadt *Gesangbuch*, 1698

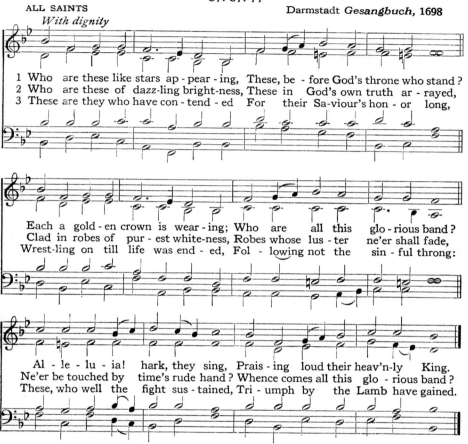

1 Who are these like stars ap - pear - ing, These, be - fore God's throne who stand?
2 Who are these of dazz-ling bright-ness, These in God's own truth ar - rayed,
3 These are they who have con - tend - ed For their Sa-viour's hon - or long,

Each a gold - en crown is wear - ing; Who are all this glo - rious band?
Clad in robes of pur - est white-ness, Robes whose lus - ter ne'er shall fade,
Wrest-ling on till life was end - ed, Fol - lowing not the sin - ful throng:

Al - le - lu - ia! hark, they sing, Prais - ing loud their heav'n-ly King.
Ne'er be touched by time's rude hand? Whence comes all this glo - rious band?
These, who well the fight sus - tained, Tri - umph by the Lamb have gained.

4 These are they whose hearts were riven,
    Sore with woe and anguish tried,
Who in prayer full oft have striven
    With the God they glorified:
      Now, their painful conflict o'er,
      God has bid them weep no more.

5 These, like priests, have watched and waited,
    Off'ring up to Christ their will,
Soul and body consecrated,
    Day and night they serve him still.
      Now in God's most holy place,
      Blest they stand before his face.

THEOBALD HEINRICH SCHENCK, 1719;
Tr. FRANCES E. COX, 1841, *alt.*

Saints' Days and Holy Days

Also the following:

131

Apostles

LITTLE CORNARD

66. 66. 88

MARTIN SHAW, 1915

With vigor

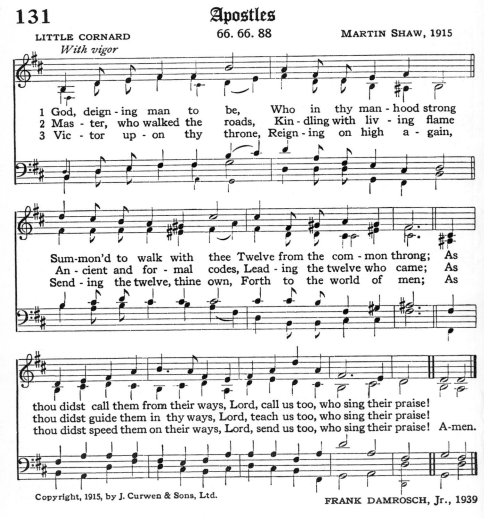

1 God, deign - ing man to be, Who in thy man - hood strong
2 Mas - ter, who walked the roads, Kin - dling with liv - ing flame
3 Vic - tor up - on thy throne, Reign - ing on high a - gain,

Sum-mon'd to walk with thee Twelve from the com - mon throng; As
An - cient and for - mal codes, Lead - ing the twelve who came; As
Send - ing the twelve, thine own, Forth to the world of men; As

thou didst call them from their ways, Lord, call us too, who sing their praise!
thou didst guide them in thy ways, Lord, teach us too, who sing their praise!
thou didst speed them on their ways, Lord, send us too, who sing their praise! A-men.

FRANK DAMROSCH, Jr., 1939

132 *First Tune*

Apostles
L. M.

AETERNA CHRISTI MUNERA   Mediaeval Plainsong, Mode VII
Unison, in flowing style

1 The e-ter - nal gifts of Christ the King, The mar-tyrs' glo -rious
2 The princ - es of the Church are they, Tri-umph-ant lead-ers
3 They braved the ter-rors of the time, No tor-ment shook their
4 Theirs is the stead-fast faith of saints, The hope that nev -er
5 In them the Fa-ther's glo ry shone, In them the Spi -rit's
6 Re-deem - er, hear us of thy love, That, with thy mar-tyr

deeds we sing; And all, with hearts of glad - ness, raise
in the fray, In hea-ven's hall a vic - tor band,
faith sub-lime; Soon, ho - ly death bro't peace and rest
yields nor faints; The per - fect love of Christ they know:
will was done, The Son him-self ex - ults in them;
host a - bove, Thy ser-vants, too, may find a place,

Due hymns of thank-ful love and praise.
True lights that light - en ev - 'ry land.
And light e - ter - nal with the blest.
These lay the prince of this world low.
Joy fills the new Je - ru - sa - lem.
And reign for ev - er through thy grace. A - men.

ST. AMBROSE, 340–397; *Hymnal Version*, 1940

Apostles
L. M.

GUIDETTI

Mediaeval Melody,
arr. GIOVANNI GUIDETTI, 1582

In unison, with spirit

1 The e - ter - nal gifts of Christ the King, The mar - tyrs' glo - rious
2 The princ - es of the Church are they, Tri - umph - ant lead - ers
3 They braved the ter - rors of the time, No tor - ment shook their

deeds we sing; And all, with hearts of glad - ness, raise
in the fray, In hea - ven's hall a vic - tor band,
faith sub - lime; Soon, ho - ly death brought peace and rest

In harmony

Due hymns of thank - ful love and praise.
True lights that light - en ev - - - 'ry land.
And light e - ter - nal with the blest. A - men.

4 Theirs is the steadfast faith of saints,
The hope that never yields nor faints;
The perfect love of Christ they know:
These lay the prince of this world low.

5 In them the Father's glory shone,
In them the Spirit's will was done,
The Son himself exults in them;
Joy fills the new Jerusalem.

6 Redeemer, hear us of thy love,
That, with thy martyr host above,
Thy servants, too, may find a place,
And reign for ever through thy grace. Amen.

ST. AMBROSE, 340–397; *Hymnal Version*, 1940

Also the following:

549 The Son of God goes forth to war

133

Evangelists
76. 76. D.

PRAETORIUS

Brightly

Melody, 1536, adapted by
MICHAEL PRAETORIUS, 1609

1 Come sing, ye choirs ex - ult - ant, Those mes - sen - gers of God,
2 In one har - mo - nious wit - ness The cho - sen four com - bine,

Through whom the liv - ing Gos - pels Came sound-ing all a - broad!
While each his own com - mis - sion Ful - fils in ev - 'ry line;

Whose voice pro-claimed sal - va - tion That poured up - on the night,
As, in the pro - phet's vi - sion, From out the am - ber flame

And drove a - way the sha - dows, And filled the world with light.
In form of vis - age di - verse Four liv - ing crea-tures came.

3 Foursquare on this foundation
The Church of Christ remains,
A house to stand unshaken
By floods or winds or rains.
O glorious happy portion
In this safe home to be,
By God, true man, united
With God eternally!

Latin, 12th cent.; Tr. JACKSON MASON, 1889

Evangelists
887. 887

COBB

GERARD F. COBB, 1838–1904

Brightly

1 Come, pure hearts, in sweet - est mea - sure Sing of those who
2 See the riv - ers four that glad - den, With their streams, the
3 O that we, thy truth con - fess - ing, And thy ho - ly

spread the trea - sure In the ho - ly Gos - pels shrined;
bet - ter E - den Plant - ed by our Lord most dear;
word pos - sess - ing, Je - sus, may thy love a - dore;

Bless - ed ti - dings of sal - va - tion, Peace on earth their
Christ the foun - tain, these the wa - ters; Drink, O Si - on's
Un - to thee our voic - es rais - ing, Thee with all thy

proc - la - ma - tion, Love from God to lost man - kind.
sons and daugh-ters, Drink, and find sal - va - tion here.
ran - somed prais - ing, Ev - er and for ev - er - more. A-men.

Latin, 12th cent.; Tr. ROBERT CAMPBELL, 1850, *alt.*

Also the following:

403 Book of books, our people's strength
253 Spread, O spread, thou mighty word

Martyrs
87. 87. D.

ALTA TRINITA BEATA

Italian Melody, 14th century,
adapted by CHARLES BURNEY, 1782

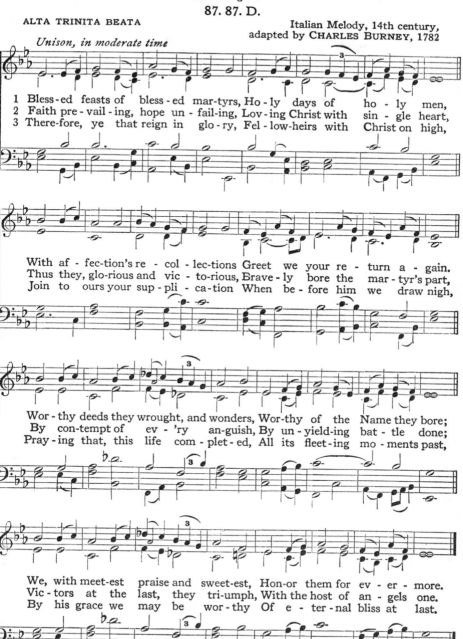

Unison, in moderate time

1 Bless-ed feasts of bless-ed mar-tyrs, Ho-ly days of ho-ly men,
2 Faith pre-vail-ing, hope un-fail-ing, Lov-ing Christ with sin-gle heart,
3 There-fore, ye that reign in glo-ry, Fel-low-heirs with Christ on high,

With af-fec-tion's re-col-lec-tions Greet we your re-turn a-gain.
Thus they, glo-rious and vic-to-rious, Brave-ly bore the mar-tyr's part,
Join to ours your sup-pli-ca-tion When be-fore him we draw nigh,

Wor-thy deeds they wrought, and wonders, Wor-thy of the Name they bore;
By con-tempt of ev-'ry an-guish, By un-yield-ing bat-tle done;
Pray-ing that, this life com-plet-ed, All its fleet-ing mo-ments past,

We, with meet-est praise and sweet-est, Hon-or them for ev-er-more.
Vic-tors at the last, they tri-umph, With the host of an-gels one.
By his grace we may be wor-thy Of e-ter-nal bliss at last.

Latin, 12th cent.; Tr. JOHN MASON NEALE, 1851, *alt.*

136 Martyrs

TEMPUS ADEST FLORIDUM   76. 76. D.   Traditional Swedish Melody,
Boldly, not fast   *Piae Cantiones*, 1582

1 Let us now our voic - es raise, Wake the day with glad - ness;
2 Nev - er flinched they from the flame, From the tor - ment nev - er;
3 Up and fol - low, Chris - tian men! Press through toil and sor - row;

God him - self to joy and praise Turns our hu - man sad - ness;
Vain the ty - rant's sharp - est aim, Vain each fierce en - dea - vor:
Spurn the night of fear, and then, O the glo - rious mor - row!

Joy that mar - tyrs won their crown, O - pen'd heav'n's bright por - tal,
For by faith they saw the land Decked in all its glo - ry,
Who will ven - ture on the strife; Who will first be - gin it?

When they laid the mor - tal down For the life im - mor - tal.
Where tri - umph-ant now they stand With the vic - tor's sto - ry.
Who will grasp the land of Life? War - riors, up and win it!

ST. JOSEPH the Hymnographer, *9th cent.*; *Tr.* J. M. NEALE, 1862, *alt.*

Also the following:

531 O valiant hearts, who to your glory came (Stanzas 4, 5, 6)
132 The eternal gifts of Christ the King (Omitting Stanza 2)
549 The Son of God goes forth to war

137 𝕿𝖍𝖆𝖓𝖐𝖘𝖌𝖎𝖛𝖎𝖓𝖌 𝕯𝖆𝖞

77. 77. 77. 77

ST. GEORGE'S WINDSOR GEORGE J. ELVEY, 1858

Brightly

1 Come, ye thank-ful peo - ple, come, Raise the song of har-vest-home:
2 All the world is God's own field, Fruit un - to his praise to yield;
3 For the Lord our God shall come, And shall take his har - vest home;

All is safe - ly gath - ered in, Ere the win - ter storms be - gin;
Wheat and tares to - geth - er sown, Un - to joy or sor - row grown:
From his field shall in that day All of - fenc - es purge a - way;

God, our Ma - ker, doth pro - vide For our wants to be sup - plied;
First the blade, and then the ear, Then the full corn shall ap - pear:
Give his an - gels charge at last In the fire the tares to cast,

Come to God's own tem - ple, come, Raise the song of har-vest-home.
Grant, O har - vest Lord, that we Whole-some grain and pure may be.
But the fruit - ful ears to store In his gar - ner ev - er - more. A-men.

4 Even so, Lord, quickly come There, for ever purified,
To thy final harvest-home; In thy presence to abide:
Gather thou thy people in, Come, with all thine angels, come,
Free from sorrow, free from sin; Raise the glorious harvest-home. Amen.

HENRY ALFORD, 1844, *alt.*

Thanksgiving Day

76. 76. D., with Refrain

CLAUDIUS

JOHANN A. P. SCHULZ, 1800

With energy

1 We plow the fields, and scat - ter The good seed on the land,
2 He on - ly is the Ma - ker Of all things near and far;
3 We thank thee, then, O Fa - ther, For all things bright and good,

But it is fed and wa - tered By God's al - migh - ty hand;
He paints the way - side flow - er, He lights the eve - ning star;
The seed-time and the har - vest, Our life, our health, our food:

He sends the snow in win - ter, The warmth to swell the grain,
The winds and waves o - bey him, By him the birds are fed;
No gifts have we to of - fer For all thy love im - parts,

The breez - es and the sun - shine, And soft re-fresh-ing rain.
Much more to us, his chil - dren, He gives our dai - ly bread.
But that which thou de - sir - est, Our hum - ble thank-ful hearts.

Thanksgiving Day

All good gifts a-round us Are sent from heav'n a-bove;

Then thank the Lord, O thank the Lord For all his love. A-men.

MATTHIAS CLAUDIUS, 1782; *Tr.* JANE M. CAMPBELL, 1861

139

L. M.

OLD HUNDREDTH

LOUIS BOURGEOIS, 1551

With great dignity

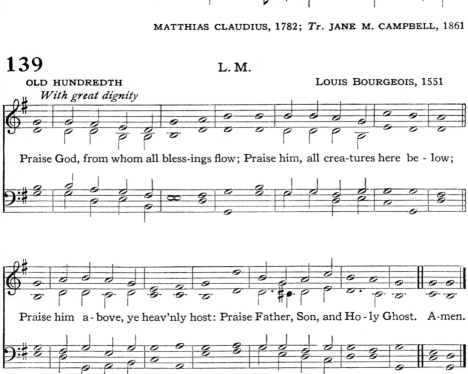

Praise God, from whom all bless-ings flow; Praise him, all crea-tures here be - low;

Praise him a - bove, ye heav'nly host: Praise Father, Son, and Ho - ly Ghost. A-men.

THOMAS KEN, 1709

140 𝕿𝖍𝖆𝖓𝖐𝖘𝖌𝖎𝖛𝖎𝖓𝖌 𝕯𝖆𝖞

77. 77. 77

DIX

CONRAD KOCHER, 1838, *alt.*

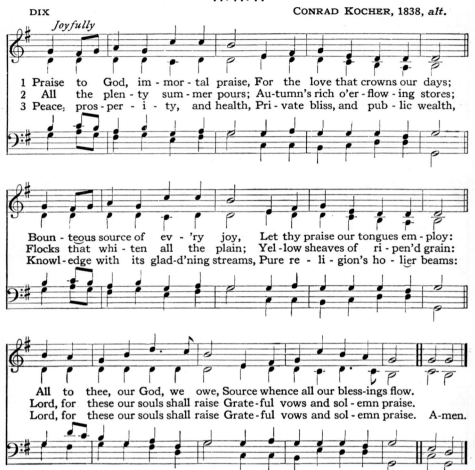

Joyfully

1 Praise to God, im - mor - tal praise, For the love that crowns our days;
2 All the plen - ty sum - mer pours; Au-tumn's rich o'er - flow - ing stores;
3 Peace, pros - per - i - ty, and health, Pri - vate bliss, and pub - lic wealth,

Boun - teous source of ev - 'ry joy, Let thy praise our tongues em - ploy:
Flocks that whi - ten all the plain; Yel - low sheaves of ri - pen'd grain:
Knowl - edge with its glad-d'ning streams, Pure re - li - gion's ho - lier beams:

All to thee, our God, we owe, Source whence all our bless-ings flow.
Lord, for these our souls shall raise Grate-ful vows and sol - emn praise.
Lord, for these our souls shall raise Grate-ful vows and sol - emn praise. A-men.

4 As thy prosp'ring hand hath blest,
 May we give thee of our best;
 And by deeds of kindly love
 For thy mercies grateful prove;
 Singing thus through all our days
 Praise to God, immortal praise.   Amen.

ANNA LAETITIA BARBAULD, 1772

Also the following:

296 For the beauty of the earth
308 Let us, with a gladsome mind
145 Not alone for mighty empire
276 Now thank we all our God
148 O God, beneath thy guiding hand

141

National Days
664. 6664

AMERICA
With breadth

In *Thesaurus Musicus,* 1740

1 My coun - try, 'tis of thee, Sweet land of
2 My na - tive coun - try, thee, Land of the

lib - er - ty, Of thee I sing; Land where my
no - ble free, Thy name I love; I love thy

fa - thers died, Land of the pil - grims' pride,
rocks and rills, Thy woods and tem - pled hills;

From ev - 'ry moun - tain - side Let free - dom ring.
My heart with rap - ture thrills Like that a - bove. A - men.

3 Let music swell the breeze,
And ring from all the trees
   Sweet freedom's song;
Let mortal tongues awake,
Let all that breathe partake,
Let rocks their silence break,
   The sound prolong.

4 Our fathers' God, to thee,
Author of liberty,
   To thee we sing;
Long may our land be bright
With freedom's holy light;
Protect us by thy might,
   Great God, our King. Amen.

SAMUEL FRANCIS SMITH, 1832

142 The National Anthem

Irregular

JOHN STAFFORD SMITH, c. 1771

1 O say can you see, by the dawn's ear - ly
2 O thus be it ev - er, when free - men shall

light, What so proud - ly we hailed at the twi - light's last
stand Be - tween their loved homes and the war's des - o -

gleam - ing, Whose broad stripes and bright stars, through the per - il - ous
la - tion! Blest with vic - t'ry and peace, may the heav'n-res - cued

fight, O'er the ram - parts we watched, were so gal - lant - ly
land Praise the Power that hath made and pre - served us a

The National Anthem

stream - ing? And the rock - ets' red glare, the bombs burst - ing in
na - tion! Then con - quer we must, when our cause it is

air, Gave proof through the night that our flag was still there.
just, And this be our mot - to, "In God is our trust."

O say does that star - span-gled ban - ner yet wave
And the star - span - gled ban - ner in tri - umph shall wave

O'er the land of the free and the home of the brave?
O'er the land of the free and the home of the brave!

FRANCIS SCOTT KEY, 1814

10 10. 10 10

NATIONAL HYMN   GEORGE WILLIAM WARREN, 1892

With vigor

1 God of our fa - thers, whose al-migh-ty hand Leads forth in beau - ty
2 Thy love di - vine hath led us in the past, In this free land by

all the star - ry band Of shin - ing worlds in splen-dor through the
thee our lot is cast; Be thou our rul - er, guar - dian, guide, and

skies, Our grate - ful songs be - fore thy throne a - rise.
stay, Thy word our law, thy paths our cho - sen way. A-men.

3 From war's alarms, from deadly pestilence,
   Be thy strong arm our ever sure defence;
   Thy true religion in our hearts increase,
   Thy bounteous goodness nourish us in peace.

4 Refresh thy people on their toilsome way,
   Lead us from night to never-ending day;
   Fill all our lives with love and grace divine,
   And glory, laud, and praise be ever thine.
                           Amen.

DANIEL CRANE ROBERTS, 1876

144 **National Days**

67. 67. 66. 66

NUN DANKET

In unison, majestically

JOHANN CRUEGER, 1647,
adapted by FELIX MENDELSSOHN, 1840

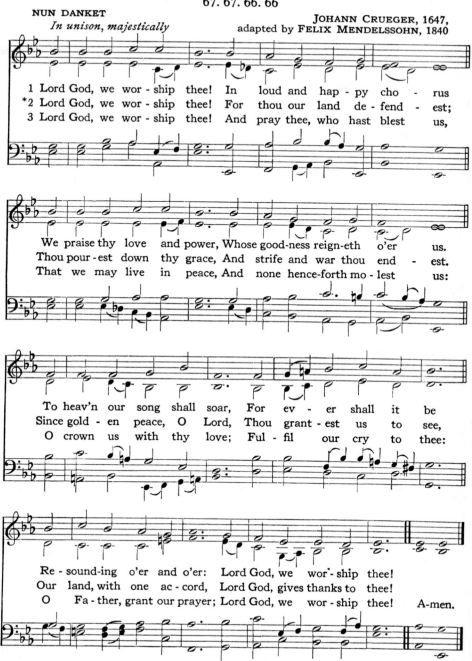

1 Lord God, we wor - ship thee! In loud and hap - py cho - rus

*2 Lord God, we wor - ship thee! For thou our land de - fend - est;

3 Lord God, we wor - ship thee! And pray thee, who hast blest us,

We praise thy love and power, Whose good-ness reign-eth o'er us.

Thou pour - est down thy grace, And strife and war thou end - est.

That we may live in peace, And none hence-forth mo - lest us:

To heav'n our song shall soar, For ev - er shall it be

Since gold - en peace, O Lord, Thou grant - est us to see,

O crown us with thy love; Ful - fil our cry to thee:

Re - sound-ing o'er and o'er: Lord God, we wor - ship thee!

Our land, with one ac - cord, Lord God, gives thanks to thee!

O Fa - ther, grant our prayer; Lord God, we wor - ship thee! A-men.

JOHANN FRANCK, 1653; *Tr.* CATHERINE WINKWORTH, 1863

National Days

87. 87. D.

GENEVA

GEORGE HENRY DAY, 1940

With strong rhythm

1 Not a - lone for migh - ty em - pire Stretch-ing far o'er land and sea,
2 Not for bat - tle-ship and for-tress, Not for conquests of the sword,
3 For the ar - mies of the faith-ful, Souls that passed and left no name;
4 God of jus - tice, save the peo - ple From the clash of race and creed,

Not a - lone for boun-teous harvests, Lift we up our hearts to thee:
But for conquests of the spi - rit Give we thanks to thee, O Lord;
For the glo - ry that il - lu-mines Pa - triot lives of death-less fame;
From the strife of class and fac-tion, Make our na - tion free in-deed;

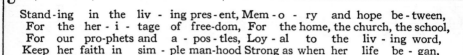

Stand-ing in the liv - ing pres - ent, Mem - o - ry and hope be - tween,
For the her - i - tage of free-dom, For the home, the church, the school,
For our pro-phets and a - pos-tles, Loy - al to the liv - ing word,
Keep her faith in sim - ple man-hood Strong as when her life be - gan,

National Days

Lord, we would with deep thanks-giving Praise thee most for things unseen.
For the o - pen door to man-hood In a land the peo-ple rule.
For all he - roes of the spi - rit, Give we thanks to thee, O Lord.
Till it find its full fru - i - tion In the broth-er - hood of man! A-men.

WILLIAM PIERSON MERRILL, 1909

146

664. 6664

AMERICA

Thesaurus Musicus, 1740

With breadth

1 God bless our na - tive land; Firm may she ev - er stand Thro' storm and
2 For her our prayers shall rise To God, a - bove the skies; On him we
3 And not to us a - lone, But be thy mer - cies known From shore to

night: When the wild tem - pests rave, Rul - er of wind and wave,
wait; Thou who art ev - er nigh, Guard-ing with watch - ful eye,
shore. Lord, make the na - tions see That men should broth - ers be

Do thou our coun - try save By thy great might.
To thee a - loud we cry, God save the state!
And form one fam - i - ly The wide world o'er. A - men.

St. 1, 2, SIEGFRIED A. MAHLMANN, 1815; *St. 3,* WILLIAM E. HICKSON, 1835

88. 88. 88

OLD HUNDRED TWELFTH

With dignity

Anonymous German Melody, 1530,
harmonized by W. D., 1937

1 God of our fa-thers, known of old, Lord of our far-flung bat-tle line, Be-neath whose aw-ful hand we hold Do-min-ion o-ver palm and pine— Lord God of hosts, be with us yet, Lest we for-get— lest we for-get!

2 The tu-mult and the shout-ing dies; The cap-tains and the kings de-part; Still stands thine an-cient sac-ri-fice, An hum-ble and a con-trite heart. Lord God of hosts, be with us yet, Lest we for-get— lest we for-get!

3 Far-called, our na-vies melt a-way; On dune and head-land sinks the fire: Lo, all our pomp of yes-ter-day Is one with Nin-e-veh and Tyre! Judge of the na-tions, spare us yet, Lest we for-get— lest we for-get!

A-men.

4 If, drunk with sight of power, we loose
Wild tongues that have not thee in awe,
Such boastings as the Gentiles use,
Or lesser breeds without the law—
Lord God of hosts, be with us yet,
Lest we forget — lest we forget!

National Days

5 For heathen heart that puts her trust
In reeking tube and iron shard,
All valiant dust that builds on dust,
And guarding, calls not thee to guard,
For frantic boast and foolish word—
Thy mercy on thy people, Lord! Amen.

RUDYARD KIPLING, 1897

From "The Five Nations," by permission of Mrs. Rudyard Kipling. From "Rudyard Kipling's Verse,"
Inclusive Edition, 1885, 1932, copyright 1891, 1934, reprinted by permission of Doubleday, Doran and Company, Inc.

148

L. M.

DUKE STREET

JOHN HATTON, 1793

With breadth

1 O God, be-neath thy guid - ing hand Our ex - iled
2 Thou heard'st, well pleased, the song, the prayer: Thy bless - ing
3 Laws, free - dom, truth, and faith in God Came with those

fa - thers crossed the sea; And when they trod the
came; and still its power Shall on - ward, through all
ex - iles o'er the waves; And where their pil - grim

win - try strand, With prayer and psalm they wor-shipped thee.
a - ges, bear The mem-'ry of that ho - ly hour.
feet have trod, The God they trust - ed guards their graves.

4 And here thy Name, O God of love,
Their children's children shall adore,
Till these eternal hills remove,
And spring adorns the earth no more.

LEONARD BACON, 1833

National Days

Also the following:

MORNING AND EVENING

149   Morning

77. 77

SELNECKER   *Cheerfully*   NICOLAUS SELNECKER, 1587

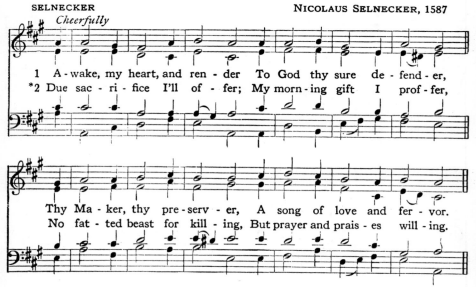

1 A-wake, my heart, and ren-der To God thy sure de-fend-er,
*2 Due sac-ri-fice I'll of-fer; My morn-ing gift I prof-fer,

Thy Ma-ker, thy pre-serv-er, A song of love and fer-vor.
No fat-ted beast for kill-ing, But prayer and prais-es will-ing.

3 Confirm my deeds and guide me:
  My day, with thee beside me,
  Beginning, middle, ending,
  Will all be upward tending.

4 My heart shall be thy dwelling,
  With joy and gladness swelling;
  Thy word my nurture, given
  To bring me on toward heaven. Amen.

A-men.

PAULUS GERHARDT, 1647; *Tr.* WINFRED DOUGLAS, 1939

150 Morning
L. M.

PIXHAM

HORATIO PARKER, 1901

Moderately quick

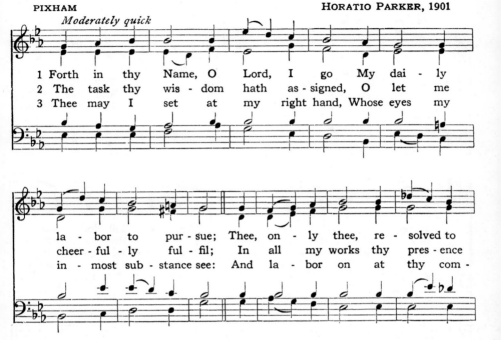

1 Forth in thy Name, O Lord, I go My dai - ly
2 The task thy wis - dom hath as - signed, O let me
3 Thee may I set at my right hand, Whose eyes my

la - bor to pur - sue; Thee, on - ly thee, re - solved to
cheer - ful - ly ful - fil; In all my works thy pres - ence
in - most sub - stance see: And la - bor on at thy com -

know, In all I think, or speak, or do.
find, And prove thy good and per - fect will.
mand, And of - fer all my works to thee. A - men.

4 Give me to bear thy easy yoke,
　And every moment watch and pray,
　And still to things eternal look,
　And hasten to thy glorious day.

5 Fain would I still for thee employ
　Whate'er thy bounteous grace hath giv'n,
　Would run my course with even joy,
　And closely walk with thee to heav'n. Amen.

CHARLES WESLEY, 1749

Alternative Tune, ANGEL'S SONG, No. 573

Morning

L. M.

MORNING HYMN   FRANÇOIS H. BARTHÉLEMON, 1785

In moderate time

1 A - wake, my soul, and with the sun Thy dai - ly
*2 Re - deem thy mis - spent mo - ments past; And live this
3 Let all thy con - verse be sin - cere, Thy con - science

stage of du - ty run; Shake off dull sloth, and
day as if thy last: Im - prove thy tal - ent
as the noon - day clear; Think how all - see - ing

joy - ful rise To pay thy morn - ing sac - ri - fice.
with due care; For the great day thy - self pre - pare.
God thy ways And all thy se - cret thoughts sur - veys. A - men.

4 Wake, and lift up thyself, my heart,
  And with the angels bear thy part,
  Who all night long unwearied sing
  High praise to the eternal King.

152 Part II of Hymn 151

5 All praise to thee, who safe hast kept
  And hast refreshed me while I slept;
  Grant, Lord, when I from death shall wake,
  I may of endless light partake.

6 Lord, I my vows to thee renew;
  Disperse my sins as morning dew;
  Guard my first springs of thought and will,
  And with thyself my spirit fill.

Morning

7 Direct, control, suggest, this day,
   All I design, or do, or say;
   That all my powers, with all their might,
   In thy sole glory may unite.

8 Praise God, from whom all blessings flow;
   Praise him, all creatures here below;
   Praise him above, ye heav'nly host:
   Praise Father, Son, and Holy Ghost. Amen.

THOMAS KEN, 1695, 1709, *alt.*

153

RATISBON

77. 77. 77

Adapted by JOHANN G. WERNER, 1815

In moderate time

1 Christ, whose glo-ry fills the skies, Christ, the true, the on-ly Light,
2 Dark and cheer-less is the morn Un-ac-com-pa-nied by thee;
3 Vis-it then this soul of mine! Pierce the gloom of sin and grief!

Sun of Right-eous-ness, a-rise! Tri-umph o'er the shades of night:
Joy-less is the day's re-turn, Till thy mer-cy's beams I see;
Fill me, ra-dian-cy di-vine; Scat-ter all my un-be-lief;

Day-spring from on high, be near; Day-star, in my heart ap-pear.
Till they in-ward light im-part, Glad my eyes, and warm my heart.
More and more thy-self dis-play, Shin-ing to the per-fect day. A-men.

CHARLES WESLEY, 1740

𝕸𝖔𝖗𝖓𝖎𝖓𝖌
847. 847

RICHTER
With vigor

JOHANN A. FREYLINGHAUSEN, 1706

1 Come, my soul, thou must be wa-king. Now is break-ing
2 Glad-ly hail the sun re-turn-ing, Rea-dy burn-ing
3 Pray that he may pros-per ev-er Each en-dea-vor,

O'er the earth an-oth-er day: Come, to him who made this
Be the in-cense of thy powers; For the night is safe-ly
When thine aim is good and true; But that he may ev-er

splen-dor See thou ren-der All thy fee-ble strength can pay.
end-ed, God hath tend-ed With his care thy help-less hours.
thwart thee, And con-vert thee, When thou e-vil wouldst pur-sue.

4 Mayest thou on life's last morrow,
  Free from sorrow,
    Pass away in slumber sweet;
And, released from death's dark sadness,
  Rise in gladness
    That far brighter sun to greet.

5 Only God's free gifts abuse not,
  Light refuse not,
    But his Spirit's voice obey;
Thou with him shalt dwell, beholding
  Light enfolding
    All things in unclouded day.

FRIEDRICH RUDOLPH LUDWIG VON CANITZ, 1654–99;
Tr. HENRY J. BUCKOLL, *alt.*

𝔐orning
847. 847

CARMAN

PETER CHRISTIAN LUTKIN, 1895

In moderate time

1 Come, my soul, thou must be wa - king. Now is break - ing
2 Glad - ly hail the sun re - turn - ing, Rea - dy burn - ing
3 Pray that he may pros - per ev - er Each en - dea - vor,

O'er the earth an - oth - er day: Come, to him who made this
Be the in - cense of thy powers; For the night is safe - ly
When thine aim is good and true; But that he may ev - er

splen - dor See thou ren - der All thy fee - ble strength can pay.
end - ed, God hath tend - ed With his care thy help - less hours.
thwart thee, And con - vert thee, When thou e - vil wouldst pur - sue.

4 Mayest thou on life's last morrow,
   Free from sorrow,
      Pass away in slumber sweet;
   And, released from death's dark sadness,
   Rise in gladness
      That far brighter sun to greet.

5 Only God's free gifts abuse not,
   Light refuse not,
      But his Spirit's voice obey;
   Thou with him shalt dwell, beholding
   Light enfolding
      All things in unclouded day.

FRIEDRICH RUDOLPH LUDWIG VON CANITZ, 1654–99;
Tr. HENRY J. BUCKOLL, *alt.*

155

Morning
L. M.

MELCOMBE
Deliberately

SAMUEL WEBBE, 1782

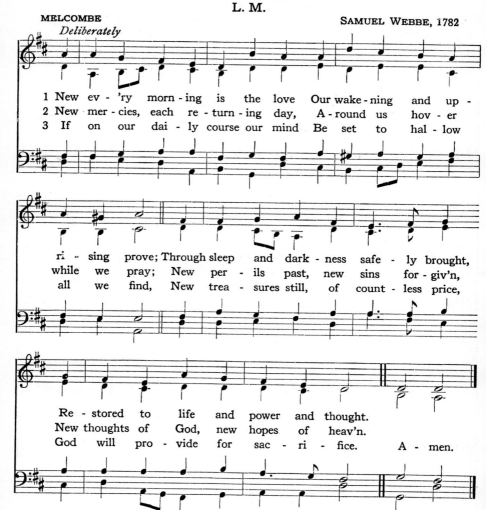

1 New ev - 'ry morn - ing is the love Our wake - ning and up -
2 New mer - cies, each re - turn - ing day, A - round us hov - er
3 If on our dai - ly course our mind Be set to hal - low

ri - sing prove; Through sleep and dark - ness safe - ly brought,
while we pray; New per - ils past, new sins for - giv'n,
all we find, New trea - sures still, of count - less price,

Re - stored to life and power and thought.
New thoughts of God, new hopes of heav'n.
God will pro - vide for sac - ri - fice. A - men.

4 Old friends, old scenes, will lovelier be,
   As more of heav'n in each we see;
   Some soft'ning gleam of love and prayer
   Shall dawn on every cross and care.

5 The trivial round, the common task,
   Will furnish all we ought to ask;
   Room to deny ourselves — a road
   To bring us daily nearer God.

Morning

6 Only, O Lord, in thy dear love,
　Fit us for perfect rest above;
　And help us, this and every day,
　To live more nearly as we pray.　Amen.

JOHN KEBLE, 1822, alt.

156

MORNING SONG

86. 86. 86

Melody, *The Union Harmony*, Virginia, 1848,
harmonized by W. D., 1940

In moderate time

1 A-wake, a-wake to love and work! The lark is in the sky,
2 Come, let thy voice be one with theirs, Shout with their shout of praise;

The fields are wet with dia-mond dew, The worlds a-wake to cry
See how the gi-ant sun soars up, Great lord of years and days!

Their bless-ings on the Lord of life, As he goes meek-ly by.
So let the love of Je-sus come And set thy soul a-blaze,

3 To give and give, and give again,
　What God hath given thee;
　To spend thyself nor count the cost;
　To serve right gloriously
　The God who gave all worlds that are,
　And all that are to be.

GEOFFREY ANKETELL STUDDERT-KENNEDY, 1921

157 *First Tune*

Morning

Office Hymn, Matins
11 11. 11 5

NOCTE SURGENTES

Sarum Plainsong, Mode VI

With movement

1 Fa - ther, we praise thee, now the night is o - ver, Ac - tive and
2 Mon-arch of all things, fit us for thy man-sions; Ban - ish our
3 All - ho - ly Fa - ther, Son, and e - qual Spi - rit, Trin - i - ty

watch - ful, stand we all be - fore thee; Sing - ing we of - fer
weak - ness, health and whole - ness send - ing; Bring us to hea - ven,
bless - ed, send us thy sal - va - tion; Thine is the glo - ry,

prayer and med - i - ta - tion: Thus we a - dore thee.
where thy saints u - ni - ted Joy with - out end - ing.
gleam - ing and re - sound - ing Through all cre - a - tion. A - men.

Latin, 10th cent.; Tr. PERCY DEARMER, 1906

By permission of the Oxford University Press

157 *Second Tune*

Morning
11 11. 11 5

CHRISTE SANCTORUM

French Church Melody, 1782,
har. by R. VAUGHAN WILLIAMS, 1906

In unison, with spirit

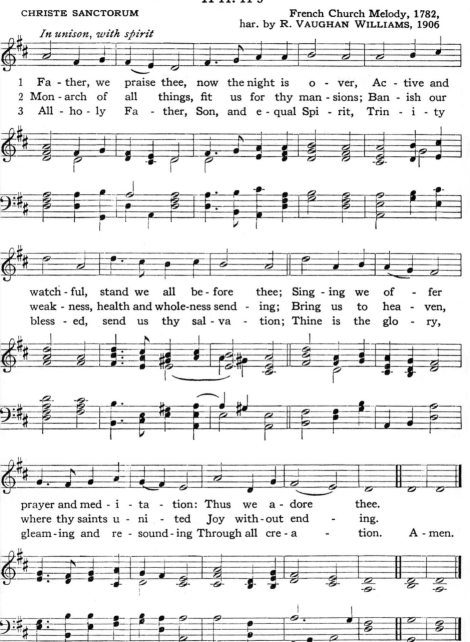

1 Fa - ther, we praise thee, now the night is o - ver, Ac - tive and
2 Mon - arch of all things, fit us for thy man - sions; Ban - ish our
3 All - ho - ly Fa - ther, Son, and e - qual Spi - rit, Trin - i - ty

watch - ful, stand we all be - fore thee; Sing - ing we of - fer
weak - ness, health and whole-ness send - ing; Bring us to hea - ven,
bless - ed, send us thy sal - va - tion; Thine is the glo - ry,

prayer and med - i - ta - tion: Thus we a - dore thee.
where thy saints u - ni - ted Joy with-out end - ing.
gleam-ing and re - sound-ing Through all cre - a - tion. A - men.

Morning
Office Hymn, Lauds
L. M.

SPLENDOR PATERNAE

Sarum Plainsong, Mode I

With dignity

1 O Splen - dor of God's glo - ry bright, O thou that bring - est
2 O thou true Sun, on us thy glance Let fall in roy - al
3 The Fa - ther, too, our prayers im - plore, Fa - ther of glo - ry

light from light, O Light of Light, light's liv - ing spring,
ra - di - ance, The Spi - rit's sanc - ti - fy - ing beam
ev - er - more, The Fa - ther of all grace and might,

O Day, all days il - lu - min - ing;
Up - on our earth - ly sens - es stream.
To ban - ish sin from our de - light: A - men.

Morning

4 To guide whate'er we nobly do,
   With love all envy to subdue,
   To make ill-fortune turn to fair,
   And give us grace our wrongs to bear.

5 All laud to God the Father be;
   All praise, eternal Son, to thee;
   All glory, as is ever meet,
   To God the holy Paraclete.   Amen.

ST. AMBROSE, 340–397; *Tr.* ROBERT BRIDGES, 1899

By permission of The Clarendon Press, Oxford

158 *Second Tune*   L. M.

PUER NOBIS
Adapted by MICHAEL PRAETORIUS, 1609

Moderately fast

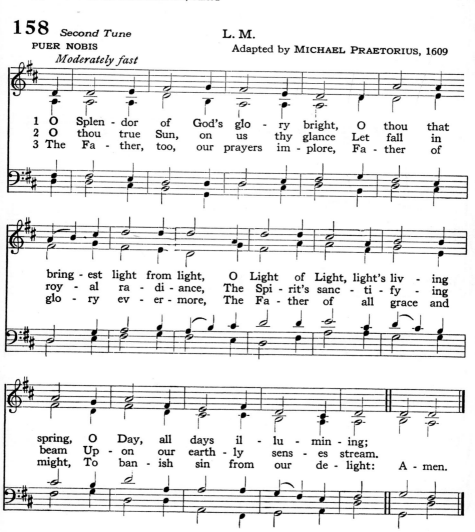

1 O Splen - dor of God's glo - ry bright, O thou that
2 O thou true Sun, on us thy glance Let fall in
3 The Fa - ther, too, our prayers im - plore, Fa - ther of

bring - est light from light, O Light of Light, light's liv - ing
roy - al ra - di - ance, The Spi - rit's sanc - ti - fy - ing
glo - ry ev - er - more, The Fa - ther of all grace and

spring, O Day, all days il - lu - min - ing;
beam Up - on our earth - ly sens - es stream.
might, To ban - ish sin from our de - light: A - men.

Morning

Office Hymn, Prime
L. M.

JAM LUCIS ORTO SIDERE   Benedictine Plainsong, Mode VIII

Fluently

1 Now that the day-light fills the sky, We lift our hearts to
2 Would guard our hearts and tongues from strife; From an-ger's din would
3 Would keep our in-most con-science pure; Our souls from fol - ly

God on high,   That he, in all we do or say,
hide our life;   From all ill sights would turn our eyes;
would se-cure;   Would bid us check the pride of sense

Would keep us free from harm to - day:
Would close our ears from van - i - ties:
With due and ho - ly ab - sti - nence.   A - men.

Alternative Tune, JAM LUCIS, No. 164

Morning

4 So we, when this new day is gone,
And night in turn is drawing on,
With conscience by the world unstained
Shall praise his Name for vict'ry gained.

5 All laud to God the Father be;
All praise, eternal Son, to thee;
All glory, as is ever meet,
To God the holy Paraclete. Amen.

Latin, 6th cent.; Tr. JOHN MASON NEALE, 1851

159 *Second Tune*   **L. M.**
HERR JESU CHRIST

Melody, pub. Goerlitz, 1648,
arr. and har. J. S. BACH, 1765

In moderate time

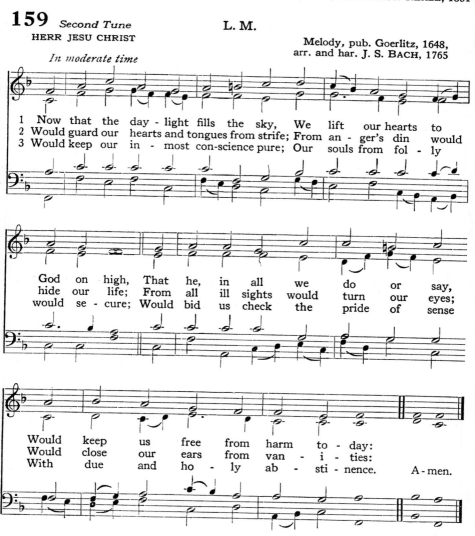

1 Now that the day-light fills the sky, We lift our hearts to
2 Would guard our hearts and tongues from strife; From an-ger's din would
3 Would keep our in-most con-science pure; Our souls from fol-ly

God on high, That he, in all we do or say,
hide our life; From all ill sights would turn our eyes;
would se-cure; Would bid us check the pride of sense

Would keep us free from harm to-day:
Would close our ears from van-i-ties:
With due and ho-ly ab-sti-nence. A-men.

Morning

Office Hymn, Terce
L. M.

NUNC SANCTE

Early Plainsong, Mode VIII

Unison, in chant style

1 Come, Ho - ly Ghost, with God the Son   And God the Fa - ther, ev - er One;
2 By   ev - 'ry power, by heart and tongue, By act and deed, thy praise be sung;

Shed forth thy grace with-in our breast, And dwell with us,   a   rea - dy guest.
In - flame with per - fect love each sense, That oth - ers' souls may kin - dle thence.

3 O Father, that we ask be done,
   Through Jesus Christ, thine only Son,
   Who, with the Holy Ghost and thee,
   Doth live and reign eternally.   Amen.

A - men.

ST. AMBROSE, 340–97; *Tr.* JOHN MASON NEALE

VETTER   Adapted from DANIEL VETTER, 1713

With movement

1 Come, Ho - ly Ghost, with God the Son   And God the   Fa - ther, ev - er One;
2 By   ev - 'ry power, by heart and tongue, By act and deed, thy praise be sung;

Noon, Afternoon

Shed forth thy grace with-in our breast, And dwell with us, a rea-dy guest.
In-flame with per-fect love each sense, That oth-ers' souls may kindle thence. Amen.

161

NUNC SANCTE
or
VETTER

Noon

Office Hymn, Sext

L. M.

1 O God of truth, O Lord of might,
Who ord'rest time and change aright,
And send'st the early morning ray,
And light'st the glow of perfect day:

2 Extinguish thou each sinful fire,
And banish every ill desire;
And while thou keep'st the body whole,
Shed forth thy peace upon the soul.

3 O Father, that we ask be done,
Through Jesus Christ, thine only Son,
Who, with the Holy Ghost and thee,
Doth live and reign eternally.   Amen.

ST. AMBROSE, 340–97; *Tr.* JOHN MASON NEALE

162

NUNC SANCTE
or
VETTER

Afternoon

Office Hymn, None

L. M.

1 O God, creation's secret force,
Thyself unmoved, all motion's source,
Who from the morn till evening ray
Through all its changes guid'st the day:

2 Grant us, when this short life is past,
The glorious evening that shall last;
That, by a holy death attained,
Eternal glory may be gained.

3 O Father, that we ask be done,
Through Jesus Christ, thine only Son,
Who, with the Holy Ghost and thee,
Doth live and reign eternally.   Amen.

ST. AMBROSE, 340–97; *Tr.* JOHN MASON NEALE

163 *First Tune*

Evening

Office Hymn, Vespers
L. M.

LUCIS CREATOR

With serenity

Sarum Plainsong, Mode VIII

1 O blest Cre - a - tor of the light, Who mak'st the
2 Whose wis - dom joined in meet ar - ray The morn and
3 Lest, sunk in sin, and whelm'd with strife, They lose the

day with ra - diance bright, And o'er the form - ing
eve, and named them day: Night comes with all its
gift of end - less life; While think - ing but the

world didst call The light from cha - os first of all;
dark - ling fears; Re - gard thy peo - ple's prayers and tears,
thoughts of time, They weave new chains of woe and crime. A - men.

Evening

4 But grant them grace that they may strain
The heav'nly gate and prize to gain:
Each harmful lure aside to cast,
And purge away each error past.

5 O Father, that we ask be done,
Through Jesus Christ, thine only Son,
Who, with the Holy Ghost and thee,
Doth live and reign eternally. Amen.

Latin, 6th cent.; Tr. JOHN MASON NEALE, 1851

163 *Second Tune*   L. M.

BROMLEY   JEREMIAH CLARK, 1700

Slowly and quietly

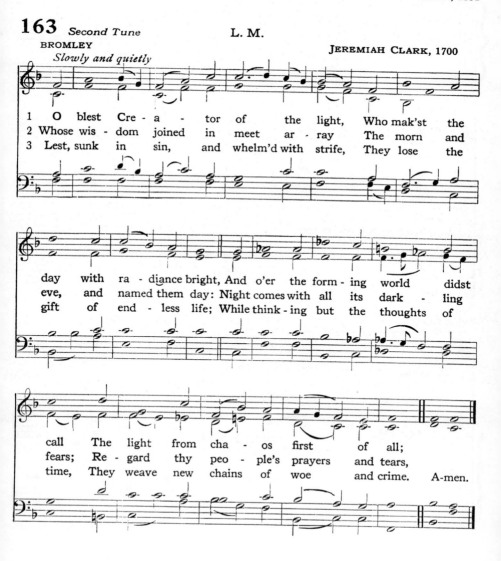

1 O blest Cre - a - tor of the light, Who mak'st the
2 Whose wis - dom joined in meet ar - ray The morn and
3 Lest, sunk in sin, and whelm'd with strife, They lose the

day with ra - diance bright, And o'er the form - ing world didst
eve, and named them day: Night comes with all its dark - ling
gift of end - less life; While think - ing but the thoughts of

call The light from cha - os first of all;
fears; Re - gard thy peo - ple's prayers and tears,
time, They weave new chains of woe and crime. A-men.

164 *First Tune*   𝕰bening
Office Hymn, Compline
L. M.

TE LUCIS   Sarum Plainsong, Mode VIII
In chant style, with motion

1 To thee be - fore the close of day, Cre - a - tor of the
2 From all ill dreams de - fend our sight, From fears and ter - rors
3 O Fa - ther, that we ask be done, Through Je - sus Christ, thine

world, we pray That, with thy wont - ed fa - vor, thou
of the night; With - hold from us our ghost - ly foe,
on - ly Son, Who, with the Ho - ly Ghost and thee,

Wouldst be our guard and keep - er now.
That spot of sin we may not know.
Doth live and reign e - ter - nal - ly.   A - men.

Latin, c. 7th cent.; Tr. JOHN MASON NEALE, 1852, *alt.*

164 *Second Tune*

Evening
L. M.

JAM LUCIS   Benedictine Plainsong, Mode VI

In chant style, with motion

1 To thee be - fore the close of day, Cre - a - tor of the
2 From all ill dreams de - fend our sight, From fears and ter - rors
3 O Fa - ther, that we ask be done, Through Je - sus Christ, thine

world, we pray That, with thy wont - ed fa - vor, thou
of the night; With - hold from us our ghost - ly foe,
on - ly Son, Who, with the Ho - ly Ghost and thee,

Wouldst be our guard and keep - er now.
That spot of sin we may not know.
Doth live and reign e - ter - nal - ly. A - men.

Latin, c. 7th cent.; Tr. JOHN MASON NEALE, *1852, alt.*

165

Evening
L. M.

TALLIS' CANON
With dignity

THOMAS TALLIS, c. 1567

Women and boys

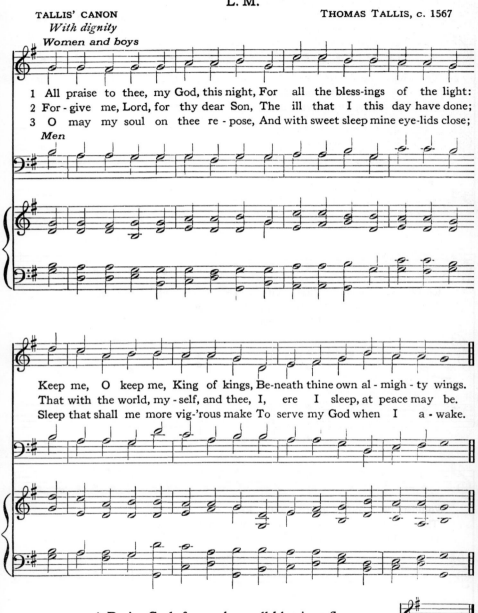

1 All praise to thee, my God, this night, For all the bless-ings of the light:
2 For-give me, Lord, for thy dear Son, The ill that I this day have done;
3 O may my soul on thee re-pose, And with sweet sleep mine eye-lids close;

Men

Keep me, O keep me, King of kings, Be-neath thine own al-migh-ty wings.
That with the world, my-self, and thee, I, ere I sleep, at peace may be.
Sleep that shall me more vig-'rous make To serve my God when I a-wake.

4 Praise God, from whom all blessings flow;
Praise him, all creatures here below;
Praise him above, ye heav'nly host:
Praise Father, Son, and Holy Ghost. Amen.

A - men.

THOMAS KEN, 1709

166 **Evening**
L. M.

HURSLEY
Quietly

Melody pub. Vienna, c. 1774,
adapted Dublin, c. 1844

1 Sun of my soul, thou Sa - viour dear, It is not
2 When the soft dews of kind - ly sleep My wea - ry
3 A - bide with me from morn till eve, For with - out

night if thou be near; O may no earth - born cloud a -
eye - lids gen - tly steep, Be my last thought, how sweet to
thee I can - not live; A - bide with me when night is

rise To hide thee from thy ser - vant's eyes.
rest For ev - er on my Sa - viour's breast.
nigh, For with - out thee I dare not die. A - men.

4 If some poor wand'ring child of thine
Have spurned to-day the voice divine,
Now, Lord, the gracious work begin;
Let him no more lie down in sin.

5 Watch by the sick; enrich the poor
With blessings from thy boundless store;
Be every mourner's sleep to-night,
Like infant's slumbers, pure and light.

6 Come near and bless us when we wake,
Ere through the world our way we take,
Till in the ocean of thy love
We lose ourselves in heav'n above. Amen.

JOHN KEBLE, 1820

167 **Evening**

11 11. 11 5

DIVA SERVATRIX

French Church Melody, Bayeux,
har. by GEORGE R. WOODWARD, 1904

In moderate time

1 Now it is eve - ning; time to rest from la - bor; Fa - ther, ac -
2 Far from our homes, Lord, drive a - way temp - ta - tion; Be thou our
3 As thy be - lov - ed, care for all who suf - fer; Com - fort the

cord - ing to thy will and plea - sure, Through the night-sea - son
guar - dian through the hours of dark - ness; Un - der the sha - dow
pris - on'd, those in lone - ly trou - ble, Wi - dows and or - phans;

have thy whole cre - a - tion Safe in thy keep - ing.
of thy wings de - fend us, Send us thine an - gel.
from the power of mal - ice Keep them in safe - ty. A - men.

4 Hallowed, O Father, be thy Name; thy kingdom
   Come as in heaven; let thy will direct us.
   Feed us, forgive us, free us from all evil,
      Save us, redeem us. Amen.

PETRUS HERBERT, 1566; *Hymnal Version*, 1940

168

Evening
L. M.

ANGELUS

Cantica Spiritualia, 1847,
arr. from GEORG JOSEPH, 1657

In moderate time

1 At e - ven, when the sun was set, The sick, O
2 Once more 'tis e - ven - tide, and we Op - pressed with
*3 O Sa - viour Christ, our woes dis - pel; For some are

Lord, a - round thee lay. O in what di - vers
va - rious ills draw near. What if thy form we
sick, and some are sad, And some have nev - er

pains they met; O with what joy they went a - way.
can - not see? We know and feel that thou art here.
loved thee well, And some have lost the love they had, A - men.

*4 And none, O Lord, have perfect rest,
    For none are wholly free from sin;
    And they who fain would love thee best
    Are conscious most of wrong within.

5 O Saviour Christ, thou too art man;
    Thou hast been troubled, tempted, tried;
    Thy kind but searching glance can scan
    The very wounds that shame would hide.

6 Thy touch has still its ancient power;
    No word from thee can fruitless fall;
    Hear, in this solemn evening hour,
    And in thy mercy heal us all. Amen.

HENRY TWELLS, 1868, *alt.*

169 *First Tune*

Evening

84. 84. 88. 84

AR HYD Y NOS

Traditional Welsh Melody

With tranquillity

1 God, that ma - dest earth and hea - ven, Dark - ness and light;
  Who the day for toil hast giv - en, For rest the night,
2 Guard us wa - king, guard us sleep - ing, And, when we die,
  May we in thy migh - ty keep - ing, All peace - ful lie:

May thine an - gel-guards de - fend us, Slum-ber sweet thy mer - cy send us,
And when death to life shall wake us, Thou wilt in thy like - ness make us;

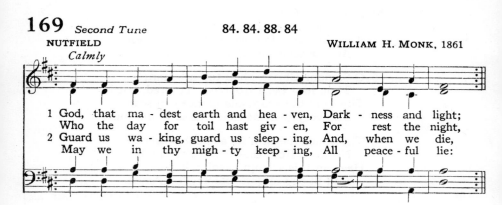

Ho - ly dreams and hopes at - tend us, This live-long night.
Then to reign in glo - ry take us With thee on high. A-men.

St. 1, REGINALD HEBER, 1827; St. 2, RICHARD WHATELEY, 1855, *alt.*

169 *Second Tune*   84. 84. 88. 84

NUTFIELD

WILLIAM H. MONK, 1861

Calmly

1 God, that ma - dest earth and hea - ven, Dark - ness and light;
  Who the day for toil hast giv - en, For rest the night,
2 Guard us wa - king, guard us sleep - ing, And, when we die,
  May we in thy migh - ty keep - ing, All peace - ful lie:

Evening

May thine an - gel-guards de - fend us, Slum-ber sweet thy mer - cy send us,
And when death to life shall wake us, Thou wilt in thy like - ness make us;

Ho - ly dreams and hopes at - tend us, This live - long night.
Then to reign in glo - ry take us With thee on high. A - men.

170   C. M.

NAOMI

JOHANN G. NAEGELI,
arr. by LOWELL MASON, 1836

Quietly

1 Now from the al - tar of my heart Let in - cense flames a - rise;
2 Min - utes and mer - cies mul - ti - plied Have made up all this day;
3 New time, new fa - vor, and new joys Do a new song re - quire;

As - sist me, Lord, to of - fer up Mine eve - ning sac - ri - fice.
Min-utes came quick, but mer-cies were More fleet and free than they.
Till I shall praise thee as I would, Ac - cept my heart's de-sire. A-men.

JOHN MASON, 1683

171 *First Tune*   𝔈𝔳𝔢𝔫𝔦𝔫𝔤
L. M.

O LUX BEATA TRINITAS   Sarum Plainsong, Mode VIII
With flowing rhythm

1 O   Tri -   ni - ty   of   bless - ed   light,
2 To   thee . . . . our morn - ing song   of   praise,
3 All   laud . . . . to God the Fa - ther   be,

O   U - - - ni - ty   of   prince - ly   might,
To   thee . . . . our eve - ning prayer   we   raise;
All   praise, ... e - ter - nal   Son,   to   thee,

The   fier - y   sun now   goes   his . . . . . way;
O   grant us   with thy   saints on . . . . . high
All   glo - ry,   as is   ev - er . . . . . meet,

Shed thou . . . . . with-in our hearts thy ray.
To praise . . . . . thee thro' e - ter - ni - ty.
To God . . . . . the ho-ly Pa - ra - clete. A - men.

Latin, c. 6th cent.; Tr. J. M. NEALE, 1852

171 *Second Tune*   L. M.

BROMLEY   JEREMIAH CLARK, 1700

Slowly and quietly

1 O Tri - ni - ty of bless - ed light, O U - ni -
2 To thee our morn - ing song of praise, To thee our
3 All laud to God the Fa - ther be, All praise, e -

ty of prince - ly might, The fier - y sun now goes his
eve - ning prayer we raise; O grant us with thy saints on
ter - nal Son, to thee, All glo - ry, as is ev - er

way; Shed thou with - in our hearts thy ray.
high To praise thee through e - ter - ni - ty.
meet, To God the ho - ly Pa - ra - clete. A-men.

172 *First Tune* **Evening**
65. 65

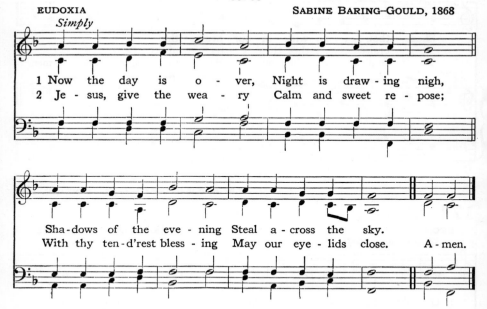

EUDOXIA
Simply

SABINE BARING–GOULD, 1868

1 Now the day is o - ver, Night is draw - ing nigh,
2 Je - sus, give the wea - ry Calm and sweet re - pose;

Sha - dows of the eve - ning Steal a - cross the sky.
With thy ten - d'rest bless - ing May our eye - lids close. A - men.

3 Grant to little children
  Visions bright of thee;
  Guard the sailors tossing
  On the deep, blue sea.

4 Comfort every suff'rer
  Watching late in pain;
  Those who plan some evil
  From their sin restrain.

5 Through the long night watches
  May thine angels spread
  Their white wings above me,
  Watching round my bed.

6 When the morning wakens,
  Then may I arise
  Pure, and fresh, and sinless
  In thy holy eyes.   Amen.

SABINE BARING–GOULD, 1865

By permission of A. W. Ridley and Co.

172 *Second Tune* 65. 65

MERRIAL
Quietly

JOSEPH BARNBY, 1868

1 Now the day is o - ver, Night is draw - ing nigh,
2 Je - sus, give the wea - ry Calm and sweet re - pose;

Evening

Sha-dows of the eve — ning Steal a-cross the sky.
With thy ten-d'rest bless — ing May our eye-lids close. A-men.

eve-ning Steal a-cross the sky.
bless-ing May our eye - - lids close.

173

10 6. 10 6

ST. NICHOLAS
Without dragging

CLEMENT C. SCHOLEFIELD, 1870

1 O Bright-ness of the im-mor-tal Fa-ther's face, Most
2 The sun is sink-ing now, and one by one The
3 Wor-thy art thou at all times to re-ceive Our

ho — ly, heav'n-ly, blest, Lord Je-sus Christ, in
lamps of eve-ning shine; We hymn the e-ter-nal
hal-lowed prais-es, Lord. O Son of God, be

whom his truth and grace Are vis-i-bly ex-pressed:
Fa-ther, and the Son, And Ho-ly Ghost di-vine.
thou, in whom we live, Through all the world a-dored. A-men.

Greek, 3rd cent.; Tr. EDWARD W. EDDIS, 1864

174

Evening
S. M.

COMBE MARTIN

BASIL HARWOOD, 1908

Calmly

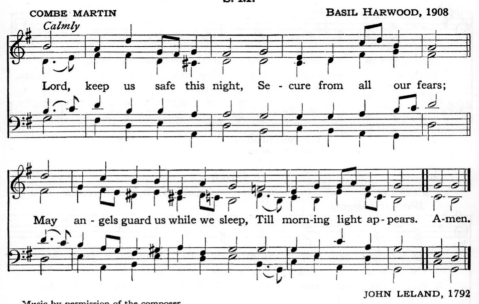

Lord, keep us safe this night, Se - cure from all our fears;

May an - gels guard us while we sleep, Till morn-ing light ap-pears. A-men.

JOHN LELAND, 1792

Music by permission of the composer

175

S. M.

GARDEN CITY

HORATIO PARKER, 1893

In moderate time

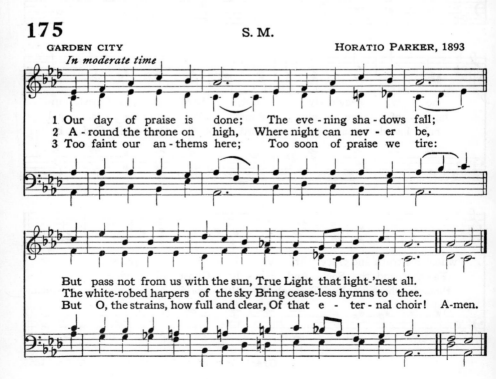

1 Our day of praise is done; The eve - ning sha - dows fall;
2 A - round the throne on high, Where night can nev - er be,
3 Too faint our an - thems here; Too soon of praise we tire:

But pass not from us with the sun, True Light that light-'nest all.
The white-robed harpers of the sky Bring cease-less hymns to thee.
But O, the strains, how full and clear, Of that e - ter - nal choir! A-men.

Evening

4 Yet, Lord, to thy dear will
  If thou attune the heart,
We in thine angels' music still
  May bear our lower part.

5 'Tis thine each soul to calm,
  Each wayward thought reclaim,
And make our life a daily psalm
  Of glory to thy Name. Amen.

JOHN ELLERTON, 1871, alt.

176

667. 667

NUNC DIMITTIS
With serenity

Melody, LOUIS BOURGEOIS, 1549,
har. by CLAUDE GOUDIMEL

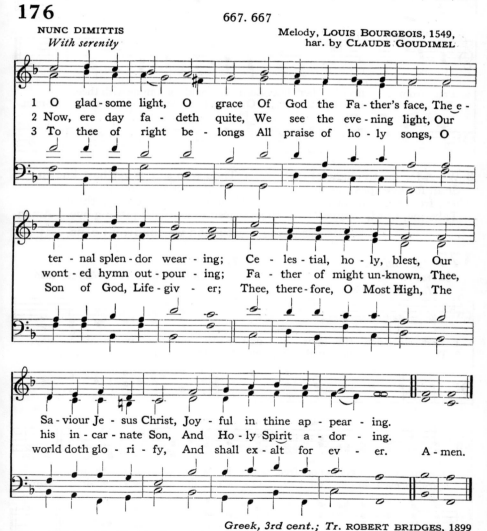

1 O glad-some light, O grace Of God the Fa-ther's face, The e-
2 Now, ere day fa-deth quite, We see the eve-ning light, Our
3 To thee of right be-longs All praise of ho-ly songs, O

ter-nal splen-dor wear-ing; Ce-les-tial, ho-ly, blest, Our
wont-ed hymn out-pour-ing; Fa-ther of might un-known, Thee,
Son of God, Life-giv-er; Thee, there-fore, O Most High, The

Sa-viour Je-sus Christ, Joy-ful in thine ap-pear-ing.
his in-car-nate Son, And Ho-ly Spirit a-dor-ing.
world doth glo-ri-fy, And shall ex-alt for ev-er. A-men.

Greek, 3rd cent.; Tr. ROBERT BRIDGES, 1899

By permission of the Clarendon Press, Oxford

177 *First Tune*

Evening
77. 77

LEW TRENCHARD

Moderately slow

Traditional English Melody
harmonized by W. D., 1918

1 Soft - ly now the light of day Fades up - on my sight a - way;
2 Thou, whose all - per - vad - ing eye Naught es - capes, with-out, with - in,

Free from care, from la - bor free, Lord, I would com-mune with thee.
Par - don each in - fir - mi - ty, O - pen fault and se - cret sin. A-men.

3 When for me the light of day
   Shall for ever pass away,
Then, from sin and sorrow free,
   Take me, Lord, to dwell with thee;

4 Thou who sinless yet hast known
   All of man's infirmity;
Then, from thine eternal throne,
   Jesus, look with pitying eye. Amen.

GEORGE WASHINGTON DOANE, 1824, *alt.*

177 *Second Tune*

77. 77

SEYMOUR

CARL MARIA VON WEBER, 1826

In moderate time

1 Soft - ly now the light of day Fades up - on my sight a - way;
2 Thou, whose all - per - vad - ing eye Naught es - capes, with-out, with - in,

Free from care, from la - bor free, Lord, I would com-mune with thee.
Par-don each in - fir - mi - ty, O - pen fault and se - cret sin. A-men.

178

Evening

87. 87. D.

VESPER HYMN

Arr. by J. A. Stevenson
from Dmitri S. Bortniansky, 1818

Quietly

1 Sa-viour, breathe an eve-ning bless-ing, Ere re - pose our spi - rits seal;
2 Though de - struc - tion walk a - round us, Though the ar -rows past us fly,

Sin and want we come con-fess - ing; Thou canst save, and thou canst heal.
An - gel-guards from thee sur-round us; We are safe, if thou art nigh.

Though the night be dark and drea - ry, Dark-ness can - not hide from thee;
Be thou nigh, should death o'er-take us; Je - sus, then our ref - uge be,

Thou art he who, nev-er wea - ry, Watch-est where thy peo-ple be.
And in pa - ra - dise a-wake us, There to rest in peace with thee. A-men.

JAMES EDMESTON, 1820

Alternative Tune, PLEADING SAVIOUR, No. 117

179 *First Tune*

Evening
98. 98

COMMANDMENTS

LOUIS BOURGEOIS, 1543

Quietly

1 The day thou ga - vest, Lord, is end - ed, The dark - ness falls at
2 We thank thee that thy Church, un - sleep - ing While earth rolls on - ward
3 As o'er each con - ti - nent and is - land The dawn leads on an -

thy be - hest; To thee our morn - ing hymns as - cend - ed,
in - to light, Through all the world her watch is keep - ing,
oth - er day, The voice of prayer is nev - er si - lent,

Thy praise shall sanc - ti - fy our rest.
And rests not now by day or night.
Nor dies the strain of praise a - way. A - men.

4 The sun that bids us rest is waking
   Our brethren 'neath the western sky,
   And hour by hour fresh lips are making
   Thy wondrous doings heard on high.

5 So be it, Lord; thy throne shall never,
   Like earth's proud empires, pass away:
   Thy kingdom stands, and grows for ever,
   Till all thy creatures own thy sway. Amen.

JOHN ELLERTON, 1870

179 *Second Tune* Evening
98. 98

ST. CLEMENT
In moderate time
CLEMENT C. SCHOLEFIELD, 1874

1 The day thou ga - vest, Lord, is end - ed, The dark - ness falls at thy be - hest; To thee our morn - ing hymns as - cend - ed, Thy praise shall sanc - ti - fy our rest.

2 We thank thee that thy Church, un - sleep - ing While earth rolls on - ward in - to light, Through all the world her watch is keep - ing, And rests not now by day or night.

3 As o'er each con - ti - nent and is - land The dawn leads on an - oth - er day, The voice of prayer is nev - er si - lent, Nor dies the strain of praise a - way. A - men.

4 The sun that bids us rest is waking
  Our brethren 'neath the western sky,
And hour by hour fresh lips are making
  Thy wondrous doings heard on high.

5 So be it, Lord; thy throne shall never,
  Like earth's proud empires, pass away:
Thy kingdom stands, and grows for ever,
  Till all thy creatures own thy sway. Amen.

JOHN ELLERTON, 1870

180

Evening
88. 84

ST. GABRIEL

Quietly

F. A. GORE OUSELEY, 1868

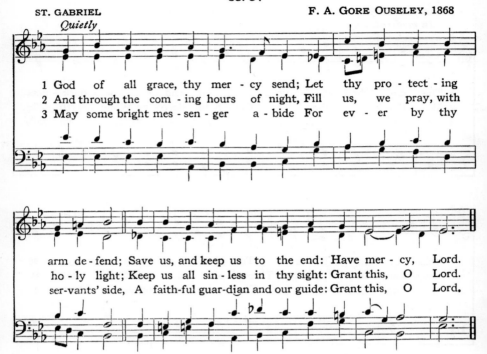

1 God of all grace, thy mer - cy send; Let thy pro - tect - ing
2 And through the com - ing hours of night, Fill us, we pray, with
3 May some bright mes - sen - ger a - bide For ev - er by thy

arm de - fend; Save us, and keep us to the end: Have mer - cy, Lord.
ho - ly light; Keep us all sin - less in thy sight: Grant this, O Lord.
ser - vants' side, A faith-ful guar-dian and our guide: Grant this, O Lord.

4 From every sin, in mercy free,
   Let heart and conscience stainless be,
   That we may live henceforth for thee:
         Grant this, O Lord.

5 We would not be by care opprest,
   But in thy love and wisdom rest;
   Give what thou seest to be best:
         Grant this, O Lord.

6 While we of every sin repent,
   Let our remaining years be spent
   In holiness and sweet content:
         Grant this, O Lord.

7 And when the end of life is near,
   May we, unshamed and void of fear,
   Wait for the judgment to appear:
         Grant this, O Lord.   Amen.

A - men.

Greek; Tr. JOHN BROWNLIE

181

Evening
776. 778

INNSBRUCK

With dignity; may be sung in unison

Traditional German Melody, pub. 1539;
adapted and har. by J. S. BACH

1 The du-teous day now clos-eth, Each flower and tree re-
2 Now all the heav'n-ly splen-dor Breaks forth in star-light
3 A-while his mor-tal blind-ness May miss God's lov-ing-

pos-eth, Shade creeps o'er wild and wood: Let us, as
ten-der From myr-iad worlds un-known; And man, the
kind-ness, And grope in faith-less strife: But when life's

night is fall-ing, On God our Ma-ker
mar-vel see-ing, For-gets his self-ish
day is o-ver Shall death's fair night dis-

call-ing, Give thanks to him, the Giv-er good.
be-ing, For joy of beau-ty not his own.
cov-er The fields of ev-er-last-ing life.

PAULUS GERHARDT, 1648; *Paraphrase by* ROBERT BRIDGES, 1899

182 Evening
88. 88. 88

ST. MATTHIAS   WILLIAM H. MONK, 1861

With movement

1 O Sa - viour, bless us ere we go; Thy word in - to our
2 The day is gone, its hours have run; And thou hast ta - ken
3 Grant us, dear Lord, from e - vil ways True ab - so - lu - tion

minds in - stil, And make our luke - warm hearts to glow With
count of all, The scan - ty tri - umphs grace hath won, The
and re - lease; And bless us, more than in past days, With

Refrain

low - ly love and fer - vent will.
bro - ken vow, the fre - quent fall. Through life's long day and
pu - ri - ty and in - ward peace.

death's dark night, O gen - tle Je - sus, be . . . our light. A - men.

Evening

4 For all we love, the poor, the sad,
   The sinful, unto thee we call;
   O let thy mercy make us glad;
   Thou art our Saviour and our all. *Refrain*

5 O Saviour, bless us; night is come;
   Through night and darkness near us be;
   Good angels watch about our home,
   And we are one day nearer thee. *Refrain*
   Amen.

FREDERICK WILLIAM FABER, 1849

183

64. 66

IRONS

HERBERT S. IRONS, 1861

In moderate time

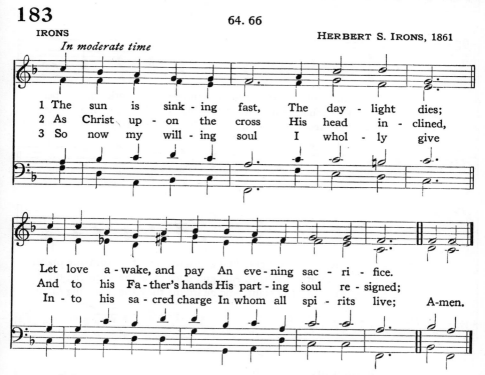

1 The sun is sink - ing fast, The day - light dies;
2 As Christ up - on the cross His head in - clined,
3 So now my will - ing soul I whol - ly give

Let love a - wake, and pay An eve - ning sac - ri - fice.
And to his Fa - ther's hands His part - ing soul re - signed;
In - to his sa - cred charge In whom all spi - rits live; A - men.

4 So now beneath his care
   I calmly rest
   Without another wish
   Abiding in the breast,

5 Save that his will be done,
   Whate'er betide;
   Dead to myself, and dead
   In him to all beside.

6 Thus would I live; yet now
   Not I, but he,
   In all his power and love,
   Henceforth alive in me.

7 One sacred Trinity,
   One Lord divine;
   May I be ever his,
   And he for ever mine. Amen.

Latin, 1805; *Hymnal Version,* 1939, *after* EDWARD CASWALL, 1838

184

Evening

76. 76. 88

ST. ANATOLIUS   ARTHUR H. BROWN, 1862

In moderate time

1 The day is past and o - ver: All thanks, O Lord, to thee!
2 The joys of day are o - ver: I lift my heart to thee,
3 The toils of day are o - ver: I raise the hymn to thee,

I pray thee that of - fence - less The hours of dark may be.
And call on thee that sin - less The hours of night may be.
And ask that free from per - il The hours of fear may be.

O Je - sus, keep me in thy sight, And guard me thro' the com - ing night.
O Je - sus, make their dark - ness light, And guard me thro' the com - ing night.
O Je - sus, keep me in thy sight, And guard me thro' the com - ing night.

4 Be thou my soul's preserver,
   O God, for thou dost know
How many are the perils
   Through which I have to go.
Lover of men, O hear my call,
And guard and save me from them all!   Amen.

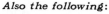
A-men.

ST. ANATOLIUS; *Tr.* JOHN MASON NEALE, 1853, *alt.*

Also the following:
467 Abide with me: fast falls the eventide
275 Holy Father, cheer our way

SACRAMENTS AND OTHER RITES
OF THE CHURCH

185 𝕳𝖔𝖑𝖞 𝕭𝖆𝖕𝖙𝖎𝖘𝖒

88. 88. 88

ST. CATHERINE
With vigor

HENRI F. HEMY, 1864,
and JAMES G. WALTON, 1870

1 O Je - sus Christ, our Lord most dear, As thou wast once an
2 As in thy heav'n - ly king - dom, Lord, Thy mes - sen - gers o -
3 And all *his* life, let an - gels keep *Him* safe from harm, a -

in - fant here, So give this child of thine, we pray,
bey thy word, Send forth the suc - cor of thy might
wake, a - sleep; May *he* not bear the cross in vain,

Refrain

Thy grace and bless - ing day by day.
To shield this child both day and night. O ho - ly Je - sus,
But with thy saints a crown at - tain.

Lord di - vine, We pray thee guard this child of thine. A - men.

HEINRICH VON LAUFENBURG, 1429; *Tr.* CATHERINE WINKWORTH, 1869, **alt.**

186

Holy Baptism
78. 78. 88

LIEBSTER JESU   JOHANN RUDOLPH AHLE, 1664

In unison, slow and quiet

Bless - ed Je - sus, here are we, Thy be - lov - ed word o - bey - ing.

Now these chil - dren come to thee As thou bid - dest in thy say - ing,
(this child doth)

"Let the lit - tle ones be giv - en Un - to me; of such is hea - ven." A-men.

BENJAMIN SCHMOLCK, 1706; *Tr.* WINFRED DOUGLAS, 1939

Hymns suitable for Adult Baptism:

375 Breathe on me, Breath of God
466 God be in my head
268 I bind unto myself to-day
404 My God, accept my heart this day
552 Soldiers of Christ, arise
408 Take my life, and let it be

187 Confirmation

76. 76. D.

ELLACOMBE

Boldly

Wirtemberg, 1784

1 As when, in far Sa-ma-ri-a, The two a-pos-tles prayed
2 O let thy grace sur-round them With glad-ness of thy love,

That there the Ho-ly Ghost might come To those on whom were laid
Thy ten-der mer-cy ev-er shine Up-on them from a-bove,

The hands, by Je-sus bid-den To point the heav'n-ly way,
Un-til, with thee u-nit-ed In hap-py realms di-vine,

So now to these thy chil-dren, Lord, Give boundless strength, we pray!
They see, a-cross the earth-ly years, This day as vic-tory's sign. A-men.

LEIGH MITCHELL HODGES, 1939

188 Confirmation
11 10. 11 10

CHARTERHOUSE

DAVID EVANS, 1927

Unison, in moderate time

1 O heav'n-ly grace in ho-ly rite de-scend - ing ....
2 Here as they pledge to fol-low thee as Sa - viour, ...
3 May they con - tin - ue thine, O God, for ev - er, ...

To those who kneel for lay - ing on of hands; ....
Je - sus their Lord, who for the Church hath died; ....
Dai - ly in - creas - ing in the Spi - rit's gift, ...

Thine be the strength, O Lord, for their de - fend - ing; ....
So may they live with - in that blest be - ha - vior ....
Un - til they bring the gift un - to the Giv - er, ...

Confirmation

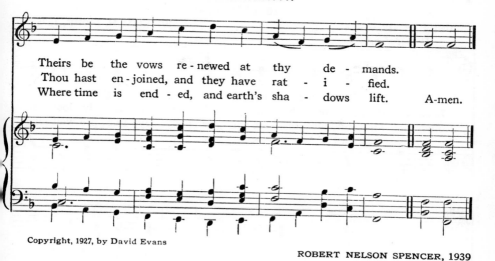

Theirs be the vows re-newed at thy de - mands.
Thou hast en-joined, and they have rat - i - fied.
Where time is end - ed, and earth's sha - dows lift. A-men.

Copyright, 1927, by David Evans

ROBERT NELSON SPENCER, 1939

Also the following:

550 Am I a soldier of the cross
577 Awake, my soul, stretch every nerve
418 Blest are the pure in heart
375 Breathe on me, Breath of God
376 Come down, O Love divine
378 Come, gracious Spirit, heavenly Dove
217 Come, Holy Ghost, our souls inspire
109 Come, thou Holy Spirit, come
371 Creator Spirit, by whose aid
560 Fight the good fight with all thy might
553 Go forward, Christian soldier
563 He who would valiant be
377 Holy Spirit, Truth divine
268 I bind unto myself to-day
425 Jesus, lead the way
554 Lead on, O King eternal
567 Lead us, heavenly Father, lead us
433 Lead us, O Father, in the paths of peace
449 My faith looks up to thee
404 My God, accept my heart this day
555 My soul, be on thy guard
108 O come, Creator Spirit, come
372 O Holy Spirit, God
570 O Jesus, I have promised
374 O King enthroned on high
572 O Master, let me walk with thee
463 O thou who camest from above
552 Soldiers of Christ, arise
408 Take my life, and let it be
427 Thine for ever! God of love

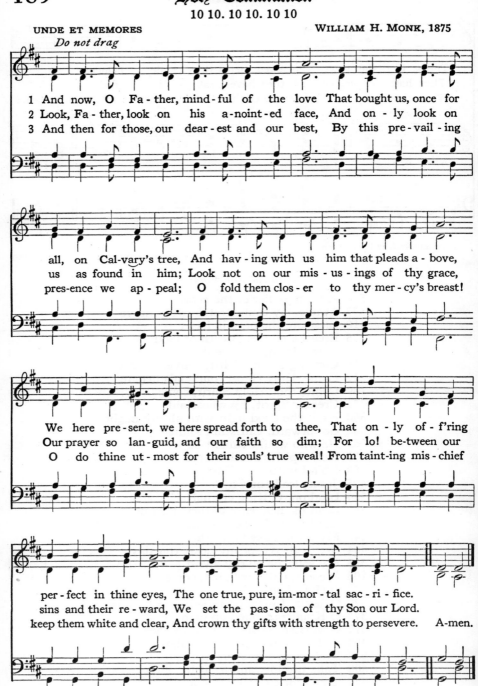

189 𝕳𝖔𝖑𝖞 𝕮𝖔𝖒𝖒𝖚𝖓𝖎𝖔𝖓

10 10. 10 10. 10 10

UNDE ET MEMORES — *Do not drag* — WILLIAM H. MONK, 1875

1 And now, O Fa-ther, mind-ful of the love That bought us, once for
2 Look, Fa-ther, look on his a-noint-ed face, And on-ly look on
3 And then for those, our dear-est and our best, By this pre-vail-ing

all, on Cal-vary's tree, And hav-ing with us him that pleads a-bove,
us as found in him; Look not on our mis-us-ings of thy grace,
pres-ence we ap-peal; O fold them clos-er to thy mer-cy's breast!

We here pre-sent, we here spread forth to thee, That on-ly of-f'ring
Our prayer so lan-guid, and our faith so dim; For lo! be-tween our
O do thine ut-most for their souls' true weal! From taint-ing mis-chief

per-fect in thine eyes, The one true, pure, im-mor-tal sac-ri-fice.
sins and their re-ward, We set the pas-sion of thy Son our Lord.
keep them white and clear, And crown thy gifts with strength to persevere. A-men.

Holy Communion

4 And so we come; O draw us to thy feet,
   Most patient Saviour, who canst love us still!
And by this food, so awful and so sweet,
   Deliver us from every touch of ill:
In thine own service make us glad and free,
And grant us nevermore to part with thee.   Amen.

WILLIAM BRIGHT, 1874

Alternative Tune, SONG 1, No. 470

190

78. 78. 77

LUISE

In moderate time

JOHANN CRUEGER'S
Praxis Pietatis Melica, 1653

1 Let thy Blood in mer - cy poured, Let thy gra - cious Bo - dy bro - ken,
2 Thou didst die that I might live; Bless-ed Lord, thou cam'st to save me:
3 By the thorns that crowned thy brow, By the spear-wound and the nail - ing,

Be to me, O gra - cious Lord, Of thy bound-less love the to - ken.
All that love of God could give Je - sus by his sor - rows gave me.
By the pain and death, I now Claim, O Christ, thy love un - fail - ing.

Refrain

Thou didst give thy - self for me, Now I give my - self to thee.   A - men.

4 Wilt thou own the gift I bring?
   All my penitence I give thee;
Thou art my exalted King,
   Of thy matchless love forgive me.

Refrain

Amen.

Greek; Tr. JOHN BROWNLIE, 1907

191 Holy Communion

10 10. 10 10. 10 10

SACRAMENTUM UNITATIS   CHARLES H. LLOYD, 1885

With movement

1 Thou, who at thy first Eu - cha - rist didst pray   That all thy Church might
2 For all thy Church, O Lord, we in - ter - cede;   Make thou our sad di -
*3 We pray thee too for wan-d'rers from thy fold;   O bring them back, good

be for ev - er one, Grant us at ev - 'ry Eu - cha - rist to say
vi - sions soon to cease; Draw us the near - er each to each, we plead,
Shep-herd of the sheep, Back to the faith which saints be-lieved of old,

With long - ing heart and soul, "Thy will be done." O may we all one
By draw-ing all to thee, O Prince of Peace; Thus may we all one
Back to the Church which still that faith doth keep; Soon may we all one

May be sung in unison

bread, one bo - dy be, Thro' this blest sac - ra-ment of u - ni-ty.
bread, one bo - dy be, Thro' this blest sac - ra-ment of u - ni-ty.
bread, one bo - dy be, Thro' this blest sac - ra-ment of u - ni-ty. A-men.

Holy Communion

4 So, Lord, at length when sacraments shall cease,
May we be one with all thy Church above,
One with thy saints in one unbroken peace,
One with thy saints in one unbounded love;
More blessèd still, in peace and love to be
One with the Trinity in Unity.   Amen.

WILLIAM HARRY TURTON, 1881

192

776. D.

O ESCA VIATORUM

LOUIS BOURGEOIS, 1549

Quietly; may be sung in unison

1 O Food of men way-far - ing, The bread of an - gels shar - ing, O Man-na from on high! We hun-ger; Lord, sup-ply us, Nor thy de-lights de - ny us, Whose hearts to thee draw nigh.

2 O stream of love past tell - ing, O pur-est foun-tain, well - ing From out the Sa-viour's side! We faint with thirst; re - vive us, Of thine a-bun-dance give us, And all we need pro - vide.

3 O Je-sus, by thee bid - den, We here a - dore thee, hid - den 'Neath forms of bread and wine. Grant when the veil is riv - en, We may be-hold, in hea - ven, Thy coun-te-nance di - vine. A-men.

Latin, 1661; *Tr.* J. ATHELSTAN L. RILEY, 1906

By permission of the Oxford University Press

193 Part I

Holy Communion
887. 887

First Tune

LAUDA SION

Plainsong Sequence, Mode VII,
12th century

In unison, light and moderately fast

1 Si - on, praise thy Sa-viour, sing-ing Hymns with ex - ul - ta - tion ring - ing,
Hon - or him, thy voice up - rais-ing, Who sur-pass-eth all thy   prais - ing;
3 What he did, at sup - per seat-ed, Christ or-dained to be re - peat - ed,
His com-mand for guid-ance ta -king, Bread and wine we hal-low, ma - king

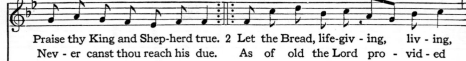

Praise thy King and Shep-herd true. 2 Let the Bread, life-giv - ing,   liv - ing,
Nev - er canst thou reach his due.   As of old the Lord pro - vid - ed
His me - mo - rial ne'er to cease; 4 Full and clear ring out   thy chant-ing,
Thus our sac - ri - fice of peace. For to - day the new ob - la - tion

Be   our theme of glad thanks-giv-ing, Now in - deed be - fore thee set;
When the twelve, di - vine - ly guid-ed, At the ho - ly ta - ble met.
Joy nor sweet - est grace be want-ing To thy heart and soul to - day:
Of   the new King's rev - e - la - tion Bids us feast in glad ar - ray.

First Tune　　　　　　　　　88. 887

BONE PASTOR

Plainsong Sequence concluded,
Mode VII, 12th century

In unison, light and moderately fast

5 Ve - ry Bread, good Shep-herd, tend　us,　Je - sus, of thy love be -
6 Thou, who all things canst and　know - est, Who on earth such food be -

friend us, Thou re - fresh us, thou de - fend us, Thine e - ter - nal
stow - est, Grant us, with thy saints, though low-est, Where the　heav'n - ly

good - ness send us　In the land of life to　see:
feast thou show - est, Fel - low-heirs and guests to　be.　A - men.

ST. THOMAS AQUINAS, 1263; *Hymnal Version*, 1939

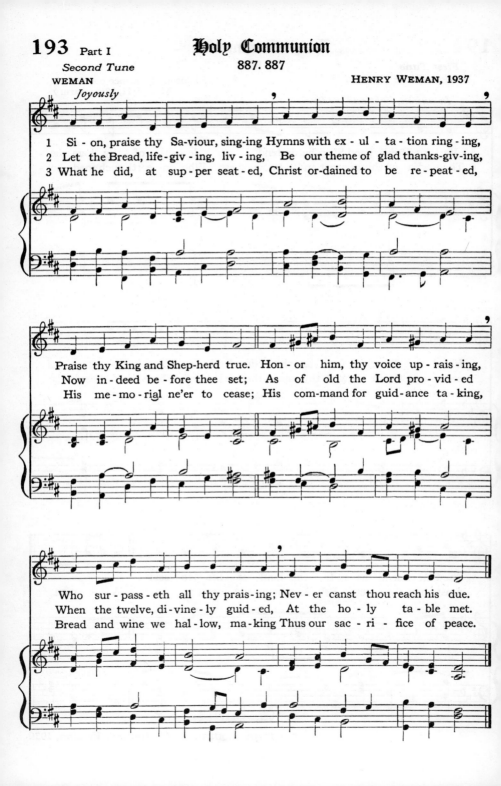

Holy Communion

4 Full and clear ring out thy chanting,
Joy nor sweetest grace be wanting
To thy heart and soul to-day:
For to-day the new oblation
Of the new King's revelation
Bids us feast in glad array.

194 Part II of Hymn 193   88. 887
Second Tune
UNITAS FRATRUM
Prayerfully
Bohemian Brethren, 1566
harmonized by W. D., 1941

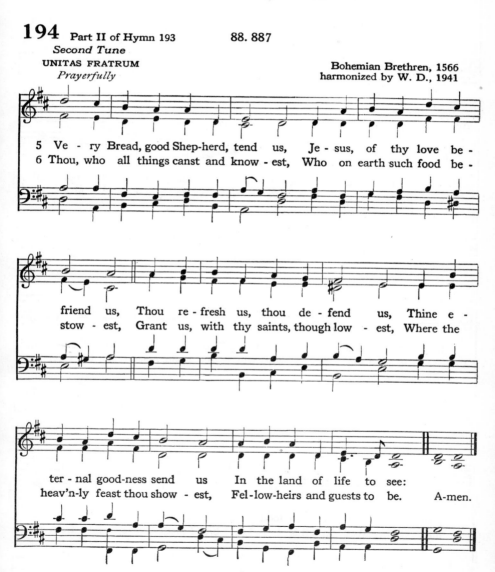

5 Ve - ry Bread, good Shep-herd, tend us, Je - sus, of thy love be -
6 Thou, who all things canst and know - est, Who on earth such food be -

friend us, Thou re - fresh us, thou de - fend us, Thine e -
stow - est, Grant us, with thy saints, though low - est, Where the

ter - nal good-ness send us In the land of life to see:
heav'n-ly feast thou show - est, Fel-low-heirs and guests to be. A-men.

ST. THOMAS AQUINAS, 1263; *Hymnal Version*, 1939

195 Holy Communion

98. 98. D.

RENDEZ A DIEU

With dignity

LOUIS BOURGEOIS, 1543

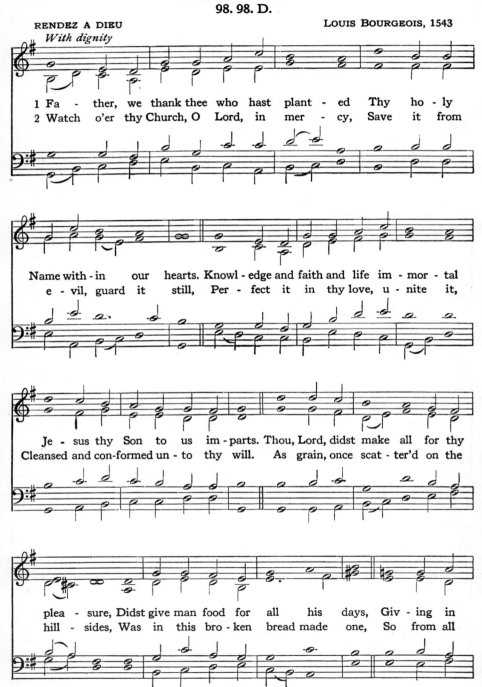

1 Fa - ther, we thank thee who hast plant - ed Thy ho - ly
2 Watch o'er thy Church, O Lord, in mer - cy, Save it from

Name with - in our hearts. Knowl - edge and faith and life im - mor - tal
e - vil, guard it still, Per - fect it in thy love, u - nite it,

Je - sus thy Son to us im - parts. Thou, Lord, didst make all for thy
Cleansed and con-formed un - to thy will. As grain, once scat - ter'd on the

plea - sure, Didst give man food for all his days, Giv - ing in
hill - sides, Was in this bro - ken bread made one, So from all

Holy Communion

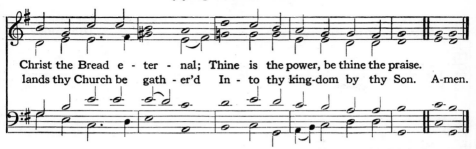

Christ the Bread e - ter - nal; Thine is the power, be thine the praise.
lands thy Church be gath - er'd In - to thy king-dom by thy Son. A-men.

Greek, from the Didache, c. 110; Tr. F. BLAND TUCKER, 1941

196

98. 98

EUCHARISTIC HYMN

JOHN S. B. HODGES, 1868

Quietly

1 Bread of the world, in mer - cy bro - ken, Wine of the soul, in

mer - cy shed, By whom the words of life were spo - ken,

And in whose death our sins are dead: A - men.

2 Look on the heart by sorrow broken,
   Look on the tears by sinners shed;
   And be thy feast to us the token
   That by thy grace our souls are fed. **Amen.**

REGINALD HEBER, *pub.* 1827

Alternative Tune, RENDEZ À DIEU, No. 195

Holy Communion
87. 87. 87

PICARDY

Traditional French Melody, 17th century

Unison, in strict rhythm, slowly

1 Let all mor - tal flesh keep si - lence, and with fear and trem - bling stand;
2 King of kings, yet born of Ma - ry, as of old on earth he stood,
3 Rank on rank the host of hea - ven spreads its van-guard on the way,

Pon-der noth-ing earth - ly - mind - ed, for with bless-ing in his hand
Lord of lords in hu - man ves - ture, in the Bo - dy and the Blood
As the Light of Light de - scend - eth from the realms of end - less day,

Christ our God to earth de - scend - eth, our full hom-age to de - mand.
He will give to all the faith - ful his own self for heav'n-ly food.
That the powers of hell may van - ish as the dark-ness clears a - way.

4 At his feet the six-winged seraph;
   cherubim with sleepless eye,
Veil their faces to the Presence,
   as with ceaseless voice they cry,
    " Alleluia, Alleluia, Alleluia, Lord most high! "
          Amen.

In harmony

A - men.

Liturgy of St. James; Para. GERARD MOULTRIE, 1864

ST. FLAVIAN   JOHN DAY'S *Psalter*, 1562
Moderately slow

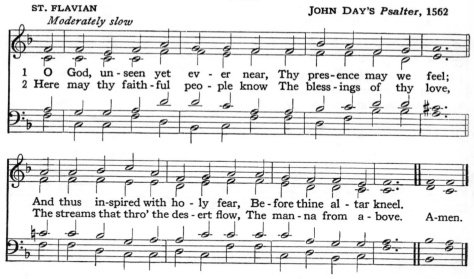

1 O God, un-seen yet ev-er near, Thy pres-ence may we feel;
2 Here may thy faith-ful peo-ple know The bless-ings of thy love,

And thus in-spired with ho-ly fear, Be-fore thine al-tar kneel.
The streams that thro' the des-ert flow, The man-na from a-bove. A-men.

3 We come, obedient to thy word,
    To feast on heav'nly food;
Our meat the Body of the Lord,
Our drink his precious Blood.

4 Thus may we all thy word obey,
    For we, O God, are thine;
And go rejoicing on our way,
    Renewed with strength divine.
                     Amen.
EDWARD OSLER, 1836, *alt.*

198 *Second Tune*   C. M.

MEDITATION   JOHN H. GOWER, 1890
Simply

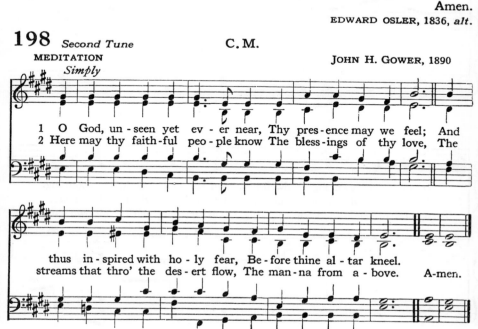

1 O God, un-seen yet ev-er near, Thy pres-ence may we feel; And
2 Here may thy faith-ful peo-ple know The bless-ings of thy love, The

thus in-spired with ho-ly fear, Be-fore thine al-tar kneel.
streams that thro' the des-ert flow, The man-na from a-bove. A-men.

Holy Communion
87. 87. 87

PANGE LINGUA

Sarum Plainsong,
Mode III, trans.

Unison, with stately movement

1 Now, my tongue, the mys-t'ry tell - ing Of the glo-rious Bo-dy sing,
2 Giv'n for us, and con - de - scend-ing To be born for us be - low,
3 That last night at sup - per ly - ing Mid the twelve, his cho-sen band,

And the Blood, all price ex - cell - ing, Which the Gen-tiles' Lord and King,
He with men in con-verse blend-ing Dwelt, the seed of truth to sow,
Je - sus, with the Law com - ply - ing, Keeps the feast its rites de - mand;

Once on earth a - mong us dwell-ing, Shed for this world's ran-som-ing.
Till he closed with wondrous end-ing His most pa - tient life of woe.
Then, more pre-cious food sup - ply - ing, Gives him-self with his own hand.

Holy Communion

A - men.

4 Word-made-flesh, true bread he maketh
  By his word his Flesh to be,
  Wine his Blood; when man partaketh,
  Though his senses fail to see,
  Faith alone, when sight forsaketh,
  Shows true hearts the mystery.

199
Second Tune　　　　87. 87. 87
ST. THOMAS　　　　J. F. WADE'S *Cantus Diversi*, 1751
Majestically

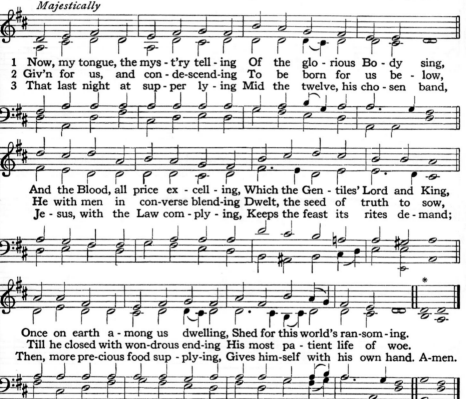

1 Now, my tongue, the mys - t'ry tell - ing Of the glo - rious Bo - dy sing,
2 Giv'n for us, and con - de - scend - ing To be born for us be - low,
3 That last night at sup - per ly - ing Mid the twelve, his cho - sen band,

And the Blood, all price ex - cell - ing, Which the Gen - tiles' Lord and King,
He with men in con - verse blend - ing Dwelt, the seed of truth to sow,
Je - sus, with the Law com - ply - ing, Keeps the feast its rites de - mand;

Once on earth a - mong us dwelling, Shed for this world's ran - som - ing.
Till he closed with won - drous end - ing His most pa - tient life of woe.
Then, more pre - cious food sup - ply - ing, Gives him - self with his own hand. A - men.

200
Part II of Hymn 199

5 Therefore we, before him bending,
　This great Sacrament revere;
　Types and shadows have their ending,
　For the newer rite is here;
　Faith, our outward sense befriending,
　Makes our inward vision clear.

6 Glory let us give and blessing
　To the Father and the Son,
　Honor, thanks, and praise addressing,
　While eternal ages run;
　Ever too his love confessing
　Who from both with both is One.
　　　　　　　　　　　Amen.

Amen only after stanza 6　ST. THOMAS AQUINAS, 1263; *Hymnal Version*, 1940

Third Tune   87. 87. 87

TANTUM ERGO   Spanish Plainsong, Mode **V**

In unison, very smoothly, without hurry

5 There-fore we, be-fore him bend - ing, ...
6 Glo - ry let us give and bless - ing . . . .

This great Sac - ra - ment re - vere; Types and sha-dows have their end - ing,
To the Fa - ther and the Son, Hon - or, thanks, and praise ad-dress - ing,

For the new - er rite is here; . . . . Faith, our out-ward sense be -
While e - ter - nal a - ges run; . . . . Ev - er too his love con -

Holy Communion

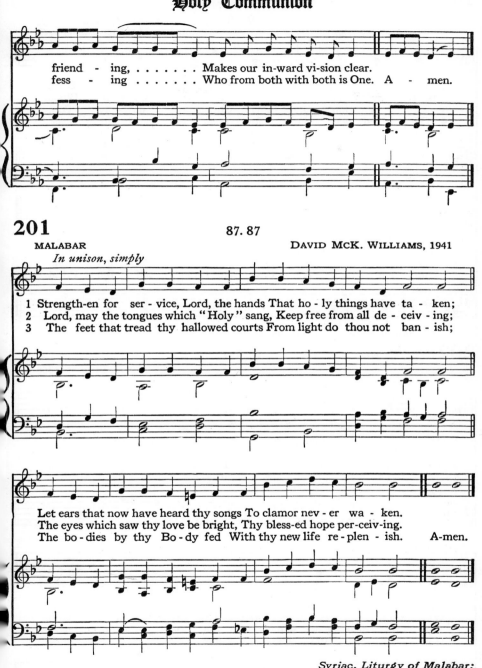

friend - ing, ... Makes our in-ward vi-sion clear.
fess - ing . . . . Who from both with both is One. A - men.

201

87. 87

MALABAR

DAVID McK. WILLIAMS, 1941

In unison, simply

1 Strength-en for ser - vice, Lord, the hands That ho - ly things have ta - ken;
2 Lord, may the tongues which "Holy" sang, Keep free from all de - ceiv - ing;
3 The feet that tread thy hallowed courts From light do thou not ban - ish;

Let ears that now have heard thy songs To clamor nev - er wa - ken.
The eyes which saw thy love be bright, Thy bless-ed hope per-ceiv-ing.
The bo - dies by thy Bo - dy fed With thy new life re - plen - ish. A-men.

Syriac, Liturgy of Malabar;
Tr. C. W. HUMPHREYS, *alt.* PERCY DEARMER, 1906

GARDEN   10. 10   Traditional English Melody,
In moderate time   adapted by MARTIN SHAW, 1929

1 Draw nigh and take the Bo - dy of the Lord,
2 Saved by that Bo - dy and that ho - ly Blood,
3 Sal - va - tion's giv - er, Christ, the on - ly Son,
4 Of - fered was he for great - est and for least,

And drink the ho - ly Blood for you out - poured.
With souls re - freshed, we ren - der thanks to God.
By his dear cross and blood the vic - tory won.
Him - self the Vic - tim, and him - self the Priest.

Copyright, 1929, by the Oxford University Press

202 *Second Tune*   10. 10

LAMMAS   ARTHUR H. BROWN, 1868
In moderate time

1 Draw nigh and take the Bo - dy of the Lord,
2 Saved by that Bo - dy and that ho - ly Blood,
3 Sal - va - tion's giv - er, Christ, the on - ly Son,
4 Of - fered was he for great - est and for least,

And drink the ho - ly Blood for you out - poured.
With souls re - freshed, we ren - der thanks to God.
By his dear cross and blood the vic - tory won.
Him - self the Vic - tim, and him - self the Priest.

Holy Communion

5 Approach ye then with faithful hearts sincere,
  And take the pledges of salvation here.

6 He that his saints in this world rules and shields
  To all believers life eternal yields;

7 With heav'nly bread makes them that hunger whole,
  Gives living waters to the thirsting soul.

8 Alpha and Omega, to whom shall bow
  All nations at the doom, is with us now.

Bangor Antiphoner, c. 690; *Tr.* J. M. NEALE, 1851, *alt.*

203
ROCKINGHAM

L. M.

Melody adapted by EDWARD MILLER, 1790,
harmonized by SAMUEL WEBBE, 1820

Slow and quiet

1 My God, thy ta - ble now is spread, Thy cup with
2 O let thy ta - ble hon - or'd be, And fur - nished
3 Drawn by thy quick-'ning grace, O Lord, In count - less
4 Nor let thy spread-ing Gos - pel rest, Till through the

love doth o - ver - flow; Be all thy chil - dren
well with joy - ful guests: And may each soul sal -
num - bers let them come, And gath - er from their
world thy truth has run; Till with this Bread all

thi - ther led, And let them thy sweet mer - cies know.
va - tion see, That here its sa - cred pledg - es tastes.
Fa - ther's board The Bread that lives be - yond the tomb.
men be blest, Who see the light or feel the sun.

A simpler harmony at No. 337

PHILIP DODDRIDGE, 1755, *alt.*

Holy Communion
11 11. 11 11

ADORO DEVOTE
In unison, moderately slow

Benedictine Plainsong,
Mode V, 13th century

1 Hum - bly I a - dore thee, Ve - ri - ty un - seen, Who thy glo - ry
2 Taste, and touch, and vi - sion, to dis - cern thee fail; Faith, that comes by
3 O me - mo - rial won - drous of the Lord's own death; Liv - ing Bread, that

hid - est 'neath these sha - dows mean; Lo, to thee sur - ren - dered,
hear - ing, pierc - es through the veil. I be - lieve what - e'er the
giv - est all thy crea - tures breath, Grant my spi - rit ev - er

my whole heart is bowed, Tranced as it be - holds thee, shrined with - in the cloud.
Son of God hath told; What the Truth hath spo - ken, that for truth I hold.
by thy life may live, To my taste thy sweet - ness nev - er - fail - ing give.

Holy Communion

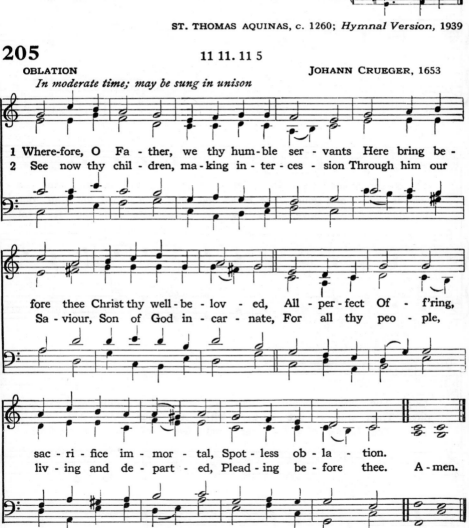

4 Jesus, whom now veilèd, I by faith descry,
   What my soul doth thirst for, do not, Lord, deny,
   That thy face unveilèd, I at last may see,
   With the blissful vision blest, my God, of thee.
                                                    Amen.

ST. THOMAS AQUINAS, c. 1260; *Hymnal Version*, 1939

205   11 11. 11 5

OBLATION   JOHANN CRUEGER, 1653

In moderate time; may be sung in unison

1 Where-fore, O Fa - ther, we thy hum-ble ser - vants Here bring be -
2 See now thy chil - dren, ma - king in - ter - ces - sion Through him our

fore thee Christ thy well - be - lov - ed, All - per - fect Of - f'ring,
Sa - viour, Son of God in - car - nate, For all thy peo - ple,

sac - ri - fice im - mor - tal, Spot - less ob - la - tion.
liv - ing and de - part - ed, Plead - ing be - fore thee. A - men.

WILLIAM H. H. JERVOIS, 1906

By permission of Mr. Peter Martineau and the Oxford University Press
Alternative Tune, ECCE JAM NOCTIS, No. 71

206 ## Holy Communion

10 10. 10 10

CANTICUM REFECTIONIS   DAVID McK. WILLIAMS, 1941

In unison, with solemn joy

1 This is the hour of ban-quet and of song; This is the heav'n-ly
2 Too soon we rise; we go our sev-eral ways; The feast, tho' not the
3 Feast aft-er feast thus comes and pass-es by, Yet, pass-ing, points to

ta-ble spread for me; Here let me feast, and, feast-ing, still pro-
love, is past and gone, The bread and wine con-sumed: yet all our
the glad feast a-bove, Giv-ing us fore-taste of the fes-tal

long The brief, bright hour of fel-low-ship with thee.
days Thou still art here with us — our shield and sun.
joy, The Lord's e-ter-nal feast of bliss and love.

HORATIUS BONAR, 1855, *alt.*

207 *First Tune* 𝔥𝔬𝔩𝔶 𝔠𝔬𝔪𝔪𝔲𝔫𝔦𝔬𝔫

10 10. 10 10

EDSALL
Quietly

GEORGE HENRY DAY, 1940

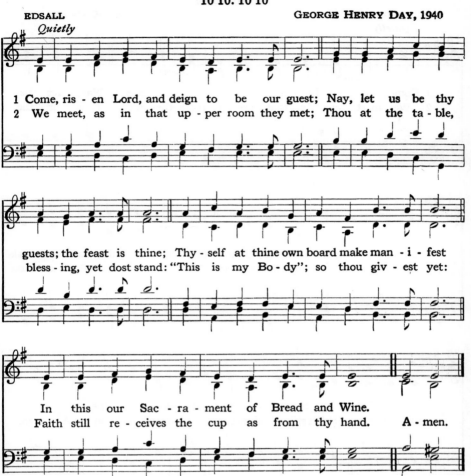

1 Come, ris - en Lord, and deign to be our guest; Nay, let us be thy
2 We meet, as in that up - per room they met; Thou at the ta - ble,

guests; the feast is thine; Thy - self at thine own board make man - i - fest
bless - ing, yet dost stand: "This is my Bo - dy"; so thou giv - est yet:

In this our Sac - ra - ment of Bread and Wine.
Faith still re - ceives the cup as from thy hand. A - men.

3 One body we, one Body who partake,
    One Church united in communion blest;
One name we bear, one Bread of life we break,
    With all thy saints on earth and saints at rest.

4 One with each other, Lord, for one in thee,
    Who art one Saviour and one living Head;
Then open thou our eyes, that we may see;
    Be known to us in breaking of the Bread. Amen.

GEORGE WALLACE BRIGGS. 1933

Alternative Tune, CANTICUM REFECTIONIS, No. 206

𝕳𝖔𝖑𝖞 𝕮𝖔𝖒𝖒𝖚𝖓𝖎𝖔𝖓
10 10. 10 10

KNICKERBOCKER

FRANK K. OWEN, 1941

Quietly

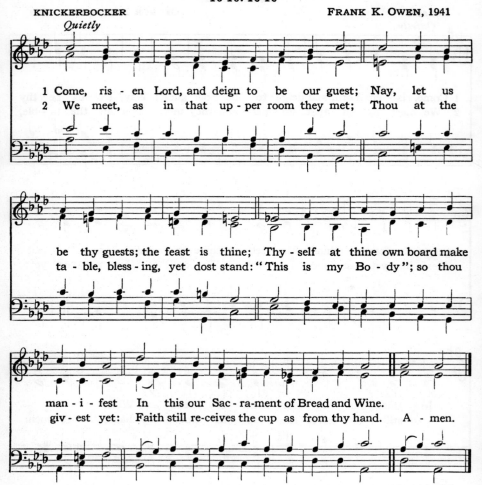

1 Come, ris-en Lord, and deign to be our guest; Nay, let us
2 We meet, as in that up-per room they met; Thou at the

be thy guests; the feast is thine; Thy-self at thine own board make
ta-ble, bless-ing, yet dost stand: "This is my Bo-dy"; so thou

man-i-fest In this our Sac-ra-ment of Bread and Wine.
giv-est yet: Faith still re-ceives the cup as from thy hand. A-men.

3 One body we, one Body who partake,
　　One Church united in communion blest;
　One name we bear, one Bread of life we break,
　　With all thy saints on earth and saints at rest.

4 One with each other, Lord, for one in thee,
　　Who art one Saviour and one living Head;
　Then open thou our eyes, that we may see;
　　Be known to us in breaking of the Bread.　Amen.

GEORGE WALLACE BRIGGS, 1933

𝕳𝖔𝖑𝖞 𝕮𝖔𝖒𝖒𝖚𝖓𝖎𝖔𝖓
10 10. 10 10

PENITENTIA   EDWARD DEARLE, 1880
Moderately slow

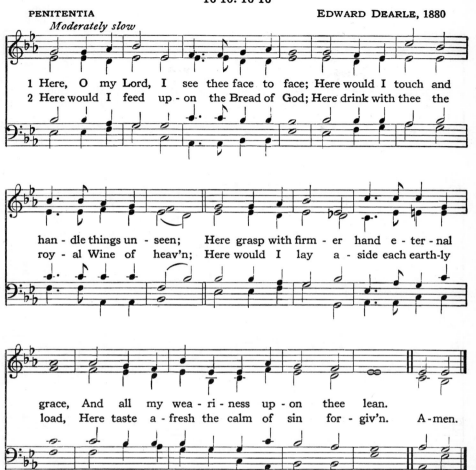

1 Here, O my Lord, I see thee face to face; Here would I touch and
2 Here would I feed up-on the Bread of God; Here drink with thee the

han-dle things un - seen; Here grasp with firm - er hand e - ter - nal
roy - al Wine of heav'n; Here would I lay a - side each earth-ly

grace, And all my wea - ri - ness up - on thee lean.
load, Here taste a - fresh the calm of sin for - giv'n. A-men.

3 I have no help but thine; nor do I need
   Another arm save thine to lean upon;
   It is enough, my Lord, enough indeed;
   My strength is in thy might, thy might alone.

4 Mine is the sin, but thine the righteousness;
   Mine is the guilt, but thine the cleansing Blood.
   Here is my robe, my refuge, and my peace;
   Thy Blood, thy righteousness, O Lord, my God.   Amen.

HORATIUS BONAR, 1855

Alternative Tune, KNICKERBOCKER, No. 207

208 *Second Tune* 𝔥𝔬𝔩𝔶 ℭ𝔬𝔪𝔪𝔲𝔫𝔦𝔬𝔫

10 10. 10 10

PEEL CASTLE
Prayerfully; may be sung in unison

Traditional Manx Melody,
School Worship, 1926

1 Here, O my Lord, I see thee face to face;
2 Here would I feed up - on the Bread of God;
3 I have no help but thine; nor do I need

Here would I touch and han - dle things un - seen;
Here drink with thee the roy - al Wine of heav'n;
An - oth - er arm save thine to lean up - on;

Here grasp with firm - er hand e - ter - nal grace,
Here would I lay a - side each earth - ly load,
It is e - nough, my Lord, e - nough in - deed;

And all my wea - ri - ness up - on thee lean.
Here taste a - fresh the calm of sin for - giv'n.
My strength is in thy might, thy might a - lone. A - men.

4 Mine is the sin, but thine the righteousness;
   Mine is the guilt, but thine the cleansing Blood.
   Here is my robe, my refuge, and my peace;
   Thy Blood, thy righteousness, O Lord, my God.   Amen.

HORATIUS BONAR, 1855

209 *First Tune* 𝕳𝖔𝖑𝖞 𝕮𝖔𝖒𝖒𝖚𝖓𝖎𝖔𝖓
L. M.

MARTYR DEI

Mediaeval Plainsong, Mode VI

In unison, with movement

1 O sav - ing Vic - tim, ope - ning wide The gate of heav'n to man
2 All praise and thanks to thee as - cend For ev - er-more, blest One

be - low, Our foes press on from ev - 'ry side,
in Three; O grant us life that shall not end,

Thine aid sup - ply, thy strength be - stow.
In our true na - tive land with thee. A - men.

ST. THOMAS AQUINAS, 1263; *Tr.* EDWARD CASWALL, 1849

Holy Communion
L. M.

ST. VINCENT

SIGISMUND NEUKOMM
arr. by JAMES UGLOW, 1868

Quietly

1 O sav - ing Vic - tim, ope - ning wide The gate of
2 All praise and thanks to thee as - cend For ev - er -

heav'n to man be - low, Our foes press on from ev - 'ry
more, blest One in Three; O grant us life that shall not

side, Thine aid sup - ply, thy strength be - stow.
end, In our true na - tive land with thee. A - men.

ST. THOMAS AQUINAS, 1263; *Tr.* EDWARD CASWALL, 1849

Alternative Tune, MELCOMBE, No. 155

210
88. 88. 88. 88

SCHMUECKE DICH

Melody by JOHANN CRUEGER, 1649

Moderately slow

1 Deck thy - self, my soul, with glad - ness, Leave the gloom-y haunts of
2 Sun, who all my life dost bright - en; Light, who dost my soul en -
3 Je - sus, Bread of Life, I pray thee, Let me glad - ly here o -

Holy Communion

sad - ness, Come in - to the day-light's splen - dor, There with
light - en; Joy, the sweet-est man e'er know - eth; Fount, whence
bey thee; Nev - er to my hurt in - vit - ed, Be thy

joy thy prais-es ren - der Un - to him whose grace un - bound-ed
all my be - ing flow - eth: At thy feet I cry, my Ma - ker,
love with love re - quit - ed; From this ban-quet let me mea - sure,

Hath this won-drous ban-quet found - ed; High o'er all the heav'ns he
Let me be a fit par - ta - ker Of this bless-ed food from
Lord, how vast and deep its trea - sure; Through the gifts thou here dost

reign - eth, Yet to dwell with thee he deign - eth.
hea - ven, For our good, thy glo - ry, giv - en.
give me, As thy guest in heav'n re - ceive me. A-men.

JOHANN FRANCK, 1649; *Tr.* CATHERINE WINKWORTH, 1863

211

Holy Communion

87. 87. 76. 86

JESU JOY OF MAN'S DESIRING

Melody by JOHANN SCHOP, 1642,
arr. and har. by J. S. BACH, 1716

Simply; may be sung in unison

Come with us, O bless-ed Je-sus, With us ev-er-

more to be; And in leav-ing now thine al-tar, Let us

nev-er-more leave thee! O let thine an-gel cho-rus

Cease not the heav'n-ly strain, But in us, thy lov-ing

Holy Communion

chil - dren, Bring peace, good will to men. A - men.

JOHN HENRY HOPKINS, Jr., 1882, *alt.*

212 77. 77. 77

BREAD OF HEAVEN WILLIAM D. MACLAGAN, 1875

In flowing style

1 Bread of heav'n, on thee we feed, For thy Flesh is meat in - deed;
2 Vine of heav'n, thy Blood sup - plies This blest cup of sac - ri - fice;

Ev - er may our souls be fed With this true and liv - ing Bread;
Lord, thy wounds our heal - ing give, To thy cross we look and live:

Day by day with strength supplied, Thro' the life of him who died.
Je - sus, may we ev - er be Graft - ed, root - ed, built in thee. A-men.

JOSIAH CONDER, 1824, *alt.*

ST. AGNES JOHN B. DYKES, 1866
Quietly

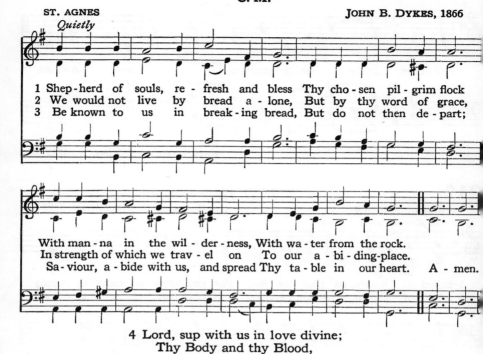

1 Shep-herd of souls, re - fresh and bless Thy cho - sen pil - grim flock
2 We would not live by bread a - lone, But by thy word of grace,
3 Be known to us in break-ing bread, But do not then de - part;

With man - na in the wil - der - ness, With wa - ter from the rock.
In strength of which we trav - el on To our a - bi - ding-place.
Sa - viour, a - bide with us, and spread Thy ta - ble in our heart. A - men.

4 Lord, sup with us in love divine;
Thy Body and thy Blood,
That living bread, that heav'nly wine,
Be our immortal food. Amen.

JAMES MONTGOMERY, 1825, *alt.*

Also the following:

214

Matrimony

11 10. 11 10

SANDRINGHAM

Not slow

JOSEPH BARNBY, 1889

1 O per - fect Love, all hu - man thought tran - scend - ing,
2 O per - fect Life, be thou their full as - sur - ance

Low - ly we kneel in prayer be - fore thy throne,
Of ten - der cha - ri - ty and stead - fast faith,

That theirs may be the love that knows no end - ing,
Of pa - tient hope, and qui - et, brave en - dur - ance,

Whom thou for ev - er - more dost join in one.
With child - like trust that fears nor pain nor death. A - men.

3 Grant them the joy which brightens earthly sorrow;
　　Grant them the peace which calms all earthly strife,
　And to life's day the glorious unknown morrow
　　That dawns upon eternal love and life. Amen.

DOROTHY F. GURNEY, 1883

215

Matrimony
C. M. D.

CHARLOTTE

Joyfully

ARTHUR H. BIGGS, 1941

1 Lord, who at Ca - na's wed - ding feast Didst as a guest ap - pear,
2 The ho - liest vow that man can make, The gold - en thread in life,

Thou dear - er far than earth - ly guest, Vouch-safe thy pres - ence here;
The bond that none may dare to break, That bind - eth man and wife;

For ho - ly thou in - deed dost prove The mar - riage vow to be,
Which, blest by thee, what-e'er be - tides, No e - vil shall de - stroy,

Pro - claim-ing it a type of love Be-tween the Church and thee.
Through anx-ious days each care di - vides, And doub-les ev - 'ry joy. A-men.

Matrimony

3 On those who at thine altar kneel,
  O Lord, thy blessing pour,
That each may wake the other's zeal
  To love thee more and more:
O grant them here in peace to live,
  In purity and love,
And, this world leaving, to receive
  A crown of life above.   Amen.

ADELAIDE THRUPP, 1853, *and* GODFREY THRING, 1882

216 87. 87

PETERSEN
In flowing style

Melody, pub. Halle, 1697,
har. by CHARLES WOOD, 1910

1 May the grace of Christ our Sa - viour, And the
2 Thus may they a - bide in un - ion With each

Fa - ther's bound-less love, With the Ho - ly Spi - rit's
oth - er and the Lord, And pos - sess, in sweet com -

fa - vor, Rest up - on them from a - bove.
mun - ion, Joys which earth can - not af - ford.   A - men.

JOHN NEWTON, 1779, *alt.*

217

First Tune

L. M.

VENI CREATOR

Sarum Plainsong, Mode VIII

In unison, smoothly and fluently

1 Come, Ho - ly Ghost, our souls in - spire, And light - en
3 Thy bless - ed unc - tion from a - bove Is com - fort,
5 A - noint and cheer our soil - ed face With the a -
7 Teach us to know the Fa - ther, Son, And thee, of

with ce - les - tial fire. 2 Thou the a - noint - ing
life, and fire of love. 4 En - a - ble with per -
bun - dance of thy grace. 6 Keep far our foes, give
both, to be but One, 8 That through the a - ges

Spi - rit art, Who dost thy sev'n - fold gifts im - part.
pet - ual light The dull - ness of our blind - ed sight.
peace at home: Where thou art guide, no ill can come.
all a - long, This may be our end - less song:

†Omit these two notes in stanza 8

Ember Days and Ordination

9 Praise to thy e - ter - nal mer - it, Fa - ther,

Son, and Ho - ly Spi - rit. A - men.

Latin, 9th cent.; Tr. JOHN COSIN, 1627

217 *Second Tune*　　　　88

COME HOLY GHOST　　　　JOHN HENRY HOPKINS, Jr., pub. 1865

Without dragging

1 Come, Ho - ly Ghost, our souls in - spire, And light - en with ce - les - tial fire.
2 　　Thou the a - noint - ing Spi - rit art, Who dost thy sev'n-fold gifts im - part.
3 Thy bless - ed unc - tion from a - bove Is com - fort, life, and fire of love.
4 En - a - ble with per - pet - ual light The dull - ness of our blind-ed sight.

Ember Days and Ordination

5 A - noint and cheer our soil - ed face With the a - bun - dance
6 Keep far our foes, give peace at home: Where thou art guide, no
7 Teach us to know the Fa - ther, Son, And thee, of both, to
8 That through the a - ges all a - long, This may be our

of thy grace.
ill can come.
be but One,
end - less song: 9 Praise to thy e - ter - nal mer - it,

Fa - ther, Son, and Ho - ly Spi - rit. A - men.

Latin, 9th cent.; Tr. JOHN COSIN, 1627

L. M.

MENDON

Traditional German Melody
arr. by SAMUEL DYER, 1828

In moderate time

1 Come, Ho - ly Ghost, Cre - a - tor blest, Vouch - safe with -
2 To thee, the Com - fort - er, we cry; To thee, the
3 The sev'n - fold gifts of grace are thine, O Fin - ger

in our souls to rest; Come with thy grace and heav'n - ly
Gift of God most high; The Fount of life, the Fire of
of the Hand Di - vine; True Prom - ise of the Fa - ther

aid, And fill the hearts which thou hast made.
love, The soul's A - noint - ing from a - bove.
thou, Who dost the tongue with speech en - dow. A - men.

4 Thy light to every sense impart,
And shed thy love in every heart;
Thine own unfailing might supply
To strengthen our infirmity.

5 Drive far away our ghostly foe,
And thine abiding peace bestow;
If thou be our preventing Guide,
No evil can our steps betide. Amen.

Latin, 9th cent.; Ordinal Version, 1929
Alternative Translation and Tune, VENI CREATOR, No. 108

Ember Days and Ordination

L. M.

HAMBURG

Arr. by LOWELL MASON, 1824

In moderate time

1 Lord, pour thy Spi - rit from on high, And thine or -
2 With - in thy tem - ple when they stand To teach the
3 Wis - dom, and zeal, and faith im - part, Firm - ness and

dain - ed ser - vants bless; Grac - es and gifts to
truth as taught by thee, Sa - viour, like stars in
meek - ness from a - bove, To bear thy peo - ple

each sup - ply, And clothe thy priests with right - eous - ness.
thy right hand, Let all thy Church's pas - tors be.
in their heart, And love the souls whom thou dost love; A-men.

4 To watch, and pray, and never faint,
    By day and night strict guard to keep,
To warn the sinner, cheer the saint,
    To feed thy lambs, and fold thy sheep.

5 So, when their work is finished here,
    They may in hope their charge resign;
So, when their Master shall appear,
    They may with crowns of glory shine. Amen.

JAMES MONTGOMERY, 1833

220 Ember Days and Ordination
10 10. 10 10

TOULON

Abbreviated from Melody
by LOUIS BOURGEOIS, 1551

Slow

1 God of the pro - phets, bless the pro-phets' sons; E - li-jah's man - tle o'er E - li - sha cast: Each age its sol - emn task may claim but once; Make each one no - bler, strong-er than the last.

2 A-noint them pro - phets! Make their ears at - tent To thy di - vin - est speech; their hearts a - wake To hu - man need; their lips make el - o - quent For right-eous - ness that shall all e - vil break.

3 A-noint them priests! Strong in - ter - ces-sors they For par-don, and for cha - ri - ty and peace! O that with them, the world, so far a - stray, Might pass in - to Christ's life of sac - ri - fice! A-men.

4 Anoint them kings! Aye, kingly kings, O Lord!
   Anoint them with the Spirit of thy Son:
   Theirs not a jeweled crown, a blood-stained sword;
   Theirs by the love of Christ a kingdom won.

5 Make them apostles, heralds of thy cross;
   Forth may they go to tell all realms thy grace:
   Inspired of thee, may they count all but loss,
   And stand at last with joy before thy face.

DENIS WORTMAN, 1884, *alt.*

221 𝕰mber 𝕯ays and 𝕺rdination

L. M.

MISSIONARY CHANT

HEINRICH C. ZEUNER, 1832

With vigor

1 Ye Chris-tian her - alds, go, pro - claim Sal - va - tion in Em -
2 God shield you with a wall of fire, With ho - ly zeal your
3 And when our la - bors all are o'er, Then may we meet to

man - uel's Name: To dis - tant climes the ti - dings
hearts in - spire, Bid ra - ging winds their fu - ry
part no more, Meet, with the ran - somed throng to

bear, And plant the Rose of Shar - on there.
cease, And calm the sav - age breast to peace.
fall, And crown the Sa - viour Lord of all. A - men.

BOURNE HALL DRAPER, 1803, *alt.*

Alternative Tune, DUKE STREET, No. 148

Also the following:

109 Come, thou Holy Spirit, come
371 Creator Spirit, by whose aid
573 Go, labor on! spend and be spent
131 God, deigning man to be
377 Holy Spirit, Truth divine
268 I bind unto myself to-day
574 Lord, speak to me, that I may speak
575 Lord, who didst send, by two and two before thee
108 O come, Creator Spirit, come
256 O Spirit of the living God
535 Rise up, O men of God

222

For the Departed
88. 84

GAZA

Traditional Jewish Melody,
adapted 1919

With serenity

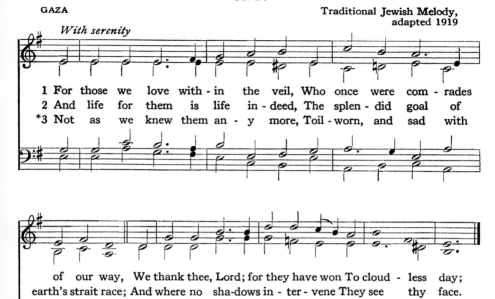

1 For those we love with - in the veil, Who once were com - rades
2 And life for them is life in - deed, The splen - did goal of
*3 Not as we knew them an - y more, Toil - worn, and sad with

of our way, We thank thee, Lord; for they have won To cloud - less day;
earth's strait race; And where no sha-dows in - ter - vene They see thy face.
bur-den'd care: E - rect, clear-eyed, up - on their brows Thy Name they bear.

4 Free from the fret of mortal years,
   And knowing now thy perfect will,
With quickened sense and heightened joy,
   They serve thee still.

5 O fuller, sweeter is that life,
   And larger, ampler is the air:
Eye cannot see nor heart conceive
   The glory there;

6 Nor know to what high purpose thou
   Dost yet employ their ripened powers,
Nor how at thy behest they touch
   This life of ours.

7 There are no tears within their eyes;
   With love they keep perpetual tryst;
And praise and work and rest are one
   With thee, O Christ.

WILLIAM CHARTER PIGGOTT, 1915

223

For the Departed
For Holy Communion at the Burial of the Dead
11 11. 11 11

ADORO DEVOTE
In unison, moderately slow

Benedictine Plainsong,
Mode V, 13th century

1 Je - sus, Son of Ma - ry, Fount of life a - lone, Here we hail thee
2 Think, O Lord, in mer - cy On the souls of those Who, in faith gone
3 Of - ten were they wound - ed In the dead - ly strife; Heal them, Good Phy-

pres - ent On thine al - tar-throne. Humbly we a - dore thee,
from us, Now in death re - pose. Here 'mid stress and con - flict
si - cian, With the balm of life. Ev - 'ry taint of e - vil,

Lord of end - less might, In the mys - tic sym - bols Veiled from earthly sight.
Toils can nev - er cease; There, the war-fare end - ed, Bid them rest in peace.
Frail-ty and de - cay, Good and gra-cious Sa - viour, Cleanse and purge away.

For the Departed

4 Rest eternal grant them,
  After weary fight;
  Shed on them the radiance
  Of thy heav'nly light.
  Lead them onward, upward,
  To the holy place,
  Where thy saints made perfect
  Gaze upon thy face.   Amen.

Written in Swahili; Tr. EDMUND S. PALMER, *pub.* 1906
By permission of the Oxford University Press

224 *First Tune*   77. 77. 88

PAX   *The Public School Hymn Book,* 1929

Quietly

1 Now the la-borer's task is o'er; Now the bat-tle day is past;
2 There the tears of earth are dried; There its hid-den things are clear;
3 There the pen-i-tents, that turn To the cross their dy-ing eyes,
4 There no more the powers of hell Can pre-vail to mar their peace;
5 "Earth to earth, and dust to dust," Calm-ly now the words we say,

Now up-on the far-ther shore Lands the voy-a-ger at last.
There the work of life is tried By a just-er judge than here.
All the love of Je-sus learn At his feet in pa-ra-dise.
Christ the Lord shall guard them well, He who died for their re-lease.
Left be-hind, we wait in trust For the re-sur-rec-tion day.

Refrain

Fa-ther, in thy gracious keeping Leave we now thy ser-vant sleep - ing.   A-men.

By permission of Novello and Company

JOHN ELLERTON, 1870

224 *Second Tune*

For the Departed
77. 77. 88

REQUIESCAT   JOHN B. DYKES, 1875

Quietly, without dragging

1 Now the la-borer's task is o'er; Now the bat - tle day is past;
2 There the tears of earth are dried; There its hid - den things are clear;
3 There the pen - i - tents, that turn To the cross their dy - ing eyes,

Now up - on the far - ther shore Lands the voy - a - ger at last.
There the work of life is tried By a just - er judge than here.
All the love of Je - sus learn At his feet in pa - ra - dise.

Refrain

Fa - ther, in thy gra-cious keep-ing Leave we now thy ser-vant sleep - ing.

4 There no more the powers of hell
    Can prevail to mar their peace;
Christ the Lord shall guard them well,
    He who died for their release.
                                 Refrain

5 "Earth to earth, and dust to dust,"
    Calmly now the words we say,
Left behind, we wait in trust
    For the resurrection day.

A - men.

                              Refrain

JOHN ELLERTON, 1870

225 For the Departed
88. 88. 88

OLD HUNDRED TWELFTH
With dignity

Anonymous German Melody, 1530,
, harmonized by W. D., 1937

1 God of the liv-ing, in whose eyes Un-veiled thy whole cre-
2 Re-leased from earth-ly toil and strife, With thee is hid-den
*3 Thy word is true, thy will is just; To thee we leave them,

a-tion lies, All souls are thine; we must not say That
still their life; Thine are their thoughts, their works, their powers, All
Lord, in trust; And bless thee for the love which gave Thy

those are dead who pass a-way; From this our world of
thine, and yet most tru-ly ours; For well we know, wher-
Son to fill a hu-man grave, That none might fear that

flesh set free, We know them liv-ing un-to thee.
e'er they be, Our dead are liv-ing un-to thee.
world to see Where all are liv-ing un-to thee. A-men.

4 O Breather into man of breath,
  O Holder of the keys of death,
  O Giver of the life within,
  Save us from death, the death of sin,
  That body, soul, and spirit be
  For ever living unto thee. Amen.

JOHN ELLERTON, 1858, alt.

226

For the Departed

88. 88. 88

WINKWORTH

JOSEPH BARNBY, 1869

In moderate time

1 O Lord, to whom the spi - rits live Of all the faith - ful
2 Bless thou the dead who die in thee; As thou hast giv - en
3 In thy green, plea - sant pas - tures feed The sheep that thou hast

passed a - way, Un - to their path that bright-ness give Which shin - eth
them re - lease, So quick - en them thy face to see, And give them
sum-moned hence; And by the still, cool wa - ters lead Thy flock in

Refrain

to the per - fect day. O Lamb of God, Re - deem - er blest,
ev - er - last - ing peace.
lov - ing prov - i - dence.

Grant them e - ter - nal light and rest. A-men.

4 Direct us with thine arm of might,
And bring us, perfected, with them
To dwell within thy city bright,
The heavenly Jerusalem.

Refrain

Amen.

RICHARD FREDERICK LITTLEDALE, 1864

For the Departed

227 Consecration of a Church
L. M.

GARDINER
With stately vigor

WILLIAM GARDINER'S
Sacred Melodies, 1815

1 All things are thine; no gift have we, Lord of all
2 Thy will was in the build - ers' thought; Thy hand un-
3 In weak - ness and in want we call On thee for
4 O Fa - ther, deign these walls to bless; Fill with thy

gifts, to of - fer thee; And hence with grate - ful hearts to-
seen a - midst us wrought; Through mor-tal mo - tive, scheme, and
whom the heav'ns are small; Thy glo - ry is thy chil - dren's
love their emp - ti - ness; And let their door a gate - way

day Thine own be - fore thy feet we lay.
plan, Thy wise e - ter - nal pur - pose ran.
good, Thy joy thy ten - der fa - ther - hood.
be To lead us from our - selves to thee. A - men.

By permission of Houghton Mifflin Company

JOHN GREENLEAF WHITTIER, 1872

228 *First Tune* 𝕮onsecration of a 𝕮hurch

11 11. 11 5

ISTE CONFESSOR

Mediaeval Plainsong, Mode VIII

In unison, not fast, flowing

1 On - ly - be - got - ten, Word of God e - ter - nal, Lord of cre -
2 This is thy tem - ple; here thy pres - ence - cham - ber; Here may thy
3 Here in our sick - ness, heal - ing grace a - bound - eth, Light in our
*4 Hal - lowed this dwell - ing where the Lord a - bid - eth, This is none
5 Lord, we be - seech thee, as we throng thy tem - ple, By thy past
6 God in three Per - sons, Fa - ther ev - er - last - ing, Son co - e -

a - tion, mer - ci - ful and migh - ty, Hear now thy ser - vants,
ser - vants, at the mys - tic ban - quet, Hum - bly a - dor - ing,
blind - ness, in our toil re - fresh - ment: Sin is for - giv - en,
oth - er than the gate of hea - ven; Stran - gers and pil - grims,
bless - ings, by thy pres - ent boun - ty, Fa - vor thy chil - dren,
ter - nal, ev - er - bless - ed Spi - rit, Thine be the glo - ry,

when their joy - ful voic - es Rise to thy pres - ence.
take thy Bo - dy bro - ken, Drink of thy chal - ice.
hope o'er fear pre - vail - eth, Joy o - ver sor - row.
seek - ing homes e - ter - nal, Pass thro' its por - tals.
and with ten - der mer - cy Hear our pe - ti - tions.
praise, and a - do - ra - tion, Now and for ev - er. A - men.

Latin, c. 9th cent.; Tr. MAXWELL J. BLACKER, *alt.*

Consecration of a Church

ROUEN

Unison, with dignity.

Rouen Church Melody,
har. by HEALEY WILLAN, 1918

1 On - ly - be - got - ten, Word of God e - ter - nal, Lord of cre -
a - tion, mer - ci - ful and migh - ty, Hear now thy ser - vants,
when their joy - ful voic - es Rise to thy pres - ence.

2 This is thy tem - ple; here thy pres-ence - cham - ber; Here may thy
ser - vants, at the mys - tic ban - quet, Hum - bly a - dor - ing,
take thy Bo - dy bro - ken, Drink of thy chal - ice.

3 Here in our sick - ness, heal - ing grace a - bound-eth, Light in our
blind - ness, in our toil re - fresh - ment: Sin is for - giv - en,
hope o'er fear pre - vail - eth, Joy o - ver sor - row. A - men.

By permission of the arranger

*4 Hallowed this dwelling where the Lord abideth,
This is none other than the gate of heaven;
Strangers and pilgrims, seeking homes eternal,
Pass through its portals.

5 Lord, we beseech thee, as we throng thy temple,
By thy past blessings, by thy present bounty,
Favor thy children, and with tender mercy
Hear our petitions.

6 God in three Persons, Father everlasting,
Son co-eternal, ever-blessèd Spirit,
Thine be the glory, praise, and adoration,
Now and for ever. Amen.

Latin, c. 9th cent.; Tr. MAXWELL J. BLACKER, 1884, *alt.*

Consecration of a Church

Also the following:

LITANIES

The stanzas of these hymns may be sung alternately by the minister (or a chorister) and the congregation, the last line of each stanza being sung always by the congregation.

229 Part I   77. 76

LEBBAEUS

St. Alban's Tune Book, 1866,
har. ARTHUR S. SULLIVAN, 1874

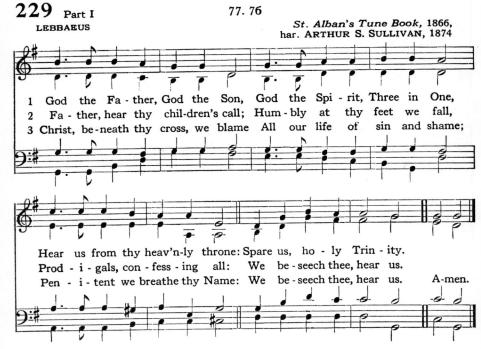

1 God the Fa-ther, God the Son, God the Spi-rit, Three in One,
2 Fa-ther, hear thy chil-dren's call; Hum-bly at thy feet we fall,
3 Christ, be-neath thy cross, we blame All our life of sin and shame;

Hear us from thy heav'n-ly throne: Spare us, ho-ly Trin-ity.
Prod-i-gals, con-fess-ing all: We be-seech thee, hear us.
Pen-i-tent we breathe thy Name: We be-seech thee, hear us.   A-men.

4 Holy Spirit, grieved and tried,
  Oft forgotten and defied,
  Now we mourn our stubborn pride:
    We beseech thee, hear us.

5 Love, that caused us first to be,
  Love, that bled upon the tree,
  Love, that draws us lovingly:
    We beseech thee, hear us.

Litanies

6 We thy call have disobeyed,
  Into paths of sin have strayed,
  And repentance have delayed:
    We beseech thee, hear us.

7 Sick, we come to thee for cure,
  Guilty, seek thy mercy sure,
  Evil, long to be made pure:
    We beseech thee, hear us.

8 Blind, we pray that we may see;
  Bound, we pray to be made free;
  Stained, we pray for sanctity:
    We beseech thee, hear us.

9 Thou who hear'st each contrite sigh,
  Bidding sinful souls draw nigh,
  Willing not that one should die:
    We beseech thee, hear us. Amen.

230 Part II of Hymn 229   77. 76

WESTERLY
JOHN HENRY HOPKINS, 1941

In unison

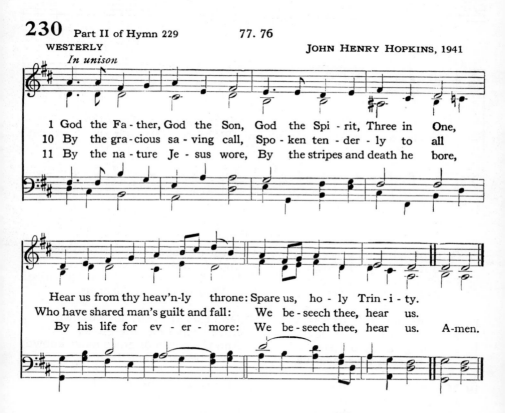

1 God the Fa-ther, God the Son, God the Spi-rit, Three in One,
10 By the gra-cious sa-ving call, Spo-ken ten-der-ly to all
11 By the na-ture Je-sus wore, By the stripes and death he bore,

Hear us from thy heav'n-ly throne: Spare us, ho-ly Trin-i-ty.
Who have shared man's guilt and fall: We be-seech thee, hear us.
By his life for ev-er-more: We be-seech thee, hear us. A-men.

12 By the love that longs to bless,
  Pitying our sore distress,
  Leading us to holiness:
    We beseech thee, hear us.

13 By the love so calm and strong,
  Patient still to suffer wrong
  And our day of grace prolong:
    We beseech thee, hear us.

14 By the love that speaks within,
  Calling us to flee from sin,
  And the joy of goodness win:
    We beseech thee, hear us.

15 By the love that bids thee spare,
  By the heav'n thou dost prepare,
  By thy promises to prayer:
    We beseech thee, hear us. Amen.

Litanies
77. 76

FARNABY

Traditional English Melody

In unison

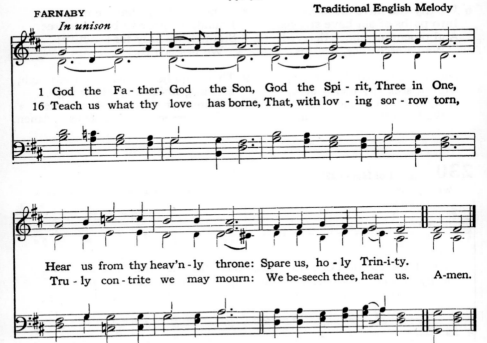

1 God the Fa - ther, God the Son, God the Spi - rit, Three in One,
16 Teach us what thy love has borne, That, with lov - ing sor - row torn,

Hear us from thy heav'n - ly throne: Spare us, ho - ly Trin-i-ty.
Tru - ly con - trite we may mourn: We be-seech thee, hear us. A-men.

17 Gifts of light and grace bestow;
Help us to resist the foe,
Fearing what alone is woe:
    We beseech thee, hear us.

18 Let not sin within us reign;
May we gladly suffer pain,
If it purge away our stain:
    We beseech thee, hear us.

19 May we to all evil die,
Fleshly longings crucify;
Fix our hearts and thoughts on
    high:
    We beseech thee, hear us.

20 Grant us faith to know thee near,
Hail thy grace, thy judgment fear,
And through trial persevere:
    We beseech thee, hear us.

21 Grant us hope from earth to rise,
And to strain with eager eyes
Towards the promised heav'nly prize:
    We beseech thee, hear us.

22 Grant us love, thy love to own,
Love to live for thee alone,
And the power of grace make known:
    We beseech thee, hear us.

23 All our weak endeavors bless,
As we ever forward press;
Lead us on to holiness:
    We beseech thee, hear us.

24 Lead us daily nearer thee
Till at last thy face we see,
Crowned with thine own purity:
    We beseech thee, hear us. Amen.

THOMAS BENSON POLLOCK, 1871, *alt.*

Litanies
77. 76

PEACEFIELD

Ancient Irish Melody,
har. by DAVID F. R. WILSON, 1919

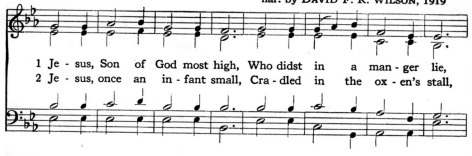

1 Je - sus, Son of God most high, Who didst in a man - ger lie,
2 Je - sus, once an in - fant small, Cra - dled in the ox - en's stall,

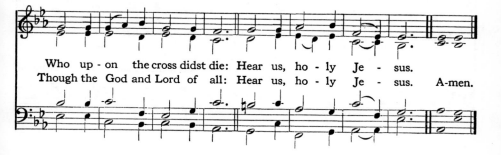

Who up - on the cross didst die: Hear us, ho - ly Je - sus.
Though the God and Lord of all: Hear us, ho - ly Je - sus. A-men.

3 Be thou with us every day,
In our work and in our play,
When we learn and when we pray:
Hear us, holy Jesus.

4 When we lie asleep at night,
Ever may thy angels bright
Keep us safe till morning light:
Hear us, holy Jesus.

5 Make us brave without a fear,
Make us happy, full of cheer,
Sure that thou art always near:
Hear us, holy Jesus.

6 May we prize our Christian name,
May we guard it free from blame,
Hating all that causes shame:
Hear us, holy Jesus.

7 May we grow from day to day,
Glad to learn each holy way,
Ever ready to obey:
Hear us, holy Jesus.

8 May we ever try to be
From all angry tempers free,
Pure and gentle, Lord, like thee:
Hear us, holy Jesus.

9 May our thoughts be undefiled,
May our words be true and mild,
Make us each a holy child:
Hear us, holy Jesus.

10 Jesus, from thy heav'nly throne,
Watching o'er each little one,
Till our life on earth is done:
Hear us, holy Jesus. Amen.

THOMAS BENSON POLLOCK, 1871, *alt.*

233 *First Tune*

Litanies
77. 76

LITANY OF THE PASSION

JOHN B. DYKES

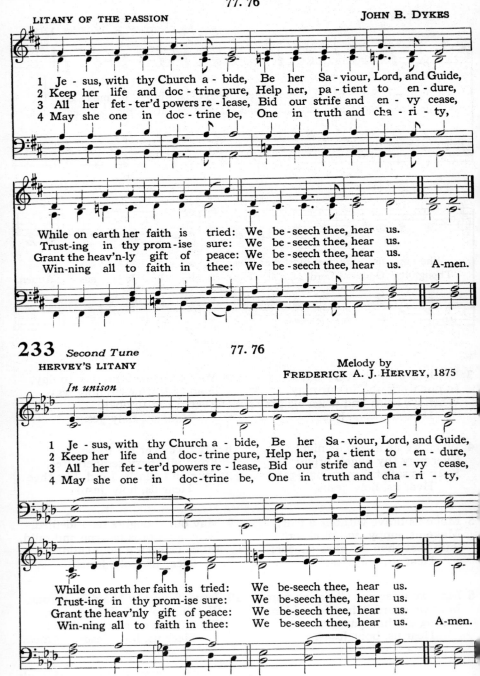

1 Je - sus, with thy Church a - bide, Be her Sa - viour, Lord, and Guide,
2 Keep her life and doc - trine pure, Help her, pa - tient to en - dure,
3 All her fet - ter'd powers re - lease, Bid our strife and en - vy cease,
4 May she one in doc - trine be, One in truth and cha - ri - ty,

While on earth her faith is tried: We be - seech thee, hear us.
Trust - ing in thy prom - ise sure: We be - seech thee, hear us.
Grant the heav'n - ly gift of peace: We be - seech thee, hear us.
Win - ning all to faith in thee: We be - seech thee, hear us. A - men.

233 *Second Tune*

77. 76

HERVEY'S LITANY

Melody by
FREDERICK A. J. HERVEY, 1875

In unison

1 Je - sus, with thy Church a - bide, Be her Sa - viour, Lord, and Guide,
2 Keep her life and doc - trine pure, Help her, pa - tient to en - dure,
3 All her fet - ter'd powers re - lease, Bid our strife and en - vy cease,
4 May she one in doc - trine be, One in truth and cha - ri - ty,

While on earth her faith is tried: We be - seech thee, hear us.
Trust - ing in thy prom - ise sure: We be - seech thee, hear us.
Grant the heav'nly gift of peace: We be - seech thee, hear us.
Win - ning all to faith in thee: We be - seech thee, hear us. A - men.

Litanies

5 May she guide the poor and blind,
Seek the lost until she find,
And the broken-hearted bind:
We beseech thee, hear us.

6 May her priests thy people feed,
Shepherds of the flock indeed,
Ready, where thou call'st, to lead:
We beseech thee, hear us.

7 Judge her not for work undone,
Judge her not for fields unwon,
Bless her works in thee begun:
We beseech thee, hear us.

8 All that she has lost, restore;
May her strength and zeal be more
Than in brightest days of yore:
We beseech thee, hear us.

9 Raise her to her calling high,
Let the nations far and nigh
Hear thy heralds' warning cry:
We beseech thee, hear us.

10 May she holy triumphs win,
Overthrow the hosts of sin,
Gather all the nations in:
We beseech thee, hear us.   Amen.

THOMAS BENSON POLLOCK, 1871, alt.

234 *First Tune*   77. 76
SCHEFFLER   JOHANN SCHEFFLER'S *Heilige Seelenlust*, 1657

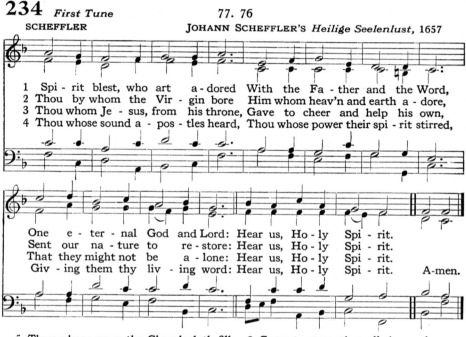

1 Spi - rit blest, who art a-dored With the Fa - ther and the Word,
2 Thou by whom the Vir - gin bore Him whom heav'n and earth a - dore,
3 Thou whom Je - sus, from his throne, Gave to cheer and help his own,
4 Thou whose sound a - pos - tles heard, Thou whose power their spi - rit stirred,

One e - ter - nal God and Lord: Hear us, Ho - ly Spi - rit.
Sent our na - ture to re - store: Hear us, Ho - ly Spi - rit.
That they might not be a - lone: Hear us, Ho - ly Spi - rit.
Giv - ing them thy liv - ing word: Hear us, Ho - ly Spi - rit.   A-men.

5 Thou whose grace the Church doth fill,
Showing her God's perfect will,
Making Jesus present still:
Hear us, Holy Spirit.

6 All thy gracious gifts bestow,
Gifts of wisdom God to know,
Gifts of strength to meet the foe:
Hear us, Holy Spirit.

7 All our evil passions kill,
Bend aright our stubborn will;
Though we grieve thee, patient still:
Hear us, Holy Spirit.

8 Come to strengthen all the weak,
Give thy courage to the meek,
Teach our falt'ring tongues to speak:
Hear us, Holy Spirit.

9 Keep us in the narrow way,
Warn us when we go astray,
Plead within us when we pray:
Hear us, Holy Spirit.

10 Holy, loving, as thou art,
Come, and live within our heart;
Nevermore from us depart:
Hear us, Holy Spirit.   Amen.

RICHARD FREDERICK LITTLEDALE, 1867, alt.

Litanies
77. 76

EVELYN

ARTHUR S. SULLIVAN, 1874

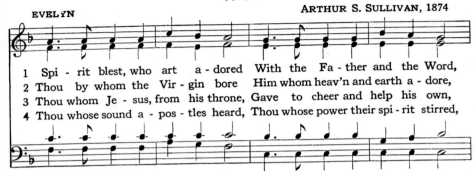

1 Spi - rit blest, who art a - dored With the Fa - ther and the Word,
2 Thou by whom the Vir - gin bore Him whom heav'n and earth a - dore,
3 Thou whom Je - sus, from his throne, Gave to cheer and help his own,
4 Thou whose sound a - pos - tles heard, Thou whose power their spi - rit stirred,

One e - ter - nal God and Lord: Hear us, Ho - ly Spi - rit.
Sent our na - ture to re - store: Hear us, Ho - ly Spi - rit.
That they might not be a - lone: Hear us, Ho - ly Spi - rit.
Giv - ing them thy liv - ing word: Hear us, Ho - ly Spi - rit. A - men.

5 Thou whose grace the Church doth
  fill,
  Showing her God's perfect will,
  Making Jesus present still:
      Hear us, Holy Spirit.

6 All thy gracious gifts bestow,
  Gifts of wisdom God to know,
  Gifts of strength to meet the foe:
      Hear us, Holy Spirit.

7 All our evil passions kill,
  Bend aright our stubborn will;
  Though we grieve thee, patient still:
      Hear us, Holy Spirit.

8 Come to strengthen all the weak,
  Give thy courage to the meek,
  Teach our falt'ring tongues to
  speak:
      Hear us, Holy Spirit.

9 Keep us in the narrow way,
  Warn us when we go astray,
  Plead within us when we pray:
      Hear us, Holy Spirit.

10 Holy, loving, as thou art,
   Come, and live within our heart;
   Nevermore from us depart:
       Hear us, Holy Spirit. Amen.

RICHARD FREDERICK LITTLEDALE, 1867, *alt.*

Also the following:
180 God of all grace, thy mercy send

HYMNS FOR CHILDREN

235

77. 77

INNOCENTS

Traditional Melody,
pub. *The Parish Choir*, 1850

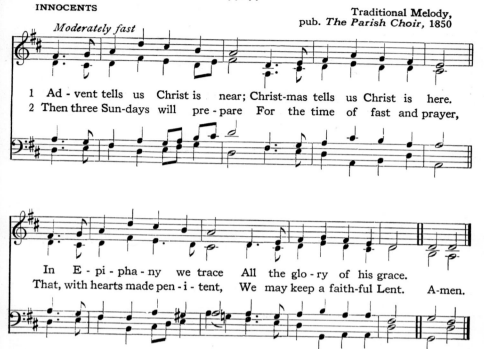

1 Ad - vent tells us Christ is near; Christ-mas tells us Christ is here.
2 Then three Sun-days will pre - pare For the time of fast and prayer,

In E - pi - pha - ny we trace All the glo - ry of his grace.
That, with hearts made pen - i - tent, We may keep a faith-ful Lent. A-men.

3 Holy Week and Easter then
Tell who died and rose again:
O that happy Easter Day!
" Christ is ris'n indeed," we say.

4 Yes, and Christ ascended, too,
To prepare a place for you;
So we give him special praise
After those great forty days.

5 Then he sent the Holy Ghost
On the day of Pentecost,
With us ever to abide:
Well may we keep Whitsuntide.

6 Last of all, we humbly sing
Glory to our God and King,
Glory to the One in Three,
On the Feast of Trinity. Amen.

KATHERINE HANKEY, 1888, *alt.*

Hymns for Children
87. 87. 77

IRBY

HENRY J. GAUNTLETT, 1858

Cheerfully

1 Once in roy - al Da - vid's ci - ty Stood a low - ly cat - tle shed,
2 He came down to earth from hea-ven, Who is God and Lord of all,
*3 And, thro' all his won - drous childhood, He would hon-or and o - bey,

Where a moth - er laid her ba - by In a man - ger for his bed:
And his shel - ter was a sta - ble, And his cra - dle was a stall;
Love, and watch the low - ly maid-en In whose gen - tle arms he lay;

Ma - ry was that moth-er mild, Je - sus Christ her lit - tle child.
With the poor, and mean, and low - ly, Lived on earth our Sa - viour ho - ly.
Chris-tian chil - dren all must be Mild, o - be - dient, good as he.

*4 For he is our childhood's pattern;
    Day by day like us he grew;
He was little, weak, and helpless,
    Tears and smiles like us he knew;
And he feeleth for our sadness,
And he shareth in our gladness.

5 And our eyes at last shall see him,
    Through his own redeeming love;
For that child so dear and gentle
    Is our Lord in heav'n above;
And he leads his children on
To the place where he is gone.

Hymns for Children

6 Not in that poor lowly stable,
With the oxen standing by,
We shall see him; but in heaven,
Set at God's right hand on high;
When like stars his children crowned,
All in white shall wait around.

CECIL FRANCES ALEXANDER, 1848

237

66. 66. 88

ARTHUR'S SEAT

JOHN GOSS, 1874

With movement

1 Be - hold a lit - tle child, Laid in a man - ger bed; The
2 A - las! in what poor state The Son of God is seen; Why
3 Where Jo - seph plies his trade, Lo, Je - sus la - bors too; The
4 A - mong the doc - tors see The boy so full of grace; Say,
5 Christ, once thy - self a boy, Our child-hood guard and guide; Be

win - try blasts blow wild A - round his in - fant head. But who is
doth the Lord so great Choose out a home so mean? That we may
hands that all things made An earth - ly craft pur - sue, That wea - ry
where - fore ta - keth he The schol - ar's low - ly place? That Chris-tian
thou its light and joy, And still with us a - bide, That thy dear

this so low - ly laid? 'Tis he by whom the worlds were made.
learn from pride to flee, And fol - low his hu - mil - i - ty.
men in him may rest, And faith - ful toil through him be blest.
boys, with rev'rence meet, May sit and learn at Je - sus' feet.
love, so great and free, May draw us ev - er-more to thee. A-men.

WILLIAM WALSHAM HOW, 1872

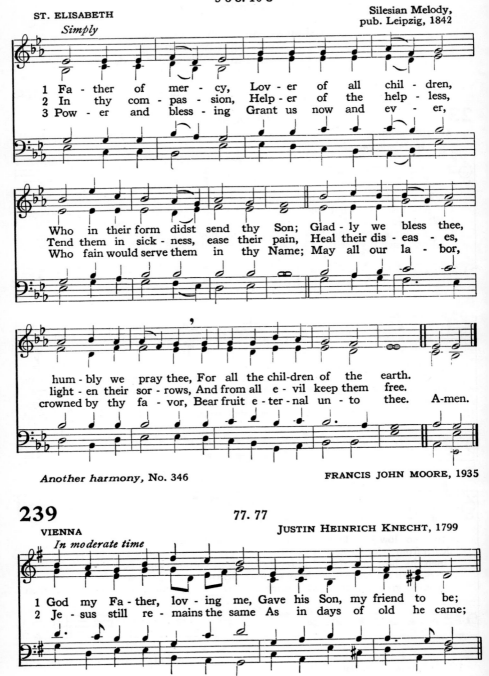

238

Hymns for Children
5 6 8. 10 8

ST. ELISABETH

Simply

Silesian Melody,
pub. Leipzig, 1842

1 Fa - ther of mer - cy, Lov - er of all chil - dren,
2 In thy com - pas - sion, Help - er of the help - less,
3 Pow - er and bless - ing Grant us now and ev - er,

Who in their form didst send thy Son; Glad - ly we bless thee,
Tend them in sick - ness, ease their pain, Heal their dis - eas - es,
Who fain would serve them in thy Name; May all our la - bor,

hum - bly we pray thee, For all the chil-dren of the earth.
light - en their sor - rows, And from all e - vil keep them free.
crowned by thy fa - vor, Bear fruit e - ter - nal un - to thee. A-men.

Another harmony, No. 346

FRANCIS JOHN MOORE, 1935

239

77. 77

JUSTIN HEINRICH KNECHT, 1799

VIENNA

In moderate time

1 God my Fa - ther, lov - ing me, Gave his Son, my friend to be;
2 Je - sus still re - mains the same As in days of old he came;

Gave his Son, my form to take, Bear-ing all things for my sake.
As my broth-er by my side, Still he seeks my steps to guide. A-men.

3 How can I repay thy love,
Lord of all the hosts above?
What have I, a child, to bring
Unto thee, thou heav'nly King?

4 I have but myself to give:
Let me to thy glory live;
Let me follow, day by day,
Where thou showest me the way. Amen.

GEORGE WALLACE BRIGGS, 1930

240

L. M.
Morning

WAINWRIGHT
Simply

RICHARD WAINWRIGHT, 1790

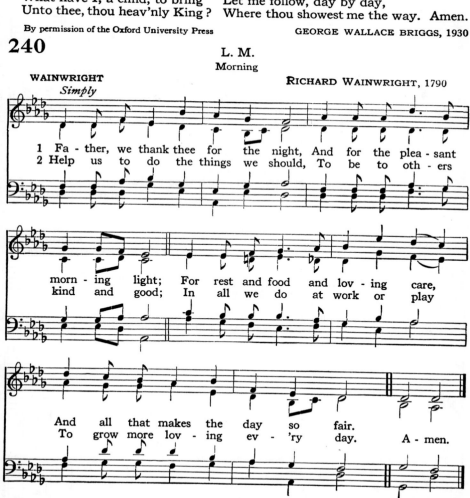

1 Fa - ther, we thank thee for the night, And for the plea - sant
2 Help us to do the things we should, To be to oth - ers

morn - ing light; For rest and food and lov - ing care,
kind and good; In all we do at work or play

And all that makes the day so fair.
To grow more lov - ing ev - 'ry day. A - men.

REBECCA J. WESTON, c. 1890

87. 87

Evening

EVENING PRAYER

JOHN STAINER, 1898, *alt.*

In unison, simply

1 Je - sus, ten - der Shep-herd, hear me; Bless thy lit - tle lamb to - night:
2 All this day thy hand has led me, And I thank thee for thy care;

Through the dark-ness be thou near me, Keep me safe till morn-ing light.
Thou hast warmed me, clothed, and fed me; Lis-ten to my eve-ning prayer. A-men.

3 Let my sins be all forgiven;
   Bless the friends I love so well:
Take us all at last to heaven,
   Happy there with thee to dwell. Amen.

MARY DUNCAN, 1839

241 *Second Tune*   87. 87

BROCKLESBURY

Melody by

CHARLOTTE A. BARNARD, 1868

In unison, simply

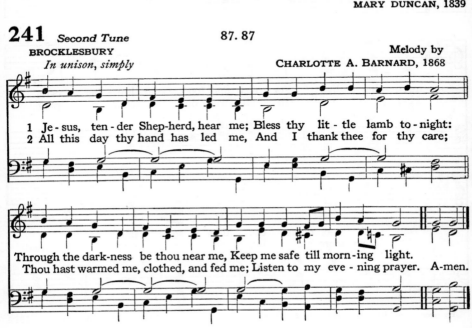

1 Je - sus, ten - der Shep-herd, hear me; Bless thy lit - tle lamb to - night:
2 All this day thy hand has led me, And I thank thee for thy care;

Through the dark-ness be thou near me, Keep me safe till morn-ing light.
Thou hast warmed me, clothed, and fed me; Listen to my eve - ning prayer. A-men.

87. 87

CRADLE HYMN

In unison, tenderly

Melody, *Harmonia Sacra*, 1753,
harmonized by LEO SOWERBY, 1940

1 Hush! my dear, lie still and slum - ber; Ho - ly
2 How much bet - ter thou'rt at - tend - ed Than the

an - gels guard thy bed, Heav'n - ly bless - ings
Son of God could be, When from hea - ven

with - out num - ber Gen - tly fall - ing on thy head.
he de - scend - ed And be - came a child like thee.

3 Soft and easy is thy cradle;
 Coarse and hard thy Saviour lay,
When his birthplace was a stable
 And his softest bed was hay.

4 May'st thou live to know and fear
 him,
 Trust and love him all thy days;
Then go dwell for ever near him,
 See his face and sing his praise.

ISAAC WATTS, 1715, *alt.*

Alternative Tune, BROCKLESBURY, No. 241

Hymns for Children
Irregular

GRAND ISLE
With vigor

JOHN HENRY HOPKINS, 1940

1 I sing a song of the saints of God .... Pa-tient and brave and true,
2 They loved their Lord so dear, so dear, And his love made them strong;
3 They lived not on-ly in a-ges past, There are hun-dreds of thou-sands still,

Who toiled and fought and lived and died For the Lord they loved and
And they fol-lowed the right, for Je-sus' sake, The whole of their good lives
The world is bright with the joy-ous saints Who love to do Je-sus'

knew. And one was a doc-tor, and one was a queen, And
long. And one was a sol-dier, and one was a priest, And
will. You can meet them in school, or in lanes, or at sea, In

Hymns for Children

one was a shep-herd-ess on the green: They were all of them
one was slain by a fierce wild beast: And there's not a - ny
church, or in trains, or in shops, or at tea, For the saints of . .

saints of God—and I mean, God help - ing, to be one too.
rea - son— no, not the least— Why I shouldn't be one too.
God are just folk like me, And I mean to be one too.

By permission of Morehouse–Gorham Co.

LESBIA SCOTT, 1929, *alt.*

244   55. 55

HASLEMERE   *Songs and Tunes for Education,* 1861
harmonized by MARTIN SHAW, 1931

In unison, simply

A-men.

1 God whose Name is Love, happy children we;
  Listen to the hymn that we sing to thee.

2 Help us to be good, always kind and true,
  In the games we play or the work we do.

3 Bless us every one singing here to thee.
  God whose Name is Love, loving may we be! Amen.

FLORENCE HOATSON, 1908

245

Hymns for Children
87. 87. 88. 77

TWINKLING STARS

Traditional German Melody
har. by LEO SOWERBY, 1941

In unison, lightly

1 Can you count the stars that bright-ly Twin-kle in the mid-night sky?
2 Do you know how ma-ny chil-dren Rise each morn-ing blithe and gay?

Can you count the clouds, so light-ly O'er the mea-dows float-ing by?
Can you count their jol-ly voic-es, Sing-ing sweet-ly day by day?

God, the Lord, doth mark their num-ber With his eyes that nev-er
God hears all the hap-py voic-es, In their mer-ry songs re-

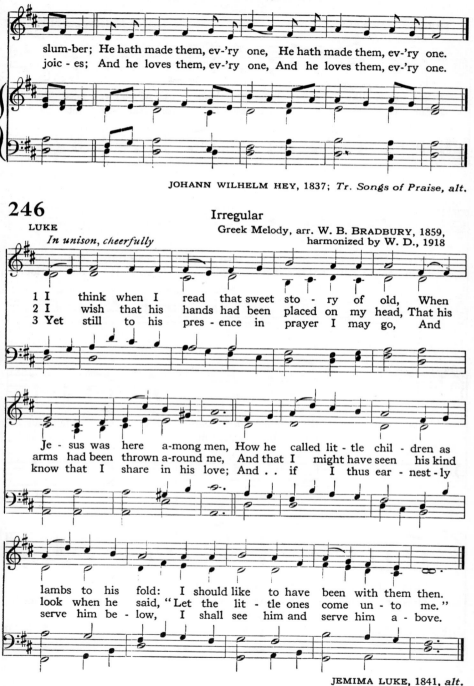

slum-ber; He hath made them, ev-'ry one, He hath made them, ev-'ry one.
joic - es; And he loves them, ev-'ry one, And he loves them, ev-'ry one.

JOHANN WILHELM HEY, 1837; *Tr. Songs of Praise, alt.*

246

LUKE

Irregular

Greek Melody, arr. W. B. BRADBURY, 1859,
harmonized by W. D., 1918

In unison, cheerfully

1 I think when I read that sweet sto - ry of old, When
2 I wish that his hands had been placed on my head, That his
3 Yet still to his pres - ence in prayer I may go, And

Je - sus was here a-mong men, How he called lit - tle chil - dren as
arms had been thrown a-round me, And that I might have seen his kind
know that I share in his love; And .. if I thus ear - nest - ly

lambs to his fold: I should like to have been with them then.
look when he said, "Let the lit - tle ones come un - to me."
serve him be - low, I shall see him and serve him a - bove.

JEMIMA LUKE, 1841, alt.

Hymns for Children
87. 87. 87

SICILIAN MARINERS
Moderately slow

Sicilian Melody, pub. 1794

1 Sa - viour, like a shep - herd lead us, Much we need thy
2 Ear - ly let us seek thy fa - vor, Ear - ly let us

ten - der care; In thy plea - sant pas - tures feed us;
learn thy will; Do thou, Lord, our on - ly Sa - viour,

For our use thy folds pre - pare: Bless - ed Je - sus,
With thy love our bo - soms fill: Bless - ed Je - sus,

bless - ed Je - sus! Thou hast bought us, thine we are.
bless - ed Je - sus! Thou hast loved us: love us still. A-men.

DOROTHY ANN THRUPP'S *Hymns for the Young*, 1836, alt

56. 64

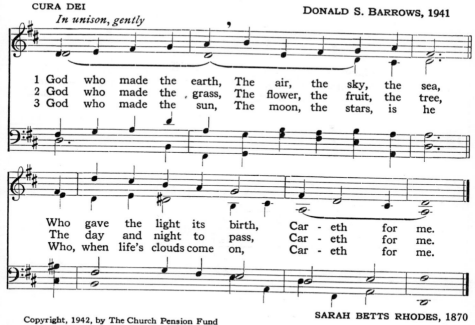

CURA DEI

DONALD S. BARROWS, 1941

In unison, gently

1 God who made the earth, The air, the sky, the sea,
2 God who made the grass, The flower, the fruit, the tree,
3 God who made the sun, The moon, the stars, is he

Who gave the light its birth, Car - eth for me.
The day and night to pass, Car - eth for me.
Who, when life's clouds come on, Car - eth for me.

Copyright, 1942, by The Church Pension Fund

SARAH BETTS RHODES, 1870

249

Before the Gospel at Holy Communion

C. M.

ST. STEPHEN

WILLIAM JONES, 1789

In moderate time

Thy Gos - pel, Je - sus, we be - lieve, And for thy help we pray,

That we in thought and word and deed, Thy Gos - pel may o - bey. A - men.

Anonymous

WORSHIP   Traditional German Melody

Joyously

1 Lord Je - sus, from thy throne a - bove Be - hold us kneel - ing
2 Be - fore thy throne in hea - ven's height A - dor - ing an - gels
3 So now we lift our hearts to thee, And in our wor - ship

here, And help us now by faith and love To know thy pres - ence
sing; But we be - lieve thou dost de - light In gifts thy chil - dren
raise, With all the com - pa - ny of heav'n, An of - fer - ing of

near, To know thy pres - ence near.
bring, In gifts thy chil - dren bring.
praise, An of - fer - ing of praise. A - men.

JOHN RUSSELL DARBYSHIRE

By permission of E. C. Schirmer Music Company

251   77. 77

GENTLE JESUS   MARTIN SHAW, 1915

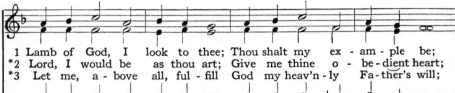

In moderate time

1 Lamb of God, I look to thee; Thou shalt my ex - am - ple be;
*2 Lord, I would be as thou art; Give me thine o - be - dient heart;
*3 Let me, a - bove all, ful - fill God my heav'n - ly Fa - ther's will;

Hymns for Children

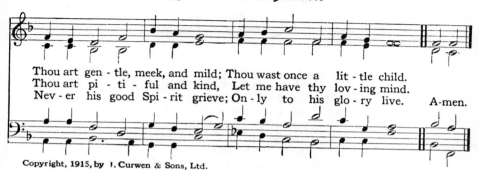

Thou art gen - tle, meek, and mild; Thou wast once a   lit - tle child.
Thou art pi - ti - ful and kind, Let me have thy lov - ing mind.
Nev - er his good Spi - rit grieve; On - ly to his glo - ry live.   A-men.

4 Loving Jesus, gentle Lamb,
In thy gracious hands I am;
Make me, Saviour, what thou art,
Like thyself within my heart.

*5 I shall then show forth thy praise,
Serve thee all my happy days;
Then the world shall always see
Christ the holy Child in me.   Amen.

CHARLES WESLEY, 1742, *alt.*

252

76. 76

At Holy Communion

CHRIST IS MY LIFE

Melody by MELCHIOR VULPIUS, 1609

Simply

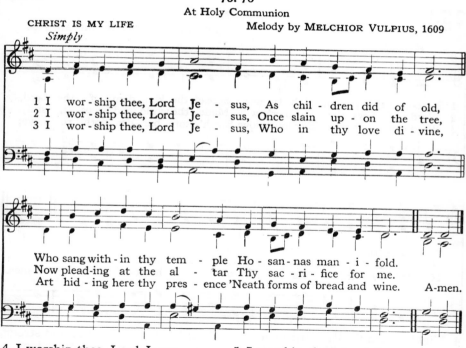

1 I wor - ship thee, Lord Je - sus, As chil - dren did of old,
2 I wor - ship thee, Lord Je - sus, Once slain up - on the tree,
3 I wor - ship thee, Lord Je - sus, Who in thy love di - vine,

Who sang with - in thy tem - ple Ho - san - nas man - i - fold.
Now plead-ing at the al - tar Thy sac - ri - fice for me.
Art hid - ing here thy pres - ence 'Neath forms of bread and wine.   A-men.

4 I worship thee, Lord Jesus,
And kneeling unto thee,
As thou didst come to Mary,
I pray thee come to me.

5 I worship thee, Lord Jesus,
My King and Saviour mild:
Thou hast blest other children;
Bless also me, thy child.   Amen.

RICHARD FREDERICK LITTLEDALE, *alt.*

Hymns for Children

Also the following:

MISSIONS

253

77. 77

LUEBECK

JOHANN A. FREYLINGHAUSEN, 1704

With spirit

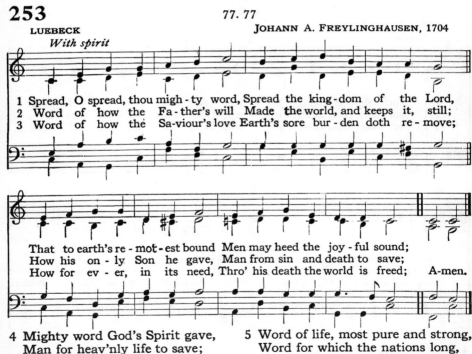

1 Spread, O spread, thou migh - ty word, Spread the king - dom of the Lord,
2 Word of how the Fa - ther's will Made the world, and keeps it, still;
3 Word of how the Sa - viour's love Earth's sore bur - den doth re - move;

That to earth's re - mot - est bound Men may heed the joy - ful sound;
How his on - ly Son he gave, Man from sin and death to save;
How for ev - er, in its need, Thro' his death the world is freed; A-men.

4 Mighty word God's Spirit gave,
Man for heav'nly life to save;
Word through whose all-holy might
Man can will and do the right;

5 Word of life, most pure and strong,
Word for which the nations long,
Spread abroad, until from night
All the world awakes to light.

Amen.

JONATHAN FRIEDRICH BAEHNMAIER, 1827;
Tr. ARTHUR W. FARLANDER *and* WINFRED DOUGLAS, 1938

Missions

76. 76. D.

MISSIONARY HYMN

With motion

LOWELL MASON, 1823

1 From Green-land's i - cy moun-tains, From In - dia's cor - al strand,
2 Can we, whose souls are light - ed With wis - dom from on high,
3 Waft, waft, ye winds, his sto - ry, And you, ye wa - ters, roll,

Where Af - ric's sun - ny foun-tains Roll down their gold - en sand,
Can we to men be - night - ed The lamp of life de - ny?
Till, like a sea of glo - ry, It spreads from pole to pole;

From ma - ny an an - cient riv - er, From ma - ny a palm - y plain,
Sal - va - tion, O sal - va - tion! The joy - ful sound pro - claim,
Till o'er our ran-somed na - ture The Lamb for sin - ners slain,

They call us to de - liv - er Their land from er - ror's chain.
Till each re - mot - est na - tion Has learnt Mes - si - ah's name.
Re - deem - er, King, Cre - a - tor, In bliss re - turns to reign.

REGINALD HEBER, 1819

255

Missions

9 10. 9 10. 10 10

CRASSELIUS

With vigor; may be sung in unison

Melody pub. Halle, 1704

1 A - wake, thou Spi - rit of the watch-men Who nev - er held their
2 O Lord, now let thy fire en - kin - dle Our hearts, that ev - 'ry -
3 The prayer thy Son him - self hath taught us We of - fer now to

peace by day or night, Con - tend-ing from the walls of Si - on A -
where its flame may go, And spread the glo - ry of re-demp-tion Till
thee at his com - mand; Be - hold and heark-en, Lord; thy chil - dren Im -

gainst the foe, con - fid - ing in thy might. Through-out the world their
all the world thy sav - ing grace shall know. O har - vest Lord, look
plore thee for the souls of ev - 'ry land: With yearn-ing hearts they

cry is ring - ing still, And bring-ing peo - ples to thy ho - ly will.
down on us and view How white the fields; the la - bor-ers, how few!
make their ar - dent plea; O hear us, Lord, and say, "Thus shall it be."

Missions

4 Send forth, O Lord, thy strong Evangel
By many messengers, all hearts to win;
Make haste to help us in our weakness;
Break down the realm of Satan, death, and sin:
The circle of the earth shall then proclaim
Thy kingdom, and the glory of thy Name.   Amen.

A - men.

KARL HEINRICH VON BOGATZKY, 1749;
Tr. WINFRED DOUGLAS *and* ARTHUR W. FARLANDER, 1939

256   L. M.

MELCOMBE   SAMUEL WEBBE, 1782
Deliberately

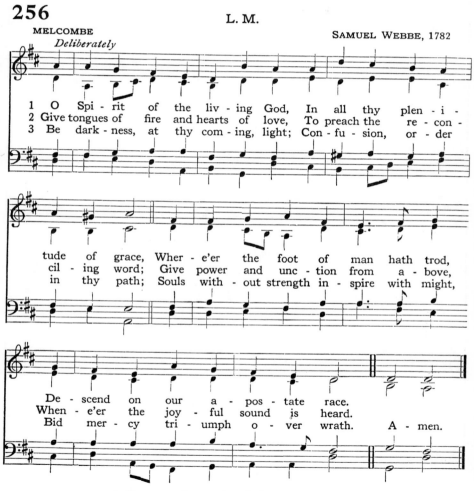

1 O Spi - rit of the liv - ing God, In all thy plen - i -
2 Give tongues of fire and hearts of love, To preach the re - con -
3 Be dark - ness, at thy com - ing, light; Con - fu - sion, or - der

tude of grace, Wher - e'er the foot of man hath trod,
cil - ing word; Give power and unc - tion from a - bove,
in thy path; Souls with - out strength in - spire with might,

De - scend on our a - pos - tate race.
When - e'er the joy - ful sound is heard.
Bid mer - cy tri - umph o - ver wrath.   A - men.

4 Convert the nations! far and nigh
The triumphs of the cross record;
The Name of Jesus glorify,
Till every people call him Lord.   Amen.

JAMES MONTGOMERY, 1823

257

Missions

76. 76. D.

LANCASHIRE   HENRY SMART, 1836

In moderate time

1 Hast - en the time ap - point - ed, By pro - phets long fore - told,
2 Let Jew and Gen - tile, meet - ing From ma - ny a dis - tant shore,
3 Let all that now u - nites us More sweet and last - ing prove,

When all shall dwell to - geth - er, One Shep - herd and one fold.
A - round one al - tar kneel - ing, One com - mon Lord a - dore.
A - clos - er bond of un - ion, In a blest land of love.

Let ev - 'ry i - dol per - ish: Thy truth to all make known
Let all that now di - vides us Re - move and pass a - way,
Let war be learned no long - er, Let strife and tu - mult cease,

Till ev - 'ry prayer be of - fered To God in Christ a - lone.
Like sha - dows of the morn - ing Be - fore the blaze of day.
All earth his bless - ed king - dom, The Lord and Prince of Peace. A - men.

4 O long-expected dawning,
  Come with thy cheering ray!
When shall the morning brighten,
  The shadows flee away?

O sweet anticipation!
  It cheers the watchers on,
To pray, and hope, and labor,
  Till the dark night be gone.

JANE BORTHWICK, 1859, *alt.*

258

Missions
67. 67. 66. 66

ST. JOAN
Sturdily

PERCY E. B. COLLER, 1941

1 Christ is the world's true Light, Its Cap-tain of sal - va - tion,
2 In Christ all ra - ces meet, Their an - cient feuds for - get - ting,

The Day - star clear and bright Of ev - 'ry man and na - tion;
The whole round world com-plete, From sun - rise to its set - ting:

New life, new hope a - wakes, Wher - e'er men own his sway:
When Christ is throned as Lord, Men shall for - sake their fear,

Free - dom her bond - age breaks, And night is turned to day.
To plough-share beat the sword, To prun-ing - hook the spear. A - men.

Copyright, 1942, by The Church Pension Fund

3 One Lord, in one great Name
    Unite us all who own thee;
Cast out our pride and shame
    That hinder to enthrone thee;
The world has waited long,
    Has travailed long in pain;
To heal its ancient wrong,
    Come, Prince of Peace, and reign.   Amen.

GEORGE WALLACE BRIGGS, 1933

259 *First Tune*   **Missions**

PALMARUM   L. M.   J. FRED. WOLLE, 1923

Resolutely

1 Fling out the ban - ner! let it float Sky-
2 Fling out the ban - ner! hea - then lands Shall
3 Fling out the ban - ner! sin - sick souls That
4 Fling out the ban - ner! let it float Sky-

ward and sea - ward, high and wide; The sun that lights its
see from far the glo - rious sight, And na - tions, crowd - ing
sink and per - ish in the strife, Shall touch in faith its
ward and sea - ward, high and wide, Our glo - ry, on - ly

shin - ing folds, The cross, on which the Sa - viour died.
to be born, Bap - tize their spi - rits in its light.
ra - diant hem, And spring im - mor - tal in - to life.
in the cross; Our on - ly hope, the Cru - ci - fied!

By permission of Mrs. Prescott Baker

259 *Second Tune*   L. M.

WALTHAM   J. BAPTISTE CALKIN, 1872

With spirit

1 Fling out the ban - ner! let it float Sky-ward and sea-ward, high and wide;
2 Fling out the ban - ner! hea - then lands Shall see from far the glo - rious sight,
3 Fling out the ban - ner! sin - sick souls That sink and per - ish in the strife,
4 Fling out the ban - ner! let it float Sky-ward and sea-ward, high and wide,

Missions

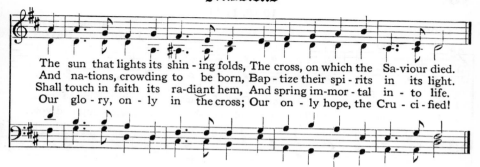

The sun that lights its shin-ing folds, The cross, on which the Sa-viour died.
And na-tions, crowding to be born, Bap-tize their spi-rits in its light.
Shall touch in faith its ra-diant hem, And spring im-mor-tal in-to life.
Our glo-ry, on-ly in the cross; Our on-ly hope, the Cru-ci-fied!

5 Fling out the banner! wide and high,
   Seaward and skyward, let it shine:
   Nor skill, nor might, nor merit ours;
   We conquer only in that sign.

GEORGE WASHINGTON DOANE, 1848, *alt.*

260 *First Tune* 10 10. 11 11
OLD HUNDRED FOURTH

THOMAS RAVENSCROFT'S
Whole Book of Psalmes, 1621

With majesty

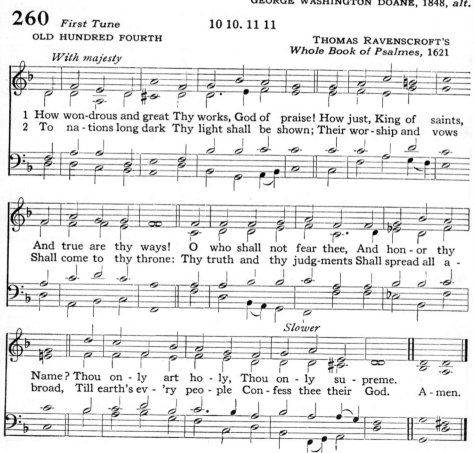

1 How won-drous and great Thy works, God of praise! How just, King of saints,
2 To na-tions long dark Thy light shall be shown; Their wor-ship and vows

And true are thy ways! O who shall not fear thee, And hon-or thy
Shall come to thy throne: Thy truth and thy judg-ments Shall spread all a-

Slower

Name? Thou on-ly art ho-ly, Thou on-ly su-preme.
broad, Till earth's ev-'ry peo-ple Con-fess thee their God. A-men.

HENRY USTIC ONDERDONK, 1826

260 *Second Tune* **Missions**
10 10. 11 11

Arranged 1822,
from J. MICHAEL HAYDN

LYONS
With energy

1 How won-drous and great Thy works, God of praise! How just, King of saints,
2 To na-tions long dark Thy light shall be shown; Their wor-ship and vows

And true are thy ways! O who shall not fear thee, And hon-or thy Name?
Shall come to thy throne: Thy truth and thy judg-ments Shall spread all a-broad,

Thou on-ly art ho-ly, Thou on-ly su-preme. A - men.
Till earth's ev-'ry peo-ple Con-fess thee their God.

HENRY USTIC ONDERDONK, 1826

261 11 10. 11 10, with Refrain

JAMES WALCH, 1876

TIDINGS
In moderate time

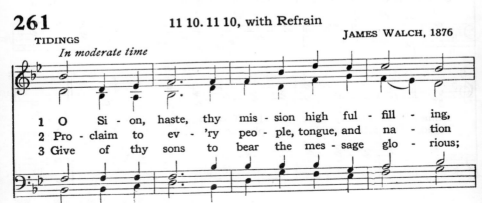

1 O Si - on, haste, thy mis-sion high ful - fill - ing,
2 Pro - claim to ev - 'ry peo-ple, tongue, and na - tion
3 Give of thy sons to bear the mes-sage glo - rious;

Missions

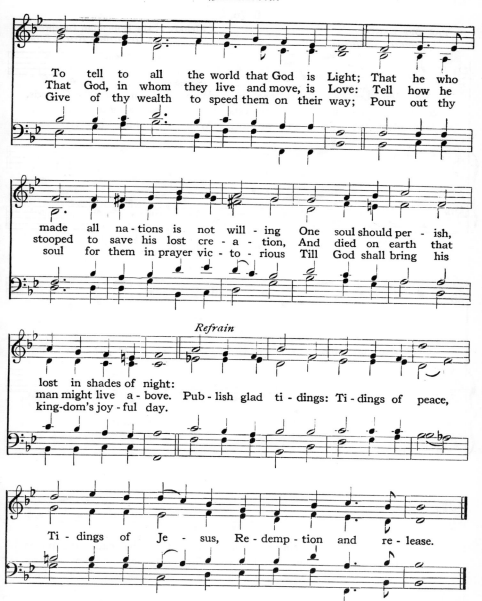

To tell to all the world that God is Light; That he who
That God, in whom they live and move, is Love: Tell how he
Give of thy wealth to speed them on their way; Pour out thy

made all na-tions is not will-ing One soul should per - ish,
stooped to save his lost cre - a - tion, And died on earth that
soul for them in prayer vic - to - rious Till God shall bring his

Refrain

lost in shades of night:
man might live a - bove. Pub - lish glad ti - dings: Ti - dings of peace,
king-dom's joy - ful day.

Ti - dings of Je - sus, Re - demp - tion and re - lease.

4 He comes again! O Sion, ere thou meet him,
   Make known to every heart his saving grace;
   Let none whom he hath ransomed fail to greet him,
   Through thy neglect, unfit to see his face.

Refrain

MARY ANN THOMSON, 1870, **alt.**

Missions

76. 76. D.

FAR OFF LANDS

Melody of the Bohemian Brethren,
in *Hemmets Koral Bok*

Brightly, in unison

1 Re - mem - ber all the peo - ple Who live in far off lands,
2 Some work in sul - try for - ests Where apes swing to and fro,
3 God bless the men and wo - men Who serve him o - ver - sea;

In strange and lone - ly ci - ties, Or roam the des - ert sands,
Some fish in migh - ty riv - ers, Some hunt a - cross the snow.
God raise up more to help them To set the na - tions free,

Or farm the moun - tain pas - tures, Or till the end - less plains
Re - mem - ber all God's chil - dren, Who yet have nev - er heard
Till all the dis - tant peo - ple In ev - 'ry for - eign place

Missions

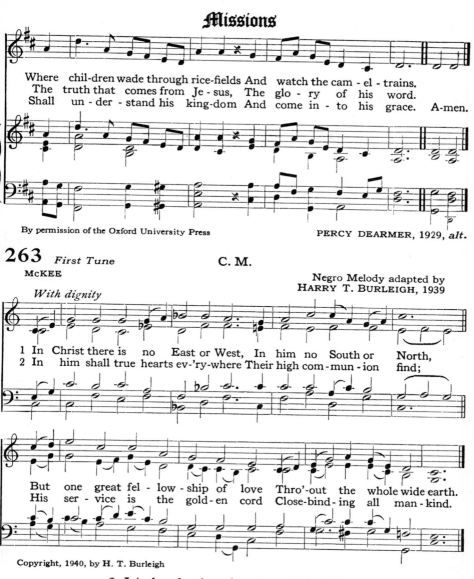

Where chil-dren wade through rice-fields And watch the cam-el-trains.
The truth that comes from Je-sus, The glo-ry of his word.
Shall un-der-stand his king-dom And come in-to his grace. A-men.

By permission of the Oxford University Press

PERCY DEARMER, 1929, *alt.*

263 *First Tune*   C. M.

McKEE

Negro Melody adapted by
HARRY T. BURLEIGH, 1939

With dignity

1 In Christ there is no East or West, In him no South or North,
2 In him shall true hearts ev-'ry-where Their high com-mun-ion find;

But one great fel-low-ship of love Thro'-out the whole wide earth.
His ser-vice is the gold-en cord Close-bind-ing all man-kind.

Copyright, 1940, by H. T. Burleigh

3 Join hands, then, brothers of the faith,
    Whate'er your race may be!
Who serves my Father as a son
    Is surely kin to me.

4 In Christ now meet both East and West,
    In him meet South and North,
All Christly souls are one in him,
    Throughout the whole wide earth.

JOHN OXENHAM, 1908

263 *Second Tune*

Missions

C. M. D.

BOURNE

EVERETT R. CURRIER, 1941

In moderate time

1 In Christ there is no East or West, In him no South or North,
3 Join hands, then, broth-ers of the faith, What-e'er your race may be!

But one great fel-low-ship of love Throughout the whole wide earth.
Who serves my Fa-ther as a son Is sure-ly kin to me.

2 In him shall true hearts ev - 'ry-where Their high com-mun-ion find;
4 In Christ now meet both East and West, In him meet South and North,

His ser - vice is the gold-en cord Close-bind - ing all man-kind.
All Christ-ly souls are one in him, Through-out the whole wide earth.

JOHN OXENHAM, 1908

264

Missions

76. 76. D.

WEBB

GEORGE J. WEBB, 1837

Brightly

1 The morn - ing light is break - ing; The dark - ness dis - ap - pears;
2 See hea - then na - tions bend - ing Be - fore the God we love,
3 Blest riv - er of sal - va - tion, Pur - sue thy on - ward way;

The sons of earth are wa - king To pen - i - ten - tial tears;
And thou-sand hearts as - cend - ing In grat - i - tude a - bove;
Flow thou to ev - 'ry na - tion, Nor in thy rich - ness stay:

Each breeze that sweeps the o - cean Brings ti - dings from a - far
While sin - ners, now con - fess - ing, The Gos - pel call o - bey,
Stay not till all the low - ly Tri - umph-ant reach their home;

Of na - tions in com - mo - tion, Pre - pared for Si - on's war.
And seek the Sa - viour's bless - ing, A na - tion in a day.
Stay not till all the ho - ly Pro - claim, "The Lord is come!"

SAMUEL FRANCIS SMITH, 1832

265   𝕸𝖎𝖘𝖘𝖎𝖔𝖓𝖘
C. M. D.

WELLINGTON SQUARE

In moderate time

GUY WARRACK, 1931

1 E - ter - nal God, whose power up-holds Both flower and flam - ing star,
2 O God of love, whose spi - rit wakes In ev - 'ry hu - man breast,
3 O God of truth, whom sci - ence seeks And rev - 'rent souls a - dore,

To whom there is no here nor there, No time, no near nor far,
Whom love, and love a - lone, can know, In whom all hearts find rest,
Who light - est ev - 'ry ear - nest mind Of ev - 'ry clime and shore,

No a - lien race, no for - eign shore, No child un-sought, un - known,
Help us to spread thy gra-cious reign, Till greed and hate shall cease,
Dis - pel the gloom of er - ror's night, Of ig - no - rance and fear,

O send us forth, thy pro-phets true, To make all lands thine own!
And kind-ness dwell in hu - man hearts, And all the earth find peace!
Un - til true wis-dom from a - bove Shall make life's path-way clear! A - men.

By permission of the composer

Missions

4 O God of beauty, oft revealed
   In dreams of human art,
In speech that flows to melody,
   In holiness of heart;
Teach us to ban all ugliness
   That blinds our eyes to thee,
Till all shall know the loveliness
   Of lives made fair and free.

5 O God of righteousness and grace,
   Seen in the Christ, thy Son,
Whose life and death reveal thy face,
   By whom thy will was done,
Inspire thy heralds of good news
   To live thy life divine,
Till Christ is formed in all mankind
   And every land is thine! Amen.

HENRY HALLAM TWEEDY, 1929

By permission of The Hymn Society

Alternative Tune, MATERNA, No. 584

Also the following:

GENERAL HYMNS

266

11 12. 12 10

NICAEA

JOHN B. DYKES, 1861

With dignity

1 Ho - ly, Ho - ly, Ho - ly! Lord God Al - migh - ty!
*2 Ho - ly, Ho - ly, Ho - ly! all the saints a - dore thee,
3 Ho - ly, Ho - ly, Ho - ly! though the dark - ness hide thee,

Ear - ly in the morn - ing our song shall rise to thee:
Cast - ing down their gold - en crowns a - round the glass - y sea;
Though the eye of sin - ful man thy glo - ry may not see,

Ho - ly, Ho - ly, Ho - ly! mer - ci - ful and migh - ty,
Cher - u - bim and ser - a - phim fall - ing down be - fore thee,
On - ly thou art ho - ly; there is none be - side thee,

God in three Per - sons, bless - ed Tri - ni - ty.
Which wert, and art, and ev - er - more shalt be.
Per - fect in power, in love, and pu - ri - ty. A - men.

4 Holy, Holy, Holy! Lord God Almighty!
  All thy works shall praise thy Name, in earth, and sky, and sea;
  Holy, Holy, Holy! merciful and mighty,
  God in three Persons, blessèd Trinity. Amen.

REGINALD HEBER, 1827

REGENT SQUARE

HENRY SMART, 1867

In moderate time

1 Ho - ly Fa - ther, great Cre - a - tor, Source of mer - cy, love, and peace,
2 Ho - ly Je - sus, Lord of glo - ry, Whom an - gel - ic hosts pro - claim,
3 Ho - ly Spi - rit, Sanc - ti - fi - er, Come with unc - tion from a - bove,

Look up - on the Me - di - a - tor, Clothe us with his right-eous-ness;
While we hear thy won-drous sto - ry, Meet and wor - ship in thy Name,
Raise our hearts to rap - tures high - er, Fill them with the Sa-viour's love.

Heav'n-ly Fa-ther, heav'n-ly Fa-ther, Through the Sa-viour hear and bless.
Dear Re-deem-er, dear Re-deem - er, In our hearts thy peace pro-claim.
Source of com-fort, Source of com-fort, Cheer us with the Sa-viour's love. Amen.

4 God the Lord, through every nation
    Let thy wondrous mercies shine.
  In the song of thy salvation
    Every tongue and race combine.
    ‖ Great Jehovah, ‖
  Form our hearts and make them thine.   Amen.

ALEXANDER VIETS GRISWOLD, 1835

ST. PATRICK

Traditional Irish Melody

In unison, with energy

1 I bind un-to my-self to-day The strong Name
2 I bind this day to me for ev-er, By power of
*3 I bind un-to my-self the power Of the great
*4 I bind un-to my-self to-day The vir-tues
*5 I bind un-to my-self to-day The power of

1 of the Tri-ni-ty, By in-vo-ca-tion
2 faith, Christ's In-car-na-tion; His bap-tism in the
3 love of cher-u-bim; The sweet "Well done" in
4 of the star-lit heav'n, The glo-rious sun's life-
5 God to hold and lead, His eye to watch, his

1 of the same, The Three in One, and One in Three.†
2 Jor-dan riv-er; His death on cross for my sal-va-tion;
3 judg-ment hour; The ser-vice of the ser-a-phim;
4 giv-ing ray, The white-ness of the moon at even,
5 might to stay, His ear to heark-en to my need;

†*Stanza 1 ends here; the following stanzas continue on the next page*

General Hymns

2 His burst - ing from the spi - ced tomb; His ri - ding
3 Con - fess - ors' faith, a - pos - tles' word, The pa - triarchs'
4 The flash - ing of the light - ning free, The whirl - ing
5 The wis - dom of my God to teach, His hand to

2 up the heav'n - ly way; His com - ing at the
3 prayers, the pro - phets' scrolls; All good deeds done un -
4 wind's tem - pes - tuous shocks, The sta - ble earth, the
5 guide, his shield to ward; The word of God to

2 day of doom: I bind un - to my - self to - day.
3 to the Lord, And pu - ri - ty of vir - gin souls.
4 deep salt sea, A - round the old e - ter - nal rocks.
5 give me speech, His heav'n - ly host to be my guard.

88. 88

DEIRDRE   Traditional Irish Melody

In harmony, with breadth

6 Christ be with me, Christ with-in me, Christ be-hind me, Christ be - fore me,
Christ be-neath me, Christ a - bove me, Christ in qui - et, Christ in dan - ger,

Christ be-side me, Christ to win me, Christ to com - fort and re - store me,
Christ in hearts of all that love me, Christ in mouth of friend and stranger.

ST. PATRICK

7 I bind un - to my - self the Name, The strong Name

of the Tri - ni - ty; By in - vo - ca - tion

General Hymns

of the same, The Three in One, and One in Three.

Of whom all na - ture hath cre - a - tion; E - ter - nal

Fa - ther, Spi - rit, Word: Praise to the Lord of

In harmony

my sal - va - tion, Sal - va - tion is of Christ the Lord. A-men.

ST. PATRICK, 372–466; *Tr.* CECIL FRANCES ALEXANDER, 1889

MOULTRIE
In moderate time

GERARD F. COBB,
1838–1904

1 Round the Lord in glo - ry seat - ed Cher - u - bim and ser - a - phim
2 Heav'n is still with glo - ry ring - ing, Earth takes up the an - gels' cry,

Filled his tem - ple, and re - peat - ed Each to each the al - ter - nate hymn:
"Ho - ly, Ho - ly, Ho - ly," sing - ing, "Lord of hosts, the Lord Most High."

"Lord, thy glo - ry fills the hea - ven, Earth is with thy full - ness stored;
With his ser - aph train be - fore him, With his ho - ly Church be - low,

Un - to thee be glo - ry giv - en, Ho - ly, Ho - ly, Ho - ly Lord."
Thus u - nite we to a - dore him, Bid we thus our an - them flow:

A - men.

3 "Lord, thy glory fills the heaven,
     Earth is with thy fullness stored;
Unto thee be glory given,
     Holy, Holy, Holy Lord."
Thus thy glorious Name confessing,
     With thine angel hosts we cry
"Holy, Holy, Holy," blessing
     Thee, the Lord of hosts Most High. Amen.

RICHARD MANT, 1837, *alt.*

77. 77. 77

ST. ATHANASIUS
With animation

EDWARD J. HOPKINS, 1872

1 Ho - ly, Ho - ly, Ho - ly, Lord God of Hosts, e - ter - nal King,
2 Since by thee were all things made, And in thee do all things live,

By the heav'ns and earth a - dored; An - gels and arch - an - gels sing,
Be to thee all hon - or paid, Praise to thee let all things give,

Chant - ing ev - er - last - ing - ly To the bless - ed Tri - ni - ty.
Sing - ing ev - er - last - ing - ly To the bless - ed Tri - ni - ty. A-men.

3 Thousands, tens of thousands stand,
   Spirits blest before thy throne,
Speeding thence at thy command;
   And when thy command is done,
     Singing everlastingly
     To the blessèd Trinity.

4 Cherubim and seraphim
   Veil their faces with their wings;
Eyes of angels are too dim
   To behold the King of kings,
     While they sing eternally
     To the blessèd Trinity.

5 Thee, apostles, prophets, thee,
   Thee, the noble martyr band,
Praise with solemn jubilee,
   Thee, the Church in every land;
     Singing everlastingly
     To the blessèd Trinity.

6 Alleluia! Lord, to thee,
   Father, Son, and Holy Ghost,
Three in One, and One in Three,
   Join we with the heav'nly host,
     Singing everlastingly
     To the blessèd Trinity. Amen.

CHRISTOPHER WORDSWORTH, 1862

664. 6664

MOSCOW

FELICE DE GIARDINI, 1769

With vigor

1 Come, thou al - migh - ty King, Help us thy Name to sing,
2 Come, thou In - car - nate Word, By heav'n and earth a - dored;

Help us to praise. Fa - ther whose love un-known All things cre -
Our prayer at - tend: Come, and thy peo - ple bless; Come, give thy

a - ted own, Build in our hearts thy throne, An-cient of Days.
word suc-cess; Stab-lish thy right-eous - ness, Sa-viour and friend. A - men.

3 Come, Holy Comforter,
Thy sacred witness bear
   In this glad hour:
Thou, who almighty art,
Now rule in every heart,
And ne'er from us depart,
   Spirit of power.

4 To thee, great One in Three,
The highest praises be,
   Hence evermore;
Thy sov'reign majesty
May we in glory see,
And to eternity
   Love and adore.   Amen.

Anonymous, c. 1757, alt.

272   664. 6664

Tune, MOSCOW

1 Thou, whose almighty word
Chaos and darkness heard,
   And took their flight;
Hear us, we humbly pray,
And, where the Gospel day
Sheds not its glorious ray,
   Let there be light!

2 Thou who didst come to bring
On thy redeeming wing
   Healing and sight,
Health to the sick in mind,
Sight to the inly blind,
O now, to all mankind,
   Let there be light!

General Hymns

3 Spirit of truth and love,
  Life-giving, holy Dove,
    Speed forth thy flight!
  Move on the waters' face
  Bearing the gifts of grace,
  And, in earth's darkest place,
    Let there be light!

4 Holy and blessèd Three,
  Glorious Trinity,
    Wisdom, love, might;
  Boundless as ocean's tide,
  Rolling in fullest pride,
  Through the world, far and wide,
    Let there be light! Amen.

JOHN MARRIOTT, 1813, *alt.*

273

78. 78. 77

TE DEUM

Boldly, *with motion*

Later form,
Melody, pub. Vienna, c. 1774

1 Ho - ly God, we praise thy Name; Lord Al - migh-ty we con-fess thee;
2 Cher - u - bim and ser - a - phim, Ev - 'ry crea-ture that can praise thee,
3 Ho - ly Fa - ther, Ho - ly Son, Ho - ly Spi - rit, Three we name thee,

All the earth doth thee ac - claim And in awe and won-der bless thee.
All, for ev - er, join the hymn An - gels and arch - an - gels raise thee,
Though in es - sence on - ly One; Un - di - vi - ded God we claim thee,

Thou, who wast be - fore all time, Art e - ter - nal, high, sub-lime.
Cry - ing out with one ac-cord, Ho - ly, Ho - ly, Ho - ly Lord.
Then a - dor - ing bend the knee, While we own the mys-ter-y. A - men.

IGNAZ FRANZ, c. 1774; *Hymnal Version,* 1940

General Hymns

11 10. 11 10

ALBANY

J. ALBERT JEFFERY, 1886

In unison, with dignity

Before stanza 1 only

1 An - cient of Days, who sit - test throned in
2 O ho - ly Fa - ther, who hast led thy
3 O ho - ly Je - sus, Prince of Peace and
4 O Ho - ly Ghost, the Lord and the Life
5 O Tri - une God, with heart and voice a -

glo - ry, To thee all knees are bent, all voic - es pray;
chil - dren In all the a - ges with the fire and cloud,
Sa - viour, To thee we owe the peace that shall pre - vail,
giv - er, Thine is the quick - 'ning power that gives in - crease:
dor - ing, Praise we the good - ness that doth crown our days;

Thy love has blessed the wide world's won - drous sto - ry
Through seas dry - shod, through wea - ry wastes be - wil - d'ring,
Still - ing the rude wills of men's wild be - ha - vior,
From thee have flowed, as from a might - y riv - er,
Pray we that thou wilt hear us, still im - plor - ing

General Hymns

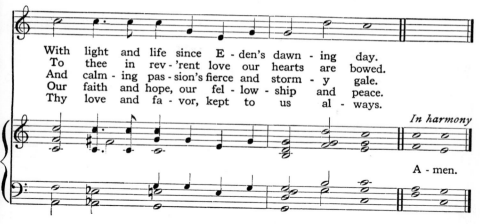

With light and life since E - den's dawn - ing day.
To thee in rev - 'rent love our hearts are bowed.
And calm - ing pas - sion's fierce and storm - y gale.
Our faith and hope, our fel - low - ship and peace.
Thy love and fa - vor, kept to us al - ways.

In harmony

A - men.

WILLIAM CROSWELL DOANE, 1886, *alt.*

275

77. 75

CAPETOWN

FRIEDRICH FILITZ, 1847

In moderate time

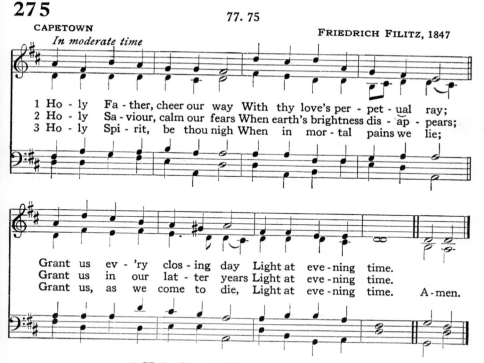

1 Ho - ly Fa - ther, cheer our way With thy love's per - pet - ual ray;
2 Ho - ly Sa - viour, calm our fears When earth's brightness dis - ap - pears;
3 Ho - ly Spi - rit, be thou nigh When in mor - tal pains we lie;

Grant us ev - 'ry clos - ing day Light at eve - ning time.
Grant us in our lat - ter years Light at eve - ning time.
Grant us, as we come to die, Light at eve - ning time.

A - men.

4 Holy, blessèd Trinity,
   Darkness is not dark with thee;
   Those thou keepest always see
   Light at evening time.   Amen.

RICHARD HAYES ROBINSON, 1869

67. 67. 66. 66

NUN DANKET   JOHANN CRUEGER, 1647
In unison, majestically   adapted by FELIX MENDELSSOHN, 1840

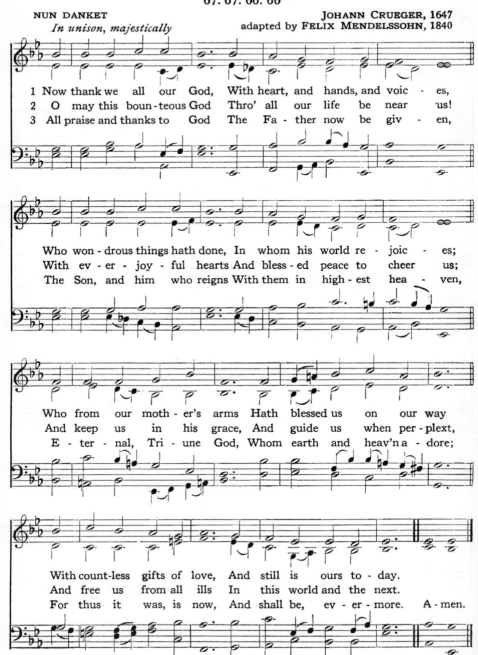

1 Now thank we all our God, With heart, and hands, and voic - es,
2 O may this boun - teous God Thro' all our life be near us!
3 All praise and thanks to God The Fa - ther now be giv - en,

Who won - drous things hath done, In whom his world re - joic - es;
With ev - er - joy - ful hearts And bless - ed peace to cheer us;
The Son, and him who reigns With them in high - est hea - ven,

Who from our moth - er's arms Hath blessed us on our way
And keep us in his grace, And guide us when per - plext,
E - ter - nal, Tri - une God, Whom earth and heav'n a - dore;

With count-less gifts of love, And still is ours to - day.
And free us from all ills In this world and the next.
For thus it was, is now, And shall be, ev - er - more. A - men.

MARTIN RINKART, c. 1630; *Tr.* CATHERINE WINKWORTH, 1858, *alt.*

277   **General Hymns**

L. M.

OLD HUNDREDTH   LOUIS BOURGEOIS, 1551

With great dignity

1 From all that dwell be-low the skies Let the Cre-a-tor's praise a-rise!
2 E-ter-nal are thy mer-cies, Lord, And truth e-ter-nal is thy word:
3 Praise God, from whom all bless-ings flow; Praise him, all crea-tures here be-low;

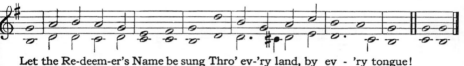

Let the Re-deem-er's Name be sung Thro' ev'ry land, by ev-'ry tongue!
Thy praise shall sound from shore to shore Till suns shall rise and set no more.
Praise him a-bove, ye heav'n-ly host: Praise Fa-ther, Son, and Ho-ly Ghost. A-men.

ISAAC WATTS, 1719; *based on Psalm 117;*
Doxology, THOMAS KEN, 1709

278   **L. M.**

Tune, OLD HUNDREDTH

1 All people that on earth do dwell,
    Sing to the Lord with cheerful voice:
    Him serve with fear, his praise forth tell,
    Come ye before him and rejoice.

2 Know that the Lord is God indeed;
    Without our aid he did us make:
    We are his folk, he doth us feed,
    And for his sheep he doth us take.

3 O enter then his gates with praise,
    Approach with joy his courts unto;
    Praise, laud, and bless his Name always,
    For it is seemly so to do.

4 For why? the Lord our God is good,
    His mercy is for ever sure;
    His truth at all times firmly stood,
    And shall from age to age endure.   **Amen.**

WILLIAM KETHE, 1561; *based on Psalm 100*

279

General Hymns

14 14. 478

PRAISE TO THE LORD

Joyfully, with dignity

Stralsund Gesangbuch, 1665
The Chorale Book for England, 1863

1 Praise to the Lord, the Al - migh - ty, the King of cre -
2 Praise to the Lord; o - ver all things he glo - rious - ly
3 Praise to the Lord, who doth pros - per thy way and de -

a - - tion; O my soul, praise him, for he is thy
reign - eth: Borne as on ea - gle - wings, safe - ly his
fend thee; Sure - ly his good - ness and mer - cy shall

health and sal - va - - tion: Join the great throng, Psal - ter - y,
saints he sus - tain - eth. Hast thou not seen How all thou
ev - er at - tend thee; Pon - der a - new What the Al -

or - gan, and song, Sound - ing in glad ad - o - ra - tion.
need - est hath been Grant - ed in what he or - dain - eth?
migh - ty can do, Who with his love doth be - friend thee.

General Hymns

4 Praise to the Lord! O let all that is in me adore him!
   All that hath breath join with Abraham's seed to adore him!
      Let the "Amen"
      Sum all our praises again
   Now as we worship before him.   Amen.

JOACHIM NEANDER, 1680;
based on Psalms 103 and 150; Hymnal Version, 1939

280

87. 87

STUTTGART

Adapted from a Melody by
C. F. WITT, Gotha, 1715

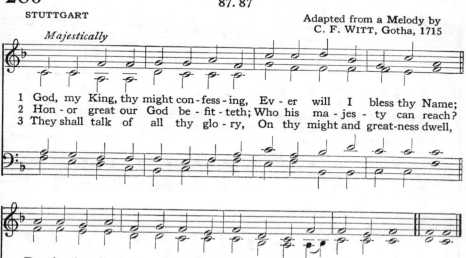

Majestically

1 God, my King, thy might con-fess-ing, Ev - er will I bless thy Name;
2 Hon - or great our God be - fit - teth; Who his ma - jes - ty can reach?
3 They shall talk of all thy glo - ry, On thy might and great-ness dwell,

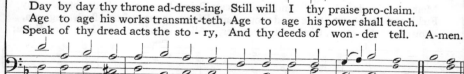

Day by day thy throne ad-dress-ing, Still will I thy praise pro-claim.
Age to age his works transmit-teth, Age to age his power shall teach.
Speak of thy dread acts the sto - ry, And thy deeds of won - der tell.   A-men.

4 Nor shall fail from memory's treasure
   Works by love and mercy wrought,
   Works of love surpassing measure,
   Works of mercy passing thought.

5 Full of kindness and compassion,
   Slow to anger, vast in love,
   God is good to all creation;
   All his works his goodness prove.

6 All thy works, O Lord, shall bless thee;
   Thee shall all thy saints adore:
   King supreme shall they confess thee,
   And proclaim thy sov'reign power.   Amen.

RICHARD MANT, 1824; based on Psalm 14𝟝

87. 87. D.

ALLELUIA   SAMUEL S. WESLEY, 1868

With joyful dignity

1 Joy - ful, joy - ful, we a - dore thee, God of glo - ry, Lord of love;
2 All thy works with joy sur - round thee, Earth and heav'n re - flect thy rays,
3 Thou art giv - ing and for - giv - ing, Ev - er bless - ing, ev - er blest,

Hearts un - fold like flowers be - fore thee, Prais - ing thee, their sun a - bove.
Stars and an - gels sing a - round thee, Cen - ter of un - bro - ken praise:
Well - spring of the joy of liv - ing, O - cean-depth of hap - py rest!

Melt the clouds of sin and sad - ness; Drive the dark of doubt a - way;
Field and for - est, vale and moun-tain, Bloom-ing mead-ow, flash - ing sea,
Thou our Fa - ther, Christ our Broth-er,—All who live in love are thine;

Giv - er of im - mor - tal glad-ness, Fill us with the light of day.
Chant-ing bird and flow - ing foun-tain, Call us to re - joice in thee.
Teach us how to love each oth - er, Lift us to the joy di - vine. A - men.

4 Mortals join the mighty chorus,   Ever singing march we onward,
    Which the morning stars began;   Victors in the midst of strife;
Father-love is reigning o'er us,   Joyful music lifts us sunward
    Brother-love binds man to man.   In the triumph song of life. Amen.

HENRY VAN DYKE, 1907

282

87. 87. 87

LAUDA ANIMA

JOHN GOSS, 1869

With movement

1 Praise, my soul, the King of hea - ven; To his feet thy
2 Praise him for his grace and fa - vor To our fa - thers
3 Fa - ther-like he tends and spares us; Well our fee - ble

trib - ute bring; Ran - somed, healed, re - stored, for - giv - en,
in dis - tress; Praise him still the same as ev - er,
frame he knows; In his hand he gen - tly bears us,

Ev - er - more his prais - es sing: Al - le - lu - ia!
Slow to chide, and swift to bless: Al - le - lu - ia!
Res - cues us from all our foes. Al - le - lu - ia!

Al - le - lu - ia! Praise the ev - er - last - ing King.
Al - le - lu - ia! Glo - rious in his faith - ful - ness.
Al - le - lu - ia! Wide - ly yet his mer - cy flows.

4 Angels, help us to adore him;   Dwellers all in time and space.
    Ye behold him face to face;   Alleluia! Alleluia!
  Sun and moon, bow down before him,   Praise with us the God of grace.

HENRY FRANCIS LYTE, 1834, *alt.; based on Psalm 103*

283

General Hymns

67. 67. 66. 66

STEADFAST

Melody pub. Hanover, 1646,
harmony after J. S. BACH

Stately

1 Our God, to whom we turn When wea - ry with il - lu - sion,
2 Thou art thy - self the truth; Though we who fain would find thee,
3 All beau - ty speaks of thee: The moun-tains and the riv - ers,

Whose stars se - rene - ly burn A - bove this earth's con - fu - sion,
Have tried, with thoughts un-couth, In fee - ble words to bind thee,
The line of lift - ed sea, Where spread-ing moon - light quiv - ers,

Thine is the migh - ty plan, The stead - fast or - der sure
It is be - cause thou art We're driv - en to the quest;
The deep-toned or - gan blast That rolls through arch - es dim

In which the world be - gan, En - dures, and shall en - dure.
Till truth from false-hood part, Our souls can find no rest.
Hints of the mu - sic vast Of thy e - ter - nal hymn.   A-men.

General Hymns

4 Wherever goodness lurks
   We catch thy tones appealing;
Where man for justice works
   Thou art thyself revealing;
The blood of man, for man
   On friendship's altar spilt,
Betrays the mystic plan
   On which thy house is built.

*5 Thou hidden fount of love,
   Of peace, and truth, and beauty,
Inspire us from above
   With joy and strength for duty.
May thy fresh light arise
   Within each clouded heart,
And give us open eyes
   To see thee as thou art.   Amen.

EDWARD GRUBB, 1925

284

C. M.

WINDSOR

M. WILLIAM DAMON'S
Booke of Musicke, 1591

With dignity

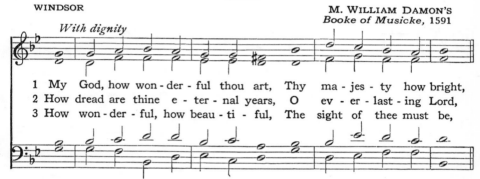

1 My God, how won - der - ful thou art, Thy ma - jes - ty how bright,
2 How dread are thine e - ter - nal years, O ev - er - last - ing Lord,
3 How won - der - ful, how beau - ti - ful, The sight of thee must be,

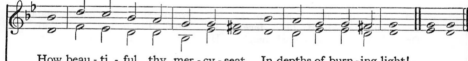

How beau - ti - ful thy mer - cy - seat, In depths of burn - ing light!
By pros-trate spi - rits day and night In - cess - ant - ly a - dored!
Thine end - less wisdom, boundless power, And awe - ful pu - ri - ty!   A - men

4 O how I fear thee, living God,
   With deepest, tenderest fears,
And worship thee with trembling hope
   And penitential tears!

5 Yet I may love thee too, O Lord,
   Almighty as thou art,
For thou hast stooped to ask of me
   The love of my poor heart.   Amen.

FREDERICK WILLIAM FABER, 1849

LEONI

Traditional Melody,
arr. MEYER LYON, c. 1770

With vigor; may be sung in unison

1 The God of A-braham praise, Who reigns en-throned a-bove;
2 He by him-self hath sworn: I on his oath de-pend;
3 There dwells the Lord, our King, The Lord, our Right-eous-ness,

An-cient of ev-er-last-ing days, And God of love;
I shall, on ea-gle-wings up-borne, To heav'n as-cend:
Tri-umph-ant o'er the world and sin, The Prince of Peace;

To him up-lift your voice, At whose su-preme com-mand
I shall be-hold his face, I shall his power a-dore,
On Si-on's sa-cred height His king-dom he main-tains,

From earth we rise, and seek the joys At his right hand.
And sing the won-ders of his grace For ev-er-more.
And, glo-rious with his saints in light, For ev-er reigns. A-men.

4 The God who reigns on high
   The great archangels sing,
And "Holy, Holy, Holy," cry,
   "Almighty King!

Who was, and is, the same,
   And evermore shall be:
Eternal Father, great I AM,
   We worship thee."

General Hymns

5 The whole triumphant host
   Give thanks to God on high;
  "Hail, Father, Son, and Holy Ghost!"
   They ever cry;

Hail, Abraham's God and mine!
   I join the heav'nly lays;
All might and majesty are thine,
   And endless praise.   Amen.

Jewish Doxology; Para. THOMAS OLIVERS, c. 1770; *alt.*

285 *Second Tune*   66. 84. D.

COVENANT   JOHN STAINER, 1889

With animation

1 The God of A-braham praise, Who reigns en-throned a - bove;
2 He by him - self hath sworn: I on his oath de - pend;
3 There dwells the Lord, our King, The Lord, our Right-eous - ness,

An - cient of ev - er - last - ing days, And God of love;
I shall, on ea - gle - wings up - borne, To heav'n as - cend:
Tri - umph-ant o'er the world and sin, The Prince of Peace;

To him up - lift your voice, At whose su - preme com - mand
I shall be - hold his face, I shall his power a - dore,
On Si - on's sa - cred height His king - dom he main - tains,

From earth we rise, and seek the joys At his right hand.
And sing the won - ders of his grace For ev - er - more.
And, glo - rious with his saints in light, For ev - er reigns. A-men.

66. 84. D.

LEONI

With vigor; may be sung in unison

Traditional Melody,
arr. MEYER LYON, c. 1770

1 Praise to the liv - ing God! All prais - ed be his Name
2 Form - less, all love - ly forms De - clare his love - li - ness;
3 His Spi - rit flow - eth free, High surg - ing where it will:

Who was, and is, and is to be, For aye the same.
Ho - ly, no ho - li - ness of earth Can his ex - press.
In pro - phet's word he spake of old; He speak - eth still.

The one e - ter - nal God Ere aught that now ap - pears:
Lo, he is Lord of all. Cre - a - tion speaks his praise,
Es - tab - lished is his law, And change-less it shall stand,

The First, the Last, be - yond all thought His time - less years!
And ev - 'ry-where, a - bove, be - low, His will o - beys.
Deep writ up - on the hu - man heart, On sea, on land. A - men.

4 Eternal life hath he
    Implanted in the soul;
His love shall be our strength and stay
    While ages roll.

Praise to the living God!
    All praisèd be his Name
Who was, and is, and is to be,
    For aye the same. Amen.

Jewish Doxology; Tr. MAX LANDSBERG *and* NEWTON MANN, 1914

General Hymns
87. 87. 887

ELBING

Not slow

PETER SOHREN, 1668

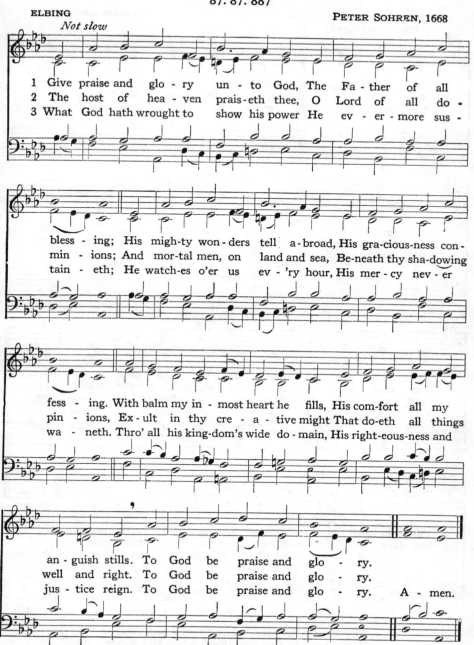

1 Give praise and glo - ry un - to God, The Fa - ther of all
2 The host of hea - ven prais - eth thee, O Lord of all do -
3 What God hath wrought to show his power He ev - er - more sus -

bless - ing; His migh-ty won - ders tell a-broad, His gra-cious-ness con -
min - ions; And mor-tal men, on land and sea, Be-neath thy sha-dowing
tain - eth; He watch-es o'er us ev - 'ry hour, His mer - cy nev - er

fess - ing. With balm my in - most heart he fills, His com-fort all my
pin - ions, Ex - ult in thy cre - a - tive might That do-eth all things
wa - neth. Thro' all his king-dom's wide do - main, His right-eous-ness and

an - guish stills. To God be praise and glo - ry.
well and right. To God be praise and glo - ry.
jus - tice reign. To God be praise and glo - ry. A - men.

JOHANN JACOB SCHUETZ, 1675;
Tr. ARTHUR W. FARLANDER *and* WINFRED DOUGLAS, 1939

10 10. 11 11

HANOVER   WILLIAM CROFT, 1708

With great dignity

1 O wor - ship the King, all glo - rious a - bove!
2 O tell of his might! O sing of his grace!
3 The earth, with its store of won - ders un - told,

O grate - ful - ly sing his power and his love!
Whose robe is the light, whose can - o - py space.
Al - migh - ty, thy power hath found - ed of old,

Our shield and de - fend - er, the An - cient of Days,
His char - iots of wrath the deep thun - der - clouds form,
Hath stab - lished it fast by a change - less de - cree,

Pa - vil - ioned in splen - dor, and gird - ed with praise.
And dark is his path on the wings of the storm.
And round it hath cast, like a man - tle, the sea.   A - men.

4 Thy bountiful care, what tongue can recite?
   It breathes in the air; it shines in the light;
   It streams from the hills; it descends to the plain,
   And sweetly distils in the dew and the rain.

General Hymns

5 Frail children of dust, and feeble as frail,
In thee do we trust, nor find thee to fail;
Thy mercies, how tender! how firm to the end!
Our Maker, Defender, Redeemer, and Friend! Amen.

ROBERT GRANT, 1833; *based on Psalm 104*

289

C. M.

ST. ANNE
Majestically

WILLIAM CROFT, 1708

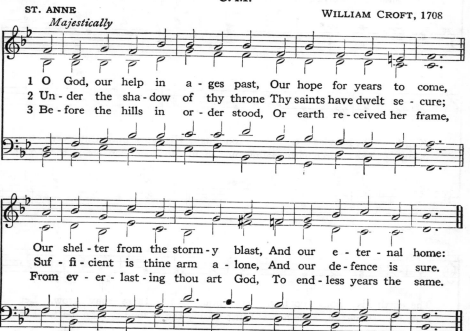

1 O God, our help in a-ges past, Our hope for years to come,
2 Un-der the sha-dow of thy throne Thy saints have dwelt se-cure;
3 Be-fore the hills in or-der stood, Or earth re-ceived her frame,

Our shel-ter from the storm-y blast, And our e-ter-nal home:
Suf-fi-cient is thine arm a-lone, And our de-fence is sure.
From ev-er-last-ing thou art God, To end-less years the same.

4 A thousand ages in thy sight
Are like an evening gone;
Short as the watch that ends the night
Before the rising sun.

5 Time, like an ever-rolling stream,
Bears all its sons away;
They fly, forgotten, as a dream
Dies at the opening day.

6 O God, our help in ages past,
Our hope for years to come,
Be thou our guide while life shall last,
And our eternal home. Amen.

A-men.

ISAAC WATTS, 1719; *based on Psalm 90*

General Hymns

10 4. 66. 66. 10 4

HIGH ROAD

Moderately fast

MARTIN SHAW, 1915

1 Let all the world in ev - 'ry cor - ner sing, My God and King! The heav'ns are not too high, His praise may thith - er fly; The earth is not too low, His prais - es there may grow. Let all the world in ev - 'ry cor - ner sing, My God and King!

2 Let all the world in ev - 'ry cor - ner sing, My God and King! The Church with psalms must shout, No door can keep them out; But, a - bove all, the heart Must bear the long - est part. Let all the world in ev - 'ry cor - ner sing, My God and King! A - men.

GEORGE HERBERT, 1633

UNIVERSAL PRAISE

W. G. WHINFIELD, 1906

1 Let all the world in ev-'ry cor-ner sing, My God and King!
2 Let all the world in ev-'ry cor-ner sing, My God and King!

The heav'ns are not too high, His praise may thith-er fly;
The Church with psalms must shout, No door can keep them out;

The earth is not too low, His prais-es there may grow.
But, a-bove all, the heart Must bear the long-est part.

Let all the world in ev-'ry cor-ner sing, My God and King!
Let all the world in ev-'ry cor-ner sing, My God and King! A-men.

GEORGE HERBERT, 1633

General Hymns

L. M.

MENDON

Traditional German Melody
arr. by SAMUEL DYER, 1828

In moderate time

1 Lord of all be - ing, throned a - far, Thy glo - ry
2 Sun of our life, thy quick - 'ning ray Sheds on our
3 Our mid - night is thy smile with - drawn; Our noon - tide

flames from sun and star; Cen - ter and soul of ev - 'ry
path the glow of day; Star of our hope, thy sof - ten'd
is thy gra - cious dawn; Our rain - bow arch, thy mer - cy's

sphere, Yet to each lov - ing heart how near!
light Cheers the long watch - es of the night.
sign; All, save the clouds of sin, are thine. A - men.

4 Lord of all life, below, above,
  Whose light is truth, whose warmth is love,
  Before thy ever-blazing throne
  We ask no luster of our own.

5 Grant us thy truth to make us free,
  And kindling hearts that burn for thee,
  Till all thy living altars claim
  One holy light, one heav'nly flame.   Amen.

OLIVER WENDELL HOLMES, 1848

292 *First Tune* 𝔊eneral 𝔥𝔶mns
77. 77. D.

RILEY
Brightly

MARTIN SHAW, 1915

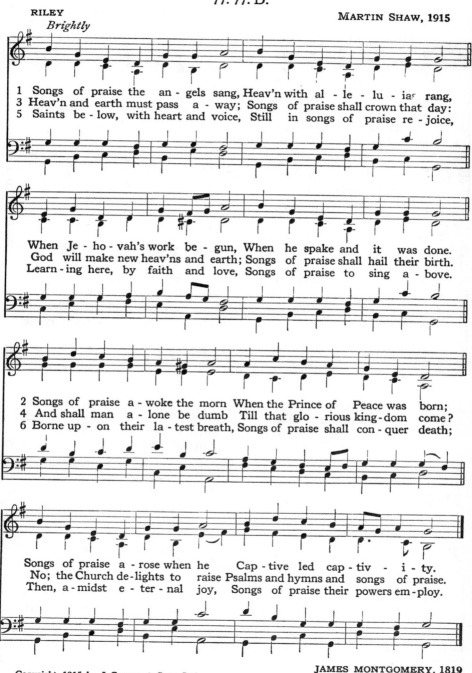

1 Songs of praise the an-gels sang, Heav'n with al-le-lu-ias rang,
3 Heav'n and earth must pass a-way; Songs of praise shall crown that day:
5 Saints be-low, with heart and voice, Still in songs of praise re-joice,

When Je-ho-vah's work be-gun, When he spake and it was done.
God will make new heav'ns and earth; Songs of praise shall hail their birth.
Learn-ing here, by faith and love, Songs of praise to sing a-bove.

2 Songs of praise a-woke the morn When the Prince of Peace was born;
4 And shall man a-lone be dumb Till that glo-rious king-dom come?
6 Borne up-on their la-test breath, Songs of praise shall con-quer death;

Songs of praise a-rose when he Cap-tive led cap-tiv-i-ty.
No; the Church de-lights to raise Psalms and hymns and songs of praise.
Then, a-midst e-ter-nal joy, Songs of praise their powers em-ploy.

JAMES MONTGOMERY, 1819

INNOCENTS

Traditional Melody,
pub. *The Parish Choir,* 1850

Moderately fast

1 Songs of praise the an - gels sang, Heav'n with al - le - lu - ias rang,
2 Songs of praise a - woke the morn When the Prince of Peace was born;
3 Heav'n and earth must pass a - way; Songs of praise shall crown that day:
4 And shall man a - lone be dumb Till that glo - rious king - dom come?

When Je - ho - vah's work be - gun, When he spake and it was done.
Songs of praise a - rose when he Cap - tive led cap - tiv - i - ty.
God will make new heav'ns and earth; Songs of praise shall hail their birth.
No; the Church de - lights to raise Psalms and hymns and songs of praise.

5 Saints below, with heart and voice,
Still in songs of praise rejoice,
Learning here, by faith and love,
Songs of praise to sing above.

6 Borne upon their latest breath,
Songs of praise shall conquer death;
Then, amidst eternal joy,
Songs of praise their powers employ.

JAMES MONTGOMERY, 1819

293 S. M.

DONCASTER

SAMUEL WESLEY, 1837

In moderate time

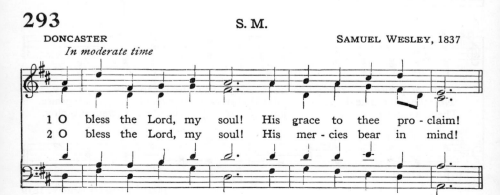

1 O bless the Lord, my soul! His grace to thee pro - claim!
2 O bless the Lord, my soul! His mer - cies bear in mind!

General Hymns

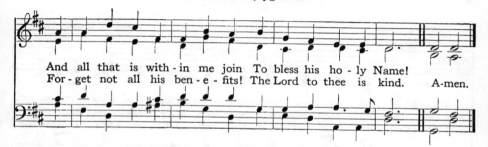

And all that is with-in me join To bless his ho-ly Name!
For-get not all his ben-e-fits! The Lord to thee is kind. A-men.

3 He will not always chide;
  He will with patience wait;
  His wrath is ever slow to rise,
  And ready to abate.

4 He pardons all thy sins;
  Prolongs thy feeble breath;
  He healeth thine infirmities,
  And ransoms thee from death.

5 He clothes thee with his love;
  Upholds thee with his truth;
  And like the eagle he renews
  The vigor of thy youth.

6 Then bless his holy Name,
  Whose grace hath made thee whole,
  Whose loving-kindness crowns thy days!
  O bless the Lord, my soul! Amen.

JAMES MONTGOMERY, 1819; *based on Psalm 103*

Alternative Tune, ST. THOMAS (WILLIAMS), No. 388

294

ST. BEES

Without dragging

77. 77

JOHN B. DYKES, 1862

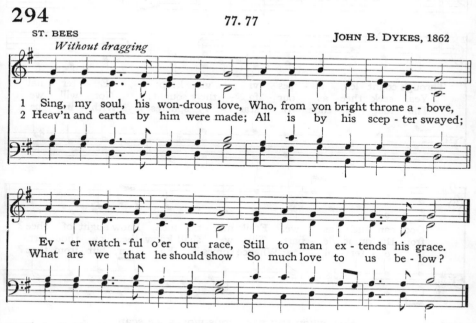

1 Sing, my soul, his won-drous love, Who, from yon bright throne a-bove,
2 Heav'n and earth by him were made; All is by his scep-ter swayed;

Ev-er watch-ful o'er our race, Still to man ex-tends his grace.
What are we that he should show So much love to us be-low?

3 God, the merciful and good,
  Bought us with the Saviour's blood,
  And, to make our safety sure,
  Guides us by his Spirit pure.

4 Sing, my soul, adore his Name!
  Let his glory be thy theme:
  Praise him till he calls thee home;
  Trust his love for all to come.

Anonymous, 1800

295

General Hymns
88. 88. 88

DAVID'S HARP
ROBERT KING, 1722

Stately

1 Lord of all ma - jes - ty and might, Whose pres - ence fills the un -
*2 Be - yond all knowl-edge thou art wise, With wis - dom that tran -
3 Frail though our form, and brief our day, Our mind has bridged the

fath - omed deep, Where - in un - count - ed worlds of light
scends all thought: Yet still we seek with strain - ing eyes,
gulf of years, Our pu - ny bal - an - ces can weigh

Through count - less a - ges vi - gil keep; E - ter - nal
Yea, seek thee as our fa - thers sought; Nor will we
The mag - ni - tude of star - ry spheres: With - in us

God, can such as we, Frail mor - tal men, know aught of thee?
from the quest de - part Till we shall know thee as thou art.
is e - ter - ni - ty; Whence comes it, Fa - ther, but from thee?

4 For, when thy wondrous works we scan,
And Mind gives answer back to mind,
Thine image stands revealed in man;
And, seeking, he shall surely find.
Thy sons, our heritage we claim:
Shall not thy children know thy Name?

General Hymns

296

77. 77. 77

ENGLAND'S LANE
With spirit; may be sung in unison

Traditional English Melody,
adapted by GEOFFREY SHAW, 1919

1 For the beau-ty of the earth, For the beau-ty of the skies,
2 For the beau-ty of each hour Of the day and of the night,
3 For the joy of ear and eye, For the heart and mind's de-light,

For the love which from our birth O-ver and a-round us lies,
Hill and vale, and tree and flower, Sun and moon, and stars of light,
For the mys-tic har-mo-ny Link-ing sense to sound and sight,

Refrain

Lord of all, to thee we raise This our hymn of grate-ful praise. A-men.

By permission of Geoffrey Shaw and the Oxford University Press

4 For the joy of human love,
Brother, sister, parent, child,
Friends on earth, and friends above,
For all gentle thoughts and mild,
                    Refrain

5 For each perfect gift of thine
To our race so freely giv'n,
Graces human and divine,
Flowers of earth and buds of heav'n,
                    Refrain
                    Amen.

Alternative Tune, DIX, No. 140   FOLLIOTT SANDFORD PIERPOINT, 1864

DURHAM

Melody, Ravenscroft's Psalter, 1621
har. by SAMUEL SEBASTIAN WESLEY

Moderately slow

1 When all thy mer - cies, O my God, My ri - sing soul sur - veys,
2 O how shall words with e - qual warmth The grat - i - tude de - clare,
3 Ten thou - sand thou-sand pre - cious gifts My dai - ly thanks em - ploy;

Trans-port - ed with the view, I'm lost In won - der, love, and praise.
That glows with - in my rav - ished heart? But thou canst read it there.
Nor is the least a cheer - ful heart That tastes those gifts with joy.

4 When nature fails, and day and night
   Divide thy works no more,
   My ever grateful heart, O Lord,
   Thy mercy shall adore.

5 Through all eternity, to thee
   A joyful song I'll raise;
   But O eternity's too short
   To utter all thy praise! Amen.

A - men.

JOSEPH ADDISON, 1712, *alt.*

Alternative Tune, TALLIS' ORDINAL, No. 298

298 *First Tune*   C. M.

TALLIS' ORDINAL

THOMAS TALLIS, c. 1567

Moderately slow

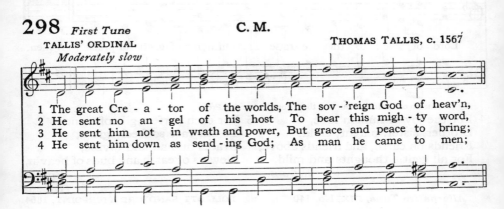

1 The great Cre - a - tor of the worlds, The sov - 'reign God of heav'n,
2 He sent no an - gel of his host To bear this migh - ty word,
3 He sent him not in wrath and power, But grace and peace to bring;
4 He sent him down as send - ing God; As man he came to men;

General Hymns

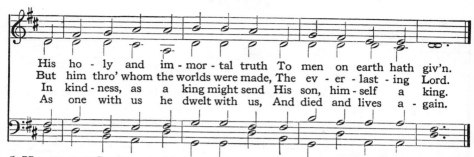

His ho - ly and im - mor - tal truth To men on earth hath giv'n.
But him thro' whom the worlds were made, The ev - er - last - ing Lord.
In kind - ness, as a king might send His son, him - self a king.
As one with us he dwelt with us, And died and lives a - gain.

5 He came as Saviour to his own,
The way of love he trod;
He came to win men by good will,
For force is not of God.

6 Not to oppress, but summon men
Their truest life to find,
In love God sent his Son to save,
Not to condemn mankind.

From Epistle to Diognetus, c. 150; Tr. F. BLAND TUCKER, 1939

298 *Second Tune* C. M.

SCARBOROUGH   FRANKLIN GLYNN, 1941
In unison, freely

1 The great Cre - a - tor of the worlds, The sov - 'reign God of heav'n,
2 He sent no an - gel of his host To bear this migh - ty word,
3 He sent him not in wrath and power, But grace and peace to bring;
4 He sent him down as send - ing God; As man he came to men;

His ho - ly and im - mor - tal truth To men on earth hath giv'n.
But him thro' whom the worlds were made, The ev - er - last - ing Lord.
In kind - ness, as a king might send His son, him - self a king.
As one with us he dwelt with us, And died and lives a - gain.

ELBING   PETER SOHREN, 1668

Not slow

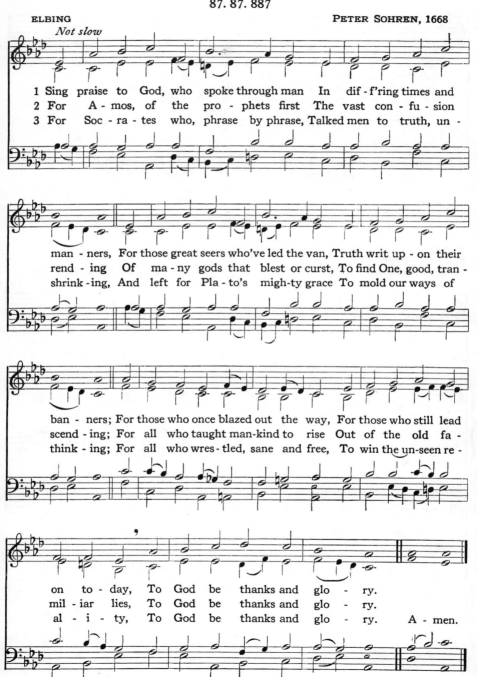

1 Sing praise to God, who spoke through man In dif-f'ring times and
2 For A-mos, of the pro-phets first The vast con-fu-sion
3 For Soc-ra-tes who, phrase by phrase, Talked men to truth, un-

man-ners, For those great seers who've led the van, Truth writ up-on their
rend-ing Of ma-ny gods that blest or curst, To find One, good, tran-
shrink-ing, And left for Pla-to's migh-ty grace To mold our ways of

ban-ners; For those who once blazed out the way, For those who still lead
scend-ing; For all who taught man-kind to rise Out of the old fa-
think-ing; For all who wres-tled, sane and free, To win the un-seen re-

on to-day, To God be thanks and glo-ry.
mil-iar lies, To God be thanks and glo-ry.
al-i-ty, To God be thanks and glo-ry. A-men.

General Hymns

4 For all the poets who have wrought
  Through music, words, and vision
To tell the beauty of God's thought
  By art's sublime precision,
Who bring our highest dreams to shape
And help the soul in her escape,
  To God be thanks and glory. Amen.

By permission of the Oxford University Press

PERCY DEARMER, 1933

300

L. M.

WINCHESTER NEW

Adapted from
Musikalisches Handbuch, Hamburg, 1690

With solemnity

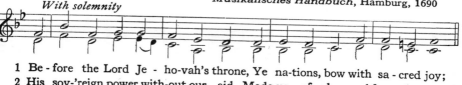

1 Be - fore the Lord Je - ho-vah's throne, Ye na-tions, bow with sa - cred joy;
2 His sov-'reign power with-out our aid Made us of clay, and formed us men;

Know that the Lord is God a - lone; He can cre - ate, and he de - stroy.
And when like wand'ring sheep we strayed, He brought us to his fold a - gain.

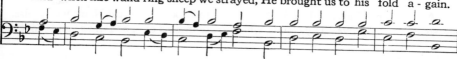

3 We are his people, we his care,
    Our souls, and all our mortal frame:
  What lasting honors shall we rear,
    Almighty Maker, to thy Name?

4 We'll crowd thy gates with thankful songs,
    High as the heav'n our voices raise;
  And earth, with her ten thousand tongues,
    Shall fill thy courts with sounding praise.

5 Wide as the world is thy command,
    Vast as eternity thy love;
  Firm as a rock thy truth must stand,
    When rolling years shall cease to move.

ISAAC WATTS, 1719, alt.; *based on Psalm 100*

ST. DENIO

Welsh Melody,
adapted 1839

In moderate time

1 Im - mor - tal, in - vis - i - ble, God on - ly wise, In light in - ac -
2 Un - rest - ing, un - hast - ing, and si - lent as light, Nor want - ing, nor

ces - si - ble hid from our eyes, Most bless - ed, most glo - rious, the
wast - ing, thou rul - est in might; Thy jus - tice like moun - tains high

An - cient of Days, Al - migh - ty, vic - to - rious, thy great Name we praise.
soar - ing a - bove Thy clouds, which are fountains of good - ness and love.

3 To all life thou givest, to both great and small;
   In all life thou livest, the true life of all;
   We blossom and flourish, like leaves on the tree,
   Then wither and perish; but naught changeth thee.

4 Great Father of glory, pure Father of light,
   Thine angels adore thee, all veiling their sight;
   All laud we would render: O help us to see
   'Tis only the splendor of light hideth thee. Amen.

A - men.

WALTER CHALMERS SMITH, 1867, *alt.*

General Hymns
98. 98. 88

MENTZER

Joyously

J. B. KOENIG'S
Harmonischer Lieder Schatz, 1738

1 O that I had a thou-sand voic-es, A thou-sand
2 Who o-ver-whelm-eth me with bless-ing? Who but thy-
3 Thy good-ness, Lord, my life com-plet-eth; O let thy

ways to praise my God! In him my in-most heart re-
self, O God of love! Who guard-eth me from fears op-
praise my tongue em-ploy, And bring thee, while my heart yet

joic-es Un-til I long to tell a-broad In songs of
press-ing? 'Tis thou, Lord God of hosts, a-bove. Thou bear-est
beat-eth, The glad thanks-giv-ing of my joy: When ebb-ing

thank-ful ec-sta-sy How much my God hath done for me.
all my guilt ab-horred, With ev-er pa-tient mer-cy, Lord.
strength all speech de-nies, Then may I breathe thy praise in sighs. A-men.

4 My God, receive these earthly praises
  So poor and weak, with gracious love;
A better tribute heaven raises
  From all thy angel choirs above:

There alleluias will I bring
A thousand-fold to thee, my
  King. Amen.

JOHANN MENTZER, 1704;
Tr. ARTHUR W. FARLANDER *and* WINFRED DOUGLAS, 1939

87. 87. 887

TO GOD ON HIGH

Adapted from Plainsong, 1539;
arr. and har. FELIX MENDELSSOHN, 1836

With dignity

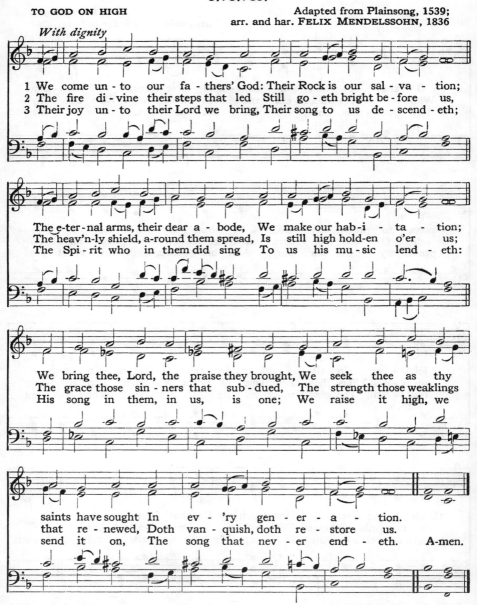

1 We come un-to our fa-thers' God: Their Rock is our sal-va-tion;
2 The fire di-vine their steps that led Still go-eth bright be-fore us,
3 Their joy un-to their Lord we bring, Their song to us de-scend-eth;

The e-ter-nal arms, their dear a-bode, We make our hab-i-ta-tion;
The heav'n-ly shield, a-round them spread, Is still high hold-en o'er us;
The Spi-rit who in them did sing To us his mu-sic lend-eth:

We bring thee, Lord, the praise they brought, We seek thee as thy
The grace those sin-ners that sub-dued, The strength those weaklings
His song in them, in us, is one; We raise it high, we

saints have sought In ev-'ry gen-er-a-tion.
that re-newed, Doth van-quish, doth re-store us.
send it on, The song that nev-er end-eth. A-men.

4 Ye saints to come, take up the strain,
   The same sweet theme endeavor;
Unbroken be the golden chain!
   Keep on the song for ever!

Safe in the same dear dwelling-place,
Rich with the same eternal grace,
Bless the same boundless Giver.
                                   Amen.

THOMAS HORNBLOWER GILL, 1868

General Hymns
87. 87. D.

BEECHER
Cheerfully

JOHN ZUNDEL, 1870

1 There's a wide-ness in God's mer-cy Like the wide-ness of the sea;
2 There is no place where earth's sor-rows Are more felt than up in heav'n;
3 For the love of God is broad-er Than the mea-sure of man's mind;

There's a kind-ness in his jus-tice, Which is more than lib - er - ty.
There is no place where earth's fail-ings Have such kind-ly judg-ment giv'n.
And the heart of the E - ter - nal Is most won-der - ful - ly kind.

There is wel-come for the sin - ner, And more gra - ces for the good;
There is plen - ti - ful re - demp-tion In the blood that has been shed;
If our love were but more sim - ple, We should take him at his word;

There is mer-cy with the Sa - viour; There is heal-ing in his blood.
There is joy for all the mem - bers In the sor-rows of the Head.
And our lives would be all sun - shine In the sweet-ness of the Lord.

FREDERICK WILLIAM FABER, 1862

ALMSGIVING

JOHN B. DYKES, 1865

In moderate time

1 O Lord of heav'n and earth and sea, To thee all
2 Thou didst not spare thine on - ly Son, But gav'st him
3 Thou giv'st the Spi - rit's bless - ed dower, Spi - rit of

praise and glo - ry be; How shall we show our
for a world un - done, And free - ly, with that
life and love and power, And dost his sev'n - fold

love to thee, Who giv - est all?
Bless - ed One, Thou giv - est all.
gra - ces shower Up - on us all. A - men.

4 For souls redeemed, for sins forgiv'n,
For means of grace and hopes of heav'n,
Father, what can to thee be giv'n,
Who givest all?

5 We lose what on ourselves we spend,
We have as treasure without end
Whatever, Lord, to thee we lend,
Who givest all;

6 To thee, from whom we all derive
Our life, our gifts, our power to give:
O may we ever with thee live,
Who givest all! Amen.

CHRISTOPHER WORDSWORTH, 1863, *alt.*

General Hymns
88. 88. 88

CAREY

HENRY CAREY, 1723

With gentle motion

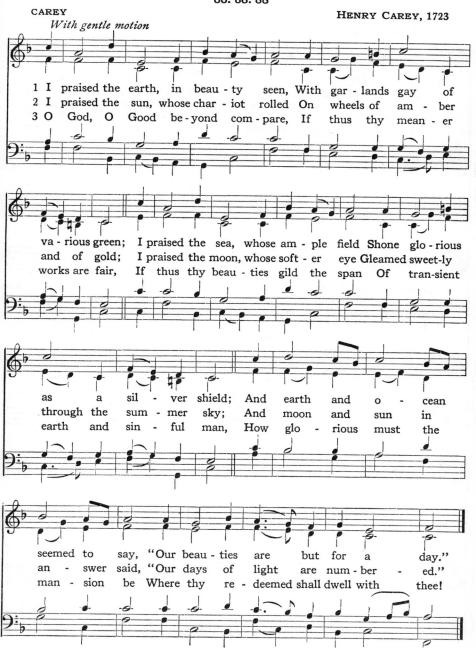

1 I praised the earth, in beau - ty seen, With gar - lands gay of
2 I praised the sun, whose char - iot rolled On wheels of am - ber
3 O God, O Good be - yond com - pare, If thus thy mean - er

va - rious green; I praised the sea, whose am - ple field Shone glo - rious
and of gold; I praised the moon, whose soft - er eye Gleamed sweet-ly
works are fair, If thus thy beau - ties gild the span Of tran-sient

as a sil - ver shield; And earth and o - cean
through the sum - mer sky; And moon and sun in
earth and sin - ful man, How glo - rious must the

seemed to say, "Our beau - ties are but for a day."
an - swer said, "Our days of light are num - ber - ed."
man - sion be Where thy re - deemed shall dwell with thee!

REGINALD HEBER, *pub.* 1827, *alt.*

General Hymns
887. 88

ALFRED M. SMITH, 1940

ASSISI

Moderately fast, in flowing style

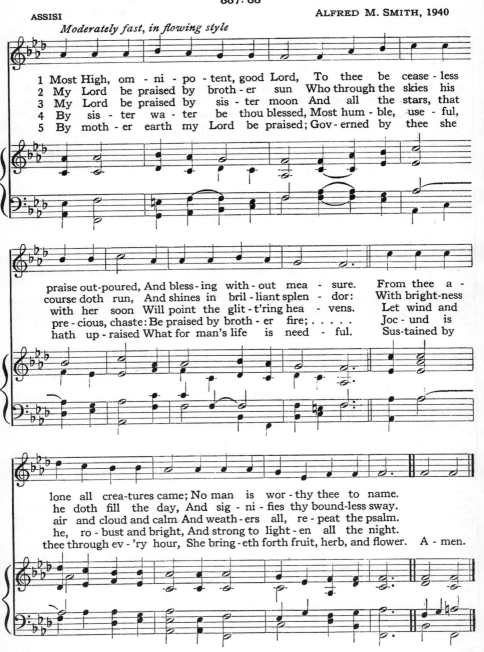

1 Most High, om - ni - po - tent, good Lord, To thee be cease - less
2 My Lord be praised by broth - er sun Who through the skies his
3 My Lord be praised by sis - ter moon And all the stars, that
4 By sis - ter wa - ter be thou blessed, Most hum - ble, use - ful,
5 By moth - er earth my Lord be praised; Gov - erned by thee she

praise out-poured, And bless - ing with - out mea - sure. From thee a -
course doth run, And shines in bril - liant splen - dor: With bright-ness
with her soon Will point the glit - t'ring hea - vens. Let wind and
pre - cious, chaste: Be praised by broth - er fire; . . . . . Joc - und is
hath up - raised What for man's life is need - ful. Sus-tained by

lone all crea-tures came; No man is wor - thy thee to name.
he doth fill the day, And sig - ni - fies thy bound-less sway.
air and cloud and calm And weath-ers all, re - peat the psalm.
he, ro - bust and bright, And strong to light - en all the night.
thee through ev - 'ry hour, She bring-eth forth fruit, herb, and flower. A - men.

This tune may be effectively sung by alternating groups; all singing the first and last stanzas

6 My Lord be praised by those who prove
In free forgivingness their love,
Nor shrink from tribulation.
Happy, who peaceably endure;
With thee, Lord, their reward is sure.

7 For death our sister, praisèd be,
From whom no man alive can flee.
Woe to the unpreparèd!
But blest be they who do thy will
And follow thy commandments still.

8 Most High, omnipotent, good Lord,
To thee be ceaseless praise outpoured,
And blessing without measure.
Let creatures all give thanks to thee,
And serve in great humility. Amen.

ST. FRANCIS OF ASSISI, 1181–1226; *Tr.* HOWARD CHANDLER ROBBINS, 1939

308

77. 77

MONKLAND

Anonymous Melody, Manchester, 1824,
arr. JOHN BERNARD WILKES, 1861

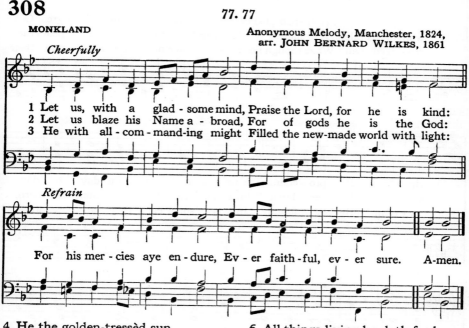

Cheerfully

1 Let us, with a glad-some mind, Praise the Lord, for he is kind:
2 Let us blaze his Name a-broad, For of gods he is the God:
3 He with all-com-mand-ing might Filled the new-made world with light:

Refrain

For his mer-cies aye en-dure, Ev-er faith-ful, ev-er sure. A-men.

4 He the golden-tressèd sun
  Caused all day his course to run:
      Refrain

5 The hornèd moon to shine by night,
  'Mid her spangled sisters bright:
      Refrain

6 All things living he doth feed,
  His full hand supplies their need:
      Refrain

7 Let us, with a gladsome mind,
  Praise the Lord, for he is kind:
      Refrain
        Amen.

JOHN MILTON, 1623, *alt.*; *Para. Psalm 136*

L. M. D.

CREATION

Adapted from
FRANZ JOSEPH HAYDN, 1798

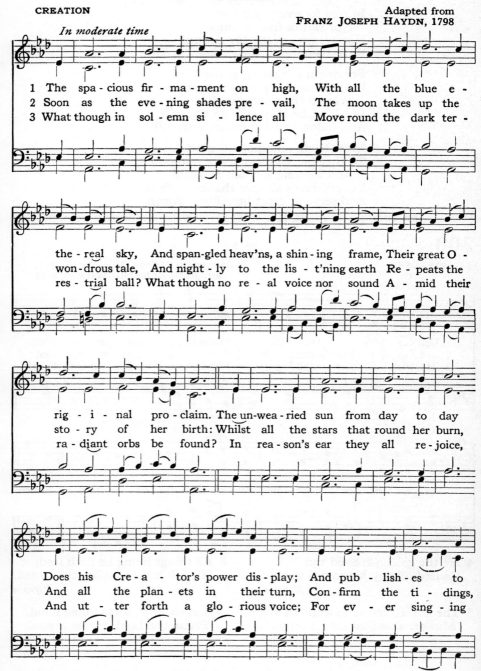

In moderate time

1 The spa - cious fir - ma - ment on high, With all the blue e -
2 Soon as the eve - ning shades pre - vail, The moon takes up the
3 What though in sol - emn si - lence all Move round the dark ter -

the - real sky, And span-gled heav'ns, a shin - ing frame, Their great O -
won - drous tale, And night - ly to the lis - t'ning earth Re - peats the
res - trial ball? What though no re - al voice nor sound A - mid their

rig - i - nal pro - claim. The un-wea - ried sun from day to day
sto - ry of her birth: Whilst all the stars that round her burn,
ra - diant orbs be found? In rea - son's ear they all re - joice,

Does his Cre - a - tor's power dis - play; And pub - lish - es to
And all the plan - ets in their turn, Con - firm the ti - dings,
And ut - ter forth a glo - rious voice; For ev - er sing - ing

General Hymns

ev - 'ry land. The work of an al - migh - ty hand.
as they roll And spread the truth from pole to pole.
as they shine, "The hand that made us is di - vine."

JOSEPH ADDISON, 1712; *based on Psalm 19*

310   C. M.

LONDON NEW

Scottish Psalter, 1635,
ad. JOHN PLAYFORD, 1671

With dignity

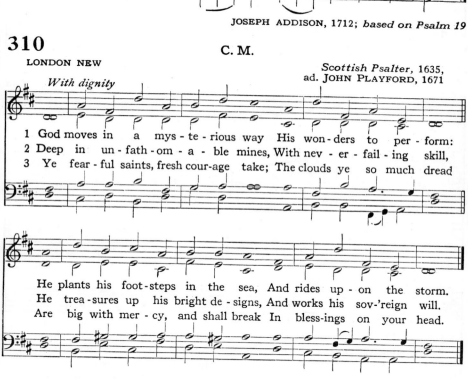

1 God moves in a mys - te - rious way His won - ders to per - form:
2 Deep in un - fath - om - a - ble mines, With nev - er - fail - ing skill,
3 Ye fear - ful saints, fresh cour - age take; The clouds ye so much dread

He plants his foot-steps in the sea, And rides up - on the storm.
He trea - sures up his bright de - signs, And works his sov - 'reign will.
Are big with mer - cy, and shall break In bless-ings on your head.

4 Judge not the Lord by feeble sense,
   But trust him for his grace;
Behind a frowning providence
   He hides a smiling face.

5 His purposes will ripen fast,
   Unfolding every hour:
The bud may have a bitter taste,
   But sweet will be the flower.

6 Blind unbelief is sure to err,
   And scan his work in vain;
God is his own interpreter,
   And he will make it plain.

Alternative Tune, DUNDEE, No. 397

WILLIAM COWPER, 1774

76. 76, with Refrain

ROYAL OAK

Traditional English Melody,
adapted by MARTIN SHAW, 1915

† *Refrain.*   *Cheerfully*

All things bright and beau-ti-ful, All crea-tures great and small,

End

All things wise and won-der-ful, The Lord God made them all.

Stanzas commence here

1 Each lit-tle flower that o-pens, Each lit-tle bird that sings,
2 The pur-ple-head-ed moun-tain, The riv-er run-ning by,
3 The cold wind in the win-ter, The plea-sant sum-mer sun,
4 He gave us eyes to see them, And lips that we might tell

† *The choir sings the Refrain first; then all repeat it, before the first stanza.*
At the close of the last repetition, the final note should be held.

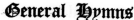

Repeat Refrain

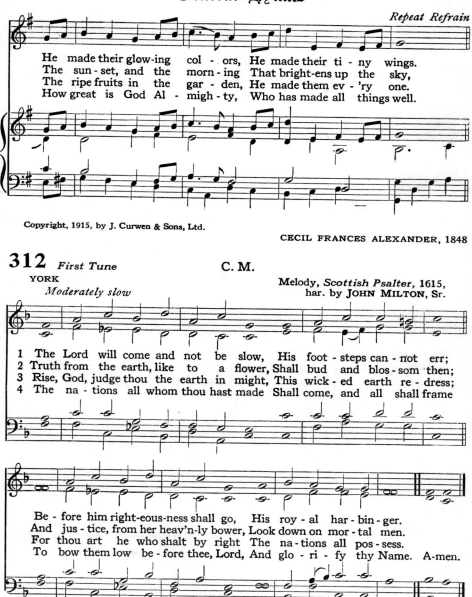

He made their glow-ing col - ors, He made their ti - ny wings.
The sun - set, and the morn - ing That bright-ens up the sky,
The ripe fruits in the gar - den, He made them ev - 'ry one.
How great is God Al - migh - ty, Who has made all things well.

CECIL FRANCES ALEXANDER, 1848

312 *First Tune*   C. M.

YORK

Moderately slow

Melody, *Scottish Psalter*, 1615,
har. by JOHN MILTON, Sr.

1 The Lord will come and not be slow, His foot - steps can - not err;
2 Truth from the earth, like to a flower, Shall bud and blos - som then;
3 Rise, God, judge thou the earth in might, This wick - ed earth re - dress;
4 The na - tions all whom thou hast made Shall come, and all shall frame

Be - fore him right-eous-ness shall go, His roy - al har - bin - ger.
And jus - tice, from her heav'n-ly bower, Look down on mor - tal men.
For thou art he who shalt by right The na - tions all pos - sess.
To bow them low be - fore thee, Lord, And glo - ri - fy thy Name. A-men.

5 For great thou art, and wonders great
By thy strong hand are done:
Thou in thy everlasting seat
Remainest God alone. Amen.

JOHN MILTON, 1648, *based on Psalms 82, 85, 86*

C. M.

BALFOUR

Melody by G. J. KNOWLES, 18th cent.;
harmonized by GEOFFREY SHAW, 1919

Moderately slow

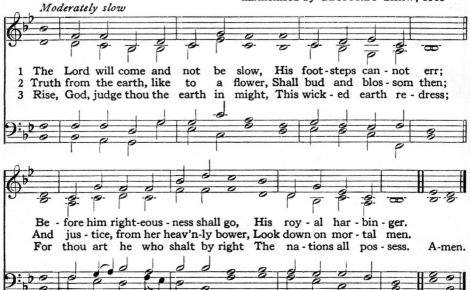

1 The Lord will come and not be slow, His foot-steps can-not err;
2 Truth from the earth, like to a flower, Shall bud and blos-som then;
3 Rise, God, judge thou the earth in might, This wick-ed earth re-dress;

Be - fore him right-eous-ness shall go, His roy - al har - bin - ger.
And jus - tice, from her heav'n-ly bower, Look down on mor - tal men.
For thou art he who shalt by right The na - tions all pos - sess. A-men.

By permission of Geoffrey Shaw and the Oxford University Press

4 The nations all whom thou hast made
Shall come, and all shall frame
To bow them low before thee, Lord,
And glorify thy Name.

5 For great thou art, and wonders great
By thy strong hand are done:
Thou in thy everlasting seat
Remainest God alone. Amen.

JOHN MILTON, 1648, *based on Psalms 82, 85, 86*

313 77. 776. D.

SHINING DAY

Melody,
JOHANN GEORG EBELING, 1666

Fast

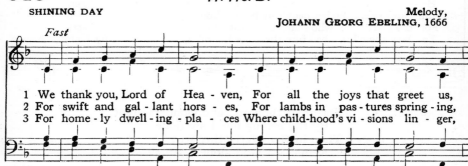

1 We thank you, Lord of Hea - ven, For all the joys that greet us,
2 For swift and gal - lant hors - es, For lambs in pas - tures spring - ing,
3 For home - ly dwell - ing - pla - ces Where child-hood's vi - sions lin - ger,

General Hymns

For all that you have giv - en To help us and de - light us
For dogs with friend-ly fa - ces, For birds with mu - sic throng - ing
For friends and kind - ly voic - es, For bread to stay our hun - ger

In earth and sky and seas; The sun - light on the mea - dows,
Their chan - tries in the trees; For herbs to cool our fe - ver,
And sleep to bring us ease; For zeal and zest of liv - ing,

The rain - bow's fleet - ing won - der, The clouds with cool - ing sha - dows,
For flowers of field and gar - den, For bees a - mong the clo - ver
For faith and un - der - stand - ing, For words to tell our lov - ing,

The stars that shine in splen - dor—We thank you, Lord, for these.
With sto - len sweet - ness la - den—We thank you, Lord, for these.
For hope of peace un - end - ing—We thank you, Lord, for these. A-men.

JAN STRUTHER, 1933

Words and music by permission of the Oxford University Press

MAGDALEN COLLEGE   WILLIAM HAYES, 1774
With spirit

1 We sing of God, the migh-ty source Of all things;
2 The world, the clus-t'ring spheres he made, The glo-rious
*3 Glo-rious the sun in mid ca-reer; Glo-rious the as-

the stu-pen-dous force On which all strength de-pends;
light, the sooth-ing shade, Dale, mea-dow, grove, and hill;
sem-bled fires ap-pear; Glo-rious the com-et's train:

From whose right arm, be-neath whose eyes, All pe-riod,
The mul-ti-tu-di-nous a-byss, Where se-cre-
Glo-rious the trum-pet and a-larm; Glo-rious the al-

power, and en-ter-prise Com-men-ces, reigns, and ends.
cy re-mains in bliss, And wis-dom hides her skill.
migh-ty stretched-out arm; Glo-rious the en-rap-tured main:

4 Glorious, most glorious is the crown
  Of him that brought salvation down
    By meekness, called man's son;
  Seers that stupendous truth believed,
  And now the matchless deed's achieved,
    Determined, dared, and done.

CHRISTOPHER SMART, 1765, *alt.*

General Hymns

12 11. 12 11

KREMSER

Traditional Netherlands Melody,
pub. 1625, arr. EDWARD KREMSER

Resolutely

1 We gath - er to - geth - er to ask the Lord's bless - ing;
2 Be - side us to guide us, our God with us join - ing,
3 We all do ex - tol thee, thou lead - er tri - umph - ant,

He chast - ens and hast - ens his will to make known;
Or - dain - ing, main - tain - ing his king - dom di - vine;
And pray that thou still our de - fend - er wilt be.

The wick - ed op - press - ing now cease from dis - tress - ing:
So from the be - gin - ning the fight we were win - ning:
Let thy con - gre - ga - tion es - cape trib - u - la - tion:

Sing prais - es to his Name; he for - gets not his own.
Thou, Lord, wast at our side: all glo - ry be thine!
Thy Name be ev - er praised! O Lord, make us free! A - men.

Anonymous, 1625; Tr. THEODORE BAKER

65. 65. D., with Refrain

PRINCE RUPERT
With vigor

English March, 1648
arr. by GUSTAV HOLST, 1925

1 Hark! the voice e - ter - nal, Robed in ma - jes - ty,
2 Bright the world and glo - rious, Calm both earth and sea,

Call - ing in - to be - ing Earth and sea and sky;
No - ble in its gran - deur Stood man's pu - ri - ty;

Hark! in count-less num - bers All the an - gel throng
Came the great trans-gres - sion, Came the sad-dening fall,

Alto and Bass

Hark! in count - less num-bers
Came the great trans-gres-sion,

Hail cre - a - tion's morn - ing With one burst of song.
Death and des - o - la - tion Breath-ing o - ver all.

Hail cre - a - tion's morn - ing
Death and des - o - la - tion

General Hymns

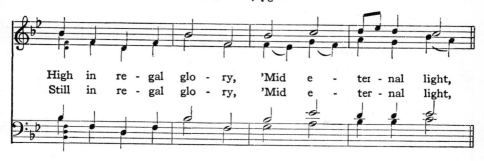

High in re - gal glo - ry, 'Mid e - ter - nal light,
Still in re - gal glo - ry, 'Mid e - ter - nal light,

Reign, O King im - mor - tal, Ho - ly, in - fi - nite.
Reigned the King im - mor - tal, Ho - ly, in - fi - nite. A-men.

3 Long the nations waited,
   Through the troubled night,
Looking, longing, yearning,
   For the promised light.
Prophets saw the morning
   Breaking far away,
Minstrels sang the splendor
   Of that opening day;
     While in regal glory,
      'Mid eternal light,
     Reigned the King immortal,
     Holy, infinite.

4 Brightly dawned the Advent
   Of the new-born King,
Joyously the watchers
   Heard the angels sing.
Sadly closed the evening
   Of his hallowed life,
As the noontide darkness
   Veiled the last dread strife.
     Lo! again in glory,
      'Mid eternal light,
     Reigns the King immortal,
     Holy, infinite.

5 Lo! again he cometh,
   Robed in clouds of light,
As the Judge eternal,
   Armed with power and might.
Nations to his footstool
   Gathered then shall be;
Earth shall yield her treasures,
   And her dead, the sea.
     Till the trumpet soundeth,
      'Mid eternal light,
     Reign, thou King immortal,
     Holy, infinite.

6 Jesus! Lord and Master,
   Prophet, Priest, and King,
To thy feet, triumphant,
   Hallowed praise we bring.
Thine the pain and weeping,
   Thine the victory;
Power, and praise, and honor,
   Be, O Lord, to thee.
     High in regal glory,
      'Mid eternal light,
     Reign, O King immortal,
     Holy, infinite.   Amen.

JOHN JULIAN, 1882

317

Irregular

ANNUNCIATION

Traditional Dutch Melody, pub. 1896,
har. by DAVID McK. WILLIAMS, 1940

In moderate time

1 A mes - sage came to a maid - en young; The
2 No great - er news could a mes - sen - ger bring; For
3 He came, God's Word to the world here be - low; And
4 And some - times trum - pets from Si - on ring out, And

an - gel stood be - side her In shin - ing robes, and with
'twas from that young moth - er He came, who walked on the
round him there did gath - er A band who found that this
tramp - ing comes, and drum - ming; "Thy king - dom come," so we

gold - en tongue He told what should be - tide her:
earth as a king, And yet was all men's broth - er:
teach - er to know Was e'en to know the Fa - ther:
cry; and they shout, "It comes!" and still 'tis com - ing.

General Hymns

The maid was lost in won - der; Her world was
His truth has spread like lea - ven; 'Twill mar - ry
He healed the sick who sought him, For - gave the
Far, far a - head, to win us, Yet with us,

rent a - sun - der; Ah! how could
earth to hea - ven, Till all a -
foes who fought him; Be - side the
nay with - in us; Till all shall

she Christ's moth - er be By God's most high de - cree!
gree In char - i - ty To dwell from sea to sea.
sea Of Gal - i - lee He set the na - tions free.
see That King is he, The Love from Gal - i - lee!

St. 1, Dutch; Para. E. B. G., 1928;
St. 2, 3, 4, PERCY DEARMER, 1928

88. 88. 11

HOSANNA   JOHN B. DYKES, 1865

With spirit

1 Ho - san - na to the liv - ing Lord! Ho - san - na to the in -
2 Ho - san - na, Lord! thine an - gels cry; Ho - san - na, Lord! thy
3 O Sa - viour, with pro - tect - ing care A - bide in this thy

car-nate Word! To Christ, Cre - a - tor, Saviour, King, Let earth, let heav'n, Ho-
saints re - ply; A - bove, be-neath us, and a-round, The dead and liv - ing
house of prayer, Where we thy part-ing prom-ise claim, As - sem-bled in thy

Refrain

san - na sing!
swell the sound; Ho - san - na, Lord! Ho - san - na in the high - est!
sa - cred Name.

4 But, chiefest, in our cleansèd breast,
   Eternal! bid thy Spirit rest;
   And make our secret soul to be
   A temple pure and worthy thee.
                        Refrain

5 So in the last and dreadful day,
   When earth and heav'n shall melt away,
   Thy flock, redeemed from sinful stain,
   Shall swell the sound of praise again.
                        Refrain
                        Amen.

A - men.

REGINALD HEBER, 1827

319

RICHMOND C. M. THOMAS HAWEIS, 1792

With movement

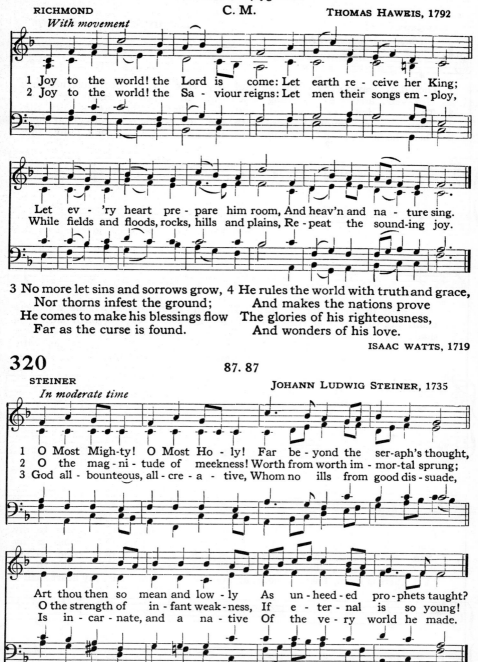

1 Joy to the world! the Lord is come: Let earth re - ceive her King;
2 Joy to the world! the Sa - viour reigns: Let men their songs em - ploy,

Let ev - 'ry heart pre - pare him room, And heav'n and na - ture sing.
While fields and floods, rocks, hills and plains, Re - peat the sound-ing joy.

3 No more let sins and sorrows grow,   4 He rules the world with truth and grace,
   Nor thorns infest the ground;   And makes the nations prove
He comes to make his blessings flow   The glories of his righteousness,
   Far as the curse is found.   And wonders of his love.

ISAAC WATTS, 1719

320 87. 87

STEINER JOHANN LUDWIG STEINER, 1735

In moderate time

1 O Most Migh-ty! O Most Ho - ly! Far be - yond the ser-aph's thought,
2 O the mag - ni - tude of meekness! Worth from worth im - mor-tal sprung;
3 God all - bounteous, all - cre - a - tive, Whom no ills from good dis - suade,

Art thou then so mean and low - ly As un - heed-ed pro-phets taught?
O the strength of in - fant weak-ness, If e - ter - nal is so young!
Is in - car - nate, and a na - tive Of the ve - ry world he made.

CHRISTOPHER SMART, 1765

321

General Hymns

Irregular

MARGARET

TIMOTHY R. MATTHEWS, 1876

Unison, in moderate time

1 Thou didst leave thy throne and thy king - ly crown When thou
2 Hea - ven's arch - es rang when the an - gels sang, Pro -
3 The .. fox - es found rest, and the birds had their nest In the
4 Thou .. ca - mest, O Lord, with the liv - ing word That should
5 When the heav'ns shall ring, and the an - gels sing At thy

ca - mest to earth for me; But in Beth - le-hem's home was there
claim - ing thy roy - al de - gree; But in low - ly birth didst thou
shade of the for - est tree; But thy couch was the sod, O thou
set thy peo - ple free; But with mock - ing scorn, and with
com - ing to vic - to - ry, Let thy voice call me home, say - ing,

found no room For thy ho - ly na - tiv - i - ty. O come to my
come to earth, And in great hu - mil - i - ty. O come to my
Son of God, In the des - ert of Gal - i - lee. O come to my
crown of thorn, They bore thee to Cal - va - ry. O come to my
"Yet there is room, There is room at my side for thee." And my heart shall re-

General Hymns

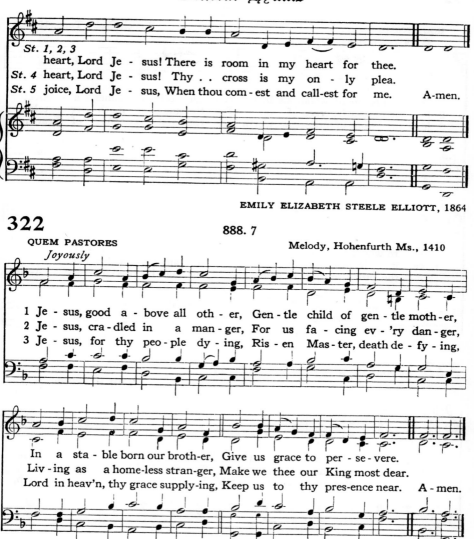

St. 1, 2, 3   heart, Lord Je - sus! There is room in my heart for thee.
St. 4   heart, Lord Je - sus! Thy .. cross is my on - ly plea.
St. 5   joice, Lord Je - sus, When thou com - est and call-est for me. A-men.

EMILY ELIZABETH STEELE ELLIOTT, 1864

322   888. 7

QUEM PASTORES   Melody, Hohenfurth Ms., 1410
Joyously

1 Je - sus, good a - bove all oth - er, Gen - tle child of gen - tle moth - er,
2 Je - sus, cra - dled in a man - ger, For us fa - cing ev - 'ry dan - ger,
3 Je - sus, for thy peo - ple dy - ing, Ris - en Mas - ter, death de - fy - ing,

In a sta - ble born our broth - er, Give us grace to per - se - vere.
Liv - ing as a home-less stran-ger, Make we thee our King most dear.
Lord in heav'n, thy grace supply-ing, Keep us to thy pres-ence near. A - men.

4 Jesus, who our sorrows bearest,
    All our thoughts and hopes thou sharest,
    Thou to man the truth declarest;
        Help us all thy truth to hear.

5 Lord, in all our doings guide us;
    Pride and hate shall ne'er divide us;
    We'll go on with thee beside us,
        And with joy we'll persevere! Amen.

By permission of the Oxford University Press

PERCY DEARMER, 1906

323 *First Tune* — **General Hymns**

77. 77

HOLY NAME

French Psalm Tune, 1562

With animation

1 Je - sus! Name of wondrous love! Name all oth - er names a - bove!
2 Je - sus! Name de-creed of old, To the maid-en moth - er told,
3 Je - sus! Name of price-less worth To the fall-en sons of earth,

Un - to which must ev - 'ry knee Bow in deep hu - mil - i - ty.
Kneel-ing in her low - ly cell, By the an - gel Ga - bri - el.
For the prom-ise that it gave, "Je - sus shall his peo - ple save." A-men.

323 *Second Tune*

77. 77

ST. BEES

JOHN B. DYKES, 1862

With movement

1 Je - sus! Name of won-drous love! Name all oth - er names a - bove!
2 Je - sus! Name de - creed of old, To the maid - en moth - er told,
3 Je - sus! Name of price - less worth To the fall - en sons of earth,

Un - to which must ev - 'ry knee Bow in deep hu - mil - i - ty.
Kneel-ing in her low - ly cell, By the an - gel Ga - bri - el.
For the prom-ise that it gave, "Je - sus shall his peo - ple save." A-men.

General Hymns

*4 Jesus! Name of mercy mild,
Given to the holy child
When the cup of human woe
First he tasted here below.

5 Jesus! only Name that's giv'n
Under all the mighty heav'n,
Whereby man, to sin enslaved,
Bursts his fetters and is saved.

6 Jesus! Name of wondrous love!
Human Name of God above;
Pleading only this we flee,
Helpless, O our God, to thee. Amen.

WILLIAM WALSHAM HOW, 1854

324

ORIENTIS PARTIBUS
With dignity

77. 77
Office de la Circoncision, Sens, c. 1210

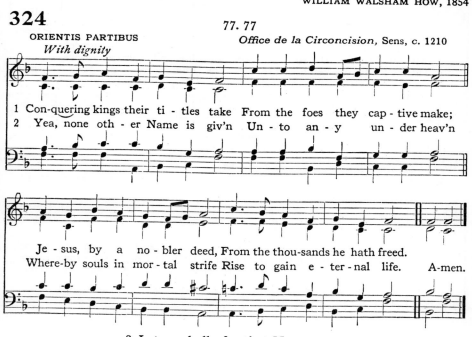

1 Con-quering kings their ti-tles take From the foes they cap-tive make;
2 Yea, none oth-er Name is giv'n Un-to an-y un-der heav'n

Je - sus, by a no-bler deed, From the thou-sands he hath freed.
Where-by souls in mor-tal strife Rise to gain e-ter-nal life. A-men.

3 Let us gladly for that Name
Bear the cross, endure the shame,
Suffer with him joyfully,
Death, through him, is victory.

4 Jesus, who dost condescend
To be called the sinner's Friend,
Hear us, as to thee we pray,
Glorying in thy Name to-day. Amen.

Nevers Breviary, 1727; *Hymnal Version*, 1940

Alternative Tune, INNOCENTS, No. 235

STRACATHRO

Melody, CHARLES HUTCHESON, 1832,
har. by GEOFFREY SHAW, 1925

In moderate time

1 O for a thou-sand tongues to sing My dear Re-deem-er's praise,
2 Je - sus, the Name that charms our fears, That bids our sor - rows cease;
3 He speaks; and, list - 'ning to his voice, New life the dead re - ceive,

The glo - ries of my God and King, The tri-umphs of his grace!
'Tis mu - sic in the sin-ner's ears, 'Tis life and health and peace.
The mourn-ful bro-ken hearts re-joice, The hum-ble poor be - lieve. A-men.

By permission of Geoffrey Shaw and the Oxford University Press

325 *Second Tune* C. M.

ARLINGTON

THOMAS A. ARNE, 1762

Joyfully

1 O for a thou-sand tongues to sing My dear Re - deem-er's praise,
2 Je - sus, the Name that charms our fears, That bids our sor - rows cease;
3 He speaks; and, list - 'ning to his voice, New life the dead re - ceive,

The glo - ries of my God and King, The tri-umphs of his grace!
'Tis mu - sic in the sin-ner's ears, 'Tis life and health and peace.
The mourn-ful bro-ken hearts re-joice, The hum-ble poor be - lieve. A-men.

General Hymns

4 Hear him, ye deaf; his praise, ye dumb,
Your loosened tongues employ;
Ye blind, behold your Saviour come;
And leap, ye lame, for joy!

5 My gracious Master and my God,
Assist me to proclaim
And spread through all the earth abroad
The honors of thy Name. Amen.

CHARLES WESLEY, 1740

326

87. 87. 87

ORIEL

CASPAR ETT, 1840

In moderate time

1 To the Name of our sal - va - tion Laud and hon - or let us pay,
2 Je - sus is the Name we trea - sure; Name be - yond what words can tell;
3 'Tis the Name that who - so preacheth Speaks like mu - sic to the ear;

Which for ma - ny a gen - er - a - tion Hid in God's fore-knowl-edge lay;
Name of glad - ness, Name of plea - sure, Ear and heart de - light-ing well;
Who in prayer this Name be - seech-eth Sweet-est com - fort find - eth near;

But with ho - ly ex - ul - ta - tion We may sing a - loud to - day.
Name of sweet - ness, pass-ing measure, Sa - ving us from sin and hell.
Who its per - fect wis - dom reacheth, Heav'nly joy pos - sess-eth here. A - men.

4 Therefore we, in love adoring,
This most blessèd Name revere,
Holy Jesus, thee imploring
So to write it in us here
That hereafter, heav'nward soaring,
We may sing with angels there. Amen.

Latin, 15th cent.; Tr. Hymns Ancient and Modern, 1861

L. M. D.

JORDAN   JOSEPH BARNBY, 1872

In moderate time

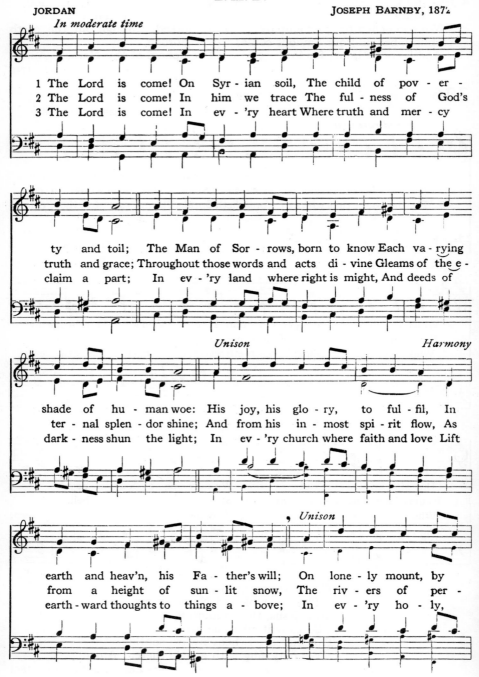

1 The Lord is come! On Syr - ian soil, The child of pov - er -
2 The Lord is come! In him we trace The ful - ness of God's
3 The Lord is come! In ev - 'ry heart Where truth and mer - cy

ty and toil; The Man of Sor - rows, born to know Each va - rying
truth and grace; Throughout those words and acts di - vine Gleams of the e -
claim a part; In ev - 'ry land where right is might, And deeds of

Unison   *Harmony*

shade of hu - man woe: His joy, his glo - ry, to ful - fil, In
ter - nal splen - dor shine; And from his in - most spi - rit flow, As
dark - ness shun the light; In ev - 'ry church where faith and love Lift

Unison

earth and heav'n, his Fa - ther's will; On lone - ly mount, by
from a height of sun - lit snow, The riv - ers of per -
earth - ward thoughts to things a - bove; In ev - 'ry ho - ly,

General Hymns

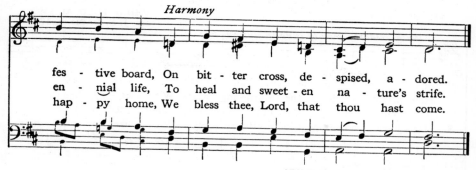

festive board, On bitter cross, despised, adored.
ennial life, To heal and sweeten nature's strife.
happy home, We bless thee, Lord, that thou hast come.

ARTHUR PENRHYN STANLEY, 1872

328

BELMONT

C. M.

Arr. from WILLIAM GARDINER'S
Sacred Melodies, 1812

In flowing style

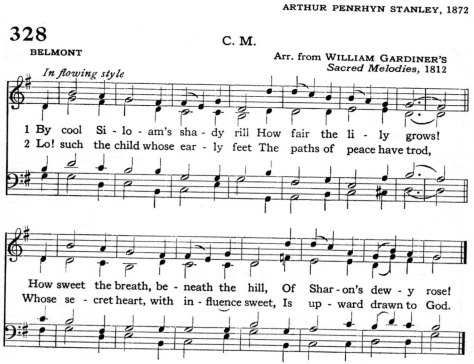

1 By cool Siloam's shady rill How fair the lily grows!
2 Lo! such the child whose early feet The paths of peace have trod,

How sweet the breath, beneath the hill, Of Sharon's dewy rose!
Whose secret heart, with influence sweet, Is upward drawn to God.

3 O thou whose infant feet were found
    Within thy Father's shrine,
Whose years, with changeless virtue crowned,
    Were all alike divine,

4 Dependent on thy bounteous breath,
    We seek thy grace alone,
In childhood, manhood, age, and death,
    To keep us still thine own.

REGINALD HEBER, 1812, *alt.*

329 **General Hymns**

887. 887. 48. 48

FRANKFORT

PHILIP NICOLAI, 1599,
arr. J. S. BACH, c. 1730

1 How bright ap-pears the Morn-ing Star, With mer-cy beam-ing from a - far; The host of heav'n re - joic - es; O Right-eous Branch, O Jes - se's Rod! Thou Son of Man and Son of God! We, too, will lift our voic - es:

2 Though cir - cled by the hosts on high, He deigned to cast a pi - tying eye Up - on his help - less crea - ture; The whole cre - a - tion's Head and Lord, By high - est ser - a - phim a - dored, As - sumed our ve - ry na - ture;

3 Re - joice, ye heav'ns; thou earth, re - ply; With praise, ye sin - ners, fill the sky, For this his In - car - na - tion. In - car - nate God, put forth thy power, Ride on, ride on, great Con - quer - or, Till all know thy sal - va - tion.

General Hymns

Je - sus, Je - sus! Ho - ly, ho - ly, yet most low - ly,
Je - sus, grant us, Through thy mer - it, to in - her - it
A - men, A - men! Al - le - lu - ia! Al - le - lu - ia!

Draw thou near us; Great Em - man - uel, come and hear us.
Thy sal - va - tion; Hear, O hear our sup - pli - ca - tion.
Praise be giv - en Ev - er - more, by earth and hea - ven. A-men.

PHILIP NICOLAI, 1597; *Para.* WILLIAM MERCER, 1859

330   C. M.

BOUWERIE   W. A. GOLDSWORTHY, 1941
Serenely

1 I know not how that Beth - l'hem's babe Could in the God - head be;
2 I know not how that Cal - vary's cross A world from sin could free;
3 I know not how that Jo - seph's tomb Could solve death's mys - ter - y;

I on - ly know the man - ger child Has brought God's life to me.
I on - ly know its match - less love Has brought God's love to me.
I on - ly know a liv - ing Christ, Our im - mor - tal - i - ty.

HARRY WEBB FARRINGTON, 1910

Alternative Tune, BISHOPTHORPE, No. 360

C. M. D.

KINGSFOLD

Traditional English Melody,
arr. by R. VAUGHAN WILLIAMS, 1906

With spirit

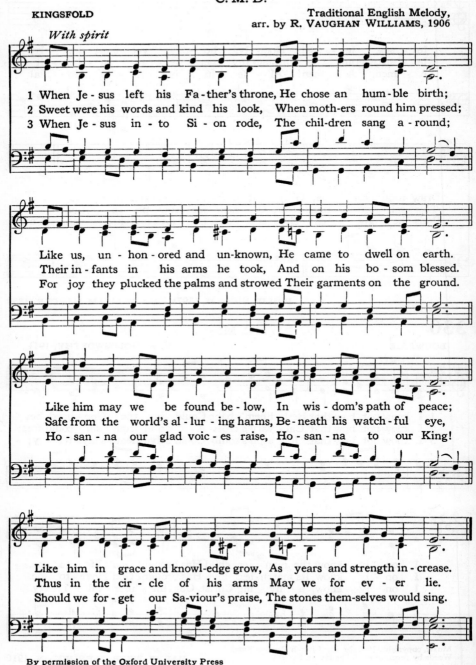

1 When Je - sus left his Fa - ther's throne, He chose an hum - ble birth;
2 Sweet were his words and kind his look, When moth-ers round him pressed;
3 When Je - sus in - to Si - on rode, The chil-dren sang a - round;

Like us, un - hon - ored and un-known, He came to dwell on earth.
Their in - fants in his arms he took, And on his bo - som blessed.
For joy they plucked the palms and strowed Their garments on the ground.

Like him may we be found be - low, In wis - dom's path of peace;
Safe from the world's al - lur - ing harms, Be - neath his watch - ful eye,
Ho - san - na our glad voic - es raise, Ho - san - na to our King!

Like him in grace and knowl-edge grow, As years and strength in - crease.
Thus in the cir - cle of his arms May we for ev - er lie.
Should we for - get our Sa-viour's praise, The stones them-selves would sing.

JAMES MONTGOMERY, 1816, alt.

77. 77. D.

SPANISH CHANT

Arr. by BENJAMIN CARR, 1824

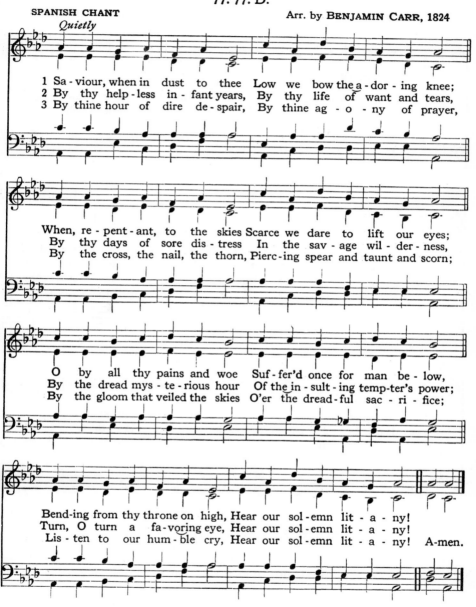

1 Sa-viour, when in dust to thee Low we bow the a-dor-ing knee;
2 By thy help-less in-fant years, By thy life of want and tears,
3 By thine hour of dire de-spair, By thine ag-o-ny of prayer,

When, re-pent-ant, to the skies Scarce we dare to lift our eyes;
By thy days of sore dis-tress In the sav-age wil-der-ness,
By the cross, the nail, the thorn, Pierc-ing spear and taunt and scorn;

O by all thy pains and woe Suf-fer'd once for man be-low,
By the dread mys-te-rious hour Of the in-sult-ing temp-ter's power;
By the gloom that veiled the skies O'er the dread-ful sac-ri-fice;

Bend-ing from thy throne on high, Hear our sol-emn lit-a-ny!
Turn, O turn a fa-vor-ing eye, Hear our sol-emn lit-a-ny!
Lis-ten to our hum-ble cry, Hear our sol-emn lit-a-ny! A-men.

4 By thy deep expiring groan,
By the sad sepulchral stone,
By the vault, whose dark abode
Held in vain the rising God;

O from earth to heav'n restored,
Mighty, re-ascended Lord,
Listen, listen to the cry
Of our solemn litany! Amen.

ROBERT GRANT, 1815, *alt.*

L. M.

INTERCESSION   Arr. by JOHN B. DYKES, 1853

In moderate time

1 O Je - sus, cru - ci - fied for man, O Lamb, all
2 We pray thee, grant us strength to take Our dai - ly
3 As on our dai - ly way we go, Through light or

glo - rious on thy throne, Teach thou our won - d'ring
cross, what - e'er it be, And glad - ly for thine
shade, in calm or strife, O may we bear thy

souls to scan The mys - t'ry of thy love un - known.
own dear sake In paths of pain to fol - low thee.
marks be - low In con - quer'd sin and chast-en'd life. A - men.

† 4 And week by week this day we ask
     That holy memories of thy cross
     May sanctify each common task,
     And turn to gain each earthly loss.

5 Grant us, dear Lord, our cross to bear
     Till at thy feet we lay it down;
     Win through thy blood our pardon there,
     And through the cross attain the crown. Amen.

WILLIAM WALSHAM HOW, 1871

† *For Friday only*

334

General Hymns
65. 65. D.

PENITENCE
Simply

SPENCER LANE, 1875

1 In the hour of tri - al, Je - sus, plead for me,
2 With for - bid - den plea - sures Would this vain world charm,
3 Should thy mer - cy send me Sor - row, toil, and woe,

Lest by base de - ni - al I de - part from thee.
Or its sor - did trea - sures Spread to work me harm,
Or should pain at - tend me On my path be - low,

When thou seest me wa - ver, With a look re - call,
Bring to my re - mem - brance Sad Geth - sem - a - ne,
Grant that I may nev - er Fail thy hand to see;

Nor for fear or fa - vor Suf - fer me to fall.
Or, in dark - er sem - blance, Cross-crowned Cal - va - ry.
Grant that I may ev - er Cast my care on thee.
A - men.

4 When my last hour cometh,
   Fraught with strife and pain,
When my dust returneth
   To the dust again,

On thy truth relying,
   Through that mortal strife,
Jesus, take me, dying,
   To eternal life. Amen.

JAMES MONTGOMERY, 1834, *alt.*

CASWALL   65. 65   FRIEDRICH FILITZ, 1847

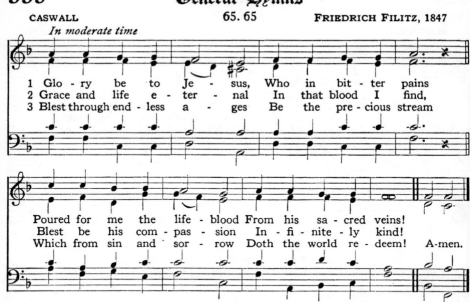

1 Glo - ry be to Je - sus, Who in bit - ter pains
2 Grace and life e - ter - nal In that blood I find,
3 Blest through end - less a - ges Be the pre - cious stream

Poured for me the life - blood From his sa - cred veins!
Blest be his com - pas - sion In - fi - nite - ly kind!
Which from sin and sor - row Doth the world re - deem! A - men.

4 Oft as earth exulting   5 Lift ye then your voices;
  Wafts its praise on high,   Swell the mighty flood;
Angel hosts, rejoicing,   Louder still and louder
  Make their glad reply.   Praise the precious blood.   Amen.

Italian, 18th cent.; Tr. EDWARD CASWALL, *alt.*

336 RATHBUN   87. 87   ITHAMAR CONKEY, 1851

With breadth

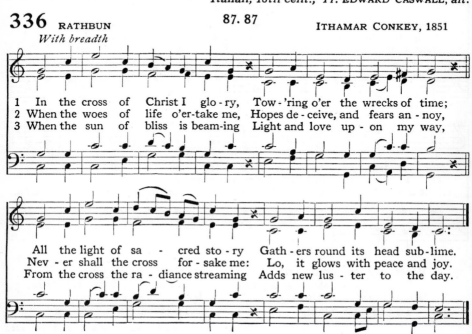

1 In the cross of Christ I glo - ry, Tow - 'ring o'er the wrecks of time;
2 When the woes of life o'er - take me, Hopes de - ceive, and fears an - noy,
3 When the sun of bliss is beam-ing Light and love up - on my way,

All the light of sa - cred sto - ry Gath - ers round its head sub - lime.
Nev - er shall the cross for - sake me: Lo, it glows with peace and joy.
From the cross the ra - diance streaming Adds new lus - ter to the day.

General Hymns

4 Bane and blessing, pain and pleasure,
 By the cross are sanctified;
 Peace is there that knows no measure,
 Joys that through all time abide.

5 In the cross of Christ I glory,
 Tow'ring o'er the wrecks of time;
 All the light of sacred story
 Gathers round its head sublime.

JOHN BOWRING, 1825

337

L. M.

ROCKINGHAM
In moderate time

Arr. by EDWARD MILLER, 1790

1 When I sur - vey the won - drous cross Where the young
2 For - bid it, Lord, that I should boast, Save in the
3 See, from his head, his hands, his feet, Sor - row and

Prince of Glo - ry died, My rich - est gain I
cross of Christ, my God: All the vain things that
love flow min - gled down! Did e'er such love and

count but loss, And pour con - tempt on all my pride.
charm me most, I sac - ri - fice them to his blood.
sor - row meet, Or thorns com - pose so rich a crown?

4 Were the whole realm of nature mine,
 That were an off'ring far too small;
 Love so amazing, so divine,
 Demands my soul, my life, my all.

Alternative Tune, HAMBURG, No. 219

ISAAC WATTS, 1707

6664. 884

WIGAN   SAMUEL SEBASTIAN WESLEY, 1872

With deep feeling

1 Be - hold the Lamb of God! O thou for sin - ners slain,
2 Be - hold the Lamb of God! All hail, in - car - nate Word,
3 Be - hold the Lamb of God! Wor - thy is he a - lone

Let it not be in vain That thou hast died:
Thou ev - er - last - ing Lord, Sa - viour most blest;
That sit - teth on the throne Of God a - bove;

Thee for my Sa - viour let me take, My on - ly ref - uge
Fill us with love that nev - er faints, Grant us with all thy
One with the An - cient of all days, One with the Com - fort -

let me make Thy pierc - ed side.
bless - ed saints E - ter - nal rest.
er in praise, All light and love. A - men.

MATTHEW BRIDGES, 1848, *alt.*

ST. CHRISTOPHER
Not too slow

FREDERICK C. MAKER, 1881

1 O Lamb of God, still keep me Near to thy wound-ed side;
2 'Tis on-ly in thee hi - ding, I feel my life se - cure;
3 Soon shall my eyes be-hold thee, With rap - ture, face to face;

'Tis on - ly there in safe - ty And peace I can a - bide.
In thee a - lone a - bi - ding, The con - flict can en - dure:
One half hath not been told me Of all thy power and grace;

What foes and snares sur - round me; What lusts and fears with - in!
Thine arm the vic - to-ry gain - eth O'er ev - 'ry hurt - ful foe;
Thy beau - ty, Lord, and glo - ry, The won - ders of thy love,

The grace that sought and found me A - lone can keep me clean.
Thy love my heart sus - tain - eth In all its care and woe.
Shall be the end - less sto - ry Of all thy saints a - bove. A-men.

JAMES GEORGE DECK, 1842, *alt.*

Alternative Tune, MEIRIONYDD, No. 598

L. M.

BRESLAU

Melody pub. Leipzig, 1625
Modern form

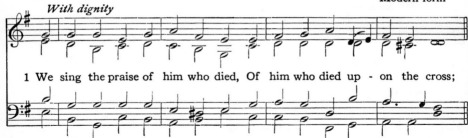

With dignity

1 We sing the praise of him who died, Of him who died up - on the cross;

The sin-ner's hope let men de - ride: For this we count the world but loss.

2 Inscribed upon the cross we see
   In shining letters, God is love:
He bears our sins upon the tree:
   He brings us mercy from above.

3 The cross, it takes our guilt away;
   It holds the fainting spirit up;
It cheers with hope the gloomy day,
   And sweetens every bitter cup.

4 It makes the coward spirit brave,
   And nerves the feeble arm for fight;
It takes its terror from the grave,
   And gilds the bed of death with light.

5 The balm of life, the cure of woe,
   The measure and the pledge of love,
The sinner's refuge here below,
   The angels' theme in heav'n above.

THOMAS KELLY, 1815

76. 86. 86. 86

ST. CHRISTOPHER
Not too slow

FREDERICK C. MAKER, 1881

1 Be - neath the cross of Je - sus I fain would take my stand,
2 Up - on the cross of Je - sus Mine eyes at times can see
3 I take, O cross, thy sha - dow For my a - bi - ding place;

The sha - dow of a migh - ty rock With - in a wea - ry land,
The ve - ry dy - ing form of one Who suf - fer'd there for me;
I ask no oth - er sun-shine than The sun - shine of his face;

A home with - in the wil - der - ness, A rest up - on the way,
And from my smit - ten heart with tears Two won - ders I con - fess:
Con - tent to let the world go by, To know no gain nor loss,

From the burn - ing of the noon-tide heat, And the bur - den of the day.
The won - ders of re - deem - ing love, And my own worth-less-ness.
My sin - ful self my on - ly shame, My glo - ry all the cross.

ELIZABETH CECILIA CLEPHANE; *pub.* 1872

76. 76. 88. 77

ST. THEOCTISTUS

FREDERICK A. GORE OUSELEY, 1882

In moderate time

1 Je - sus, Name all names a - bove; Je - sus, best and dear - est;
2 Je - sus, crowned with bit - ter thorn, By man - kind for - sa - ken,
3 Je - sus, o - pen me the gate That of old he en - ter'd

Je - sus, fount of per - fect love, Ho - liest, ten - derest, near - est; Thou the
Je - sus, who through scourge and scorn Held thy faith un - sha - ken, Je - sus,
Who, in that most lost es - tate, Whol - ly on thee ven - tured; Thou, whose

source of grace com - ple - test, Thou the pur - est, thou the sweet - est,
clad in pur - ple rai - ment, For man's fail - ure ma - king pay - ment;
wounds are ev - er plead - ing, And thy pas - sion in - ter - ce - ding,

Thou the well of power di - vine, Make me, keep me, seal me thine!
Let not all thy woe and pain, Let not Cal - vary be in vain!
From my weak - ness let me rise To a home in pa - ra - dise! A - men.

ST. THEOCTISTUS, c. 890;
Tr. JOHN MASON NEALE, 1862, alt.

NEWMAN   RICHARD RUNCIMAN TERRY, 1912

In unison, fervently

1 Praise to the Ho - liest in the height, And in the depth be praise;
2 O lov - ing wis - dom of our God! When all was sin and shame,
3 O wi - sest love! that flesh and blood, Which did in Ad - am fail,

In all his words most won - der - ful, Most sure in all his ways!
A sec - ond Ad - am to the fight And to the res - cue came.
Should strive a - fresh a - gainst the foe, Should strive, and should pre-vail;

4 And that a higher gift than grace
   Should flesh and blood refine:
   God's presence and his very self,
   And essence all-divine.

5 O generous love! that he who smote
   In Man for man the foe,
   The double agony in Man
   For man should undergo;

6 And in the garden secretly,
   And on the cross on high,
   Should teach his brethren, and inspire
   To suffer and to die.

A - men.

7 Praise to the Holiest in the height,
   And in the depth be praise;
   In all his words most wonderful,
   Most sure in all his ways! Amen.

JOHN HENRY NEWMAN, 1865

343 *Second Tune*   **General Hymns**
C. M.

GERONTIUS   JOHN B. DYKES, 1868

In moderate time

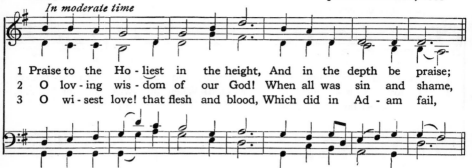

1 Praise to the Ho - liest in the height, And in the depth be praise;
2 O lov - ing wis - dom of our God! When all was sin and shame,
3 O wi - sest love! that flesh and blood, Which did in Ad - am fail,

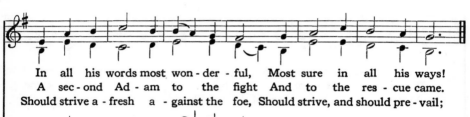

In all his words most won - der - ful, Most sure in all his ways!
A sec - ond Ad - am to the fight And to the res - cue came.
Should strive a - fresh a - gainst the foe, Should strive, and should pre - vail;

4 And that a higher gift than grace
   Should flesh and blood refine:
God's presence and his very self,
   And essence all-divine.

5 O generous love! that he who smote
   In Man for man the foe,
The double agony in Man
   For man should undergo;

6 And in the garden secretly,
   And on the cross on high,
Should teach his brethren, and inspire
   To suffer and to die.

7 Praise to the Holiest in the height,
   And in the depth be praise;
In all his words most wonderful,
   Most sure in all his ways! Amen.

A - men.

JOHN HENRY NEWMAN, 1865

L. M.

DEUS TUORUM MILITUM

Grenoble Church Melody

In unison, with stately dignity

1 O love, how deep, how broad, how high, How pass - ing
2 For us bap - tized, for us he bore His ho - ly
3 For us he prayed, for us he taught, For us his

thought and fan - ta - sy, That God, the Son of God, should
fast, and hun - ger'd sore; For us temp - ta - tions sharp he
dai - ly works he wrought, By words and signs and ac - tions,

take Our mor - tal form for mor - tals' sake.
knew; For us the temp - ter o - ver - threw.
thus Still seek - ing not him - self, but us.   A - men.

4 For us to wicked men betrayed,
   Scourged, mocked, in purple robe arrayed,
   He bore the shameful cross and death;
   For us gave up his dying breath.

5 For us he rose from death again,
   For us he went on high to reign;
   For us he sent his Spirit here
   To guide, to strengthen, and to cheer.

6 All glory to our Lord and God
   For love so deep, so high, so broad;
   The Trinity whom we adore
   For ever and for evermore.   Amen.

Latin, 15th cent.; Tr. BENJAMIN WEBB, 1854, *alt.*

ST. COLUMBA   Traditional Irish Melody

In flowing style

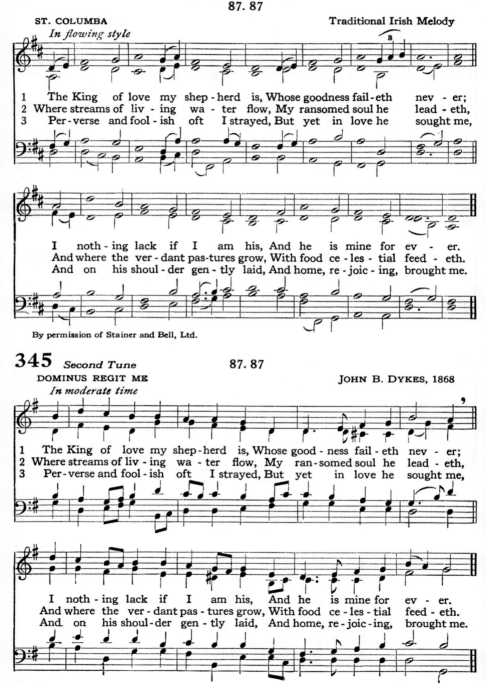

1 The King of love my shep-herd is, Whose goodness fail-eth nev - er;
2 Where streams of liv - ing wa - ter flow, My ransomed soul he lead - eth,
3 Per - verse and fool-ish oft I strayed, But yet in love he sought me,

I noth - ing lack if I am his, And he is mine for ev - er.
And where the ver-dant pas-tures grow, With food ce - les - tial feed - eth.
And on his shoul-der gen - tly laid, And home, re - joic - ing, brought me.

By permission of Stainer and Bell, Ltd.

345 *Second Tune*   87. 87

DOMINUS REGIT ME
JOHN B. DYKES, 1868
In moderate time

1 The King of love my shep-herd is, Whose good - ness fail - eth nev - er;
2 Where streams of liv - ing wa - ter flow, My ran-somed soul he lead - eth,
3 Per - verse and fool-ish oft I strayed, But yet in love he sought me,

I noth - ing lack if I am his, And he is mine for ev - er.
And where the ver-dant pas-tures grow, With food ce - les - tial feed - eth.
And on his shoul-der gen - tly laid, And home, re - joic-ing, brought me.

4 In death's dark vale I fear no ill
    With thee, dear Lord, beside me;
  Thy rod and staff my comfort still,
    Thy cross before to guide me.

1st Tune

A - men.

5 Thou spread'st a table in my sight;
    Thy unction grace bestoweth;
  And O what transport of delight
    From thy pure chalice floweth!

6 And so through all the length of days
    Thy goodness faileth never:
  Good Shepherd, may I sing thy praise
    Within thy house for ever.   Amen.

2nd Tune

A - men.

HENRY WILLIAMS BAKER, 1868; *based on Psalm 23*

346 *First Tune*   568. 558

FAIREST LORD JESUS   *Münster Gesangbuch, 1677*
With breadth

1 Fair - est Lord Je - sus, Rul - er of all na - ture,
2 Fair are the mea - dows, Fair - er still the wood - lands,
3 Fair is the sun - shine, Fair - er still the moon - light, And

O thou of God and man the Son; Thee will I cher - ish,
Robed in the bloom - ing garb of spring: Je - sus is fair - er,
all the twink - ling, star - ry host: Je - sus shines bright - er,

Thee will I hon - or, Thou, my soul's glo - ry, joy, and crown.
Je - sus is pur - er, Who makes the woe - ful heart to sing.
Je - sus shines pur - er, Than all the an - gels heav'n can boast.

St. 1, 3, Münster, 1677; St. 2, Leipzig, 1842; Tr. pub. Philadelphia, 1850

568. 558

ST. ELISABETH

Silesian Melody, pub. Leipzig, 1842;
har. by T. TERTIUS NOBLE, 1918

Simply

1 Fair - est Lord Je - sus, Rul - er of all na - ture,
2 Fair are the mea - dows, Fair - er still the wood - lands,
3 Fair is the sun - shine, Fair - er still the moon - light,

O thou of God and man the Son; Thee will I
Robed in the bloom - ing garb of spring: Je - sus is
And all the twink - ling, star - ry host: Je - sus shines

Org.

cher - ish, Thee will I hon - or, Thou, my soul's glo - ry, joy, and crown.
fair - er, Je - sus is pur - er, Who makes the woe-ful heart to sing.
bright-er, Je - sus shines pur - er, Than all the an - gels heav'n can boast.

A simpler harmony, No. 238

347 *First Tune*   87. 87. D.

ALLELUIA

SAMUEL SEBASTIAN WESLEY, 1868

With joyful dignity

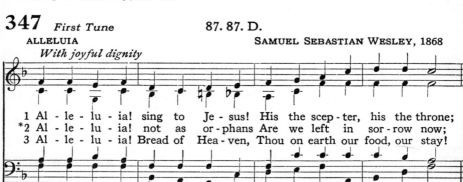

1 Al - le - lu - ia! sing to Je - sus! His the scep - ter, his the throne;
*2 Al - le - lu - ia! not as or - phans Are we left in sor - row now;
3 Al - le - lu - ia! Bread of Hea - ven, Thou on earth our food, our stay!

General Hymns

Al - le - lu - ia! his the tri - umph, His the vic - to - ry a - lone;
Al - le - lu - ia! he is near us, Faith be - lieves, nor ques - tions how:
Al - le - lu - ia! here the sin - ful Flee to thee from day to day:

Hark! the songs of peace - ful Si - on Thun - der like a migh - ty flood;
Though the cloud from sight re - ceived him, When the for - ty days were o'er,
In - ter - ces - sor, friend of sin - ners, Earth's Re - deem - er, plead for me,

Je - sus out of ev - 'ry na - tion Hath re - deemed us by his blood.
Shall our hearts for - get his prom - ise, "I am with you ev - er - more"?
Where the songs of all the sin - less Sweep a - cross the crys - tal sea.

4 Alleluia! King eternal,
　　Thee the Lord of lords we own:
Alleluia! born of Mary,
　　Earth thy footstool, heav'n thy throne:
Thou within the veil hast entered,
　　Robed in flesh, our great High Priest:
Thou on earth both Priest and Victim
　　In the eucharistic feast.

5 Alleluia! sing to Jesus!
　　His the scepter, his the throne;
Alleluia! his the triumph,
　　His the victory alone;
Hark! the songs of holy Sion
　　Thunder like a mighty flood;
Jesus out of every nation
　　Hath redeemed us by his blood.

A-men.

WILLIAM CHATTERTON DIX, 1866

87. 87. D.

HVFRYDOL

ROWLAND HUGH PRICHARD, c. 1830

With dignity

1 Al - le - lu - ia! sing to Je - sus! His the scep - ter, his the throne;
*2 Al - le - lu - ia! not as or - phans Are we left in sor - row now;
3 Al - le - lu - ia! Bread of Hea - ven, Thou on earth our food, our stay!

Al - le - lu - ia! his the tri - umph, His the vic - to - ry a - lone;
Al - le - lu - ia! he is near us, Faith be - lieves, nor ques-tions how:
Al - le - lu - ia! here the sin - ful Flee to thee from day to day:

Hark! the songs of peace-ful Si - on Thun - der like a migh-ty flood;
Though the cloud from sight re - ceived him, When the for - ty days were o'er,
In - ter - ces - sor, friend of sin - ners, Earth's Re - deem-er, plead for me,

Je - sus out of ev - 'ry na - tion Hath re - deemed us by his blood.
Shall our hearts for-get his prom - ise, "I am with you ev - er-more"?
Where the songs of all the sin - less Sweep a - cross the crys-tal sea.

General Hymns

4 Alleluia! King eternal,
   Thee the Lord of lords we own:
Alleluia! born of Mary,
   Earth thy footstool, heav'n thy throne:
Thou within the veil hast entered,
   Robed in flesh, our great High Priest:
Thou on earth both Priest and Victim
   In the eucharistic feast.

5 Alleluia! sing to Jesus!
   His the scepter, his the throne;
Alleluia! his the triumph,
   His the victory alone;
Hark! the songs of holy Sion
   Thunder like a mighty flood;
Jesus out of every nation
   Hath redeemed us by his blood. Amen.

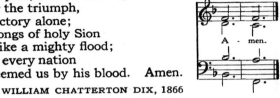

WILLIAM CHATTERTON DIX, 1866

348

65. 65

EUDOXIA

SABINE BARING-GOULD, 1868

Simply

1 Je - sus, gen - tlest Sa - viour, God of might and power,
2 Na - ture can - not hold thee, Heav'n is all too strait
3 Out be - yond the shin - ing Of the far - thest star,

Thou thy - self art dwell - ing With us at this hour.
For thine end - less glo - ry And thy roy - al state.
Thou art ev - er stretch - ing In - fi - nite - ly far. A-men.

4 Yet the hearts of children
   Hold what worlds can not,
And the God of wonders
   Loves the lowly spot.

5 Jesus, gentlest Saviour,
   Thou art with us now;
Fill us with thy goodness
   Till our hearts o'erflow.

6 Multiply our graces;
   Give us love and fear,
And, dear Lord, the chiefest,
   Grace to persevere!

7 O how can we thank thee
   For a gift like this,
Gift that truly maketh
   Heav'n's eternal bliss? Amen.

FREDERICK WILLIAM FABER, 1854, *alt.*

76. 76. D.

WATERMOUTH   ARTHUR HENRY MANN, 1889

In moderate time

1 O Sa - viour, pre - cious Sa - viour, Whom yet un - seen we love;
2 O bring - er of sal - va - tion, Who won-drous - ly hast wrought,
3 In thee all full - ness dwell - eth, All grace and power di - vine;

O Name of might and fa - vor All oth - er names a - bove;
Thy - self the rev - e - la - tion Of love be - yond our thought;
The glo - ry that ex - cel - leth, O Son of God, is thine;

Refrain

We wor - ship thee, we bless thee, To thee, O Christ, we sing;

We praise thee, and con - fess thee Our ho - ly Lord and King.   A-men.

4 O grant the consummation   Then shall we praise and bless thee
   Of this our song above,   Where perfect praises ring,
In endless adoration   And evermore confess thee
   And everlasting love;   Our Saviour and our King.   Amen.

FRANCES RIDLEY HAVERGAL, 1870

Alternative Tune, MEIRIONYDD, No. 598

350 *First Tune* — **General Hymns**

66. 66. 88. 88

JUBILATE
With vigor

HORATIO PARKER, 1894

1 Re - joice, the Lord is King! Your Lord and King a - dore!
2 The Lord the Sa - viour reigns, The God of truth and love:
3 His king - dom can - not fail; He rules o'er earth and heav'n;

Mor - tals, give thanks and sing, And tri - umph ev - er - more.
When he had purged our stains, He took his seat a - bove.
The keys of death and hell To Christ the Lord are giv'n.

Refrain

Lift up your heart! lift up your voice! Re - joice! a - gain I say, re - joice!

Lift up your heart! lift up your voice! Re - joice! a - gain I say, re - joice!

4 Rejoice in glorious hope!
  Our Lord the Judge shall come,
  And take his servants up
  To their eternal home.
  Refrain

CHARLES WESLEY, 1746, *alt.*

66. 66. 88

RESURRECTION

Jubilant, but not fast

Harmonia Sacra, 1753,
har. by W. D., 1941

1 Re - joice, the Lord is King! Your Lord and King a - dore!
2 The Lord the Sa - viour reigns, The God of truth and love:
3 His king - dom can - not fail; He rules o'er earth and heav'n;
4 Re - joice in glo - rious hope! Our Lord the Judge shall come,

Mor - tals, give thanks and sing, And tri - umph ev - er - more.
When he had purged our stains, He took his seat a - bove.
The keys of death and hell To Christ the Lord are giv'n.
And take his ser - vants up To their e - ter - nal home.

Refrain

Lift up your heart! lift up your voice! Re - joice! a - gain I say, re - joice!

CHARLES WESLEY, 1746, *alt.*

351

898. 898. 664. 448

SLEEPERS, WAKE

Melody, PHILIP NICOLAI, 1599,
arr. and har. by J. S. BACH, 1731

Broad and solemn; may be sung in unison

1 { Praise the Lord through ev - 'ry na - tion; His ho - ly arm hath
   { Praise your King, ye Chris - tian le - gions, Who now pre - pares in
2 { Je - sus, Lord, our Cap - tain glo - rious, O'er sin, and death, and
   { We con - fess, pro - claim, a - dore thee; We bow the knee, we

General Hymns

wrought sal - va - tion; Ex - alt him on his Fa-ther's throne.
heav'n - ly re - gions Un - fail - ing man - sions for his own:
hell vic - to - rious, Wis - dom and might to thee be - long:
fall be - fore thee; Thy love hence-forth shall be our song.

With voice and min-strel - sy Ex - tol his ma - jes - ty:
The cross mean - while we bear, The crown ere - long to wear:

Al - le - lu - ia! His praise shall sound all na - ture round,
Al - le - lu - ia! Thy reign ex - tend world with - out end;

Wher - e'er the race of man is found.
Let praise from all to thee as - cend. A - men.

RHIJNVIS FEITH, 1806; *Para.* JAMES MONTGOMERY, 1828

DIADEMATA   GEORGE J. ELVEY, 1868

With vigor

1 Crown him with ma - ny crowns, The Lamb up - on his throne;
2 Crown him the Son of God Be - fore the worlds be - gan,
3 Crown him the Lord of life, Who tri - umphed o'er the grave,

Hark! how the heav'n - ly an - them drowns All mu - sic but its own:
And ye, who tread where he hath trod, Crown him the Son of man;
And rose vic - to - rious in the strife For those he came to save;

A - wake, my soul, and sing Of him who died for thee,
Who ev - 'ry grief hath known That wrings the hu - man breast,
His glo - ries now we sing Who died, and rose on high,

And hail him as thy match-less King Through all e - ter - ni - ty.
And takes and bears them for his own, That all in him may rest.
Who died, e - ter - nal life to bring, And lives that death may die.

General Hymns

4 Crown him of lords the Lord,
Who over all doth reign,
Who once on earth, the incarnate Word,
For ransomed sinners slain,
Now lives in realms of light,
Where saints with angels sing
Their songs before him day and night,
Their God, Redeemer, King.

5 Crown him the Lord of heav'n,
Enthroned in worlds above;
Crown him the King, to whom is giv'n
The wondrous name of Love.
Crown him with many crowns,
As thrones before him fall,
Crown him, ye kings, with many crowns,
For he is King of all.

MATTHEW BRIDGES, 1851

353   C. M.

CAITHNESS   Melody in *Scottish Psalter*, 1635

Moderately slow

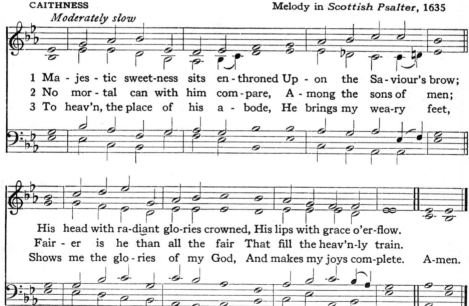

1 Ma - jes - tic sweet-ness sits en - throned Up - on the Sa - viour's brow;
2 No mor - tal can with him com - pare, A - mong the sons of men;
3 To heav'n, the place of his a - bode, He brings my wea-ry feet,

His head with ra-diant glo-ries crowned, His lips with grace o'er-flow.
Fair - er is he than all the fair That fill the heav'n-ly train.
Shows me the glo - ries of my God, And makes my joys com-plete. A-men.

4 Since from his bounty I receive
Such proofs of love divine,
Had I a thousand hearts to give,
Lord, they should all be thine. Amen.

SAMUEL STENNETT, 1787, *alt.*

Alternative Tune, HORSLEY, No. 65

354 *First Tune*   𝔊eneral 𝔥ymns
C. M. D.

TREGARON   PHILIP JAMES, 1941
Triumphantly

1 And have the bright im - men - si - ties Re-ceived our ris - en Lord, Where
2 The heav'n that hides him from our sight Knows nei-ther near nor far: An

light-years frame the Plei - a - des And point O - ri - on's sword? Do
al - tar can - dle sheds its light As sure - ly as a star; And

fla - ming suns his foot-steps trace Through cor - ri - dors sub - lime, The
where his lov - ing peo - ple meet To share the gift di - vine, There

Lord of in - ter - stel - lar space And Con - quer - or of time?
stands he with un - hur - rying feet; There heav'n - ly splen-dors shine.

HOWARD CHANDLER ROBBINS, 1932

354 *Second Tune* 𝕲𝖊𝖓𝖊𝖗𝖆𝖑 𝕳𝖞𝖒𝖓𝖘
C. M. D.

HALIFAX

Melody, GEORGE FREDERICK HANDEL, 1748,
arr. and har. by W. D., 1941

With breadth and majesty

1 And have the bright im - men - si - ties Re - ceived our ris - en Lord,
2 The heav'n that hides him from our sight Knows nei - ther near nor far:

Where light-years frame the Plei - a - des And point O - ri - on's sword?
An al - tar can - dle sheds its light As sure - ly as a star;

Do fla - ming suns his foot-steps trace Through cor-ri - dors sub - lime,
And where his lov - ing peo -ple meet To share the gift di - vine,

In unison *rit.*

The Lord of in - ter-stel - lar space And Con - quer-or of time?
There stands he with un-hur-rying feet; There heav'n-ly splen - dors shine.

rit.

HOWARD CHANDLER ROBBINS, 1932

CORONATION   OLIVER HOLDEN, 1793

Majestically, in strict time throughout

1 All hail the power of Je - sus' Name! Let an - gels pros-trate fall;
2 Crown him, ye mar - tyrs of our God, Who from his al - tar call:
3 Hail him, the Heir of Da - vid's line, Whom Da - vid Lord did call,

Bring forth the roy - al di - a - dem, And crown him Lord of all!
Praise him whose way of pain ye trod, And crown him Lord of all!
The God in - car-nate, Man di - vine, And crown him Lord of all!

Bring forth the roy - al di - a - dem, And crown him Lord of all!
Praise him whose way of pain ye trod, And crown him Lord of all!
The God in - car-nate, Man di - vine, And crown him Lord of all!

*4 Ye seed of Israel's chosen race,
Ye ransomed of the fall,
Hail him who saves you by his grace,
And crown him Lord of all!

*5 Sinners, whose love can ne'er forget
The wormwood and the gall,
Go, spread your trophies at his feet,
And crown him Lord of all!

6 Let every kindred, every tribe,
On this terrestrial ball,
To him all majesty ascribe,
And crown him Lord of all!

EDWARD PERRONET, 1779, *alt.*

355 *Second Tune*   **General Hymns**
868, with Refrain

MILES' LANE   WILLIAM SHRUBSOLE, 1779

1 All hail the power of Je - sus' Name! Let an - gels
2 Crown him, ye mar - tyrs of our God, Who from his
3 Hail him, the Heir of Da - vid's line, Whom Da - vid

pros - trate fall; Bring forth the roy - al di - a - dem,
al - tar call: Praise him whose way of pain ye trod,
Lord did call, The God in - car - nate, Man di - vine,

Refrain

And crown him, crown him, crown him, crown him Lord of all!

*4 Ye seed of Israel's chosen race,
Ye ransomed of the fall,
Hail him who saves you by his grace,
And crown him Lord of all!

*5 Sinners, whose love can ne'er forget
The wormwood and the gall,
Go, spread your trophies at his feet,
And crown him Lord of all!

6 Let every kindred, every tribe,
On this terrestrial ball,
To him all majesty ascribe,
And crown him Lord of all!

EDWARD PERRONET, 1779, *alt.*

356 *First Tune*   𝕲eneral 𝕳ymns

65. 65. D.

KING'S WESTON

R. VAUGHAN WILLIAMS, 1925

In unison, with vigor

1 At the Name of Je - sus Ev - 'ry knee shall bow,
2 Hum-bled for a sea - son, To re - ceive a Name
3 Bore it up tri - umph - ant, With its hu - man light,

Ev - 'ry tongue con - fess him King of glo - ry now;
From the lips of sin - ners, Un - to whom he came,
Through all ranks of crea - tures, To the cen - tral height,

'Tis the Fa - ther's plea - sure We should call him Lord,
Faith-ful - ly he bore it Spot - less to the last,
To the throne of God - head, To the Fa - ther's breast;

Who from the be - gin - ning Was the migh - ty Word.
Brought it back vic - to - rious, When from death he passed;
Filled it with the glo - ry Of that per - fect rest.

General Hymns

4 In your hearts enthrone him;
   There let him subdue
All that is not holy,
   All that is not true:
Crown him as your Captain
   In temptation's hour;
Let his will enfold you
   In its light and power.

5 Brothers, this Lord Jesus
   Shall return again,
With his Father's glory
   O'er the earth to reign;
For all wreaths of empire
   Meet upon his brow,
And our hearts confess him
   King of glory now.

CAROLINE MARIA NOEL, 1870, *alt.*

356 *Second Tune* 65. 65. D.

EVELYNS

WILLIAM H. MONK, 1875

In moderate time

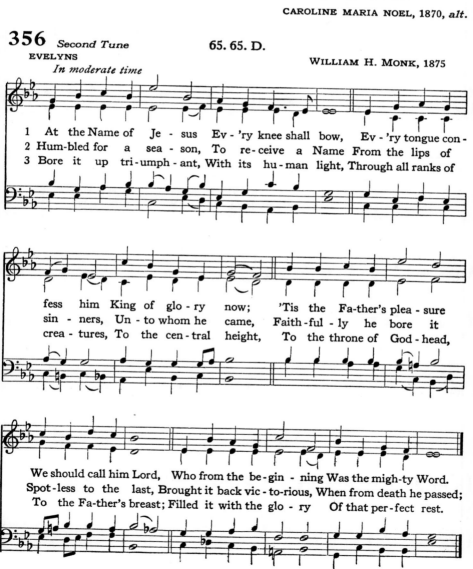

1 At the Name of Je - sus Ev - 'ry knee shall bow, Ev - 'ry tongue con-
2 Hum-bled for a sea - son, To re - ceive a Name From the lips of
3 Bore it up tri-umph - ant, With its hu - man light, Through all ranks of

fess him King of glo - ry now; 'Tis the Fa-ther's plea - sure
sin - ners, Un - to whom he came, Faith - ful - ly he bore it
crea - tures, To the cen - tral height, To the throne of God - head,

We should call him Lord, Who from the be - gin - ning Was the migh-ty Word.
Spot - less to the last, Brought it back vic - to-rious, When from death he passed;
To the Fa-ther's breast; Filled it with the glo - ry Of that per - fect rest.

87. 87. D.

IN BABILONE

Traditional Dutch Melody
har. by T. TERTIUS NOBLE, 1918

In unison, with breadth

1 Hail, thou once de - spi - sed Je - sus! Hail, thou
2 Pas - chal Lamb, by God ap - point - ed, All our
3 Je - sus, hail! en - throned in glo - ry, There for
4 Wor - ship, hon - or, power, and bless - ing Thou art

Gal - i - le - an King! Thou didst suf - fer
sins on thee were laid: By al - migh - ty
ev - er to a - bide; All the heav'n - ly
wor - thy to re - ceive: High - est prais - es,

to re - lease us; Thou didst free sal - va - tion bring.
love a - noint - ed, Thou hast full a - tone - ment made.
hosts a - dore thee, Seat - ed at thy Fa - ther's side.
with - out ceas - ing, Meet it is for us to give.

General Hymns

Hail, thou u - ni - ver - sal Sa - viour, Bear - er
All thy peo - ple are for - giv - en Through the
There for sin - ners thou art plead - ing: There thou
Help, ye bright an - gel - ic spi - rits, Bring your

of our sin and shame! By thy mer - it
vir - tue of thy blood: O - pen'd is the
dost our place pre - pare; Ev - er for us
sweet - est, no - blest lays; Help to sing our

we find fa - vor: Life is giv - en through thy Name.
gate of hea - ven, Peace is made 'twixt man and God.
in - ter - ce - ding, Till in glo - ry we ap - pear.
Sa - viour's mer - its, Help to chant Em - man - uel's praise! A - men.

JOHN BAKEWELL, 1757; MARTIN MADAN, 1760; *alt.*

A simpler harmonization will be found at No. 103

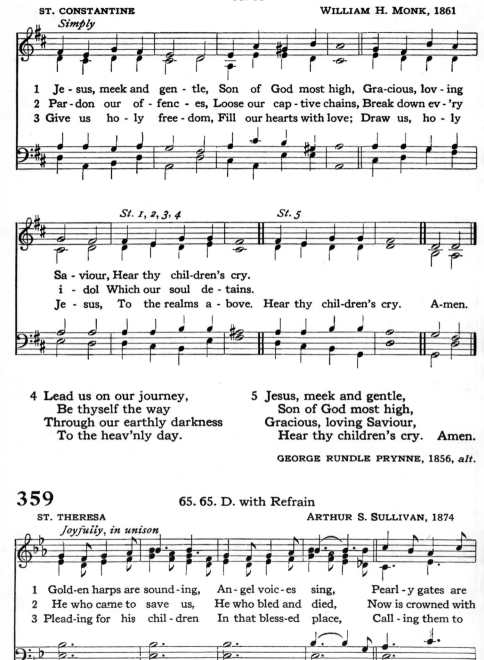

358

65. 65

ST. CONSTANTINE

WILLIAM H. MONK, 1861

Simply

1 Je - sus, meek and gen - tle, Son of God most high, Gra - cious, lov - ing
2 Par - don our of - fenc - es, Loose our cap - tive chains, Break down ev - 'ry
3 Give us ho - ly free - dom, Fill our hearts with love; Draw us, ho - ly

St. 1, 2, 3, 4   *St. 5*

Sa - viour, Hear thy chil-dren's cry.
i - dol Which our soul de - tains.
Je - sus, To the realms a - bove. Hear thy chil-dren's cry. A-men.

4 Lead us on our journey,
　Be thyself the way
Through our earthly darkness
　To the heav'nly day.

5 Jesus, meek and gentle,
　Son of God most high,
Gracious, loving Saviour,
　Hear thy children's cry. Amen.

GEORGE RUNDLE PRYNNE, 1856, *alt.*

359   65. 65. D. with Refrain

ST. THERESA

ARTHUR S. SULLIVAN, 1874

Joyfully, in unison

1 Gold-en harps are sound-ing, An - gel voic - es sing, Pearl - y gates are
2 He who came to save us, He who bled and died, Now is crowned with
3 Plead-ing for his chil - dren In that bless-ed place, Call - ing them to

General Hymns

o - pen'd, O - pen'd for the King; Je - sus, King of glo - ry,
glo - ry At his Fa - ther's side. From the grave a - ris - en,
glo - ry, Send - ing them his grace; His bright home pre - par - ing,

Je - sus, King of love, Is gone up in tri - umph To his throne a - bove.
Nev - er - more to die; Je - sus, King of glo - ry, Is gone up on high.
Faith - ful ones, for you; Je - sus ev - er liv - eth, Ev - er lov - eth too.

Refrain

All his suf - f'ring end - ed, Joy - ful - ly we sing,

Je - sus hath as - cend - ed! Glo - ry to our King! A - men.

FRANCES RIDLEY HAVERGAL, 1871, alt.

BISHOPTHORPE   JEREMIAH CLARK, 1700
With motion

1 Im - mor - tal Love, for ev - er full, For ev - er
2 Our out - ward lips con - fess the Name All oth - er
3 We may not climb the heav'n - ly steeps To bring the

flow - ing free, For ev - er shared, for ev - er
names a - bove; Love on - ly know - eth whence it
Lord Christ down; In vain we search the low - est

whole, A nev - er ebb - ing sea!
came, And com - pre - hend - eth love.
deeps, For him no depths can drown: A - men.

4 But warm, sweet, tender, even yet
   A present help is he;
And faith has still its Olivet,
   And love its Galilee.

5 The healing of his seamless dress
   Is by our beds of pain;
We touch him in life's throng and
   press,
And we are whole again.

6 Through him the first fond prayers are
   said
Our lips of childhood frame;
The last low whispers of our dead
Are burdened with his Name.

7 O Lord, and Master of us all,
   Whate'er our name or sign,
We own thy sway, we hear thy call,
We test our lives by thine.   Amen.

JOHN GREENLEAF WHITTIER, 1856

360 *Second Tune* **General Hymns**

ALBANO C. M. VINCENT NOVELLO, 1800

In moderate time

1 Im - mor - tal Love, for ev - er full, For ev - er flow - ing free, For
2 Our out - ward lips con - fess the Name All oth - er names a - bove; Love
3 We may not climb the heav'n - ly steeps To bring the Lord Christ down; In

ev - er shared, for ev - er whole, A nev - er ebb - ing sea!
on - ly know - eth whence it came, And com - pre - hend - eth love.
vain we search the low - est deeps, For him no depths can drown: A-men.

361 C. M.

ST. JAMES RAPHAEL COURTEVILLE, 1697

With dignity

1 Thou art the Way, to thee a - lone From sin and death we flee; And
2 Thou art the Truth, thy word a - lone True wis - dom can im - part; Thou
3 Thou art the Life, the rend - ing tomb Pro - claims thy con - qu'ring arm; And

he who would the Fa - ther seek, Must seek him, Lord, by thee.
on - ly canst in - form the mind And pu - ri - fy the heart.
those who put their trust in thee Nor death nor hell shall harm. A-men.

4 Thou art the Way, the Truth, the Life:
Grant us that way to know,
That truth to keep, that life to win,
Whose joys eternal flow. Amen.

GEORGE WASHINGTON DOANE, 1824, *alt.*

11 11. 12 11

MONKS GATE

Traditional Sussex Melody,
arr. by R. VAUGHAN WILLIAMS, 1904

Brightly

1 Mas - ter of ea - ger youth, Con - trol - ling, guid - ing,
2 Thou art our migh - ty Lord, Our strength in sad - ness,
3 Good Shep - herd of thy sheep, Thine own de - fend - ing,

Lift - ing our hearts to truth, New power pro - vid - ing;
The Fa - ther's con - quering Word, True source of glad - ness;
In love thy chil - dren keep To life un - end - ing.

Shep - herd of in - no - cence, Thou art our Con - fi -
Thy Name we glo - ri - fy, O Je - sus, throned on
Thou art thy - self the Way: Lead us then day by

dence; To thee, our sure De - fence, We bring our prais - es.
high, Who gav'st thy - self to die For man's sal - va - tion.
day In thine own steps, we pray, O Lord most ho - ly. A-men.

General Hymns

4 Glorious their life who sing,
   With glad thanksgiving,
  True hymns to Christ the King
    In all their living:

Ye who confess his Name,
Come then with hearts aflame;
Let word and life acclaim
  Our Lord and Saviour.   Amen.

Alternative Tune, ST. DUNSTAN'S, No. 563

ST. CLEMENT of Alexandria, c. 200;
Para., F. BLAND TUCKER, 1939

363

10 11. 11 12

SLANE

Traditional Irish Melody

In unison, with movement

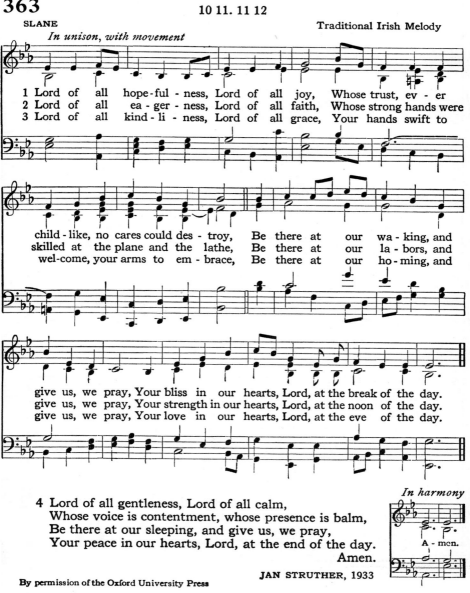

1 Lord of all hope-ful - ness, Lord of all joy, Whose trust, ev - er
2 Lord of all ea - ger - ness, Lord of all faith, Whose strong hands were
3 Lord of all kind - li - ness, Lord of all grace, Your hands swift to

child - like, no cares could des - troy, Be there at our wa - king, and
skilled at the plane and the lathe, Be there at our la - bors, and
wel-come, your arms to em - brace, Be there at our ho - ming, and

give us, we pray, Your bliss in our hearts, Lord, at the break of the day.
give us, we pray, Your strength in our hearts, Lord, at the noon of the day.
give us, we pray, Your love in our hearts, Lord, at the eve of the day.

4 Lord of all gentleness, Lord of all calm,
  Whose voice is contentment, whose presence is balm,
  Be there at our sleeping, and give us, we pray,
  Your peace in our hearts, Lord, at the end of the day.
                                       Amen.

In harmony

A - men.

JAN STRUTHER, 1933

11 10. 11 10

CHARTERHOUSE   DAVID EVANS, 1927

Unison, in moderate time

1 O Son of man, our he - ro strong and ten - der, . . .
2 O feet so strong to climb the path of du - ty, . . .
3 Lov - er of chil - dren, boy-hood's in - spi - ra - tion, . .
4 Not in our fail - ures on - ly and our sad - ness, . .

Whose ser - vants are the brave in all the earth, ...
O lips di - vine that taught the words of truth, ...
Of all man - kind the ser - vant and the king, ...
We seek thy pres - ence, com - fort - er and friend; . . . . . .

Our liv - ing sac - ri - fice to thee we ren - der, ...
Kind eyes that marked the li - lies in their beau - ty, ...
O Lord of joy and hope and con - so - la - tion, . . .
O rich man's guest, be with us in our glad - ness! . . .

General Hymns

Who shar - est all our sor - row, all our mirth.
And heart that kin - dled at the zeal of youth,
To thee our fears and joys and hopes we bring.
O poor man's mate, our low - liest tasks at - tend! A - men.

FRANK FLETCHER, c. 1924

365

L. M.

PALISADES

LEO SOWERBY, 1941

With breadth

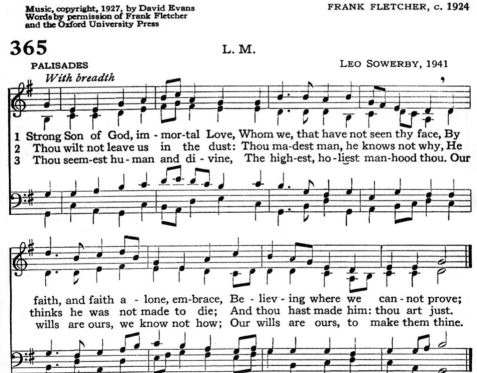

1 Strong Son of God, im - mor-tal Love, Whom we, that have not seen thy face, By
2 Thou wilt not leave us in the dust: Thou ma-dest man, he knows not why, He
3 Thou seem-est hu - man and di - vine, The high-est, ho - liest man-hood thou. Our

faith, and faith a - lone, em-brace, Be - liev - ing where we can - not prove;
thinks he was not made to die; And thou hast made him: thou art just.
wills are ours, we know not how; Our wills are ours, to make them thine.

4 Our little systems have their day;
They have their day and cease to be;
They are but broken lights of thee,
And thou, O Lord, art more than they.

ALFRED TENNYSON, 1850

General Hymns

10 10 10, with Alleluia

ENGELBERG

CHARLES VILLIERS STANFORD, 1904

Triumphantly, in unison

1 All praise to thee, for thou, O King di - vine, Didst yield the
2 Thou cam'st to us in low - li - ness of thought; By thee the
3 Let this mind be in us which was in thee, Who wast a
4 Where-fore, by God's e - ter - nal pur - pose, thou Art high ex -
5 Let ev - 'ry tongue con - fess with one ac - cord In heav'n and

glo - ry that of right was thine, That in our dark-en'd hearts thy
out - cast and the poor were sought, And by thy death was God's sal -
ser - vant that we might be free, Hum-bling thy - self to death on
alt - ed o'er all crea-tures now, And giv'n the Name to which all
earth that Je - sus Christ is Lord; And God the Fa - ther be by

grace might shine.
va - tion wrought. Al - le - lu - ia! Al - le - lu - ia!
Cal - va - ry.
knees shall bow.
all a - dored.

St. 1, 2, 3, 4 St. 5 *In harmony*

A - men.

Copyright, Stainer and Bell, Ltd.
Alternative Tune, SINE NOMINE, No. 126

F. BLAND TUCKER, 1938

LAUDES DOMINI   JOSEPH BARNBY, 1868

Briskly

1 When morn-ing gilds the skies, My heart, a-wa-king, cries, May
2 When mirth for mu-sic longs, This is my song of songs: May
3 No love-lier an-ti-phon In all high heav'n is known Than,

Je-sus Christ be praised! When eve-ning sha-dows fall, This
Je-sus Christ be praised! God's ho-ly house of prayer Hath
Je-sus Christ be praised! There to the e-ter-nal Word The e-

rings my cur-few call, May Je - sus Christ be praised!
none that can com - pare With: Je - sus Christ be praised!
ter - nal psalm is heard: May Je - sus Christ be praised!

4 Ye nations of mankind,
In this your concord find:
  May Jesus Christ be praised!
Let all the earth around
Ring joyous with the sound:
  May Jesus Christ be praised!

5 Sing, suns and stars of space,
Sing, ye that see his face,
  Sing, Jesus Christ be praised!
God's whole creation o'er,
For aye and evermore
  Shall Jesus Christ be praised!

German, c. 1800; Tr. ROBERT BRIDGES, 1899

86. 84

ST. CUTHBERT   JOHN B. DYKES, 1861

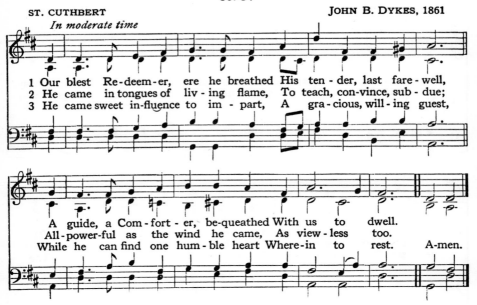

1 Our blest Re-deem-er, ere he breathed His ten - der, last fare - well,
2 He came in tongues of liv - ing flame, To teach, con-vince, sub - due;
3 He came sweet in-fluence to im - part, A gra - cious, will-ing guest,

A guide, a Com - fort - er, be-queathed With us to dwell.
All-power-ful as the wind he came, As view-less too.
While he can find one hum-ble heart Where-in to rest. A-men.

4 And his that gentle voice we hear,
    Soft as the breath of even,
That checks each fault, that calms each fear,
    And speaks of heav'n.

5 And every virtue we possess,
    And every victory won,
And every thought of holiness
    Are his alone.

6 Spirit of purity and grace,
    Our weakness, pitying, see;
O make our hearts thy dwelling-place,
    And worthier thee. Amen.

HARRIET AUBER, 1829, *alt.*

369   C. M.

ST. AGNES   JOHN B. DYKES, 1866

1 Come, Ho - ly Spi - rit, heav'n-ly Dove, With all thy quick-'ning powers;
2 See how we tri - fle here be - low, Fond of these earth - ly toys;
3 In vain we tune our for - mal songs, In vain we strive to rise:

General Hymns

Kin - dle a flame of sa - cred love In these cold hearts of ours.
Our souls, how hea - vi - ly they go, To reach e - ter - nal joys.
Ho - san - nas lan-guish on our tongues, And our de - vo - tion dies. A - men.

4 Come, Holy Spirit, heav'nly Dove,
   With all thy quick'ning powers;
  Come, shed abroad a Saviour's love,
   And that shall kindle ours. Amen.

ISAAC WATTS, 1707, alt.

370

C. M.

GRAEFENBERG
Moderately slow

JOHANN CRUEGER, 1653

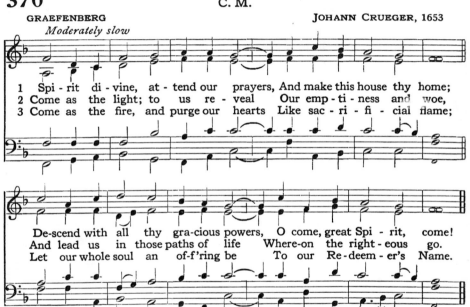

1 Spi - rit di - vine, at - tend our prayers, And make this house thy home;
2 Come as the light; to us re - veal Our emp - ti - ness and woe,
3 Come as the fire, and purge our hearts Like sac - ri - fi - cial flame;

De-scend with all thy gra-cious powers, O come, great Spi - rit, come!
And lead us in those paths of life Where-on the right-eous go.
Let our whole soul an of-f'ring be To our Re-deem - er's Name.

4 Come as the dove, and spread thy wings,
   The wings of peaceful love;
  And let thy Church on earth become
   Blest as the Church above.

5 Spirit divine, attend our prayers;
   Make a lost world thy home;
  Descend with all thy gracious powers;
   O come, great Spirit, come! Amen.

A-men.

ANDREW REED, 1829

371

General Hymns
88. 88. 888

ATTWOOD
Serenely

THOMAS ATTWOOD, 1831

1 Cre - a - tor Spi - rit, by whose aid The world's foun-da - tions
2 O Source of un - cre - a - ted light, The Fa - ther's prom-ised
3 Plen - teous of grace, come from on high, Rich in thy sev'n - fold

first were laid, Come, vis - it ev - 'ry hum - ble mind;
Pa - ra - clete, Thrice ho - ly Fount, thrice ho - ly Fire,
en - er - gy; Make us e - ter - nal truth re - ceive,

Come, pour thy joys on hu - man kind; From sin and
Our hearts with heav'n - ly love in - spire; Come, and thy
And prac - tise all that we be - lieve; Give us thy -

sor - row set us free, And make thy tem - ples wor - thy
sa - cred unc - tion bring To sanc - ti - fy us while we
self, that we may see The Fa - ther and the Son by

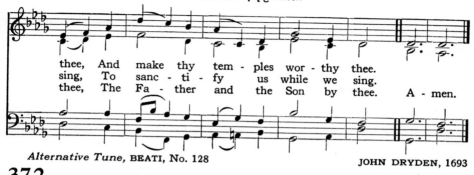

thee, And make thy tem - ples wor - thy thee.
sing, To sanc - ti - fy us while we sing.
thee, The Fa - ther and the Son by thee. A - men.

Alternative Tune, BEATI, No. 128

JOHN DRYDEN, 1693

372   S. M.

VENICE

WILLIAM AMPS, 1858

In flowing style

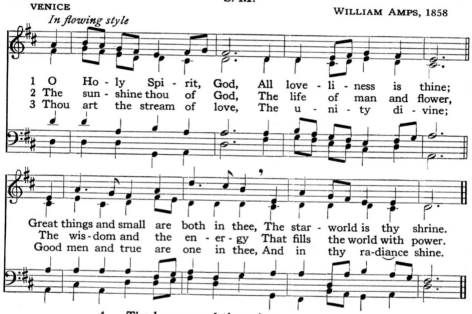

1 O Ho - ly Spi - rit, God, All love - li - ness is thine;
2 The sun - shine thou of God, The life of man and flower,
3 Thou art the stream of love, The u - ni - ty di - vine;

Great things and small are both in thee, The star - world is thy shrine.
The wis - dom and the en - er - gy That fills the world with power.
Good men and true are one in thee, And in thy ra - diance shine.

4   The heroes and the saints
      Thy messengers became:
And all the lamps that guide the world
      Were kindled at thy flame.

5   The calls that come to us
      Upon thy winds are brought;
The light that gleams beyond our dreams
      Is something thou hast thought.

6   Give fellowship, we pray,
      In love and joy and peace,
That we in counsel, knowledge, might,
      And wisdom, may increase. Amen.

A - men.

PERCY DEARMER, 1933

CULBACH   77. 77   From JOHANN SCHEFFLER'S
Heilige Seelenlust, 1657

In moderate time

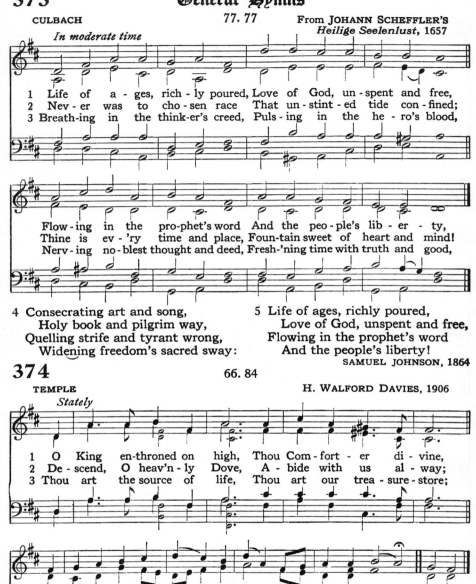

1 Life of a - ges, rich - ly poured, Love of God, un - spent and free,
2 Nev - er was to cho - sen race That un - stint - ed tide con - fined;
3 Breath-ing in the think-er's creed, Puls - ing in the he - ro's blood,

Flow - ing in the pro-phet's word And the peo - ple's lib - er - ty,
Thine is ev - 'ry time and place, Foun-tain sweet of heart and mind!
Nerv-ing no - blest thought and deed, Fresh-'ning time with truth and good,

4 Consecrating art and song,
    Holy book and pilgrim way,
Quelling strife and tyrant wrong,
    Widening freedom's sacred sway:

5 Life of ages, richly poured,
    Love of God, unspent and free,
Flowing in the prophet's word
    And the people's liberty!

SAMUEL JOHNSON, 1864

374   66. 84

TEMPLE   H. WALFORD DAVIES, 1906

Stately

1 O King en-throned on high, Thou Com - fort - er di - vine,
2 De - scend, O heav'n - ly Dove, A - bide with us al - way;
3 Thou art the source of life, Thou art our trea - sure-store;

Blest Spi - rit of all truth, be nigh And make us thine.
And in the full - ness of thy love Cleanse us, we pray.
Give us thy peace, and end our strife For ev - er - more. A-men.

Greek, c. 8th cent.; Tr. JOHN BROWNLIE

SWABIA
In moderate time

JOHANN MARTIN SPIESS, 1745,
arr. by W. H. HAVERGAL, 1847

1 Breathe on me, Breath of God, Fill me with life a-new,
2 Breathe on me, Breath of God, Un-til my heart is pure,

That I may love what thou dost love, And do what thou wouldst do.
Un-til with thee I will one will, To do or to en-dure. A-men.

3 Breathe on me, Breath of God,
  Till I am wholly thine,
  Till all this earthly part of me
  Glows with thy fire divine.

4 Breathe on me, Breath of God,
  So shall I never die;
  But live with thee the perfect life
  Of thine eternity. Amen.

EDWIN HATCH, 1878

375 *Second Tune* S. M.

NOVA VITA
In moderate time

LISTER R. PEACE, 1914

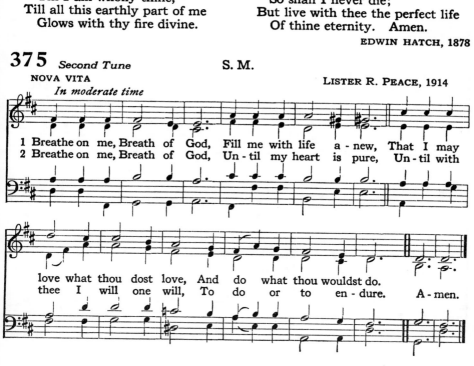

1 Breathe on me, Breath of God, Fill me with life a-new, That I may
2 Breathe on me, Breath of God, Un-til my heart is pure, Un-til with

love what thou dost love, And do what thou wouldst do.
thee I will one will, To do or to en-dure. A-men.

DOWN AMPNEY
Moderately slow

R. VAUGHAN WILLIAMS, 1906

1 Come down, O Love di - vine, Seek thou this soul of mine, And vis - it it with thine own ar - dor glow - ing; O Com - fort - er, draw near, With - in my heart ap - pear, And kin - dle it, thy ho - ly flame be - stow - ing.

2 O let it free - ly burn, Till earth - ly pas - sions turn To dust and ash - es in its heat con - sum - ing; And let thy glo - rious light Shine ev - er on my sight, And clothe me round, the while my path il - lum - ing.

3 And so the yearn - ing strong, With which the soul will long, Shall far out - pass the power of hu - man tell - ing; For none can guess its grace, Till he be - come the place Where - in the Ho - ly Spi - rit makes his dwell - ing. A-men.

BIANCO DA SIENA, d. 1434; Tr. R. F. LITTLEDALE, 1867

77. 77

LEW TRENCHARD

Traditional English Melody
harmonized by W. D., 1918

Moderately slow

1 Ho - ly Spi - rit, Truth di - vine, Dawn up - on this soul of mine;
2 Ho - ly Spi - rit, Love di - vine, Glow with - in this heart of mine;
3 Ho - ly Spi - rit, Power di - vine, Fill and nerve this will of mine;

Breath of God, and in - ward Light, Wake my spi - rit, clear my sight.
Kin - dle ev - 'ry high de - sire; Per - ish self in thy pure fire!
By thee may I strong - ly live, Brave - ly bear, and no - bly strive.

4 Holy Spirit, Right divine,
   King within my conscience reign;
   Be my law, and I shall be
   Firmly bound, for ever free.

5 Holy Spirit, Peace divine,
   Still this restless heart of mine;
   Speak to calm this tossing sea,
   Stayed in thy tranquillity.

6 Holy Spirit, Joy divine,
   Gladden thou this heart of mine;
   In the desert ways I sing,

"Spring, O Well, for ev - er spring!" A - men.

SAMUEL LONGFELLOW, 1864

GOOD SHEPHERD, ROSEMONT   **L. M.**   ROBERT B. MILLER, 1940

Calmly

1 Come, gra - cious Spi - rit, heav'n - ly Dove, With light and
2 The light of truth to us dis - play, And make us
3 Lead us to Christ, the liv - ing Way, Nor let us

com - fort from a - bove; Be thou our guard - ian, thou our
know and choose thy way; Plant ho - ly fear in ev - 'ry
from his pre - cepts stray; Lead us to ho - li - ness, the

guide; O'er ev - 'ry thought and step pre - side.
heart, That we from thee may ne'er de - part.
road That we must take to dwell with God. A-men.

4 Lead us to heav'n, that we may share
Fulness of joy for ever there;
Lead us to God, our final rest,
To be with him for ever blest. Amen.

SIMON BROWNE, 1720, *alt.*

378 *Second Tune*   **L. M.**

MENDON   Traditional German Melody
arr. by SAMUEL DYER, 1828

With breadth

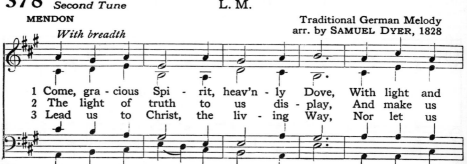

1 Come, gra - cious Spi - rit, heav'n - ly Dove, With light and
2 The light of truth to us dis - play, And make us
3 Lead us to Christ, the liv - ing Way, Nor let us

General Hymns

com - fort from a - bove; Be thou our guard - ian, thou our
know and choose thy way; Plant ho - ly fear in ev - 'ry
from his pre - cepts stray; Lead us to ho - li - ness, the

guide; O'er ev - 'ry thought and step pre - side.
heart, That we from thee may ne'er de - part.
road That we must take to dwell with God.   A - men.

379   77. 75

CAPETOWN   FRIEDRICH FILITZ, 1847

In moderate time

1 Gra - cious Spi - rit, Ho - ly Ghost, Taught by thee we cov - et most,
2 Love is kind, and suf - fers long, Love is meek, and thinks no wrong,
3 Pro - phe - cy will fade a - way, Melt - ing in the light of day;

Of thy gifts at Pen - te - cost, Ho - ly, heav'n-ly love.
Love than death it - self more strong; There-fore, give us love.
Love will ev - er with us stay; There-fore, give us love.   A - men.

4 Faith and hope and love we see,
Joining hand in hand, agree,
But the greatest of the three,
And the best, is love.   Amen.

CHRISTOPHER WORDSWORTH, 1862, *alt.*

380

CHELSEA SQUARE
C. M.
HOWARD C. ROBBINS, 1941,
har. by RAY F. BROWN, 1941

With dignity

1 Put forth, O God, thy Spi - rit's might And bid thy Church in - crease,
2 Let works of dark - ness dis - ap - pear Be - fore thy con-quer-ing light;
3 Let what a - pos - tles learned of thee Be ours from age to age;
4 O judge di - vine of hu - man strife! O van - quish-er of pain!

In breadth and length, in depth and height, Her u - ni - ty and peace.
Let ha - tred and tor-ment-ing fear Pass with the pass-ing night.
Their stead-fast faith our u - ni - ty, Their peace our her - i - tage.
To know thee is e - ter - nal life, To serve thee is to reign. A-men.

By permission of the author

HOWARD CHANDLER ROBBINS, 1937

381 WAREHAM
L. M.
WILLIAM KNAPP, 1738

In moderate time

1 Tri - umph - ant Si - on, lift thy head From dust and
2 Put all thy beau - teous gar - ments on, And let thine
3 No more shall foes un - clean in - vade, And fill thy

dark - ness and the dead; Though hum - bled long, a -
ex - cel - lence be known: Decked in the robes of
hal - lowed walls with dread; No more shall hell's in -

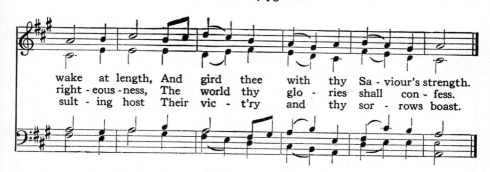

wake at length, And gird thee with thy Saviour's strength.
right-eous-ness, The world thy glo - ries shall con - fess.
sult - ing host Their vic - t'ry and thy sor - rows boast.

4 God from on high has heard thy prayer,
His hand thy ruins shall repair:
Nor will thy watchful Monarch cease
To guard thee in eternal peace.

PHILIP DODDRIDGE, 1755, *alt.*

382　　　　　　C. M.

TALLIS' ORDINAL　　　　　　　　　THOMAS TALLIS, c. 1567
Moderately slow

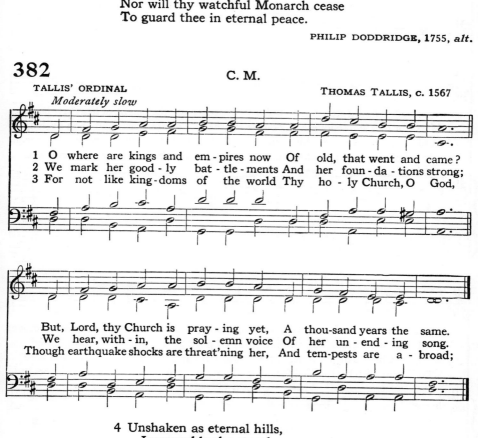

1 O where are kings and em-pires now Of old, that went and came?
2 We mark her good-ly bat-tle-ments And her foun-da-tions strong;
3 For not like king-doms of the world Thy ho-ly Church, O God,

But, Lord, thy Church is pray-ing yet, A thou-sand years the same.
We hear, with-in, the sol-emn voice Of her un-end-ing song.
Though earthquake shocks are threat'ning her, And tem-pests are a-broad;

4 Unshaken as eternal hills,
Immovable she stands,
A mountain that shall fill the earth,
A house not made by hands.

ARTHUR CLEVELAND COXE, 1839

URBS BEATA

Sarum Plainsong, Mode II

In unison, with spirit

1 Bless-ed ci - ty, heav'n-ly Sa - lem, Vi - sion dear of peace and love,
2 From ce - les - tial realms de-scend-ing, Bri - dal glo - ry round thee shed,
3 Bright thy gates of pearl are shin - ing; They are o - pen ev - er - more;
4 Ma - ny a blow and bi - ting sculp-ture Pol-ished well those stones e - lect,

Who of liv - ing stones art build - ed In the height of heav'n a-bove,
Meet for him whose love es - poused thee, To thy Lord shalt thou be led;
And by vir - tue of his mer - its Thith-er faith - ful souls do soar,
In their pla - ces now com - pact - ed By the heav'n-ly Ar - chi-tect,

And, with an - gel hosts en-cir-cled, As a bride dost earth-ward move;
All thy streets and all thy bulwarks Of pure gold are fash-ion-ed.
Who, for Christ's dear Name, in this world Pain and trib-u - la-tion bore.
Who there-with hath willed for ev-er That his pal - ace should be decked.

General Hymns

5 Laud and honor to the Father,
Laud and honor to the Son,
Laud and honor to the Spirit,
Ever Three, and ever One,
Consubstantial, co-eternal,
While unending ages run.   Amen.

Latin, c. 7th cent.; Tr. JOHN MASON NEALE, 1851, *alt.*

A - men.

383 *Second Tune*   87. 87. 87

ORIEL   CASPAR ETT, 1840

In moderate time

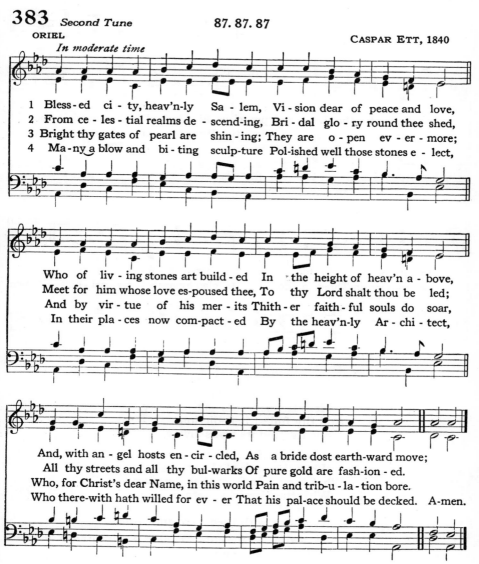

1 Bless-ed ci - ty, heav'n-ly Sa - lem, Vi - sion dear of peace and love,
2 From ce - les - tial realms de - scend-ing, Bri - dal glo - ry round thee shed,
3 Bright thy gates of pearl are shin - ing; They are o - pen ev - er - more;
4 Ma - ny a blow and bi - ting sculp-ture Pol-ished well those stones e - lect,

Who of liv - ing stones art build - ed In the height of heav'n a - bove,
Meet for him whose love es-poused thee, To thy Lord shalt thou be led;
And by vir - tue of his mer - its Thith - er faith - ful souls do soar,
In their pla - ces now com-pact - ed By the heav'n-ly Ar - chi - tect,

And, with an - gel hosts en - cir - cled, As a bride dost earth-ward move;
All thy streets and all thy bul-warks Of pure gold are fash-ion - ed.
Who, for Christ's dear Name, in this world Pain and trib-u - la - tion bore.
Who there-with hath willed for ev - er That his pal-ace should be decked.   A-men.

87. 87. 87

REGENT SQUARE   HENRY SMART, 1867

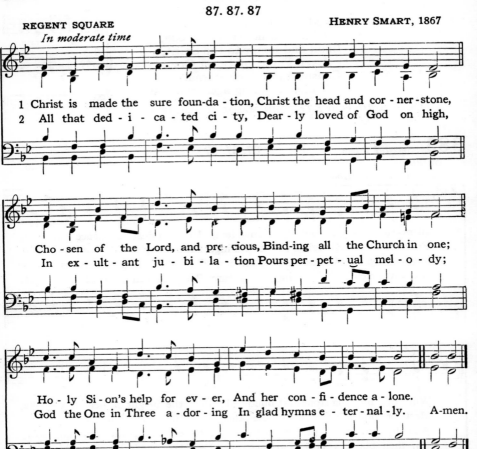

In moderate time

1 Christ is made the sure foun-da-tion, Christ the head and cor-ner-stone,
2 All that ded-i-ca-ted ci-ty, Dear-ly loved of God on high,

Cho-sen of the Lord, and pre-cious, Bind-ing all the Church in one;
In ex-ult-ant ju-bi-la-tion Pours per-pet-ual mel-o-dy;

Ho-ly Si-on's help for ev-er, And her con-fi-dence a-lone.
God the One in Three a-dor-ing In glad hymns e-ter-nal-ly.   A-men.

3 To this temple, where we call thee,
    Come, O Lord of Hosts, to-day;
With thy wonted loving-kindness
    Hear thy servants as they pray,
And thy fullest benediction
    Shed within its walls alway.

4 Here vouchsafe to all thy servants
    What they ask of thee to gain;
What they gain from thee, for ever
    With the blessèd to retain,
And hereafter in thy glory
    Evermore with thee to reign.   Amen.

Latin, c. 7th cent.; Tr. JOHN MASON NEALE, 1851, *alt.*

Alternative Tunes. URBS BEATA *and* ORIEL. No. 383

385

General Hymns

87. 87. D.

AUSTRIA

FRANZ JOSEPH HAYDN, 1797

With majesty

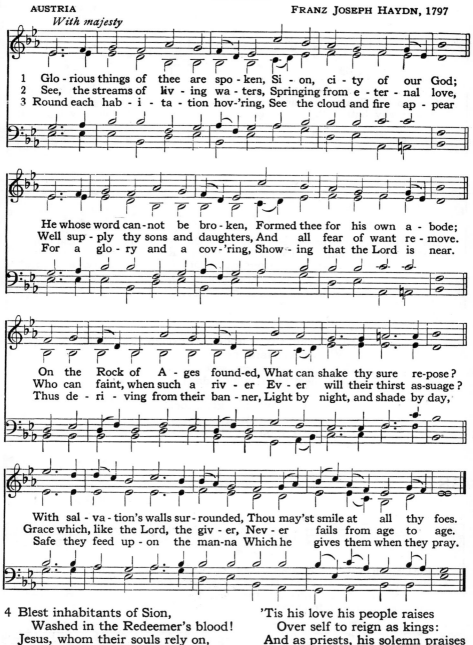

1 Glo - rious things of thee are spo - ken, Si - on, ci - ty of our God;
2 See, the streams of liv - ing wa - ters, Springing from e - ter - nal love,
3 Round each hab - i - ta - tion hov-'ring, See the cloud and fire ap - pear

He whose word can - not be bro - ken, Formed thee for his own a - bode;
Well sup - ply thy sons and daughters, And all fear of want re - move.
For a glo - ry and a cov-'ring, Show - ing that the Lord is near.

On the Rock of A - ges found-ed, What can shake thy sure re-pose?
Who can faint, when such a riv - er Ev - er will their thirst as-suage?
Thus de - ri - ving from their ban - ner, Light by night, and shade by day,

With sal - va - tion's walls sur - rounded, Thou may'st smile at all thy foes.
Grace which, like the Lord, the giv - er, Nev - er fails from age to age.
Safe they feed up - on the man-na Which he gives them when they pray.

4 Blest inhabitants of Sion,
   Washed in the Redeemer's blood!
Jesus, whom their souls rely on,
   Makes them kings and priests to God.

'Tis his love his people raises
Over self to reign as kings:
And as priests, his solemn praises
Each for a thank-off'ring brings.

Alternative Tune, EBENEZER, No. 519

JOHN NEWTON, 1779, alt.

RICHMOND   THOMAS HAWEIS, 1792

With movement

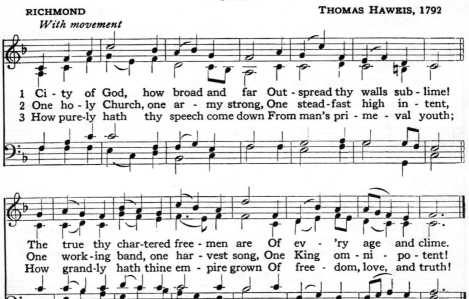

1 Ci - ty of God, how broad and far Out - spread thy walls sub - lime!
2 One ho - ly Church, one ar - my strong, One stead-fast high in - tent,
3 How pure-ly hath thy speech come down From man's pri - me - val youth;

The true thy char-tered free - men are Of ev - 'ry age and clime.
One work-ing band, one har - vest song, One King om - ni - po - tent!
How grand-ly hath thine em - pire grown Of free - dom, love, and truth!

4 How gleam thy watchfires through the night
    With never-fainting ray!
How rise thy towers, serene and bright,
    To meet the dawning day!

5 In vain the surge's angry shock,
    In vain the drifting sands:
Unharmed upon the eternal rock
    The eternal city stands.

SAMUEL JOHNSON, 1860

387   C. M.

ST. BAVON   CHARLES EDWARD HORSLEY, 1857

In moderate time

1 The Church of God a king - dom is, Where Christ in power doth reign,
2 Glad com - pa - nies of saints pos - sess This Church be - low, a - bove;
3 An al - tar stands with - in the shrine Where - on, once sac - ri - ficed,
4 There rich and poor, from count - less lands, Praise Christ on mys - tic rood;

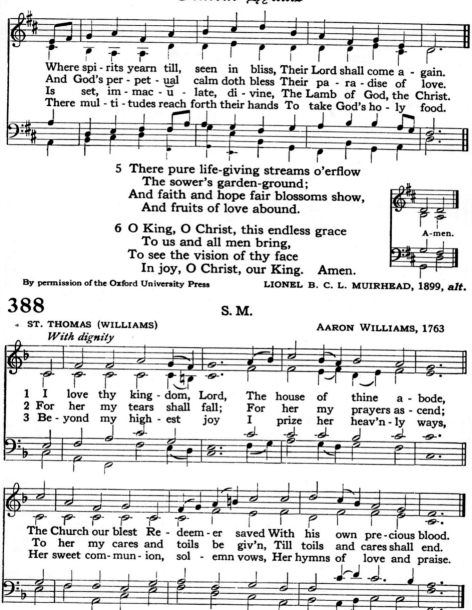

Where spi - rits yearn till, seen in bliss, Their Lord shall come a - gain.
And God's per - pet - ual calm doth bless Their pa - ra - dise of love.
Is set, im - mac - u - late, di - vine, The Lamb of God, the Christ.
There mul - ti - tudes reach forth their hands To take God's ho - ly food.

5 There pure life-giving streams o'erflow
   The sower's garden-ground;
   And faith and hope fair blossoms show,
   And fruits of love abound.

6 O King, O Christ, this endless grace
   To us and all men bring,
   To see the vision of thy face
   In joy, O Christ, our King.   Amen.

A-men.

By permission of the Oxford University Press   LIONEL B. C. L. MUIRHEAD, 1899, *alt.*

388   S. M.

ST. THOMAS (WILLIAMS)   AARON WILLIAMS, 1763

With dignity

1 I love thy king - dom, Lord,   The house of thine a - bode,
2 For her my tears shall fall;   For her my prayers as - cend;
3 Be - yond my high - est joy   I prize her heav'n - ly ways,

The Church our blest Re - deem - er saved With his own pre - cious blood.
To her my cares and toils be giv'n, Till toils and cares shall end.
Her sweet com - mun - ion, sol - emn vows, Her hymns of love and praise.

4 Jesus, thou friend divine,
   Our Saviour and our King,
Thy hand from every snare and foe
Shall great deliverance bring.

5 Sure as thy truth shall last,
   To Sion shall be giv'n
The brightest glories earth can yield,
And brighter bliss of heav'n.

TIMOTHY DWIGHT, 1800, *alt.*

10 10. 10 10

WOODLANDS   WALTER GREATOREX, 1919

Unison, in moderate time

1 Rise, crowned with light, im - pe - rial Sa - lem, rise! Ex - alt thy
2 See a long race thy spa - cious courts a - dorn: See fu - ture
3 See bar-barous na - tions at thy gates at - tend, Walk in thy
4 The seas shall waste, the skies to smoke de - cay, Rocks fall to

tower-ing head and lift thine eyes! See heav'n its spark - ling
sons, and daugh-ters yet un - born, In crowd-ing ranks on
light, and in thy tem - ple bend: See thy bright al - tars
dust, and moun-tains melt a - way; But fixed his word, his

por - tals wide dis - play, And break up - on thee in a flood of day.
ev - 'ry side a - rise, De-mand-ing life, im - pa-tient for the skies.
thronged with prostrate kings, While ev - 'ry land its joy-ous trib - ute brings.
sa - ving power re - mains; Thy realm shall last, thy own Mes-si - ah reigns.

By permission of W. Greatorex   ALEXANDER POPE, 1712

NATIONAL HYMN
With vigor

GEORGE WILLIAM WARREN, 1892

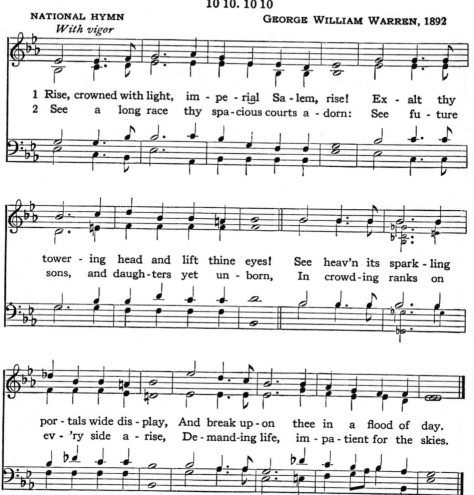

1 Rise, crowned with light, im - pe - ri̱al Sa - lem, rise! Ex - alt thy
2 See a long race thy spa - cious courts a - dorn: See fu - ture

tower - ing head and lift thine eyes! See heav'n its spark - ling
sons, and daugh-ters yet un - born, In crowd-ing ranks on

por - tals wide dis - play, And break up - on thee in a flood of day.
ev - 'ry side a - rise, De - mand-ing life, im - pa - tient for the skies.

3 See barbarous nations at thy gates attend,
Walk in thy light, and in thy temple bend:
See thy bright altars thronged with prostrate kings,
While every land its joyous tribute brings.

4 The seas shall waste, the skies to smoke decay,
Rocks fall to dust, and mountains melt away;
But fixed his word, his saving power remains;
Thy realm shall last, thy own Messiah reigns.

ALEXANDER POPE, 1712

MOUNT SION

Triumphantly

HORATIO PARKER, 1886

1 O 'twas a joy - ful sound to hear Our tribes de -
2 O ev - er pray for Sa - lem's peace; For they shall
3 For my dear breth - ren's sake, and friends No less than

vout - ly say, Up, Is - rael! to the tem - ple haste,
pros - p'rous be, Thou ho - ly ci - ty of our God,
breth - ren dear, I'll pray: May peace in Sa - lem's towers

And keep your fes - tal day. At Sa - lem's courts we
Who bear true love to thee. May peace with - in thy
A con - stant guest ap - pear. But most of all I'll

must ap - pear, With our as - sem - bled powers, In strong and
sa - cred walls A con - stant guest be found; With plen - ty
seek thy good, And ev - er wish thee well, For Si - on

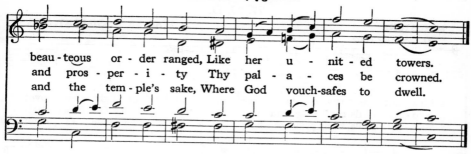

beau - teous or - der ranged, Like her u - nit - ed towers.
and pros - per - i - ty Thy pal - a - ces be crowned.
and the tem - ple's sake, Where God vouch-safes to dwell.

TATE *and* BRADY, 1698; *based on Psalm 122*

391

C. M.

ST. FLAVIAN
Moderately slow

JOHN DAY'S *Psalter*, 1562

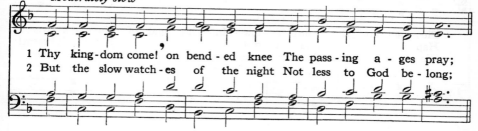

1 Thy king - dom come! on bend - ed knee The pass - ing a - ges pray;
2 But the slow watch - es of the night Not less to God be - long;

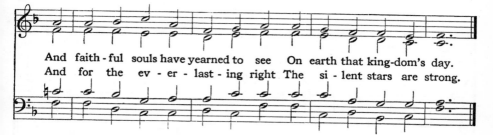

And faith - ful souls have yearned to see On earth that king-dom's day.
And for the ev - er - last - ing right The si - lent stars are strong.

3 And lo, already on the hills
　The flags of dawn appear;
Gird up your loins, ye prophet souls,
　Proclaim the day is near:

4 The day in whose clear-shining light
　All wrong shall stand revealed,
When justice shall be throned in might,
　And every hurt be healed;

5 When knowledge, hand in hand with peace,
　Shall walk the earth abroad;
The day of perfect righteousness,
　The promised day of God.

FREDERICK LUCIAN HOSMER, 1891

77. 77. D.

MAIDSTONE

WALTER B. GILBERT, 1862

In flowing style

1 Plea-sant are thy courts a-bove In the land of light and love;
2 Hap-py birds that sing and fly Round thy al-tars, O Most High;
3 Hap-py souls, their prais-es flow Ev-er in this vale of woe;

Plea-sant are thy courts be-low In this land of sin and woe.
Hap-pier souls that find a rest In a heav'nly Fa-ther's breast!
Wa-ters in the des-ert rise, Man-na feeds them from the skies:

O my spi-rit longs and faints For the con-verse of thy saints, For the
Like the wan-d'ring dove that found No re-pose on earth a-round, They can
On they go from strength to strength Till they reach thy throne at length, At thy

bright-ness of thy face, For thy full-ness, God of grace.
to their ark re-pair And en-joy it ev-er there.
feet a-dor-ing fall, Who hast led them safe through all. A-men.

4 Lord, be mine this prize to win;   Sun and shield alike thou art;
  Guide me thro' a world of sin;   Guide and guard my erring heart.
  Keep me by thy saving grace;   Grace and glory flow from thee;
  Give me at thy side a place.   Shower, O shower them, Lord, on me. Amen.

HENRY FRANCIS LYTE, 1834; *based on Psalm 84*

ST. CATHERINE
With vigor

HENRI F. HEMY, 1864,
and JAMES G. WALTON, 1870

1 Faith of our fa - thers! liv - ing still In spite of dun - geon,
2 Our fa - thers, chained in pris - ons dark, Were still in heart and
3 Faith of our fa - thers! faith and prayer Shall win all na - tions

fire, and sword: O how our hearts beat high with joy,
con - science free: And tru - ly blest would be our fate,
un - to thee; And through the truth that comes from God,

Refrain

When-e'er we hear that glo - rious word:
If we, like them, should die for thee.
Man - kind shall then in - deed be free.

Faith of our fa - thers,

ho - ly faith! We will be true to thee till death.

4 Faith of our fathers! we will love
Both friend and foe in all our strife:
And preach thee, too, as love knows how,
By kindly deeds and virtuous life.

Refrain

FREDERICK WILLIAM FABER, 1849, *alt.*

General Hymns
87. 87. D.

WILLIAM S. BAMBRIDGE

ST. ASAPH

In march time

1 Through the night of doubt and sor - row On - ward goes the pil - grim band,
2 One the light of God's own pres-ence, O'er his ran-somed peo-ple shed,
3 One the strain the lips of thou-sands Lift as from the heart of one;

Sing-ing songs of ex - pec - ta - tion, March-ing to the prom-ised land.
Cha-sing far the gloom and ter - ror, Bright-'ning all the path we tread:
One the con - flict, one the per - il, One the march in God be - gun:

Clear be - fore us through the dark-ness Gleams and burns the guid-ing light:
One the ob - ject of our jour-ney, One the faith which nev-er tires,
One the glad-ness of re - joic-ing On the far e - ter-nal shore,

Broth-er clasps the hand of broth-er, Step-ping fear-less through the night.
One the ear - nest look-ing for-ward, One the hope our God in - spires.
Where the one Al - migh-ty Fa - ther Reigns in love for ev - er - more.

BERNARD SEVERIN INGEMANN, 1825;
Tr. SABINE BARING–GOULD, 1867

General Hymns
11 11. 11 5

CLOISTERS

JOSEPH BARNBY, 1868

Moderately fast, in strict time

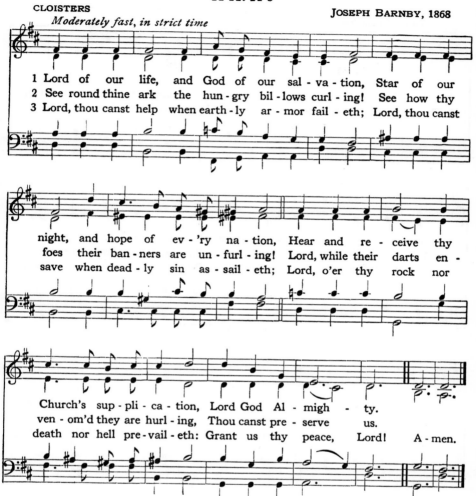

1 Lord of our life, and God of our sal - va - tion, Star of our
2 See round thine ark the hun - gry bil - lows curl - ing! See how thy
3 Lord, thou canst help when earth - ly ar - mor fail - eth; Lord, thou canst

night, and hope of ev - 'ry na - tion, Hear and re - ceive thy
foes their ban - ners are un - furl - ing! Lord, while their darts en -
save when dead - ly sin as - sail - eth; Lord, o'er thy rock nor

Church's sup - pli - ca - tion, Lord God Al - migh - ty.
ven - om'd they are hurl - ing, Thou canst pre - serve us.
death nor hell pre - vail - eth: Grant us thy peace, Lord! A - men.

4 Peace, in our hearts, our evil thoughts assuaging,
　Peace, in thy Church, where brothers are engaging,
　Peace, when the world its busy war is waging;
　　Calm thy foes raging!

5 Grant us thy help till backward they are driven;
　Grant them thy truth, that they may be forgiven;
　Grant peace on earth, and after we have striven,
　　Peace in thy heaven.　Amen.

PHILIP PUSEY, 1834;
based on MATTHAUS A. VON LOEWENSTERN, 1644

Alternative Tune, ROUEN, No. 228

General Hymns

76. 76. D.

SAMUEL SEBASTIAN WESLEY, 1864

AURELIA

In moderate time

1 The Church's one foun-da-tion Is Je-sus Christ her Lord;
2 E-lect from ev-'ry na-tion, Yet one o'er all the earth,
3 Though with a scorn-ful won-der Men see her sore op-prest,

She is his new cre-a-tion By wa-ter and the word:
Her char-ter of sal-va-tion, One Lord, one faith, one birth;
By schisms rent a-sun-der, By her-e-sies dis-trest;

From heav'n he came and sought her To be his ho-ly bride;
One ho-ly Name she bless-es, Par-takes one ho-ly food,
Yet saints their watch are keep-ing, Their cry goes up, "How long?"

With his own blood he bought her, And for her life he died.
And to one hope she press-es, With ev-'ry grace en-dued.
And soon the night of weep-ing Shall be the morn of song. A-men.

General Hymns

4 'Mid toil and tribulation,
    And tumult of her war,
  She waits the consummation
    Of peace for evermore;
  Till with the vision glorious
    Her longing eyes are blest,
  And the great Church victorious
    Shall be the Church at rest.

5 Yet she on earth hath union
    With God, the Three in One,
  And mystic sweet communion
    With those whose rest is won.
  O happy ones and holy!
    Lord, give us grace that we
  Like them, the meek and lowly,
    On high may dwell with thee.   Amen.

SAMUEL JOHN STONE, 1866

397

C. M.

 DUNDEE

With dignity

Scottish Psalter, 1615

1 Let saints on earth in con-cert sing With those whose work is done;
2 One fam-i-ly we dwell in him, One Church, a-bove, be-neath,
3 One ar-my of the liv-ing God, To his com-mand we bow;

For all the ser-vants of our King In heav'n and earth are one.
Though now di-vi-ded by the stream, The nar-row stream of death.
Part of the host have crossed the flood, And part are cross-ing now.   A-men.

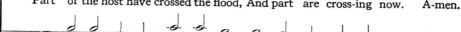

4 E'en now by faith we join our hands
    With those that went before,
  And greet the ever-living bands
    On the eternal shore.

5 Jesus, be thou our constant Guide;
    Then, when the word is giv'n,
  Bid Jordan's narrow stream divide,
    And bring us safe to heav'n.   Amen.

CHARLES WESLEY, 1759, alt.

66. 66 *(Iambic)*

QUAM DILECTA

HENRY L. JENNER, 1861

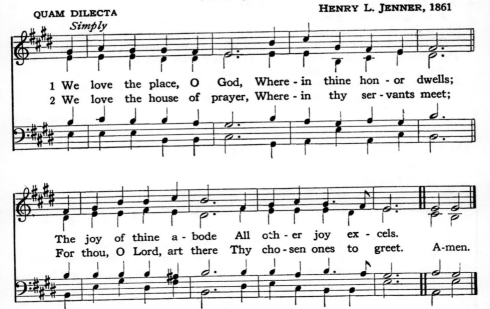

1 We love the place, O God, Where-in thine hon-or dwells;
2 We love the house of prayer, Where-in thy ser-vants meet;

The joy of thine a-bode All oth-er joy ex-cels.
For thou, O Lord, art there Thy cho-sen ones to greet. A-men.

3 We love the sacred font,
   Wherein the holy Dove
Bestows, as ever wont,
   His blessing from above.

4 We love thine altar, Lord,
   Its mysteries revere;
For there, in faith adored,
   We find thy presence near.

5 We love thy holy word,
   The lamp thou gav'st to guide
All wand'rers home, O Lord,
   Home to their Father's side.

6 Then let us sing the love
   To us so freely giv'n,
Until we sing above
   The triumph song of heav'n! Amen.

WILLIAM BULLOCK, 1854, *alt.*

399

66. 66 *(Trochaic)*

RAVENSHAW

Ave Hierarchia, 1531,
arr. WILLIAM H. MONK, 1861

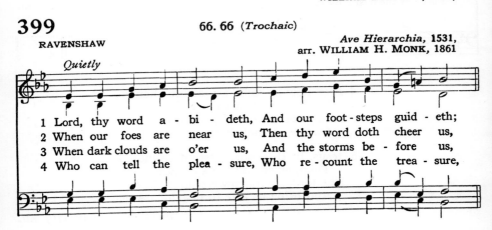

1 Lord, thy word a-bi-deth, And our foot-steps guid-eth;
2 When our foes are near us, Then thy word doth cheer us,
3 When dark clouds are o'er us, And the storms be-fore us,
4 Who can tell the plea-sure, Who re-count the trea-sure,

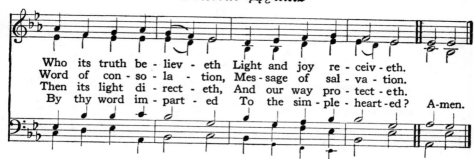

Who its truth be - liev - eth Light and joy re - ceiv - eth.
Word of con - so - la - tion, Mes - sage of sal - va - tion.
Then its light di - rect - eth, And our way pro - tect - eth.
By thy word im - part - ed To the sim - ple - heart - ed? A - men.

5 Word of mercy, giving
   Succor to the living;
   Word of life, supplying
   Comfort to the dying!

6 O that we, discerning
   Its most holy learning,
   Lord, may love and fear thee,
   Evermore be near thee! Amen.

HENRY WILLIAMS BAKER, 1861, *alt.*

400   C. M.

GRAEFENBERG
Moderately slow

JOHANN CRUEGER, 1653

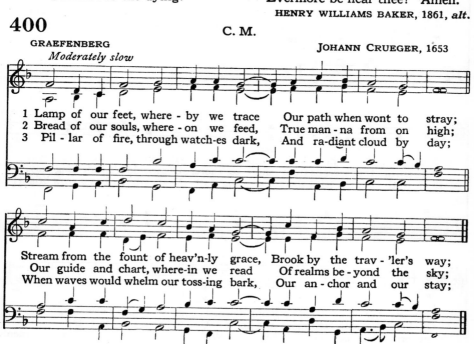

1 Lamp of our feet, where - by we trace   Our path when wont to stray;
2 Bread of our souls, where - on we feed,   True man - na from on high;
3 Pil - lar of fire, through watch - es dark,   And ra - diant cloud by day;

Stream from the fount of heav'n - ly grace, Brook by the trav - 'ler's way;
Our guide and chart, where - in we read   Of realms be - yond the sky;
When waves would whelm our toss - ing bark,   Our an - chor and our stay;

4 Word of the ever-living God,
   Will of his glorious Son;
   Without thee how could earth be trod,
   Or heav'n itself be won?

5 Lord, grant us all aright to learn
   The wisdom it imparts;
   And to its heav'nly teaching turn,
   With simple, childlike hearts. Amen.

A-men.

BERNARD BARTON, 1826

WEYMOUTH
C. M. D.
THEODORE P. FERRIS, 1941

With animation

1 Be-hold a Sow-er! from a - far He go-eth forth with might;
2 O Lord of life, to thee we lift Our hearts in praise for those,
3 Shine forth, O Light, that we may see, With hearts all un - a - fraid,

The roll-ing years his fur-rows are, His seed the grow-ing light;
Thy pro-phets, who have shown thy gift Of grace that ev - er grows,
The mean-ing and the mys - ter - y Of things that thou hast made:

For all the just his word is sown, It spring-eth up al - way;
Of truth that spreads from shore to shore, Of wis-dom's wide-ning ray,
Shine forth, and let the dark-ling past Be-neath thy beam grow bright;

The ten - der blade is hope's young dawn, The har-vest, love's new day.
Of light that shin - eth more and more Un-to thy per - fect day.
Shine forth, and touch the fu - ture vast With thine un-troub-led light. A-men.

4 Light up thy word; the fettered page O Light of Light! within us dwell,
  From killing bondage free: Through us thy radiance pour,
Light up our way; lead forth this age That word and life thy truths may tell,
  In love's large liberty. And praise thee evermore. Amen.

WASHINGTON GLADDEN, 1904

76. 76. D.

MUNICH
In moderate time

Meiningen Gesangbuch, 1693

1 O Word of God in-car-nate, O Wis-dom from on high,
2 The Church from her dear Mas-ter Re-ceived the gift di-vine,
3 It float-eth like a ban-ner Be-fore God's host un-furled;

O Truth, un-changed, un-chang-ing, O Light of our dark sky;
And still that light she lift-eth O'er all the earth to shine.
It shin-eth like a bea-con A-bove the dark-ling world;

We praise thee for the ra-diance That from the hal-lowed page,
It is the gold-en cas-ket Where gems of truth are stored;
It is the chart and com-pass That o'er life's surg-ing sea,

A lan-tern to our foot-steps, Shines on from age to age.
It is the heav'n-drawn pic-ture Of Christ, the liv-ing Word.
'Mid mists and rocks and quick-sands, Still guides, O Christ, to thee. A-men.

4 O make thy Church, dear Saviour,
  A lamp of purest gold,
  To bear before the nations
  Thy true light as of old;

O teach thy wand'ring pilgrims
  By this their path to trace,
Till, clouds and darkness ended,
  They see thee face to face. Amen.

WILLIAM WALSHAM HOW, 1867

78. 78. 88

LIEBSTER JESU
JOHANN RUDOLPH AHLE, 1664

Slow and quiet

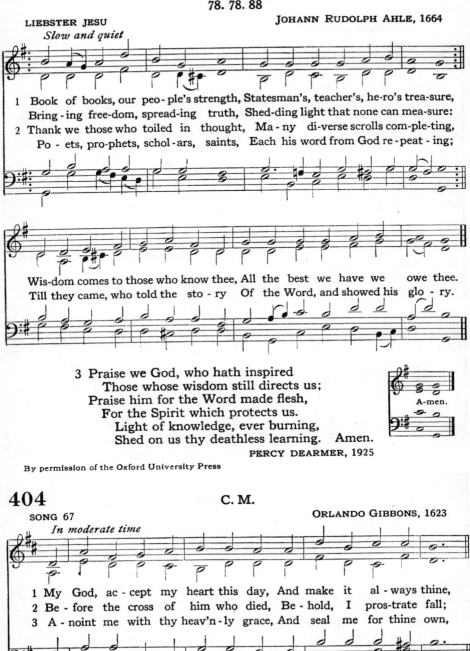

1 Book of books, our peo- ple's strength, Statesman's, teacher's, he-ro's trea-sure,
Bring-ing free-dom, spread-ing truth, Shed-ding light that none can mea-sure:
2 Thank we those who toiled in thought, Ma-ny di-verse scrolls com-ple-ting,
Po- ets, pro-phets, schol-ars, saints, Each his word from God re-peat-ing;

Wis-dom comes to those who know thee, All the best we have we owe thee.
Till they came, who told the sto-ry Of the Word, and showed his glo-ry.

3 Praise we God, who hath inspired
   Those whose wisdom still directs us;
   Praise him for the Word made flesh,
   For the Spirit which protects us.
   Light of knowledge, ever burning,
   Shed on us thy deathless learning. Amen.

A-men.

PERCY DEARMER, 1925

By permission of the Oxford University Press

404 C. M.

SONG 67
ORLANDO GIBBONS, 1623

In moderate time

1 My God, ac-cept my heart this day, And make it al-ways thine,
2 Be-fore the cross of him who died, Be-hold, I pros-trate fall;
3 A-noint me with thy heav'n-ly grace, And seal me for thine own,

General Hymns

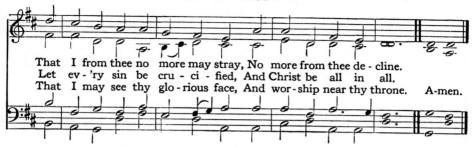

That I from thee no more may stray, No more from thee de - cline.
Let ev - 'ry sin be cru - ci - fied, And Christ be all in all.
That I may see thy glo - rious face, And wor - ship near thy throne. A - men.

4 Let every thought and work and word,
   To thee be ever giv'n;
   Then life shall be thy service, Lord,
   And death the gate of heav'n. Amen.

MATTHEW BRIDGES, 1848, *alt.*

405 ARTAVIA 10 10. 10 6 EDWARD J. HOPKINS, 1887

With deep feeling

1 I sought the Lord, and af - ter - ward I knew He moved my
2 Thou didst reach forth thy hand and mine en - fold; I walked and
3 I find, I walk, I love, but O the whole Of love is

soul to seek him, seek - ing me; It was not I that found, O
sank not on the storm-vexed sea; 'Twas not so much that I on
but my an - swer, Lord, to thee; For thou wert long be - fore - hand

Sa - viour true; No, I was found of thee.
thee took hold, As thou, dear Lord, on me.
with my soul, Al - ways thou lov - edst me. A - men.

Anonymous, c. 1878

406

General Hymns
85. 83

STEPHANOS

HENRY W. BAKER, 1868

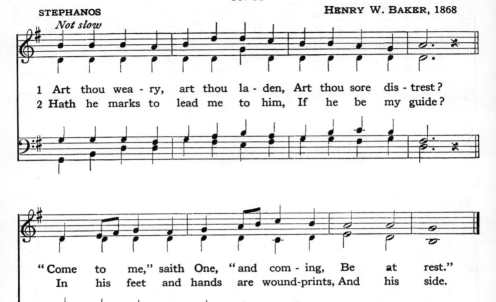

1 Art thou wea - ry, art thou la - den, Art thou sore dis - trest?
2 Hath he marks to lead me to him, If he be my guide?

"Come to me," saith One, "and com - ing, Be at rest."
In his feet and hands are wound-prints, And his side.

3 Is there diadem, as monarch,
    That his brow adorns?
  Yea, a crown, in very surety,
    But of thorns.

4 If I still hold closely to him,
    What hath he at last?
  Sorrow vanquished, labor ended,
    Jordan past.

5 If I ask him to receive me,
    Will he say me nay?
  Not till earth, and not till heaven
    Pass away.

6 Finding, following, keeping, struggling,
    Is he sure to bless?
  Saints, apostles, prophets, martyrs,
    Answer, "Yes."

JOHN MASON NEALE, 1862, *alt.*

76. 76. D.

ST. HILDA

JUSTIN H. KNECHT, 1799,
and EDWARD HUSBAND, 1871

In moderate time

1 O Je - sus, thou art stand - ing Out - side the fast-closed door,
2 O Je - sus, thou art knock - ing: And lo! that hand is scarred,
3 O Je - sus, thou art plead - ing In ac - cents meek and low:

In low - ly pa - tience wait - ing To pass the thresh-old o'er:
And thorns thy brow en - cir - cle, And tears thy face have marred;
"I died for you, my chil - dren, And will ye treat me so?"

Shame on us, Chris - tian broth - ers, His Name and sign who bear,
O love that pass - eth knowl - edge, So pa - tient - ly to wait!
O Lord, with shame and sor - row We o - pen now the door:

O shame, thrice shame up - on us, To keep him stand - ing there!
O sin that hath no e - qual, So fast to bar the gate!
Dear Sa - viour, en - ter, en - ter, And leave us nev - er - more. A-men.

WILLIAM WALSHAM HOW, 1867

408

77. 77. D.

HOLLINGSIDE

JOHN B. DYKES, 1861

In moderate time

1 Take my life, and let it be Con - se - cra - ted, Lord, to thee;
2 Take my voice, and let me sing Al - ways, on - ly, for my King;

Take my mo-ments and my days, Let them flow in cease-less praise.
Take my in - tel - lect, and use Ev - 'ry power as thou shalt choose.

Take my hands, and let them move At the im - pulse of thy love;
Take my will, and make it thine: It shall be no long - er mine.

Take my feet, and let them be Swift and beau-ti - ful for thee.
Take my - self, and I will be Ev - er, on - ly, all for thee. A-men.

FRANCES RIDLEY HAVERGAL, 1874

SAFFRON WALDEN
Moderately slow   ARTHUR HENRY BROWN, 1890

1 Just as I am, with-out one plea, But that thy
2 Just as I am, though tossed a-bout With ma-ny a
*3 Just as I am, poor, wretch-ed, blind; Sight, rich-es,

blood was shed for me, And that thou
con - flict, ma - ny a doubt; Fight - ings and
heal - ing of the mind, Yea, all I

bidd'st me come to thee, O Lamb of God, I come.
fears with - in, with - out, O Lamb of God, I come.
need, in thee to find, O Lamb of God, I come. A - men.

4 Just as I am: thou wilt receive;
Wilt welcome, pardon, cleanse, relieve,
Because thy promise I believe,
     O Lamb of God, I come.

5 Just as I am, thy love unknown
Has broken every barrier down;
Now to be thine, yea, thine alone,
     O Lamb of God, I come.

6 Just as I am, of thy great love
The breadth, length, depth, and height to prove,
Here for a season, then above:
     O Lamb of God, I come. Amen.

CHARLOTTE ELLIOTT, 1836, *alt.*

General Hymns
L. M.

ST. CRISPIN

GEORGE J. ELVEY, 1862

Not slow

1 Just as I am, with - out one plea, But that thy
2 Just as I am, though tossed a - bout With ma - ny a
*3 Just as I am, poor, wretch - ed, blind; Sight, rich - es,

blood was shed for me, And that thou bidd'st me come to
con - flict, ma - ny a doubt; Fight-ings and fears with - in, with -
heal - ing of the mind, Yea, all I need, in thee to

thee, O Lamb of God, I come, I come.
out, O Lamb of God, I come, I come.
find, O Lamb of God, I come, I come. A - men.

4 Just as I am: thou wilt receive;
  Wilt welcome, pardon, cleanse, relieve,
  Because thy promise I believe,
    O Lamb of God, I come.

5 Just as I am, thy love unknown
  Has broken every barrier down;
  Now to be thine, yea, thine alone,
    O Lamb of God, I come.

6 Just as I am, of thy great love
  The breadth, length, depth, and height to prove,
  Here for a season, then above:
    O Lamb of God, I come. Amen.

CHARLOTTE ELLIOTT, 1836, *alt.*

L. M.

WOODWORTH

Without dragging

WILLIAM B. BRADBURY, 1849

1 Just as I am, with-out one plea, But that thy
2 Just as I am, though tossed a-bout With ma-ny a
*3 Just as I am, poor, wretch-ed, blind; Sight, rich - es,

blood was shed for me, And that thou bidd'st me
con - flict, ma - ny a doubt; Fight - ings and fears with -
heal - ing of the mind, Yea, all I need, in

come to thee, O Lamb of God, I come, I come.
in, with - out, O Lamb of God, I come, I come.
thee to find, O Lamb of God, I come, I come. A - men.

4 Just as I am: thou wilt receive;
Wilt welcome, pardon, cleanse, relieve,
Because thy promise I believe,
   O Lamb of God, I come.

5 Just as I am, thy love unknown
Has broken every barrier down;
Now to be thine, yea, thine alone,
   O Lamb of God, I come.

6 Just as I am, of thy great love
The breadth, length, depth, and height to prove,
Here for a season, then above:
   O Lamb of God, I come. Amen.

CHARLOTTE ELLIOTT, 1836, *alt.*

410 *First Tune*

General Hymns

C. M.

Chetham's Psalmody, 1718

BURFORD

In moderate time

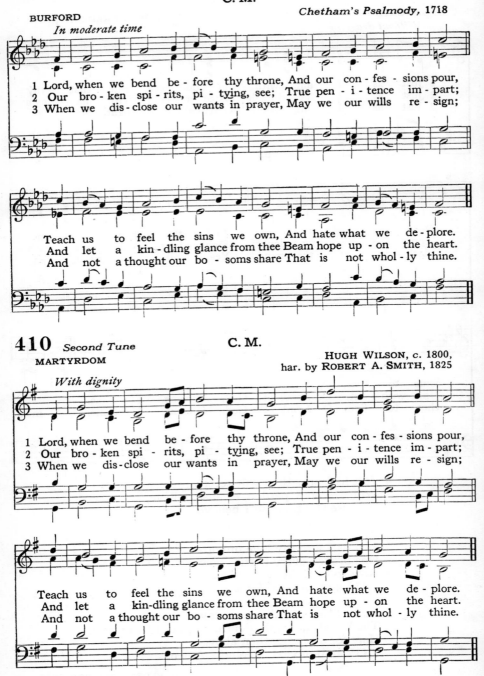

1 Lord, when we bend be - fore thy throne, And our con - fes - sions pour,
2 Our bro - ken spi - rits, pi - tying, see; True pen - i - tence im - part;
3 When we dis - close our wants in prayer, May we our wills re - sign;

Teach us to feel the sins we own, And hate what we de - plore.
And let a kin - dling glance from thee Beam hope up - on the heart.
And not a thought our bo - soms share That is not whol - ly thine.

410 *Second Tune*

C. M.

HUGH WILSON, c. 1800,
har. by ROBERT A. SMITH, 1825

MARTYRDOM

With dignity

1 Lord, when we bend be - fore thy throne, And our con - fes - sions pour,
2 Our bro - ken spi - rits, pi - tying, see; True pen - i - tence im - part;
3 When we dis - close our wants in prayer, May we our wills re - sign;

Teach us to feel the sins we own, And hate what we de - plore.
And let a kin - dling glance from thee Beam hope up - on the heart.
And not a thought our bo - soms share That is not whol - ly thine.

General Hymns

1st Tune

A - men.

4 Let faith each weak petition fill,
   And waft it to the skies,
   And teach our hearts 'tis goodness still
   That grants it, or denies.   Amen.

JOSEPH DACRE CARLYLE, 1802

2nd Tune

A - men.

411

L. M.

GRACE CHURCH
With dignity

IGNAZ J. PLEYEL, 1815

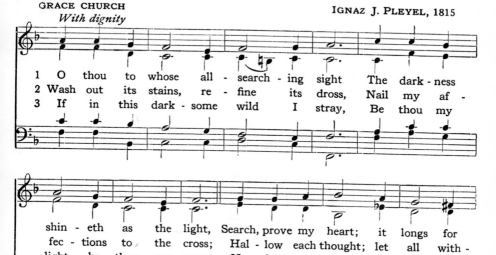

1 O thou to whose all - search - ing sight The dark - ness
2 Wash out its stains, re - fine its dross, Nail my af -
3 If in this dark - some wild I stray, Be thou my

shin - eth as the light, Search, prove my heart; it longs for
fec - tions to the cross; Hal - low each thought; let all with -
light, be thou my way; No foes, no e - vils need I

thee; O burst these bonds, and set it free!
in Be clean, as thou, my Lord, art clean.
fear, No harm, while thou, my God, art near.   A - men.

4 Saviour, where'er thy steps I see,
   Dauntless, untired, I follow thee:
   O let thy hand support me still,
   And lead me to thy holy hill!   Amen.

N. L. VON ZINZENDORF, 1721; *Tr.* JOHN WESLEY, 1738, *alt.*

88. 84

HANFORD
ARTHUR S. SULLIVAN, 1874

Quietly

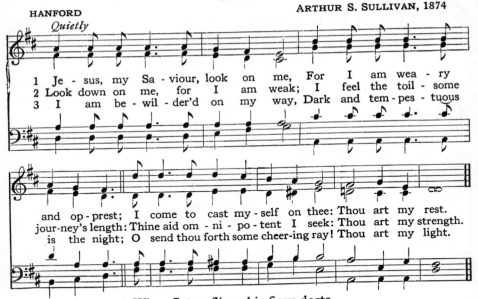

1 Je - sus, my Sa - viour, look on me, For I am wea - ry
2 Look down on me, for I am weak; I feel the toil - some
3 I am be - wil - der'd on my way, Dark and tem - pes - tuous

and op - prest; I come to cast my - self on thee: Thou art my rest.
jour-ney's length: Thine aid om - ni - po - tent I seek: Thou art my strength.
is the night; O send thou forth some cheer-ing ray! Thou art my light.

4 When Satan flings his fiery darts,
    I look to thee; my terrors cease;
    Thy cross a hiding-place imparts:
    Thou art my peace.

5 Standing alone on Jordan's brink,
    In that tremendous, latest strife,
    Thou wilt not suffer me to sink:
    Thou art my life.

A - men.

6 Thou wilt my every want supply,
    E'en to the end, whate'er befall:
    Through life, in death, eternally,
    Thou art my all. Amen.

CHARLOTTE ELLIOTT, 1869, *alt.*

413 C. M.

ST. BERNARD
Cologne, 1741,
arr. by JOHN RICHARDSON, 1851

Moderately slow

1 Lord, as to thy dear cross we flee, And plead to be for - giv'n,
2 Help us, through good re - port and ill, Our dai - ly cross to bear;
3 Let grace our self - ish - ness ex - pel, Our earth - li - ness re - fine;

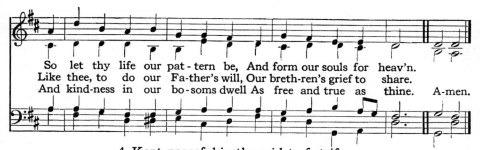

So let thy life our pat-tern be, And form our souls for heav'n.
Like thee, to do our Fa-ther's will, Our breth-ren's grief to share.
And kind-ness in our bo-soms dwell As free and true as thine. A-men.

4 Kept peaceful in the midst of strife,
    Forgiving and forgiv'n,
  O may we lead the pilgrim's life,
    And follow thee to heav'n! Amen.

JOHN HAMPDEN GURNEY, 1838, *alt.*

414

C. M.

KILMARNOCK

NEILL DOUGALL, 1831

In moderate time

1 O for a heart to praise my God, A heart from sin set free!
2 A heart re-signed, sub-mis-sive, meek, My dear Re-deem-er's throne,
3 An hum-ble, low-ly, con-trite heart, Be-liev-ing, true, and clean;

A heart that's sprin-kled with the blood So free-ly shed for me;
Where on-ly Christ is heard to speak, Where Je-sus reigns a-lone;
Which nei-ther life nor death can part From him that dwells with-in;

4 A heart in every thought renewed,
    And full of love divine,
  Perfect, and right, and pure, and good,
    A copy, Lord, of thine!

5 Thy nature, gracious Lord, impart;
    Come quickly from above;
  Write thy new name upon my heart,
    Thy new, best name of Love. Amen.

A - men.

Alternative Tune, BEATITUDO, No. 416

CHARLES WESLEY, 1742, *alt.*

ABERYSTWYTH
With movement

JOSEPH PARRY, 1879

1 Je - sus, Lov - er of my soul, Let me to thy bo - som fly,
2 Oth - er ref - uge have I none, Hangs my help - less soul on thee;
3 Plen - teous grace with thee is found, Grace to cleanse from ev - 'ry sin;

While the near - er wa - ters roll, While the tem - pest still is high:
Leave, ah! leave me not a - lone, Still sup - port and com - fort me!
Let the heal - ing streams a - bound, Make and keep me pure with - in.

Hide me, O my Sa - viour, hide, Till the storm of life be past;
All my trust on thee is stayed; All my help from thee I bring;
Thou of life the foun - tain art, Free - ly let me take of thee:

Safe in - to the ha - ven guide, O re - ceive my soul at last.
Cov - er my de - fence-less head With the sha - dow of thy wing.
Spring thou up with - in my heart, Rise to all e - ter - ni - ty. A-men.

CHARLES WESLEY, 1740, *alt.*

HOLLINGSIDE   JOHN B. DYKES, 1861

In moderate time

1 Je - sus, Lov - er of my soul, Let me to thy bo - som fly,
2 Oth - er ref - uge have I none, Hangs my help - less soul on thee;
3 Plen-teous grace with thee is found, Grace to cleanse from ev - 'ry sin;

While the near - er wa - ters roll, While the tem - pest still is high:
Leave, ah! leave me not a - lone, Still sup - port and com - fort me!
Let the heal - ing streams a - bound, Make and keep me pure with - in.

Hide me, O my Sa - viour, hide, Till the storm of life be past;
All my trust on thee is stayed; All my help from thee I bring;
Thou of life the foun - tain art, Free - ly let me take of thee:

Safe in - to the ha - ven guide, O re - ceive my soul at last.
Cov - er my de-fence-less head With the sha-dow of thy wing.
Spring thou up with - in my heart, Rise to all e - ter - ni - ty.   A-men.

CHARLES WESLEY, 1740, *alt.*

77. 77. D.

MARTYN
Without dragging

SIMEON B. MARSH, 1834

1 Je - sus, Lov - er of my soul, Let me to thy bo - som fly,
2 Oth - er ref - uge have I none, Hangs my help - less soul on thee;
3 Plen-teous grace with thee is found, Grace to cleanse from ev - 'ry sin;

While the near - er wa - ters roll, While the tem - pest still is high:
Leave, ah! leave me not a - lone, Still sup-port and com - fort me!
Let the heal - ing streams a - bound, Make and keep me pure with - in.

Hide me, O my Sa - viour, hide, Till the storm of life be past;
All my trust on thee is stayed; All my help from thee I bring;
Thou of life the foun - tain art, Free - ly let me take of thee:

Safe in - to the ha - ven guide, O re-ceive my soul at last.
Cov - er my de-fence-less head With the sha-dow of thy wing.
Spring thou up with - in my heart, Rise to all e - ter - ni - ty. A-men.

CHARLES WESLEY, 1740, *alt.*

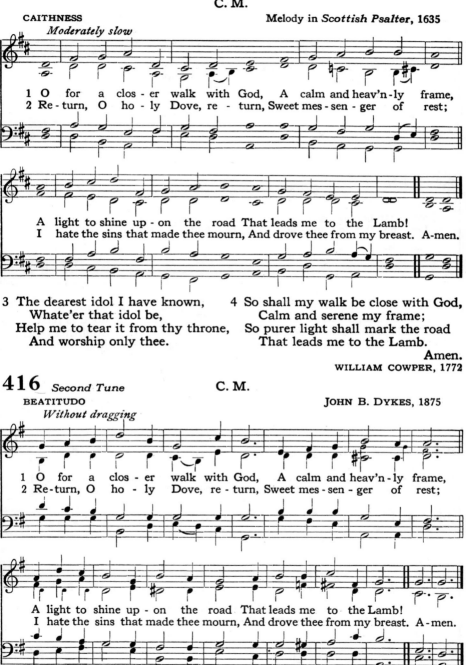

CAITHNESS   Melody in *Scottish Psalter*, 1635

Moderately slow

1 O for a clos - er walk with God, A calm and heav'n - ly frame,
2 Re - turn, O ho - ly Dove, re - turn, Sweet mes - sen - ger of rest;

A light to shine up - on the road That leads me to the Lamb!
I hate the sins that made thee mourn, And drove thee from my breast. A-men.

3 The dearest idol I have known,   4 So shall my walk be close with God,
   Whate'er that idol be,   Calm and serene my frame;
   Help me to tear it from thy throne,   So purer light shall mark the road
   And worship only thee.   That leads me to the Lamb.

Amen.
WILLIAM COWPER, 1772

416 *Second Tune*   C. M.

BEATITUDO   JOHN B. DYKES, 1875

Without dragging

1 O for a clos - er walk with God, A calm and heav'n - ly frame,
2 Re - turn, O ho - ly Dove, re - turn, Sweet mes - sen - ger of rest;

A light to shine up - on the road That leads me to the Lamb!
I hate the sins that made thee mourn, And drove thee from my breast. A-men.

417

General Hymns

S. M.

ST. BRIDE   SAMUEL HOWARD, 1762

With dignity

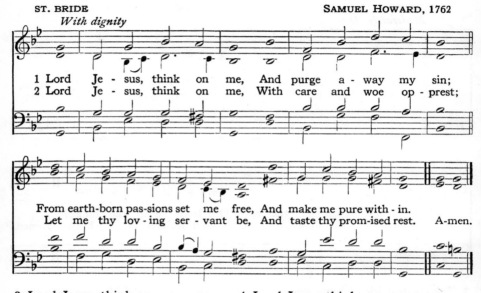

1 Lord Je - sus, think on me, And purge a - way my sin;
2 Lord Je - sus, think on me, With care and woe op - prest;

From earth-born pas-sions set me free, And make me pure with - in.
Let me thy lov-ing ser - vant be, And taste thy prom-ised rest. A-men.

3 Lord Jesus, think on me,
   Nor let me go astray;
Through darkness and perplexity
   Point thou the heav'nly way.

4 Lord Jesus, think on me,
   That, when the flood is past,
I may the eternal brightness see,
   And share thy joy at last. Amen.

SYNESIUS, c. 375–430; *Tr.* ALLEN W. CHATFIELD, 1876

418

S. M.

FRANCONIA   JOHANN B. KOENIG, 1738,
                     arr. by W. H. HAVERGAL, 1847

In moderate time

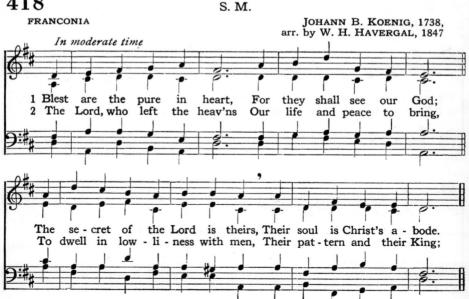

1 Blest are the pure in heart, For they shall see our God;
2 The Lord, who left the heav'ns Our life and peace to bring,

The se - cret of the Lord is theirs, Their soul is Christ's a - bode.
To dwell in low - li - ness with men, Their pat - tern and their King;

General Hymns

3 He to the lowly soul
  Doth still himself impart;
  And for his dwelling and his throne
  Chooseth the pure in heart.

4 Lord, we thy presence seek;
  May ours this blessing be;
  Give us a pure and lowly heart,
  A temple meet for thee. Amen.

A-men.

JOHN KEBLE, 1819, *alt.*

419

SHADDICK
C. M.

In moderate time

BATES G. BURT, 1941

1 Prayer is the soul's sin-cere de-sire, Un-ut-ter'd or ex-pressed,
2 Prayer is the bur-den of a sigh, The fall-ing of a tear,
3 Prayer is the sim-plest form of speech That in-fant lips can try;

The mo-tion of a hid-den fire That trem-bles in the breast.
The up-ward glan-cing of an eye When none but God is near.
Prayer the sub-lim-est strains that reach The Ma-jes-ty on high.

4 Prayer is the Christian's vital breath,
  The Christian's native air,
  His watchword at the gates of death:
  He enters heav'n with prayer.

5 O thou by whom we come to God,
  The Life, the Truth, the Way,
  The path of prayer thyself hast trod:
  Lord, teach us how to pray. Amen.

A-men.

JAMES MONTGOMERY, 1818

420 *First Tune*   **General Hymns**
88. 84

WIMBLEDON   SAMUEL SEBASTIAN WESLEY, 1864

In flowing style

1 My God, my Fa - ther, while I stray Far from my home in
*2 Though dark my path, and sad my lot, Let me be still and
*3 What though in lone - ly grief I sigh For friends be - lov'd, no

life's rough way, O teach me from my heart to say, "Thy will be done!"
mur - mur not, Or breathe the prayer di - vine - ly taught, "Thy will be done!"
long - er nigh, Sub - mis - sive still would I re - ply, "Thy will be done!"

420 *Second Tune*   88. 84

HANFORD   ARTHUR S. SULLIVAN, 1874

Quietly

1 My God, my Fa - ther, while I stray Far from my home in
*2 Though dark my path, and sad my lot, Let me be still and
*3 What though in lone - ly grief I sigh For friends be - lov'd, no

life's rough way, O teach me from my heart to say, "Thy will be done!"
mur - mur not, Or breathe the prayer di - vine - ly taught, "Thy will be done!"
long - er nigh, Sub - mis - sive still would I re - ply, "Thy will be done!"

General Hymns

*4 If thou should'st call me to resign
   What most I prize, it ne'er was mine:
   I only yield thee what is thine;
      " Thy will be done!"

*5 Let but my fainting heart be blest
   With thy good Spirit for its guest,
   My God, to thee I leave the rest;
      " Thy will be done!"

6 Renew my will from day to day,
   Blend it with thine, and take away
   All that now makes it hard to say,
      " Thy will be done!"

*7 Then, when on earth I breathe no more
   The prayer oft mixed with tears before,
   I'll sing upon a happier shore,
      " Thy will, be done!"   Amen.

CHARLOTTE ELLIOTT, 1834, *alt.*

1st Tune

A - men.

2nd Tune

A-men.

421

L. M.

RETREAT

THOMAS HASTINGS, 1842

In moderate time

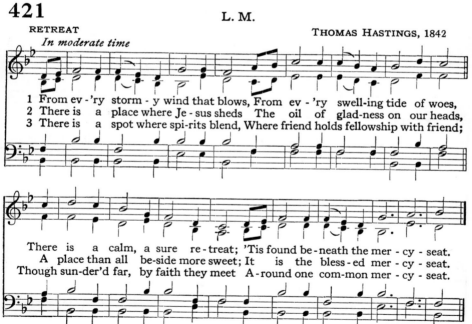

1 From ev-'ry storm-y wind that blows, From ev-'ry swell-ing tide of woes,
2 There is a place where Je-sus sheds The oil of glad-ness on our heads,
3 There is a spot where spi-rits blend, Where friend holds fellowship with friend;

There is a calm, a sure re-treat; 'Tis found be-neath the mer-cy-seat.
A place than all be-side more sweet; It is the bless-ed mer-cy-seat.
Though sun-der'd far, by faith they meet A-round one com-mon mer-cy-seat.

4 There, there, on eagle-wings we soar,
   And time and sense seem all no more;
   And heav'n comes down, our souls to greet,
   And glory crowns the mercy-seat.

HUGH STOWELL, 1828, *alt.*

ERIE

CHARLES CROZAT CONVERSE, 1868

In moderate time

1 What a friend we have in Je - sus, All our sins and griefs to bear!
2 Have we tri - als and temp-ta - tions? Is there trou - ble an - y-where?
3 Are we weak and hea - vy - la - den, Cum-bered with a load of care?

What a priv - i - lege to car - ry Ev - 'ry-thing to God in prayer!
We should nev - er be dis - cour - aged: Take it to the Lord in prayer!
Pre - cious Sa-viour, still our ref - uge—Take it to the Lord in prayer!

O what peace we of - ten for - feit, O what need-less pain we bear,
Can we find a friend so faith - ful, Who will all our sor -rows share?
Do thy friends de-spise, for-sake thee? Take it to the Lord in prayer!

All be-cause we do not car - ry Ev - 'ry-thing to God in prayer!
Je - sus knows our ev - 'ry weak-ness—Take it to the Lord in prayer!
In his arms he'll take and shield thee, Thou wilt find a sol - ace there.

JOSEPH SCRIVEN, c. 1855

FEDERAL STREET   HENRY KEMBLE OLIVER, 1832

In moderate time

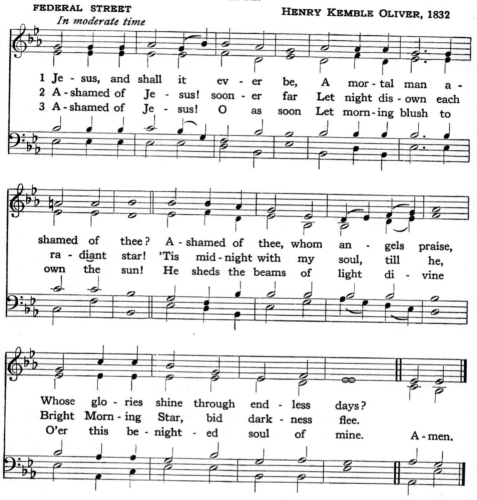

1 Je - sus, and shall it ev - er be, A mor - tal man a -
2 A - shamed of Je - sus! soon - er far Let night dis - own each
3 A - shamed of Je - sus! O as soon Let morn - ing blush to

shamed of thee? A - shamed of thee, whom an - gels praise,
ra - diant star! 'Tis mid - night with my soul, till he,
own the sun! He sheds the beams of light di - vine

Whose glo - ries shine through end - less days?
Bright Morn - ing Star, bid dark - ness flee.
O'er this be - night - ed soul of mine.   A - men.

4 Ashamed of Jesus! that dear friend
On whom my hopes of heav'n depend!
No; when I blush, be this my shame,
That I no more revere his Name.

5 Ashamed of Jesus! empty pride!
I'll boast a Saviour crucified,
And O may this my portion be,
My Saviour not ashamed of me!   Amen.

JOSEPH GRIGG, 1765, *alt.*

Alternative Tune, MELCOMBE, No. 155

424 *First Tune* **General Hymns**
C. M. D.

VOX DILECTI   JOHN B. DYKES, 1868
In moderate time

1 I heard the voice of Je - sus say, "Come un - to me and rest;
2 I heard the voice of Je - sus say, "Be - hold, I free - ly give
3 I heard the voice of Je - sus say, "I am this dark world's light;

Lay down, thou wea - ry one, lay down Thy head up - on my breast."
The liv - ing wa - ter; thirst - y one, Stoop down and drink, and live."
Look un - to me, thy morn shall rise, And all thy day be bright."

I came to Je - sus as I was, Wea - ry, and worn, and sad;
I came to Je - sus, and I drank Of that life - giv - ing stream;
I looked to Je - sus, and I found In him my Star, my Sun;

I found in him a rest - ing-place, And he has made me glad.
My thirst was quenched, my soul re - vived, And now I live in him.
And in that light of life I'll walk Till trav - 'ling days are done.

HORATIUS BONAR, 1846

424 *Second Tune* 𝔊𝔢𝔫𝔢𝔯𝔞𝔩 𝔥𝔶𝔪𝔫𝔰
C. M. D.

THIRD MODE MELODY   THOMAS TALLIS, 1567
With deep feeling

1 I heard the voice of Je - sus say, "Come un - to me and rest;
2 I heard the voice of Je - sus say, "Be - hold, I free - ly give
3 I heard the voice of Je - sus say, "I am this dark world's light;

Lay down, thou wea - ry one, lay down Thy head up - on my breast."
The liv - ing wa - ter; thirst - y one, Stoop down and drink, and live."
Look un - to me, thy morn shall rise, And all thy day be bright."

I came to Je - sus as I was, Wea - ry, and worn, and sad;
I came to Je - sus, and I drank Of that life - giv - ing stream;
I looked to Je - sus, and I found In him my Star, my Sun;

Slightly slower

I found in him a rest - ing - place, And he has made me glad.
My thirst was quench'd, my soul re - vived, And now I live in him.
And in that light of life I'll walk Till trav - 'ling days are done.

HORATIUS BONAR, 1846

ROCHELLE   55. 88. 55   ADAM DRESE, 1698

Quietly

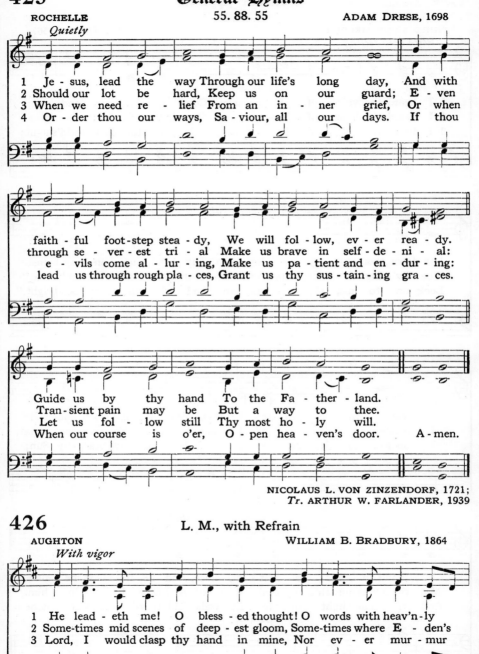

1 Je - sus, lead the way Through our life's long day, And with
2 Should our lot be hard, Keep us on our guard; E - ven
3 When we need re - lief From an in - ner grief, Or when
4 Or - der thou our ways, Sa - viour, all our days. If thou

faith - ful foot-step stea - dy, We will fol - low, ev - er rea - dy.
through se - ver - est tri - al Make us brave in self - de - ni - al:
e - vils come al - lur - ing, Make us pa - tient and en - dur - ing:
lead us through rough pla - ces, Grant us thy sus - tain - ing gra - ces.

Guide us by thy hand To the Fa - ther - land.
Tran - sient pain may be But a way to thee.
Let us fol - low still Thy most ho - ly will.
When our course is o'er, O - pen hea - ven's door. A - men.

NICOLAUS L. VON ZINZENDORF, 1721;
Tr. ARTHUR W. FARLANDER, 1939

426   L. M., with Refrain

AUGHTON   WILLIAM B. BRADBURY, 1864

With vigor

1 He lead - eth me! O bless - ed thought! O words with heav'n - ly
2 Some-times mid scenes of deep - est gloom, Some-times where E - den's
3 Lord, I would clasp thy hand in mine, Nor ev - er mur - mur

General Hymns

com-fort fraught! What-e'er I do, wher-e'er I be, Still 'tis God's
bow-ers bloom, By wa-ters calm, o'er trou-bled sea, Still 'tis his
nor re-pine; Con-tent, what-ev-er lot I see, Since 'tis my

Refrain

hand that lead-eth me.
hand that lead-eth me. He lead-eth me! He lead-eth me!
God that lead-eth me.

By his own hand he lead-eth me! His faith-ful fol-lower

I would be, For by his hand he lead-eth me.

4 And when my task on earth is done,
   When, by thy grace, the victory's won,
   E'en death's cold wave I will not flee,
   Since God through Jordan leadeth me.
                    Refrain

JOSEPH HENRY GILMORE, 1862

SAVANNAH   77. 77   *The Foundery Collection, 1742*

Moderately fast

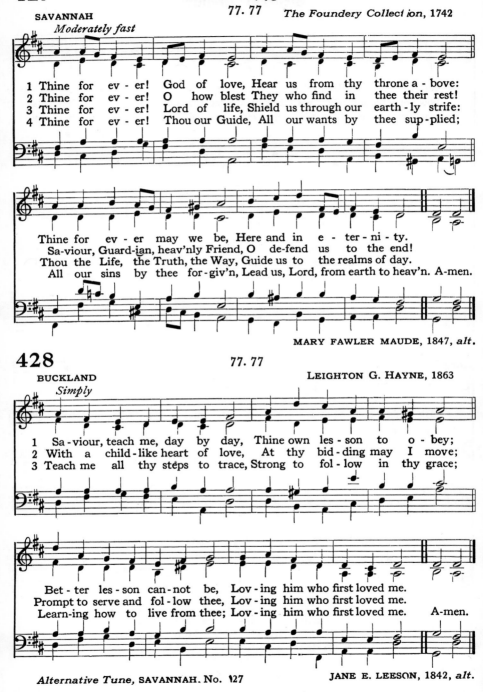

1 Thine for ev - er! God of love, Hear us from thy throne a - bove:
2 Thine for ev - er! O how blest They who find in thee their rest!
3 Thine for ev - er! Lord of life, Shield us through our earth - ly strife:
4 Thine for ev - er! Thou our Guide, All our wants by thee sup - plied;

Thine for ev - er may we be, Here and in e - ter - ni - ty.
Sa - viour, Guard-ian, heav'nly Friend, O de-fend us to the end!
Thou the Life, the Truth, the Way, Guide us to the realms of day.
All our sins by thee for-giv'n, Lead us, Lord, from earth to heav'n. A-men.

MARY FAWLER MAUDE, 1847, *alt.*

428   77. 77

BUCKLAND   LEIGHTON G. HAYNE, 1863

Simply

1 Sa - viour, teach me, day by day, Thine own les - son to o - bey;
2 With a child - like heart of love, At thy bid - ding may I move;
3 Teach me all thy steps to trace, Strong to fol - low in thy grace;

Bet - ter les - son can - not be, Lov - ing him who first loved me.
Prompt to serve and fol - low thee, Lov - ing him who first loved me.
Learn-ing how to live from thee; Lov - ing him who first loved me. A-men.

Alternative Tune, SAVANNAH. No. 127   JANE E. LEESON, 1842, *alt.*

429 *First Tune*
38. 656. 3

CHICHESTER

ALFRED E. WHITEHEAD, 1941

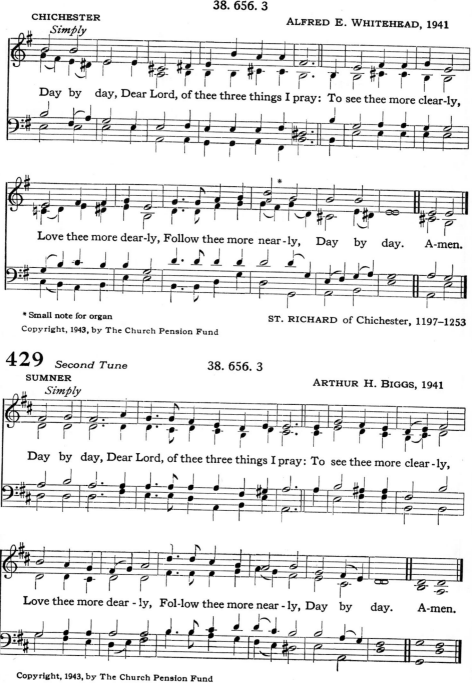

Day by day, Dear Lord, of thee three things I pray: To see thee more clear-ly,

Love thee more dear-ly, Follow thee more near-ly, Day by day. A-men.

*Small note for organ

ST. RICHARD of Chichester, 1197–1253

Copyright, 1943, by The Church Pension Fund

429 *Second Tune*
38. 656. 3

SUMNER

ARTHUR H. BIGGS, 1941

Simply

Day by day, Dear Lord, of thee three things I pray: To see thee more clear-ly,

Love thee more dear-ly, Fol-low thee more near-ly, Day by day. A-men.

Copyright, 1943, by The Church Pension Fund

430 *First Tune* 𝕲𝖊𝖓𝖊𝖗𝖆𝖑 𝕳𝖞𝖒𝖓𝖘

10 4. 10 4. 10 10

SANDON

Quietly

Melody by
CHARLES HENRY PURDAY, 1860

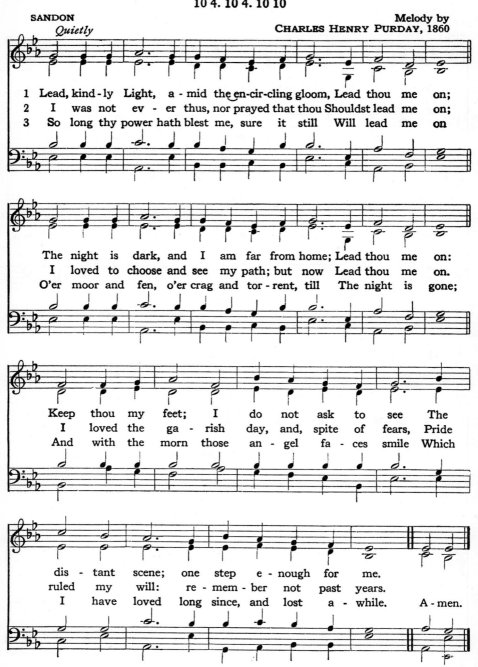

1 Lead, kind-ly Light, a-mid the en-cir-cling gloom, Lead thou me on;
2 I was not ev-er thus, nor prayed that thou Shouldst lead me on;
3 So long thy power hath blest me, sure it still Will lead me on

The night is dark, and I am far from home; Lead thou me on:
I loved to choose and see my path; but now Lead thou me on.
O'er moor and fen, o'er crag and tor-rent, till The night is gone;

Keep thou my feet; I do not ask to see The
I loved the ga-rish day, and, spite of fears, Pride
And with the morn those an-gel fa-ces smile Which

dis - tant scene; one step e - nough for me.
ruled my will: re - mem - ber not past years.
I have loved long since, and lost a - while. A - men.

JOHN HENRY NEWMAN, 1833

10 4. 10 4. 10 10

LUX BENIGNA   JOHN B. DYKES, 1865

In strict time

1 Lead, kind-ly Light, a-mid the en-cir-cling gloom, Lead thou me on;
2 I was not ev-er thus, nor prayed that thou Shouldst lead me on;
3 So long thy power hath blest me, sure it still Will lead me on

The night is dark, and I am far from home; Lead thou me on:
I loved to choose and see my path; but now Lead thou me on.
O'er moor and fen, o'er crag and tor-rent, till The night is gone;

Keep thou my feet; I do not ask to see
I loved the ga-rish day, and, spite of fears,
And with the morn those an-gel fa-ces smile

The dis-tant scene; one step e-nough for me.
Pride ruled my will: re-mem-ber not past years.
Which I have loved long since, and lost a-while. A-men.

JOHN HENRY NEWMAN, 1833

431   𝔊eneral 𝔥ymns

76. 76. D.

NYLAND

Traditional Finnish Melody
har. by DAVID EVANS, 1927

With flowing rhythm

1 In heav'n - ly love a - bi - ding, No change my heart shall fear,
2 Wher - ev - er he may guide me, No want shall turn me back;
3 Green pas - tures are be - fore me, Which yet I have not seen;

And safe is such con - fi - ding, For noth - ing chan-ges here.
My Shep - herd is be - side me, And noth - ing can I lack.
Bright skies will soon be o'er me, Where the dark clouds have been.

The storm may roar with - out me, My heart may low be laid;
His wis - dom ev - er wa - keth, His sight is nev - er dim;
My hope I can - not mea - sure, The path to life is free;

But God is round a - bout me, And can I be dis-mayed?
He knows the way he ta - keth, And I will walk with him.
My Sa - viour has my trea - sure, And he will walk with me.

By permission of the Oxford University Press   ANNA LAETITIA WARING, 1850

Alternative Tune, MEIRIONYDD, No. 598

C. M. D.

LARAMIE   ARNOLD G. H. BODE, 1941

In moderate time

1 I know not where the road will lead I fol - low day by day,
3 And some I love have reached the end, But some with me may stay,
5 The count-less hosts lead on be - fore, I must not fear nor stray;

Or where it ends: I on - ly know I walk the King's high-way.
Their faith and hope still guid - ing me: I walk the King's high-way.
With them, the pil - grims of the faith, I walk the King's high-way.

2 I know not if the way is long, And no one else can say;
4 The way is truth, the way is love, For light and strength I pray,
6 Through light and dark the road leads on Till dawns the end - less day,

But rough or smooth, up hill or down, I walk the King's high - way.
And through the years of life, to God, I walk the King's high - way.
When I shall know why in this life I walk the King's high - way.

EVELYN ATWATER CUMMINS, 1922

433 *First Tune*

SONG 22   10 10. 10 10   ORLANDO GIBBONS, 1623

With movement

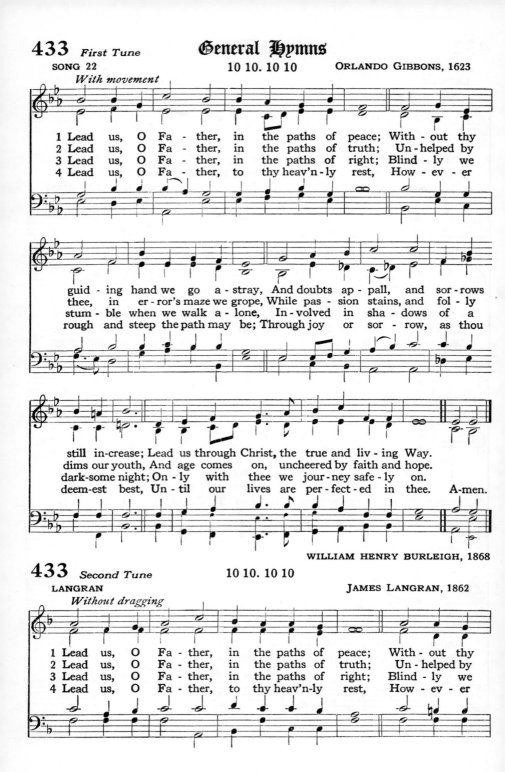

1 Lead us, O Fa - ther, in the paths of peace; With - out thy
2 Lead us, O Fa - ther, in the paths of truth; Un - helped by
3 Lead us, O Fa - ther, in the paths of right; Blind - ly we
4 Lead us, O Fa - ther, to thy heav'n - ly rest, How - ev - er

guid - ing hand we go a - stray, And doubts ap - pall, and sor - rows
thee, in er - ror's maze we grope, While pas - sion stains, and fol - ly
stum - ble when we walk a - lone, In - volved in sha - dows of a
rough and steep the path may be; Through joy or sor - row, as thou

still in - crease; Lead us through Christ, the true and liv - ing Way.
dims our youth, And age comes on, uncheered by faith and hope.
dark - some night; On - ly with thee we jour - ney safe - ly on.
deem - est best, Un - til our lives are per - fect - ed in thee. A - men.

WILLIAM HENRY BURLEIGH, 1868

433 *Second Tune*   10 10. 10 10

LANGRAN   JAMES LANGRAN, 1862

Without dragging

1 Lead us, O Fa - ther, in the paths of peace; With - out thy
2 Lead us, O Fa - ther, in the paths of truth; Un - helped by
3 Lead us, O Fa - ther, in the paths of right; Blind - ly we
4 Lead us, O Fa - ther, to thy heav'n - ly rest, How - ev - er

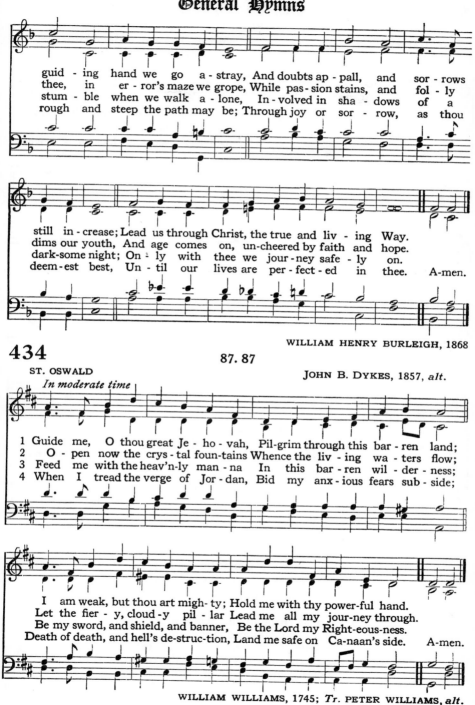

guid - ing hand we go a - stray, And doubts ap - pall, and sor - rows
thee, in er - ror's maze we grope, While pas - sion stains, and fol - ly
stum - ble when we walk a - lone, In - volved in sha - dows of a
rough and steep the path may be; Through joy or sor - row, as thou

still in - crease; Lead us through Christ, the true and liv - ing Way.
dims our youth, And age comes on, un-cheered by faith and hope.
dark-some night; On - ly with thee we jour-ney safe - ly on.
deem - est best, Un - til our lives are per - fect - ed in thee. A-men.

WILLIAM HENRY BURLEIGH, 1868

434

87. 87

ST. OSWALD

JOHN B. DYKES, 1857, *alt.*

In moderate time

1 Guide me, O thou great Je - ho - vah, Pil-grim through this bar - ren land;
2 O - pen now the crys - tal foun-tains Whence the liv - ing wa - ters flow;
3 Feed me with the heav'n-ly man - na In this bar - ren wil - der - ness;
4 When I tread the verge of Jor - dan, Bid my anx - ious fears sub - side;

I am weak, but thou art migh - ty; Hold me with thy power-ful hand.
Let the fier - y, cloud - y pil - lar Lead me all my jour-ney through.
Be my sword, and shield, and banner, Be the Lord my Right-eous-ness.
Death of death, and hell's de-struc - tion, Land me safe on Ca-naan's side. A-men.

WILLIAM WILLIAMS, 1745; *Tr.* PETER WILLIAMS, *alt.*

435 *First Tune*

86. 886

HERMANN

Melody, NIKOLAUS HERMANN, 1554,
harmonized by W. D., 1940

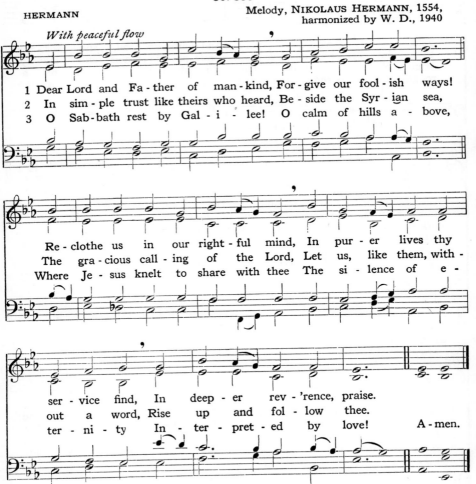

With peaceful flow

1 Dear Lord and Fa - ther of man - kind, For - give our fool - ish ways!
2 In sim - ple trust like theirs who heard, Be - side the Syr - ian sea,
3 O Sab-bath rest by Gal - i - lee! O calm of hills a - bove,

Re - clothe us in our right - ful mind, In pur - er lives thy
The gra - cious call - ing of the Lord, Let us, like them, with -
Where Je - sus knelt to share with thee The si - lence of e -

ser - vice find, In deep - er rev - 'rence, praise.
out a word, Rise up and fol - low thee.
ter - ni - ty In - ter - pret - ed by love! A - men.

4 Drop thy still dews of quietness,
  Till all our strivings cease:
Take from our souls the strain and stress,
And let our ordered lives confess
  The beauty of thy peace.

5 Breathe through the heats of our desire
  Thy coolness and thy balm;
Let sense be dumb, let flesh retire;
Speak through the earthquake, wind, and fire,
  O still, small voice of calm. Amen.

JOHN GREENLEAF WHITTIER, 1872

FREDERICK C. MAKER, 1887

REST

Quietly

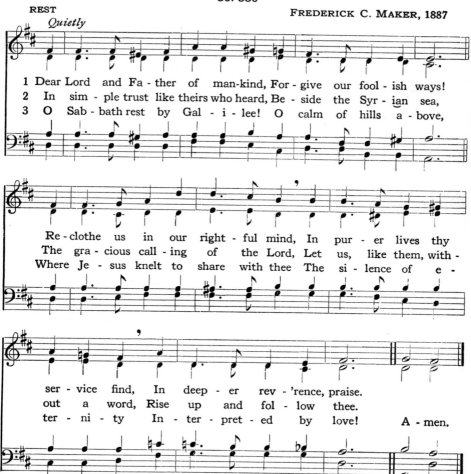

1 Dear Lord and Fa - ther of man-kind, For - give our fool - ish ways!
2 In sim - ple trust like theirs who heard, Be - side the Syr - ian sea,
3 O Sab - bath rest by Gal - i - lee! O calm of hills a - bove,

Re - clothe us in our right - ful mind, In pur - er lives thy
The gra - cious call - ing of the Lord, Let us, like them, with -
Where Je - sus knelt to share with thee The si - lence of e -

ser - vice find, In deep - er rev - 'rence, praise.
out a word, Rise up and fol - low thee.
ter - ni - ty In - ter - pret - ed by love!   A - men.

4 Drop thy still dews of quietness,
    Till all our strivings cease:
Take from our souls the strain and stress,
And let our ordered lives confess
    The beauty of thy peace.

5 Breathe through the heats of our desire
    Thy coolness and thy balm;
Let sense be dumb, let flesh retire;
Speak through the earthquake, wind, and fire,
    O still, small voice of calm.   Amen.

JOHN GREENLEAF WHITTIER, 1872

SONG 46   ORLANDO GIBBONS, 1623

Not fast

1 Peace, per - fect peace, in this dark world of sin?
2 Peace, per - fect peace, by throng - ing du - ties pressed?
3 Peace, per - fect peace, with sor - rows surg - ing round?

The blood of Je - sus whis - pers peace with - in.
To do the will of Je - sus, this is rest.
On Je - sus' bo - som naught but calm is found.

436 *Second Tune*   10. 10

PAX TECUM   CHARLES VINCENT and
                     G. T. CALDBECK, 1877

Do not drag

1 Peace, per - fect peace, in this dark world of sin?
2 Peace, per - fect peace, by throng - ing du - ties pressed?
3 Peace, per - fect peace, with sor - rows surg - ing round?

The blood of Je - sus whis - pers peace with - in.
To do the will of Je - sus, this is rest.
On Je - sus' bo - som naught but calm is found.

General Hymns

4 Peace, perfect peace, with loved ones far away?
In Jesus' keeping we are safe, and they.

5 Peace, perfect peace, our future all unknown?
Jesus we know, and he is on the throne.

6 Peace, perfect peace, death shadowing us and ours?
Jesus has vanquished death and all its powers.

7 It is enough: earth's struggles soon shall cease,
And Jesus call us to heav'n's perfect peace.

EDWARD HENRY BICKERSTETH, 1875

437

C. M.

GEORGETOWN

DAVID McK. WILLIAMS, 1941

In unison, with movement

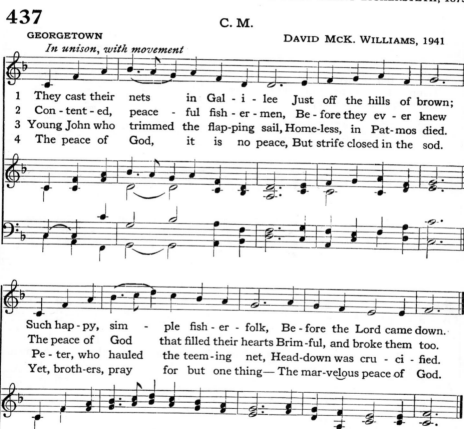

1 They cast their nets in Gal-i-lee Just off the hills of brown;
2 Con-tent-ed, peace-ful fish-er-men, Be-fore they ev-er knew
3 Young John who trimmed the flap-ping sail, Home-less, in Pat-mos died.
4 The peace of God, it is no peace, But strife closed in the sod.

Such hap-py, sim-ple fish-er-folk, Be-fore the Lord came down.
The peace of God that filled their hearts Brim-ful, and broke them too.
Pe-ter, who hauled the teem-ing net, Head-down was cru-ci-fied.
Yet, broth-ers, pray for but one thing— The mar-vel-ous peace of God.

WILLIAM ALEXANDER PERCY, 1924, *alt.*

NEED

ROBERT LOWRY, 1872

Without dragging

1 I need thee ev - 'ry hour, Most gra - cious Lord;
2 I need thee ev - 'ry hour; Stay thou near by;
3 I need thee ev - 'ry hour, In joy or pain;

No ten - der voice like thine Can peace af - ford.
Temp - ta - tions lose their power When thou art nigh.
Come quick - ly and a - bide, Or life is vain.

Refrain

I need thee, O I need thee, Ev - 'ry hour I need thee;

O bless me now, my Sa - viour, I come to thee. A - men.

4 I need thee every hour;
    Teach me thy will;
    And thy rich promises
    In me fulfil.   *Refrain*
            Amen.

ANNIE SHERWOOD HAWKS, 1872;
Refrain, ROBERT LOWRY, 1872

PARRATT   64. 64   WALTER PARRATT, 1904

Quietly

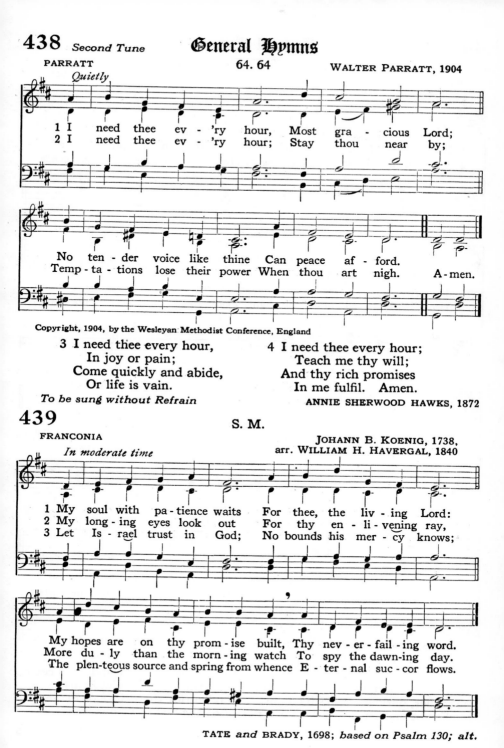

1 I need thee ev - 'ry hour, Most gra - cious Lord;
2 I need thee ev - 'ry hour; Stay thou near by;

No ten - der voice like thine Can peace af - ford.
Temp - ta - tions lose their power When thou art nigh. A - men.

Copyright, 1904, by the Wesleyan Methodist Conference, England

3 I need thee every hour,
   In joy or pain;
   Come quickly and abide,
     Or life is vain.

4 I need thee every hour;
   Teach me thy will;
   And thy rich promises
     In me fulfil. Amen.

To be sung without Refrain   ANNIE SHERWOOD HAWKS, 1872

439   S. M.

FRANCONIA   JOHANN B. KOENIG, 1738,
                arr. WILLIAM H. HAVERGAL, 1840

In moderate time

1 My soul with pa - tience waits For thee, the liv - ing Lord:
2 My long - ing eyes look out For thy en - li - vening ray,
3 Let Is - rael trust in God; No bounds his mer - cy knows;

My hopes are on thy prom - ise built, Thy nev - er - fail - ing word.
More du - ly than the morn - ing watch To spy the dawn-ing day.
The plen-teous source and spring from whence E - ter - nal suc - cor flows.

TATE and BRADY, 1698; *based on Psalm 130; alt.*

440 *First Tune*   𝔊𝔢𝔫𝔢𝔯𝔞𝔩 𝔥𝔶𝔪𝔫𝔰
77. 77. D.

WATCHMAN   LOWELL MASON, 1830
With movement

1 Watch-man, tell us of the night, What its signs of prom-ise are.
2 Watch-man, tell us of the night; High - er yet that star as - cends.

Trav - 'ler, o'er yon moun-tain's height, See that glo - ry - beam-ing star.
Trav - 'ler, bless - ed - ness and light, Peace and truth its course por - tends.

Watch - man, does its beau - teous ray Aught of joy or hope fore - tell?
Watch - man, will its beams a - lone Gild the spot that gave them birth?

Trav - 'ler, yes; it brings the day, Prom - ised day of Is - ra - el.
Trav - 'ler, a - ges are its own; See, it bursts o'er all the earth.

3 Watchman, tell us of the night,   Watchman, let thy wand'rings cease;
  For the morning seems to dawn.   Hie thee to thy quiet home.
Trav'ler, darkness takes its flight,   Trav'ler, lo! the Prince of Peace,
  Doubt and terror are withdrawn.   Lo! the Son of God is come!

JOHN BOWRING, 1825

General Hymns

Alternative unison setting, St. 3

Har. by T. TERTIUS NOBLE, 1917

3 Watch-man, tell us of the night, For the morn - ing seems to dawn.

Trav - 'ler, dark-ness takes its flight, Doubt and ter - ror are with-drawn.

Watch-man, let thy wand'rings cease; Hie thee to thy qui - et home.

Trav - 'ler, lo! the Prince of Peace, Lo! the Son of God is come!

77. 77. D.

ABERYSTWYTH   JOSEPH PARRY, 1879

With movement

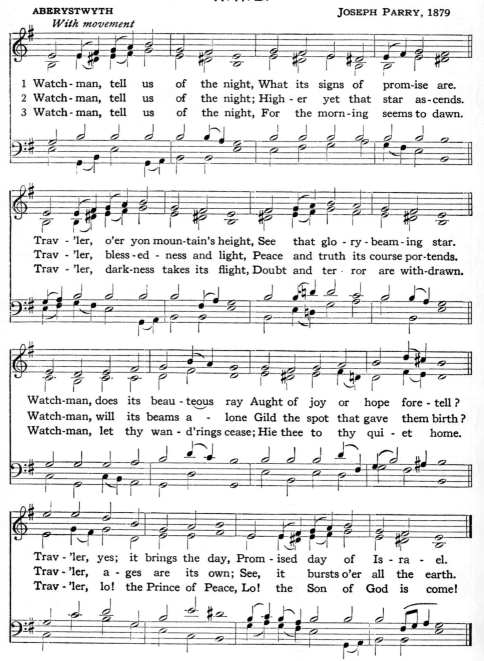

1 Watch-man, tell us of the night, What its signs of prom-ise are.
2 Watch-man, tell us of the night; High-er yet that star as-cends.
3 Watch-man, tell us of the night, For the morn-ing seems to dawn.

Trav-'ler, o'er yon moun-tain's height, See that glo-ry-beam-ing star.
Trav-'ler, bless-ed-ness and light, Peace and truth its course por-tends.
Trav-'ler, dark-ness takes its flight, Doubt and ter-ror are with-drawn.

Watch-man, does its beau-teous ray Aught of joy or hope fore-tell?
Watch-man, will its beams a-lone Gild the spot that gave them birth?
Watch-man, let thy wan-d'rings cease; Hie thee to thy qui-et home.

Trav-'ler, yes; it brings the day, Prom-ised day of Is-ra-el.
Trav-'ler, a-ges are its own; See, it bursts o'er all the earth.
Trav-'ler, lo! the Prince of Peace, Lo! the Son of God is come!

JOHN BOWRING, 1825

WILTSHIRE

GEORGE SMART, *c.* 1795

With flowing rhythm

1 I know not what the fu - ture hath Of
2 And if my heart and flesh are weak To
3 No of - f'ring of my own I have, Nor

mar - vel or sur - prise, As - sured a - lone that
bear an un - tried pain, The bruis - ed reed he
works my faith to prove; I can but give the

life and death God's mer - cy un - der - lies.
will not break, But strength - en and sus - tain.
gifts he gave, And plead his love for love.

4 And so beside the silent sea
    I wait the muffled oar;
  No harm from him can come to me
    On ocean or on shore.

5 I know not where his islands lift
    Their fronded palms in air;
  I only know I cannot drift
    Beyond his love and care.

JOHN GREENLEAF WHITTIER, 1867

BANGOR

WILLIAM TANS'UR, 1734

Moderately slow

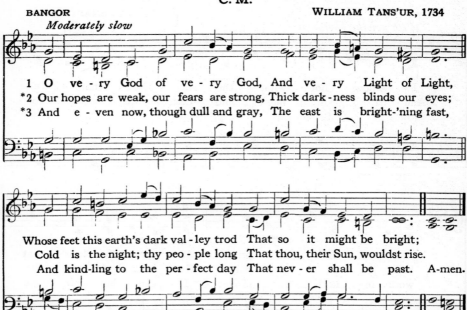

1 O ve-ry God of ve-ry God, And ve-ry Light of Light,
*2 Our hopes are weak, our fears are strong, Thick dark-ness blinds our eyes;
*3 And e-ven now, though dull and gray, The east is bright-'ning fast,

Whose feet this earth's dark val-ley trod That so it might be bright;
Cold is the night; thy peo-ple long That thou, their Sun, wouldst rise.
And kind-ling to the per-fect day That nev-er shall be past. A-men.

4 O guide us till our path is done,
And we have reached the shore
Where thou, our everlasting Sun,
Art shining evermore!

5 We wait in faith, and turn our face
To where the daylight springs,
Till thou shalt come our gloom to chase,
With healing in thy wings. Amen.

JOHN MASON NEALE, 1846

443

76. 76. D.

LIGHT

The Christian Lyre, 1832,
harmonized by W. D., 1941

With breadth

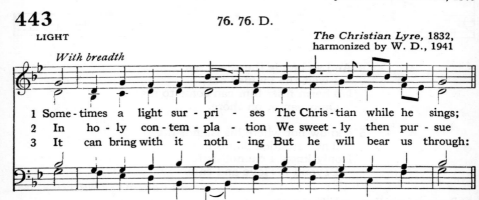

1 Some-times a light sur-pri-ses The Chris-tian while he sings;
2 In ho-ly con-tem-pla-tion We sweet-ly then pur-sue
3 It can bring with it noth-ing But he will bear us through:

General Hymns

It is the Lord who ri - ses With heal - ing in his wings:
The theme of God's sal - va - tion, And find it ev - er new;
Who gives the li - lies cloth - ing Will clothe his peo - ple, too:

When com-forts are de - clin - ing, He grants the soul a - gain
Set free from pres - ent sor - row, We cheer - ful - ly can say,
Be - neath the spread-ing hea - vens No crea-ture but is fed;

In unison

A sea - son of clear shin - ing, To cheer it af - ter rain.
Let the un-known to - mor - row Bring with it what it may.
And he who feeds the ra - vens Will give his chil - dren bread.

4 Though vine nor fig-tree neither
　　Their wonted fruit should bear,
Though all the fields should wither,
　　Nor flocks nor herds be there;
Yet, God the same abiding,
　　His praise shall tune my voice;
For, while in him confiding,
　　I cannot but rejoice.

Alternative Tune, MEIRIONYDD, No. 598　　　　WILLIAM COWPER, 1779

IRISH C. M. Melody pub. Dublin, 1749

In moderate time

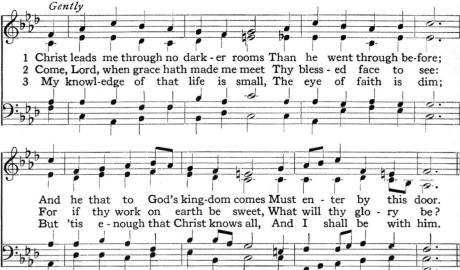

1 O thou in all thy might so far, In all thy love so near;
2 What heart can com-pre-hend thy Name, Or search-ing find thee out,

Be - yond the range of sun and star, And yet be - side us here:
Who art with - in a quick - 'ning flame, A pres - ence round a - bout?

3 Yet though I know thee but in part,
  I ask not, Lord, for more:
Enough for me to know thou art;
  To love thee, and adore.

   Alternative Tune, ST. PETER, No. 455

4 And dearer than all things I know
  Is childlike faith to me,
That makes the darkest way I go
  An open path to thee.

FREDERICK LUCIAN HOSMER, 1876

445 C. M.

STURGES ERNEST J. PARSONS, 1941

Gently

1 Christ leads me through no dark - er rooms Than he went through be-fore;
2 Come, Lord, when grace hath made me meet Thy bless - ed face to see:
3 My knowl-edge of that life is small, The eye of faith is dim;

And he that to God's king-dom comes Must en - ter by this door.
For if thy work on earth be sweet, What will thy glo - ry be?
But 'tis e - nough that Christ knows all, And I shall be with him.

Copyright, 1943, by The Church Pension Fund RICHARD BAXTER, 1681

76. 76. D.

PASSION CHORALE

HANS LEO HASSLER, 1601,
adapted and har. by J. S. BACH, 1729

Solemnly, but not too slow; may be sung in unison

1 Com - mit thou all that grieves thee And fills thy heart with care
2 O trust the Lord then whol - ly, If thou would'st be se - cure;

To him whose faith - ful mer - cy The skies a - bove de - clare,
His work must thou con - sid - er For thy work to en - dure.

Who gives the winds their cours - es, Who points the clouds their way;
What prof - it doth it bring thee To pine in grief and care?

'Tis he will guide thy foot - steps And be thy staff and stay.
God on - ly sends his bless - ing In an - swer to thy prayer.

3 Thy lasting truth and mercy,
   O Father, see aright
The needs of all thy children,
   Their anguish or delight:
What loving wisdom chooseth,
   Redeeming might will do,
And bring to sure fulfilment
   Thy counsel good and true.

4 Hope on, then, broken spirit;
   Hope on, be not afraid:
Fear not the griefs that plague thee
   And keep thy heart dismayed:
Thy God, in his great mercy,
   Will save thee, hold thee fast,
And in his own time grant thee
   The sun of joy at last.

PAULUS GERHARDT, 1646;
Tr. ARTHUR W. FARLANDER *and* WINFRED DOUGLAS, 1939

C. M.

LYSTRA
CHARLES WESLEY, Jr., 1757–1834

Quietly

1 Fa - ther, what-e'er of earth-ly bliss Thy sov-'reign will de - nies,
2 Give me a calm and thank-ful heart, From ev - 'ry mur-mur free;

Ac - cept - ed at thy throne of grace Let this pe - ti - tion rise:
The bless-ings of thy grace im - part, And make me live to thee.

3 Let the firm hope that thou art mine
   My path of life attend:
   Thy presence through my journey shine,
   And crown my journey's end. Amen.

A - men.

ANNE STEELE, 1760, *alt.*

Alternative Tune, NAOMI, No. 170

448 TRUST
87. 87
FELIX MENDELSSOHN, 1840

With dignity

1 Call Je - ho - vah thy sal - va - tion, Rest be-neath the Al-migh-ty's shade;
2 There no tu - mult can a - larm thee; Thou shalt dread no hid - den snare;
3 God shall charge his an - gel le - gions Watch and ward o'er thee to keep,

In his se - cret hab - i - ta - tion Dwell, and nev - er be dis-mayed.
Guile nor vi - o - lence can harm thee, In e - ter - nal safe-guard there.
Though thou walk through hos - tile re-gions, Though in des - ert wilds thou sleep.

General Hymns

4 Since, with pure and firm affection,
  Thou on God hast set thy love,
  With the wings of his protection,
  He will shield thee from above.

5 Thou shalt call on him in trouble,
  He will hearken, he will save;
  Here for grief reward thee double,
  Crown with life beyond the grave.

JAMES MONTGOMERY, 1822; *based on Psalm 91*

449 664. 6664

OLIVET

Without dragging

LOWELL MASON, 1833

1 My faith looks up to thee, Thou Lamb of Cal - va - ry,
2 May thy rich grace im - part Strength to my faint - ing heart,
3 While life's dark maze I tread, And griefs a - round me spread,

Sa - viour di - vine! Now hear me while I pray, Take all my
My zeal in - spire; As thou hast died for me, O may my
Be thou my guide; Bid dark - ness turn to day; Wipe sor - row's

guilt a - way; O let me from this day Be whol - ly thine.
love to thee Pure, warm, and change-less be, A liv - ing fire.
tears a - way; Nor let me ev - er stray From thee a - side. A-men.

*4 When ends life's transient dream,
  When death's cold, sullen stream
      Shall o'er me roll;
  Blest Saviour, then in love,
  Fear and distrust remove;
  O bear me safe above,
      A ransomed soul. Amen.

RAY PALMER, 1830

MARTYRDOM
C. M.
HUGH WILSON, c. 1800,
har. by ROBERT A. SMITH, 1825

With dignity

1 As pants the hart for cool - ing streams When heat - ed in the chase,
2 For thee, my God, the liv - ing God, My thirst - y soul doth pine:
3 Why rest - less, why cast down, my soul? Hope still, and thou shalt sing
4 To Fa - ther, Son, and Ho - ly Ghost, The God whom we a - dore,

So longs my soul, O God, for thee, And thy re - fresh - ing grace.
O when shall I be - hold thy face, Thou Ma - jes - ty di - vine?
The praise of him who is thy God, Thy health's e - ter - nal spring.
Be glo - ry, as it was, is now, And shall be ev - er - more. A-men.

TATE *and* BRADY, 1696; *based on Psalm 42*

451
SONG 13
77. 77
ORLANDO GIBBONS, 1623

Quietly

1 Lord, for ev - er at thy side Let my place and por - tion be:
2 Meek - ly may my soul re - ceive All thy Spi - rit hath re - vealed;

Strip me of the robe of pride, Clothe me with hu - mil - i - ty.
Thou hast spo - ken; I be - lieve, Though the or - a - cle be sealed.

3 Humble as a little child,
   Weanèd from the mother's breast,
By no subtleties beguiled,
   On thy faithful word I rest.

4 Israel, now and evermore
   In the Lord Jehovah trust;
Him, in all his ways, adore,
   Wise, and wonderful, and just.

JAMES MONTGOMERY, 1819; *based on Psalm 131*

General Hymns
S. M. D.

CHALVEY
In moderate time

LEIGHTON G. HAYNE, 1868

1 Je - sus, my strength, my hope, On thee I cast my care;
2 Give me a true re - gard, A sin - gle, stea - dy aim,

With hum - ble con - fi - dence look up, And know thou hear'st my prayer.
Un - moved by threat-'ning or re - ward, To thee and thy great Name;

Give me on thee to wait, Till I can all things do;
A jeal - ous, just con - cern For thine im - mor - tal praise;

On thee, al - migh - ty to cre - ate, Al - migh - ty to re - new.
A pure de - sire that all may learn And glo - ri - fy thy grace.

3 I rest upon thy word;
   The promise is for me;
 My succor and salvation, Lord,
   Shall surely come from thee:
 But let me still abide,
   Nor from my hope remove,
 Till thou my patient spirit guide
   Into thy perfect love. Amen.

CHARLES WESLEY, 1742

A-men.

665. 665. 786

JESUS, ALL MY GLADNESS

JOHANN CRUEGER, 1653,
har. by J. S. BACH, 1723

Slow and with dignity; may be sung in unison

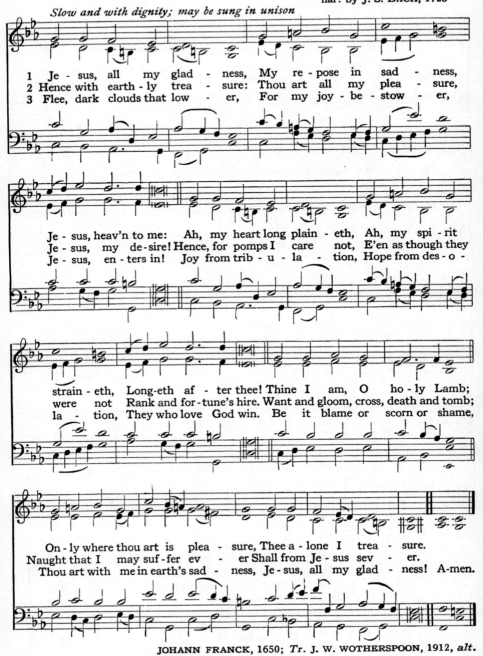

1 Je - sus, all my glad - ness, My re - pose in sad - ness,
2 Hence with earth - ly trea - sure: Thou art all my plea - sure,
3 Flee, dark clouds that low - er, For my joy - be - stow - er,

Je - sus, heav'n to me: Ah, my heart long plain - eth, Ah, my spi - rit
Je - sus, my de - sire! Hence, for pomps I care not, E'en as though they
Je - sus, en - ters in! Joy from trib - u - la - tion, Hope from des - o -

strain - eth, Long - eth af - ter thee! Thine I am, O ho - ly Lamb;
were not Rank and for - tune's hire. Want and gloom, cross, death and tomb;
la - tion, They who love God win. Be it blame or scorn or shame,

On - ly where thou art is plea - sure, Thee a - lone I trea - sure.
Naught that I may suf - fer ev - er Shall from Je - sus sev - er.
Thou art with me in earth's sad - ness, Je - sus, all my glad - ness! A - men.

JOHANN FRANCK, 1650; *Tr.* J. W. WOTHERSPOON, 1912, *alt.*

87. 87. D.

ST. CHAD
In moderate time

RICHARD REDHEAD, 1820–1901

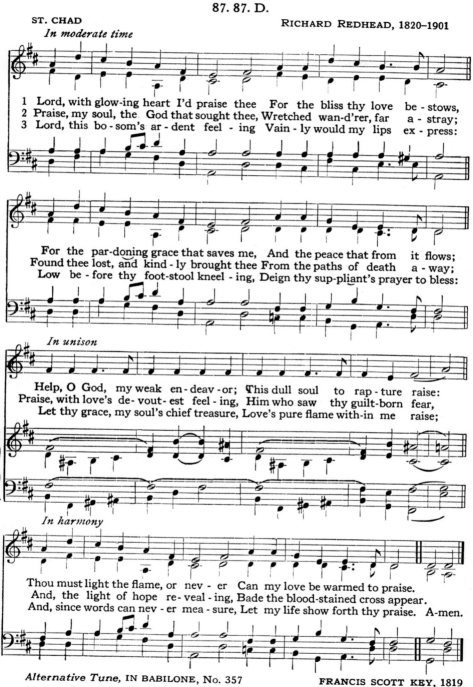

1 Lord, with glow-ing heart I'd praise thee For the bliss thy love be - stows,
2 Praise, my soul, the God that sought thee, Wretched wan-d'rer, far a - stray;
3 Lord, this bo - som's ar - dent feel - ing Vain - ly would my lips ex - press:

For the par-don-ing grace that saves me, And the peace that from it flows;
Found thee lost, and kind - ly brought thee From the paths of death a - way;
Low be - fore thy foot-stool kneel - ing, Deign thy sup-pliant's prayer to bless:

In unison

Help, O God, my weak en - deav - or; This dull soul to rap - ture raise:
Praise, with love's de - vout - est feel - ing, Him who saw thy guilt-born fear,
Let thy grace, my soul's chief treasure, Love's pure flame with-in me raise;

In harmony

Thou must light the flame, or nev - er Can my love be warmed to praise.
And, the light of hope re - veal - ing, Bade the blood-stained cross appear.
And, since words can nev - er mea - sure, Let my life show forth thy praise. A-men.

Alternative Tune, IN BABILONE, No. 357   FRANCIS SCOTT KEY, 1819

C. M.

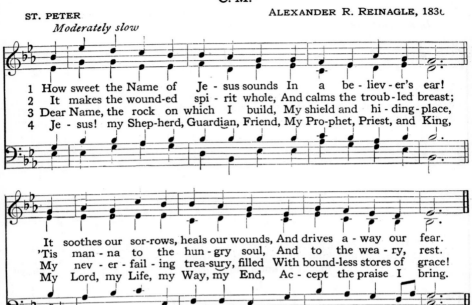

ST. PETER

ALEXANDER R. REINAGLE, 183c

Moderately slow

1 How sweet the Name of Je - sus sounds In a be - liev - er's ear!
2 It makes the wound-ed spi - rit whole, And calms the troub-led breast;
3 Dear Name, the rock on which I build, My shield and hi - ding-place,
4 Je - sus! my Shep-herd, Guardian, Friend, My Pro-phet, Priest, and King,

It soothes our sor-rows, heals our wounds, And drives a - way our fear.
'Tis man - na to the hun-gry soul, And to the wea - ry, rest.
My nev - er - fail - ing trea-sury, filled With bound-less stores of grace!
My Lord, my Life, my Way, my End, Ac - cept the praise I bring.

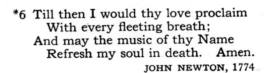

A-men.

*5 Weak is the effort of my heart,
   And cold my warmest thought;
   But when I see thee as thou art,
   I'll praise thee as I ought.

*6 Till then I would thy love proclaim
   With every fleeting breath;
   And may the music of thy Name
   Refresh my soul in death.   Amen.

JOHN NEWTON, 1774

456 C. M.

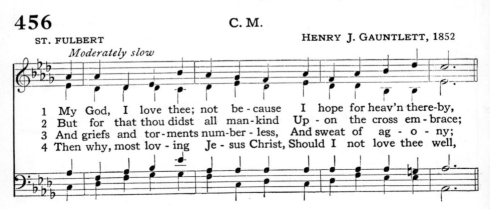

ST. FULBERT

HENRY J. GAUNTLETT, 1852

Moderately slow

1 My God, I love thee; not be - cause I hope for heav'n there-by,
2 But for that thou didst all man-kind Up - on the cross em-brace;
3 And griefs and tor-ments num-ber - less, And sweat of ag - o - ny;
4 Then why, most lov - ing Je - sus Christ, Should I not love thee well,

General Hymns

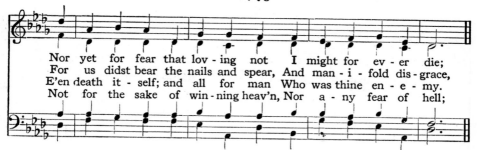

Nor yet for fear that lov-ing not I might for ev-er die;
For us didst bear the nails and spear, And man-i-fold dis-grace,
E'en death it-self; and all for man Who was thine en-e-my.
Not for the sake of win-ning heav'n, Nor a-ny fear of hell;

5 Not with the hope of gaining aught,
Not seeking a reward;
But as thyself hast lovèd me,
O ever-loving Lord!

*6 E'en so I love thee, and will love,
And in thy praise will sing,
Solely because thou art my God
And my eternal King. Amen.

A-men.

Spanish, 17th cent.; Tr. EDWARD CASWALL, 1849, *alt.*
Version from Enlarged Songs of Praise, by permission of the Oxford University Press

Alternative Tune, ST. BERNARD, No. 413

457
66. 66

MOSELEY
HENRY SMART, 1881
Quietly

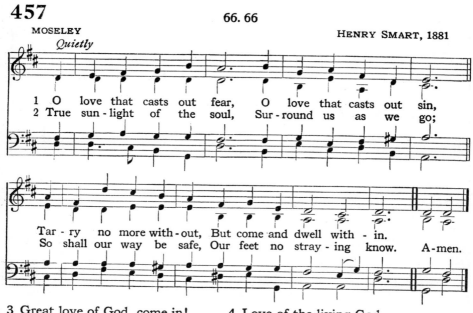

1 O love that casts out fear, O love that casts out sin,
2 True sun-light of the soul, Sur-round us as we go;

Tar-ry no more with-out, But come and dwell with-in.
So shall our way be safe, Our feet no stray-ing know. A-men.

3 Great love of God, come in!
Wellspring of heav'nly peace;
Thou Living Water, come!
Spring up, and never cease.

4 Love of the living God,
Of Father and of Son;
Love of the Holy Ghost,
Fill thou each needy one. Amen.

HORATIUS BONAR, 1861

CONSECRATION
88. 886
ANNA J. MORSE, 1941

With quiet flow

1 O Love that wilt not let me go, I rest my wea - ry
2 O Light that fol - lowest all my way, I yield my flick - 'ring
3 O Joy that seek - est me through pain, I can - not close my
4 O Cross that lift - est up my head, I dare not ask to

soul in thee; I give thee back the life I owe, That
torch to thee; My heart re - stores its bor - rowed ray, That
heart to thee; I trace the rain - bow through the rain, And
fly from thee; I lay in dust life's glo - ry dead, And

in thine o - cean depths its flow May rich - er, full - er be.
in thy sun - shine's blaze its day May bright - er, fair - er be.
feel the prom - ise is not vain That morn shall tear - less be.
from the ground there blossoms red Life that shall end - less be. A-men.

GEORGE MATHESON, 1882

458 *Second Tune* 88. 886

ST. MARGARET
ALBERT LISTER PEACE, 1885

In moderate time

1 O Love that wilt not let me go, I rest my wea - ry
2 O Light that fol - lowest all my way, I yield my flick - 'ring
3 O Joy that seek - est me through pain, I can - not close my
4 O Cross that lift - est up my head, I dare not ask to

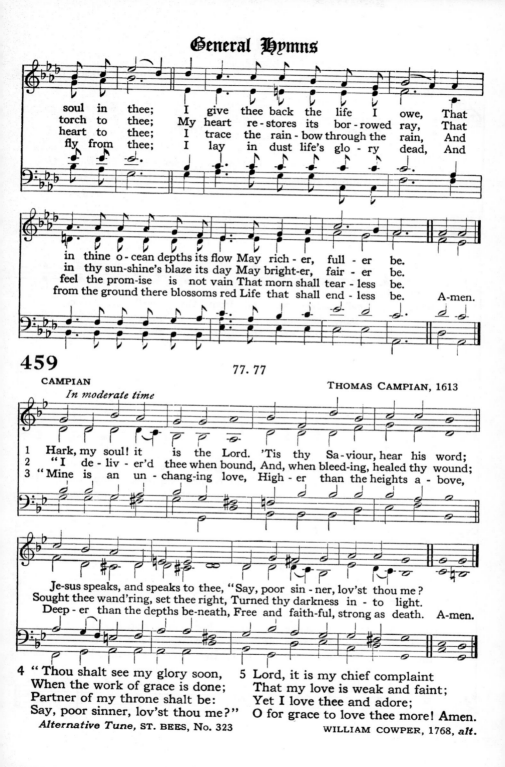

soul in thee; I give thee back the life I owe, That
torch to thee; My heart re-stores its bor-rowed ray, That
heart to thee; I trace the rain-bow through the rain, And
fly from thee; I lay in dust life's glo-ry dead, And

in thine o-cean depths its flow May rich-er, full-er be.
in thy sun-shine's blaze its day May bright-er, fair-er be.
feel the prom-ise is not vain That morn shall tear-less be.
from the ground there blossoms red Life that shall end-less be. A-men.

459 77. 77

CAMPIAN   THOMAS CAMPIAN, 1613

In moderate time

1 Hark, my soul! it   is the Lord. 'Tis thy Sa-viour, hear his word;
2 "I de-liv-er'd thee when bound, And, when bleed-ing, healed thy wound;
3 "Mine is an un-chang-ing love, High-er than the heights a-bove,

Je-sus speaks, and speaks to thee, "Say, poor sin-ner, lov'st thou me?
Sought thee wand'ring, set thee right, Turned thy darkness in-to light.
Deep-er than the depths be-neath, Free and faith-ful, strong as death. A-men.

4 " Thou shalt see my glory soon,   5 Lord, it is my chief complaint
   When the work of grace is done;   That my love is weak and faint;
   Partner of my throne shalt be: Yet I love thee and adore;
   Say, poor sinner, lov'st thou me?"   O for grace to love thee more! Amen.
Alternative Tune, ST. BEES, No. 323   WILLIAM COWPER, 1768, alt.

88. 88. 88

ST. CHRYSOSTOM   JOSEPH BARNBY, 1871

Not slow

1 Je - sus, my Lord, my God, my all, Hear me, blest Sa - viour,
2 Je - sus, too late I thee have sought; How can I love thee
3 Je - sus, what didst thou find in me That thou hast dealt so

when I call; Hear me, and from thy dwell - ing place Pour
as I ought, And how ex - tol thy match - less fame, The
lov - ing - ly? How great the joy that thou hast brought! O

down the rich - es of thy grace. Je - sus, my Lord, I
glo - rious beau - ty of thy Name? Je - sus, my Lord, I
far ex - ceed - ing hope or thought! Je - sus, my Lord, I

thee a - dore; O make me love thee more and more!
thee a - dore; O make me love thee more and more!
thee a - dore; O make me love thee more and more! A - men.

* Parts transposed

4 Jesus, of thee shall be my song;
　To thee my heart and soul belong:
　All that I am or have is thine;
　And thou, my Saviour, thou art mine.
　　Jesus, my Lord, I thee adore;
　　O make me love thee more and more! Amen.

HENRY COLLINS, 1854, *alt.*

461

64. 64. 66. 44

PROPIOR DEO

ARTHUR SEYMOUR SULLIVAN, 1872

In moderate time

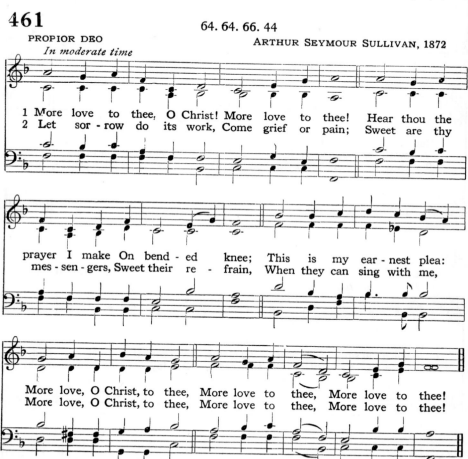

1 More love to thee, O Christ! More love to thee! Hear thou the
2 Let sor - row do its work, Come grief or pain; Sweet are thy

prayer I make On bend - ed knee; This is my ear - nest plea:
mes - sen - gers, Sweet their re - frain, When they can sing with me,

More love, O Christ, to thee, More love to thee, More love to thee!
More love, O Christ, to thee, More love to thee, More love to thee!

3 Then shall my latest breath
　Whisper thy praise;
This be the parting cry
　My heart shall raise,
This still its prayer shall be:
More love, O Christ, to thee,
　‖More love to thee!‖ Amen.

ELIZABETH PRENTISS, 1869

A - men.

462 *First Tune* — **General Hymns** — C. M.

WINDSOR

With dignity

M. WILLIAM DAMON'S
Booke of Musicke, 1591

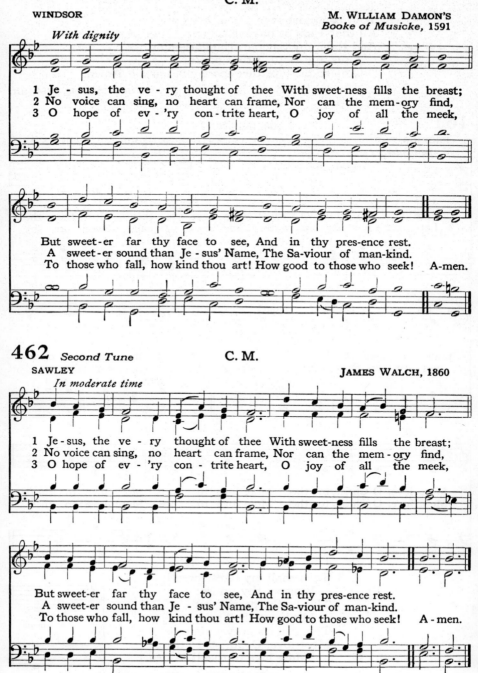

1 Je - sus, the ve - ry thought of thee With sweet-ness fills the breast;
2 No voice can sing, no heart can frame, Nor can the mem - ory find,
3 O hope of ev - 'ry con - trite heart, O joy of all the meek,

But sweet - er far thy face to see, And in thy pres - ence rest.
A sweet - er sound than Je - sus' Name, The Sa - viour of man - kind.
To those who fall, how kind thou art! How good to those who seek! A - men.

462 *Second Tune* — C. M.

SAWLEY

In moderate time

JAMES WALCH, 1860

1 Je - sus, the ve - ry thought of thee With sweet-ness fills the breast;
2 No voice can sing, no heart can frame, Nor can the mem - ory find,
3 O hope of ev - 'ry con - trite heart, O joy of all the meek,

But sweet-er far thy face to see, And in thy pres-ence rest.
A sweet-er sound than Je - sus' Name, The Sa-viour of man-kind.
To those who fall, how kind thou art! How good to those who seek! A - men.

General Hymns

Alternative Tune, ST. AGNES, No. 213

4 But what to those who find? Ah, this
  Nor tongue nor pen can show;
  The love of Jesus, what it is,
  None but who love him know.

5 Jesus, our only joy be thou,
  As thou our prize wilt be;
  In thee be all our glory now,
  And through eternity. Amen.

Latin, 12th cent.; Tr. EDWARD CASWALL, 1849, *alt.*

463

L. M.

HEREFORD

SAMUEL SEBASTIAN WESLEY, 1872

In flowing style

1 O thou who ca - mest from a - bove The fire ce -
2 There let it for thy glo - ry burn With ev - er -
3 Je - sus, con - firm my heart's de - sire To work, and

les - tial to im - part, Kin - dle a flame of
bright, un - dy - ing blaze, And trem - bling to its
speak, and think for thee; Still let me guard the

sa - cred love On the mean al - tar of my heart.
source re - turn In hum - ble prayer and fer - vent praise.
ho - ly fire And still stir up the gift in me.

4 Still let me prove thy perfect will,
  My acts of faith and love repeat,
  Till death thy endless mercies seal,
  And make the sacrifice complete. Amen.

CHARLES WESLEY, 1762, *alt.*

A - men.

Alternative Tune, MENDON, No. 218

ST. CATHERINE
With vigor

HENRI F. HEMY, 1864,
and JAMES G. WALTON, 1870

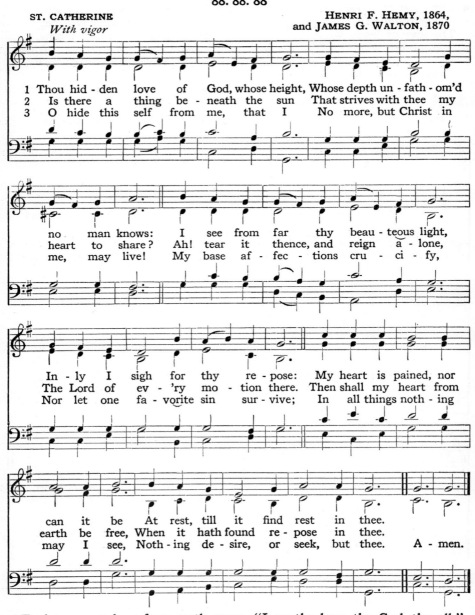

1 Thou hid - den love of God, whose height, Whose depth un - fath - om'd
2 Is there a thing be - neath the sun That strives with thee my
3 O hide this self from me, that I No more, but Christ in

no man knows: I see from far thy beau - teous light,
heart to share? Ah! tear it thence, and reign a - lone,
me, may live! My base af - fec - tions cru - ci - fy,

In - ly I sigh for thy re - pose: My heart is pained, nor
The Lord of ev - 'ry mo - tion there. Then shall my heart from
Nor let one fa - vorite sin sur - vive; In all things noth - ing

can it be At rest, till it find rest in thee.
earth be free, When it hath found re - pose in thee.
may I see, Noth - ing de - sire, or seek, but thee. A - men.

4 Each moment draw from earth away   "I am thy love, thy God, thy all."
My heart, that lowly waits thy call!   To feel thy power, to hear thy voice,
Speak to my inmost soul, and say,   To taste thy love, be all my choice!
                                                      Amen.

GERHARDT TERSTEEGEN, 1729; *Tr.* JOHN WESLEY, 1738, *alt.*

BETHANY   LOWELL MASON, 1856
Fast and joyful

1 Near - er, my God, to thee, Near - er to thee! E'en though it
2 Though like the wan - der - er, The sun gone down, Dark - ness be
3 There let the way ap - pear Steps un - to heav'n; All that thou

be a cross That rais - eth me; Still all my song would be,
o - ver me, My rest a stone; Yet in my dreams I'd be
send - est me In mer - cy giv'n; An - gels to beck - on me

Near - er, my God, to thee, Near - er, my God, to thee, Near - er to thee.

4 Then, with my waking thoughts
  Bright with thy praise,
Out of my stony griefs
  Bethel I'll raise;
So by my woes to be
‖Nearer, my God, to thee,‖
  Nearer to thee.

5 Or if on joyful wing,
  Cleaving the sky,
Sun, moon, and stars forgot,
  Upwards I fly,
Still all my song shall be,
‖Nearer, my God, to thee,‖
  Nearer to thee. Amen.

A - men.

SARAH ADAMS, 1841

Irregular

LYTLINGTON   SYDNEY H. NICHOLSON, b. 1875

Slow, with serenity

God be in my head, And in my un-der-stand-ing; God be in mine eyes, And in my look-ing; God be in my mouth, And in my speak-ing; God be in my heart, And in my think-ing; God be at mine end, And at my de-part-ing. A-men.

By permission of Sydney H. Nicholson; his copyright

Sarum Primer, 1558

467

General Hymns
10 10. 10 10

EVENTIDE
Not too slow

WILLIAM H. MONK, 1861

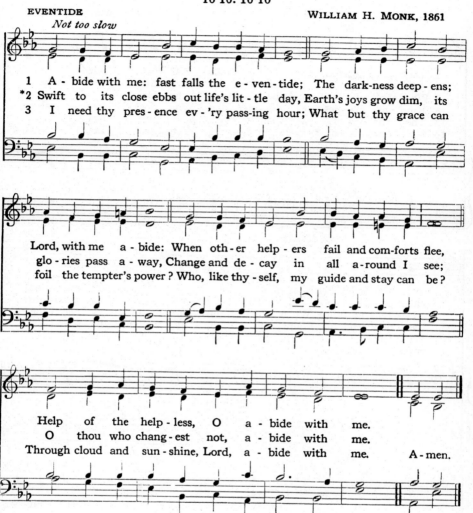

1 A - bide with me: fast falls the e - ven - tide; The dark-ness deep - ens;
*2 Swift to its close ebbs out life's lit - tle day, Earth's joys grow dim, its
3 I need thy pres - ence ev - 'ry pass-ing hour; What but thy grace can

Lord, with me a - bide: When oth - er help - ers fail and com-forts flee,
glo - ries pass a - way, Change and de - cay in all a-round I see;
foil the tempter's power? Who, like thy - self, my guide and stay can be?

Help of the help - less, O a - bide with me.
O thou who chang - est not, a - bide with me.
Through cloud and sun - shine, Lord, a - bide with me. A - men.

4 I fear no foe, with thee at hand to bless;
Ills have no weight, and tears no bitterness.
Where is death's sting? where, grave, thy victory?
I triumph still, if thou abide with me.

5 Hold thou thy cross before my closing eyes;
Shine through the gloom, and point me to the skies;
Heav'n's morning breaks, and earth's vain shadows flee:
In life, in death, O Lord, abide with me. Amen.

HENRY FRANCIS LYTE, 1847

468 Part I — General Hymns — 888

DIES IRAE — Plainsong Sequence, 13th cent.

General Hymns

it ring-eth; All be - fore the throne it bring-eth.
a - wa-king, To its Judge an an-swer ma - king.
car - na - tion; Leave me not to rep - ro - ba - tion!
f'ring bought me. Shall such grace be vain - ly brought me?
a - base me, But to thy right hand up-raise me.
un-bound-ed, Call me with thy saints sur-round-ed.

5 Lo! the book, ex - act - ly word - ed, Where-in all hath
6 When the Judge his seat at - tain - eth And each hid-den
11 Right-eous Judge! for sin's pol - lu - tion Grant thy gift of
12 Guil - ty, now I pour my moan - ing, All my shame with
17 Low I kneel, with heart sub - mis - sion: See, like ash - es,

been re - cord - ed: Thence shall judgment be a - ward - ed.
deed ar - raign - eth, Noth-ing un - a-venged re - main - eth.
ab - so - lu - tion, Ere the day of ret - ri - bu - tion.
an-guish own - ing; Spare, O God, thy sup-pliant groan-ing!
my con - tri - tion; Help me in my last con - di - tion.

Latin, 13th cent.; possibly by THOMAS *of Celano; Tr.* WILLIAM J. IRONS, 1849
It is suggested that alternate groups sing alternate stanzas

18 †Ah! that day of tears and mourn-ing! From the dust of

earth re-turn-ing, Man for judg-ment must pre-

pare him; Spare, O God, in mer - - - cy spare him!

†*Stanzas 18 and 19 should be sung by all*

General Hymns

19 Lord, all-pi-tying, Jesus blest, Grant them thine e-ter-nal rest. A - men.

Latin, 12th cent.; Stanza 19, Tr. ISAAC WILLIAMS

469 HESPERUS   L. M.   HENRY BAKER, 1866

In moderate time

1 Sa - viour, when night in - volves the skies, My soul, a -
2 On thee my wa - king rap - tures dwell, When crim - son
3 When noon her throne in light ar - rays, To thee my
4 O'er earth, when shades of eve - ning steal, To death and

dor - ing, turns to thee, Thee, self - a - based in
gleams the east a - dorn, Thee, vic - tor of the
soul tri - umph - ant springs, Thee, throned in glo - ry's
thee my thoughts I give: To death, whose power I

mor - tal guise And wrapt in shades of death for me.
grave and hell, Thee, source of life's e - ter - nal morn.
end - less blaze, Thee, Lord of lords and King of kings.
soon must feel, To thee, with whom I trust to live.

THOMAS GISBORNE, 1805

10 10. 10 10. 10 10

SONG 1
ORLANDO GIBBONS, 1623

With movement

1 Where is death's sting? We were not born to die, Nor on - ly
*2 Laugh - ter is thine, the laugh-ter free from scorn, And thine the
3 Ful - ness of life, in bo - dy, mind, and soul; "Who saves his

for the life be - yond the grave; All that is beau - ti -
smile up - on a cheer - ful face: Thine, too, the tears, when
life shall lose it," thou hast said: A great ad - ven - ture

ful in earth and sky, All skill, all knowl - edge,
love for love must mourn, And death brings si - lence
with a glo - rious goal; Noth - ing that lives in

all the powers we have, Are of thy giv - ing, and in
for a lit - tle space. Thou ga - vest, and thou dost not
thee is ev - er dead: Brave liv - ing here: and then, be -

General Hymns

them we see   No   dust   and   ash - es,   but   a   part   of   thee.
take a - way: The part - ing   is   but   here, and   for   a   day.
yond the grave, More life   and   more ad - ven - ture   for   the   brave.

GODFREY FOX BRADBY, 1929

471 *First Tune*   77. 77. 77

PETRA   RICHARD REDHEAD, 1853

In moderate time

1 Rock of   a - ges, cleft for   me, Let me hide my - self in thee;
2 Should my tears for   ev - er flow, Should my zeal no   lan - guor know,
3 While I   draw this fleet - ing breath, When mine eye - lids close in death,

Let   the   wa - ter and   the blood From thy side, a heal - ing flood,
All   for   sin could not   a - tone: Thou must save, and thou a - lone;
When I   rise to worlds un - known And be - hold thee on   thy throne,

Be   of   sin the dou - ble cure, Cleanse me from its guilt and power.
In   my hand no price I bring, Sim - ply to   thy cross I cling.
Rock of   a - ges, cleft for   me, Let me hide my - self in   thee.   A-men.

AUGUSTUS MONTAGUE TOPLADY, 1776, *alt.*

TOPLADY
77. 77. 77
THOMAS HASTINGS, 1830

In moderate time

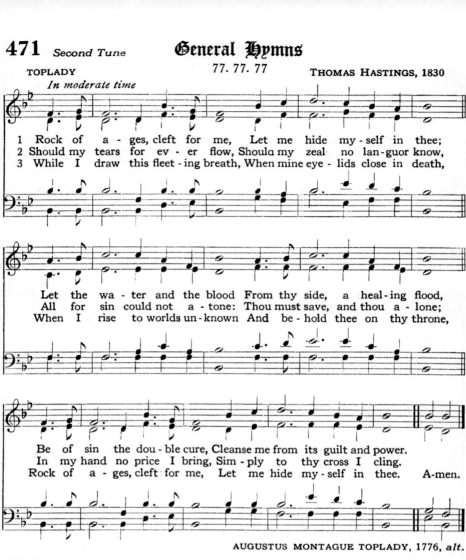

1 Rock of a - ges, cleft for me, Let me hide my-self in thee;
2 Should my tears for ev - er flow, Should my zeal no lan-guor know,
3 While I draw this fleet-ing breath, When mine eye-lids close in death,

Let the wa - ter and the blood From thy side, a heal-ing flood,
All for sin could not a - tone: Thou must save, and thou a - lone;
When I rise to worlds un-known And be-hold thee on thy throne,

Be of sin the dou-ble cure, Cleanse me from its guilt and power.
In my hand no price I bring, Sim-ply to thy cross I cling.
Rock of a - ges, cleft for me, Let me hide my-self in thee. A-men.

AUGUSTUS MONTAGUE TOPLADY, 1776, *alt.*

472
11 10. 11 10, with Refrain
HENRY SMART, 1868

PILGRIMS

Not slow

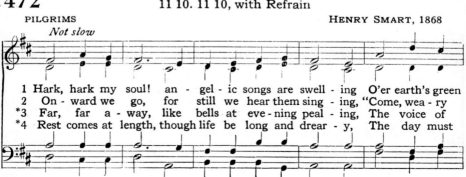

1 Hark, hark my soul! an - gel - ic songs are swell - ing O'er earth's green
2 On - ward we go, for still we hear them sing - ing, "Come, wea - ry
*3 Far, far a - way, like bells at eve - ning peal - ing, The voice of
*4 Rest comes at length, though life be long and drear - y, The day must

General Hymns

fields and o-cean's wave-beat shore; How sweet the truth those bless-ed
souls, for Je - sus bids you come;" And through the dark, its ech-oes
Je - sus sounds o'er land and sea, And la - den souls, by thou-sands
dawn, and dark-some night be past; Faith's jour - neys end in wel-come

strains are tell - ing Of that new life when sin shall be no more!
sweet-ly ring - ing, The mu - sic of the Gos - pel leads us home.
meek-ly steal - ing, Kind Shep-herd, turn their wea - ry steps to thee.
to the wea - ry, And heav'n, the heart's true home, will come at last.

Refrain

An - gels of Je - sus, an - gels of light,

Sing - ing to wel - come the pil - grims of the night.

5 Angels, sing on! your faithful watches keeping;
Sing us sweet fragments of the songs above;
Till morning's joy shall end the night of weeping,
And life's long shadows break in cloudless love.

Refrain

FREDERICK WILLIAM FABER, 1854, *alt*

DAWN   T. H. INGHAM, 1931

In moderate time

1 High o'er the lone - ly hills Black turns to gray,
2 So, o'er the hills of life, Storm - y, for - lorn,
3 Hear we no beat of drums, Fan - fare nor cry,

Organ

Bird - song the val - ley fills, Mists fold a - way;
Out of the cloud and strife Sun - rise is born;
When Christ the her - ald comes Qui - et - ly nigh;

Gray wakes to green a - gain, Beau - ty is seen a - gain,
Swift grows the light for us; End - ed is night for us;
Splen - dor he makes on earth; Col - or a - wakes on earth;

Gold and se - rene a - gain Dawn - eth the day.
Sound - less and bright for us Break - eth God's morn.
Sud - den - ly breaks on earth Light from the sky.

4 Bid then farewell to sleep: Now shall you find at last
     Rise up and run!   Night's left behind at last,
What though the hill be steep?   And for mankind at last
     Strength's in the sun.   Day has begun!

76. 76. D.

WOODBIRD
Cheerfully

Traditional German Melody

1 O day of rest and glad - ness, O day of joy and light,
2 On thee, at the cre - a - tion, The light first had its birth;
3 To - day on wea - ry na - tions The heav'n - ly man - na falls;

O balm of care and sad - ness, Most beau - ti - ful, most bright;
On thee for our sal - va - tion Christ rose from depths of earth;
To ho - ly con - vo - ca - tions The sil - ver trum - pet calls,

On thee the high and low - ly, Through a - ges joined in tune,
On thee our Lord vic - to - rious The Spi - rit sent from heav'n,
Where Gos - pel - light is glow - ing With pure and ra - diant beams,

Sing, Ho - ly, Ho - ly, Ho - ly, To the great God Tri - une.
And thus on thee most glo - rious A trip - le light was giv'n.
And liv - ing wa - ter flow - ing With soul - re - fresh - ing streams. A-men.

4 New graces ever gaining
   From this our day of rest,
We reach the rest remaining
   To spirits of the blest.

To Holy Ghost be praises,
   To Father, and to Son;
The Church her voice upraises
   To thee, blest Three in One. Amen.

CHRISTOPHER WORDSWORTH, 1862, *alt.*

6665. D.

MAXON   FRANKLIN GLYNN, 1941

In unison, not hurried; the pauses only slight

1 Sing, men and an - gels, sing, For God our Life and King Has
2 Sing, crea - tures, sing; the dust That lives by lure and lust Is
3 Af - ter the win - ter snows A wind of heal - ing blows, And

giv'n us light and spring And morn - ing break - ing.
kin - dled by the thrust Of life un - dy - ing;
thorns put forth a rose, And li - lies cheer us;

Now may man's soul a - rise As kins - man to the skies,
This hope our Mas - ter bare Has made all for - tunes fair,
Life's ev - er - last - ing spring Hath robbed death of his sting,

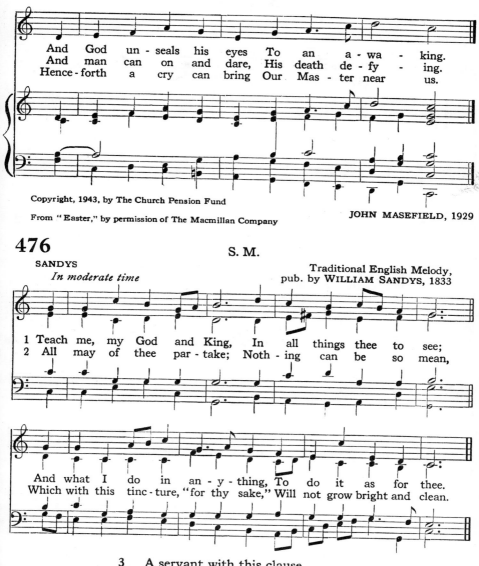

And God un-seals his eyes To an a-wa-king.
And man can on and dare, His death de-fy-ing.
Hence-forth a cry can bring Our Mas-ter near us.

JOHN MASEFIELD, 1929

476   S. M.

SANDYS
In moderate time

Traditional English Melody,
pub. by WILLIAM SANDYS, 1833

1 Teach me, my God and King, In all things thee to see;
2 All may of thee par-take; Noth-ing can be so mean,

And what I do in an-y-thing, To do it as for thee.
Which with this tinc-ture, "for thy sake," Will not grow bright and clean.

3 A servant with this clause
   Makes drudgery divine:
   Who sweeps a room, as for thy laws,
   Makes that and the action fine.

4 This is the famous stone
   That turneth all to gold;
   For that which God doth touch and own
   Cannot for less be told. Amen.

A-men.

GEORGE HERBERT, 1633

668. 668. 3366

TYSK

German Melody,
sung in Tysk Church, Stockholm, 1718

Reverently

1 God him-self is with us; Let us all a - dore him,
2 Thou per-va-dest all things: Let thy ra-diant beau-ty
3 Come, a - bide with-in me; Let my soul, like Ma-ry,
*4 Glad-ly we sur-ren - der Earth's de-ceit-ful trea-sures,

And with awe ap - pear be - fore him. God is here with-
Light mine eyes to see my du - ty. As the ten - der
Be thine earth - ly sanc-tu - a - ry. Come, in - dwell-ing
Pride of life, and sin - ful plea - sures: Glad - ly, Lord, we

in us; Soul, in si - lence fear him, Hum - bly, fer - vent-
flow - ers Ea - ger - ly un - fold them, To the sun - light
Spi - rit, With trans-fig - ured splen - dor; Love and hon - or
of - fer Thine to be for ev - er, Soul and life and

ly draw near him. Now his own Who have known
calm - ly hold them, So let me Qui - et - ly
will I ren - der. Where I go Here be - low,
each en - deav - or. Thou a - lone Shalt be known

God, in wor-ship low - ly, Yield their spi-rits whol - ly.
In thy rays im - bue me; Let thy light shine through me.
Let me bow be - fore thee, Know thee, and a - dore thee.
Lord of all our be - ing, Life's true way de - cree - ing. A-men.

GERHARDT TERSTEEGEN, 1729;
Hymnal Version, 1940; *St. 2*, HENRY SLOANE COFFIN

478

86. 886

ETERNAL LIGHT

KENNETH E. RUNKEL, 1941

In moderate time

1 E - ter - nal Light! e - ter - nal Light! How pure that
2 O how shall I, whose na - tive sphere Is dark, whose
3 There is a way for man to rise To that sub -
4 These, these pre - pare us for the sight Of ho - li -

soul must be, When, placed with - in thy search - ing sight, It
mind is dim, Be - fore the In - ef - fa - ble ap - pear, And
lime a - bode: An of - f'ring and a sac - ri - fice, A
ness a - bove: The sons of ig - no - rance and night May

shrinks not, but with calm de - light Can live, and look on thee.
on my na - ked spi - rit bear The un - cre - a - ted beam?
Ho - ly Spi - rit's en - er - gies, An Ad - vo - cate with God:
dwell in the e - ter - nal Light, Through the e - ter - nal Love!

Copyright, 1941, by The H. W. Gray Co.
Alternative Tune, HERMANN, No. 435

THOMAS BINNEY, c. 1826, *alt.*

87. 87. D.

HYFRYDOL
With dignity   ROWLAND HUGH PRICHARD, c. 1830

1 Love di - vine, all loves ex - cel - ling, Joy of heav'n, to earth come down,
2 Come, al - migh - ty to de - liv - er, Let us all thy life re - ceive;
3 Fin - ish then thy new cre - a - tion; Pure and spot - less let us be:

Fix in us thy hum - ble dwell - ing, All thy faith - ful mer - cies crown.
Sud - den - ly re - turn, and nev - er, Nev - er - more thy tem - ples leave.
Let us see thy great sal - va - tion Per - fect - ly re - stored in thee:

Je - sus, thou art all com - pas - sion, Pure, un - bound - ed love thou art;
Thee we would be al - way bless - ing, Serve thee as thy hosts a - bove,
Changed from glo - ry in - to glo - ry, Till in heav'n we take our place,

Vis - it us with thy sal - va - tion, En - ter ev - 'ry trembling heart.
Pray, and praise thee without ceas - ing, Glo - ry in thy perfect love.
Till we cast our crowns be - fore thee, Lost in wonder, love, and praise. A - men.

CHARLES WESLEY, 1747

LOVE DIVINE
With movement   GEORGE F. LeJEUNE, 1887

1 Love di - vine, all loves ex - cel - ling, Joy of heav'n, to earth come down,
2 Come, al - migh - ty to de - liv - er, Let us all thy life re - ceive;
3 Fin - ish then thy new cre - a - tion; Pure and spot - less let us be:

Fix in us thy hum - ble dwell - ing, All thy faith - ful mer - cies crown.
Sud - den - ly re - turn, and nev - er, Nev - er - more thy tem - ples leave.
Let us see thy great sal - va - tion Per - fect - ly re - stored in thee:

Je - sus, thou art all com - pas - sion, Pure, un - bound - ed love thou art;
Thee we would be al - way bless - ing, Serve thee as thy hosts a - bove,
Changed from glo - ry in - to glo - ry, Till in heav'n we take our place,

Vis - it us with thy sal - va - tion, En - ter ev - 'ry trem - bling heart.
Pray, and praise thee without ceas - ing, Glo - ry in thy per - fect love.
Till we cast our crowns be - fore thee, Lost in won - der, love, and praise.   A-men.

CHARLES WESLEY, 1747

Alternative Tune, BEECHER, No. 304

480

General Hymns
77. 77. 88. 88

HOLY OFFERINGS

RICHARD REDHEAD, 1870

With movement

1 Ho - ly of - f'rings, rich and rare, Of - fer - ings of praise and prayer,
2 Hom-age of each hum - ble heart, Ere we from thy house de - part;

Pur - er life and pur - pose high, Clasp - ed hands, up - lift - ed eye,
Wor - ship fer - vent, deep and high, Ad - o - ra - tion, ec - sta - sy;

Low - ly acts of ad - o - ra - tion To the God of
All that child - like love can ren - der Of de - vo - tion

our sal - va - tion; On his al - tar laid, we leave them:
true and ten - der; On thine al - tar laid, we leave them:

Christ, pre - sent them! God, re - ceive them!
Christ, pre - sent them! God, re - ceive them! A - men.

3 To the Father, and the Son,
And the Spirit, Three in One,
Though our mortal weakness raise
Off'rings of imperfect praise,
Yet with hearts bowed down most lowly,
Crying, Holy! Holy! Holy!
On thine altar laid, we leave them:
Christ, present them! God, receive them! Amen.

JOHN SAMUEL BEWLEY MONSELL, 1867

481

S. M.

YATTENDON 46
With dignity

HARRY ELLIS WOOLDRIDGE, 1899

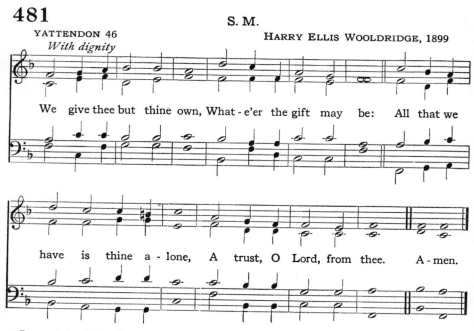

We give thee but thine own, What - e'er the gift may be: All that we

have is thine a - lone, A trust, O Lord, from thee. A - men.

By permission of The Clarendon Press, Oxford

WILLIAM WALSHAM HOW, 1858

482 *First Tune* 𝕲eneral 𝕳ymns

10 10. 10 10

SURSUM CORDA

ALFRED M. SMITH, 1941

In unison, fervently

1 "Lift up your hearts!" We lift them, Lord, to thee; Here at thy
2 A - bove the lev - el of the for - mer years, The mire of
3 Lift ev - 'ry gift that thou thy - self hast giv'n; Low lies the
4 Then, as the trum - pet - call in af - ter years, "Lift up your

feet none oth - er may we see. "Lift up your hearts!" E'en
sin, the weight of guilt - y fears, The mist of doubt, the
best till lift - ed up to heav'n: Low lie the bound - ing
hearts!", rings peal - ing in our ears, Still shall those hearts re -

so, with one ac - cord, We lift them up, we lift them to the Lord.
blight of love's de - cay, O Lord of Light, lift all our hearts to - day!
heart, the teem-ing brain, Till, sent from God, they mount to God a - gain.
spond with full ac - cord, "We lift them up, we lift them to the Lord!"

HENRY MONTAGU BUTLER, 1881, *alt.*

10 10. 10 10

MAGDA
R. VAUGHAN WILLIAMS, 1925

In moderate time, not too slow

1 "Lift up your hearts!" We lift them, Lord, to thee;
2 A - bove the lev - el of the for - mer years,
3 Lift ev - 'ry gift that thou thy - self hast giv'n;

Here at thy feet none oth - er may we see.
The mire of sin, the weight of guilt - y fears,
Low lies the best till lift - ed up to heav'n:

"Lift up your hearts!" E'en so, with one ac - cord,
The mist of doubt, the blight of love's de - cay,
Low lie the bound - ing heart, the teem - ing brain,

We lift them up, we lift them to the Lord.
O Lord of Light, lift all our hearts to - day!
Till, sent from God, they mount to God a - gain.

Copyright, 1925, by R. Vaughan Williams

4 Then, as the trumpet-call in after years,
   "Lift up your hearts!", rings pealing in our ears,
   Still shall those hearts respond with full accord,
   "We lift them up, we lift them to the Lord!"

HENRY MONTAGU BUTLER, 1881, *alt.*

483   𝔊eneral 𝔥𝔶mns

11 10. 11 10

CONSOLATION   Arr. from SAMUEL WEBBE, 1792

Not too slow

1 Come, ye dis - con - so - late, wher - e'er ye lan - guish,
2 Joy of the des - o - late, light of the stray - ing,
3 Here see the Bread of life; see wa - ters flow - ing

Come to the mer - cy - seat, fer - vent - ly kneel:
Hope of the pen - i - tent, fade - less and pure!
Forth from the throne of God, pure from a - bove:

Here bring your wound - ed hearts, here tell your an - guish;
Here speaks the Com - fort - er, ten - der - ly say - ing,
Come to the feast of love; come, ev - er know - ing

Earth has no sor - row that heav'n can - not heal.
"Earth has no sor - row that heav'n can - not cure."
Earth has no sor - row but heav'n can re - move.

THOMAS MOORE, 1816; *St. 3*, THOMAS HASTINGS, 1831

General Hymns
L. M.

TRURO

With spirit

Psalmodia Evangelica, 1789

1 Lift up your heads, ye migh-ty gates; Be-hold the King of
2 O blest the land, the ci - ty blest, Where Christ the rul - er
3 Fling wide the por - tals of your heart; Make it a tem - ple,

glo - ry waits! The King of kings is draw - ing
is con - fest! O hap - py hearts and hap - py
set a - part From earth - ly use for heav'n's em -

near; The Sa - viour of the world is here.
homes To whom this King of tri - umph comes!
ploy, A - dorned with prayer and love and joy. A - men.

*4 Redeemer, come! I open wide
  My heart to thee: here, Lord, abide!
  Let me thy inner presence feel:
  Thy grace and love in me reveal.

5 So come, my Sov'reign; enter in!
  Let new and nobler life begin;
  Thy Holy Spirit guide us on,
  Until the glorious crown be won. Amen.

GEORGE WEISSEL, 1642, *based on Psalm 24;*
Tr. CATHERINE WINKWORTH, *alt.*

Alternative Tune, WAREHAM, No. 119

ABENDS

Melody by
HERBERT S. OAKELEY, 1873

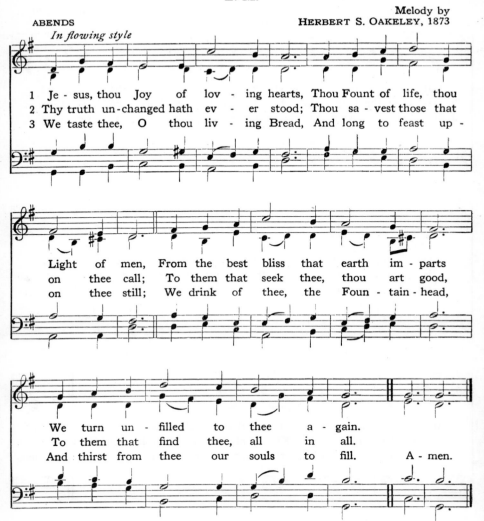

1 Je - sus, thou Joy of lov - ing hearts, Thou Fount of life, thou
2 Thy truth un - changed hath ev - er stood; Thou sa - vest those that
3 We taste thee, O thou liv - ing Bread, And long to feast up -

Light of men, From the best bliss that earth im - parts
on thee call; To them that seek thee, thou art good,
on thee still; We drink of thee, the Foun - tain - head,

We turn un - filled to thee a - gain.
To them that find thee, all in all.
And thirst from thee our souls to fill. A - men.

4 Our restless spirits yearn for thee,
 Where'er our changeful lot is cast;
Glad, when thy gracious smile we see,
 Blest, when our faith can hold thee fast.

5 O Jesus, ever with us stay,
 Make all our moments calm and bright;
Chase the dark night of sin away,
 Shed o'er the world thy holy light. Amen.

Latin, 12th cent.; Tr. RAY PALMER, 1858

485 *Second Tune* 𝕲𝖊𝖓𝖊𝖗𝖆𝖑 𝕳𝖞𝖒𝖓𝖘
L. M.

CHRISTE REDEMPTOR   Sarum Plainsong, Mode I

In moderate time, very smoothly

1 Je - sus, thou Joy of lov - ing hearts, Thou Fount of
2 Thy truth un - changed hath ev - er stood; Thou sa - vest
3 We taste thee, O thou liv - ing Bread, And long to
4 Our rest - less spi - rits yearn for thee, Wher - e'er our
5 O Je - sus, ev - er with us stay, Make all our

life, thou Light of men, From the best bliss that earth im - parts
those that on thee call; To them that seek thee, thou art good,
feast up - on thee still; We drink of thee, the Foun - tain-head,
change-ful lot is cast; Glad, when thy gra - cious smile we see,
mo - ments calm and bright; Chase the dark night of sin a - way,

We turn un - filled to thee a - gain.
To them that find thee, all in all.
And thirst from thee our souls to fill.
Blest, when our faith can hold thee fast.
Shed o'er the world thy ho - ly light. A - men.

11 10. 11 10

WELWYN   ALFRED SCOTT-GATTY, 1902

With movement

1 Now once a - gain for help that nev - er fail - eth,
2 That we may rise and go forth from thine al - tar,
3 Know - ing there will not be so dark a val - ley

We bring our griev - ous bur - den un - to thee.
To bear the load we could not bear be - fore,
But those who watch may find thy guid - ing ray,

Pour down thy strength, for noth - ing else a - vail - eth,
With mind se - rene, with step that does not fal - ter,
Know - ing there will not be so blind an al - ley

Bless thou the bow - ing head, the bend - ing knee,
Know - ing thy hand will o - pen ev - 'ry door;
But it will o - pen on thy broad high - way.

By permission of the Abbot of Downside

4 O Light that led the saints through all the ages,
    O Hope that lifted up the martyr's head,
    O Comforter of children and of sages,
    Lead on! lead on, as thou hast always led!

MILDRED WHITNEY STILLMAN, 1939

10 10. 10 10

ELLERS   EDWARD J. HOPKINS, 1869

In unison, with dignity

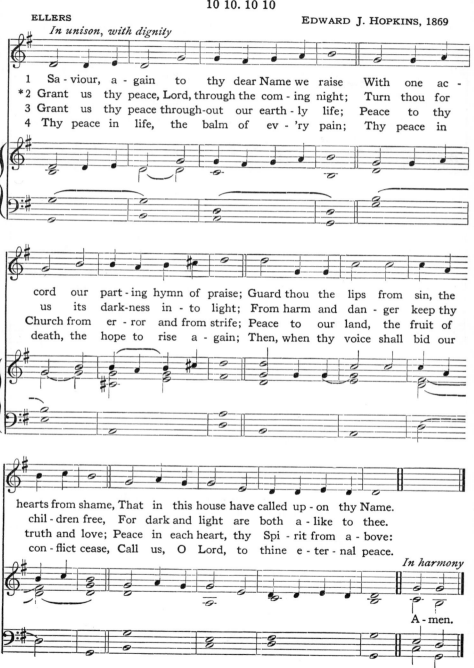

1 Sa - viour, a - gain to thy dear Name we raise With one ac -
*2 Grant us thy peace, Lord, through the com - ing night; Turn thou for
3 Grant us thy peace through-out our earth - ly life; Peace to thy
4 Thy peace in life, the balm of ev - 'ry pain; Thy peace in

cord our part - ing hymn of praise; Guard thou the lips from sin, the
us its dark - ness in - to light; From harm and dan - ger keep thy
Church from er - ror and from strife; Peace to our land, the fruit of
death, the hope to rise a - gain; Then, when thy voice shall bid our

hearts from shame, That in this house have called up - on thy Name.
chil - dren free, For dark and light are both a - like to thee.
truth and love; Peace in each heart, thy Spi - rit from a - bove:
con - flict cease, Call us, O Lord, to thine e - ter - nal peace.

In harmony

A - men.

JOHN ELLERTON, 1866

STRACATHRO   Melody, CHARLES HUTCHESON, 1832,
har. by GEOFFREY SHAW, 1925

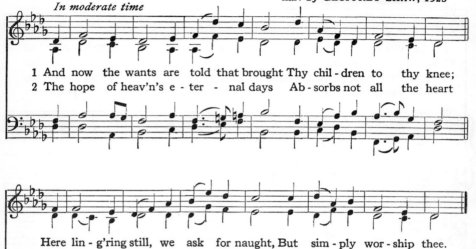

In moderate time

1 And now the wants are told that brought Thy chil - dren to thy knee;
2 The hope of heav'n's e - ter - nal days Ab - sorbs not all the heart

Here lin - g'ring still, we ask for naught, But sim - ply wor - ship thee.
That gives thee glo - ry, love, and praise, For be - ing what thou art.

By permission of Geoffrey Shaw and the Oxford University Press

3 For thou art God, the One, the same,
   O'er all things high and bright,
And round us, when we speak thy Name,
   There spreads a heav'n of light.

4 O wondrous peace, in thought to dwell
   On excellence divine;
To know that naught in man can tell
   How fair thy beauties shine!

5 O thou above all blessing blest,
   O'er thanks exalted far,
Thy very greatness is a rest
   To weaklings as we are;

6 For when we feel the praise of thee
   A task beyond our powers,
We say, "A perfect God is he,
   And he is fully ours."

WILLIAM BRIGHT, 1866

489 *First Tune* 𝔊eneral 𝔥ymns
87. 87. 87

SICILIAN MARINERS
Moderately slow
Sicilian Melody, pub. 1794

1 Lord, dis - miss us with thy bless - ing; Fill our hearts with
2 Thanks we give and ad - o - ra - tion For thy Gos - pel's
3 So that when thy love shall call us, Sa - viour, from the

joy and peace; Let us each, thy love pos - sess - ing,
joy - ful sound: May the fruits of thy sal - va - tion
world a - way, Fear of death shall not ap - pall us,

Tri - umph in re - deem - ing grace: O re - fresh us,
In our hearts and lives a - bound: May thy pres - ence,
Glad thy sum - mons to o - bey. May we ev - er,

O re - fresh us, Trav - 'ling thro' this wil - der - ness.
may thy pres - ence With us ev - er - more be found;
may we ev - er Reign with thee in end - less day. A - men.

Ascribed to JOHN FAWCETT, 1773, *alt.*

DISMISSAL WILLIAM LETTON VINER, 1845

In moderate time

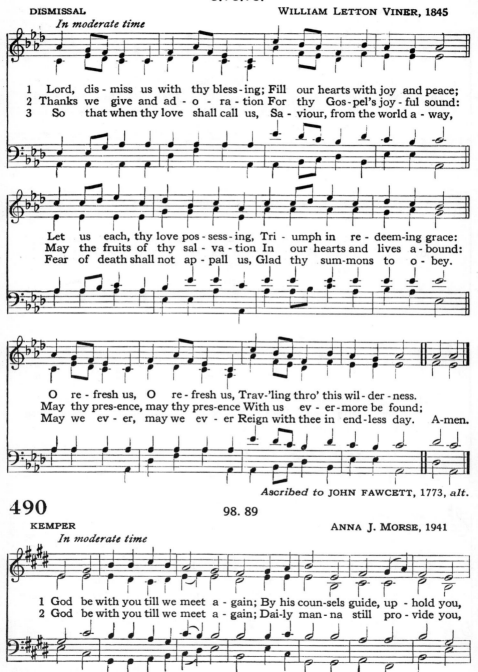

1 Lord, dis - miss us with thy bless-ing; Fill our hearts with joy and peace;
2 Thanks we give and ad - o - ra-tion For thy Gos-pel's joy-ful sound:
3 So that when thy love shall call us, Sa - viour, from the world a - way,

Let us each, thy love pos-sess-ing, Tri - umph in re - deem-ing grace:
May the fruits of thy sal - va-tion In our hearts and lives a - bound:
Fear of death shall not ap - pall us, Glad thy sum-mons to o - bey.

O re - fresh us, O re - fresh us, Trav-'ling thro' this wil - der - ness.
May thy pres-ence, may thy pres-ence With us ev - er-more be found;
May we ev - er, may we ev - er Reign with thee in end-less day. A-men.

Ascribed to JOHN FAWCETT, 1773, alt.

490 98. 89

KEMPER ANNA J. MORSE, 1941

In moderate time

1 God be with you till we meet a - gain; By his coun-sels guide, up - hold you,
2 God be with you till we meet a - gain; Dai-ly man - na still pro - vide you,

General Hymns

With his sheep se-cure-ly fold you: God be with you till we meet a - gain.
'Neath his wings protecting hide you: God be with you till we meet a - gain.

JEREMIAH EAMES RANKIN, 1882, *alt.*

491   66. 66. 66

OLD HUNDRED TWENTIETH

Melody from THOMAS EST'S
Whole Book of Psalmes, 1592

In moderate time

1 Ci - ty not made with hands, Not throned a - bove the skies,
2 Wher - e'er the gen - tle heart Finds cour - age from a - bove;
3 Thou art wher - e'er the proud In hum - ble - ness melts down;
4 Where in life's com - mon ways With cheer - ful feet we go;

Nor walled with shin - ing walls, Nor framed with stones of price,
Wher - e'er the heart for - sook Warms with the breath of love;
Where self it - self yields up; Where mar - tyrs win their crown;
Where in his steps we tread, Who trod the way of woe;

More bright than gold or gem, God's own Je - ru - sa - lem!
Where faith bids fear de - part, Ci - ty of God, thou art.
Where faith - ful souls pos - sess Them - selves in per - fect peace;
Where he is in the heart, Ci - ty of God, thou art.

FRANCIS TURNER PALGRAVE, 1867, *alt.*

ST. KEVERNE   CRAIG SELLAR LANG, 1936

In unison, with spirit

1 From glo-ry to glo-ry ad-van-cing, we praise thee, O Lord;
3 Thanks-giv-ing, and glo-ry and wor-ship, and bless-ing and love,

Thy Name with the Fa-ther and Spi-rit be ev-er a-dored.
One heart and one song have the saints up-on earth and a-bove.

2 From strength un-to strength we go for-ward on Si-on's high-way,
4 O Lord, ev-er-more to thy ser-vants thy pres-ence be nigh;

General Hymns

To ap-pear be-fore God in the ci - ty of in - fi - nite day.
Ev - er fit us by ser - vice on earth for thy ser - vice on high. A - men.

By permission

Liturgy of St. James; Tr. C. W. HUMPHREYS, 1906

493

11 10. 11 10

INTERCESSOR

C. HUBERT H. PARRY, 1904

With dignity

1 O broth - er man, fold to thy heart thy broth - er: Where pi - ty
2 Fol - low with rev - 'rent steps the great ex - am - ple Of him whose
3 Then shall all shack - les fall: the storm - y clan - gor Of wild war -

dwells, the peace of God is there; To wor - ship right - ly is to
ho - ly work was do - ing good: So shall the wide earth seem our
mu - sic o'er the earth shall cease; Love shall tread out the bale - ful

love each oth - er, Each smile a hymn, each kind - ly deed a prayer.
Fa - ther's tem - ple, Each lov - ing life a psalm of grat - i - tude.
fire of an - ger, And in its ash - es plant the tree of peace.

Music copyright, 1904, by the Proprietors of Hymns Ancient and Modern
Words by permission of Houghton Mifflin Company

JOHN GREENLEAF WHITTIER, 1848

86. 86. 86

MORNING SONG

Melody, *The Union Harmony*, Virginia, 1848,
harmonized by W. D., 1940

In moderate time

1 O ho - ly ci - ty, seen of John, Where Christ, the Lamb, doth reign,
*2 Hark, how from men whose lives are held More cheap than mer - chan - dise;
3 O shame to us who rest con - tent While lust and greed for gain

With - in whose four-square walls shall come No night, nor need, nor pain,
From wo - men strug-gling sore for bread, From lit - tle chil-dren's cries,
In street and shop and ten - e - ment Wring gold from hu - man pain,

And where the tears are wiped from eyes That shall not weep a - gain!
There swells the sob-bing hu - man plaint That bids thy walls a - rise!
And bit - ter lips in blind de - spair Cry, "Christ hath died in vain!"

4 Give us, O God, the strength to build
   The city that hath stood
   Too long a dream, whose laws are love,
   Whose ways are brotherhood,
   And where the sun that shineth is
   God's grace for human good.

5 Already in the mind of God
   That city riseth fair:
   Lo, how its splendor challenges
   The souls that greatly dare —
   Yea, bids us seize the whole of life
   And build its glory there.

WALTER RUSSELL BOWIE, 1910

495 *First Tune*   **General Hymns**
S. M.

BOYLSTON
Not slow
LOWELL MASON, 1832

1 Blest be the tie that binds Our hearts in Je - sus' love:
2 Be - fore our Fa - ther's throne We pour u - ni - ted prayers;
3 We share our mu - tual woes, Our mu - tual bur - dens bear;

The fel - low-ship of Chris-tian minds Is like to that a - bove.
Our fears, our hopes, our aims are one; Our com-forts and our cares.
And of - ten for each oth - er flows The sym - pa - thi - zing tear.

4 When we at death must part,   5 From sorrow, toil, and pain,
   Not like the world's, our pain;   And sin, we shall be free;
But one in Christ, and one in heart,   And perfect love and friendship reign
   We part to meet again.   Throughout eternity.

JOHN FAWCETT, 1782, *alt.*

495 *Second Tune*   S. M.

DENNIS
Calmly
Adapted by LOWELL MASON, 1845
from JOHANN GEORG NAEGELI

1 Blest be the tie that binds Our hearts in Je - sus' love: The
2 Be - fore our Fa - ther's throne We pour u - ni - ted prayers; Our
3 We share our mu - tual woes, Our mu - tual bur - dens bear; And

fel - low - ship of Chris-tian minds Is like to that a - bove.
fears, our hopes, our aims are one; Our com - forts and our cares.
of - ten for each oth - er flows The sym - pa - thi - zing tear.

76. 76. 88. 85

KENDAL   ARTHUR SOMERVELL, 1906

Boldly

1 When wilt thou save the peo - ple? O God of mer - cy, when?   Not
2 Shall crime bring crime for ev - er, Strength aid - ing still the strong?   Is
3 When wilt thou save the peo - ple? O God of mer - cy, when?   The

kings and lords, but na - tions; Not thrones and crowns, but men!
it thy will, O Fa - ther, That man shall toil for wrong?
peo - ple, Lord, the peo - ple, Not thrones and crowns, but men!

Flowers of thy heart, O God, are they; Let them not pass, like weeds, a - way,
"No," say thy moun-tains; "No," thy skies; Man's clouded sun shall bright - ly rise,
God save the peo - ple; thine they are, Thy chil-dren, as thy an - gels fair:

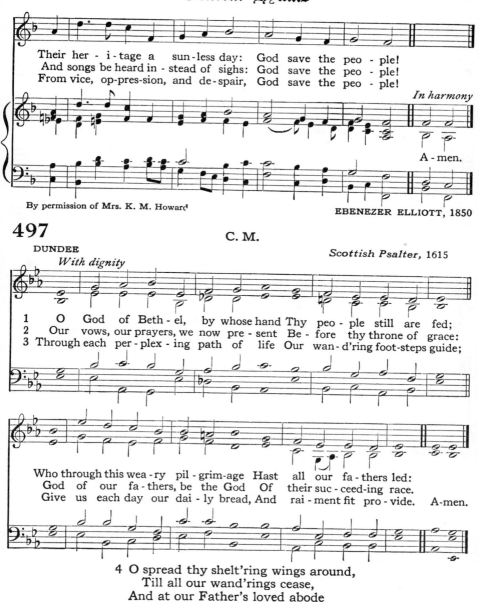

Their her - i - tage a   sun - less day: God save the peo - ple!
And songs be heard in - stead of sighs: God save the peo - ple!
From vice, op-pres-sion, and de-spair,   God save the peo - ple!

In harmony

A - men.

By permission of Mrs. K. M. Howard

EBENEZER ELLIOTT, 1850

497

C. M.

DUNDEE

With dignity

Scottish Psalter, 1615

1 O   God   of Beth - el, by whose hand Thy peo - ple still are fed;
2 Our   vows, our prayers, we now pre - sent Be - fore thy throne of grace:
3 Through each per - plex - ing path of   life Our wan- d'ring foot-steps guide;

Who through this wea - ry pil - grim-age Hast all our fa - thers led:
God   of our fa - thers, be the God Of their suc - ceed-ing race.
Give us each day our dai - ly bread, And rai - ment fit pro - vide.   A-men.

4 O spread thy shelt'ring wings around,
   Till all our wand'rings cease,
   And at our Father's loved abode
   Our souls arrive in peace!

5 Such blessings from thy gracious hand
   Our humble prayers implore;
   And thou shalt be our chosen God
   And portion evermore.   Amen.

PHILIP DODDRIDGE, 1736; JOHN LOGAN, 1781

L. M.

GARDINER

WILLIAM GARDINER'S
Sacred Melodies, 1815

With stately vigor

1 Where cross the crowd - ed ways of life, Where sound the
2 In haunts of wretch - ed - ness and need, On sha - dowed
*3 From ten - der child - hood's help - less - ness, From wo - man's

cries of race and clan, A - bove the noise of self - ish
thresh - olds dark with fears, From paths where hide the lures of
grief, man's bur - den'd toil, From fam - ished souls, from sor - row's

strife, We hear thy voice, O Son of man.
greed, We catch the vi - sion of thy tears.
stress, Thy heart hath nev - er known re - coil. A - men.

*4 The cup of water giv'n for thee
   Still holds the freshness of thy grace;
   Yet long these multitudes to see
   The sweet compassion of thy face.

5 O Master, from the mountain side,
   Make haste to heal these hearts of pain;
   Among these restless throngs abide,
   O tread the city's streets again;

6 Till sons of men shall learn thy love,
   And follow where thy feet have trod;
   Till glorious from thy heav'n above,
   Shall come the city of our God. Amen.

FRANK MASON NORTH, 1905

88. 88. 88

ST. PETERSBURG   Arr. from DMITRI S. BORTNIANSKY, 1825

With simple dignity

1 Be - fore thy throne, O God, we kneel; Give us a con - science
2 Search out our hearts and make us true, Wish - ful to give to
3 For sins of heed - less word and deed, For pride am - bi - tious
4 Let the fierce fires which burn and try, Our in - most spi - rits

quick to feel, A rea - dy mind to un - der - stand The
all their due; From love of plea - sure, lust of gold, From
to suc - ceed, For craft - y trade and sub - tle snare To
pu - ri - fy: Con - sume the ill; purge out the shame; O

mean - ing of thy chast - 'ning hand; What - e'er the pain and
sins which make the heart grow cold, Wean us and train us
catch the sim - ple un - a - ware, For lives be - reft of
God, be with us in the flame; A new - born peo - ple

shame may be, Bring us, O Fa - ther, near - er thee.
with thy rod; Teach us to know our faults, O God.
pur - pose high, For - give, for - give, O Lord, we cry.
may we rise, More pure, more true, more no - bly wise. A - men.

WILLIAM BOYD CARPENTER, 1841–1918

87. 87. D.

SUPPLICATION   WILLIAM H. MONK, 1823–1899

With breadth

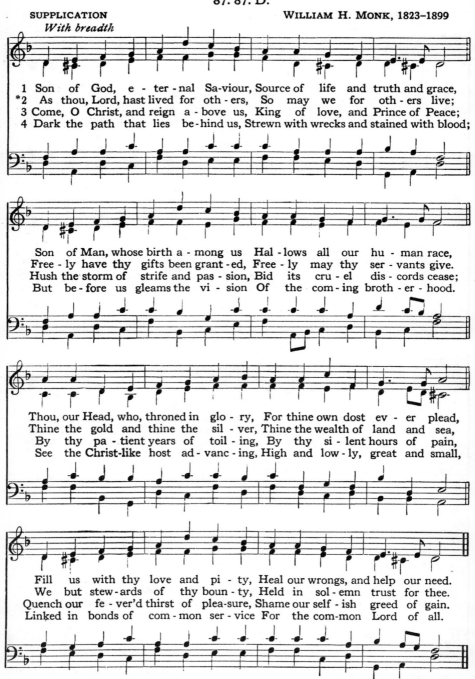

1 Son of God, e - ter - nal Sa-viour, Source of life and truth and grace,
*2 As thou, Lord, hast lived for oth - ers, So may we for oth - ers live;
3 Come, O Christ, and reign a - bove us, King of love, and Prince of Peace;
4 Dark the path that lies be-hind us, Strewn with wrecks and stained with blood;

Son of Man, whose birth a - mong us Hal -lows all our hu - man race,
Free - ly have thy gifts been grant-ed, Free - ly may thy ser - vants give.
Hush the storm of strife and pas - sion, Bid its cru - el dis - cords cease;
But be - fore us gleams the vi - sion Of the com - ing broth - er - hood.

Thou, our Head, who, throned in glo - ry, For thine own dost ev - er plead,
Thine the gold and thine the sil - ver, Thine the wealth of land and sea,
By thy pa - tient years of toil - ing, By thy si - lent hours of pain,
See the Christ-like host ad - vanc - ing, High and low - ly, great and small,

Fill us with thy love and pi - ty, Heal our wrongs, and help our need.
We but stew - ards of thy boun - ty, Held in sol - emn trust for thee.
Quench our fe - ver'd thirst of plea-sure, Shame our self - ish greed of gain.
Linked in bonds of com - mon ser - vice For the com-mon Lord of all.

5 Son of God, eternal Saviour,
　　Source of life and truth and grace,
　Son of Man, whose birth among us
　　Hallows all our human race,
　Thou who prayedst, thou who willest
　　That thy people should be one,
　Grant, O grant our hope's fruition:
　　Here on earth thy will be done.　Amen.

SOMERSET CORRY LOWRY, 1893

Alternative Tune, IN BABILONE, No. 103

A - men.

501　　　　　　C. M.

WALSALL　　　　　　　　　　　English Melody, pub. c. 1721

In unison, with deep feeling

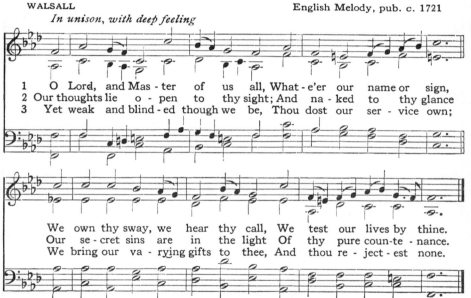

1　O Lord, and Mas - ter of us all, What - e'er our name or sign,
2　Our thoughts lie o - pen to thy sight; And na - ked to thy glance
3　Yet weak and blind - ed though we be, Thou dost our ser - vice own;

We own thy sway, we hear thy call, We test our lives by thine.
Our se - cret sins are in the light Of thy pure coun - te - nance.
We bring our va - rying gifts to thee, And thou re - ject - est none.

4　To thee our full humanity,
　　Its joys and pains belong;
　The wrong of man to man on thee
　　Inflicts a deeper wrong.

5　Who hates, hates thee; who loves, becomes
　　Therein to thee allied:
　All sweet accords of hearts and homes
　　In thee are multiplied.

6　Apart from thee all gain is loss,
　　All labor vainly done;
　The solemn shadow of the cross
　　Is better than the sun.

　　　　JOHN GREENLEAF WHITTIER, 1856

WOKING   FRANKLIN GLYNN, 1941

Jubilant

1 O some-times gleams up - on our sight, Through pres - ent
2 That all of good the past hath had Re - mains to
3 Through the harsh nois - es of our day A low, sweet
4 Hence-forth my heart shall sigh no more For old - en

wrong, the e - ter - nal **right**; And step by step since time be -
make our own time **glad**, Our com-mon dai - ly life di -
prel - ude finds its **way**; Through clouds of doubt and creeds of
time and ho - lier **shore**: God's love and bless - ing, then and

gan We see the stea - dy gain of man:
vine, And ev - 'ry land a Pal - es - tine.
fear, A light is break - ing calm and clear.
there, Are now, and here, and ev - 'ry - where.

JOHN GREENLEAF WHITTIER, 1852

503

66. 66. D.

NON NOBIS DOMINE

In unison, boldly

DAVID McK. WILLIAMS, 1942

1 Non no - bis, Do - mi - ne! Not un - to us, O Lord,
2 And we con - fess our blame, How all too high we hold
3 O power by whom we live, Cre - a - tor, judge and friend,

The praise and glo - ry be Of an - y deed or word:
That noise which men call fame, That dross which men call gold.
Up - hold - ing - ly for - give, Nor leave us at the end;

For in thy judg-ment lies To crown or bring to naught
For these we un - der - go Our hot and god - less days;
But grant us yet to see In all our pit - e - ous ways,

All knowl-edge and de - vice That man has reached or wrought.
But in our souls we know, Not un - to us the praise.
Non no - bis, Do - mi - ne, Not un - to us the praise. A - men.

Music copyright, 1943, by The Church Pension Fund

RUDYARD KIPLING, 1934

66. 66. 888

RHOSYMEDRE

JOHN DAVID EDWARDS, c. 1840

With tranquillity

1 Our Fa - ther, by whose Name All fa - ther - hood is known,
2 O Christ, thy - self a child With - in an earth - ly home,
3 O Spi - rit, who dost bind Our hearts in u - ni - ty,

Who dost in love pro - claim Each fam - i - ly thine own,
With heart still un - de - filed, Thou didst to man - hood come;
Who teach - est us to find The love from self set free,

Bless thou all par - ents, guard - ing well, With con - stant love as
Our chil - dren bless, in ev - 'ry place, That they may all be -
In all our hearts such love in - crease, That ev - 'ry home, by

sen - ti - nel, The homes in which thy peo - ple dwell.
hold thy face, And know - ing thee may grow in grace.
this re - lease, May be the dwell - ing place of peace. A-men.

F. BLAND TUCKER, 1941

76. 76. D.

COMMEMORATION   Melody, BARTHOLOMAEUS GESIUS, 1605,
In moderate time   arr. by JOHANN SEBASTIAN BACH, 1769

1 Our Fa - ther, by whose ser - vants Our house was built of old,
2 The change-ful years un - rest - ing Their si - lent course have sped,
3 They reap not where they la - bored; We reap what they have sown;

Whose hand hath crowned her chil - dren With bless - ings man - i - fold,
New com-rades ev - er bring - ing In com-rades' steps to tread:
Our har - vest may be gar - ner'd By a - ges yet un - known.

For thine un - fail - ing mer - cies Far - strewn a - long our way,
And some are long for - got - ten, Long spent their hopes and fears;
The days of old have dower'd us With gifts be - yond all praise:

With all who passed be - fore us, We praise thy Name to - day.
Safe rest they in thy keep - ing, Who chang-est not with years.
Our Fa - ther, make us faith - ful To serve the com - ing days. A-men.

4 Before us and beside us,   One family unbroken,
   Still holden in thine hand   We join, with one acclaim,
A cloud unseen of witness,   One heart, one voice uplifting,
   Our elder comrades stand: To glorify thy Name. Amen.

GEORGE WALLACE BRIGGS, 1920

By permission of The Grammar School, Loughborough

General Hymns

"The Children's Song"

(Land of our birth, we pledge to thee
Our love and toil in the years to be,
When we are grown and take our place
As men and women with our race.)

506

L. M.

LLEDROD

Welsh Hymn Melody, 1859

With vigor; may be sung in unison

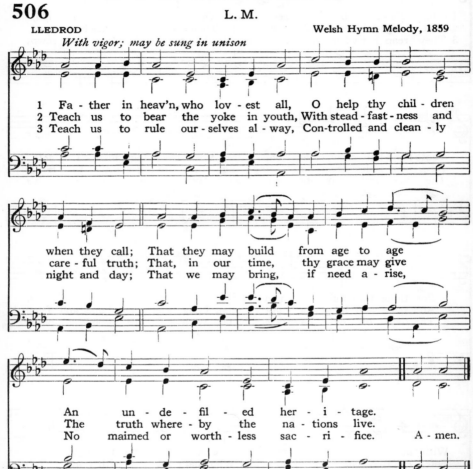

1 Fa - ther in heav'n, who lov - est all, O help thy chil - dren
2 Teach us to bear the yoke in youth, With stead - fast - ness and
3 Teach us to rule our - selves al - way, Con-trolled and clean - ly

when they call; That they may build from age to age
care - ful truth; That, in our time, thy grace may give
night and day; That we may bring, if need a - rise,

An un - de - fil - ed her - i - tage.
The truth where - by the na - tions live.
No maimed or worth - less sac - ri - fice. A - men.

4 Teach us to look in all our ends
   On thee for Judge and not our friends;
   That we, with thee, may walk uncowed
   By fear or favor of the crowd.

5 Teach us the strength that cannot seek,
   By deed or thought, to hurt the weak;
   That, under thee, we may possess
   Man's strength to comfort man's distress.

General Hymns

6 Teach us delight in simple things,
   And mirth that has no bitter springs;
   Forgiveness free of evil done,
   And love to all men 'neath the sun.   Amen.

(Land of our birth, our faith, our pride,
For whose dear sake our fathers died;
O Motherland, we pledge to thee
Head, heart, and hand through the years to be.)

Alternative Tune, PIXHAM, No. 150   RUDYARD KIPLING, 1906

From "Puck of Pook's Hill," by permission of Mrs. Rudyard Kipling. From "Rudyard Kipling's Verse," Inclusive Edition, 1885, 1932, copyright 1891, 1934, reprinted by permission of Doubleday, Doran and Company, Inc.

507
C. M.

ST. MAGNUS   JEREMIAH CLARK, 1709

In moderate time

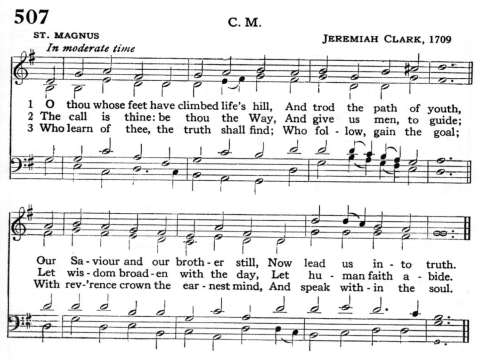

1 O thou whose feet have climbed life's hill, And trod the path of youth,
2 The call is thine: be thou the Way, And give us men, to guide;
3 Who learn of thee, the truth shall find; Who fol - low, gain the goal;

Our Sa - viour and our broth - er still, Now lead us in - to truth.
Let wis - dom broad - en with the day, Let hu - man faith a - bide.
With rev-'rence crown the ear - nest mind, And speak with - in the soul.

4 Awake the purpose high which strives,
   And, falling, stands again;
   Confirm the will of eager lives
   To quit themselves like men:

5 Thy life the bond of fellowship,
   Thy love the law that rules,
   Thy Name, proclaimed by every lip,
   The Master of our schools.   Amen.

A - men.

LOUIS FITZGERALD BENSON, 1894

By permission of Mrs. Robert E. Jeffreys

LYNNE   BATES G. BURT, 1940

In unison, spirited

1 O God of youth, whose Spi - rit in our hearts is stir - ring
2 Fill thou our hearts with zeal in ev - 'ry brave en - dea - vor
3 Teach us to know the way of Je - sus Christ, our Mas - ter,
4 May we be true to him, our Cap - tain of sal - va - tion,

Hope and de - sire for no - ble lives and true,
To right the wrongs that shame this mor - tal life;
Give us his clear - eyed faith, his fear - less heart,
Bear - ing his cross in ser - vice glad and free,

Keep us, we pray thee, stead - fast and un - err - ing;
Give us the val - iant spi - rit that shall nev - er
And through life's dark - ness, dan - ger, and dis - as - ter,
Win - ning the world to that last con - sum - ma - tion

With light and love di - vine our souls en - due.
Fal - ter or fail how - ev - er long the strife.
O may we nev - er from his side de - part.
When all its king-doms shall his king - dom be. A-men.

Music and words by permission of the author   BATES G. BURT, 1940

509

General Hymns

11 10. 11 10

ST. OSYTH

THOMAS WOOD, 1925

In unison, with vigor

1 Fa - ther, we come, with youth and vig - or press - ing,
2 Be with us, Lord; we kneel in sup - pli - ca - tion,
3 Feed us, O Lord, that we may rise vic - to - rious,

Glad - ly to serve, our loy - al - ty to own;
In bonds of fel - low - ship be - fore thy throne;
Filled with the power that comes from thee a - lone,

Grant that we may, thy ho - ly Name con - fess - ing,
By fer - vent prayer, by will - ing con - se - cra - tion,
In - spired with zeal to face life's chal - lenge glo - rious,

Know thy Son Christ, and seek to make him known.
Help us to know the Christ and make him known.
Ea - ger to know the Christ and make him known. A-men.

Music copyright, 1925, by the Oxford University Press

Words by permission of the author

EDITH CLAYTON, 1922, *alt.*

Alternative Tune, WELWYN, No. 486

LABOR   ALFRED M. SMITH, 1941

In unison, with movement

1 All la - bor gained new dig - ni - ty Since he who all cre - a - tion made
2 No work is com - mon-place, if all Be done as un - to him a - lone;

Toiled with his hands for dai - ly bread Right man - ful - ly.
Life's sim - plest toil to him is known Who know - eth all.

3 Each smallest common thing he makes
  Serves him with its minutest part;
  Man only with his wand'ring heart
    His way forsakes.

4 His service is life's highest joy,
  It yields fair fruit a hundred fold:
  Be this our prayer — "Not fame, nor gold,
    But — thine employ ! "

JOHN OXENHAM, 1920

511

General Hymns

87. 87. D.

PLEADING SAVIOUR
Somewhat slowly

Plymouth Collection,
New York, 1855

1 Je - sus, thou di - vine Com-pan-ion, By thy low - ly hu - man birth
2 Where the ma - ny toil to - geth - er, There art thou a - mong thine own;
3 Ev - 'ry task, how - ev - er sim - ple, Sets the soul that does it free;

Thou hast come to join the work-ers, Bur - den-bear - ers of the earth.
Where the tired . . work-man sleep-eth, There art thou with him a - lone:
Ev - 'ry deed of love and kind-ness Done to man is done to thee.

Thou, the car - pen - ter of Naz-areth, Toil - ing for thy dai - ly food,
Thou, the peace that pass - eth knowl-edge, Dwellest in the dai - ly strife;
Je - sus, thou di - vine Com-pan - ion, Help us all to work our best;

By thy patience and thy courage, Thou hast taught us toil is good.
Thou, the Bread of heav'n, art bro-ken In the sac - ra - ment of life.
Bless us in our dai - ly la - bor, Lead us to our Sab-bath rest. A-men.

HENRY VAN DYKE, 1909, *alt.*

512 ## General Hymns
88. 88. 88

JOHN B. DYKES, 1861

MELITA
In moderate time

1 E - ter - nal Fa - ther, strong to save, Whose arm hath bound the
2 O Christ, whose voice the wa - ters heard And hushed their ra - ging

rest - less wave, Who bidd'st the migh - ty o - cean deep Its
at thy word, Who walk - edst on the foam - ing deep, And

own ap - point - ed lim - its keep: O hear us when we
calm a - mid its rage didst sleep: O hear us when we

cry to thee For those in per - il on the sea.
cry to thee For those in per - il on the sea. A-men.

General Hymns

3 Most Holy Spirit, who didst brood
  Upon the chaos dark and rude,
  And bid its angry tumult cease,
  And give, for wild confusion, peace;
    O hear us when we cry to thee
    For those in peril on the sea.

4 O Trinity of love and power,
  Our brethren shield in danger's hour;
  From rock and tempest, fire and foe,
  Protect them wheresoe'er they go;
    Thus evermore shall rise to thee
    Glad hymns of praise from land and sea.   Amen.

WILLIAM WHITING, 1860, *alt.*

513

Tune, MELITA

1 Almighty Father, strong to save,
  Whose arm hath bound the restless wave,
  Who bidd'st the mighty ocean deep
  Its own appointed limits keep:
    O hear us when we cry to thee
    For those in peril on the sea.

2 O Christ, the Lord of hill and plain
  O'er which our traffic runs amain
  By mountain pass or valley low;
  Wherever, Lord, thy brethren go,
    Protect them by thy guarding hand
    From every peril on the land.

3 O Spirit, whom the Father sent
  To spread abroad the firmament;
  O Wind of heaven, by thy might
  Save all who dare the eagle's flight,
    And keep them by thy watchful care
    From every peril in the air.

4 O Trinity of love and power,
  Our brethren shield in danger's hour;
  From rock and tempest, fire and foe,
  Protect them wheresoe'er they go;
    Thus evermore shall rise to thee
    Glad praise from air and land and sea.   Amen.

Hymnal Version, from A Missionary Service Book, 1937;
Stanzas 1 and 4, WILLIAM WHITING, 1860, *alt.*

85. 83

WESTRIDGE

MARTIN SHAW, 1929

In unison, not too quick

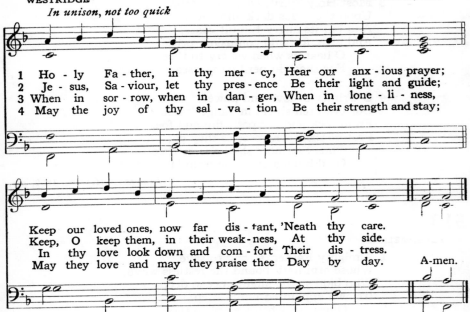

1 Ho - ly Fa - ther, in thy mer - cy, Hear our anx - ious prayer;
2 Je - sus, Sa - viour, let thy pres - ence Be their light and guide;
3 When in sor - row, when in dan - ger, When in lone - li - ness,
4 May the joy of thy sal - va - tion Be their strength and stay;

Keep our loved ones, now far dis - tant, 'Neath thy care.
Keep, O keep them, in their weak - ness, At thy side.
In thy love look down and com - fort Their dis - tress.
May they love and may they praise thee Day by day. A-men.

Copyright, 1929, by the Oxford University Press

5 Holy Spirit, let thy teaching
   Sanctify their life;
   Send thy grace that they may conquer
    In the strife.

6 Father, Son, and Holy Spirit,
   God the One in Three,
   Bless them, guide them, save them, keep them
    Near to thee. Amen.

By permission of the Oxford University Press

ISABEL S. STEVENSON, 1869

515

C. M.

VINCENT NOVELLO, 1800

ALBANO

In moderate time

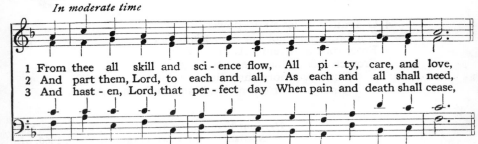

1 From thee all skill and sci - ence flow, All pi - ty, care, and love,
2 And part them, Lord, to each and all, As each and all shall need,
3 And hast - en, Lord, that per - fect day When pain and death shall cease,

General Hymns

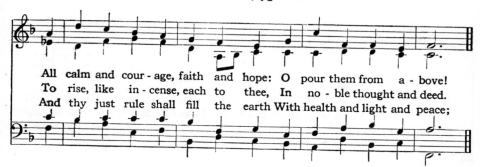

All calm and cour-age, faith and hope: O pour them from a-bove!
To rise, like in-cense, each to thee, In no-ble thought and deed.
And thy just rule shall fill the earth With health and light and peace;

4 When ever blue the sky shall gleam,
  And ever green the sod,
  And man's rude work deface no more
  The paradise of God. Amen.

CHARLES KINGSLEY, 1871

A - men.

516

STOERL C. M.

JOHANN G. CHR. STOERL, 1710

In moderate time

1 Fa - ther, whose will is life and good For all of mor-tal breath, Bind
2 Em-power the hands and hearts and wills Of friends both near and far, Who
3 Wher-e'er they heal the maimed and blind, Let love of Christ at-tend: Pro -

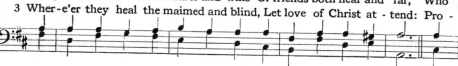

strong the bond of broth-er-hood Of those who fight with death.
bat - tle with the bo - dy's ills, And wage thy ho - ly war.
claim the Good Phy - si - cian's mind, And prove the Sa-viour friend. A-men.

4 O Father, look from heav'n and bless,
  Where'er thy servants be,
  Their works of pure unselfishness,
  Made consecrate to thee. Amen.

HARDWICKE DRUMMOND RAWNSLEY, 1851–1920

517   𝕲𝖊𝖓𝖊𝖗𝖆𝖑 𝕳𝖞𝖒𝖓𝖘

C. M. D.

ST. MATTHEW   *Supplement to the New Version,* 1708

With vigor

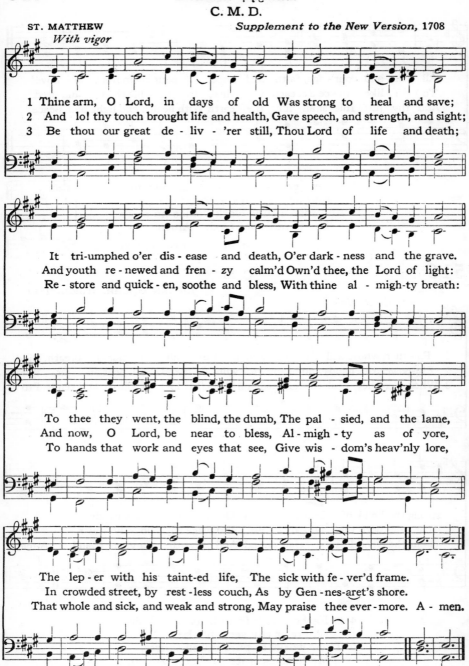

1 Thine arm, O Lord, in days of old Was strong to heal and save;
2 And lo! thy touch brought life and health, Gave speech, and strength, and sight;
3 Be thou our great de - liv - 'rer still, Thou Lord of life and death;

It tri-umphed o'er dis - ease and death, O'er dark - ness and the grave.
And youth re - newed and fren - zy calm'd Own'd thee, the Lord of light:
Re - store and quick - en, soothe and bless, With thine al - migh-ty breath:

To thee they went, the blind, the dumb, The pal - sied, and the lame,
And now, O Lord, be near to bless, Al - migh - ty as of yore,
To hands that work and eyes that see, Give wis - dom's heav'nly lore,

The lep - er with his taint-ed life, The sick with fe - ver'd frame.
In crowded street, by rest - less couch, As by Gen - nes-aret's shore.
That whole and sick, and weak and strong, May praise thee ever - more. A - men.

EDWARD HAYES PLUMPTRE, 1864

518

ST. LEONARD

Melody by
JOHANN CHRISTOPH BACH, 1693

With movement

1 Judge e - ter - nal, throned in splen-dor, Lord of lords and King of kings,

With thy liv - ing fire of judg-ment Purge this land of bit - ter things;

Sol - ace all its wide do - min-ion With the heal - ing of thy wings.

2 Still the weary folk are pining
 For the hour that brings release,
And the city's crowded clangor
 Cries aloud for sin to cease;
And the homesteads and the woodlands
 Plead in silence for their peace.

3 Crown, O God, thine own endeavor;
 Cleave our darkness with thy sword;
Feed the faint and hungry heathen
 With the richness of thy word;
Cleanse the body of this nation
 Through the glory of the Lord. Amen.

HENRY SCOTT HOLLAND, 1902

A - men.

87. 87. D.

EBENEZER (TON-Y-BOTEL)   THOMAS JOHN WILLIAMS, 1890

In unison, slowly, with dignity

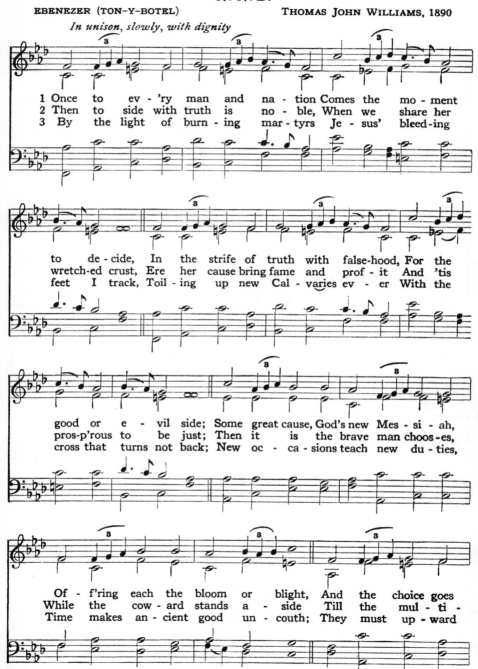

1 Once to ev - 'ry man and na - tion Comes the mo - ment
2 Then to side with truth is no - ble, When we share her
3 By the light of burn - ing mar - tyrs Je - sus' bleed-ing

to de - cide, In the strife of truth with false-hood, For the
wretch-ed crust, Ere her cause bring fame and prof - it And 'tis
feet I track, Toil - ing up new Cal - varies ev - er With the

good or e - vil side; Some great cause, God's new Mes - si - ah,
pros-p'rous to be just; Then it is the brave man choos-es,
cross that turns not back; New oc - ca - sions teach new du - ties,

Of - f'ring each the bloom or blight, And the choice goes
While the cow - ard stands a - side Till the mul - ti -
Time makes an - cient good un - couth; They must up - ward

by	for	ev - er	'Twixt	that	dark - ness	and	that	light.
tude	make	vir - tue	Of	the	faith they	had	de - nied.
still	and	on - ward	Who	would	keep a -	breast	of	truth.

4 Though the cause of evil prosper,
   Yet 'tis truth alone is strong;
Though her portion be the scaffold,
   And upon the throne be wrong,

Yet that scaffold sways the future,
   And, behind the dim unknown,
Standeth God within the shadow
   Keeping watch above his own.

JAMES RUSSELL LOWELL, 1845

520   L. M.

WAREHAM   WILLIAM KNAPP, 1738

In moderate time

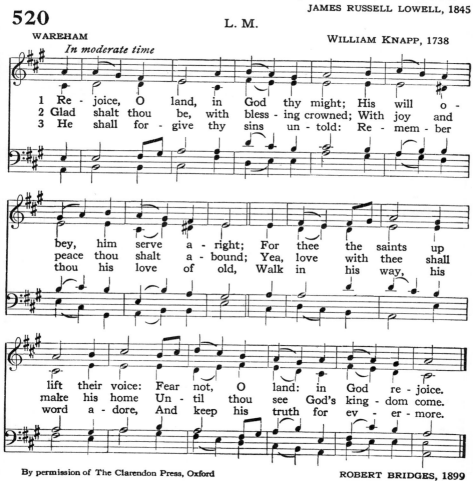

1 Re -	joice,	O	land,	in	God	thy	might;	His	will	o -
2 Glad	shalt	thou	be,	with	bless - ing	crowned;	With	joy	and
3 He	shall	for - give	thy	sins	un - told:	Re - mem - ber

bey,	him	serve	a - right;	For	thee	the	saints	up
peace	thou	shalt	a - bound;	Yea,	love	with	thee	shall
thou	his	love	of	old,	Walk	in	his	way,	his

lift	their	voice:	Fear	not,	O	land:	in	God	re - joice.
make	his	home	Un - til	thou	see	God's	king - dom	come.
word	a - dore,	And	keep	his	truth	for	ev - er - more.

By permission of The Clarendon Press, Oxford   ROBERT BRIDGES, 1899

76. 76. D.

KING'S LYNN

In unison, with dignity

Traditional English Melody,
arr. by R. VAUGHAN WILLIAMS, 1906

1 O God of earth and al - tar, Bow down and hear our cry,
2 From all that ter - ror teach - es, From lies of tongue and pen,
3 Tie in a liv - ing teth - er The prince and priest and thrall,

Our earth - ly rul - ers fal - ter, Our peo - ple drift and die;
From all the eas - y speech - es That com - fort cru - el men,
Bind all our lives to - geth - er, Smite us and save us all;

The walls of gold en - tomb us, The swords of scorn di - vide,
From sale and prof - a - na - tion Of hon - or, and the sword,
In ire and ex - ul - ta - tion A - flame with faith, and free,

Take not thy thun-der from us, But take a - way our pride.
From sleep and from dam - na - tion, De - liv - er us, good Lord!
Lift up a liv - ing na - tion, A sin - gle sword to thee. A-men.

GILBERT KEITH CHESTERTON, 1906

87. 87. 887

BOHEMIAN BRETHREN   Melody of the Unitas Fratrum, pub. 1566

Unison, in moderate time

1 Lord Christ, when first thou cam'st to men, Up - on a cross they
2 O awe - ful Love, which found no room In life where sin de -
3 New ad - vent of the love of Christ, Shall we a - gain re -
4 O wound-ed hands of Je - sus, build In us thy new cre -

bound thee, And mock'd thy sa - ving king-ship then By thorns with which
nied thee, And, doomed to death, must bring to doom The power which cru -
fuse thee, Till in the night of hate and war We per - ish as
a - tion; Our pride is dust, our vaunt is stilled, We wait thy rev -

they crowned thee: And still our wrongs may weave thee now New
ci - fied thee, Till not a stone was left on stone, And
we lose thee? From old un - faith our souls re - lease To
e - la - tion: O love that tri - umphs o - ver loss, We

thorns to pierce that stea - dy brow, And robe of sor - row round thee.
all a na - tion's pride, o'erthrown, Went down to dust be - side thee!
seek the king-dom of thy peace, By which a - lone we choose thee.
bring our hearts be - fore thy cross, To fin - ish thy sal - va - tion.

By permission of the author
and of the Oxford University Press   WALTER RUSSELL BOWIE, 1928

523 **General Hymns**

11 10. 11 9

RUSSIA   ALEXIS LVOV, 1833

1 God the Om - ni - po-tent! King, who or - dain - est Thun - der thy
2 God the All - mer - ci - ful! earth hath for - sa - ken Thy ways all

clar - ion, the light - ning thy sword; Show forth thy pi - ty on
ho - ly, and slight - ed thy word; Bid not thy wrath in its

high where thou reign - est: Give to us peace in our time, O Lord.
ter - rors a - wa - ken: Give to us peace in our time, O Lord.

3 God the All-righteous One! man hath defied thee;
   Yet to eternity standeth thy word,
Falsehood and wrong shall not tarry beside thee:
   Give to us peace in our time, O Lord.

4 God the All-provident! earth by thy chast'ning,
   Yet shall to freedom and truth be restored;
Through the thick darkness thy kingdom is hast'ning:
   Thou wilt give peace in thy time, O Lord.   Amen.

A-men.

St. 1, 2, HENRY FOTHERGILL CHORLEY, 1842;
St. 3, 4, JOHN ELLERTON, 1870; alt.

87. 87. 87

MANNHEIM

Congregational Church Music, 1853
adapted from FRIEDRICH FILITZ, 1847

Moderately slow

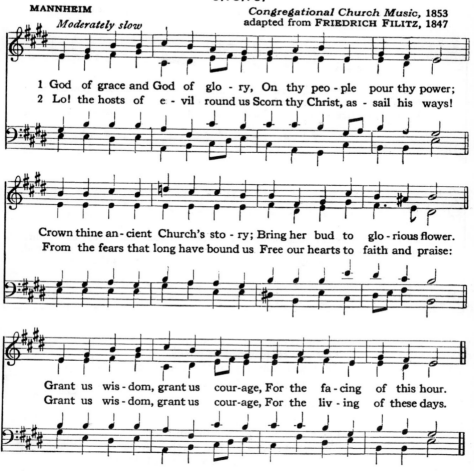

1 God of grace and God of glo - ry, On thy peo - ple pour thy power;
2 Lo! the hosts of e - vil round us Scorn thy Christ, as - sail his ways!

Crown thine an - cient Church's sto - ry; Bring her bud to glo - rious flower.
From the fears that long have bound us Free our hearts to faith and praise:

Grant us wis - dom, grant us cour-age, For the fa - cing of this hour.
Grant us wis - dom, grant us cour-age, For the liv - ing of these days.

3 Cure thy children's warring madness,
    Bend our pride to thy control;
Shame our wanton, selfish gladness,
    Rich in things and poor in soul.
Grant us wisdom, grant us courage,
    Lest we miss thy kingdom's goal.

4 Set our feet on lofty places;
    Gird our lives that they may be
Armored with all Christ-like graces
    In the fight to set men free.
Grant us wisdom, grant us courage,
    That we fail not man nor thee. Amen.

A - men.

HARRY EMERSON FOSDICK, 1930, *alt.*

BELLWOODS   JAMES HOPKIRK, 1938

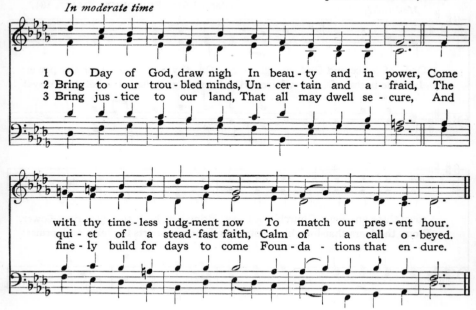

In moderate time

1 O Day of God, draw nigh In beau-ty and in power, Come
2 Bring to our trou-bled minds, Un-cer-tain and a-fraid, The
3 Bring jus-tice to our land, That all may dwell se-cure, And

with thy time-less judg-ment now   To   match our pres-ent hour.
qui-et of a stead-fast faith, Calm of a call o-beyed.
fine-ly build for days to come Foun-da-tions that en-dure.

4 Bring to our world of strife
Thy sov'reign word of peace,
That war may haunt the earth no more
And desolation cease.

5 O Day of God, draw nigh
As at creation's birth,
Let there be light again, and set
Thy judgments on the earth. Amen.

A-men.

R. B. Y. SCOTT, 1937, *alt.*

526   *First Tune*   C. M.

VERMONT   ANNE L. MILLER, 1941

In moderate time

1 Give peace, O God, the na-tions cry, From e-vil man and deed;
2 Yet not thy peace, O God, they ask, The peace that grace be-stows:
3 But peace they ask from war's a-larms, Sur-cease from earth-y care,

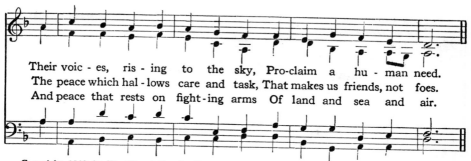

Their voic-es, ris-ing to the sky, Pro-claim a hu-man need.
The peace which hal-lows care and task, That makes us friends, not foes.
And peace that rests on fight-ing arms Of land and sea and air.

4 We need the peace of heart and mind
  In men from hate set free,
Who by their love for human kind
  Show deeper love for thee.

5 O cleanse all hearts of pride and greed,
  Remove all lust and sin,
That man from chains of wrath be freed,
  Eternal peace to win. Amen.

JOHN W. NORRIS, 1939

A - men.

526 *Second Tune*   C. M.

LYNCHBURG   HENRY HALLSTROM, 1941

In unison, solemnly

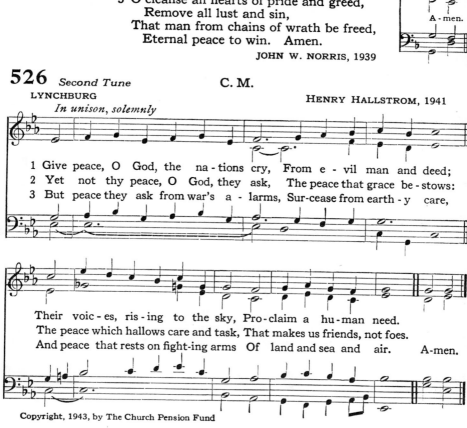

1 Give peace, O God, the na-tions cry, From e-vil man and deed;
2 Yet not thy peace, O God, they ask, The peace that grace be-stows:
3 But peace they ask from war's a-larms, Sur-cease from earth-y care,

Their voic-es, ris-ing to the sky, Pro-claim a hu-man need.
The peace which hallows care and task, That makes us friends, not foes.
And peace that rests on fight-ing arms Of land and sea and air. A-men.

TAYLOR HALL   LEO SOWERBY, 1941

In moderate time

1 Peace in our time, O Lord, To all the peo-ples—Peace!
2 Too long mis-trust and fear Have held our souls in thrall;
3 O shall we nev-er learn The truth all time has taught,—

Peace sure-ly based up-on thy will And built in right-eous-ness.
Sweep through the earth, keen breath of heav'n, And sound a no-bler call!
That with-out God as ar-chi-tect Our build-ing comes to naught?

Thy power a-lone can break The fet-ters that en-chain The
Come, as thou didst of old, In love so great that men Shall
Lord, help us, and in-spire Our hearts and lives, that we May

sore-ly-strick-en soul of life, And make it live a-gain.
cast a-side all oth-er gods And turn to thee a-gain!
build, with all thy won-drous gifts, A king-dom meet for thee! A-men.

General Hymns

4 Peace in our time, O Lord,
   To all the peoples — Peace!
   Peace that shall build a glad new world
   And make for life's increase.
   O Living Christ, who still
   Dost all our burdens share,
   Come now and dwell within the hearts
   Of all men everywhere!   Amen.

JOHN OXENHAM, 1938

By permission of the author

528
L. M.

HESPERUS

HENRY BAKER, 1866

In moderate time

1 O God of love, O King of peace, Make wars through-
2 Re-mem-ber, Lord, thy works of old, The won-ders
3 Whom shall we trust but thee, O Lord? Where rest but

out the world to cease; The wrath of sin - ful
that our fa - thers told; Re - mem - ber not our
on thy faith - ful word? None ev - er called on

man re - strain, Give peace, O God, give peace a - gain!
sin's dark stain, Give peace, O God, give peace a - gain!
thee in vain, Give peace, O God, give peace a - gain!   A - men.

HENRY WILLIAMS BAKER, 1861, *alt.*

RACINE   ROLAND DIGGLE, 1941

With dignity

1 Lord God of hosts, whose migh - ty hand Do - min - ion holds on
2 For those who weak and bro - ken lie In wea - ri - ness and
3 For those to whom the call shall come, We pray thy ten - der

sea and land, In peace and war thy will we see . . .
ag - o - ny, Great Heal - er, to their beds of pain Come,
wel - come home; The toil, the bit - ter - ness, all past, We

Sha - ping the lar - ger lib - er - ty; Na - tions may rise and
touch and make them whole a - gain. O hear a peo - ple's
trust them to thy love at last. O hear a peo - ple's

na - tions fall, Thy change-less pur - pose rules them all.
prayers, and bless Thy ser - vants in their hour of stress!
prayers for all Who, no - bly stri - ving, no - bly fall! A - men.

General Hymns

4 For those who minister and heal,
   And spend themselves, their skill, their zeal;
   Renew their hearts with Christ-like faith,
   And guard them from disease and death;
     And in thine own good time, Lord, send
     Thy peace on earth till time shall end. Amen.

By permission of the author   JOHN OXENHAM, 1914

530
L. M.

PATER OMNIPOTENS

MARK DICKEY, 1941

In moderate time

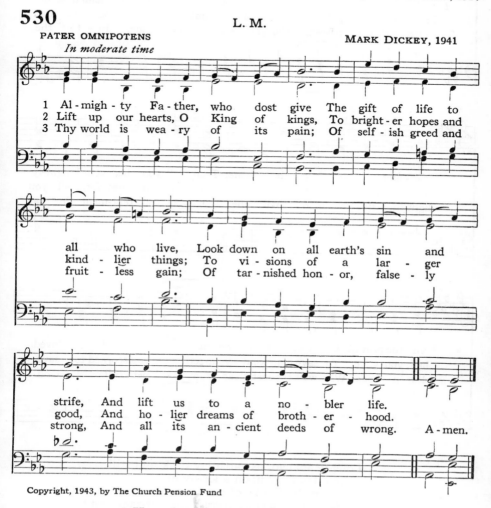

1 Al - migh - ty Fa - ther, who dost give The gift of life to all who live, Look down on all earth's sin and strife, And lift us to a no - bler life.

2 Lift up our hearts, O King of kings, To bright - er hopes and kind - lier things; To vi - sions of a lar - ger good, And ho - lier dreams of broth - er - hood.

3 Thy world is wea - ry of its pain; Of self - ish greed and fruit - less gain; Of tar - nished hon - or, false - ly strong, And all its an - cient deeds of wrong. A - men.

Copyright, 1943, by The Church Pension Fund

4 Hear thou the prayer thy servants pray,
   Uprising from all lands to-day,
   And o'er the vanquished powers of sin,
   O bring thy great salvation in. Amen.

By permission of Mrs. J. H. B. Masterman   JOHN HOWARD BERTRAM MASTERMAN, 1922

BIRMINGHAM

FRANCIS CUNNINGHAM'S
A Selection of Psalm Tunes, 1834

With spirit

1 O val - iant hearts, who to your glo - ry came Through dust of
*2 Proud - ly you gath - er'd, rank on rank, to war, As who had
*3 Splen - did you passed, the great sur - ren - der made, In - to the

con - flict and thro' bat - tle flame; Tran-quil you lie, your knight-ly
heard God's mes-sage from a - far; All you had hoped for, all you
light that nev - er more shall fade; Deep your con - tent-ment in that

vir - tue proved, Your mem-o-ry hal-lowed in the land you loved.
had, you gave To save man-kind—your-self you scorned to save.
blest a - bode, Who wait the last clear trum - pet - call of God.

4 Long years ago, as earth lay dark and still,
  Rose a loud cry upon a lonely hill,
  While in the frailty of our human clay,
  Christ our Redeemer passed the self-same way.

5 Still stands his cross from that dread hour to this,
  Like some bright star above the dark abyss;
  Still, through the veil, the victor's pitying eyes
  Look down to bless our lesser Calvaries.

6 These were his servants; in his steps they trod,
  Following through death the martyred Son of God:
  Victor he rose; victorious too shall rise
  They who have drunk his cup of sacrifice.

7 O risen Lord, O Shepherd of our dead,
  Whose cross has brought them and whose staff has led,
  In glorious hope their proud and sorrowing land
  Commits her children to thy gracious hand.

JOHN STANHOPE ARKWRIGHT, 1919
By permission of the author and of Skeffington & Son, Ltd., publishers

531 *Second Tune*   10 10. 10 10

VALIANT HEARTS

GUSTAV HOLST, 1925

In moderate time

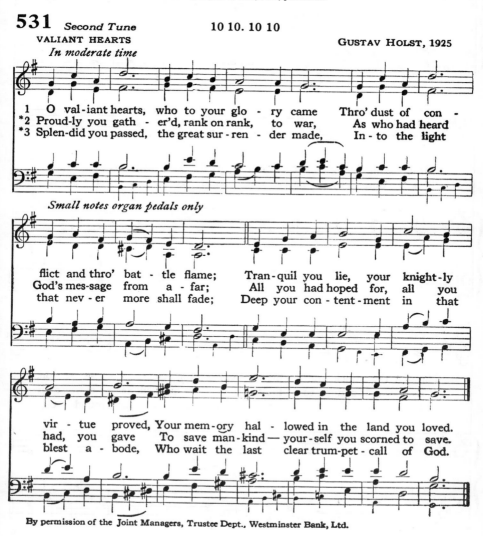

Small notes organ pedals only

1 O val-iant hearts, who to your glo - ry came Thro' dust of con -
*2 Proud-ly you gath - er'd, rank on rank, to war, As who had heard
*3 Splen-did you passed, the great sur - ren - der made, In - to the light

flict and thro' bat - tle flame; Tran - quil you lie, your knight-ly
God's mes-sage from a - far; All you had hoped for, all you
that nev - er more shall fade; Deep your con - tent-ment in that

vir - tue proved, Your mem-ory hal - lowed in the land you loved.
had, you gave To save man-kind — your-self you scorned to save.
blest a - bode, Who wait the last clear trum-pet - call of God.

By permission of the Joint Managers, Trustee Dept., Westminster Bank, Ltd.

11 10. 11 10. 10

LANGHAM

GEOFFREY SHAW, 1925

In unison, moderately slow

1 Fa - ther e - ter - nal, Rul - er of cre - a - tion,
2 Ra - ces and peo - ples, lo, we stand di - vi - ded,
3 En - vious of heart, blind - eyed, with tongues con - found - ed,

Spi - rit of life, which moved ere form was made,
And, shar - ing not our griefs, no joy can share;
Na - tion by na - tion still goes un - for - giv'n,

Through the thick dark - ness cov - 'ring ev - 'ry na - tion,
By wars and tu - mults love is mocked, de - ri - ded;
In wrath and fear, by jeal - ous - ies sur - round - ed,

General Hymns

Light   to man's blind - ness,   O   be thou our   aid:
His   conquering cross   no   king - dom wills   to   bear:
Build - ing proud towers which shall   not reach to   heav'n:

Refrain

Thy   king - dom come,   O   Lord, thy   will   be   done.

*4 Lust of possession worketh desolations;
    There is no meekness in the sons of earth;
    Led by no star, the rulers of the nations
    Still fail to bring us to the blissful birth:
                                                    Refrain

5 How shall we love thee, holy hidden Being,
    If we love not the world which thou hast made?
    O give us brother-love for better seeing
    Thy Word made flesh, and in a manger laid.
                                                    Refrain

LAURENCE HOUSMAN, 1919

C. M. D.

BETHLEHEM   GOTTFRIED W. FINK, 1842

In moderate time

1 Our Fa - ther, thy dear Name doth show The great-ness of thy love;
2 A - like we share thy ten - der care; We trust one heav'n-ly friend;
3 Bring in, we pray, the glo - rious day When bat - tle cries are stilled,
4 Close knit the warm fra - ter - nal tie That makes the whole world one;

All are thy chil - dren here be - low As in thy heav'n a - bove.
Be - fore one mer - cy - seat in prayer In con - fi - dence we bend;
When bit - ter strife is swept a - way, And hearts with love are filled.
Our dis - cords change to har - mo - ny Like an - gel - songs be - gun:

One fam - i - ly on earth are we Through-out its wi - dest span:
A - like we hear thy lov - ing call; One heav'n-ly vi - sion scan,
O help us ban - ish pride and wrong, Which since the world be - gan
At last, up - on that bright-er shore Com-plete thy glo - rious plan,

O help us ev - 'ry-where to see The broth-er - hood of man.
One Lord, one faith, one hope for all, The broth-er - hood of man.
Have marred its peace; help us make strong The broth-er - hood of man.
And heav'n shall crown for ev - er-more The broth-er - hood of man. A-men.

CHARLES HERBERT RICHARDS, 1910

HOSMER
66. 66 *Psalteriolum Harmonicum,* 1642

In moderate time

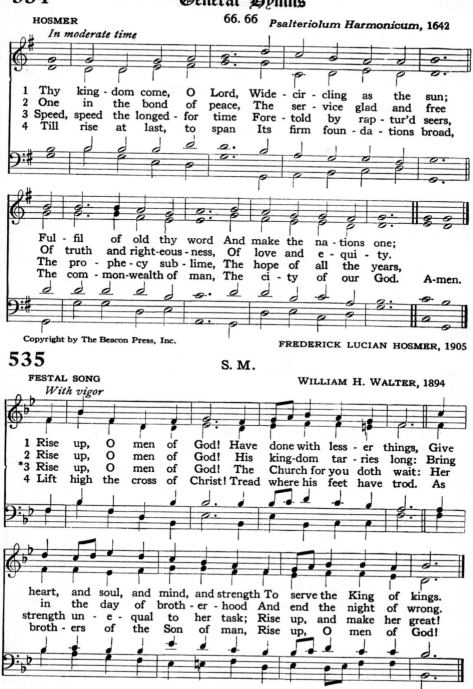

1 Thy king - dom come, O Lord, Wide - cir - cling as the sun;
2 One in the bond of peace, The ser - vice glad and free
3 Speed, speed the longed - for time Fore - told by rap - tur'd seers,
4 Till rise at last, to span Its firm foun - da - tions broad,

Ful - fil of old thy word And make the na - tions one;
Of truth and right-eous - ness, Of love and e - qui - ty.
The pro - phe - cy sub - lime, The hope of all the years,
The com - mon-wealth of man, The ci - ty of our God. A-men.

Copyright by The Beacon Press, Inc.

FREDERICK LUCIAN HOSMER, 1905

535
S. M.

FESTAL SONG
With vigor

WILLIAM H. WALTER, 1894

1 Rise up, O men of God! Have done with less - er things, Give
2 Rise up, O men of God! His king-dom tar - ries long: Bring
*3 Rise up, O men of God! The Church for you doth wait: Her
4 Lift high the cross of Christ! Tread where his feet have trod. As

heart, and soul, and mind, and strength To serve the King of kings.
in the day of broth - er - hood And end the night of wrong.
strength un - e - qual to her task; Rise up, and make her great!
broth - ers of the Son of man, Rise up, O men of God!

By permission of the author

WILLIAM PIERSON MERRILL, 1911

10 10. 10 10. 10

OLD HUNDRED TWENTY FOURTH   Louis Bourgeois, 1551

Slow

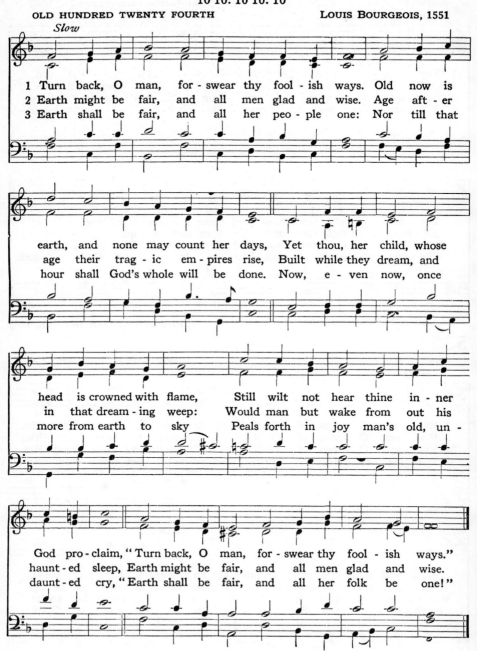

1 Turn back, O man, for-swear thy fool-ish ways. Old now is
2 Earth might be fair, and all men glad and wise. Age aft-er
3 Earth shall be fair, and all her peo-ple one: Nor till that

earth, and none may count her days, Yet thou, her child, whose
age their trag-ic em-pires rise, Built while they dream, and
hour shall God's whole will be done. Now, e-ven now, once

head is crowned with flame, Still wilt not hear thine in-ner
in that dream-ing weep: Would man but wake from out his
more from earth to sky Peals forth in joy man's old, un-

God pro-claim, "Turn back, O man, for-swear thy fool-ish ways."
haunt-ed sleep, Earth might be fair, and all men glad and wise.
daunt-ed cry, "Earth shall be fair, and all her folk be one!"

CLIFFORD BAX, 1919

By permission of A. D. Peters

MOSCOW   FELICE DE GIARDINI, 1769

With vigor

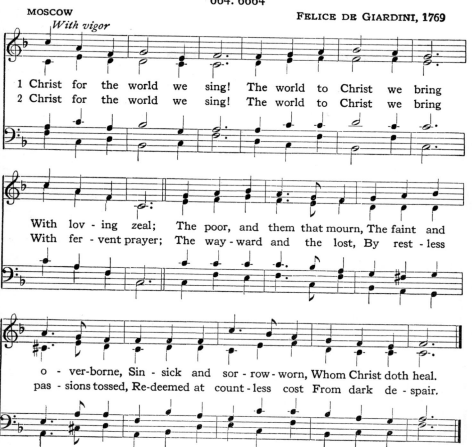

1 Christ for the world we sing! The world to Christ we bring
2 Christ for the world we sing! The world to Christ we bring

With lov - ing zeal; The poor, and them that mourn, The faint and
With fer - vent prayer; The way - ward and the lost, By rest - less

o - ver-borne, Sin - sick and sor - row-worn, Whom Christ doth heal.
pas - sions tossed, Re-deemed at count - less cost From dark de - spair.

3 Christ for the world we sing!
  The world to Christ we bring
    With one accord;
  With us the work to share,
  With us reproach to dare,
  With us the cross to bear,
    For Christ our Lord.

4 Christ for the world we sing!
  The world to Christ we bring
    With joyful song;
  The new-born souls, whose days,
  Reclaimed from error's ways,
  Inspired with hope and praise,
    To Christ belong.

SAMUEL WOLCOTT, 1869

Irregular

MARTIN SHAW, 1931

PURPOSE

With breadth

1 God is work - ing his pur - pose out As year suc -
2 From ut - most east to ut - most west, Wher - e'er man's
3 March we forth in the strength of God, With the ban - ner of
4 All we can do is noth - ing worth Un - less God

Octaves to the end

ceeds to year: . . . . . God is work - ing his
foot hath trod, By the mouth of ma - ny
Christ un - furled, That the light of the glo - rious
bless - es the deed; . . . . . Vain - ly we hope for the

pur - pose out, And the time is draw - ing near; Near - er and
mes - sen - gers Goes forth the voice of God; Give ear to
gos - pel of truth May shine throughout the world: Fight we the
har - vest - tide Till God gives life to the seed; Yet near - er and

General Hymns

near - er draws the time, The time that shall sure - ly be,
me, ye con - ti - nents, Ye isles, give ear to me,
fight with sorrow and sin To set their cap - tives free,
near - er draws the time, The time that shall sure - ly be,

When the earth shall be filled with the glo - ry of God
That the earth may be filled with the glo - ry of God
That the earth may be filled with the glo - ry of God
When the earth shall be filled with the glo - ry of God

St. 1, 2, 3 | St. 4

As the wa - ters cov - er the sea.
As the wa - ters cov - er the sea.
As the wa - ters cov - er the sea.
As the wa - ters cov - er the sea. . . . . . .

ARTHUR CAMPBELL AINGER, 1894

L. M.

ARMES   PHILIP ARMES, 1875

Boldly

1 Soon may the last glad song a - rise Through all the
2 Let thrones and powers and king - doms be O - be - dient,
3 O that the an - them now might swell, And host to

mil - lions of the skies, That song of tri - umph which re -
migh - ty God, to thee; And o - ver land and stream and
host the tri - umph tell, That not one reb - el heart re -

cords That all the earth is now the Lord's.
main Wave thou the scep - ter of thy reign.
mains, But o - ver all the Sa - viour reigns! A - men.

Ascribed *to* MRS. VOKES, 1816

539 *Second Tune*   **L. M.**

TRURO   *Psalmodia Evangelica*, 1789

With spirit

1 Soon may the last glad song a - rise Through all the mil - lions
2 Let thrones and powers and king - doms be O - be - dient, migh - ty
3 O that the an - them now might swell, And host to host the

General Hymns

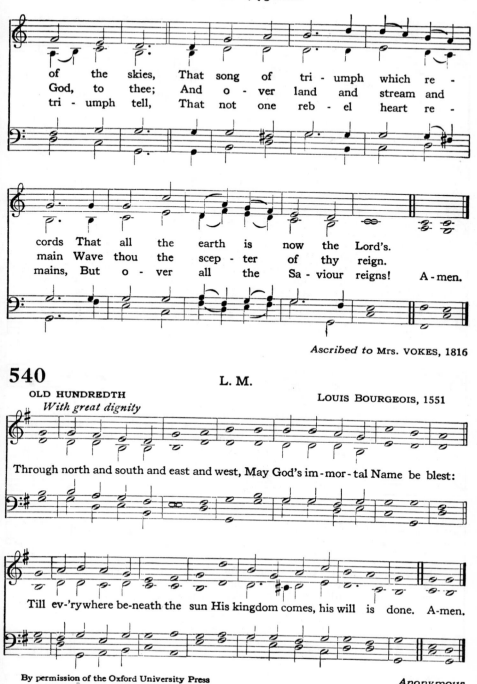

of the skies, That song of tri - umph which re -
God, to thee; And o - ver land and stream and
tri - umph tell, That not one reb - el heart re -

cords That all the earth is now the Lord's.
main Wave thou the scep - ter of thy reign.
mains, But o - ver all the Sa - viour reigns! A - men.

Ascribed to Mrs. VOKES, 1816

540

L. M.

OLD HUNDREDTH

LOUIS BOURGEOIS, 1551

With great dignity

Through north and south and east and west, May God's im-mor-tal Name be blest:

Till ev-'ry where be-neath the sun His kingdom comes, his will is done. A-men.

Anonymous

541   𝕲eneral 𝕳ymns

86. 86. 88

CONQUEST   DONALD S. BARROWS, 1941

Moderately fast

1 O North, with all thy vales of green! O South, with
2 Lo, in the clouds of heav'n ap - pears God's well - be -
3 O Fa - ther, haste the prom - is'd hour, When at his
4 When all shall heed the words he said, A - mid their

all thy palms! From peo - pl'd towns and vales be - tween,
lov - ed Son; He brings a train of bright - er years;
feet shall lie All rule, au - thor - i - ty, and power
dai - ly cares, And by the lov - ing life he led

Up - lift the voice of psalms; Raise, an - cient East, the an - them
His king-dom is be - gun. He comes, a guilt - y world to
Be - neath the am - ple sky; When he shall reign from pole to
Shall seek to pat - tern theirs; And he who con - quer'd death shall

high, And let the youth - ful West re - ply.
bless With mer - cy, truth, and right - eous - ness.
pole, The Lord of ev - 'ry hu - man soul:
win The migh - tier con - quest o - ver sin. A - men.

WILLIAM CULLEN BRYANT, 1869

L. M.

DUKE STREET   JOHN HATTON, 1793

With breadth

1 Je - sus shall reign wher - e'er the sun Doth his suc -
2 To him shall end - less prayer be made, And prais - es
3 Peo - ple and realms of ev - 'ry tongue Dwell on his

ces - sive jour - neys run; His king - dom stretch from
throng to crown his head; His Name like sweet per -
love with sweet - est song; And in - fant voic - es

shore to shore, Till moons shall wax and wane no more.
fume shall rise With ev - 'ry morn - ing sac - ri - fice.
shall pro - claim Their ear - ly bless - ings on his Name.

4 Blessings abound where'er he reigns;
   The prisoner leaps to lose his chains,
   The weary find eternal rest,
   And all the sons of want are blest.

5 Let every creature rise and bring
   Peculiar honors to our King;
   Angels descend with songs again,
   And earth repeat the loud Amen.

ISAAC WATTS, 1719

CHRISTUS REX　　　　　　　　　DAVID McK. WILLIAMS, 1941

In unison, with vigor

1 Christ is the King! O friends up - raise An - thems of
2 O Chris - tian wo - men, Chris - tian men, All the world
3 Let Love's un - con - quer - a - ble might Your scat - ter'd

joy and ho - ly praise For his brave saints of an - cient days,
o - ver, seek a - gain The Way dis - ci - ples fol - low'd then.
com - pa - nies u - nite In ser - vice to the Lord of light:

Who with a faith for ev - er new Fol - lowed the King, and
Christ through all a - ges is the same: Place the same hope in
So shall God's will on earth be done, New lamps be lit, new

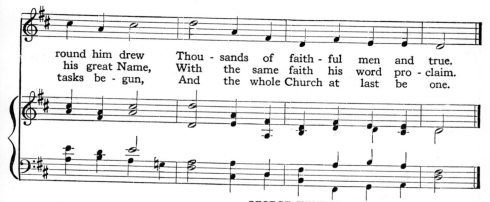

round him drew   Thou - sands of faith - ful men and true.
his great Name,   With the same faith his word pro - claim.
tasks be - gun,   And the whole Church at last be one.

GEORGE KENNEDY ALLEN BELL, 1933, *alt.*

Music copyright, 1943, by The Church Pension Fund
Words by special permission of the author
and of the Oxford University Press

544

66. 66

ST. CECILIA

LEIGHTON G. HAYNE, 1863

In moderate time

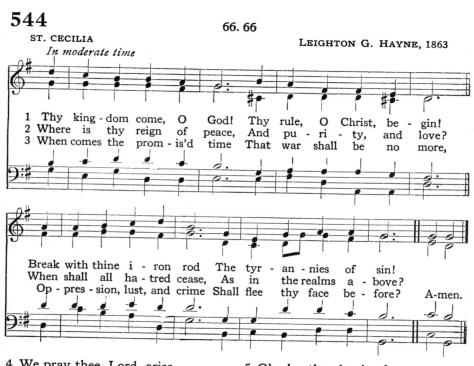

1 Thy king - dom come, O God! Thy rule, O Christ, be - gin!
2 Where is thy reign of peace, And pu - ri - ty, and love?
3 When comes the prom - is'd time That war shall be no more,

Break with thine i - ron rod The tyr - an - nies of sin!
When shall all ha - tred cease, As in the realms a - bove?
Op - pres - sion, lust, and crime Shall flee thy face be - fore? A-men.

4 We pray thee, Lord, arise,
    And come in thy great might;
Revive our longing eyes,
    Which languish for thy sight.

5 O'er heathen lands afar
    Thick darkness broodeth yet:
Arise, O Morning Star,
    Arise, and never set! Amen.

LEWIS HENSLEY, 1867

WOODBIRD — *Cheerfully*

Traditional German Melody

1 Hail to the Lord's A - noint - ed, Great Da - vid's great - er Son!
2 He comes with suc - cor speed - y To those who suf - fer wrong,
*3 He shall come down like show - ers Up - on the fruit - ful earth,

Hail, in the time ap - point - ed, His reign on earth be - gun!
To help the poor and need - y, And bid the weak be strong;
And love, joy, hope, like flow - ers, Spring in his path to birth:

He comes to break op - pres - sion, To set the cap - tive free;
To give them songs for sigh - ing, Their dark - ness turn to light,
Be - fore him on the moun - tains Shall peace, the her - ald, go;

To take a - way trans - gres - sion, And rule in e - qui - ty.
Whose souls, con - demned and dy - ing, Were pre - cious in his sight.
And right - eous - ness in foun - tains From hill to val - ley flow.

4 Kings shall bow down before him,
    And gold and incense bring;
All nations shall adore him,
    His praise all people sing;

To him shall prayer unceasing
    And daily vows ascend;
His kingdom still increasing,
    A kingdom without end.

5 O'er every foe victorious,
　　He on his throne shall rest;
　From age to age more glorious,
　　All-blessing and all-blest:

The tide of time shall never
　His covenant remove;
His Name shall stand for ever,
　His changeless Name of Love.

JAMES MONTGOMERY, 1821, *based on Psalm 72*

545 *Second Tune*　　　76. 76. D.

ZOAN

WILLIAM H. HAVERGAL, 1859

With vigor

1 Hail to the Lord's A-noint-ed, Great Da-vid's great-er Son!
2 He comes with suc-cor speed-y To those who suf-fer wrong,
*3 He shall come down like show-ers Up-on the fruit-ful earth,

Hail, in the time ap-point-ed, His reign on earth be-gun!
To help the poor and need-y, And bid the weak be strong;
And love, joy, hope, like flow-ers, Spring in his path to birth:

He comes to break op-pres-sion, To set the cap-tive free;
To give them songs for sigh-ing, Their dark-ness turn to light,
Be-fore him on the moun-tains Shall peace, the her-ald, go;

To take a-way trans-gres-sion, And rule in e-qui-ty.
Whose souls, con-demned and dy-ing, Were pre-cious in his sight.
And right-eous-ness in foun-tains From hill to val-ley flow.

65. 65. D., with Refrain

BLENCATHRA   ARTHUR SOMERVELL, 1925

With vigor

1 For - ward through the a - ges, In un - bro - ken line,
2 Wi - der grows the king - dom, Reign of love and light;

Move the faith - ful spi - rits At the call di - vine:
For it we must la - bor Till our faith is sight.

Gifts in dif - f'ring mea - sure, Hearts in one ac - cord,
Pro - phets have pro-claimed it, Mar - tyrs tes - ti - fied,

Man - i - fold the ser - vice, One the sure re - ward.
Po - ets sung its glo - ry, He - roes for it died.

General Hymns

Refrain, in unison

For - ward through the a - ges, In un - bro - ken line,

Move the faith - ful spi - rits At the call di - vine.

3 Not alone we conquer,
  Not alone we fall;
In each loss or triumph
  Lose or triumph all.
Bound by God's far purpose
  In one living whole,
Move we on together
  To the shining goal!

Refrain

FREDERICK LUCIAN HOSMER, 1908

Alternative Tune, ST. BONIFACE, No. 561

547 *First Tune* **General Hymns**
C. M.

MARTYRS
In unison, with noble austerity
Scottish Psalter, 1615

1 O God of truth, whose liv - ing Word Up - holds what - e'er hath breath,
2 Set up thy stan - dard, Lord, that we Who claim a heav'n - ly birth

Look down on thy cre - a - tion, Lord, En - slaved by sin and death.
May march with thee to smite the lies That vex thy groan - ing earth.

547 *Second Tune* C. M.

MARLOW
With movement
Arr. from JOHN CHETHAM'S *Psalmody, 1718*

1 O God of truth, whose liv - ing Word Up - holds what - e'er hath breath,
2 Set up thy stan - dard, Lord, that we Who claim a heav'n - ly birth

Look down on thy cre - a - tion, Lord, En - slaved by sin and death.
May march with thee to smite the lies That vex thy groan - ing earth.

General Hymns

3 We fight for truth? we fight for God?
 Poor slaves of lies and sin!
 He who would fight for thee on earth
 Must first be true within.

4 Then, God of truth for whom we long,
 Thou who wilt hear our prayer,
 Do thine own battle in our hearts,
 And slay the falsehood there.

5 Yea, come; then, tried as in the fire,
 From every lie set free,
 Thy perfect truth shall dwell in us,
 And we shall live in thee.   Amen.

THOMAS HUGHES, 1859

1st Tune

A - men.

2nd Tune

A - men.

548

L. M.

SEABURY

CLAUDE MEANS, 1941

In moderate time

1 Cre - a - tion's Lord, we give thee thanks That this thy world is in - com-plete;
2 That thou hast not yet fin-ished man; That we are in the ma - king still,

That bat - tle calls our marshaled ranks; That work awaits our hands and feet;
As friends who share the Maker's plan, As sons who know the Fa-ther's will.

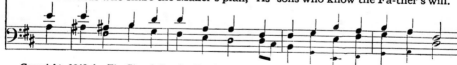

3 What though the kingdom long delay,
 And still with haughty foes must cope?
 It gives us that for which to pray,
 A field for toil and faith and hope.

4 Since what we choose is what we are,
 And what we love we yet shall be,
 The goal may ever shine afar;
 The will to win it makes us free.

WILLIAM DE WITT HYDE, 1903

ALL SAINTS NEW   HENRY S. CUTLER, 1872

With vigor

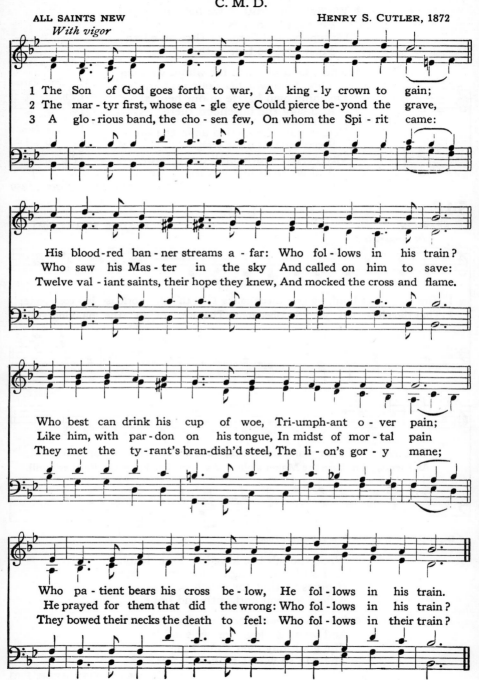

1 The Son of God goes forth to war, A king-ly crown to gain;
2 The mar-tyr first, whose ea-gle eye Could pierce be-yond the grave,
3 A glo-rious band, the cho-sen few, On whom the Spi-rit came:

His blood-red ban-ner streams a-far: Who fol-lows in his train?
Who saw his Mas-ter in the sky And called on him to save:
Twelve val-iant saints, their hope they knew, And mocked the cross and flame.

Who best can drink his cup of woe, Tri-umph-ant o-ver pain;
Like him, with par-don on his tongue, In midst of mor-tal pain
They met the ty-rant's bran-dish'd steel, The li-on's gor-y mane;

Who pa-tient bears his cross be-low, He fol-lows in his train.
He prayed for them that did the wrong: Who fol-lows in his train?
They bowed their necks the death to feel: Who fol-lows in their train?

4 A noble army, men and boys,
   The matron and the maid,
   Around the Saviour's throne rejoice,
   In robes of light arrayed.
   They climbed the steep ascent of heav'n
   Through peril, toil, and pain:
   O God, to us may grace be giv'n
   To follow in their train.   Amen.

REGINALD HEBER, 1812

550

C. M.

MARLOW

Arr. from JOHN CHETHAM'S *Psalmody*, 1718

With movement

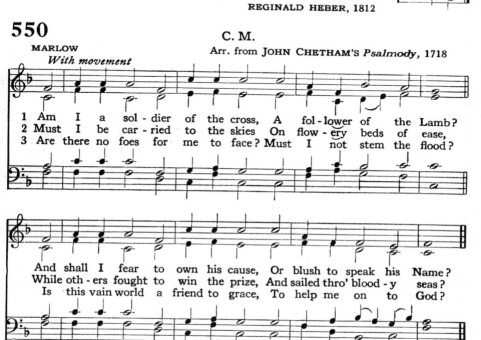

1 Am I a sol-dier of the cross, A fol-lower of the Lamb?
2 Must I be car-ried to the skies On flow-ery beds of ease,
3 Are there no foes for me to face? Must I not stem the flood?

And shall I fear to own his cause, Or blush to speak his Name?
While oth-ers fought to win the prize, And sailed thro' blood-y seas?
Is this vain world a friend to grace, To help me on to God?

4 Sure I must fight if I would reign;
   Increase my courage, Lord;
   I'll bear the cross, endure the pain,
   Supported by thy word.

5 Thy saints, in all this glorious war,
   Shall conquer, though they die;
   They view the triumph from afar,
   And seize it with their eye.

6 When that illustrious day shall rise,
   And all thy armies shine
   In robes of victory through the skies,
   The glory shall be thine.   Amen.

ISAAC WATTS, 1724, *alt.*

87. 87. 66. 667

EIN' FESTE BURG   Melody, MARTIN LUTHER, 1529

With vigor; may be sung in unison

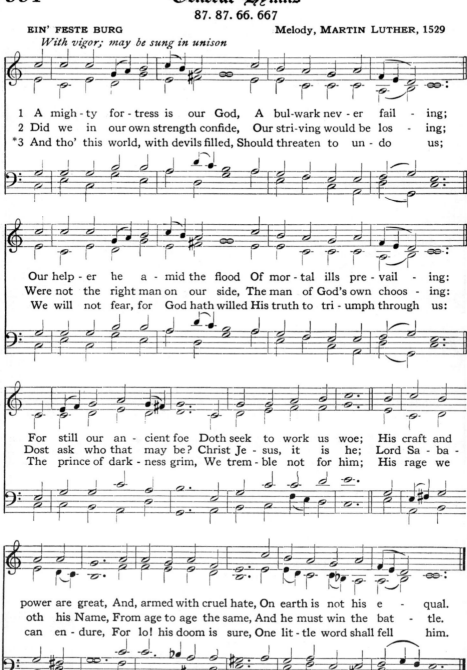

1 A migh-ty for-tress is our God, A bul-wark nev-er fail - ing;
2 Did we in our own strength confide, Our stri-ving would be los - ing;
*3 And tho' this world, with devils filled, Should threaten to un-do us;

Our help-er he a-mid the flood Of mor-tal ills pre-vail - ing:
Were not the right man on our side, The man of God's own choos - ing:
We will not fear, for God hath willed His truth to tri-umph through us:

For still our an-cient foe Doth seek to work us woe; His craft and
Dost ask who that may be? Christ Je-sus, it is he; Lord Sa-ba-
The prince of dark-ness grim, We trem-ble not for him; His rage we

power are great, And, armed with cruel hate, On earth is not his e - qual.
oth his Name, From age to age the same, And he must win the bat - tle.
can en-dure, For lo! his doom is sure, One lit-tle word shall fell him.

General Hymns

*4 That word above all earthly powers,
    No thanks to them, abideth;
  The Spirit and the gifts are ours
    Through him who with us sideth:
    Let goods and kindred go,
    This mortal life also;
  The body they may kill:
  God's truth abideth still,
    His kingdom is for ever.

MARTIN LUTHER, 1529; *Tr.* FREDERICK HENRY HEDGE, 1852

552   S. M.

SILVER STREET   ISAAC SMITH, c. 1770
With dignity

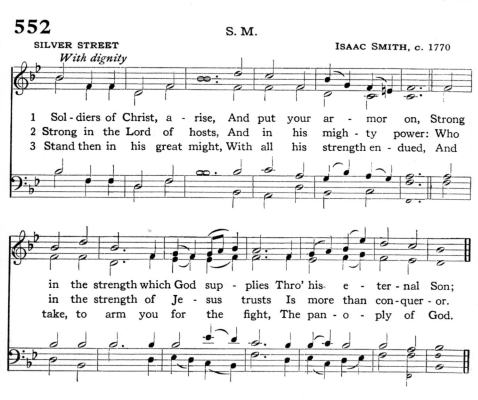

1 Sol - diers of Christ, a - rise, And put your ar - mor on, Strong
2 Strong in the Lord of hosts, And in his migh - ty power: Who
3 Stand then in his great might, With all his strength en - dued, And

in the strength which God sup - plies Thro' his e - ter - nal Son;
in the strength of Je - sus trusts Is more than con - quer - or.
take, to arm you for the fight, The pan - o - ply of God.

4 From strength to strength go on,
  Wrestle, and fight, and pray:
  Tread all the powers of darkness down,
  And win the well-fought day.

5 That, having all things done,
  And all your conflicts past,
  Ye may o'ercome, through Christ alone,
  And stand complete at last. Amen.

A-men.

CHARLES WESLEY, 1749

76. 76. D.

LANCASHIRE   HENRY SMART, 1836

In moderate time

1 Go for - ward, Chris - tian sol - dier, Be - neath his ban - ner true:
2 Go for - ward, Chris - tian sol - dier, Fear not the se - cret foe;
3 Go for - ward, Chris - tian sol - dier, Nor dream of peace - ful rest,
4 Go for - ward, Chris - tian sol - dier, Fear not the gath - 'ring night:

The Lord him - self, thy Lead - er, Shall all thy foes sub - due.
Far more o'er thee are watch - ing Than hu - man eyes can know:
Till Sa - tan's host is van-quished And heav'n is all pos - sess'd;
The Lord has been thy shel - ter; The Lord will be thy light.

His love fore - tells thy tri - als; He knows thine hour - ly need;
Trust on - ly Christ, thy Cap - tain; Cease not to watch and pray;
Till Christ him - self shall call thee To lay thine ar - mor by,
When morn his face re - veal - eth, Thy dan - gers all are past:

He can with bread of hea - ven Thy faint - ing spi - rit feed.
Heed not the treach-'rous voic - es That lure thy soul a - stray.
And wear in end - less glo - ry The crown of vic - to - ry.
O pray that faith and vir - tue May keep thee to the last!

LAURENCE TUTTIETT, 1861

76. 76. D.

Tune, LANCASHIRE

1 Lead on, O King eternal,
   The day of march has come;
Henceforth in fields of conquest
   Thy tents shall be our home:
Through days of preparation
   Thy grace has made us strong,
And now, O King eternal,
   We lift our battle-song.

2 Lead on, O King eternal,
   Till sin's fierce war shall cease,
And holiness shall whisper
   The sweet Amen of peace;
For not with swords loud clashing,
   Nor roll of stirring drums,
But deeds of love and mercy,
   The heav'nly kingdom comes.

3 Lead on, O King eternal:
   We follow, not with fears;
For gladness breaks like morning
   Where'er thy face appears.
Thy cross is lifted o'er us;
   We journey in its light:
The crown awaits the conquest;
   Lead on, O God of might! Amen.

ERNEST WARBURTON SHURTLEFF, 1887

A - men.

555   S. M.

HEATH

In moderate time

MASON and WEBB'S
Cantica Laudis, 1850

1 My soul, be on thy guard; Ten thou-sand foes a - rise;
2 O watch and fight and pray! The bat - tle ne'er give o'er;
3 Ne'er think the vic - tory won, Nor lay thine ar - mor down:
4 Fight on, my soul, till death Shall bring thee to thy God!

A host of sins are press-ing hard To draw thee from the skies.
Re - new it bold - ly ev - 'ry day, And help di - vine im - plore.
Thy ar-duous work will not be done Till thou ob - tain thy crown.
He'll take thee, at thy part - ing breath, Up to his blest a - bode.

GEORGE HEATH, 1781

General Hymns

65. 65. D.

SOHREN

WINFRED DOUGLAS, 1938,
after a phrase by PETER SOHREN, 1668

In unison, with energy

1 Chris - tian, dost thou see them On the ho - ly ground,
2 Chris - tian, dost thou feel them, How they work with - in,
3 Chris - tian, dost thou hear them, How they speak thee fair?
4 "Well I know thy trou - ble, O my ser - vant true;

How the powers of dark - ness Rage thy steps a - round?
Stri - ving, tempt - ing, lur - ing, Goad - ing in - to sin?
"Al - ways fast and vi - gil? Al - ways watch and prayer?"
Thou art ve - ry wea - ry, I was wea - ry too;

In harmony

Chris - tian, up and smite them, Count - ing gain but loss,
Chris - tian, nev - er trem - ble; Nev - er be down - cast;
Chris - tian, an - swer bold - ly: "While I breathe I pray!"
But that toil shall make thee Some day all mine own,

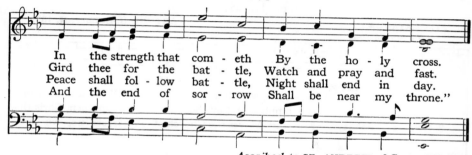

In the strength that com - eth By the ho - ly cross.
Gird thee for the bat - tle, Watch and pray and fast.
Peace shall fol - low bat - tle, Night shall end in day.
And the end of sor - row Shall be near my throne."

Ascribed to ST. ANDREW of Crete, 660–732;
Tr. JOHN MASON NEALE

556 *Second Tune*   65. 65. D.

ST. ANDREW OF CRETE

JOHN B. DYKES, 1868

In moderate time

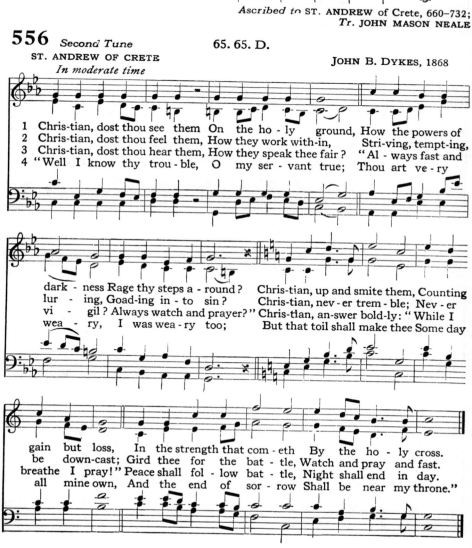

1 Chris-tian, dost thou see them On the ho - ly ground, How the powers of
2 Chris-tian, dost thou feel them, How they work with-in, Stri-ving, tempt-ing,
3 Chris-tian, dost thou hear them, How they speak thee fair? "Al - ways fast and
4 "Well I know thy trou - ble, O my ser - vant true; Thou art ve - ry

dark - ness Rage thy steps a - round? Chris-tian, up and smite them, Counting
lur - ing, Goad-ing in - to sin? Chris-tian, nev - er trem - ble; Nev - er
vi - gil? Always watch and prayer?" Chris-tian, an-swer bold-ly: "While I
wea - ry, I was wea - ry too; But that toil shall make thee Some day

gain but loss, In the strength that com - eth By the ho - ly cross.
be down-cast; Gird thee for the bat - tle, Watch and pray and fast.
breathe I pray!" Peace shall fol - low bat - tle, Night shall end in day.
all mine own, And the end of sor - row Shall be near my throne."

65. 65. D., with Refrain

ST. GERTRUDE   ARTHUR S. SULLIVAN, 1871

In march time

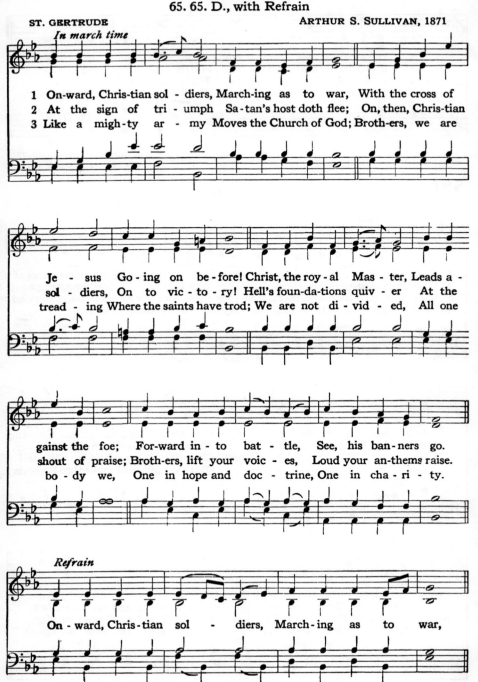

1 On-ward, Chris-tian sol - diers, March-ing as to war, With the cross of
2 At the sign of tri - umph Sa-tan's host doth flee; On, then, Chris-tian
3 Like a migh-ty ar - my Moves the Church of God; Broth-ers, we are

Je - sus Go-ing on be-fore! Christ, the roy-al Mas - ter, Leads a -
sol - diers, On to vic-to-ry! Hell's foun-da-tions quiv - er At the
tread - ing Where the saints have trod; We are not di - vid - ed, All one

gainst the foe; For-ward in-to bat - tle, See, his ban-ners go.
shout of praise; Broth-ers, lift your voic - es, Loud your an-thems raise.
bo - dy we, One in hope and doc - trine, One in cha - ri - ty.

Refrain

On - ward, Chris-tian sol - diers, March-ing as to war,

With the cross of Je - sus Go - ing on be - fore! A-men.

4 Crowns and thrones may perish,
   Kingdoms rise and wane,
But the Church of Jesus
   Constant will remain;
Gates of hell can never
   'Gainst that Church prevail;
We have Christ's own promise,
   And that cannot fail.
                        Refrain

5 Onward, then, ye people,
   Join our happy throng;
Blend with ours your voices
   In the triumph song:
Glory, laud, and honor,
   Unto Christ the King;
This through countless ages
   Men and angels sing.
                        Refrain
                        Amen.

SABINE BARING-GOULD, 1864

558

77. 77

UNIVERSITY COLLEGE   HENRY J. GAUNTLETT, 1852

With vigor

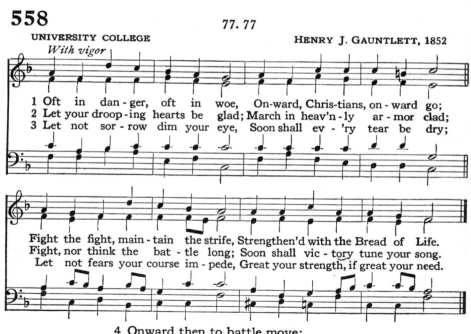

1 Oft in dan - ger, oft in woe, On-ward, Chris-tians, on - ward go;
2 Let your droop-ing hearts be glad; March in heav'n-ly ar - mor clad;
3 Let not sor - row dim your eye, Soon shall ev - 'ry tear be dry;

Fight the fight, main - tain the strife, Strengthen'd with the Bread of Life.
Fight, nor think the bat - tle long; Soon shall vic - tory tune your song.
Let not fears your course im - pede, Great your strength, if great your need.

4 Onward then to battle move;
   More than conquerors ye shall prove;
Though opposed by many a foe,
   Christian soldiers, onward go.

St. 1, HENRY KIRKE WHITE, 1806, *alt.*;
St. 2, 3, 4, FRANCES S. FULLER-MAITLAND, 1827

65. 65. D., with Refrain

SION   HENRY SMART, 1872

In march time

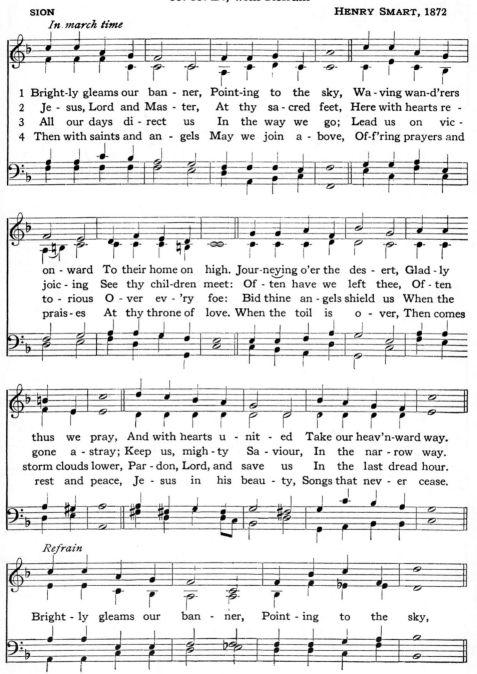

1 Bright-ly gleams our ban - ner, Point-ing to the sky, Wa - ving wand'rers
2 Je - sus, Lord and Mas - ter, At thy sa - cred feet, Here with hearts re -
3 All our days di - rect us In the way we go; Lead us on vic -
4 Then with saints and an - gels May we join a - bove, Of-f'ring prayers and

on - ward To their home on high. Jour-neying o'er the des - ert, Glad - ly
joic - ing See thy chil-dren meet: Of - ten have we left thee, Of - ten
to - rious O - ver ev - 'ry foe: Bid thine an - gels shield us When the
prais - es At thy throne of love. When the toil is o - ver, Then comes

thus we pray, And with hearts u - nit - ed Take our heav'n-ward way.
gone a - stray; Keep us, migh - ty Sa - viour, In the nar - row way.
storm clouds lower, Par - don, Lord, and save us In the last dread hour.
rest and peace, Je - sus in his beau - ty, Songs that nev - er cease.

Refrain

Bright - ly gleams our ban - ner, Point - ing to the sky,

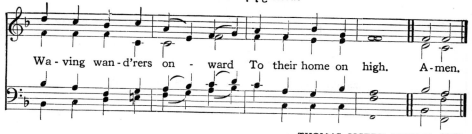

Wa - ving wan - d'rers on - ward To their home on high. A - men.

THOMAS JOSEPH POTTER, 1860,
and WILLIAM WALSHAM HOW, 1867

560 *First Tune*   **L. M.**

RUSHFORD

HENRY G. LEY, 1936

In unison, with spirit

1 Fight the good fight with all thy might, Christ is thy
2 Run the straight race through God's good grace, Lift up thine
3 Cast care a - side, lean on thy Guide; His bound - less
4 Faint not nor fear, his arms are near; He chang - eth

strength and Christ thy right; Lay hold on life, and it shall be Thy
eyes and seek his face; Life with its way be - fore us lies, . .
mer - cy will pro - vide; Trust, and thy trust - ing soul shall prove .
not, and thou art dear; On - ly be - lieve, and thou shalt see That

joy . . . . and crown e - ter - nal - ly.
Christ is the path and Christ the prize.
Christ is its life and Christ its love.
Christ . . . . is all in all to thee.

By permission of The Year Book Press

JOHN SAMUEL BEWLEY MONSELL, 1863, *alt.*

PENTECOST
WILLIAM BOYD, 1864

With spirit

1 Fight the good fight with all thy might, Christ is thy
2 Run the straight race through God's good grace, Lift up thine
3 Cast care a - side, lean on thy Guide; His bound - less
4 Faint not nor fear, his arms are near; He chang - eth

strength and Christ thy right; Lay hold on life, and it shall
eyes and seek his face; Life with its way be - fore us
mer - cy will pro - vide; Trust, and thy trust - ing soul shall
not, and thou art dear; On - ly be - lieve, and thou shalt

be Thy joy and crown e - ter - nal - ly.
lies, Christ is the path and Christ the prize.
prove Christ is its life and Christ its love.
see That Christ is all in all to thee.

JOHN SAMUEL BEWLEY MONSELL, 1863, *alt.*

Alternative Tune, DUKE STREET, No. 148

561 ST. BONIFACE 65. 65. Triple HENRY GADSBY, 1875

Cheerfully

1 For - ward! be our watch-word, Steps and voic - es joined; Seek the things be -
2 Glo - ries up - on glo - ries Hath our God pre-pared, By the souls that
3 Far o'er yon ho - ri - zon Rise the ci - ty towers Where our God a -
4 To the e - ter - nal Fa - ther Loud-est an-thems raise; To the Son and

General Hymns

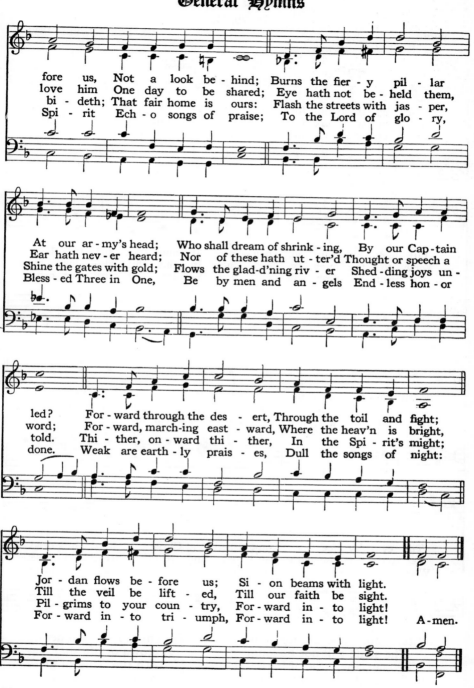

fore us, Not a look be - hind; Burns the fier - y pil - lar
love him One day to be shared; Eye hath not be - held them,
bi - deth; That fair home is ours: Flash the streets with jas - per,
Spi - rit Ech - o songs of praise; To the Lord of glo - ry,

At our ar - my's head; Who shall dream of shrink - ing, By our Cap - tain
Ear hath nev - er heard; Nor of these hath ut - ter'd Thought or speech a
Shine the gates with gold; Flows the glad-d'ning riv - er Shed - ding joys un -
Bless - ed Three in One, Be by men and an - gels End - less hon - or

led? For - ward through the des - ert, Through the toil and fight;
word; For - ward, march - ing east - ward, Where the heav'n is bright,
told. Thi - ther, on - ward thi - ther, In the Spi - rit's might;
done. Weak are earth - ly prais - es, Dull the songs of night:

Jor - dan flows be - fore us; Si - on beams with light.
Till the veil be lift - ed, Till our faith be sight.
Pil - grims to your coun - try, For - ward in - to light!
For - ward in - to tri - umph, For - ward in - to light! A - men.

HENRY ALFORD, 1871

76. 76. D.

WEBB   GEORGE J. WEBB, 1837

With stately dignity

1 Stand up, stand up, for Je - sus, Ye sol - diers of the cross;
2 Stand up, stand up, for Je - sus; The trum - pet call o - bey;
3 Stand up, stand up, for Je - sus; Stand in his strength a - lone;

Lift high his roy - al ban - ner, It must not suf - fer loss:
Forth to the migh - ty con - flict In this his glo - rious day:
The arm of flesh will fail you, Ye dare not trust your own:

From vic - to - ry un - to vic - tory His ar - my shall he lead,
Ye that are men now serve him A - gainst un - num-ber'd foes;
Put on the gos - pel ar - mor, And watch-ing un - to prayer,

Till ev - 'ry foe is van-quished And Christ is Lord in - deed.
Let cour - age rise with dan - ger, And strength to strength op - pose.
When du - ty calls, or dan - ger, Be nev - er want - ing there.

4 Stand up, stand up, for Jesus;   To him that overcometh,
   The strife will not be long;   A crown of life shall be;
This day, the noise of battle;   He with the King of glory
   The next, the victor's song.   Shall reign eternally.

GEORGE DUFFIELD, Jr., 1858

563

ST. DUNSTAN'S
Sturdily

WINFRED DOUGLAS, 1917

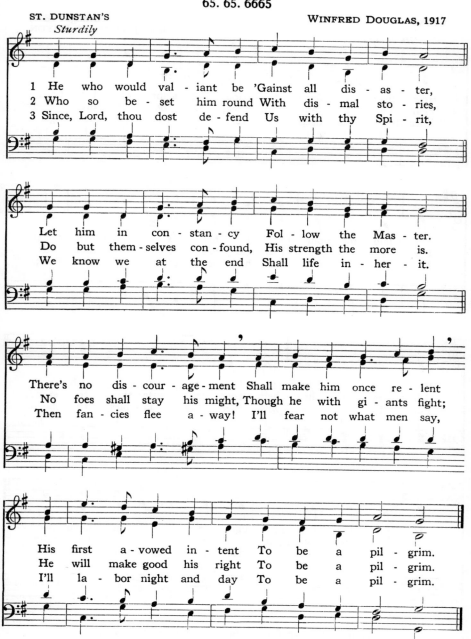

1 He who would val - iant be 'Gainst all dis - as - ter,
2 Who so be - set him round With dis - mal sto - ries,
3 Since, Lord, thou dost de - fend Us with thy Spi - rit,

Let him in con - stan - cy Fol - low the Mas - ter.
Do but them - selves con - found, His strength the more is.
We know we at the end Shall life in - her - it.

There's no dis - cour - age - ment Shall make him once re - lent
No foes shall stay his might, Though he with gi - ants fight;
Then fan - cies flee a - way! I'll fear not what men say,

His first a - vowed in - tent To be a pil - grim.
He will make good his right To be a pil - grim.
I'll la - bor night and day To be a pil - grim.

Music by permission of the composer
Words by permission of the Oxford University Press

JOHN BUNYAN, 1684, *alt.*;
English Hymnal Version, 1906

Alternative Tune, MONKS GATE, No. 362

11 11. 11 11

LYONS

With energy

Arranged 1822,
from J. MICHAEL HAYDN

1 How firm a foun - da - tion, ye saints of the Lord,
2 "Fear not, I am with thee; O be not dis - mayed!
3 "When through the deep wa - ters I call thee to go,

Is laid for your faith in his ex - cel - lent word!
For I am thy God, and will still give thee aid;
The riv - ers of woe shall not thee o - ver - flow;

What more can he say than to you he hath said,
I'll strength - en thee, help thee, and cause thee to stand,
For I will be with thee, thy trou - bles to bless,

To you that for ref - uge to Je - sus have fled?
Up - held by my right - eous, om - ni - po - tent hand.
And sanc - ti - fy to thee thy deep - est dis - tress.

4 "When through fiery trials thy pathway shall lie,
   My grace, all-sufficient, shall be thy supply;
   The flame shall not hurt thee; I only design
   Thy dross to consume, and thy gold to refine.

General Hymns

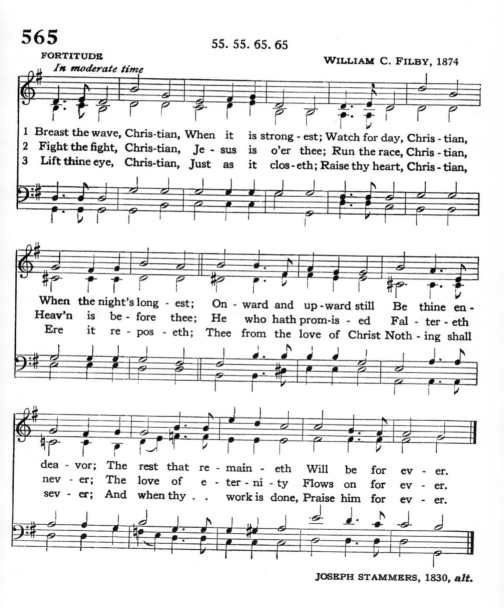

5 "The soul that to Jesus hath fled for repose,
I will not, I will not desert to his foes;
That soul, though all hell shall endeavor to shake,
I'll never, no, never, no, never forsake."

K. in JOHN RIPPON'S *Selection of Hymns*, 1787, **alt.**

Alternative Tune, ST. DENIO, No. 301

565   55. 55. 65. 65

FORTITUDE   WILLIAM C. FILBY, 1874
In moderate time

1 Breast the wave, Christian, When it is strong - est; Watch for day, Christian,
2 Fight the fight, Christian, Je - sus is o'er thee; Run the race, Christian,
3 Lift thine eye, Christian, Just as it clos-eth; Raise thy heart, Chris - tian,

When the night's long - est; On - ward and up-ward still Be thine en -
Heav'n is be - fore thee; He who hath prom-is - ed Fal - ter - eth
Ere it re - pos - eth; Thee from the love of Christ Noth - ing shall

dea - vor; The rest that re - main - eth Will be for ev - er.
nev - er; The love of e - ter - ni - ty Flows on for ev - er.
sev - er; And when thy . . work is done, Praise him for ev - er.

JOSEPH STAMMERS, 1830, **alt.**

CHESTER · WILLIAM SIDELL CHESTER, 1898

Resolutely; may be sung in unison

1 Je-sus calls us; o'er the tu-mult Of our life's wild, rest-less sea,
2 As, of old, Saint An-drew heard it By the Gal-i-le-an lake,
3 Je-sus calls us from the wor-ship Of the vain world's gold-en store;

Day by day his clear voice sound-eth, Say-ing, "Chris-tian, fol-low me;"
Turned from home and toil and kin-dred, Leav-ing all for his dear sake.
From each i-dol that would keep us, Say-ing, "Chris-tian, love me more."

566 *Second Tune* 87. 87

GALILEE · WILLIAM H. JUDE, 1887

With dignity

1 Je-sus calls us; o'er the tu-mult Of our life's wild, rest-less sea,
2 As, of old, Saint An-drew heard it By the Gal-i-le-an lake,
3 Je-sus calls us from the wor-ship Of the vain world's gold-en store;

Day by day his clear voice sound-eth, Say-ing, "Christian, fol-low me;"
Turned from home and toil and kin-dred, Leav-ing all for his dear sake.
From each i-dol that would keep us, Say-ing, "Christian, love me more."

General Hymns

1st Tune

A - men.

4 In our joys and in our sorrows,
    Days of toil and hours of ease,
  Still he calls, in cares and pleasures,
    " Christian, love me more than these."

5 Jesus calls us! By thy mercies,
    Saviour, make us hear thy call,
  Give our hearts to thine obedience,
    Serve and love thee best of all.   Amen.

2nd Tune

A - men.

CECIL FRANCES ALEXANDER, 1852, *alt.*

567

DULCE CARMEN

With joyful dignity

87. 87. 87

An Essay on the Church Plain Chant, 1782

1 Lead us, heav'n-ly Fa - ther, lead us O'er the world's tem-pes-tu-ous sea;
2 Sa-viour, breathe for-give-ness o'er us; All our weak-ness thou dost know;
3 Spi - rit of our God, de-scend-ing, Fill our hearts with heav'n-ly joy;

Guard us, guide us, keep us, feed us, For we have no help but thee,
Thou didst tread this earth be - fore us; Thou didst feel its keen - est woe;
Love with ev - 'ry pas - sion blend-ing, Plea-sure that can nev - er cloy;

Yet pos - sess - ing ev - 'ry bless-ing, If our God our Fa-ther be.
Lone and drea - ry, faint and wea - ry, Thro' the des-ert thou didst go.
Thus pro - vid - ed, pardon'd, guid-ed, Noth-ing can our peace de-stroy.   A-men.

JAMES EDMESTON, 1821

65. 65. D., with Refrain

HERMAS   FRANCES RIDLEY HAVERGAL, 1871

In march time

1 On our way re - joic - ing Glad - ly let us go; Con-quer'd hath our
2 If with hon - est - heart - ed Love for God and man, Day by day thou
3 Un - to God the Fa - ther Joy - ful songs we sing, Un - to God the

Lead - er, Vanquish'd is the foe. Christ with-out, our safe - ty; Christ with-
find us Do - ing what we can, Thou who giv'st the seed - time Wilt give
Sa - viour Thank-ful hearts we bring, Un - to God the Spi - rit Bow we

in, our joy; Who, if we be faith - ful, Can our hope de - stroy?
large in - crease, Crown the head with bless - ings, Fill the heart with peace.
and a - dore, On our way re - joic - ing Now and ev - er - more.

Refrain

On our way re - joic - ing As we for - ward move,

General Hymns

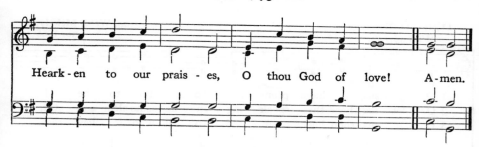

Heark - en to our prais - es, O thou God of love! A - men.

JOHN SAMUEL BEWLEY MONSELL, 1863, *alt.*

569

C. M.

ST. FLAVIAN
Moderately slow

JOHN DAY'S *Psalter*, 1562

1 Lo! what a cloud of wit - ness - es En - com-pass us a - round!
2 Let us, with zeal like theirs in - spired, Strive in the Chris - tian race;
3 Be - hold a Wit - ness no - bler still, Who trod af - flic - tion's path;

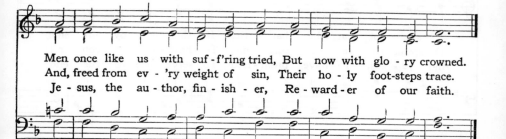

Men once like us with suf - f'ring tried, But now with glo - ry crowned.
And, freed from ev - 'ry weight of sin, Their ho - ly foot-steps trace.
Je - sus, the au - thor, fin - ish - er, Re - ward - er of our faith.

4 He, for the joy before him set,
   And moved by pitying love,
Endured the cross, despised the shame,
   And now he reigns above.

5 Thither, forgetting things behind,
   Press we to God's right hand;
There, with the Saviour and his saints,
   Triumphantly to stand.

Scottish Paraphrase, 1745, *alt.*

570 *First Tune*   𝕲eneral 𝕳ymns

76. 76. D.

LLANFYLLIN   Traditional Welsh Melody,
With spirit   pub. 1865

1 O Je - sus, I have prom - ised To serve thee to the end:
2 O let me hear thee speak - ing In ac - cents clear and still,
3 O Je - sus, thou hast prom - ised To all who fol - low thee,

Be thou for ev - er near me, My Mas - ter and my friend;
A - bove the storms of pas - sion, The mur-murs of self - will;
That where thou art in glo - ry There shall thy ser - vant be;

I shall not fear the bat' - tle, If thou art by my side,
O speak to re - as - sure me, To hast - en or con - trol;
And, Je - sus, I have prom - ised To serve thee to the end;

Nor wan - der from the path - way, If thou wilt be my guide.
O speak, and make me lis - ten, Thou guar-dian of my soul.
O give me grace to fol - low, My Mas-ter and my friend. A-men.

JOHN ERNEST BODE, 1869, *alt.*

DAY OF REST JAMES WILLIAM ELLIOTT, 1874
With spirit

1 O Je - sus, I have prom - ised To serve thee to the end:
2 O let me hear thee speak - ing In ac - cents clear and still,
3 O Je - sus, thou hast prom - ised To all who fol - low thee,

Be thou for ev - er near me, My Mas - ter and my friend;
A - bove the storms of pas - sion, The mur - murs of self - will;
That where thou art in glo - ry There shall thy ser - vant be;

I shall not fear the bat - tle, If thou art by my side,
O speak to re - as - sure me, To hast - en or con - trol;
And, Je - sus, I have prom - ised To serve thee to the end;

Unison *Harmony*

Nor wan - der from the path - way, If thou wilt be my guide.
O speak, and make me lis - ten, Thou guar - dian of my soul.
O give me grace to fol - low, My Mas - ter and my friend. A-men.

JOHN ERNEST BODE, 1869, *alt.*

MONT RICHARD   PERCY CARTER BUCK, 20th cent.

Unison, in moderate time

1 Not al - ways on the mount may we Rapt in the
2 "Lord, it is good a - bi - ding here," We cry, the
3 Yet hath one such ex - alt - ed hour Up - on the
4 Till all the low - ly vale grows bright, Trans - fig - ured
5 The mount for vi - sion: but be - low The paths of

heav'n-ly vi - sion be: The shores of thought and feel - ing
heav'n-ly pres - ence near: The vi - sion van - ish - es, our
soul re - deem - ing power, And in its strength, thro' af - ter
in re - mem - ber'd light, And in un - tir - ing souls we
dai - ly du - ty go, And no - bler life there - in shall

know The Spi - rit's ti - dal ebb and flow.
eyes Are lift - ed in - to va - cant skies.
days, We trav - el our ap - point - ed ways,
bear The fresh - ness of the up - per air.
own The pat - tern on the moun - tain shown.

By permission of the composer   FREDERICK LUCIAN HOSMER, 1885

ONEONTA

In moderate time

WALTER HENRY HALL, 1918

1 Not al - ways on the mount may we Rapt in the
2 "Lord, it is good a - bi - ding here," We cry, the

heav'n - ly vi - sion be: The shores of thought and
heav'n - ly pres - ence near: The vi - sion van - ish -

feel - ing know The Spi - rit's ti - dal ebb and flow.
es, our eyes Are lift - ed in - to va - cant skies.

3 Yet hath one such exalted hour
  Upon the soul redeeming power,
  And in its strength, through after days,
  We travel our appointed ways,

4 Till all the lowly vale grows bright,
  Transfigured in remembered light,
  And in untiring souls we bear
  The freshness of the upper air.

5 The mount for vision: but below
  The paths of daily duty go,
  And nobler life therein shall own
  The pattern on the mountain shown.

FREDERICK LUCIAN HOSMER, 1885

L. M.

MARYTON   H. PERCY SMITH, 1874

1 O Mas - ter, let me walk with thee In low - ly
2 Help me the slow of heart to move By some clear,

paths of ser - vice free; Tell me thy se - cret; help me
win - ning word of love; Teach me the way - ward feet to

bear The strain of toil, the fret of care.
stay, And guide them in the home - ward way. A - men.

3 Teach me thy patience; still with thee
In closer, dearer company,
In work that keeps faith sweet and strong,
In trust that triumphs over wrong,

4 In hope that sends a shining ray
Far down the future's broad'ning way,
In peace that only thou canst give,
With thee, O Master, let me live. Amen.

WASHINGTON GLADDEN, 1879

573

L. M.

ANGEL'S SONG (SONG 34)

ORLANDO GIBBONS, 1623

Not too slow

1 Go, la - bor on! spend and be spent! Thy joy to
2 Go, la - bor on! e - nough, while here, If he shall
3 Go, la - bor on, while it is day! The world's dark

do the Fa - ther's will: It is the way the
praise thee, if he deign The will - ing heart to
night is hast - 'ning on: Speed, speed thy work! cast

Mas - ter went; Should not the ser - vant tread it still?
mark and cheer: No toil for him shall be in vain.
sloth a - way! It is not thus that souls are won.

4 Toil on, faint not, keep watch, and pray;
　　Be wise the erring soul to win;
　　Go forth into the world's highway,
　　Compel the wanderer to come in.

5 Toil on, and in thy toil rejoice;
　　For toil comes rest, for exile home;
　　Soon shalt thou hear the Bridegroom's voice,
　　The midnight cry, "Behold, I come!"

HORATIUS BONAR, 1843, *alt.*

Alternative Tune, WILDERNESS, No. 574

WILDERNESS

REGINALD S. THATCHER,
from *The Clarendon Hymn Book,* 1936

In unison, with breadth

1 Lord, speak to me, that I may speak In liv - ing
*2 O lead me, Lord, that I may lead The wan-d'ring
3 O strength-en me, that while I stand Firm on the
4 O teach me, Lord, that I may teach The pre - cious

ech - oes of thy tone; As thou hast sought, so let me seek
and the wa - vering feet; O feed me, Lord, that I may feed
Rock, and strong in thee, I may stretch out a lov - ing hand
things thou dost im - part; And wing my words, that they may reach

Last stanza

Thy err - ing chil - dren lost and lone.
Thy hun-g'ring ones with man - na sweet.
To wres - tlers with the troub - led sea. [joy, thy glo - ry share.
The hid - den depths of ma - ny a heart.

Last stanza

General Hymns

*5 O give thine own sweet rest to me,
    That I may speak with soothing power
A word in season, as from thee,
    To weary ones in needful hour.

6 O fill me with thy fulness, Lord,
    Until my very heart o'erflow
In kindling thought and glowing word,
    Thy love to tell, thy praise to show.

*7 O use me, Lord, use even me,
    Just as thou wilt, and when, and where;
Until thy blessèd face I see,
    Thy rest, thy joy, thy glory share. Amen.

In harmony
A - men.

FRANCES RIDLEY HAVERGAL, 1872

574 *Second Tune*   L. M.

HOLLEY   GEORGE HEWS, 1835

With movement

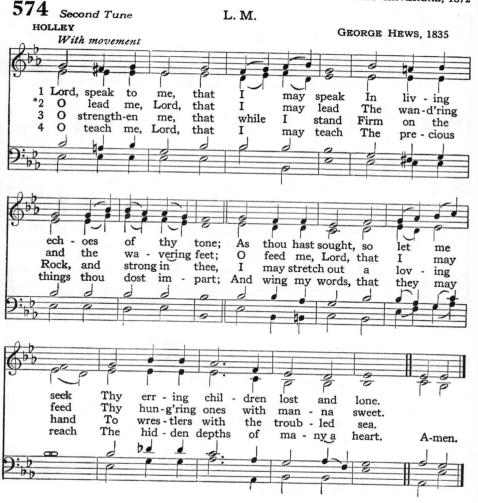

1 Lord, speak to me, that I may speak In liv - ing
*2 O lead me, Lord, that I may lead The wan - d'ring
3 O strength-en me, that while I stand Firm on the
4 O teach me, Lord, that I may teach The pre - cious

ech - oes of thy tone; As thou hast sought, so let me
and the wa - vering feet; O feed me, Lord, that I may
Rock, and strong in thee, I may stretch out a lov - ing
things thou dost im - part; And wing my words, that they may

seek Thy err - ing chil - dren lost and lone.
feed Thy hun - g'ring ones with man - na sweet.
hand To wres - tlers with the troub - led sea.
reach The hid - den depths of ma - ny a heart. A-men.

575 **General Hymns**
11 10. 11 10

LOMBARD STREET   FREDERICK GEORGE RUSSELL, 1929
In unison, with breadth

1 Lord, who didst send, by two and two be - fore thee, Thine own dis -
2 Make us to see the light that shines in all men, Help us to

ci - ples, those three score and ten, That they should show the
learn how thorns can make a crown, Show us how love will

lost ones where the path was And bring the light to eyes of blind-ed men:
keep ourselves from fall - ing And pi - ty lift up oth - ers who are down.

By permission of the Executors of the late F. G. Russell

3 Thou art our Captain: teach us to be like thee,
    And where thou leadest we will follow on;
  We do not know what orders may await us,
    Save the great order, "Let thy will be done."

4 It shall be done, if we be strong to follow
    The path which led thee to that aweful day;
  It shall be done, if true to thy example
    We guide ourselves and others in thy way.
                                    Amen.

A - men.

STEUART WILSON, 1930
From Enlarged Songs of Praise, by permission of the author

576

4. 10 10. 10 4

ORA LABORA

T. TERTIUS NOBLE, 1918

In unison, very broadly

1 Come, la - bor on. Who dares stand i - dle on the har-vest plain,
2 Come, la - bor on. The en - e - my is watch-ing night and day,
3 Come, la - bor on. A - way with gloom - y doubts and faithless fear!
4 Come, la - bor on. Claim the high call - ing an-gels can-not share—
5 Come, la - bor on. No time for rest, till glows the west-ern sky,

While all a-round him waves the gold-en grain? And to each ser - vant
To sow the tares, to snatch the seed a - way; While we in sleep our
No arm so weak but may do ser-vice here: By fee-blest a - gents
To young and old the gos - pel gladness bear: Re - deem the time; its
Till the long sha - dows o'er our path-way lie, And a glad sound comes

does the Mas - ter say, "Go work to - day."
du - ty have for - got, He slum - - - ber'd not.
may our God ful - fil His right - - - eous will.
hours too swift - ly fly. The night - - - draws nigh.
with the set - ting sun, . . "Ser - - - vants, well done."

JANE BORTHWICK, 1859, alt.

86. 866

CHRISTMAS   GEORGE FREDERICK HANDEL, 1728

1 A - wake, my soul, stretch ev - 'ry nerve, And
2 A cloud of wit - ness - es a - round Hold

press with vig - or on; A heav'n-ly race de-mands thy zeal,
thee in full sur - vey; For-get the steps al - rea - dy trod,

And an im - mor - tal crown, And an im - mor - tal crown.
And on - ward urge thy way, And on - ward urge thy way.

3 'Tis God's all-animating voice
    That calls thee from on high;
    'Tis his own hand presents the prize
    ‖ To thine aspiring eye. ‖

4 Then wake, my soul, stretch every nerve,
    And press with vigor on;
    A heav'nly race demands thy zeal,
    ‖ And an immortal crown. ‖

PHILIP DODDRIDGE, 1755

BRASTED

77. 77

GEORG P. WEIMAR, 1780

Joyously

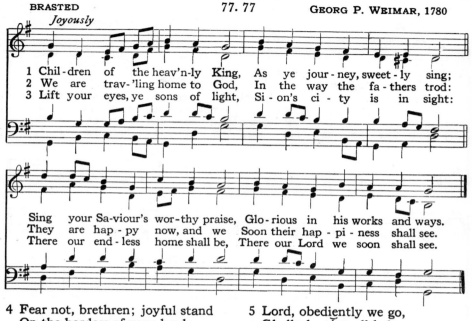

1 Chil - dren of the heav'n-ly King, As ye jour - ney, sweet - ly sing;
2 We are trav- 'ling home to God, In the way the fa - thers trod:
3 Lift your eyes, ye sons of light, Si - on's ci - ty is in sight:

Sing your Sa-viour's wor-thy praise, Glo - rious in his works and ways.
They are hap - py now, and we Soon their hap - pi - ness shall see.
There our end - less home shall be, There our Lord we soon shall see.

4 Fear not, brethren; joyful stand
On the borders of your land;
Jesus Christ, your Father's Son,
Bids you undismayed go on.

5 Lord, obediently we go,
Gladly leaving all below;
Only thou our leader be,
And we will still follow thee.

JOHN CENNICK, 1742

578 *Second Tune*

77. 77

Melody arr. 1791,
from IGNAZ PLEYEL

PLEYEL'S HYMN

Joyously

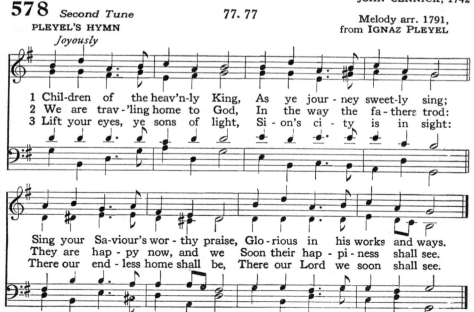

1 Chil-dren of the heav'n-ly King, As ye jour - ney sweet-ly sing;
2 We are trav -'ling home to God, In the way the fa - thers trod:
3 Lift your eyes, ye sons of light, Si - on's ci - ty is in sight:

Sing your Sa-viour's wor - thy praise, Glo - rious in his works and ways.
They are hap - py now, and we Soon their hap - pi - ness shall see.
There our end - less home shall be, There our Lord we soon shall see.

579 *First Tune* ### 𝕲eneral ℌymnş
S. M.

CARLISLE   CHARLES LOCKHART, 1769

In moderate time

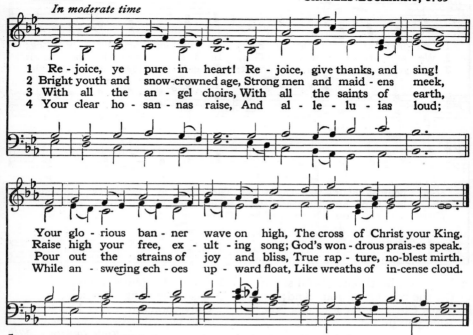

1 Re - joice, ye pure in heart! Re - joice, give thanks, and sing!
2 Bright youth and snow-crowned age, Strong men and maid - ens meek,
3 With all the an - gel choirs, With all the saints of earth,
4 Your clear ho - san - nas raise, And al - le - lu - ias loud;

Your glo - rious ban - ner wave on high, The cross of Christ your King.
Raise high your free, ex - ult - ing song; God's won - drous prais-es speak.
Pour out the strains of joy and bliss, True rap - ture, no-blest mirth.
While an - swering ech - oes up - ward float, Like wreaths of in-cense cloud.

5 Yes, on through life's long path,
  Still chanting as ye go,
From youth to age, by night and day,
  In gladness and in woe.

6 Still lift your standard high,
  Still march in firm array,
As warriors through the darkness toil,
  Till dawns the golden day.

7 At last the march shall end;
  The wearied ones shall rest;
The pilgrims find their Father's house,
  Jerusalem the blest.

8 Then on, ye pure in heart!
  Rejoice, give thanks, and sing!
Your glorious banner wave on high,
  The cross of Christ your King.

EDWARD HAYES PLUMPTRE, 1865

579 *Second Tune*   S. M., with Refrain

MARION   ARTHUR H. MESSITER, 1883

With movement

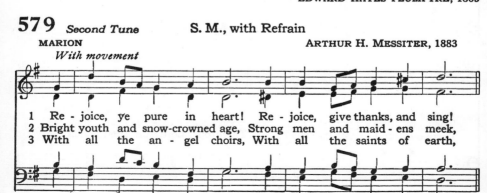

1 Re - joice, ye pure in heart! Re - joice, give thanks, and sing!
2 Bright youth and snow-crowned age, Strong men and maid - ens meek,
3 With all the an - gel choirs, With all the saints of earth,

General Hymns

Your glo - rious ban - ner wave on high, The cross of Christ your King.
Raise high your free, ex - ult - ing song; God's won-drous prais-es speak.
Pour out the strains of joy and bliss, True rap - ture, no - blest mirth.

Refrain

Re - joice, re - joice, re - joice, give thanks and sing!

Re - joice, re - joice,

4 Your clear hosannas raise,
   And alleluias loud;
   While answering echoes upward float,
   Like wreaths of incense cloud.
   Refrain

5 Yes, on through life's long path,
   Still chanting as ye go,
   From youth to age, by night and day,
   In gladness and in woe.
   Refrain

6 Still lift your standard high,
   Still march in firm array,
   As warriors through the darkness toil,
   Till dawns the golden day.
   Refrain

7 At last the march shall end;
   The wearied ones shall rest;
   The pilgrims find their Father's house,
   Jerusalem the blest.
   Refrain

8 Then on, ye pure in heart!
   Rejoice, give thanks, and sing!
   Your glorious banner wave on high,
   The cross of Christ your King.
   Refrain

EDWARD HAYES PLUMPTRE, 1865

65. 65. D.

EDINA   HERBERT S. OAKELEY, 1868

In moderate time

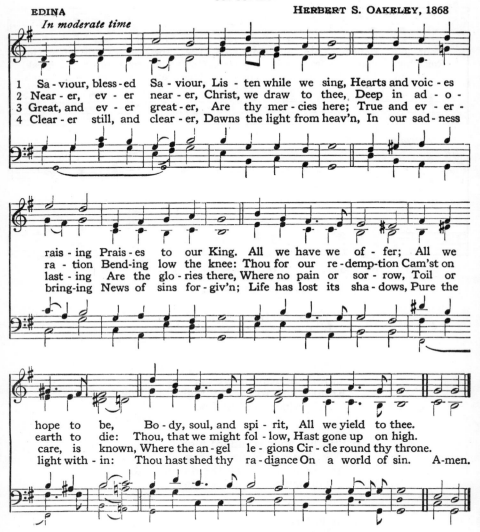

1 Sa - viour, bless - ed Sa - viour, Lis - ten while we sing, Hearts and voic - es
2 Near - er, ev - er near - er, Christ, we draw to thee, Deep in ad - o -
3 Great, and ev - er great - er, Are thy mer - cies here; True and ev - er -
4 Clear - er still, and clear - er, Dawns the light from heav'n, In our sad - ness

rais - ing Prais - es to our King. All we have we of - fer; All we
ra - tion Bend - ing low the knee: Thou for our re - demp - tion Cam'st on
last - ing Are the glo - ries there, Where no pain or sor - row, Toil or
bring - ing News of sins for - giv'n; Life has lost its sha - dows, Pure the

hope to be, Bo - dy, soul, and spi - rit, All we yield to thee.
earth to die: Thou, that we might fol - low, Hast gone up on high.
care, is known, Where the an - gel le - gions Cir - cle round thy throne.
light with - in: Thou hast shed thy ra - diance On a world of sin. A - men.

5 Onward, ever onward,
    Journeying o'er the road
Worn by saints before us,
    Journeying on to God!
Leaving all behind us,
    May we hasten on,
Backward never looking
    Till the prize is won.

6 Bliss, all bliss excelling,
    When the ransomed soul,
Earthly toils forgetting,
    Finds its promised goal,
Where in joys unheard of
    Saints with angels sing,
Never weary raising
    Praises to their King. Amen.

GODFREY THRING, 1862, *alt.*

Alternative Tune, ST. ALBAN'S, No. 581

581

65. 65. D.

ST. ALBAN'S

In moderate time

THOMAS MORLEY, 1867

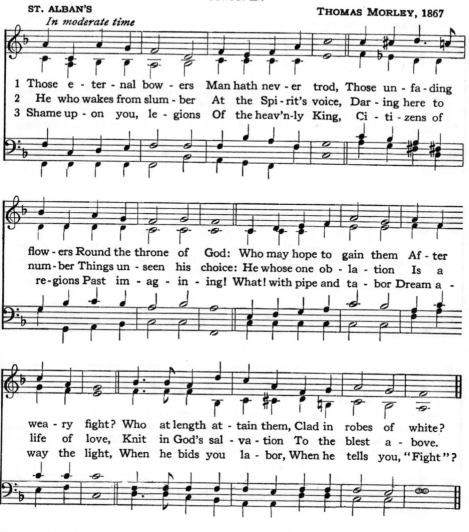

1 Those e - ter - nal bow - ers Man hath nev - er trod, Those un - fa - ding
2 He who wakes from slum - ber At the Spi - rit's voice, Dar - ing here to
3 Shame up - on you, le - gions Of the heav'n - ly King, Ci - ti - zens of

flow - ers Round the throne of God: Who may hope to gain them Af - ter
num - ber Things un - seen his choice: He whose one ob - la - tion Is a
re - gions Past im - ag - in - ing! What! with pipe and ta - bor Dream a -

wea - ry fight? Who at length at - tain them, Clad in robes of white?
life of love, Knit in God's sal - va - tion To the blest a - bove.
way the light, When he bids you la - bor, When he tells you, "Fight"?

4 Jesus, Lord of glory,
    As we breast the tide,
Whisper thou the story
    Of the other side;
Where the saints are casting
    Crowns before thy feet,
Safe for everlasting,
    In thyself complete. Amen.

A - men.

St. 1, 3, ascribed to ST. JOHN *of Damascus, 8th cent.;*
Tr. JOHN MASON NEALE, 1862, *alt.*

77. 77. D.

ANIMA CHRISTI

Traditional English Melody,
adapted 1906

In unison, with vigor

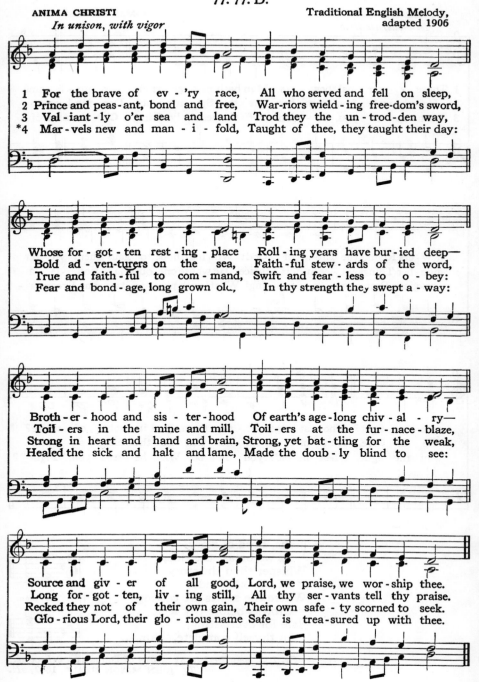

1 For the brave of ev - 'ry race, All who served and fell on sleep,
2 Prince and peas - ant, bond and free, War-riors wield - ing free-dom's sword,
3 Val - iant - ly o'er sea and land Trod they the un - trod-den way,
*4 Mar - vels new and man - i - fold, Taught of thee, they taught their day:

Whose for - got - ten rest - ing - place Roll - ing years have bur - ied deep—
Bold ad - ven-turers on the sea, Faith-ful stew - ards of the word,
True and faith - ful to com - mand, Swift and fear - less to o - bey:
Fear and bond - age, long grown old, In thy strength they swept a - way:

Broth - er - hood and sis - ter - hood Of earth's age - long chiv - al - ry—
Toil - ers in the mine and mill, Toil - ers at the fur - nace - blaze,
Strong in heart and hand and brain, Strong, yet bat - tling for the weak,
Healed the sick and halt and lame, Made the doub - ly blind to see:

Source and giv - er of all good, Lord, we praise, we wor - ship thee.
Long for - got - ten, liv - ing still, All thy ser - vants tell thy praise.
Recked they not of their own gain, Their own safe - ty scorned to seek.
Glo - rious Lord, their glo - rious name Safe is trea-sured up with thee.

General Hymns

5 Evermore their life abides
  Who have lived to do thy will:
High above the restless tides
  Stands their city on the hill:
Lord and Light of every age,
  By thy same sure counsel led,
Heirs of their great heritage
  In their footsteps will we tread.

GEORGE WALLACE BRIGGS, 1920

By permission of Loughborough College, England

583

MARTINS

10 10. 7

PERCY CARTER BUCK, 1913

Unison, in moderate time

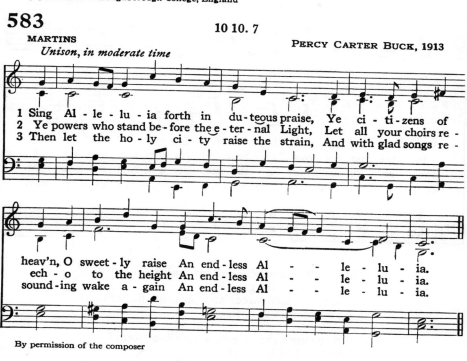

1 Sing Al - le - lu - ia forth in du - teous praise, Ye ci - ti - zens of
2 Ye powers who stand be - fore the e - ter - nal Light, Let all your choirs re -
3 Then let the ho - ly ci - ty raise the strain, And with glad songs re -

heav'n, O sweet - ly raise An end - less Al - - - le - lu - ia.
ech - o to the height An end - less Al - - - le - lu - ia.
sound - ing wake a - gain An end - less Al - - - le - lu - ia.

By permission of the composer

4 Ye who have fought and joined the starry throng,
  Ye victors, now take up the eternal song,
    An endless Alleluia.

5 Your songs of triumph shall for ever ring,
  The hymns which tell the honor of your King,
    An endless Alleluia.

6 Such song is rest and food and deep delight
  To saints forgiven; let them all unite
    In endless Alleluia.

7 Almighty Christ, to thee our voices sing
  Glory for evermore; to thee we bring
    An endless Alleluia. Amen.

Latin, 5th–8th cent.; Hymnal Version, 1940

SOUTHWELL   HERBERT S. IRONS, 1861
Quietly

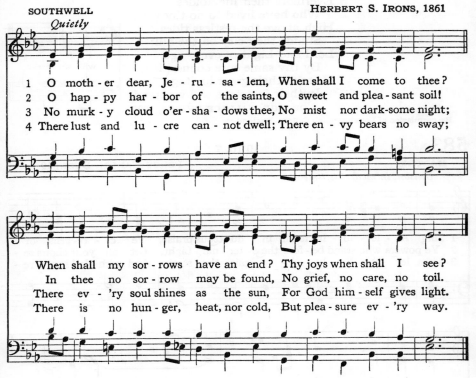

1 O moth - er dear, Je - ru - sa - lem, When shall I come to thee?
2 O hap - py har - bor of the saints, O sweet and plea - sant soil!
3 No murk - y cloud o'er - sha - dows thee, No mist nor dark-some night;
4 There lust and lu - cre can - not dwell; There en - vy bears no sway;

When shall my sor - rows have an end? Thy joys when shall I see?
In thee no sor - row may be found, No grief, no care, no toil.
There ev - 'ry soul shines as the sun, For God him - self gives light.
There is no hun - ger, heat, nor cold, But plea - sure ev - 'ry way.

5 Thy gardens and thy gallant walks
    Continually are green;
There grow such sweet and pleasant flowers
    As nowhere else are seen.

6 Quite through the streets with silver sound
    The flood of life doth flow,
Upon whose banks on every side
    The wood of life doth grow.

7 There trees for evermore bear fruit,
    And evermore do spring;
There evermore the angels be,
    And evermore do sing.

8 Jerusalem, Jerusalem,
    God grant that I may see
Thine endless joy, and of the same
    Partaker ever be!

Alternative Tune, DIANA, No. 585

F. B. P., c. *16th cent.*

584 *Second Tune* 𝔊𝔢𝔫𝔢𝔯𝔞𝔩 𝔥𝔶𝔪𝔫𝔰
C. M. D.

MATERNA
With spirit

SAMUEL A. WARD, 1882

1 O moth - er dear, Je - ru - sa - lem, When shall I come to thee?
3 No murk - y cloud o'er - sha - dows thee, No mist nor dark - some night;

When shall my sor - rows have an end? Thy joys when shall I see?
There ev - 'ry soul shines as the sun, For God him - self gives light.

2 O hap - py har - bor of the saints, O sweet and plea - sant soil!
4 There lust and lu - cre can - not dwell; There en - vy bears no sway;

In thee no sor - row may be found, No grief, no care, no toil.
There is no hun - ger, heat, nor cold, But plea - sure ev - 'ry way.

585 *First Tune*   𝕲eneral 𝕳ymns

C. M.

LAND OF REST

Traditional American Melody,
coll. and har. by ANNABEL MORRIS BUCHANAN

With unhurried simplicity

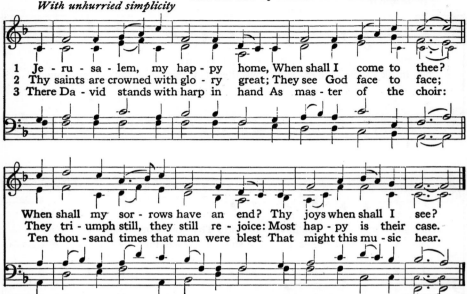

1 Je - ru - sa - lem, my hap - py home, When shall I come to thee?
2 Thy saints are crowned with glo - ry great; They see God face to face;
3 There Da - vid stands with harp in hand As mas - ter of the choir:

When shall my sor - rows have an end? Thy joys when shall I see?
They tri - umph still, they still re - joice: Most hap - py is their case.
Ten thou - sand times that man were blest That might this mu - sic hear.

Copyright, 1938, by J. Fischer & Bro.

585 *Second Tune*   C. M.

DIANA

Traditional English Melody, 16th cent.,
harmonized by W. D., 1939

Quietly, with deep feeling

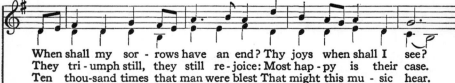

1 Je - ru - sa - lem, my hap - py home, When shall I come to thee?
2 Thy saints are crowned with glo - ry great; They see God face to face;
3 There Da - vid stands with harp in hand As mas - ter of the choir:

When shall my sor - rows have an end? Thy joys when shall I see?
They tri - umph still, they still re - joice: Most hap - py is their case.
Ten thou - sand times that man were blest That might this mu - sic hear.

General Hymns

4 Our Lady sings Magnificat
  With tune surpassing sweet;
And all the virgins bear their part,
  Sitting about her feet.

5 There Magdalen hath left her moan,
  And cheerfully doth sing
With blessèd saints, whose harmony
  In every street doth ring.

6 Jerusalem, Jerusalem,
  God grant that I may see
Thine endless joy, and of the same
  Partaker ever be!

F. B. P., c. *16th cent.*

586

C. M.

CAPEL

In moderate time

Traditional English Melody,
arr. R. VAUGHAN WILLIAMS, 1906

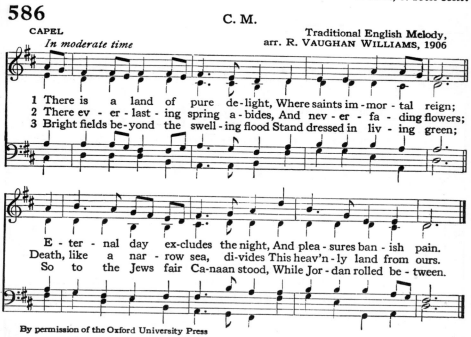

1 There is a land of pure de-light, Where saints im-mor-tal reign;
2 There ev-er-last-ing spring a-bides, And nev-er-fa-ding flowers;
3 Bright fields be-yond the swell-ing flood Stand dressed in liv-ing green;

E-ter-nal day ex-cludes the night, And plea-sures ban-ish pain.
Death, like a nar-row sea, di-vides This heav'n-ly land from ours.
So to the Jews fair Ca-naan stood, While Jor-dan rolled be-tween.

By permission of the Oxford University Press

4 But timorous mortals start and shrink
  To cross the narrow sea;
And linger, trembling on the brink,
  And fear to launch away.

5 O could we make our doubts remove,
  Those gloomy doubts that rise,
And see the Canaan that we love,
  With faith's illumined eyes:

6 Could we but climb where Moses stood,
  And view the landscape o'er,
Not Jordan's stream, nor death's cold flood,
  Should fright us from the shore!

ISAAC WATTS, 1709, *alt.*

587 *First Tune*   **General Hymns**
87. 87. 87

REGENT SQUARE   HENRY SMART, 1867
In moderate time

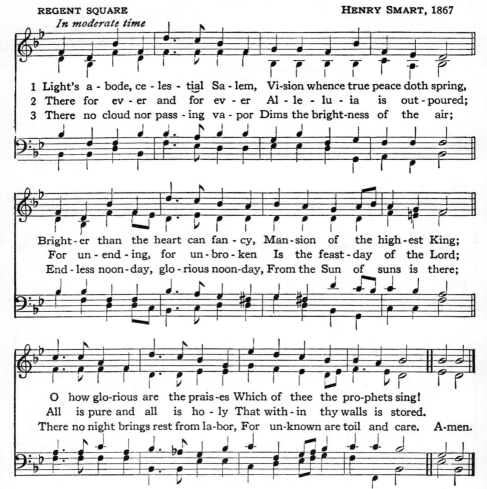

1 Light's a - bode, ce - les - tial Sa - lem, Vi-sion whence true peace doth spring,
2 There for ev - er and for ev - er Al - le - lu - ia is out - poured;
3 There no cloud nor pass - ing va - por Dims the bright-ness of the air;

Bright - er than the heart can fan - cy, Man - sion of the high - est King;
For un - end - ing, for un - bro - ken Is the feast - day of the Lord;
End - less noon - day, glo - rious noon-day, From the Sun of suns is there;

O how glo-rious are the prais - es Which of thee the pro-phets sing!
All is pure and all is ho - ly That with - in thy walls is stored.
There no night brings rest from la-bor, For un-known are toil and care. A-men.

*4 O how glorious and resplendent,
    Fragile body, shalt thou be,
When endued with heav'nly beauty,
    Full of health, and strong, and free,
Full of vigor, full of pleasure
    That shall last eternally!

5 Now with gladness, now with courage,
    Bear the burden on thee laid,
That hereafter these thy labors
    May with endless gifts be paid,
And in everlasting glory
    Thou with brightness be arrayed.

General Hymns

6 Laud and honor to the Father,
Laud and honor to the Son,
Laud and honor to the Spirit,
Ever Three, and ever One,
Consubstantial, co-eternal,
While unending ages run.   Amen.

Latin, 15th cent.; Tr. JOHN MASON NEALE, *alt.*

587 *Second Tune*   87. 87. 87
AD PERENNIS   French Church Melody, c. 16th cent.
Joyously, in unison

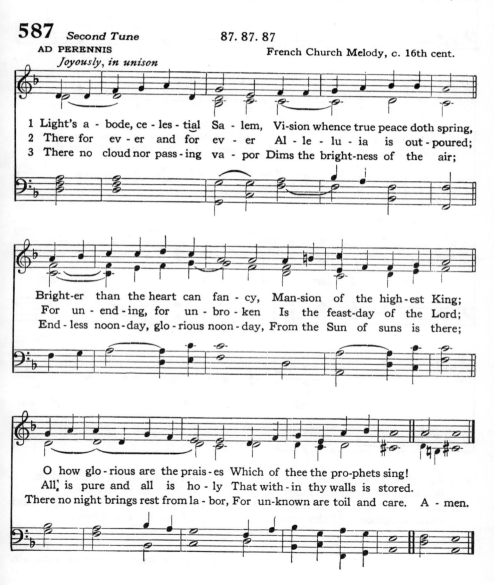

1 Light's a - bode, ce - les - tial Sa - lem, Vi-sion whence true peace doth spring,
2 There for ev - er and for ev - er Al - le - lu - ia is out - poured;
3 There no cloud nor pass - ing va - por Dims the bright-ness of the air;

Bright-er than the heart can fan - cy, Man-sion of the high - est King;
For un - end - ing, for un - bro - ken Is the feast-day of the Lord;
End - less noon-day, glo - rious noon - day, From the Sun of suns is there;

O how glo - rious are the prais - es Which of thee the pro-phets sing!
All is pure and all is ho - ly That with - in thy walls is stored.
There no night brings rest from la - bor, For un-known are toil and care.   A - men.

86. 86. 66. 66

PARADISE   JOSEPH BARNBY, 1856

In moderate time

1 O Par - a - dise, O Par - a - dise, Who doth not crave for rest?
2 O Par - a - dise, O Par - a - dise, The world is grow-ing old;
3 O Par - a - dise, O Par - a - dise, We long to sin no more;

Who would not seek the hap - py land Where they that loved are blest;
Who would not be at rest and free Where love is nev - er cold?
We long to be as pure on earth As on thy spot - less shore;

Refrain

Where loy - al hearts and true Stand ev - er in the light,

All rap - ture, thro' and thro', In God's most ho - ly sight. A-men.

4 O Paradise, O Paradise,
   We shall not wait for long;
   E'en now the loving ear may catch
   Faint fragments of thy song;
           Refrain

5 Lord Jesus, King of Paradise,
   O keep us in thy love,
   And guide us to that happy land
   Of perfect rest above;
           Refrain
           Amen.

FREDERICK WILLIAM FABER, 1862, *alt.*

589   **General Hymns**

10 10. 10 10

O QUANTA QUALIA   Ad. 1854, from *Méthode du Plain Chant,* 1808;
har. by JOHN B. DYKES, 1868

With dignity

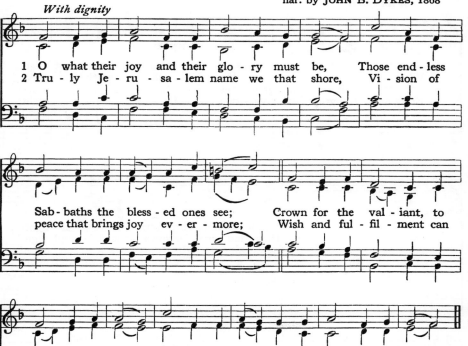

1 O what their joy and their glo - ry must be, Those end - less
2 Tru - ly Je - ru - sa - lem name we that shore, Vi - sion of

Sab - baths the bless - ed ones see; Crown for the val - iant, to
peace that brings joy ev - er - more; Wish and ful - fil - ment can

wea - ry ones rest: God shall be all, and in all ev - er blest.
sev - er'd be ne'er, Nor the thing prayed for come short of the prayer.

3 There, where no troubles distraction can bring,
We the sweet anthems of Sion shall sing;
While for thy grace, Lord, their voices of praise
Thy blessèd people eternally raise.

4 Now, in the meanwhile, with hearts raised on high,
We for that country must yearn and must sigh,
Seeking Jerusalem, dear native land,
Through our long exile on Babylon's strand.

A-men.

5 Low before him with our praises we fall,
Of whom, and in whom, and through whom are all;
Of whom, the Father; and in whom, the Son;
Through whom, the Spirit, with them ever One. Amen.

PETER ABELARD, c. 1129;
Tr. JOHN MASON NEALE, 1854, *alt.*

ALFORD   JOHN B. DYKES, 1875

With spirit

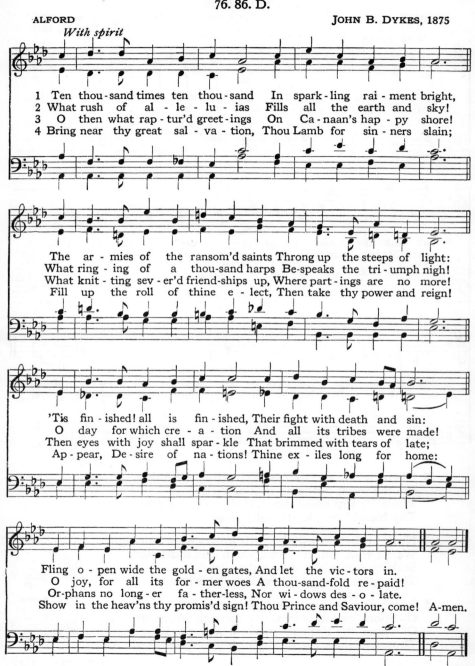

1 Ten thou-sand times ten thou-sand In spark-ling rai - ment bright,
2 What rush of al - le - lu - ias Fills all the earth and sky!
3 O then what rap - tur'd greet-ings On Ca-naan's hap - py shore!
4 Bring near thy great sal - va - tion, Thou Lamb for sin - ners slain;

The ar - mies of the ransom'd saints Throng up the steeps of light:
What ring - ing of a thou-sand harps Be-speaks the tri - umph nigh!
What knit - ting sev - er'd friend-ships up, Where part - ings are no more!
Fill up the roll of thine e - lect, Then take thy power and reign!

'Tis fin - ished! all is fin - ished, Their fight with death and sin:
O day for which cre - a - tion And all its tribes were made!
Then eyes with joy shall spar - kle That brimmed with tears of late;
Ap - pear, De - sire of na - tions! Thine ex - iles long for home:

Fling o - pen wide the gold - en gates, And let the vic - tors in.
O joy, for all its for - mer woes A thou-sand-fold re - paid!
Or-phans no long - er fa - ther-less, Nor wi - dows des - o - late.
Show in the heav'ns thy promis'd sign! Thou Prince and Saviour, come! A-men.

HENRY ALFORD, 1867

66. 66. D.

BEULAH
In moderate time
Melody by HENRI F. HEMY, 1864

1 There is a bless-ed home Be-yond this land of woe,
2 There is a land of peace: Good an-gels know it well;

Where tri-als nev-er come, Nor tears of sor-row flow;
Glad songs that nev-er cease With-in its por-tals swell;

Where faith is lost in sight, And pa-tient hope is crowned,
A-round its glo-rious throne Ten thou-sand saints a-dore

And ev-er-last-ing light Its glo-ry throws a-round.
Christ, with the Fa-ther One, And Spi-rit, ev-er-more.

3 O joy all joys beyond,
  To see the Lamb who died,
And count each sacred wound
  In hands, and feet, and side!
To give to him the praise
  Of every triumph won,
And sing through endless days
  The great things he hath done!

4 Look up, ye saints of God!
  Nor fear to tread below
The path your Saviour trod
  Of daily toil and woe!
Wait but a little while
  In uncomplaining love!
His own most gracious smile
  Shall welcome you above.

HENRY WILLIAMS BAKER, 1861

CHRIST IS MY LIFE   Melody by MELCHIOR VULPIUS, 1609

Serenely

1 O hea - ven - ly Je - ru - sa - lem Of ev - er - last - ing halls,
2 Thou art the gold - en man - sion Where saints for ev - er sing,
3 There God for ev - er sit - teth, Him - self of all the crown;
4 Naught to this seat ap - proach - eth Their sweet peace to mo - lest;

Thrice bless-ed are the peo - ple Thou stor-est in thy walls.
The seat of God's own cho - sen, The pal - ace of the King.
The Lamb, the Light that shin - eth And nev - er go - eth down.
They sing their God for ev - er, Nor day nor night they rest. A-men.

5 Sure hope doth thither lead us;
    Our longings thither tend;
    May short-lived toil ne'er daunt us
    For joys that cannot end.

6 To Christ, the Sun that lightens
    His Church above, below;
    To Father, and to Spirit
    All things created bow.   Amen.

Latin, 18th cent.; Tr. ISAAC WILLIAMS, 1839

592 *Second Tune*   76. 76. D.

ALL HALLOWS   GEORGE C. MARTIN, 1892

In unison, triumphantly

1 O hea - ven - ly Je - ru - sa - lem Of ev - er - last - ing halls,
3 There God for ev - er sit - teth, Him-self of all the crown;

General Hymns

Thrice bless - ed are the peo - ple Thou stor - est in thy walls.
The Lamb, the Light that shin - eth And nev - er go - eth down.

2 Thou art the gold - en man - sion Where saints for ev - er sing,
4 Naught to this seat ap - proach - eth Their sweet peace to mo - lest;

In harmony

The seat of God's own cho - sen, The pal - ace of the King.
They sing their God for ev - er, Nor day nor night they rest. A-men.

593 *First Tune*   # 𝕲eneral 𝕳ymns
76. 86. D.

GRESHAM   GEOFFREY SHAW, 1915

Unison, in moderate time

1 I heard a sound of voic-es A-round the great white throne, With
2 From ev-'ry clime and kin-dred, And na-tions from a-far, As
3 I saw the ho-ly ci-ty, The New Je-ru-sa-lem, Come

harp-ers harp-ing on their harps To him that sat there-on:
ser-ried ranks re-turn-ing home In tri-umph from a war,
down from heav'n, a bride a-dorned With jew-el'd di-a-dem;

"Sal-va-tion, glo-ry, hon-or!" I heard the song a-rise, As
I heard the saints up-rais-ing, The myr-iad hosts a-mong, In
The flood of crys-tal wa-ters Flowed down the gold-en street; And

General Hymns

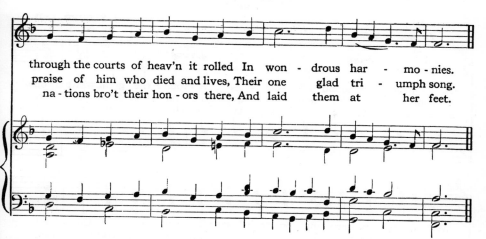

through the courts of heav'n it rolled In won - drous har - mo - nies.
praise of him who died and lives, Their one glad tri - umph song.
na - tions bro't their hon - ors there, And laid them at her feet.

4 And there no sun was needed,
   Nor moon to shine by night,
God's glory did enlighten all,
   The Lamb himself the light;
And there his servants serve him,
   And, life's long battle o'er,
Enthroned with him, their Saviour, King,
   They reign for evermore.

5 O great and glorious vision!
   The Lamb upon his throne;
O wondrous sight for man to see!
   The Saviour with his own:
To drink the living waters
   And stand upon the shore,
Where neither sorrow, sin, nor death
   Shall ever enter more.

6 O Lamb of God who reignest!
   Thou bright and morning Star,
Whose glory lightens that new earth
   Which now we see from far!
O worthy Judge eternal!
   When thou dost bid us come,
Then open wide the gates of pearl
   And call thy servants home. Amen.

In harmony

A - men.

GODFREY THRING, 1886

76. 86. D.

PATMOS

HENRY J. STORER, 1891

In moderate time

1 I heard a sound of voic - es A - round the great white throne,
2 From ev - 'ry clime and kin - dred, And na - tions from a - far,
3 I saw the ho - ly ci - ty, The New Je - ru - sa - lem,

With harp - ers harp - ing on their harps To him that sat there - on:
As ser - ried ranks re - turn - ing home In tri - umph from a war,
Come down from heav'n, a bride a - dorned With jew - el'd di - a - dem;

"Sal - va - tion, glo - ry, hon - or!" I heard the song a - rise,
I heard the saints up - rais - ing, The myr - iad hosts a - mong,
The flood of crys - tal wa - ters Flowed down the gold - en street;

As through the courts of heav'n it rolled In won - drous har - mo - nies.
In praise of him who died and lives, Their one glad tri - umph song.
And na - tions brought their hon - ors there, And laid them at her feet.

4 And there no sun was needed,
Nor moon to shine by night,
God's glory did enlighten all,
The Lamb himself the light;
And there his servants serve him,
And, life's long battle o'er,
Enthroned with him, their Saviour, King,
They reign for evermore.

5 O great and glorious vision!
The Lamb upon his throne;
O wondrous sight for man to see!
The Saviour with his own:
To drink the living waters
And stand upon the shore,
Where neither sorrow, sin, nor death
Shall ever enter more.

General Hymns

6 O Lamb of God who reignest!
  Thou bright and morning Star,
  Whose glory lightens that new earth
  Which now we see from far!

O worthy Judge eternal!
  When thou dost bid us come,
  Then open wide the gates of pearl
  And call thy servants home.
                Amen.

GODFREY THRING, 1886

594

10 6. 10 6. 76. 76

MELCHIOR

Broadly, but with spirit

Erfurt, 1663; har. by
CHARLES WOOD, 1904

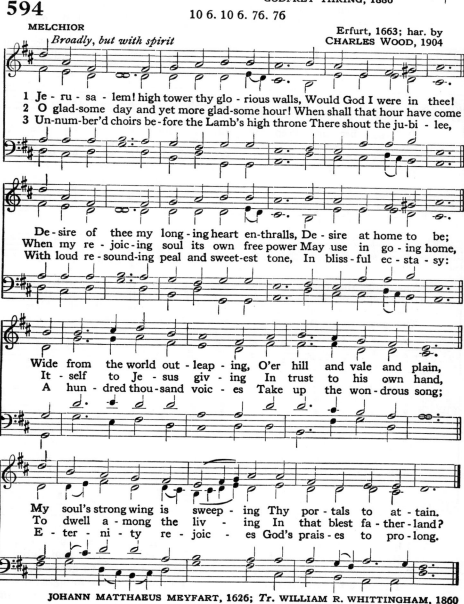

1 Je - ru - sa - lem! high tower thy glo - rious walls, Would God I were in thee!
2 O glad-some day and yet more glad-some hour! When shall that hour have come
3 Un-num-ber'd choirs be-fore the Lamb's high throne There shout the ju-bi - lee,

De - sire of thee my long - ing heart en-thralls, De - sire at home to be;
When my re - joic-ing soul its own free power May use in go - ing home,
With loud re - sound-ing peal and sweet-est tone, In bliss - ful ec - sta - sy:

Wide from the world out - leap - ing, O'er hill and vale and plain,
It - self to Je - sus giv - ing In trust to his own hand,
A hun - dred thou-sand voic - es Take up the won - drous song;

My soul's strong wing is sweep - ing Thy por - tals to at - tain.
To dwell a - mong the liv - ing In that blest fa - ther - land?
E - ter - ni - ty re - joic - es God's prais - es to pro - long.

JOHANN MATTHAEUS MEYFART, 1626; *Tr.* WILLIAM R. WHITTINGHAM, 1860

PEARSALL   76. 76. D.   ROBERT L. PEARSALL, 1863

1 The world is ve - ry e - vil; The times are wax - ing late;
2 A - rise, a - rise, good Chris - tian, Let right to wrong suc - ceed;
3 'Mid power that knows no lim - it, And wis - dom free from bound,
4 That peace—but who may claim it? The guile - less in their way,

Be so - ber and keep vig - il; The Judge is at the gate:
Let pen - i - ten - tial sor - row To heav'n-ly glad - ness lead:
The be - a - tif - ic vi - sion Shall glad the saints a - round;
Who keep the ranks of bat - tle, Who mean the thing they say:

The Judge that comes in mer - cy, The Judge that comes with might,
To the home of fade - less splen - dor, Of flowers that bear no thorn,
The peace of all the faith - ful, The calm of all the blest,
The peace that is for hea - ven, And shall be for the earth:

To ter - mi - nate the e - vil, To di - a - dem the right.
Where they shall dwell as chil - dren, Who here as ex - iles mourn.
In - vi - o - late, un - va - ried, Di - vin - est, sweet - est, best.
The pal - ace that re - ech - oes With fes - tal song and mirth.

5 O happy, holy portion,   Strive, man, to win that glory;
    Refection for the blest,   Toil, man, to gain that light;
True vision of true beauty,   Send hope before to grasp it,
    The cure for all distrest!   Till hope be lost in sight.

            ST. BERNARD of Cluny, c. 1145; *Tr.* JOHN MASON NEALE, 1858, *alt.*

OSLO   *First Tune*   76. 76. D.   Traditional Norwegian Melody

In moderate time

1 Brief life is here our por - tion, Brief sor - row, short-lived care;
2 There grief is turned to plea - sure; Such plea - sure as be - low

The life that knows no end - ing, The tear - less life is there.
No hu - man voice can ut - ter, No hu - man heart can know;

O hap - py ret - ri - bu - tion, Short toil, e - ter - nal rest,
And af - ter flesh - ly weak - ness, And af - ter this world's night,

For mor - tals and for sin - ners A man - sion with the blest!
And af - ter storm and whirl - wind, Are calm and joy and light.

Harmony by permission of the Oxford University Press

3 And now we fight the battle,
  But then shall wear the crown
Of full and everlasting
  And passionless renown;
And he whom now we trust in
  Shall then be seen and known,
And they that know and see him
  Shall have him for their own.

4 The morning shall awaken,
  The shadows flee away,
And each true-hearted servant
  Shall shine as doth the day;
For God our King and Portion,
  In fullness of his grace,
We then shall see for ever,
  And worship face to face.

ST. BERNARD of Cluny, c. 1145; *Tr.* JOHN MASON NEALE, 1851, *alt.*

596

ST. ALPHEGE

HENRY J. GAUNTLETT, 1852

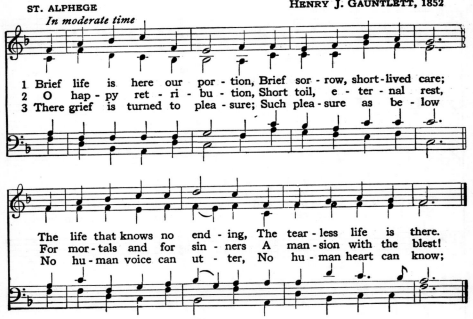

1 Brief life is here our por - tion, Brief sor - row, short - lived care;
2 O hap - py ret - ri - bu - tion, Short toil, e - ter - nal rest,
3 There grief is turned to plea - sure; Such plea - sure as be - low

The life that knows no end - ing, The tear - less life is there.
For mor - tals and for sin - ners A man - sion with the blest!
No hu - man voice can ut - ter, No hu - man heart can know;

4 And after fleshly weakness,
   And after this world's night,
   And after storm and whirlwind,
   Are calm and joy and light.

5 And now we fight the battle,
   But then shall wear the crown
   Of full and everlasting
   And passionless renown;

6 And he whom now we trust in
   Shall then be seen and known,
   And they that know and see him
   Shall have him for their own.

7 The morning shall awaken,
   The shadows flee away,
   And each true-hearted servant
   Shall shine as doth the day;

8 For God our King and Portion,
   In fullness of his grace,
   We then shall see for ever,
   And worship face to face.

ST. BERNARD of Cluny, c. 1145;
Tr. JOHN MASON NEALE, 1851, *alt.*

EWING   76. 76. D.   ALEXANDER C. EWING, 1853
With dignity

1 Je - ru - sa - lem the gold - en, With milk and hon - ey blest,
2 They stand, those halls of Si - on, All ju - bi - lant with song,

Be - neath thy con - tem - pla - tion Sink heart and voice op - prest:
And bright with ma - ny an an - gel, And all the mar - tyr throng:

I know not, O I know not, What joys a - wait us there;
The Prince is ev - er in them, The day - light is se - rene;

What ra - dian - cy of glo - ry, What bliss be - yond com-pare!
The pas - tures of the bless - ed Are decked in glo - rious sheen. A-men.

3 There is the throne of David;
   And there, from care released,
The shout of them that triumph,
   The song of them that feast;
And they who with their Leader
Have conquered in the fight,
   For ever and for ever
   Are clad in robes of white.

4 O sweet and blessèd country,
   The home of God's elect!
O sweet and blessèd country
   That eager hearts expect!
Jesus, in mercy bring us
   To that dear land of rest,
Who art, with God the Father,
   And Spirit, ever blest. Amen.

ST. BERNARD of Cluny, *c.* 1145; *Tr.* JOHN MASON NEALE, 1858, *alt.*

First Tune

76. 76. D.

MEIRIONYDD

Melody by WILLIAM LLOYD, 1840

In moderate time; may be sung in unison

1 For thee, O dear, dear coun - try, Mine eyes their vig - ils keep;
2 O one, O on - ly man - sion! O Par - a - dise of joy!

For ve - ry love be - hold - ing Thy ho - ly name, they weep.
Where tears are ev - er ban - ish'd And smiles have no al - loy;

The men - tion of thy glo - ry Is unc - tion to the breast,
Thy love - li - ness op - press - es All hu - man thought and heart,

And med - i - cine in sick - ness, And love, and life, and rest.
And none, O Peace, O Si - on, Can sing thee as thou art. A-men.

3 With jasper glow thy bulwarks,
  Thy streets with emeralds blaze;
The sardius and the topaz
  Unite in thee their rays;
Thine ageless walls are bonded
  With amethyst unpriced;
The saints build up thy fabric,
  And the corner-stone is Christ.

4 The cross is all thy splendor,
  The Crucified thy praise;
His laud and benediction
  Thy ransomed people raise:
Upon the Rock of Ages
  They build thy holy tower;
Thine is the victor's laurel,
  And thine the golden dower.

General Hymns

5 O sweet and blessèd country,
   The home of God's elect!
   O sweet and blessèd country
   That eager hearts expect!

Jesus, in mercy bring us
   To that dear land of rest,
   Who art, with God the Father,
   And Spirit, ever blest.   Amen.

ST. BERNARD of Cluny, c. 1145;
Tr. JOHN MASON NEALE, 1858, *alt.*

598   Part IV of Hymn 595   76. 76. D.
          Second Tune

HOMELAND   ARTHUR S. SULLIVAN, 1867

1 For thee, O dear, dear country, Mine eyes their vig-ils keep;
2 O one, O on-ly man-sion! O Par-a-dise of joy!

For ve-ry love be-hold-ing Thy ho-ly name, they weep.
Where tears are ev-er ban-ish'd And smiles have no al-loy;

The men-tion of thy glo-ry Is unc-tion to the breast,
Thy love-li-ness op-press-es All hu-man thought and heart,

And med-i-cine in sick-ness, And love, and life, and rest.
And none, O Peace, O Si-on, Can sing thee as thou art.   A-men.

Third Tune 76. 76. D.

ELY CATHEDRAL T. TERTIUS NOBLE, 1895

With joyful dignity

1 For thee, O dear, dear coun - try, Mine eyes their vig - ils keep;
2 O one, O on - ly man - sion! O Par - a - dise of joy!
3 With jas - per glow thy bul - warks, Thy streets with em-eralds blaze;
4 The cross is all thy splen - dor, The Cru - ci - fied thy praise;
5 O sweet and bless - ed coun - try, The home of God's e - lect!

For ve - ry love be - hold - ing Thy ho - ly name, they weep.
Where tears are ev - er ban - ish'd And smiles have no al - loy;
The sar - dius and the to - paz U - nite in thee their rays;
His laud and ben - e - dic - tion Thy ran - som'd peo - ple raise:
O sweet and bless - ed coun - try That ea - ger hearts ex - pect!

General Hymns

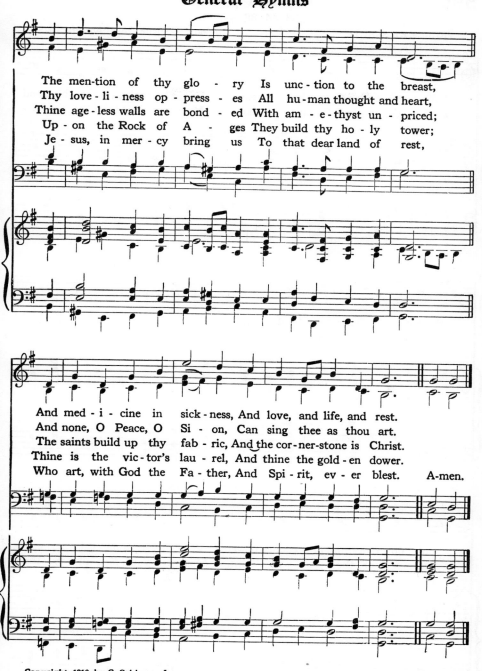

The men-tion of thy glo - ry Is unc - tion to the breast,
Thy love - li - ness op - press - es All hu - man thought and heart,
Thine age - less walls are bond - ed With am - e - thyst un - priced;
Up - on the Rock of A - ges They build thy ho - ly tower;
Je - sus, in mer - cy bring us To that dear land of rest,

And med - i - cine in sick - ness, And love, and life, and rest.
And none, O Peace, O Si - on, Can sing thee as thou art.
The saints build up thy fab - ric, And the cor - ner-stone is Christ.
Thine is the vic - tor's lau - rel, And thine the gold - en dower.
Who art, with God the Fa - ther, And Spi - rit, ev - er blest. A-men.

ST. BERNARD of Cluny, c. 1145;
Tr. JOHN MASON NEALE, 1858, alt.

88. 44. 88. 44. 444

VIGILES ET SANCTI   Melody, Cologne *Gesangbuch,* 1623
Boldly, in unison

1 Ye watch-ers and ye ho - ly ones,   Bright seraphs, cher - u - bim, and

2 O high - er than the cher - u - bim,   More glo-rious than the ser - a -

thrones,   Raise the glad strain, Al - le - lu - ia! Cry

phim,   Lead their prais - es, Al - le - lu - ia! Thou

out, do - min - ions, princedoms, powers,   Vir - tues, arch-an - gels, an - gels'

bear - er of the e - ter - nal Word,   Most gra-cious, mag - ni - fy the

General Hymns

choirs,
Lord, Al - le - lu - ia, Al - le - lu - ia, Al - le -

lu - ia, Al - le - lu - ia, Al - le - lu - - ia!

The antiphonal Alleluias may be sung either as indicated; or between Choir and Congregation; or between men's and women's voices.

3 Respond, ye souls in endless rest,
　Ye patriarchs and prophets blest,
　　Alleluia, Alleluia!
　Ye holy twelve, ye martyrs strong,
　All saints triumphant, raise the song
　Alleluia, Alleluia, Alleluia, Alleluia, Alleluia!

4 O friends, in gladness let us sing,
　Supernal anthems echoing,
　　Alleluia, Alleluia!
　To God the Father, God the Son,
　And God the Spirit, Three in One,
　Alleluia, Alleluia, Alleluia, Alleluia, Alleluia!
　　　　　　　　　　　　Amen.

In harmony

A - men.

ATHELSTAN RILEY, 1909

66. 66. 44. 44

DARWALL
With dignity

JOHN DARWALL, 1770

1 Ye ho - ly an - gels bright, Who wait at God's right hand, Or
2 Ye bless - ed souls at rest, Who ran this earth - ly race And

through the realms of light Fly at your Lord's com - mand, As - sist our
now, from sin re - leased, Be - hold the Sa - viour's face, God's prais - es

song, For else the theme Too high doth seem For mor - tal tongue.
sound, As in his sight With sweet de - light Ye do a - bound.

3 Ye saints, who toil below,
　　Adore your heav'nly King,
And onward as ye go
　　Some joyful anthem sing;
　　　Take what he gives
　　　And praise him still,
　　Through good or ill,
Who ever lives!

4 My soul, bear thou thy part,
　　Triumph in God above:
And with a well-tuned heart
　　Sing thou the songs of love!
　　　Let all thy days
　　　Till life shall end,
　　Whate'er he send,
Be filled with praise.

RICHARD BAXTER, 1672,
and JOHN HAMPDEN GURNEY, 1838

SERVICE MUSIC

𝔓rinciples of 𝔠hanting

There is today a complete consensus of opinion on all sides that good chanting is primarily good reading aloud; that the rhythms of natural speech are as essential in the singing of Psalms and Canticles as in the saying of them without music.

The notes of a chant tune have no time value of their own apart from the rhythm of the syllables to which they are sung. The chant has no fixed rhythm of its own to which the syllables are adapted, and all of its measures are of constantly changing length, sometimes of two beats, sometimes of three, sometimes of only one weak beat. The printing of a chant with a whole note for each recitation is purely conventional. If a recitation consists of only a single unstressed syllable (such as "and" in the second phrase of *Gloria Patri*), the note sung should be only as long as the unstressed syllable well read. If, on the other hand, a verse begins with a long recitation, such as the second verse of *Venite,* the whole note represents the unhurried reading of nine syllables, with their natural stresses only, and no other accent whatever.

The notes of the two cadences do not indicate the slightest break in the smooth natural reading of the words, or the slightest addition of a musical measure accent to the natural stresses of good reading.

Failure to achieve good chanting is failure on the part of the choirmaster to teach the two primary principles of chanting, which are these:

(*a*)*The pace of the reading is the same in both Recitations and Inflections.*

(*b*)*All stresses are merely those of good reading.*

A sound method of teaching these principles effectively is as follows:

Have the choir read the words of the first verse of a Canticle together, distinctly and naturally, giving the sense. Repeat, if necessary, till the verse is well read. Then let them read the words in monotone, in the same rhythm precisely, and with the same stresses.

The organist should then play the chant, preferably with the first note of each part a half-note, not the conventional whole note, as written.

Then have the choir sing the verse in precisely the same rhythm, with the same stresses, and the same care for giving the sense.

A Canticle thus learned, or rather re-learned, verse by verse, will not readily disintegrate into the old careless reiteration of a fixed mechanical rhythm unrelated to the meaning of its words. Good chanting is just good intelligent reading, in musical tones.

Directions for Anglican Chanting

The pointing here used is a careful revision of that previously set forth in the Hymnal and by the Joint Commission on Church Music. The principal change is in treating the Mediation as a semi-cadence, without the characteristic doubling of a final trochaic foot which is musically normal at the full cadence of the Ending. One, two, or three syllables may be sung to its final note. The final note of the Ending provides for one syllable only, except in the words *thanksgiving, handmaiden, forefathers,* and *night season.*

The signs used for pointing in this book are as follows:

(*a*) The upright stroke | precedes the first syllable of either Mediation or Ending, and is occasionally repeated after the first rhythmical foot of the Ending.

(*b*) The syllable in bold-faced **type** is always sung to two notes of the chant.

(*c*) The dot • is placed after, and sometimes before, two syllables to indicate that the second is to be sung to the same note, repeated with the same time value, as the first.

(*d*) The dash — indicates the omission of the Reciting Note in the three verses where it occurs on p. 741.

Breath should be taken only at the end of a line; in verses 5 and 6, p. 742, lines run over. A comma in a line is observed by slightly prolonging the previous syllable.

Be careful not to stress weak opening syllables in a line; and to sing a weak final syllable lightly and quickly.

All passing notes have been eliminated from the music, as involving a time element foreign to good chanting.

The method of singing *Gloria Patri* is illustrated below.

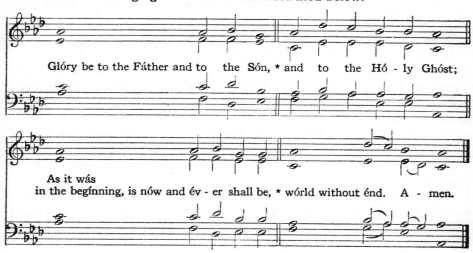

Glóry be to the Fáther and to   the Són, * and   to   the Hó - ly Ghóst;

As it wás
in the begínning, is nów and év - er shall be, * wórld without énd.   A - men.

Directions for Plainsong Chanting

The special signs used in this book for Plainsong chanting are but two.

The upright stroke | precedes the first syllable which changes in pitch from the reciting note. It is wholly unrelated to stress or accent.

The note in parentheses (♪) in the music provides for an occasional extra syllable in cadences. In such a case, the preceding note loses half of its value. Sing and play ♪ ♪ ♩ not ♩ ♪ ♩

As in Anglican chanting, breath should be taken only at the end of a line. In verse 5, No. 621, the line necessarily runs over. It should extend to the close of the verse. A comma occuring in a line is observed by slightly prolonging the previous syllable.

The final syllable of each half verse should be sung *diminuendo*; if it is unstressed, sing it lightly and quickly.

The letters (*a*), (*b*), (*c*), indicate varying accompaniments conforming to the varying rhythms of the cadences. In them, the precise notation for abbreviated or lengthened cadences is clearly noted.

The Intonation is used only in the first verse, except in *Benedictus, Magnificat*, and *Nunc dimittis*, which are noted throughout.

THE CHORAL SERVICE

The Ferial Preces

601

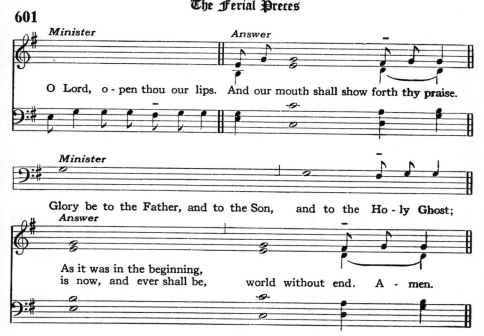

O Lord, o - pen thou our lips. And our mouth shall show forth thy praise.

Glory be to the Father, and to the Son, and to the Ho - ly Ghost;

As it was in the beginning, is now, and ever shall be, world without end. A - men.

The Choral Service

Minister Praise ye the Lord.   **Answer** The Lord's Name be prais-ed.

The Festal Preces

602

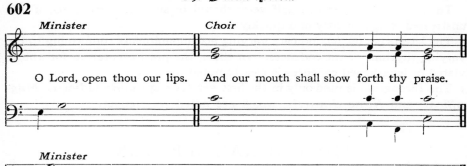

Minister O Lord, open thou our lips.   **Choir** And our mouth shall show forth thy praise.

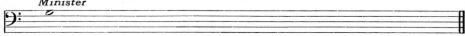

Minister

Glory be to the Father, and to the Son, and to the Holy Ghost;

Choir

As it was in the beginning, is now, and ever shall be, world with-

out end. A-men.   **Minister** Praise ye the Lord.   **Choir** The Lord's Name be prais-ed.

The Suffrages after the Creed

Minister

The Lord be with you.

601 Ferial Responses

People, in unison

And with thy spirit.

602 Festal Responses

Choir

And with thy spirit.

Minister

Let us pray. Our Father,

Minister and People, in unison

who art in heaven, *etc.*

Minister and People

. . . for ever and ever. A - men.

Choir

. . . for ever and ever. A - men.

Minister

O Lord, show thy mercy upon us.

People, in unison

And grant us thy sal - va - tion.

Choir

And grant us thy sal - va - tion.

* *The melody of the People is the same in both Ferial and Festal Responses.*

The Choral Service

O Lord, save the State.

601

And mercifully hear
us when we call up - on thee.

602

And mercifully hear us when we call up-on thee.

*Minister

Endue thy Ministers with righteousness.

And make thy chosen people joyful.

And make thy chosen people joy-ful.

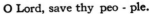

*Minister

O Lord, save thy peo - ple.

And bless thine in-her - i - tance.

And bless thine in-her - i - tance.

*Only at Evening Prayer

702

The Choral Service

Minister

Give peace in our time, O Lord.

601

People, in unison

For it is thou, Lord, only,

that makest us dwell in safety.

602

Choir

For it is thou, Lord, on-ly,

that makest us dwell in safe-ty.

*Only at Evening Prayer

Minister

O God, make clean our hearts within us.

People, in unison

And take not thy Holy Spirit from us.

Choir

And take not thy Holy Spi-rit from us.

After the sung Collects

People, in unison

A - men.

Choir

A - men.

MORNING CANTICLES
The Invitatory Antiphons

603   W. BOYCE   **605**   D. HANFORTH

604   E. G. MONK   **606**   G. A. MACFARREN

Sundays in Advent.
Our King and Saviour | draweth nigh;
* O come, let | us a**dore** him.

Christmas Day until the Epiphany.
Alleluia.   Unto us a | child is born;
* O come, let us adore him. | Alle**lu**ia.

The Epiphany Octave and the Feast of the Transfiguration.
The Lord hath manifested | forth his glory;
* O come, let | us a**dore** him.

Easter Monday until Ascension Day.
Alleluia.   The Lord is | risen · indeed;
* O come, let us adore him. | Alle**lu**ia.

Ascension Day until Whitsunday.
Alleluia.   Christ the Lord ascendeth | into heav'n;
* O come, let us adore him. | Alle**lu**ia.

Whitsunday and six days after.
Alleluia.   The Spirit of the Lord | filleth · the world;
* O come, let us adore him. | Alle**lu**ia.

Trinity Sunday.
Father, Son, and Holy Ghost, | **one** God;
* O come, let | us a**dore** him.

The Purification and the Annunciation.
The Word was made flesh, and | dwelt among us;
* O come, let | us a**dore** him.

Any Saint's Day provided with a proper Epistle and Gospel.
The Lord is glorious | in his saints;
* O come, let | us a**dore** him.

The chant of the Invitatory Antiphon should be the same as that of Venite, **exultemus** Domino.

Venite, exultemus Domino

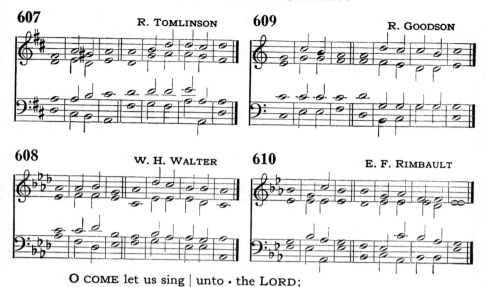

607 R. TOMLINSON
608 W. H. WALTER
609 R. GOODSON
610 E. F. RIMBAULT

O COME let us sing | unto • the LORD;
   * let us heartily rejoice in the strength of | our sal**va**tion.

2 Let us come before his presence with | **thanks**giving;
   * and show ourselves | glad in him with psalms.

3 For the LORD is a | **great** God;
   * and a great | King above all gods.

4 In his hand are all the corners | of the earth;
   * and the strength of the hills is | **his al**so.

5 The sea is | his and • he made it;
   * and his hands pre|pared • the **dry** land.

6 O come let us worship and | **fall** down,
   * and kneel before the | LORD our **Ma**ker.

7 For he is the | Lord our God;
   * and we are the people of his pasture,
   and the | sheep of **his** hand.

8 O worship the LORD in the | beauty • of holiness;
   * let the whole earth | stand in awe of him.

9 For he cometh, for he cometh to | judge the earth;
   * and with righteousness to judge the world,
   and the | peoples with his truth.

Glory be to the Father and | to the Son,
   * and | to the Holy Ghost;

As it was in the beginning, is now and | ever shall be,
   * world without | **end. A**men.

The note in parentheses used only when two syllables follow the accented note.

Sundays in Advent.	(a) Our King and Saviour draweth | nigh; * O come, let | us adore him.
Christmas Day until the Epiphany.	(b) Alleluia. Unto us a | child is born; * O come, let us adore him. | Alleluia.
The Epiphany Octave and the Feast of the Transfiguration.	(b) The Lord hath manifested forth his | glory; * O come, let | us adore him.
Easter Monday until Ascension Day.	(a) Alleluia. The Lord is risen in|deed; * O come, let us adore him. | Alleluia.
Ascension Day until Whitsunday.	(b) Alleluia. Christ the Lord ascendeth into | heaven; * O come, let us adore him. | Alleluia.
Whitsunday and six days after.	(a) Alleluia. The Spirit of the Lord filleth the | world; * O come, let us adore him. | Alleluia.
Trinity Sunday.	(a) Father, Son, and Holy Ghost, one | God; * O come, let | us adore him.
The Purification and the Annunciation.	(b) The Word was made flesh, and dwelt a|mong us; * O come, let | us adore him.
Any Saint's Day provided with a proper Epistle and Gospel.	(a) The Lord is glorious in his | saints; * O come, let | us adore him.

Individual antiphon melodies for the Invitatories and their proper chants for Venite *may be found in* The Choral Service *and* The Congregational Choral Service, *set forth by General Convention and to be had of* The H. W. Gray Company, 159 East 48th Street, New York.

Venite, exultemus Domino

612

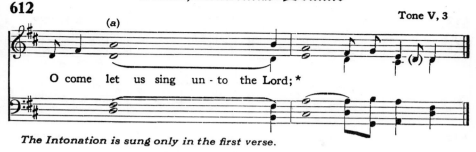

O come let us sing un-to the Lord; *

The Intonation is sung only in the first verse.

(a) O COME let us sing unto the | LORD;
  * let us heartily rejoice in the strength of | our salvation.

(b) 2 Let us come before his presence with thanks|giving;
  * and show ourselves | glad in him with psalms.

(a) 3 For the LORD is a great | God;
  * and a great King | above all gods.

(a) 4 In his hand are all the corners of the | earth;
  * and the strength of the hills | is his also.

(b) 5 The sea is his and he | made it;
  * and his hands prepar|ed the dry land.

(a) 6 O come let us worship and fall | down,
  * and kneel before the | LORD our Maker.

(a) 7 For he is the Lord our | God;
  * and we are the people of his pasture,
  and the | sheep of his hand.

(c) 8 O worship the LORD in the beauty of | holiness;
  * let the whole earth | stand in awe of him.

(a) 9 For he cometh, for he cometh to judge the | earth;
  * and with righteousness to judge the world,
  and the | peoples with his truth.

(a) Glory be to the Father and to the | Son,
  * and | to the Holy Ghost;

(b) As it was in the beginning, is now and ever | shall be,
  * world | without end.   Amen.

The Intonation before the reciting note is sung in the Invitatory, and in the first verse only of Venite.

Te Deum laudamus

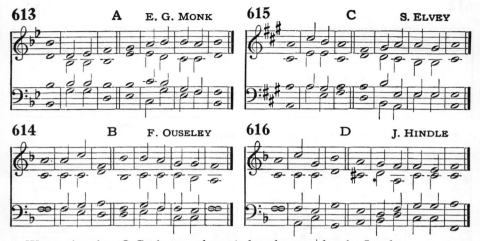

613 A E. G. MONK

615 C S. ELVEY

614 B F. OUSELEY

616 D J. HINDLE

WE praise thee O God; we acknowledge thee to | be the Lord.
   * All the earth doth worship thee, the Father | ever**last**ing.

2   To thee all Angels cry aloud;
    the Heavens and all the | Powers therein;
       * To thee Cherubim and Seraphim con|tinually do cry,

3   Holy Holy Holy Lord God of | Sabaoth;
       * Heaven and earth are full of the Majesty | of thy **glo**ry.

4   The glorious company of the Apostles | **praise** thee.
       * The goodly fellowship of the | Prophets **praise** thee.

5   The noble army of Martyrs | **praise** thee.
       * The holy Church throughout all the world | doth acknowledge thee;

6   The Father of an infinite Majesty;
    Thine adorable true and | only Son;
       * Also the Holy | Ghost the Comforter.

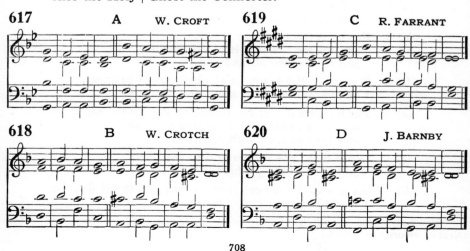

617 A W. CROFT

619 C R. FARRANT

618 B W. CROTCH

620 D J. BARNBY

Te Deum laudamus

THOU art the King of | Glory . O Christ.
   * Thou art the everlasting | Son of . the **Fa**ther.

8   When thou tookest upon thee to de|liver man,
     * thou didst humble thyself to be | born of . a **Vir**gin.

9   When thou hadst overcome the | sharpness . of death,
     * thou didst open the Kingdom of Heaven to | all be**lie**vers.

10   Thou sittest at the right | hand of God,
     * in the glory | of the **Fa**ther.

11   We believe that thou shalt come to | be our Judge.
     * We therefore pray thee help thy servants,
     whom thou hast redeemed | with thy precious blood.

12   Make them to be numbered | with thy Saints,
     * in glory | ever**last**ing.

A   E. G. MONK   C   S. ELVEY

B   F. OUSELEY   D   J. HINDLE

O LORD save thy people and bless thine | heritage.
   * Govern them and lift them | up for **ev**er.

14   Day by day we | magni•fy thee;
     * And we worship thy Name ever | world with**out** end.

15   Vouchsafe O Lord to keep us this day with|**out** sin.
     * O Lord have mercy upon us, have | mercy . up**on** us.

16   O Lord let thy mercy be upon us, as our | trust . is in . thee.
     * O Lord in thee have I trusted;
     let me never | be con**found**ed.

All of the chants for Te Deum laudamus *may be sung in unison, if so desired*

Te Deum laudamus

Tone VIII, 1

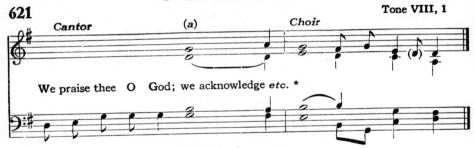

We praise thee O God; we acknowledge etc. *

The Intonation is sung only in the first verse.

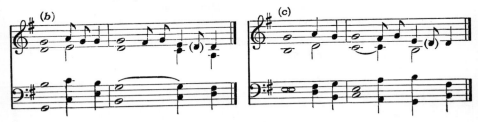

(*a*) WE praise thee O God; we acknowledge thee to be the | Lord.
    * All the earth doth worship thee, the Father | everlasting.

(*b*) 2 To thee all Angels cry aloud;
    the Heavens and all the | Powers therein;
    * To thee Cherubim and Seraphim contin|ually do cry,

(*b*) 3 Holy Holy Holy Lord God of | Sabaoth;
    * Heaven and earth are full of the Majesty | of thy glory.

(*c*) 4 The glorious company of the Apostles | praise thee.
    * The goodly fellowship of the | Prophets praise thee.

(*c*) 5 The noble army of Martyrs | praise thee.
    * The holy Church throughout all the world | doth ac·
    knowledge thee;

(*a*) 6 The Father of an infinite Majesty;
    Thine adorable true and only | Son;
    * Also the Holy | Ghost the Comforter.

Tone VII, 3

Thou art the King of Glo - ry O Christ.*

Te Deum laudamus

(a) THOU art the King of | Glory O Christ.
   * Thou art the everlasting | Son of the Father.

(b) 8 When thou tookest upon thee | to deliver man,
       * thou didst humble thyself to be | born of a Virgin.

(a) 9 When thou hadst overcome the | sharpness of death,
       * thou didst open the Kingdom of Heaven to | all believers.

(a) 10 Thou sittest at the | right hand of God,
       * in the glory | of the Father.

(c) 11 We believe that thou shalt | come to be our Judge.
       * We therefore pray thee help thy servants,
         whom thou hast redeemed | with thy precious blood.

(b) 12 Make them to be | numbered with thy Saints,
       * in glory | everlasting.

(a) O LORD save thy people and bless thine | heritage.
   * Govern them and lift them | up for ever.

(b) 14 Day by day we magnify | thee;
       * And we worship thy Name ever | world without end.

(b) 15 Vouchsafe O Lord to keep us this day without | sin.
       * O Lord have mercy upon us, have mer|cy upon us.

(b) 16 O Lord let thy mercy be upon us, as our trust is in | thee.
       * O Lord in thee have I trusted;
         let me never | be confounded.

Benedictus es, Domine

623

T. TURTON

624

R. H. STANLEY

BLESSED art thou, O Lord | God of · our fathers:
 * praised and exalted above | all for **ev**er.

2 Blessed art thou for the | Name of · thy Majesty:
 * praised and exalted above | all for **ev**er.

3 Blessed art thou in the temple | of thy holiness:
 * praised and exalted above | all for **ev**er.

4 Blessed art thou that beholdest the depths,
 and dwellest be|tween the Cherubim:
 * praised and exalted above | all for **ev**er.

5 Blessed art thou on the glorious | throne of · thy kingdom:
 * praised and exalted above | all for **ev**er.

6 Blessed art thou in the firma|ment of heaven:
 * praised and exalted above | all for **ev**er.

Glory be to the Father and | to the Son,
 * and | to the Holy Ghost;

As it was in the beginning, is now and | ever shall be,
 * world without | **end**. **A**men.

625

J. SOAPER

626

J. RANDALL

Benedicite, omnia opera Domini

627

Intonation only in the first verse Tone IV, 4

O all ye Works of the Lord, bless | ye the Lord: * . . . mag-ni | fy him for ev-er.

O ALL ye Works of the Lord, bless | ye the Lord:
   * praise him and magni | fy him for ever.
2   O ye Angels of the Lord, bless | ye the Lord:

O YE Heavens, bless | ye the Lord:
4   O ye Waters that be above the firmament, bless | ye the Lord:
5   O all ye Powers of the Lord, bless | ye the Lord:
6   O ye Sun and Moon, bless | ye the Lord:
7   O ye Stars of heaven, bless | ye the Lord:
8   O ye Showers and Dew, bless | ye the Lord:
9   O ye Winds of God, bless | ye the Lord:
10   O ye Fire and Heat, bless | ye the Lord:
11   O ye Winter and Summer, bless | ye the Lord:
12   O ye Dews and Frosts, bless | ye the Lord:
13   O ye Frost and Cold, bless | ye the Lord:
14   O ye Ice and Snow, bless | ye the Lord:
15   O ye Nights and Days, bless | ye the Lord:
16   O ye Light and Darkness, bless | ye the Lord:
17   O ye Lightnings and Clouds, bless | ye the Lord:

O LET the Earth | bless the Lord:
   * yea let it praise him and magni | fy him for ever.
19   O ye Mountains and Hills, bless | ye the Lord:
20   O all ye Green Things upon the earth, bless | ye the Lord:
21   O ye Wells, bless | ye the Lord:
22   O ye Seas and Floods, bless | ye the Lord:
23   O ye Whales and all that move in the waters, bless | ye the Lord:
24   O all ye Fowls of the air, bless | ye the Lord:
25   O all ye Beasts and Cattle, bless | ye the Lord:
26   O ye Children of Men, bless | ye the Lord:

O LET Israel | bless the Lord:
28   O ye Priests of the Lord, bless | ye the Lord:
29   O ye Servants of the Lord, bless | ye the Lord:
30   O ye Spirits and Souls of the Righteous, bless | ye the Lord:
31   O ye holy and humble Men of heart, bless | ye the Lord:

LET us bless the Father and the Son and the | Holy Ghost:

* praise him and magni | fy him for ever.

* praise him and magni | fy him for ever.

713

Benedicite, omnia opera Domini

628

G. M. GARRETT

714

Benedicite, omnia opera Domini

J. TROUTBECK

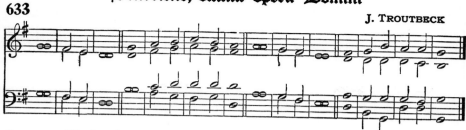

O ALL ye Works of the Lord | bless • ye the • Lord:
     * praise him and magnify | him for ever.

2   O ye Angels of the Lord | bless • ye the • Lord:

O YE Heavens | bless • ye the • Lord:

4   O ye Waters that be above the firmament | bless • ye the • Lord:

5   O all ye Powers of the Lord | bless • ye the • Lord:

6   O ye Sun and Moon | bless • ye the • Lord:

7   O ye Stars of heaven | bless • ye the • Lord:

8   O ye Showers and Dew | bless • ye the • Lord:

9   O ye Winds of God | bless • ye the • Lord:

10 O ye Fire and Heat | bless • ye the • Lord:

11 O ye Winter and Summer | bless • ye the • Lord:

12 O ye Dews and Frosts | bless • ye the • Lord:

13 O ye Frost and Cold | bless • ye the • Lord:

14 O ye Ice and Snow | bless • ye the • Lord:

15 O ye Nights and Days | bless • ye the • Lord:

16 O ye Light and Darkness | bless • ye the • Lord:

17 O ye Lightnings and Clouds | bless • ye the • Lord:

O LET the Earth | bless the Lord:
     * yea let it praise him and magnify | him for ever.

19 O ye Mountains and Hills | bless • ye the • Lord:

20 O all ye Green Things upon the earth | bless • ye the • Lord:

21 O ye Wells | bless • ye the • Lord:

22 O ye Seas and Floods | bless • ye the • Lord:

23 O ye Whales and all that move in the waters | bless • ye the • Lord:

24 O all ye Fowls of the air | bless • ye the • Lord:

25 O all ye Beasts and Cattle | bless • ye the • Lord:

26 O ye Children of Men | bless ◦ ye the • Lord:

O LET Israel | bless the Lord:

28 O ye Priests of the Lord | bless • ye the • Lord:

29 O ye Servants of the Lord | bless • ye the • Lord:

30 O ye Spirits and Souls of the Righteous | bless • ye the • Lord:

31 O ye holy and humble Men of heart | bless • ye the • Lord:

LET us bless the Father and the Son and the | Holy Ghost:

* praise him and magnify | him for ever.

* praise him and magnify | him for ever.

Benedictus

Benedictus

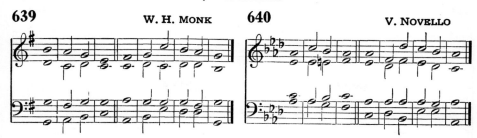

639   W. H. MONK   **640**   V. NOVELLO

BLESSED be the Lord God of | Israel;
* for he hath visited and re|deemed · his **peo**ple;

2 And hath raised up a mighty sal|vation for us,
* in the house of his | servant **Da**vid;

3 As he spake by the mouth of his | holy Prophets,
* which have | been · since the | world began;

4 That we should be saved | from our enemies,
* and from the hand of | all that **hate** us.

5 To perform the mercy promised to our | **fore**fathers,
* and to remember his | holy covenant;

6 To perform the oath which he sware to our forefather | Abraham,
* that | he would **give** us;

7 That we being delivered out of the | hand of · our enemies
* might | serve him · with**out** fear;

8 In holiness and righteous|ness before him,
* all the | days of **our** life.

9 And thou child shalt be called the prophet | of the Highest:
* for thou shalt go before the face of the | Lord · to pre|pare his ways;

10 To give knowledge of salvation | unto · his people
* for the re|mission of their sins,

11 Through the tender mercy | of our God;
* whereby the day-spring from on | high hath | visit·ed us;

12 To give light to them that sit in darkness,
and in the | shadow · of death,
* and to guide our feet | into · the way of peace.

Glory be to the Father and | to the Son,
* and | to the Holy Ghost;

As it was in the beginning, is now and | ever shall be,
* world without | **end**. **Amen**.

Benedictus

Tone VII, 5

Cantor

Choir and Congregation

Bless-ed be the Lord God of Is-ra-el; *for he hath visited and re-deem-ed his peo-ple;

2 And hath raised up a mighty sal-va-tion for us, * in the house of his ser-vant Da-vid;

3 As he spake by the mouth of his ho-ly Prophets, *which have been since the world be-gan;

4 That we should be saved from our en-e-mies, * and from the hand of all that hate us.

5 To per-form the mercy promised to our fore-fathers, * and to re-member his ho-ly cov-e-nant;

Benedictus

6 To per-form the oath
which he sware to our forefather A-bra-ham, * that he would give us;

7 That we being delivered
out of the hand of our en-e-mies * might serve him without fear;

8 In ho - li-ness and righteousness be-fore him, * all the days of our life.

9 And thou child
shalt be called the prophet of the High - est: * for thou shalt go before the
face of the

Lord to pre - pare his ways; 10 To give knowledge of salvation un - to his peo - ple

719

Benedictus

* for the re-mis-sion of their sins, 11 Through the ten-der mer-cy of our God;

* whereby the day-spring   12 To   give light to them
from on high hath vis-it-ed us;   that sit in dark-ness,

and in the shadow of death, * and to guide our feet in-to the way of peace.

Glo-ry   be to the Father and to the Son, * and to the Ho-ly Ghost; As   it

was in the beginning, is now and ev-er shall be,*world without end. A-men.

Jubilate Deo

642 OXFORD CHANT

644 G. J. ELVEY

643 A. H. BROWN

645 W. RUSSELL

O BE joyful in the LORD | all ye lands:
  * serve the LORD with gladness,
    and come before his | presence with a song.

2   Be ye sure that the LORD he is God;
    it is he that hath made us and not | we ourselves;
    * we are his people and the | sheep of · his **pas**ture.

3   O go your way into his gates with thanksgiving,
    and into his | courts with praise;
    * be thankful unto him and | **speak** | good of · his Name.

4   For the LORD is gracious, his mercy is | everlasting;
    * and his truth endureth from generation to | gene**ra**tion.

    Glory be to the Father and | to the Son,
    * and | to the Holy Ghost;

    As it was in the beginning, is now and | ever shall be,
    * world without | **end. A**men.

646 W. LAWES

EVENING CANTICLES

𝔐agnificat

656

S. WESLEY

657

J. RANDALL

MY soul doth magni|fy the Lord,
    * and my spirit hath rejoiced in | God my **Saviour.**

2 For | he · hath re·garded
    * the lowliness | of his **hand**maiden.

3 For be|hold from henceforth
    * all generations shall | call me **bless**ed.

4 For he that is mighty hath | magni·fied me;
    * and | holy is his Name.

2nd half

5 And his mercy is on | them that fear him
    * throughout | all · gene**ra**tions.

6 He hath showed | strength · with his · arm;
    * he hath scattered the proud in the imagi|nation of their hearts.

7 He hath put down the mighty | from their seat,
    * and hath ex|alted · the | humble · and meek.

8 He hath filled the hungry with | **good** things;
    * and the rich he hath | **sent** | empty · away.

9 He remembering his mercy hath holpen his servant | Israel;
    * as he promised to our forefathers,
    Abraham and his | seed for **ev**er.

Glory be to the Father and | to the Son,
    * and | to the Holy Ghost;

As it was in the beginning, is now and | ever shall **be,**
    * world without | **end. A**men.

Magnificat

658

Tone VIII, 1; Solemn form

Cantor   *Choir and Congregation*

My soul doth mag-ni-fy the Lord, * and my spi-rit hath rejoiced in God my

Saviour. 2 For he hath re-gard-ed * the low-li-ness of his handmaiden.

3 For be-hold from henceforth * all gen-e-ra-tions shall call me bless-ed.

4 For he that is migh-ty hath mag-ni-fi-ed me; *

and ho-ly is his Name. 5 And his mer-cy is on them that

Magnificat

fear him * throughout all gen - e - ra - tions. 6 He hath show - ed

strength with his arm; * he hath scat - tered the proud in the imagi -

na-tion of their hearts. 7 He hath put down the migh - ty from their seat, *

and hath ex - alt - ed the humble and meek. 8 He hath fill - ed the

hun - gry with good things; * and the rich he hath sent empty a - way.

Magnificat

9 He re - mem - ber-ing his mer-cy hath hol-pen his ser-vant Is - ra - el; * as he prom - ised to our forefathers, Abraham and his seed, for ev - er. Glo-ry be to the Fa - ther, and to the Son, * and to the Ho - ly Ghost; As it was in the be - gin-ning, is now and ev - er shall be, * world with-out end. A - men.

Cantate Domino

J. TURLE

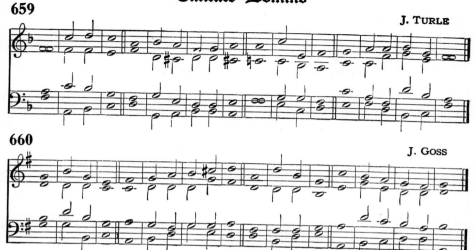

J. GOSS

O SING unto the LORD a | **new** song;
* for he hath | **done** | marvel·lous things.

2 With his own right hand and with his | holy arm,
* hath he gotten him|self the victory.

3 The LORD declar-ed | his salvation;
* his righteousness hath he openly showed
in the | sight · of the **hea**then.

4 He hath remembered his mercy and truth toward the house of | Israel;
* and all the ends of the world have seen the sal|vation of our God.

5 Show yourselves joyful unto the LORD | all ye lands;
* sing, re|joice and **give** thanks.

6 Praise the LORD up|on the harp;
* sing to the harp with a | psalm of **thanks**giving.

7 With trumpets | also · and shawms,
* O show yourselves joyful be|fore the LORD the King.

8 Let the sea make a noise and all that | therein is;
* the round world and | they that dwell therein.

9 Let the floods clap their hands,
and let the hills be joyful together be|fore the LORD;
* for he | cometh · to judge the earth.

10 With righteousness shall he | judge the world,
* and the | peoples · with equity.

Glory be to the Father and | to the Son,
* and | to the Holy Ghost;

As it was in the beginning, is now and | ever shall **be,**
* world without | **end. A**men.

Bonum est confiteri

661 G. A. MACFARREN

664 J. HEYWOOD

662 J. NAYLOR

665 T. TALLIS?

663 S. ELVEY

666 J. BATTISHILL

IT is a good thing to give thanks | unto · the LORD,
   * and to sing praises unto thy Name | O Most **High**est;

2   To tell of thy loving-kindness early | in the morning,
   * and of thy | truth · in the | **night** season;

3   Upon an instrument of ten strings and up|on the lute;
   * upon a loud instrument | and upon the harp.

4   For thou LORD hast made me | glad · through thy · works;
   * and I will rejoice in giving praise for the oper|ations of thy hands.

Glory be to the Father and | to the Son,
   * and | to the Holy Ghost;

As it was in the beginning, is now and | ever shall be,
   * world without | **end.** Amen.

Nunc dimittis

667 C. W. CORFE

668 J. NAYLOR

669 W. HINE

670 J. BLOW

671 J. BARNBY

672 R. FARRANT

LORD, now lettest thou thy servant de|part in peace,
 * ac|cording to thy word.

2 For mine | eyes have seen
 * thy | **salva**tion,

3 Which | thou · hast pre·pared
 * before the face of | **all peo**ple;

4 To be a light to | lighten · the Gentiles,
 * and to be the glory of thy | people Israel.

Glory be to the Father and | to the Son,
 * and | to the Holy Ghost;

As it was in the beginning, is now and | ever shall **be**,
 * world without | **end. A**men.

Nunc dimittis

673   Tone I, 2

Cantor   *Choir and Congregation*

Lord, now lettest thou thy servant depart in peace, * ac-cord-ing to thy word.

2 For mine eyes have seen * thy sal - va - tion, 3 Which thou hast pre - par - ed

* before the face of all peo - ple; 4 To be a light to lighten the Gen-tiles,

* and to be the glory of thy peo-ple Is - ra - el. Glo-ry be to the Father and

to the Son, * and to the Ho - ly Ghost; As it was in the beginning,

Deus misereatur

is now and ever shall be, * world with - out end. A - men.

674   OXFORD CHANT   675   H. ALDRICH

GOD be merciful unto | us and bless us,
    * and show us the light of his countenance,
    and be | merci·ful unto us;

2   That thy way may be | known up·on earth,
    * thy saving health a|mong all **na**tions.

In unison

3   Let the peoples praise | thee O God;
    * yea let all the | peoples **praise** thee.

4   O let the nations re|joice and · be glad;
    * for thou shalt judge the folk righteously,
    and govern the | nations · up**on** earth.

In unison

5   Let the peoples praise | thee O God;
    * yea let all the | peoples **praise** thee.

6   Then shall the earth bring | forth her increase;
    * and God, even our own God, shall | give us · his **bless**ing.

7   God | **shall** bless us;
    * and all the ends of the | world shall **fear** him.

Glory be to the Father and | to the Son,
    * and | to the Holy Ghost;

As it was in the beginning, is now and | ever shall **be,**
    * world without | **end. A**men.

731

Benedic, anima mea

676   G. A. MACFARREN

678   J. NAYLOR

677   F. A. G. OUSELEY

679   J. F. BURROWS

PRAISE the LORD | O my soul;
    * and all that is within me | praise his holy **Name.**

2   Praise the LORD | O my soul,
    * and forget not | all his benefits:

3   Who forgiveth | all thy sin,
    * and healeth all | thine infirmities;

4   Who saveth thy | life from · destruction,
    * and crowneth thee with mercy and | loving-**kind**ness.

5   O praise the LORD ye angels of his,
    ye that ex|cel in strength;
    * ye that fulfil his commandment,
     and hearken | unto · the | voice of · his word.

6   O praise the LORD all | ye his hosts;
    * ye servants of his that | do his **plea**sure.

7   O speak good of the LORD all ye works of his,
    in all places of | his dominion:
    * praise thou the | **LORD** O my soul.

Glory be to the Father and | to the Son,
    * and | to the Holy Ghost;

As it was in the beginning, is now and | ever shall be,
    * world without | **end. Amen.**

OCCASIONAL CANTICLES
Easter Day

680   J. Goss   **681**   W. Lee

682   W. Parratt

CHRIST our Passover is sacri|ficed for us:
   * therefore | let us keep the feast,

2   Not with old leaven,
   neither with the leaven of | malice · and wickedness;
   * but with the unleavened bread of sin|cerity and truth.

CHRIST being raised from the dead | dieth · no more;
   * death hath no more do|minion over him.

4   For in that he died, he died unto | **sin** once:
   * but in that he liveth, he | liveth unto God.

5   Likewise reckon ye also yourselves to be dead in|deed · **unto** · sin,
   * but alive unto God through | Jesus Christ our Lord.

CHRIST is risen | from the dead,
   * and become the | firstfruits · of | them that slept.

7   For since by | man came death,
   * by man came also the resur|rection of the dead.

8   For as in Adam | **all** die,
   * even so in Christ shall | all be made alive.

Glory be to the Father and | to the Son,
   * and | to the Holy Ghost;

As it was in the beginning, is now and | ever shall be,
   * world without | **end. A**men.

The Intonation is sung only in the first verse.

(a) **CHRIST** our Passover is sacrificed | for us:
  * therefore | let us keep the feast,

(b) 2 Not with old leaven,
  neither with the leaven of malice and wick|edness;
  * but with the unleavened bread of sin|cerity and truth.

(a) **CHRIST** being raised from the dead dieth | no more;
  * death hath no more do|minion over him.

(a) 4 For in that he died, he died unto | sin once:
  * but in that he liveth, he | liveth unto God.

(b) 5 Likewise reckon ye also yourselves to be dead indeed un|to sin,
  * but alive unto God through | Jesus Christ our Lord.

(c) **CHRIST** is risen from | the dead,
  * and become the first|fruits of them that slept.

(b) 7 For since by man | came death,
  * by man came also the resur|rection of the dead.

(a) 8 For as in Adam | all die,
  * even so in Christ shall | all be made alive.

(b) Glory be to the Father and to | the Son,
  * and | to the Holy Ghost;

(c) As it was in the beginning, is now and ever | shall be,
  * world | without end. Amen.

Thanksgiving Day

684   S. ARNOLD   **685**   W. H. WALTER

686   W. BOYCE

O PRAISE the LORD,
    for it is a good thing to sing praises | unto . our God;
    * yea a joyful and pleasant thing it | is to . be **thank**ful.

2   The LORD doth build | up Jerusalem,
    * and gather together the | outcasts . of Israel.

3   He healeth those that are | broken . in heart,
    * and giveth medicine to | heal their **sick**ness.

4   O sing unto the LORD with | **thanks**giving;
    * sing praises upon the | **harp** | unto . our God:

5   Who covereth the heaven with clouds,
    and prepareth | rain . for the . earth;
    * and maketh the grass to grow upon the mountains,
    and | herb . for the | use of men;

6   Who giveth fodder | unto . the cattle,
    * and feedeth the young ravens that | call up**on** him.

7   Praise the LORD | O Jerusalem;
    * praise thy | God O **Si**on.

8   For he hath made fast the | bars of . thy gates,
    * and hath blessed thy | children . with**in** thee.

2nd half
9   He maketh | peace . in thy . borders,
    * and filleth thee | with the flour of wheat.

Glory be to the Father and | to the Son,
    * and | to the Holy Ghost;

As it was in the beginning, is now and | ever shall be,
    * world without | **end**. Amen.

𝕿𝖍𝖆𝖓𝖐𝖘𝖌𝖎𝖛𝖎𝖓𝖌 𝕯𝖆𝖞

Tone VIII, 2

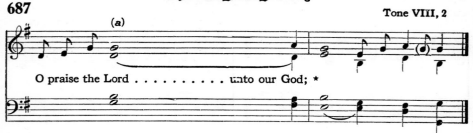

O praise the Lord . . . . unto our God; *

The Intonation is sung only in the first verse.

(*a*) O PRAISE the LORD,
   for it is a good thing to sing praises unto our | God;
   * yea a joyful and pleasant thing it is | to be thankful.

(*c*) 2 The LORD doth build up Je|rusalem,
   * and gather together the out|casts of Israel.

(*a*) 3 He healeth those that are broken in | heart,
   * and giveth medicine to | heal their sickness.

(*b*) 4 O sing unto the LORD with thanks|giving;
   * sing praises upon the harp | unto our God:

(*a*) 5 Who covereth the heaven with clouds,
   and prepareth rain for the | earth;
   * and maketh the grass to grow upon the mountains,
   and herb | for the use of men;

(*b*) 6 Who giveth fodder unto the | cattle,
   * and feedeth the young ravens that | call upon him.

(*c*) 7 Praise the LORD, O Je|rusalem;
   * praise thy | God O Sion.

(*a*) 8 For he hath made fast the bars of thy | gates,
   * and hath blessed thy chil|dren within thee.

(*b*) 9 He maketh peace in thy | borders,
   * and filleth thee | with the flour of wheat.

(*a*) Glory be to the Father and to the | Son,
   * and | to the Holy Ghost;

(*b*) As it was in the beginning, is now and ever | shall be,
   * world | without end. Amen.

Burial of the Dead

688 W. FELTON   **689**   J. BLOW

LORD let me know mine end and the number | of my days;
  * that I may be certified how | long I have to live.

2 Behold thou hast made my days as it were a span long,
  and mine age is even as nothing in re|spect of thee;
  * and verily every man living is alto|gether vanity.

3 For man walketh in a vain shadow and disquieteth him|self in vain;
  * he heapeth up riches and cannot tell | who shall gather them.

4 And now Lord | what is . my hope?
  * truly my | hope is | even . in thee.

5 Deliver me from | all . mine of.fences;
  * and make me not a rebuke | unto . the **fool**ish.

6 When thou with rebukes dost chasten man for sin,
  thou makest his beauty to consume away,
  like as it were a moth | fretting a garment:
  * every man therefore | is but vanity.

7 Hear my prayer O LORD and with thine ears con|sider my calling;
  * hold | not thy | peace at . my tears;

8 For I am a stranger with thee | and a sojourner,
  * as | all my fathers were.

9 O spare me a little that I may re|cover . my strength,
  * before I go hence and | be no **more** seen.

Glory be to the Father and | to the Son,
  * and | to the Holy Ghost;

As it was in the beginning, is now and | ever shall be,
  * world without | **end. A**men.

690   J. NAYLOR   **691**   W. R. BEXFIELD

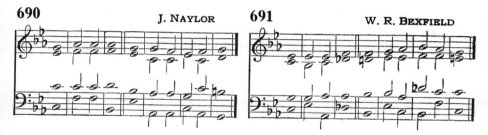

Burial of the Dead

LORD thou hast | been our refuge,
    * from one generation | to another.

2   Before the mountains were brought forth,
    or ever the earth and the | world were made,
    * thou art God from ever|lasting . and | world with.out end.

3   Thou turnest | man . to de.struction;
    * again thou sayest, Come a|gain, ye | children . of men.

4   For a thousand years in thy sight are but as yesterday,
    | when it . is past,
    * and | as a | watch in . the night.

5   As soon as thou scatterest them they are even | as a sleep;
    * and fade away | sudden.ly like the grass.

6   In the morning it is green and | groweth up;
    * but in the evening it is cut down, dried | up and wither-ed.

7   For we consume away in | thy displeasure,
    * and are afraid at thy wrathful | indignation.

8   Thou hast set our mis|deeds before thee;
    * and our secret sins in the | light of . thy countenance.

9   For when thou art angry all our | days are gone:
    * we bring our years to an end, as it | were a | tale that . is told.

10   The days of our age are threescore years and ten;
    and though men be so strong that they come to | fourscore years,
    * yet is their strength then but labour and sorrow;
    so soon passeth it a|way and we are gone.

11   So teach us to | number . our days,
    * that we may apply our hearts | unto **wis**dom.

Glory be to the Father and | to the Son,
    * and | to the Holy Ghost;

As it was in the beginning, is now and | ever shall be,
    * world without | **end. Amen.**

Burial of the Dead

E. EDWARDS

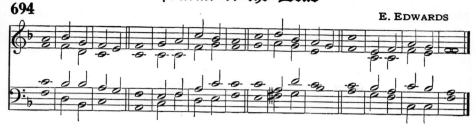

THE LORD is my light and my salvation;
whom then | shall I **fear**?
* the LORD is the strength of my life;
of whom then | shall I be afraid?

2   One thing have I desired of the LORD which I | will re**quire**;
* even that I may dwell in the house of the LORD all the days of my life,
to behold the fair beauty of the LORD and to | visit . his **tem**ple.

3   For in the time of trouble he shall hide me in his | tabernacle;
* yea in the secret place of his dwelling shall he hide me,
and set me up up|on a rock of stone.

4   And now shall he lift | up mine **head**
* above mine enemies | round a**bout** me.

5   Therefore will I offer in his dwelling an oblation with | **great** gladness:
* I will sing and speak | praises | unto . the LORD.

6   Hearken unto my voice O LORD when I | cry . unto . **thee**;
* have mercy up|on me . and **hear** me.

7   My heart hath talked of thee, | Seek ye . my **face**:
* Thy | face LORD will I seek.

8   O hide not thou thy | face from **me**,
* nor cast thy servant a|way in . dis**plea**sure.

9   Thou hast | been my succour;
* leave me not neither forsake me, O God of | my sal**va**tion.

10   I should utter|ly have fainted,
* but that I believe verily to see the goodness of the LORD
in the | land of . the **liv**ing.

2nd half

11   O tarry thou the | **LORD'S** leisure;
* be strong and he shall comfort thine heart;
and | put thou . thy | trust in . the LORD.

Glory be to the Father and | to the **Son**,
* and | to the Holy Ghost;

As it was in the beginning, is now and | ever shall be,
* world without | **end**. Amen.

Burial of the Dead

Arr. from M. LUTHER

GOD is our | hope and strength,
  * a very present | help in **trou**ble.

2 Therefore will we not fear though the | earth be moved,
  * and though the hills be carried | into . the | midst of . the sea;

2nd half

3 Though the waters thereof | rage and swell,
  * and though the mountains shake at the | tempest of the same.

4 There is a river the streams whereof make glad the | city . of God;
  * the holy place of the tabernacle of the | **Most High**est.

5 God is in the midst of her, therefore shall she | not . be re·moved;
  * God shall help her and | that right **ear**ly.

6 Be still then and know that | I am God:
  * I will be exalted among the nations,
  and I will be ex|alted in the earth.

7 The LORD of | hosts is with us;
  * the God of Jacob | is our **ref**uge.

Glory be to the Father and | to the Son,
  * and | to the Holy Ghost;

As it was in the beginning, is now and | ever shall be,
  * world without | **end. A**men.

J. T. HARRIS

I WILL lift up mine eyes | unto . the hills;
  * from | **whence** | cometh · my help?

2 My help cometh even | from the LORD,
  * who hath | **made** | heav'n and earth.

3 He will not suffer thy | foot to · be **moved**;
  * and he that | keepeth · thee will not **sleep.**

4 Behold he that keepeth | Israel
  * shall | neither | slumber · nor sleep.

Burial of the Dead

5 The LORD him|self . is thy . keeper;
  * the LORD is thy defence up|on thy **right** hand;

6 So that the sun shall not | burn thee . by day,
  * — | neither . the | moon by night.

7 The LORD shall preserve thee from | **all** evil;
  * yea it is even | he . that shall | keep thy soul.

8 The LORD shall preserve thy going out and thy | coming in,
  * from this time | forth for evermore.

  Glory be to the Father and | to the Son,
  * and | to the Holy Ghost;

  As it was in the beginning, is now and | ever shall be,
  * world without | **end. A**men.

697

J. TURLE, from H. PURCELL

OUT of the deep have I called unto thee O | LORD;
* — | **Lord** hear my voice.

2 O let thine ears consider | well
  * the | voice of my complaint.

3 If thou LORD wilt be extreme to mark what is done a|miss,
  * O Lord, | who . may a|**bide** it?

4 For there is mercy with | thee;
  * therefore shalt | thou be **fear**ed.

5 I look for the LORD; my soul doth | wait for him;
  * — | in his | word . is my . trust.

6 My soul fleeth unto the Lord before the morning | watch;
  * I say be|fore the morning watch.

7 O Israel trust in the LORD, for with the LORD there is | mercy,
  * and with him is | plenteous . re**demp**tion.

8 And he shall redeem | Israel
  * from | **all his** sins.

  Glory be to the Father and | to the Son,
  * and | to the Holy Ghost;

  As it was in the beginning, is now and ever | shall be,
  * world without | **end. A**men.

Burial of a Child

698 W. Douglas   **699**   W. Hine

700   W. T. Best

THE LORD | is my shepherd;
* therefore can | I lack **noth**ing.

2 He shall feed me in a | **green** pasture,
* and lead me forth beside the | waters · of **com**fort.

3 He shall con|vert my soul,
* and bring me forth in the paths of righteousness | for his **Name's** sake.

4 Yea though I walk through the valley of the shadow of death,
I will | fear no evil;
* for thou art with me; thy rod and thy | **staff** comfort me.

5 Thou shalt prepare a table before me
in the presence of | them that trouble me;
* thou hast anointed my head with | oil · and my | cup shall · be full.

6 Surely thy loving-kindness and mercy
shall follow me all the | days of · my life;
* and I will dwell in the house of the | LORD for **ev**er.

Glory be to the Father and | to the Son,
* and | to the Holy Ghost;

As it was in the beginning, is now and | ever shall **be**,
* world without | **end.** Amen.

The Psalm I will lift up mine eyes unto the hills *as at* No. 696

THE HOLY COMMUNION
First Communion Service
Responses to the Decalogue

701

JOHN MERBECKE and GEORGE C. MARTIN

In unison

Lord, have mer - cy up - on us, and in - cline our hearts to

After the 10th Commandment

keep this law. Lord, have mer - cy up - on us, and

write all these thy laws in our hearts, we be - seech thee.

Kyrie eleison

702

JOHN MERBECKE, 1549

In unison

Lord, have mer - cy up - on us. Christ, have mer - cy up -

on us. Lord, have mer - cy up - on us.

Each Kyrie may be sung thrice   743

First Communion Service
Credo

703

JOHN MERBECKE, 1549

Priest   **Choir and Congregation**

I be-lieve in one God the Fa-ther Al-migh-ty, Ma-ker of heav'n and earth,

And of all things vi-si-ble and in-vi-si-ble: And in one Lord Je-sus Christ,

the on-ly-be-got-ten Son of God; Be-got-ten of his Fa-ther be-fore all worlds,

God of God, Light of Light, Ve-ry God of ve-ry God; Be-got-ten, not made;

Be-ing of one sub-stance with the Fa-ther; By whom all things were made:

First Communion Service

Who for us men and for our sal-va-tion came down from heaven,

And was in-car-nate by the Ho-ly Ghost of the Vir-gin Ma-ry, And was made man:

And was cru-ci-fied al-so for us un-der Pon-tius Pi-late; He suf-fer'd and was

bur-ied: And the third day he rose a-gain ac-cord-ing to the Scriptures:

And as-cend-ed in-to heaven, And sit-teth on the right hand of the Fa-ther:

745

First Communion Service

And he shall come a-gain, with glo-ry, to judge both the quick and the dead;

Whose king-dom shall have no end. And I be-lieve in the Ho-ly Ghost,

The Lord, and Giv-er of Life, Who proceed-eth from the Fa-ther and the Son;

Who with the Fa-ther and the Son to-geth-er is worshipped and glo-ri-fied;

Who spake by the Prophets: And I believe one Cath-o-lic and Ap-os-tol-ic Church:

First Communion Service

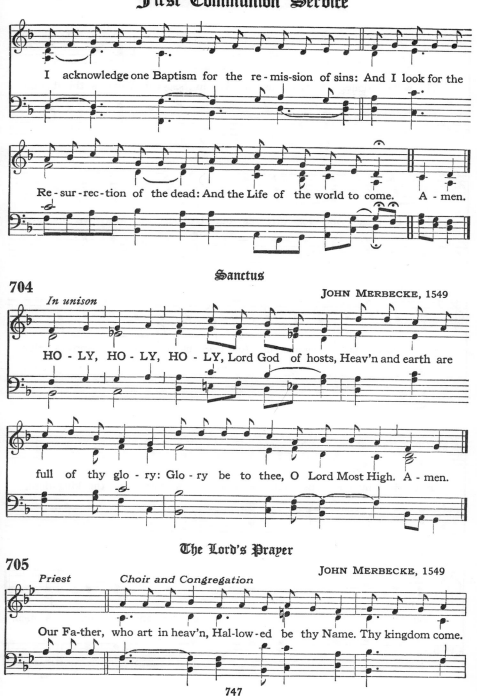

I acknowledge one Baptism for the re-mis-sion of sins: And I look for the

Re-sur-rec-tion of the dead: And the Life of the world to come. A - men.

Sanctus

704

In unison

JOHN MERBECKE, 1549

HO - LY, HO - LY, HO - LY, Lord God of hosts, Heav'n and earth are

full of thy glo - ry: Glo - ry be to thee, O Lord Most High. A - men.

The Lord's Prayer

705

Priest   *Choir and Congregation*

JOHN MERBECKE, 1549

Our Fa-ther, who art in heav'n, Hal-low-ed be thy Name. Thy kingdom come.

First Communion Service

Thy will be done, On earth as it is in hea-ven. Give us this day our dai-ly bread. And for-give us our tres-pass-es, As we for-give those who tres-pass a-gainst us. And lead us not in-to temp-ta-tion, But de-liv-er us from e-vil. For thine is the king-dom, and the power, and the glo-ry, for ev-er and ev-er. A-men.

748

First Communion Service
Agnus Dei

706

In unison

JOHN MERBECKE, 1549

O Lamb of God, that ta-kest a-way the sins of the world, have mer-cy up-on us. O Lamb of God, that ta-kest a-way the sins of the world, have mer-cy up-on us. O Lamb of God, that ta-kest a-way the sins of the world, grant us thy peace.

Gloria in excelsis

707

Priest

Choir and Congregation

JOHN MERBECKE, 1549

Glo-ry be to God on high, and on earth peace, good will towards men.

First Communion Service

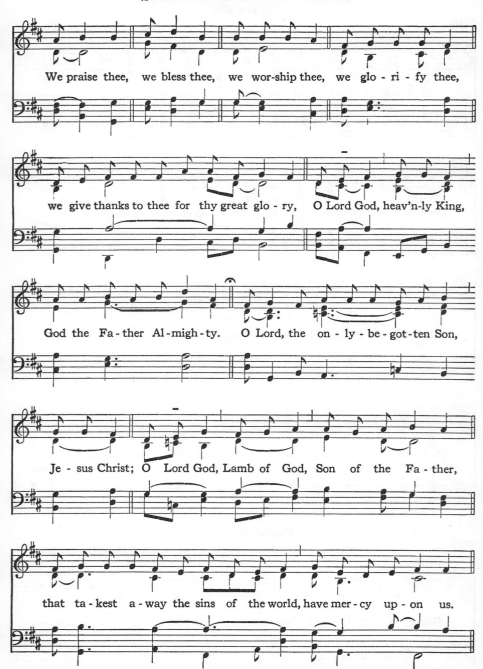

We praise thee, we bless thee, we wor-ship thee, we glo - ri - fy thee,

we give thanks to thee for thy great glo - ry, O Lord God, heav'n-ly King,

God the Fa - ther Al - migh - ty. O Lord, the on - ly - be - got - ten Son,

Je - sus Christ; O Lord God, Lamb of God, Son of the Fa - ther,

that ta - kest a - way the sins of the world, have mer - cy up - on us.

First Communion Service

Thou that ta-kest a-way the sins of the world, re-ceive our prayer.

Thou that sit-test at the right hand of God the Fa-ther,

have mer-cy up-on us. For thou on-ly art ho-ly;

thou on-ly art the Lord; thou on-ly, O Christ, with the Ho-ly Ghost,

art most high in the glo-ry of God the Fa-ther. A-men.

Second Communion Service
Responses to the Decalogue

708

In unison, moderate time

HEALEY WILLAN, 1928

Lord, have mer - cy up - on us, and in - cline our

After the 10th Commandment

hearts to keep this law. Lord, have mer - cy up - on us, and

write all these thy laws in our hearts, we be - seech thee.

Kyrie eleison, threefold

709

HEALEY WILLAN, 1928

In unison

Lord, have mer - cy up - on us. Christ, have mer - cy up -

on us. Lord, have mer - cy up - on us.

The complete Service, including the *Creed* and the *Benedictus*, is published by the Oxford University Press, London—Carl Fischer, Inc., sole agents for the U. S. A.

Second Communion Service
Kyrie eleison, ninefold

710

In unison, moderate time

HEALEY WILLAN, 1928

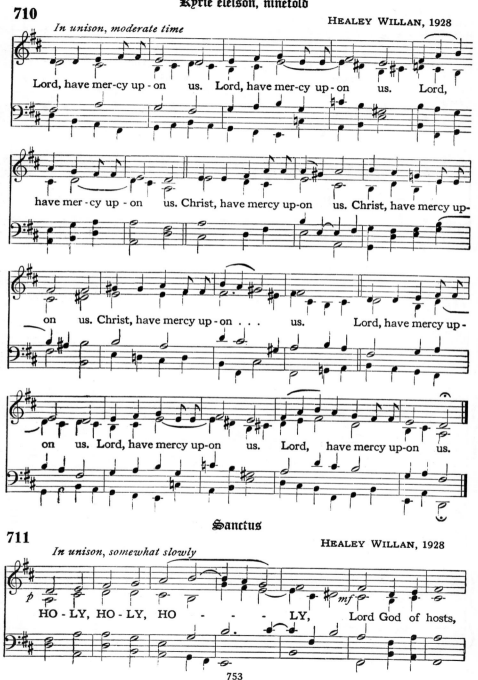

Lord, have mer-cy up-on us. Lord, have mer-cy up-on us. Lord,

have mer-cy up-on us. Christ, have mercy up-on us. Christ, have mercy up-

on us. Christ, have mercy up-on ... us. Lord, have mercy up-

on us. Lord, have mercy up-on us. Lord, have mercy up-on us.

Sanctus

711

HEALEY WILLAN, 1928

In unison, somewhat slowly

p   *mf*

HO - LY, HO - LY, HO - - - LY, Lord God of hosts,

Second Communion Service

Hea-ven and earth are full .. of thy glo-ry: Glo - - ry be to
thee, O Lord Most High. A - - - - - - men.

Agnus Dei

712

HEALEY WILLAN, 1928

In unison, slow Men

O Lamb of God, that ta-kest a-way the
sins of the world, .. have mer-cy up-on ....

Second Communion Service

755

Second Communion Service

grant . . . . us thy . . . . peace.

Gloria in excelsis

713

HEALEY WILLAN, 1928

Priest   *In unison, in moderate time*

Glo - ry be to God on high, and on earth peace, good will towards men.

We praise thee, we bless thee, we wor - ship thee, we

glo - ri - fy thee, we give thanks to thee for thy great glo - ry,

756

Second Communion Service

O . . Lord God, heav'n - ly King, God . . . the Fa - ther Al -

A little slower

migh - - - - - ty. . . . . O Lord, the

on - ly-be-got-ten Son, Je - sus Christ; O Lord God, Lamb of God,

Son of the Fa - ther, that ta - kest a - way the sins of the world, have

mer - cy up - on us. Thou that ta - kest a - way the sins of the

757

Second Communion Service

world, re - ceive our prayer. Thou that sit - test at the

right hand of God the Fa - ther, have mer - cy up - on us.

First pace

For thou on - ly art ho - ly; thou on - ly art the Lord; thou

on - ly, O Christ, with the Ho - ly Ghost, art most

high in the glo - ry of God the Fa - ther.

Second Communion Service

A - - - - - - - - - - - - - men.

Third Communion Service
Responses to the Decalogue

714

GEORGE OLDROYD, 1938

In harmony, after 1, 3, 5, 7, 9

Lord, have mercy up-on us, and in - cline our hearts to keep this law.

Men in unison, after 2, 4, 6, 8

Lord, have mer-cy up - on us, and in - cline our hearts to keep this law.

Sw.

Gt.

all Sw.

In harmony, after 10

Lord, have mer-cy up - on us. Lord, have mer - cy up -

Ped.

Ped.

The complete Service, including the *Creed* and the *Benedictus*, is published by the Oxford University Press, London—Carl Fischer, Inc., sole agents for the U. S. A.

Third Communion Service

on us, and write all these thy laws in our hearts,

Organ only — we be - seech thee...

Organ

Ped.

Kyrie eleison, ninefold

715

GEORGE OLDROYD, 1938

In moderate time, tenderly

poco rit.

Organ

Sw.

pp

Lord, have mer - cy up - on ...... us. Lord, have

Lord, have mer - cy up - on us.

mer - cy up - on ..... us. Lord, ... have mer

Lord, have mer - cy up - on us. Lord, ... have mer -

Third Communion Service

761

Third Communion Service

Third Communion Service

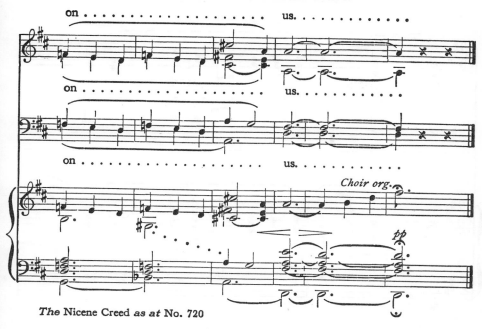

The Nicene Creed *as at* No. 720

Sanctus

716

GEORGE OLDROYD, 1938

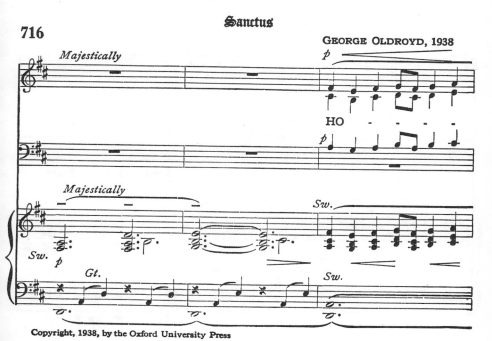

Third Communion Service

Third Communion Service

765

Third Communion Service
Agnus Dei

717

GEORGE OLDROYD, 1938

In moderate time, tenderly

O Lamb of God, . . that ta - kest a - way . . . . the sins of the world, have mer - cy up - on . . us.

O Lamb of God, that ta - kest a -

Third Communion Service

Third Communion Service

grant . . . . . us . . . . . thy . . . . . . peace. . . .

world,

thy peace.

Gloria in excelsis

718

GEORGE OLDROYD, 1938

Priest   *mp Somewhat slow*   *, mf*

Glo - ry   be   to God on high, and   on earth   peace, good will   to-wards men. We

In moderate time

praise thee, we   bless   thee, we   wor-ship thee, we   glo - ri - fy   thee, we   give

Third Communion Service

thanks to thee for thy great glo - ry, .. O Lord God, ..

heav'n-ly King, God the Fa - ther Al - migh - ty. O

Somewhat slower, with expression *rubato* - - - *a tempo*

Lord, the on - ly - be - got - ten Son .. Je - sus .. Christ; O

Lord God, Lamb of God, Son of the Fa - ther, that ta - kest a - way the

769

Third Communion Service

poco rubato - - a tempo

sins of the world, have mer - cy up - on ... us. ..... Thou that

expressively   crescendo

ta - kest a - way the sins   of the world,   re - ceive our pray - er. Thou that

Third Communion Service

sit-test at the right hand of God . . . . . the Fa-ther, have mer-cy up-

on . . us. . . . . For thou on-ly art ho - ly; thou on-ly art the

Third Communion Service

Lord; thou on - ly, O Christ, with the Ho - ly Ghost, art most

high in the glo - ry of God the Fa - ther. A - men.

772

719

Plainsong, 12th cent.

Boys

p

Lord, ... have mer - cy up - on .... us. ...

Men

p

Lord, . have mer - cy up - on . . . us.

Boys

Lord, ...

have mer - cy up - on . . . us. Christ, have mer - cy up - on . . . us.

Men

mf

Boys

mf

Christ, ... have mer - cy up - on .... us. ...

Men

Boys

mf

f

Christ, have mer - cy up - on .... us. Lord, ...

Fourth Communion Service

have mer-cy up-on.... us. Lord,............

mf

Men

have mer - cy up - on.... us... Lord,............

f

Boys

Full choir

f

rit. poco   *broader*   *rit. molto*

have mer - cy up - on... us...

Credo

720

Plainsong, 9th cent.

Priest   *Choir and Congregation*

I be-lieve in one God the Fa-ther Al-migh-ty, Ma-ker of hea-ven and earth,

774

Fourth Communion Service

And of all things vi - si - ble and in - vi - si - ble: And in one Lord Je - sus Christ,

the on - ly - be - got - ten Son of God; Be - got - ten of his Fa - ther be - fore all worlds,

God of God, Light of Light, Ve - ry God of ve - ry God; Be - got - ten, not made;

Be - ing of one sub - stance with the Fa - ther; By whom all things were made:

Who for us men and for our sal - va - tion came down from heaven,

Fourth Communion Service

And was in-carnate by the Ho-ly Ghost of the Vir-gin Ma-ry, And was made man:

And was cru-ci-fi-ed al-so for us un-der Pontius Pi-late; He suffered and was

bu-ri-ed: And the third day he rose a-gain ac-cord-ing to the Scriptures:

And as-cend-ed in-to hea-ven, And sit-teth on the right hand of the Fa-ther:

And he shall come a-gain, with glo-ry, to judge both the quick and the dead;

776

Fourth Communion Service

Whose kingdom shall have no end. And I be-lieve in the Ho-ly Ghost, The

Lord, and Giv-er of Life, Who proceed-eth from the Fa-ther and the Son;

Who with the Father and the Son to-geth-er is worshipp'd and glo-ri - fi - ed;

Who spake by the Pro-phets: And I be-lieve one Cath-o - lic and

Ap-os-tol-ic Church: I ac-knowledge one Bap-tism for the re-mis-sion of sins:

And I look for the Re-sur-rec-tion of the dead: And the Life of the

world .. to come. A - - - - - men.

721　　　　　　　　**Sanctus**　　　　　　　Plainsong, 14th cent.

In unison, with majesty

HO - - LY, HO - LY, HO - - - - LY,

Lord . . . . God . . . . of hosts, Hea-ven and

earth are full . . . . . of thy glo - ry: Glo - ry be to thee,

Fourth Communion Service

O Lord Most High. A - - - - men.

The Lord's Prayer

722

Priest   Choir and Congregation   Traditional, very ancient

Our Fa-ther, who art in heaven, Hal-low - ed be thy Name. Thy kingdom come.

Thy will be done, On earth as it is in heaven. Give us this day our daily bread.

And for-give us our tres-pass-es, As we for-give those who trespass a-gainst us.

And lead us not in - to temp-ta - tion, But de - liv-er us from e - vil. For thine

Fourth Communion Service

is the kingdom, and the power, and the glo - ry, for ev-er and ev - er. A-men.

Agnus Dei

723

Plainsong, 10th cent., 13th cent.

Boys

O . . . . Lamb of God, that . . ta - kest a - way the sins . .

Men

of the world, have mer - cy up - on . . . . us. O . . . . .

Lamb of God, that ta-kest a - way the sins of the world, have mer -

Full choir

cy up - on . . us. O . . . Lamb of God, that . . ta - kest a -

780

Fourth Communion Service

way the sins .. of the world, grant . . . . . us . . . . thy . . . peace.

Gloria in excelsis

724

English Plainsong, 15th cent.

Priest . . . *Boys*

Glo-ry be to God on high, and on earth . . peace, good will towards men.

Men . . . *Boys* . . . *Men* . . . *Boys*

We praise thee, we bless . . thee, we wor-ship thee, we glo-ri-fy thee,

Men . . . *Full choir*

we give . . . thanks to thee for thy great glo-ry, O Lord

God, . . hea-ven-ly King, God the Fa-ther Al-migh-ty.

16' Ped.

781

Fourth Communion Service

O Lord, the on-ly-be-got-ten Son, Je-sus Christ; O Lord God, Lamb of God,

Son of the Fa-ther, that ta-kest a-way the sins of the world, have mer-cy

up - on us. Thou that ta-kest a-way the sins of the world, re - ceive

our . . . prayer. Thou that sit-test at the right hand of God the Fa-ther,

have mer-cy up-on us. For thou on-ly art ho-ly; thou on-ly art the Lord;

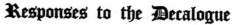

Responses to the Decalogue

thou on - ly, O Christ, with the Ho - ly Ghost, art most high in the

glo - ry of God the Fa - ther. A - - - - - men.

Responses to the Decalogue

725

EDWARD C. BAIRSTOW, 1923

In unison, quasi recit. — *Moderately quick*

Lord, have mer-cy up-on us, and in - cline our hearts to keep this law.

Organ, 1, 4, 7

Organ, 2, 5, 8

Organ, 3, 6, 9

Responses to the Decalogue

After the 10th
p Recit.

Moderately quick

Lord, have mer - cy up - on us, and write all

these thy laws in our hearts, . . we be - seech thee. . .

726

JOHN STAINER

Lord, have mer - cy up - on . . . us, and in - cline our hearts to

After the 10th

keep this law. Lord, have mer - cy up - on . . . us, and

Kyrie eleison, threefold

Slow

write all these thy laws in our hearts, we be - seech thee.

pp

727

THOMAS TALLIS, arr. by JOHN STAINER

Lord, have mer - cy up - on ... us. Christ, have mer - cy

*

up - on .. us. Lord, have mer - cy up - on .... us.

rit.

The Congregation should sing the melody in the tenor part.

728

T. TERTIUS NOBLE

p   *mf*

Lord, have mer - cy up - on .... us. .... Christ, have

f

mer - cy up - on .. us. Lord, have mer - cy up - on .... us.

Kyrie eleison, ninefold

729

T. FREDERICK H. CANDLYN, 1936

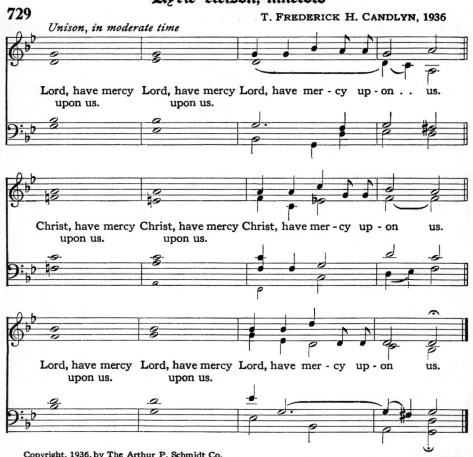

Lord, have mercy Lord, have mercy Lord, have mer - cy up - on . . us.
upon us. upon us.

Christ, have mercy Christ, have mercy Christ, have mer - cy up - on us.
upon us. upon us.

Lord, have mercy Lord, have mercy Lord, have mer - cy up - on us.
upon us. upon us.

*May be sung in harmony. For threefold Kyrie, omit first two measures of
each part.*

Gloria tibi

730 Traditional

Glo - ry be to thee, O Lord.
(Praise be to thee, O Christ.)

731 Ancient Chant

Glo - ry be to thee, O Lord.
(Praise be to thee, O Christ.)

The Nicene Creed, Nos. 701 and 720

At the Presentation of the Alms and Oblations

732

L. M.

GARDINER

WILLIAM GARDINER'S
Sacred Melodies, 1815

With stately vigor

All things are thine; no gift have we, Lord of all gifts, to of - fer thee; And hence with grate - ful hearts to - day Thine own be - fore thy feet we lay. A - men.

JOHN GREENLEAF WHITTIER, 1872

733

Anonymous

May be sung in unison

All things come of thee, O Lord, and of thine own have we giv - en thee. A - men.

Also the following:

481 We give thee but thine own
139 Praise God, from whom all blessings flow
195 Father, we thank thee who hast planted

Sursum corda

734

Priest

Choir and Congregation

Lift up your hearts. We lift . . . them up un-to the Lord.

Priest

Let us give . . . . . thanks un - to our Lord God.

Choir and Congregation

It is meet . . . . . and right so to do.

Before Sanctus No. 711 *and* No. 716, Sursum corda *should be sung a semitone higher.*

Sanctus

735

SAMUEL WESLEY, 1766–1837

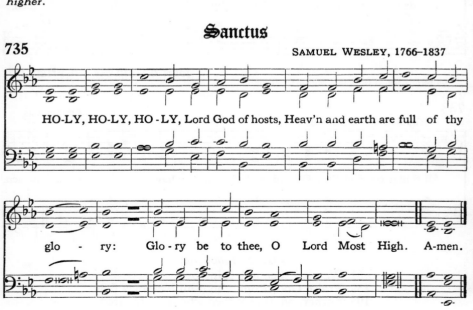

HO-LY, HO-LY, HO-LY, Lord God of hosts, Heav'n and earth are full of thy

glo - ry: Glo - ry be to thee, O Lord Most High. A-men.

Sanctus

736

PETER CHRISTIAN LUTKIN, 1920

In unison, slow and sustained

HO - - LY, HO - - LY, HO - LY, Lord God of hosts, . Heav'n and earth are full of thy glo - ry: Glo-ry be to thee, O Lord Most High. A - men.

Sanctus

737

EDWARD C. BAIRSTOW, 1923

HO - LY, HO - LY, HO - LY, Lord God of hosts,

Heav'n and earth are full of thy glo - ry: Glo - ry be to

thee, O Lord Most High. A - - - - men.

The complete Service is published by the Oxford University Press, London—Carl Fischer, Inc., sole agents for the U. S. A.

Gloria in excelsis

Ancient Melody
arranged by T. TERTIUS NOBLE, 1920

Glory be to God on high, and on earth peace, good will towards men.

We praise thee,
we bless thee, we wor - ship thee, we glorify thee, we give thanks to thee for thy great glo - ry,

O Lord God, heav'n - ly King, God the Fa - ther Al - migh - ty.

O Lord, the
only-begotten Son, Je - sus Christ; O Lord God, Lamb of God, Son of the Fa - ther,

Sopranos and altos in unison
mf

that takest away the sins of the world, have mer - cy up - on us.

Gloria in excelsis

Full choir in harmony

Thou that takest away the sins of the world, re - ceive . . . . our prayer.

Thou that sittest
at the right hand of God the Fa - ther, have mer - cy up - on us.

For thou on - ly art ho - ly; thou on - ly art the Lord;

thou only, O art most high
Christ, with the Ho - ly Ghost, in the glory of God the Fa - ther. A - men.

739
Old Scottish Chant

Glory be to God on high, and on earth peace, good will towards men.

We praise thee,
we bless thee, we wor-ship thee,
we glorify thee, we give
thanks to thee for thy great glo - ry,

792

Gloria in excelsis

O Lord God, heav'n - ly King, God the Father Al - migh - ty.

O Lord, the
only-begotten Son, Je - sus Christ;

O Lord God,
Lamb of God, Son of the Fa - ther,

that takest away the sins of the world, have mercy up - on . . us.

Thou that takest away the sins of the world, re - ceive our prayer.

Thou that sittest
at the right hand of God the Fa - ther,

have mercy up - on . . us.

For thou on - ly art ho - ly; thou on - ly art the Lord;

793

Gloria in excelsis

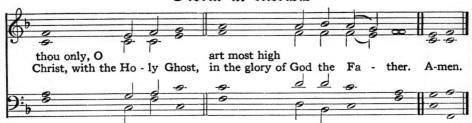

thou only, O ⎪ art most high
Christ, with the Ho - ly Ghost, ⎪ in the glory of God the Fa - ther. A-men.

Hymns in place of Gloria in excelsis *are listed in the Liturgical Index.*

Also the following:

347 Alleluia! Bread of Heaven (Stanzas 3, 4)
335 Glory be to Jesus
200 Glory let us give and blessing (Stanza 6)
204 Humbly I adore thee (Stanzas 1, 3)
  3 Lamb of God, the heavens adore thee (Stanza 3)

Amen

740

Dresden Amen

A - men, A - - - men.

741

JOHN STAINER

A - men, A - - - - -

A - men, A - men, A - - - -

men, A - - - men, A - - men, A - men.

A - men,

Index of Service Music

THE CHORAL RESPONSES Pages 699–703

CHANTS

HOLY COMMUNION

Acknowledgments and Permissions

The Joint Commission on the Revision of the Hymnal acknowledges with gratitude its indebtedness to the following authors and owners of copyrights for their kind permission to include the hymns and tunes listed below.

The Beacon Press, from "Hymns of the Spirit": 534, 546

The Book of Common Praise: 117

The Clarendon Press, Oxford, from the Yattendon Hymnal edited by Robert Bridges: 71, 75, 129, 158, 176, 181, 367, 520

The Oxford University Press. From the English Hymnal: 61, 78, 97, 112, 115, 157, 192, 201, (and Peter Martineau) 205, 223, (and representatives of the late W. Chalmers Smith) 301, 387, 492, 518, (and Walter Russell Bowie) 522. From Enlarged Songs of Praise: 34, 86, 102, 107, 122, 207, (and W. Charter Piggott) 222, 239, 258, 262, 295, 299, 313, 317, 322, 342, 363, 372, 403, 456, 473, 521, 532, 540. From Hymns of the Russian Church: 11. From the Oxford Book of Carols: 45. From the Revised Church Hymnary: 514

Also from the Oxford University Press: 66 (stanza 1), (and Frank Fletcher) 364, (and G. K. A. Bell) 543, 563, (and Steuart Wilson) 575, 599

D. Appleton-Century Company, Inc.: 42, 380, 422, (and Eric M. North) 498

The American Tract Society: 263

A. S. Barnes and Company: 494

Doubleday, Doran and Company, Inc.: 147 (from "Five Nations," Rudyard Kipling), 503 (from "Three Poems" Rudyard Kipling), 506 (from "Puck of Pook's Hill" Rudyard Kipling)

Hodder and Stoughton, Ltd.: 156

Houghton Mifflin Company: 227, 291, 360, 377, 435, 441, 493, 501, 502, 519

The Macmillan Company: 44, 365 (from "In Memoriam" by Alfred Tennyson), 475 (from "Easter" by John Masefield)

Marshall, Morgan and Scott, Ltd.: 180, 374

Morehouse-Gorham Company: 243, 354

Novello and Company, Ltd.: 458

W. A. Pond and Company, for any rights it may possess in 41

A. W. Ridley and Company: 172

Charles Scribner's Sons and Tertius Van Dyke (from The Poems of Henry Van Dyke): 281, 511

Skeffington and Sons, Ltd. (and John Stanhope Arkwright): 531

Yale University Press (and William Alexander Percy): 437

Maxwell J. Blacker, daughters of, 228 (special permission for altering 7 words in stanzas 1, 2, 4, 5); Arthur C. H. Borrer, Executor for Mrs. Alexander, 268; Godfrey Fox Bradby, 470; Bates G. Burt, 508; E. M. Butler, 482; Edith Clayton, 509; Henry Sloane Coffin, 477 (stanza 2); Alta Lind Cook, 37; Evelyn Atwater Cummins, 432; Frank Damrosch, Jr., 131; Harry Emerson Fosdick, 524; Marion Franklin Ham, 84; Leigh Mitchell Hodges, 187; Hymn

Acknowledgments and Permissions

Society of America, The, 265, 330; Mrs. Robert F. Jefferys, 507; Mrs. Rudyard Kipling, 147, 503, 506; Loughborough College, England, 582; Loughborough Grammar School, England, 505; Mary Runyon Lowry, 438, Refrain; Mrs. J. H. B. Masterman, 530; William Pierson Merrill, 145, 535; Francis John Moore, 238; National Sunday School Union, The, 244; John W. Norris, 526; John Oxenham, the late, 263, 510, 527, 529; A. D. Peters, 536; Mrs. H. D. Rawnsley, 516; Howard Chandler Robbins, 14, 81, 100, 307, 354, 380; R. B. Y. Scott, 525; Mrs. Mary Wentworth Shields, 499; Robert Nelson Spencer, 188; F. Bland Tucker, 68, 195, 298, 362, 366, 504; Sydney James Wallis, S.S.J.E., 110

Music Acknowledgments and Permissions, English

The Clarendon Press, Oxford: (Yattendon 46) 481

The Oxford University Press. From Enlarged Songs of Praise: 21, 26, 34, 39, 43 (harmony only), 45, 82[2], 86, 101, 102, 107, 126[1], 188, 202[1], 240, 296, 312[2], 325[1], 331, 356[1], 362, 364, 376, 482[2], 488, 509, 514, 521, 538, 546, 586, 596[1] (harmony only). From the English Hymnal: 157[2], 582, 599. From Revised Church Hymnary: 122, 431. From The Clarendon Hymn Book: 574[1]

Boosey and Company, Ltd.: 208[2]

J. Curwen and Sons, Ltd.: from Curwen edition No. 6300, published by J. Curwen and Sons, Ltd., 24 Berners Street, London W. 1, England: 131, 251, 290[1], 292[1], 311 (adapted from an English Traditional Melody by Dr. Martin Shaw), 593[1]

The Proprietors of Hymns Ancient and Modern: 493

Joint Managers, Trustee Department, Westminster Bank, Ltd.: 44, 316, 531[2]

The League of Nations Union, 532

Stainer and Bell, Ltd.: 268, 345[1], 366

The Year Book Press: 560[1]

The Abbot of Downside, 486; Percy Carter Buck, 571[1], 583; Executors of Sir Walford Davies, *374; Miss E. Galloway, *128[1]; Walter Greatorex, *389[1]; Basil Harwood, 174; Mrs. K. M. Howard, 496; T. H. Ingham, *473; Craig Sellar Lang, 492; National Sunday School Union, The, 244; Sydney H. Nicholson, 466; Executors of F. G. Russell, 575; Mrs. Walter S. Vale, 110; Guy Warrack, 265; Wesleyan Methodist Conference, England, *438[2]; David F. R. Wilson, 232

Music Acknowledgments and Permissions, American

The H. W. Gray Company: 29[2], 64[1], 346[2], 354[1], 357, 377, 440[1], 478, 571[2], 576, 629, 728, 738

The Oxford University Press, London — Carl Fischer, Inc., sole agents for the U.S.A.: 708, 709, 710, 711, 712, 713, 714, 715, 716, 717, 718, 725, 737

D. Appleton-Century Company: 42

J. Fischer and Brother: 81, 585[1]

Hope Publishing Company: 43 (melody only)

The Parish Press, Fond du Lac: 736

Acknowledgments and Permissions

E. C. Schirmer Music Company: 250 (From The Concord Hymnal, Concord Series No. 10, copyright by The E. C. Schirmer Music Company)

G. Schirmer, Inc.: 598[3]

The Arthur P. Schmidt Company: 729

Mrs. Prescott Baker, 259[1]; Edward Shippen Barnes, 42; Annabel Morris Buchanan, 585[1], her setting of the traditional *Land of Rest*, learned as a child from the singing of her grandmother, Mrs. S. J. (Sarah Ann Love) Foster; H. T. Burleigh, 263[1]; E. R. Currier, 263[2]; Franklin Glynn, 298[2], 502; James Hopkirk, 525; Mary Runyon Lowry, 438[1]; Hilton Rufty, 81; F. W. Snow, chant 693; Healey Willan, 228[2], 708, 709, 710, 711, 712, 713

The following copyrights are held by The Church Pension Fund in the interests of the respective composers: 46[2], 84, 112, 145, 201, 206, 207[1], 207[2], 215, 248, 258, 330, 365, 378[1], 401, 419, 429[1], 429[2], 432, 437, 445, 475, 503, 526[1], 526[2], 527, 529, 530, 541, 543, 548.

The Plainsong tunes were harmonized and the First and Fourth Communion Services were arranged and harmonized by Winfred Douglas.

The following tunes were specially composed for this edition of the Hymnal: Donald S. Barrows, 248, 541; Arthur H. Biggs, 215, 429[2]; Arnold G. H. Bode, 432; Bates G. Burt, 419, 508; Percy E. B. Coller, 258; Everett R. Currier, 263[2]; George Henry Day, 145, 207[1]; Mark Dickey, 530; Roland Diggle, 529; Winfred Douglas, 100, 556[1]; Theodore P. Ferris, 401; Graham George, 64[1]; Franklin Glynn, 298[2], 475, 502; W. A. Goldsworthy, 330; D. Vincent Gray, 112; Henry Hallstrom, 526[2]; John Henry Hopkins, 230, 243; Philip James, 354[1]; Claude Means, 548; Anne L. Miller, 526[1]; Robert B. Miller, 378[1]; Anna J. Morse, 458[1], 490; T. Tertius Noble, 84; Frank K. Owen, 207[2]; Ernest J. Parsons, 445; Howard C. Robbins and Ray F. Brown, 380; Kenneth E. Runkel, 478; Alfred M. Smith, 307, 482[1], 510; Leo Sowerby, 365, 527; Albert J. Strohm, 46[2]; Alfred E. Whitehead, 429[1]; David McK. Williams, 201, 206, 437, 503, 543.

The special thanks of the Commission are extended not only to these contributors, but also to the hundreds of anonymous composers whose generous co-operation greatly aided the acquisition of an adequate collection of present-day American tunes.

Every effort has been made to ascertain the owners of copyrights and to secure their permission for the use of their words and tunes. Starred numbers indicate that in spite of repeated letters, contact has not been established; this is largely due to the difficulties of communication during war. We hope that owners will pardon any such omissions or any errors, which will be corrected, and all resulting fees remitted, on notification.

Subject Index of General Hymns

Topical Index

799

Topical Index

Topical Index

801

Topical Index

Liturgical Index

Hymns Suggested for the Services of the Church Year

This index has been provided to meet two objectives:

1. To provide the clergy with a ready reference and guide to the selection of suitable hymns for a given day or season of the Church Kalendar:
2. To encourage the use of new hymns and tunes.

An effort has been made to use hymns that would lend some degree of liturgical unity to the services of the Church. This is a difficult task because liturgical unity does not always exist between the Collect, Epistle, and Gospel for a given day. This condition is even more pronounced in the lessons assigned by the Prayer Book Lectionary for the Divine Offices. This lectionary has been used despite the many changes that are now being made in its structure.

The hymns chosen for Holy Communion are for the most part objective. In this great act of thanksgiving it seemed more fitting to suggest hymns of praise rather than hymns of prayer or intercession. Hymns of a more subjective nature have been chosen for Morning and Evening Prayer.

Sequence hymns have been suggested for the place of the ancient Gradual and Sequence in the Holy Communion. Office hymns have not been suggested for Morning and Evening Prayer, although their use is recommended, especially at Evensong, when elaborate settings of the Canticles are to be used. An office hymn before the *Magnificat* at such a time gives additional opportunity for the congregation to share in the service.

Hymns to be used in place of the *Gloria in excelsis* have been suggested only for those seasons when the Canticle is not employed. Only one set of Ember Day hymns has been suggested, namely that for Advent, but this set may serve as a guide for the others.

	Morning Prayer			Evening Prayer			The Holy Communion					
O Omit / St. Stanza / Pt. Part Days & Seasons	Opening	General	Closing	Opening	General	Closing	Opening	Sequence	General	Communion	In place of Gloria	Closing
Advent I	1	318	316	7	165	6	153	8	312	203	212	9
Advent II	402	442	10	4	573	11	402	403	473	195	209	8
Advent III	544	219	386	518	473	391	10	256	595	201	211	1
Ember Days	7	416	573	564	572	5	219	131	575	206	211	535
Advent IV	2	3	4	316	440	442	2	4	3	197	201	5
Christmas Eve				32	33	30	27	25	19	199	...	32
Christmas Day	16	42	14	21	33 39	24	12	14	21	204	...	28
St. Stephen's Day	549	136	130	132 O St. 2	452	553	549	135	569	209	...	593 581
St. John Evangelist	126	131	125	403	124	543	130	134	437	205	...	543
Holy Innocents	130	331	593	472	451	175	112	34	418	209	...	600
1st after Christmas	28	317	40	21	35	24	13	14	17	485	...	31
The Circumcision	285	455	326	291	504	356	113	342 St.	366	205	...	326
2nd Christmas	290	34	600	476	20	321 St. 1, 2, 5	18	500 St. 1, 2, 5	20	193	...	316
The Epiphany	49	50	329	440	51	52	53	48	52	12 St. 1, 2	...	46
Epiphany I	153	465	52	258	247	47	153	331 St. 1	48	348 St. 1, 5, 7	...	53

O Omit
St. Stanza
Pt. Part

Days & Seasons	Morning Prayer			Evening Prayer			The Holy Communion					
	Opening	General	Closing	Opening	General	Closing	Opening	Sequence	General	Communion	In place of Gloria	Closing
Epiphany II	477	571	489	393	280	275	374	10	366	189	...	300
Epiphany III	566	328	150	260	263	537	319	495	296	191	...	545
Epiphany IV	156	258	546	442	448	182	532	517	53	192	...	555
Epiphany V	310	446	327	171	556	377	318	362	479	210	...	329
								St. 1, 3, 5				
Epiphany VI	564	459	54	301	216	54	596	10	271	200	...	54
Septuagesima	151	426	394	499	409	536	577	524	560	509	209	501
								St. 2, 3				
Sexagesima	492	550	553	523	448	582	315	401	297	195	211	287
Quinquagesima	155	388	498	173	379	167	456	73	558	460	209	568
								O St. 1				
Ash Wednesday	55	334	336	57	413	447	56	60	310	208	211	59
Lent I	410	60	339	575	411	175	60	55	404	196	209	61
Lent II	459	334	385	556	412	445	416	449	253	483	211	456
								St. 1, 2				
Lent III	533	293	343	435	549	303	340	161	58	194	209	477
Lent IV	159	536	335	345	547	489	284	584	570	192	211	337
Lent V	338	361	336	163	60	340	332	338	71	205	209	336
								St. 4				
Palm Sunday	64	75	70	71	58	68	62	342	75	202	209	64
Maundy Thursday							199	193	206	194	209	201
Easter Even				65	83	341						
Easter Day	90	88	92	94	99	91	85	97	89	210	...	85
							86	90		207	...	94
Easter I	94	100	96	95	98	90	87	537	88	192	...	96
Easter II	475	99	583	279	247	294	485	345	93	213	...	445
		O St. 2, 3, 4										
Easter III	92	437	591	94	90	165	592	351	494	201	...	390
								St. 1				
Easter IV	130	589	282	273	225	177	296	134	376	210	...	150
Easter V	101	277	303	276	563	554	101	497	287	195	...	303
Ascension Day							103	354	105	210	...	106
							102					
Sunday after Ascension	347	354	103	352	368	176	357	498	355	210	...	356
Whitsunday	107	371	111	256	299	370	107	109	108	457	...	110
	378											
Trinity Sunday	266	285	567	286	291	301	268	269	267	204	...	270
Trinity I	273	574	114	288	284	260	366	500	493	211	...	277
								St. 3, 4, 5				
Trinity II	556	407	434	385	370	280	367	582	506	203	...	519
Trinity III	154	433	291	310	260	538	287	405	308	198	...	523
Trinity IV	303	441	301	282	456	597	524	372	525	191	...	333
Trinity V	156	305	500	567	449	439	539	564	566	201	...	390
Trinity VI	276	541	473	273	353	275	318	524	575	190	...	489
Trinity VII	287	435	389	315	470	580	253	293	263	195	...	256
Trinity VIII	543	491	499	304	419	393	302	463	377	189	...	478
Trinity IX	286	288	520	315	558	553	368	343	552	485	...	562
								St. 1, 4				
Trinity X	492	551	434	567	321	427	274	510	147	193	...	145
Trinity XI	577	517	411	170	215	487	157	134	503	189	...	394
Trinity XII	155	458	281	543	409	183	159	540	511	201	...	267
Trinity XIII	545	375	267	143	582	173	260	299	530	212	...	270
Trinity XIV	564	131	508	165	393	355	151	380	281	210	...	489
							Pt. 2					
Trinity XV	158	563	484	555	574	414	498	337	535	200	...	562
Trinity XVI	518	536	539	314	524	492	598	366	278	193	...	282

Liturgical Index

Days & Seasons	Morning Prayer			Evening Prayer			The Holy Communion					
	Opening	General	Closing	Opening	General	Closing	Opening	Sequence	General	Communion	In place of Gloria	Closing
Trinity XVII	367	297	474	302	422	349	300	307 St. 1, 8	287	208	...	557
Trinity XVIII	482	237	367	275	416	175	316	545	317	207	...	347
Trinity XIX	154	370	280	573	516	165	158	413	567	211	...	150
Trinity XX	287	325	448	523	526	529	280	292	524	203	...	484
Trinity XXI	125	130	593	448	483	446	553	551 St. 1, 2	555	331	...	558
Trinity XXII	285	299	569	474	466	170	388	362 St. 3, 4	493	207	...	396
Trinity XXIII	457	424	294	176	343	528	496	491	583	189	...	425
Trinity XXIV	597	401	153	275	449	472	593	124	535	199	...	592
Sunday next before Advent	156	552	562	179	363	553	552	329 St. 1	351	205	...	554
St. Andrew's Day	537	566	546	257	265	264	542	260	566	543	...	253
St. Thomas' Day	99 St. 1, 5, 6, 7, 8	330	385	553	432	130	131	129 St. 1–4	99 St. 1, 5, 6, 7, 8	204	...	590
Conversion St. Paul	114	393	136	355	263	550	114	599 St. 2, 4	531	130	...	128
The Purification	115	418	116	347	493	414	116	479 St. 1, 2	389 St. 1–4	193	...	115
St. Matthias	582	136	531	124	435	130	134 St. 1, 3	583	136	195	...	127
The Annunciation	118	257	599	298	117	302	118	418	317	485	...	599
St. Mark	565	403	543	259	560	124	133	403	124	204	...	125
St. Philip & St. James	564	361	127	574	372	592	126	129	361	193	...	593
St. Barnabas	125	127	386	598	451	282	125	260	517	201	...	543
St. John Baptist	10	325	440	455	128	478	9	345	10	191	...	126
St. Peter	535	405	253	402	213	593	374	350	437	201	...	124
St. James	585	131	267	273	289	570	132	130	124	212	...	549
The Transfiguration	119	571	287	492	291	290	119	571	498	209	...	396
St. Bartholomew	546	465	567	521	493	280	136	135	131	199	...	589
St. Matthew	133	463	130	134	265	569	133	134	403	201	...	129
St. Michael & All Angels	121	444	600	270	494	472	122	123	121	193	...	599
St. Luke	131	515	134	593	516	598	133	400	515	201	...	130
St. Simon & St. Jude	125	396	410	380	451	590	131	132	127	485	...	125
All Saints	126	124	130	127	585	270	126	397	243	195	...	125
Thanksgiving Day	276	145	140	137	146	296	137	308	138	206	...	140

O   Omit
St. Stanza
Pt. Part

Index of Authors, Translators, Sources

Index of Authors, Translators, Sources

Index of Authors, Translators, Sources

Index of Composers, Sources, Arrangers

Index of Composers, Sources, Arrangers

Index of Composers, Sources, Arrangers

Metrical Index

815

Metrical Index

Metrical Index

Index of Tunes

Index of Tunes

Hymns Suitable Also for Use as Anthems

Index of First Lines

Index of First Lines

Index of First Lines

Index of First Lines

Index of First Lines

Index of First Lines

SUPPLEMENT TO THE HYMNAL 1940

Prepared by the Joint Commission on Church Music, 1960

Copyright, 1961, by The Church Pension Fund

Liturgical Index

This index has been provided as a ready reference and guide to the selection of suitable hymns for a given day or season of the Church Year.

An effort has been made to use hymns that would lend some degree of liturgical unity to the services of the Church. The Collect, Epistle and Gospel for the Day do not always express a unity of thought, nevertheless they must of necessity provide the basis of hymn choices in a Liturgical Index. The recently revised Prayer Book Lectionary for the Divine Offices has ably represented this basic principle.

The chart is set under the headings Morning Prayer, Holy Communion and Evening Prayer. However, it is intended that, except where obviously inappropriate, the selections may be readily transferred and used in any service of the Day.

It is also suggested that when a congregation is learning a new hymn, repetition for one or two Sundays following is advisable.

The Hymnal indicates, by use of the asterisk, those stanzas in certain hymns which may properly be omitted without violating the sense.

In addition to the General Index two lists are appended:
(1) Hymns appropriate in Substitution for the Gloria in Excelsis,
(2) Office and Sequence Hymns.

HYMNS IN SUBSTITUTION FOR THE GLORIA IN EXCELSIS

The Gloria in Excelsis is normally sung except during Advent and Lent at which time "some proper hymn" may be substituted for it. "Proper" means either appropriate to its position in reference to the Prayer of Thanksgiving or with reference to the Collect, Epistle and Gospel (propers) of the Day.

The following list of substitutes should be thought of as a list of hymns appropriate to the ending of a celebration of the Holy Communion, possibly but not necessarily seasonal. The omission of stanzas of certain of the hymns is appropriate here. Some hymns under "Holy Communion" in the Hymnal may also be used.

139	276	287
140	277	492, St. 2
144	279	599, St. 4
158	282, St. 1	

OFFICE AND SEQUENCE HYMNS

Office Hymns

Advent: 6, 8, 9, 10
Christmas: 20
Epiphany: 47, 48
Lent: 56, 61
Passiontide: 63, 66, 68
Eastertide: 89, 98
Whitsunday: 108
The Circumcision: 113, 324, 326, 462
Presentation of Christ in the Temple: 116

Transfiguration: 119
St. Michael and All Angels: 123
All Saints: 592
Apostles, Evangelists, Martyrs: 132
Consecration of a Church: 228, 383, 384
Throughout the Year: 157, 158, 159, 160, 161, 162, 163, 164, 171, 589

830

Liturgical Index

Sequences

(To be used between the Epistle and Gospel:)

Easter	97	Evangelists	133, 134
Whitsunday	109	Martyrs	135
Saints' Day	129	At a Burial	468

Other Sequences in the Hymnal — 76, 193, 194

(Selections under any one service may be readily transferred.)

Day	Morning Prayer	The Holy Communion	Evening Prayer
Advent I	1, 7, 153	484, 8*, 318*, 312, 9	7, 165, 6
Advent II	133, 522, 401*	253, 403*, 442*, 8*, 5*	402, 400*, 11
Advent III	518, 574*, 391	10, 256*, 573*, 476	544, 473, 312
Advent IV	4, 2, 3	7*, 9*, 11, 5, 1	316, 440, 442
Christmas Eve and Christmas Day — see Hymns 12 to 45			
St. Stephen	549, 136*, 130	546*, 135*, 569, 599	132, 452, 583
St. John Evangelist	126, 131, 125	130, 133*, 437, 543	403, 124
Holy Innocents	130, 131, 593	112, 34*, 418, 586	112, 451, 175
1st after Christmas — see Hymns 12 to 45			
The Circumcision	285, 504, 356	113*, 342 (st.1), 366, 326	324, 323*, 6
2nd Christmas	290, 19, 14	319, 500 (st.1,2,5)*, 20, 325	476, 320
The Epiphany	52, 50, 329	53, 48*, 258, 46	440, 47, 49
Epiphany I	52, 328, 258	153, 331 (st.1), 48, 237* (o.st.2), 542	46, 247, 47
Epiphany II	477, 263, 489	545, 10*, 327, 53	366, 176, 275
Epiphany III	158, 424, 365	363, 206*, 296, 543	260, 263, 537
Epiphany IV	156, 258, 548	532, 517*, 53, 555	442, 448, 182
Epiphany V	310, 290, 539	538, 462 (st.1,3,5)*, 478, 329	171, 283, 377
Epiphany VI	564, 376, 595	521, 518*, 271, 522	499, 525, 301
Septuagesima	151, 576, 555	577, 524*, 560*, 558	444, 536, 425
Sexagesima	492, 550, 563	315, 401*, 195*, 287	167, 448, 523
Quinquagesima	155, 379, 456	498, 353*, 360, 479	431, 168, 176
Ash Wednesday	55, 344, 336	56, 60*, 501, 59	57, 413, 447
Lent I	410, 55, 446	60, 55*, 477, 61	407, 466, 411
Lent II	419, 334, 488	418, 449*, 258, 253	414, 445, 335
Lent III	533, 497, 343	340, 158*, 56, 517	435, 550, 303
Lent IV	159, 584, 284	585, 201*, 504, 345	437, 547, 489
Lent V	338, 361, 336	536, 340*, 80, 71	163, 60, 335
Palm Sunday	62, 484, 64	62, 64, 63*, 337, 68	75, 70, 73
Maundy Thursday		199, 193, 189, 194, 195	
Easter Day and Easter I — see hymns 84 to 100			
Easter II	597, 475, 583	484, 345*, 437, 279	445, 247, 294
Easter III	543, 432, 463	389, 394*, 494, 492	493, 225, 346
Easter IV	506, 476, 150	361, 376*, 375, 282	273, 397, 177
Easter V, Rogation Sunday	101, 278, 311	280, 287*, 497, 303	419, 296, 511
Ascension Day	103, 102, 354, 105, 106		
Sunday after Ascension	357, 354, 103	347, 368*, 355, 356	352, 353, 350
Whitsunday	378, 371, 256	107, 109*, 108, 457, 385	111, 373, 370
Trinity	266*, 285, 274	268, 273*, 267, 272	275, 567, 269
Trinity I	499, 574, 273	366, 500 (st.1)*, 304, 277	288, 284, 260
Trinity II	367, 323, 434	582, 294*, 573, 280	171, 370, 519
Trinity III	154, 433, 289	287*, 551 (st.1,2), 345, 300	372, 260, 291
Trinity IV	303, 441, 301	524, 510*, 525, 538	282, 443, 597
Trinity V	156, 305, 500	564, 413*, 437*, 539	567, 449, 466
Trinity VI	318, 541, 473	597, 104*, 312, 489	273, 353, 275
Trinity VII	287, 435, 389	253, 347 (st.3,4)*, 263, 256	315, 470, 580
Trinity VIII	543, 499, 491	302, 376*, 377, 478	304, 419, 393
Trinity IX	286, 288, 520	385, 387*, 457, 485	315, 558, 553
Trinity X	497, 373, 434	274, 372 (st.1,3,4)*, 484, 518	567, 321, 427
Trinity XI	577, 517, 411	157, 268 (st.1,2)*, 60*, 394	170, 298, 487
Trinity XII	155, 458, 281	299, 155*, 515, 542	543, 409, 183
Trinity XIII	545, 493, 267	270, 499*, 530, 260	143, 582, 173
Trinity XIV	564, 517, 508	151 (pt.2), 377*, 281, 282	355, 393, 165
Trinity XV	158, 441, 484	482, 337*, 443, 551	555, 574, 414
Trinity XVI	518, 524, 539	598, 504*, 431, 454 (st.1,3)	314, 453, 462

* A hymn which may be sung between the Epistle and Gospel or in close connection to them. Where listed under Morning Prayer it may be transferred.

Note: The last hymn listed under Holy Communion is meant to be considered as a closing hymn.

831

𝕷iturgical 𝕴ndex

(Selections under any one service may be readily transferred.)

Day	Morning Prayer	The Holy Communion	Evening Prayer
Trinity XVII	474, 263, 297	300, 478*, 405, 396	302, 397, 349
Trinity XVIII	367, 533, 307	485, 156*, 522, 347	275, 416, 175
Trinity XIX	154, 370, 280	158, 413*, 344, 150	573, 516, 165
Trinity XX	287, 325, 448	294, 292*, 532, 484	523, 526, 529
Trinity XXI	557, 330, 449	551, 552*, 446, 558	555, 483, 448
Trinity XXII	285, 299, 569	388, 493*, 444, 578	474, 466, 170
Trinity XXIII	322, 424, 598	496, 491*, 583, 147	176, 343, 528
Trinity XXIV	597, 401, 153	593, 565*, 476, 592	275, 449, 472
Sunday next before Advent	156, 552, 560	552, 541*, 538, 554	179, 363, 553
St. Andrew's	537, 582, 546	542, 131*, 566*, 253	257, 265, 264
St. Thomas	99 (st.1,5,6,7,8), 330, 385	5, 129 (st.1–4)*, 592	553, 432, 130
Conversion St. Paul	114*, 393, 136	130, 132, 258, 590, 128	336, 263, 569
The Purification	115, 418, 585	418, 28 (st.4)*, 116*, 477	347, 176, 414
St. Matthias	582, 135, 531	134 (st.1,3), 583*, 136, 127	124, 589, 130
The Annunciation	118, 257, 304	118; 117*, 317, 599	298, 418, 20
St. Mark	565, 401, 543	133, 134*, 124, 549	583, 403, 125
St. Philip & St. James	564, 425, 578	126, 475*, 361, 597	574, 372, 592
St. Barnabas	129, 127, 386	125, 515*, 517, 543	585, 451, 282
St. John Baptist	10, 312, 440	9, 391*, 10, 126	455, 128, 478
St. Peter	131, 405, 557 (st.1,2,4)	132, 135*, 583, 437	334, 213, 593
St. James	135, 136, 564	129, 130*, 124, 549	273, 289, 570
The Transfiguration	119, 327, 287	119, 571*, 498, 396	492, 291, 290
St. Bartholomew	546, 465, 567	136, 135*, 131, 589	521, 493, 280
St. Matthew	133, 363, 130	133, 400*, 403, 129	134, 265, 569
St. Michael & All Angels	121, 444, 600	122, 123*, 121, 599	270, 494, 472
St. Luke	304, 515, 134	157, 133, 575*, 360, 130	593, 516, 598
St. Simon & St. Jude	125, 396, 410	131, 384, 543*, 125	380, 451, 590
All Saints	126, 124, 130	126, 397, 590*, 125	127, 585, 569
Thanksgiving Day	276, 145, 140	137, 308*, 138, 140, 313	137, 146, 296

* A hymn which may be sung between the Epistle and Gospel or in close connection to them. Where listed under Morning Prayer it may be transferred.

Note: The last hymn listed under Holy Communion is meant to be considered as a closing hymn.

MORNING CANTICLES
Benedictus es, Domine

742

(a)　　　　　　　　　　　　　　　Tone VI, c

Bless-ed art thou, O Lord God of our fa - thers:

(a)　Blessed art thou, O Lord God of | our fathers:
　　*praised and exalted above | all for ever.

(a) 2 Blessed art thou for the Name of | thy Majesty:
　　*praised and exalted above | all for ever.

(b) 3 Blessed art thou in the temple of | thy holiness:
　　*praised and exalted above | all for ever.

(b) 4 Blessed art thou that beholdest the depths,
　　and dwellest between | the Cherubim:
　　*praised and exalted above | all for ever.

(a) 5 Blessed art thou on the glorious throne of | thy kingdom:
　　*praised and exalted above | all for ever.

(b) 6 Blessed art thou in the firmament | of heaven:
　　*praised and exalted above | all for ever.

(c)　Glory be to the Father, and to | the Son,
　　*and | to the Holy Ghost;

(c)　As it was in the beginning, is now, and ev | er shall be,
　　*world | without end. Amen.

𝕭enedicite, omnia opera 𝕯omini

743
(Shortened Form)

TONUS PEREGRINUS

O   all ye works of the Lord, bless ye the Lord: - mag-ni-fy him for ev - er.

(a) 1   O ALL ye Works of the Lord | bless ye the Lord:
*praise him and magnify him | for ever.

(a) 2   O ye Angels of the Lord, | bless ye the Lord:
*praise him and magnify him | for ever.

(a) 3   O ye Heavens, | bless ye the Lord:
*O ye Waters that be above the firmament, bless | ye the Lord.

(b) 4   O all ye Powers of the Lord, | O ye Sun and Moon,
*O ye Stars of heaven, bless | ye the Lord.

(b) 5   O ye Showers and Dew, | O ye Winds of God,
*O ye Fire and Heat, bless | ye the Lord.

(b) 6   O ye Winter and Summer, | O ye Frost and Cold,
*O ye Ice and Snow, bless | ye the Lord.

(a) 7   O ye Nights and Days | bless ye the Lord:
*O ye Light and Darkness, bless | ye the Lord.

(a) 8   O ye Lightnings and Clouds, | bless ye the Lord:
*praise him and magnify him | for ever.

(a) 9   O let the | Earth bless the Lord:
*yea, let it praise him and magnify him | for ever.

(b) 10 O ye Mountains and Hills, O all ye Green | Things upon the earth,
*O ye Wells, O ye Seas and Floods, bless | ye the Lord.

(a) 11 O ye Whales, and all that move in the waters, | bless ye the Lord:
*O all ye Fowls of the air, O all ye Beasts and Cattle, bless | ye the Lord.

(a) 12 O ye Children of Men, | bless ye the Lord:
*praise him and magnify him | for ever.

(c) 13 O let Israel | bless the Lord:
*praise him and magnify him | for ever.

(b) 14 O ye Priests of the Lord, O ye | Servants of the Lord,
*O ye Spirits and Souls of the Righteous, bless | ye the Lord.

(a) 15 O ye holy and humble Men of heart, | bless ye the Lord:
*praise him and magnify him | for ever.

(b) 16 Let us bless the Father, and the Son, | and the Holy Ghost:
*praise him and magnify him | for ever.

834

Benedicite, omnia opera Domini

744

S. ELVEY

O ALL ye Works of the Lord, | bless • ye the • Lord:
*praise him and magnify | him for **ever**.

2   O ye Angels of the Lord, | bless • ye the • Lord:
*praise him and magnify | him for **ever**.

3   O ye Heavens, | bless • ye the • Lord:
*O ye Waters that be above the | firma • ment bless • ye the • Lord:

4   O all ye Powers of the Lord, O ye | Sun and Moon,
*O ye Stars of | heaven, bless • ye the • Lord:

5   O ye Showers and Dew, O ye | Winds of God,
*O ye Fire and | **Heat**, bless • ye the • Lord:

6   O ye Winter and Summer, O ye | Frost and Cold,
*O ye Ice and | **Snow**, bless • ye the • Lord:

7   O ye Nights and Days, | bless • ye the • Lord:
*O ye Light and | Darkness, bless • ye the • Lord:

8   O ye Lightnings and Clouds, | bless • ye the • Lord:
*praise him and magnify | him for **ever**

9   O let the Earth | bless the Lord:
*yea, let it praise him and magnify | him for **ever**

10 O ye Mountains and Hills, O all ye Green Things up | on the earth,
*O ye Wells, O ye Seas and | **Floods**, bless • ye the • Lord:

Benedicite, omnia opera Domini

11   O ye Whales, and all that move in the waters, | bless • ye the • Lord:
     *O all ye Fowls of the air, O all ye Beasts and | Cattle, bless • ye the •
     Lord:

12   O ye Children of Men, | bless • ye the • Lord:
     *praise him and magnify | him for **ev**er.

13   O let Israel | bless the Lord:
     *praise him and magnify | him for **ev**er.

14   O ye Priests of the Lord, O ye Servants | of the Lord,
     *O ye Spirits and Souls of the | Righteous, bless • ye the • Lord:

15   O ye holy and humble Men of heart, | bless • ye the • Lord:
     *praise him and magnify | him for **ev**er.

16   Let us bless the Father, and the Son, and the | Holy Ghost:
     *praise him and magnify | him for **ev**er.

745   Jubilate Deo

TONE III, A6

O   be joy - ful in the   Lord all   ye lands:

(*a*) 1   O BE joyful in the | Lord all ye lands:
     *serve the Lord with gladness,
     and come before | his presence with a song.

(*a*) 2   Be ye sure that the Lord he is God;
     it is he that hath made us, and | not we ourselves;
     *we are his people, and the | sheep of his pasture.

(*b*) 3   O go your way into his gates with thanksgiving,
     and | into his courts with praise;
     *be thankful unto him | and speak good of his Name.

(*a*) 4   For the Lord is gracious, his mercy is | everlasting;
     *and his truth endureth from generation | to generation.

(*b*)   Glory be to the | Father and to the Son,
     * | and to the Holy Ghost;

(*a*)   As it was in the beginning, is now, and | ever shall be,
     * | world without end. Amen.

EVENING CANTICLES

746 𝕸𝖆𝖌𝖓𝖎𝖋𝖎𝖈𝖆𝖙

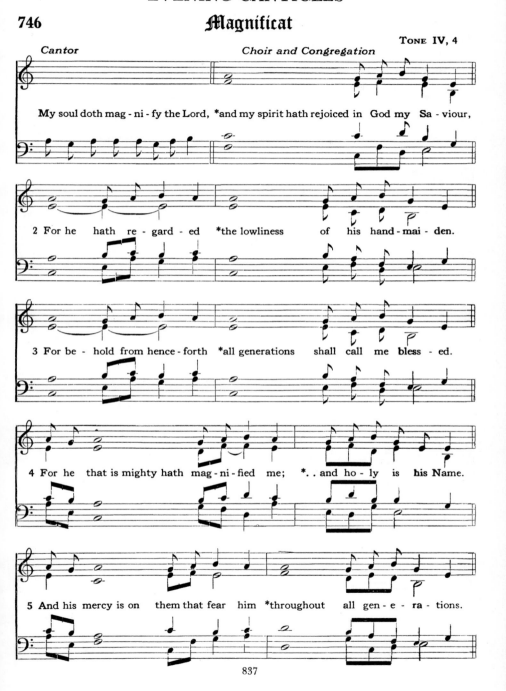

Cantor *Choir and Congregation*

My soul doth mag - ni - fy the Lord, *and my spirit hath rejoiced in God my Sa - viour,

2 For he hath re - gard - ed *the lowliness of his hand - mai - den.

3 For be - hold from hence - forth *all generations shall call me bless - ed.

4 For he that is mighty hath mag - ni - fied me; *. . and ho - ly is his Name.

5 And his mercy is on them that fear him *throughout all gen - e - ra - tions.

Magnificat

6 He hath showed strength with his arm; *he hath scattered the proud in the ima-gi - na-tion of their hearts.

7 He hath put down the mighty from their seat, *and hath exalted the hum-ble and meek.

8 He hath filled the hungry with good things; *and the rich he hath sent emp-ty a-way.

9 He re - membering his mer - cy hath holpen his ser-vant Is - ra - el;

*as he promised to our forefathers, Abraham and his seed for ev - er.

Magnificat

Glo-ry be to the Father, and to the Son, *.. and to the Ho-ly Ghost; As it

was in the begin-ning, is now, and ev-er shall be, *world with-out end. A-men.

THE HOLY COMMUNION

Fifth Communion Service
Kyrie Eleison, ninefold

747

In unison, simply

Leo Sowerby, 1957

Lord, have mer-cy up-on us, Lord have mer-cy up-on us.

Lord, have mer-cy up-on us. Christ, have mer-cy up-on us, Christ, have

mer-cy up-on us, Christ, have mer-cy up-on us. Lord, have mer-cy up-

Fifth Communion Service

on us. Lord, have mer - cy up - on us. Lord, have mer - cy up - on us.

748   Sanctus

LEO SOWERBY, 1957

HO - LY, HO - LY, HO - LY, Lord, God of Hosts,

Heav'n and earth are full of thy glo - ry. Glo - ry

be to Thee, O Lord, most high. A - men.

840

Fifth Communion Service

Agnus Dei

LEO SOWERBY, 1957

O Lamb of God, that tak - est a - way the sins of the world, have mer - cy up - on us. O Lamb of God that tak - est a - way the sins of the world, have mer - cy up - on us. O Lamb of God, that tak - est a - way the

Fifth Communion Service

sins of the world. grant us thy peace.

Sixth Communion Service

750

Kyrie eleison, ninefold

Fairly slow

WILLIS BODINE, 1958

Lord, have mer - cy up - on us; Lord, have mer - cy up -

on us; Lord, have mer - cy up - on us. Christ, have mer - cy up -

man.

842

Sixth Communion Service

on us; Christ, have mer - cy up - on us; Christ, have mer - cy up-

(man.)

poco rit.

on us. Lord, have mer - cy up - on us; Lord, have mer - cy up-

a tempo

Ped.

on us; Lord, have mer - cy up - on us.

poco rit.

Sixth Communion Service

751   Sanctus

Willis Bodine, 1958

HO - LY, HO - LY, HO - LY,

Priest

... praising Thee and say - ing:

Broadly

Ped.

Lord God of Hosts! Heav'n and earth are full of thy glo - ry.

Somewhat faster

Glo - ry be to thee, O Lord most high! A - men.

Broader

cresc. - - - - - - - - - -

Sixth Communion Service
Agnus Dei

752

WILLIS BODINE, 1958

O Lamb of God, that tak - est a - way the sins of the world, have mer - cy up - on us. O Lamb of God, that tak - est a - way the sins of the

Quietly moving

845

Sixth Communion Service
Agnus Dei

world, have mer - cy up - on us. O Lamb of God, that

tak - est a - way the sins of the world, grant us Thy peace.

Seventh Communion Service
753
Kyrie eleison, threefold

CHARLES F. WATERS, 1930

Lord, have mer - cy up - on us. Christ, have mer - cy up -

on us. Lord, have mer - cy up - on us.

846

Seventh Communion Service

Sanctus

754

CHARLES F. WATERS, 1930

Seventh Communion Service

Agnus Dei

755

CHARLES F. WATERS, 1930

p Slowly

O Lamb of God that tak - est a - way the sins of the
world, have mer - cy up - on — us.

2 *Optional Descant*
O Lamb of God that
O Lamb of

Seventh Communion Service

Copyright, 1930, by Faith Press Ltd.

Eighth Communion Service

756

Kyrie eleison, threefold

MARTIN SHAW, 1918

Eighth Communion Service

cy up - on us, Lord, have mer - cy up - on us.

757 **Sanctus**

♩ = about 69 (but quicker where suitable).
May be sung in unison and a semitone lower.

MARTIN SHAW, 1918

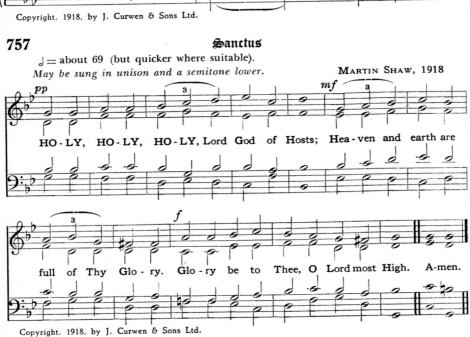

pp *mf* 3

HO - LY, HO - LY, HO - LY, Lord God of Hosts; Hea - ven and earth are

3 *f*

full of Thy Glo - ry. Glo - ry be to Thee, O Lord most High. A - men.

758 **Agnus Dei**

MARTIN SHAW, 1918

May be sung in unison. ♩ = about 69.

pp

O Lamb of God, that tak - est a - way the

pp Cantor

Eighth Communion Service

sins of the world, have mer-cy up-on us.

O Lamb of God, that tak-est a-way
Cantor

Slower

the sins of the world, grant us Thy peace.

Copyright, 1918, by J. Curwen & Sons Ltd.

759 **Credo**

Mode V

I be-lieve in one God The Fa-ther Al-migh-ty ma-ker of heav-en and earth,

And of all things vi-si-ble and in-vi-si-ble. And in one Lord Je-sus Christ,

Credo

the on - ly - be - got-ten son of God; Be-got-ten of his Fa-ther be - fore all worlds,

God of God, Light of Light, Ver - y God of Ver - y God; Be-got-ten, not made;

Be - ing of one sub-stance with the Fa - ther; By whom all things were made:

Who for us men and for our sal - va - tion came down from hea - ven.

And was in - car-nate by the Ho-ly Ghost of the Vir-gin Ma-ry, And was made man:

Credo

And was cru - ci - fied al - so for us un - der Pon-tius Pi - late:

He suf - fered and was bu - ried: And the third day he rose a - gain

ac - cord-ing to the Scrip-tures: And as - cend-ed in - to hea - ven,

And sit - teth on the right hand of the Fa - ther And he shall come a - gain, with

glo - ry, to judge both the quick and the dead, Whose king-dom shall have no end.

Credo

And I be-lieve in the Ho - ly Ghost, the Lord, and Giv - er of Life,

Who pro - ce-deth from the Fa-ther and the Son; Who with the Fa - ther

and the Son to - geth-er is wor-shipped and glo-ri - fied; Who spake by the

pro - phets: And I be-lieve one Cath-o - lic and A - pos - tol-ic Church:

I ac - know-ledge one Bap - tism for the re - mis - sion of sins:

Credo

And I look for the Re-sur-rec-tion of the dead: And the Life of the world to come. A - - - - - - - - men.

Gloria in excelsis

760

Mode I

Glo-ry be to God on high. And on earth peace, good will to-wards men.

We praise thee, We bless thee, We wor-ship thee, We glor-i-fy thee,

We give thanks to thee for thy great glo-ry, O Lord God,

855

Gloria in excelsis

hea - ven - ly King, God the Fa - ther Al - migh - ty.

O Lord, the on - ly be - got - ten Son, Je - sus Christ;

O Lord God, Lamb of God, Son of the Fa - ther.

That tak - est a - way the sins of the world, have mer - cy

up - on us. Thou that tak - est a - way the sins of the world,

Gloria in excelsis

re - ceive our prayer. Thou that sit - test at the right hand of God

the Fa - ther, have mer - cy up - on us. For thou on-ly art ho - ly:

Thou on - ly art the Lord; Thou on - ly, O Christ, with the Ho - ly Ghost,

Art most high in the glo - ry of God the Fa - ther. A - men.

857

Suggested Alternate Tunes:

4	Rejoice, rejoice, believers	Llangloffan, No. 761
37	Gentle Mary laid her child	Tempus Adest Floridum, No. 136
46	Brightest and best of the sons of the morning	Star in the East, No. 762 a, b
63	The royal banners forward go	Spires, No. 61
66	Sing, my tongue, the glorious battle	Atonement, No. 764
87	Welcome, happy morning	King's Weston, No. 763
94	Come, ye faithful, raise the strain	Hatfield, No. 765
100	The Sabbath day was by	St. Michael, No. 113
108	O come, Creator Spirit, come	St. David, No. 766
112	When Christ was born in Bethlehem	St. Magnus, No. 106
116	O Sion, open wide thy gates	Winchester Old, No. 13 (First Tune)
120	Around the throne of God a band	Wareham, No. 119
125	Hark! the sound of holy voices	Hyfrydol, No. 347 (Second Tune)
127	How bright these glorious spirits shine	Land of Rest, No. 585 (First Tune)
135	Blessed feasts of blessed martyrs	Holy Manna, No. 767 a, b
151	Awake, my soul, and with the sun	Tallis' Canon, No. 165
152	All praise to thee, who safe hast kept	Tallis' Canon, No. 165
171	O Trinity of blessed light	Wareham, No. 119
173	O Brightness of the immortal Father's face	Evening Hymn, No. 768
191	Thou, who at thy first Eucharist didst pray	Song 1, No. 470
209	O saving Victim, opening wide	Spires, No. 61
213	Shepherd of souls, refresh and bless	Windsor, No. 284
215	Lord, who at Cana's wedding feast	Kingsfold, No. 101
216	May the grace of Christ our Saviour	Stuttgart, No. 1
227	All things are thine; no gift have we	Herr Jesu Christ, No. 159 (Second Tune)
258	Christ is the world's true light	Darmstadt, No. 14
265	Eternal God, whose power upholds	Forest Green, No. 21 (First Tune)
270	Holy, Holy, Holy Lord	Dix, No. 52
274	Ancient of Days, who sittest throned in glory	Lombard Street, No. 575
281	Joyful, joyful, we adore thee	Hymn to Joy, No. 769
290	Let all the world in ev'ry corner sing	MacDougall, No. 770
292	Songs of praise the angels sang	Northampton, No. 771
294	Sing, my soul, his wondrous love	Song 13, No. 451
295	Lord of all majesty and might	Old Hundred Twelfth, No. 772
305	O Lord of heav'n and earth and sea	Layriz, No. 773
318	Hosanna to the living Lord	Vom Himmel Hoch, No. 774
319	Joy to the world! the Lord is come	Antioch, No. 775
325	O for a thousand tongues to sing	Azmon, No. 776
336	In the cross of Christ I glory	Charlestown, No. 777 a, b
342	Jesus, Name all names above	Werde Munter, No. 778
344	O love, how deep, how broad, how high	De Tar, No. 779
350	Rejoice, the Lord is King	Darwall, No. 600
371	Creator Spirit, by whose aid	Old Hundred Twelfth, No. 772
383	Blessed City, heav'nly Salem	Westminster Abbey, No. 780
384	Christ is made the sure foundation	Westminster Abbey, No. 780
394	Through the night of doubt and sorrow	Ebenezer (Ton-Y-Botel), No. 519
401	Behold a Sower! from afar	Kingsfold, No. 101
417	Lord Jesus, think on me	Southwell, No. 781
437	They cast their nets in Galilee	Dundee, No. 497
455	How sweet the name of Jesus sounds (verses 1-4)	Amazing Grace, No. 782
515	From thee all skill and science flow	St. Magnus, No. 106 or Halifax, No. 354 (Second Tune)
516	Father, whose will is life and good	St. Anne, No. 289
524	God of grace and God of glory	Cwm Rhondda, No. 783
525	O Day of God, draw nigh	Landaff, No. 784 a, b
547	O God of truth, whose living Word	Bangor, No. 442
564	How firm a foundation	Foundation, No. 785
566	Jesus calls us; o'er the tumult	Charlestown, No. 777
579	Rejoice, ye pure in heart	Vineyard Haven, No. 786

761

Llangloffan

Welsh Hymn Melody

76. 76. D.

1 Re - joice, re - joice, be - liev - ers! And let your lights ap - pear;
2 See that your lamps are burn - ing; Re - plen - ish them with oil;

The eve - ning is ad - vanc - ing, And dark - er night is near.
Look now for your sal - va - tion, The end of sin and toil.

The Bride-groom is a - ris - ing, And soon he will draw nigh;
The watch - ers on the moun - tain Pro - claim the Bride-groom near;

Up, watch in ex - pec - ta - tion! At mid-night comes the cry.
Go meet him as he com - eth, With al - le - lu - ias clear.

verses 4 & 5 over

3 O wise and holy virgins,
  Now raise your voices higher,
Until in songs of triumph
  Ye meet the angel choir.
The marriage-feast is waiting,
  The gates wide open stand;
Rise up, ye heirs of glory!
  The Bridegroom is at hand.

4 Our hope and expectation,
  O Jesus, now appear;
Arise, thou Sun so longed for,
  O'er this benighted sphere!
With hearts and hands uplifted,
  We plead, O Lord, to see
The day of earth's redemption,
  And ever be with thee! Amen.

A - men.

Laurentius Laurenti, 1700; *Tr.* Sarah B. Findlater, 1854, *alt.*

762 A

Star in the East

Southern Harmony
harm. by Alastair Cassels-Brown, 1974

11. 10. 11. 10

1. Bright - est and best of the sons of the morn - ing,
   Star of the east, the ho - ri - zon a - dorn - ing,
2. Cold on his cra - dle the dew - drops are shin - ing,
   An - gels a - dore him in slum - ber re - clin - ing,
3. Shall we then yield him, in cost - ly de - vo - tion,
   Gems of the moun - tain, and pearls of the o - cean,

Dawn on our dark - ness, and lend us thine aid;
Guide where our in - fant re - deem - er is laid.
Low lies his head with the beasts of the stall;
Ma - ker and Mon - arch and Sav - iour of all.
O - dors of E - dom, and of - f'rings di - vine,
Myrrh from the for - est, and gold from the mine?

SUPPLEMENTAL TUNES

REFRAIN

Bright - est and best of the sons of the morn - ing,

Dawn on our dark - ness, and lend us thine aid;

Star of the east, the ho - ri - zon a - dorn - ing,

Guide where our in - fant Re - deem - er is laid.

4 Vainly we offer each ample oblation,
　Vainly with gifts would his favor secure;
　Richer by far is the heart's adoration,
　Dearer to God are the prayers of the poor.
REFRAIN

Reginald Heber, 1811, *alt.*

Harmony, copyright 1975 by the Church Pension Fund

*alternate
harmonization
over*

SUPPLEMENTAL TUNES

762 B

Star in the East

Original Version
Melody in Tenor

763

King's Weston   R. Vaughan Williams, 1925

65. 65. D.

In unison

1 "Wel - come, hap - py morn - ing!" age to age shall say:
2 Earth her joy con - fess - es, cloth -ing her for spring,
3 Months in due suc - ces - sion, days of length -'ning light,
4 Ma - ker and Re - dee - mer, life and health of all,

Hell to - day is van - quished, heav'n is won to - day!
All fresh gifts re - turned with her re - turn - ing King:
Hours and pas - sing mo - ments praise thee in their flight.
Thou from heav'n be hold - ing hu - man na - ture's fall,

Lo! the dead is liv - ing God for ev - er - more!
Bloom in ev - 'ry mea - dow, leaves on ev - 'ry bough,
Bright - ness of the mor - ning, sky and fields and sea,
Of the Fa - ther's God - head true and on - ly Son,

Him, their true Cre - a - tor, all his works a - dore!
Speak his sor - row end - ed, hail his tri - umph now.
Van - quish - er of dark - ness, bring their praise to thee.
Man - hood to de - li - ver, man - hood didst put on.

2 verses over

5 Thou, of life the author, death didst undergo,
Tread the path of darkness, saving strength to show;
Come the, true and faithful now fulfil thy word
"'Tis thine own third morning! rise, O buried Lord!

6 Loose the souls long prisoned, bound with Satan's chain;
All that now is fallen to raise to life again;
Show thy face in brightness, bid the nation see;
Bring again our daylight; day returns with thee! Amen.

A - men.

**Venantius Honorius
Fortunatus, 530-609
Tr. John Ellerton, 1868**

764

Atonement

John D. O'Donnell, 1974

87. 87. 87

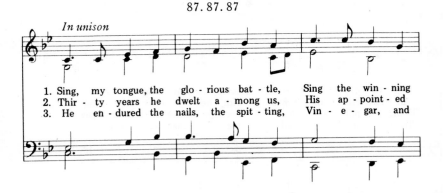

In unison

1. Sing, my tongue, the glo - rious bat - tle, Sing the win - ning
2. Thir - ty years he dwelt a - mong us, His ap - point - ed
3. He en - dured the nails, the spit - ting, Vin - e - gar, and

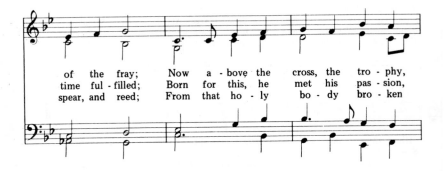

of the fray; Now a - bove the cross, the tro - phy,
time ful - filled; Born for this, he met his pas - sion,
spear, and reed; From that ho - ly bo - dy bro - ken

SUPPLEMENTAL TUNES

Sound the high tri - umph - al lay: Tell how Christ, the
This the Sa - viour free - ly willed: On the cross the
Blood and wa - ter forth pro - ceed: Earth, and stars, and

world's Re - deem - er, As a vic - tim won the day.
Lamb was lift - ed, Where his pre - cious blood was spilled.
sky, and o - cean, By that flood from stain are freed. A - men.

4 Faithful cross! above all other,
One and only noble tree!
None in foliage, none in blossom,
None in fruit thy peer may be:
Sweetest wood, and sweetest iron!
Sweetest weight is hung on thee.

5 Bend thy boughs, O tree of glory!
Thy relaxing sinews bend;
For awhile the ancient rigor
That thy birth bestowed, suspend;
And the King of heav'nly beauty
On thy bosom gently tend!

6 To the Trinity be glory
Everlasting, as is meet:
Equal to the Father, equal
To the Son, and Paraclete:
God the Three in One, whose praises
All created things repeat.

Venantius Honorius Fortunatus, 569;
Hymnal Version, 1940, *after* J. M. Neale

765

Hatfield

Clark Kimberling, 1974

76. 76. D.

in unison

flute or other instrument

1 Come, ye faith-ful, raise the strain   Of tri-umph-ant glad - ness;
2 'Tis the spring of souls to - day;   Christ hath burst his pris - on,

God hath brought his Is - ra - el   In - to joy from sad - ness;
And from three days' sleep in death   As a sun hath ris - en;

Loosed from Pha-raoh's bit-ter yoke   Ja - cob's sons and daugh - ters;
All the win - ter of our sins,   Long and dark, is fly - ing

SUPPLEMENTAL TUNES

Led them with un-moisten'd foot Through the Red Sea wa - ters.
From his light, to whom we give Laud and praise un - dy - ing.

3 Now the queen of seasons, bright
  With the day of splendor,
  With the royal feast of feasts,
  Comes its joy to render;
  Comes to glad Jerusalem,
  Who with true affection
  Welcomes in unwearied strains
  Jesus' resurrection.

4 Neither might the gates of death,
  Nor the tomb's dark portal,
  Nor the watchers, nor the seal
  Hold thee as a mortal:
  But to-day amidst thine own
  Thou didst stand, bestowing
  That thy peace which evermore
  Passeth human knowing. Amen.

A men.

St. John of Damascus, *8th cent.;*
Tr. J. M. Neale, 1853

SUPPLEMENTAL TUNES

766

St. David

Clark Kimberling, 1974

L. M.

in unison

1 O come, Cre - a - tor Spi - rit, come And make with-
2 O Gift of God, most high, thy name Is Com - fort-
3 The sev'n - fold gift of grace is thine, Thou fin - ger

in our souls thy home; Sup - ply thy grace and heav'n-ly
er; whom we ac - claim The fount of life, the fire of
of the hand di - vine; The Fa - ther's prom - ise true, to

aid To fill the hearts which thou hast made.
love, The soul's a - noint - ing from a - bove.
teach Our earth - ly tongues thy heav'n - ly speech. A - men.

4 Thy light to every sense impart;
　Pour forth thy love in every heart;
　Our weakened flesh do thou restore
　To strength and courage evermore.

5 Drive far away our spirit's foe,
　Thine own abiding peace bestow;
　If thou dost go before as guide,
　No evil can our steps betide.

6 Through thee may we the Father learn,
　And know the Son, and thee discern,
　Who art of both; and thus adore
　In perfect faith for evermore. Amen.

Latin, 9th cent.; Hymnal Version, 1939

767 A

Holy Manna

Southern Harmony
harm. by Alastair Cassels-Brown, 1974

87. 87. D.

In unison

1 Bless - ed feasts of bless - ed mar - tyr s, Ho - ly days of ho - ly men,
2 Faith pre - vail - ing, hope un - fail - ing, Lov - ing Christ with sin - gle heart,
3 There - fore, ye that reign in glo - ry, Fel - low - heirs with Christ on high,

With af - fec - tion's re - col - lec - tions Greet we your re - turn a - gain.
Thus they, glo - rious and vic - to - rious, Brave - ly bore the mar - tyr's part,
Join to ours your sup - pli - ca - tion When be - fore him we draw nigh,

Wor - thy deeds they wrought, and wonders, Wor - thy of the Name they bore;
By con-tempt of ev - 'ry an - guish, By un - yield-ing bat - tle done;
Pray - ing that, this life com-plet - ed, All its fleet -ing mo - ments past,

We, with meet - est praise and sweet - est, Hon - or them for - ev - er - more.
Vic - tors at the last, they tri - umph, With the host of an - gels one.
By his grace we may be wor - thy Of e - ter - nal bliss at last.

Latin, 12th cent.; Tr. John Mason Neale, 1851, *alt.*

Harmony, copyright 1975 by The Church Pension Fund *alt. harmonization over*

SUPPLEMENTAL TUNES

767 B

Holy Manna

SUPPLEMENTAL TUNES

768

Evening Hymn   Gerald Near, 1974

10. 6. 10. 6

In unison

1 O Bright-ness of the im- mor - tal Fa - ther's face,
2 The sun is sink - ing now, and one by one
3 Wor - thy art thou at all times to re - ceive

Most ho - ly, heav'n - ly, blest, Lord Je - sus
The lamps of eve - ning shine; We hymn the e -
Our hal - lowed prais - es, Lord. O Son of

Christ, in whom his truth and grace Are vis - i -
ter - nal Fa - ther, and the Son, And Ho - ly
God, be thou, in whom we live, Through all the

SUPPLEMENTAL TUNES

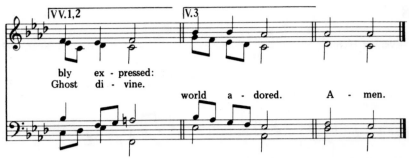

bly   ex - pressed:
Ghost   di - vine.

world   a - dored.   A - men.

Greek, 3rd cent.; Tr. Edward W. Eddis, 1864

Music, copyright 1975 by The Church Pension Fund

769

Hymn to Joy

Arr. from Beethoven
by Alastair Cassels-Brown, 1974

87. 87. D.

1. Joy - ful, joy - ful,   we a - dore thee, God of glo - ry,   Lord   of love;
2. All thy works with joy sur-round thee, Earth and heav'n re-flect   thy rays,
3. Thou art giv - ing   and for - giv - ing, Ev - er bless - ing,   ev - er blest,

Hearts un - fold like flowers be-fore thee, Prais-ing thee, their sun   a - bove.
Stars and an - gels sing a - round thee, Cen - ter of un - bro - ken praise:
Well - spring of the   joy of liv - ing, O - cean-depth of hap - py rest!

SUPPLEMENTAL TUNES

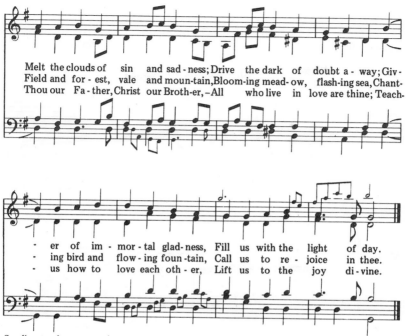

Melt the clouds of sin and sad-ness; Drive the dark of doubt a-way; Giv-
Field and for-est, vale and moun-tain, Bloom-ing mead-ow, flash-ing sea, Chant-
Thou our Fa-ther, Christ our Broth-er,—All who live in love are thine; Teach-

-er of im-mor-tal glad-ness, Fill us with the light of day.
-ing bird and flow-ing foun-tain, Call us to re-joice in thee.
-us how to love each oth-er, Lift us to the joy di-vine.

Small notes for organ only.

4 Mortals join the mighty chorus,
   Which the morning stars began;
Father-love is reigning o'er us,
   Brother-love binds man to man.
Ever singing march we onward,
   Victors in the midst of strife;
Joyful music lifts us sunward
   In the triumph song of life. Amen.

A - men.

Henry Van Dyke, 1907

770

MacDougall

Calvin Hampton, 1974

10. 4. 66. 66. 10 4

1 Let all the world in ev - 'ry cor - ner
2 Let all the world in ev - 'ry cor - ner

sing, My God and King!
sing, My God and King!

SUPPLEMENTAL TUNES

Women

Let all the world in ev - 'ry cor - ner
Let all the world in ev - 'ry cor - ner

Full

sing, My God and King! The
sing, My God and King! The

heav'ns are not too high, His praise may thith - er
Church with psalms must shout, No door can keep them

fly: The earth is not too low, His
out: But, a - bove all, the heart Must

SUPPLEMENTAL TUNES

prais - es there may grow. Let
bear the long - est part. Let

all the world in ev - 'ry cor - ner sing, My
all the world in ev - 'ry cor - ner sing, My

V.1

God and King!
God and

V.2

King! A men.

George Herbert, 1633

771

Northampton   Charles J. King

77. 77

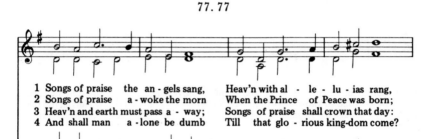

1 Songs of praise   the an - gels sang,   Heav'n with al - le - lu - ias rang,
2 Songs of praise   a - woke the morn   When the Prince of Peace was born;
3 Heav'n and earth must pass a - way;   Songs of praise shall crown that day:
4 And shall man   a - lone be dumb   Till   that glo - rious king-dom come?

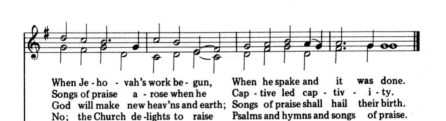

When Je - ho - vah's work be - gun,   When he spake and   it   was done.
Songs of praise   a - rose when he   Cap - tive led cap - tiv - i - ty.
God will make new heav'ns and earth;   Songs of praise shall hail   their birth.
No; the Church de -lights to raise   Psalms and hymns and songs   of praise.

5 Saints below, with heart and voice,
  Still in songs of praise rejoice,
  Learning here, by faith and love,
  Songs of praise to sing above.

6 Borne upon their latest breath,
  Songs of praise shall conquer death;
  Then, amidst eternal joy,
  Songs of praise their powers employ.

James Montgomery, 1819

Music by permission of Proprietors of Hymns Ancient and Modern

SUPPLEMENTAL TUNES

772

Old Hundred Twelfth

Anonymous German Melody, 1530
harm. by Alastair Cassels-Brown, 1974

88. 88. 88

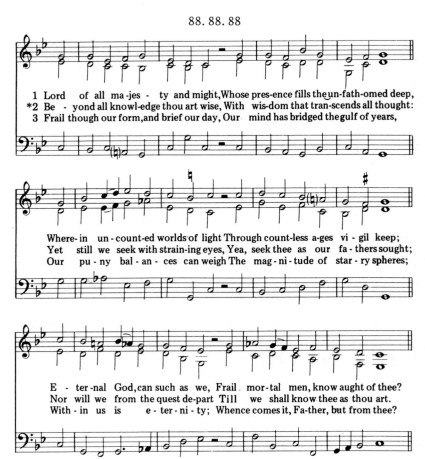

1 Lord of all ma-jes-ty and might, Whose pres-ence fills the un-fath-omed deep,
*2 Be - yond all knowl-edge thou art wise, With wis-dom that tran-scends all thought:
3 Frail though our form, and brief our day, Our mind has bridged the gulf of years,

Where-in un-count-ed worlds of light Through count-less a-ges vi-gil keep;
Yet still we seek with strain-ing eyes, Yea, seek thee as our fa-thers sought;
Our pu-ny bal-an-ces can weigh The mag-ni-tude of star-ry spheres;

E - ter-nal God, can such as we, Frail mor-tal men, know aught of thee?
Nor will we from the quest de-part Till we shall know thee as thou art.
With-in us is e - ter-ni-ty; Whence comes it, Fa-ther, but from thee?

4 For, when thy wondrous works we scan,
  And Mind gives answer back to mind,
Thine image stands revealed in man;
  And, seeking, he shall surely find.
    Thy sons, our heritage we claim:
    Shall not thy children know thy Name?

5 We know in part: enough we know
  To walk with thee, and walk aright;
And thou shalt guide us as we go,
  And lead us into fuller light,
    Till, when we stand before thy throne,
    We know at last as we are known.

George Wallace Briggs, 1933

773

Layriz

Melody from Layriz Collection, 1853
harm. by Alastair Cassels-Brown

88. 84

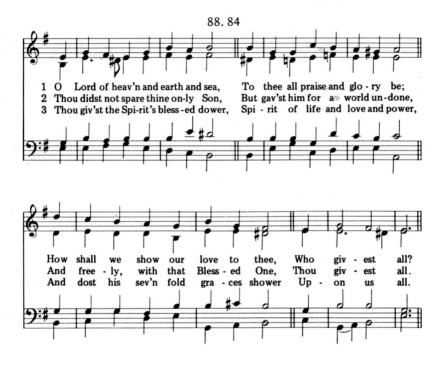

1 O Lord of heav'n and earth and sea, To thee all praise and glo - ry be;
2 Thou didst not spare thine on-ly Son, But gav'st him for a world un-done,
3 Thou giv'st the Spi-rit's bless-ed dower, Spi - rit of life and love and power,

How shall we show our love to thee, Who giv - est all?
And free - ly, with that Bless - ed One, Thou giv - est all.
And dost his sev'n fold gra - ces shower Up - on us all.

4. For souls redeemed, for sins forgiv'n,
For means of grace and hopes of heav'n,
Father, what can to thee be giv'n,
Who givest all?

5. We lose what on ourselves we spend,
We have as treasure without end
Whatever, Lord, to thee we lend,
Who givest all;

A - men

6. To thee, from whom we all derive
Our life, our gifts, our power to give:
O may we ever with thee live,
Who givest all! Amen.

Christopher Wordsworth, 1863, *alt.*

Music by permission of Oxford University Press
Harmony, copyright 1975 by The Church Pension Fund

SUPPLEMENTAL TUNES

774

Vom Himmel Hoch

Martin Luther, 1483–1546

L. M.

1 Ho - san - na to the liv - ing Lord! Ho - san - na
2 Ho - san - na, Lord! thine an - gels cry; Ho - san - na,
3 O Sa - viour, with pro - tect - ing care A - bide in

to the in - car - nate Word! To Christ, Cre - a - tor,
Lord! thy saints re - ply; A - bove, be - neath us,
this thy house of prayer, Where we thy part - ing

Sa - viour, King, Let earth, let heav'n, Ho - san - na sing!
and a - round, The dead and liv - ing swell the sound;
prom - ise claim, As - sem - bled in thy sa - cred Name.

4 But, chiefest, in our cleansed breast,
   Eternal! bid thy Spirit rest;
   And make our secret soul to be
   A temple pure and worthy thee.

5 So in the last and dreadful day,
   When earth and heav'n shall melt away,
   Thy flock, redeemed from sinful stain,
   Shall swell the sound of praise again.

A - men.

Reginald Heber, 1827

SUPPLEMENTAL TUNES

775

Antioch

Arr. from George Frederick Handel, 1685–1759
by Lowell Mason, 1792–1872

C. M.

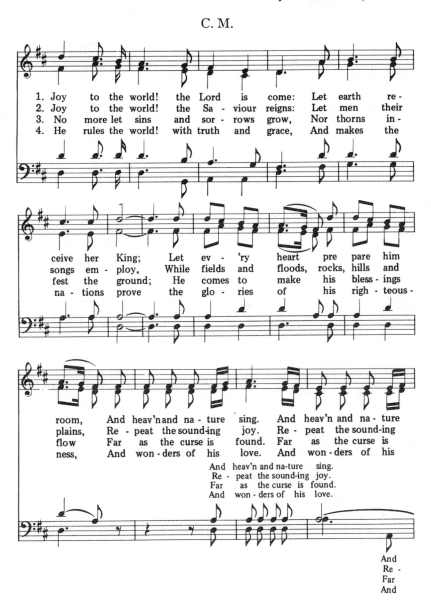

1. Joy to the world! the Lord is come: Let earth re-
2. Joy to the world! the Sa - viour reigns: Let men their
3. No more let sins and sor - rows grow, Nor thorns in-
4. He rules the world! with truth and grace, And makes the

ceive her King; Let ev - 'ry heart pre pare him
songs em - ploy, While fields and floods, rocks, hills and
fest the ground; He comes to make his bless - ings
na - tions prove the glo - ries of his righ - teous-

room, And heav'n and na - ture sing. And heav'n and na - ture
plains, Re - peat the sound-ing joy. Re - peat the sound-ing
flow Far as the curse is found. Far as the curse is
ness, And won - ders of his love. And won - ders of his

And heav'n and na-ture sing.
Re - peat the sound-ing joy.
Far as the curse is found.
And won - ders of his love.

And
Re -
Far
And

SUPPLEMENTAL TUNES

sing.   And heav'n, and heav'n and na - ture sing.
joy.   Re - peat, re - peat the sound - ing joy.
found. Far as, far as the curse is found.
love.   And won-ders, and won - ders of his love.

heav'n and na - ture sings.
peat the sound-ing joy.
as the curse is found.
won-ders of his love.

Isaac Watts, 1719

776

Azmon

Carl G. Gläser, 1784–1829
arr. by Lowell Mason, 1792–1872

C. M.

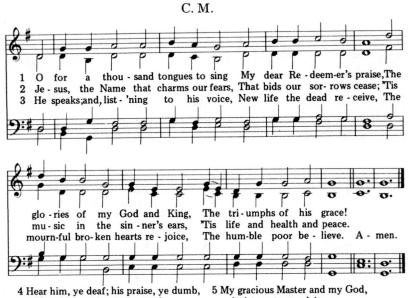

1 O for a thou - sand tongues to sing My dear Re - deem-er's praise, The
2 Je - sus, the Name that charms our fears, That bids our sor- rows cease; 'Tis
3 He speaks; and, list - 'ning to his voice, New life the dead re - ceive, The

glo - ries of my God and King, The tri - umphs of his grace!
mu - sic in the sin - ner's ears, 'Tis life and health and peace.
mourn-ful bro- ken hearts re - joice, The hum-ble poor be - lieve. A - men.

4 Hear him, ye deaf; his praise, ye dumb,   5 My gracious Master and my God,
  Your loosened tongues employ;   Assist me to proclaim
  Ye blind, behold your Saviour come;   And spread through all the earth abroad
  And leap, ye lame, for joy!   The honors of thy Name. Amen.

Charles Wesley, 1740

SUPPLEMENTAL TUNES

777 A

Charlestown

Southern Harmony
harm. by Alastair Cassels-Brown, 1974

87. 87

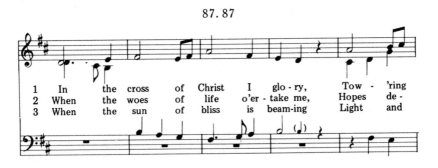

1 In the cross of Christ I glo - ry, Tow - 'ring
2 When the woes of life o'er - take me, Hopes de -
3 When the sun of bliss is beam-ing Light and

o'er the wrecks of time; All the light of
ceive, and fears an - noy, Nev - er shall the
love up - on my way, From the cross the

sa - cred sto - ry Gath - ers round its head sub - lime.
cross for - sake me: Lo, it glows with peace and joy.
ra - diance stream-ing Adds new lus - ter to the day.

4 Bane and blessing, pain and pleasure,
   By the cross are sanctified;
Peace is there that knows no measure,
   Joys that through all time abide.

5 In the cross of Christ I glory,
   Tow'ring o'er the wrecks of time;
All the light of sacred story
   Gathers round its head sublime.

John Bowring 1825

alt. harmonization over

SUPPLEMENTAL TUNES

777 B

Charlestown

Southern Harmony
harm. by Alastair Cassels-Brown

778

Werde Munter

From a melody by J. Schop, c. 1640
harm. by Alastair Cassels-Brown, 1974

76. 76. 88. 77

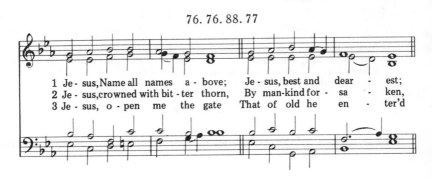

1 Je - sus, Name all names a - bove; Je - sus, best and dear - est;
2 Je - sus, crowned with bit - ter thorn, By man - kind for - sa - ken,
3 Je - sus, o - pen me the gate That of old he en - ter'd

SUPPLEMENTAL TUNES

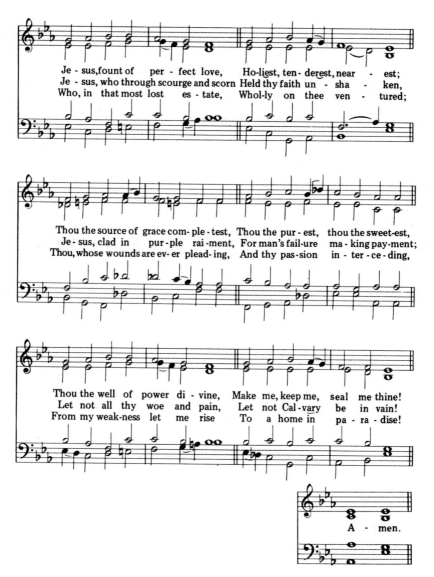

Je - sus,fount of per - fect love, Ho-liest, ten - derest, near - est;
Je - sus, who through scourge and scorn Held thy faith un - sha - ken,
Who, in that most lost es - tate, Whol-ly on thee ven - tured;

Thou the source of grace com- ple - test, Thou the pur - est, thou the sweet-est,
Je - sus, clad in pur -ple rai -ment, For man's fail-ure ma - king pay-ment;
Thou, whose wounds are ev- er plead- ing, And thy pas-sion in - ter -ce -ding,

Thou the well of power di - vine, Make me, keep me, seal me thine!
Let not all thy woe and pain, Let not Cal -vary be in vain!
From my weak-ness let me rise To a home in pa - ra -dise!

A - men.

St. Theoctistus, *c.* 890; *Tr.* John Mason Neale, 1862, *alt.*

Harmony, copyright 1975 by The Church Pension Fund

779

De Tar

Calvin Hampton, 1973

L. M.

Voice

1 O love, how deep, how broad, how high,   How pass - ing
    bore   His ho - ly
    taught,   For us his

thought and fan-ta - sy,   That God, the Son of God, should
fast, and hun- ger'd sore;   For us temp- ta - tions sharp he
dai - ly works he wrought,   By words and signs and ac - tions,

SUPPLEMENTAL TUNES

take | Our mor - tal | form for mor - tals'
knew; | For us the | temp - ter o - ver
thus | Still seek - ing | not him - self, but

First stanzas | **Last stanza**

sake. | 2 For us bap-tized, for us he
threw. | 3 For us he prayed, for us he
us. | A - men.

4 For us to wicked men betrayed,
Scourged, mocked, in purple robe arrayed,
He bore the shameful cross and death;
For us gave up his dying breath.

5 For us he rose from death again,
For us he went on high to reign;
For us he sent his Spirit here
To guide, to strengthen, and to cheer.

6 All glory to our Lord and God
For love so deep, so high, so broad;
The Trinity whom we adore
For ever and for evermore. Amen.

Latin, 15th cent., Tr. Benjamin Webb, 1854, *alt.*

SUPPLEMENTAL TUNES

780

Westminster Abbey

adapted from an anthem
of Henry Purcell (1659–1695)

8. 7. 8. 7. 8. 7

1 Christ is made the sure foun - da - tion, Christ the head and
2 All that ded - i - ca - ted cit - y, Dear - ly loved of
3 To this tem - ple, where we call thee, Come, O Lord of
4 Here vouch-safe to all thy ser - vants What they ask of

cor - ner stone, Cho - sen of the Lord, and pre - cious,
God on high, In ex - ult - ant, ju - bi - la - tion,
Hosts, to - day; With thy won - ted lov - ing kind - ness
thee to gain; What they gain from thee, for ev - er

Bind - ing all the church in one: Ho - ly Si - on's
Pours per - pet - ual mel - o - dy: God the One in
Hear thy ser - vants as they pray, And thy full - est
With the bless - ed to re - tain, And here - af - ter

SUPPLEMENTAL TUNES

help	for	ev	-	er,	And	her	con	-	fi	-	dence	a		lone.
three	a	-	dor	-	ing	In	glad	hymns	e	-	ter	-	nal	-	ly.
be	-	ne	-	dic	-	tion	Shed	with	-	in	its	walls	al	-	way.
in	thy	glo	-	ry	Ev	-	er	-	more	with	thee	to		reign.

A - men.

Latin, c. 7th cent.; Tr. John Mason Neale, 1851, alt.

Music by permission of the proprietors of Hymns Ancient & Modern

781

Southwell

Damon's Psalter, 1579
(later form of third line)

S. M

1 Lord Je - sus, think on me, And purge a - way my sin;
2 Lord Je - sus, think on me, With care and woe op - prest;

From earth-born pas - sions set me free, And make me pure with - in.
Let me thy lov - ing ser - vant be, And taste thy prom-ised rest.

verses 3 & 4 over

SUPPLEMENTAL TUNES

3 Lord Jesus, think on me,
Nor let me go astray;
Through darkness and perplexity
Point thou the heav'nly way.

4 Lord Jesus, think on me,
That, when the flood is past,
I may the eternal brightness see,
And share thy joy at last.

A - men.

Synesius, c. 375–430
Tr. Allen W. Chatfield 1876

782

Amazing Grace

Early American Melody
harm. by Alastair Cassels-Brown, 1974

C. M.

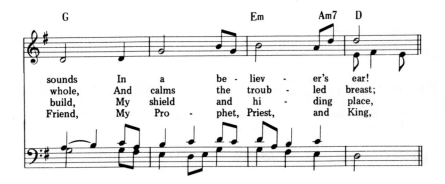

1 How sweet the Name of Je - sus
2 It makes the wound - ed spi - rit
3 Dear Name, the rock on which I
4 Je - sus! my Shep - herd, Guar - dian,

sounds In a be - liev - er's ear!
whole, And calms the troub - led breast;
build, My shield and hi - ding place,
Friend, My Pro - phet, Priest, and King,

SUPPLEMENTAL TUNES

It	soothes	our	sor - rows,	heals	our
'Tis	man - na	to	the	hun - gry
My	nev - er - fail - ing	trea - sury,
My	Lord,	my	Life,	my	Way,	my

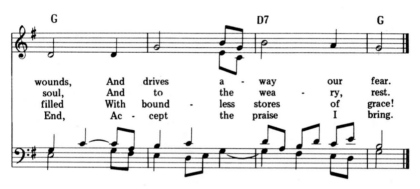

wounds,	And	drives	a - way	our	fear.
soul,	And	to	the	wea - ry,	rest.
filled	With	bound - less	stores	of	grace!
End,	Ac - cept	the	praise	I	bring.

The guitar and keyboard may be played together or separately. A drone bass on low G and the D above, alternating or played together can be added. Members of the congregation with a gift for harmonizing should be encouraged to sing their own line.

A - men.

John Newton 1774

783

Cwm Rhondda

John Hughes, 1873–1932

87. 87. 87

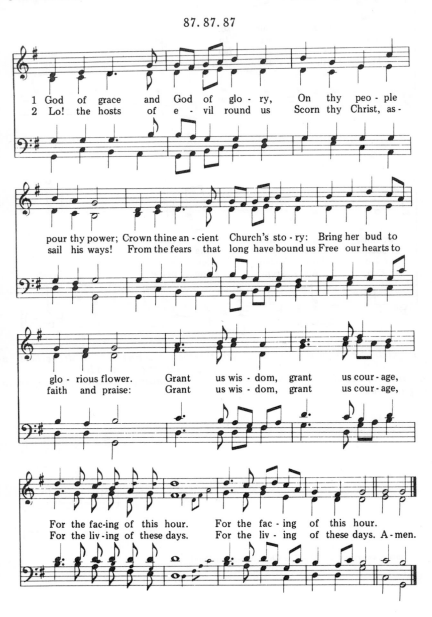

1 God of grace and God of glo - ry,
2 Lo! the hosts of e - vil round us

On thy peo - ple
Scorn thy Christ, as -

pour thy power; Crown thine an - cient Church's sto - ry: Bring her bud to
sail his ways! From the fears that long have bound us Free our hearts to

glo - rious flower. Grant us wis - dom, grant us cour - age,
faith and praise: Grant us wis - dom, grant us cour - age,

For the fac-ing of this hour. For the fac - ing of this hour.
For the liv-ing of these days. For the liv - ing of these days. A - men.

SUPPLEMENTAL TUNES

3 Cure thy children's warring madness,
   Bend our pride to thy control;
Shame our wanton, selfish gladness,
   Rich in things and poor in soul.
Grant us wisdom, grant us courage,
   Lest we miss thy kingdom's goal.

4 Set our feet on lofty places;
   Gird our lives that they may be
Armored with all Christ-like graces
   In the fight to set men free.
Grant us wisdom, grant us courage,
   That we fail not man nor thee. Amen.

Harry Emerson Fosdick, 1930, *alt.*

784 A

Landaff

Southern Harmony
harm. by Alastair Cassels-Brown, 1974

S. M.

1 O Day of God, draw nigh In beau-ty and in power,
2 Bring to our trou-bled minds, Un-cer-tain and a-fraid,
3 Bring jus-tice to our land, That all may dwell se-cure,

Come with thy time-less judg-ment now To match our pres-ent hour.
The qui-et of a stead-fast faith, Calm of a call o-beyed.
And fine-ly build for days to come Foun-da-tions that en-dure.

alternative harmonization and verses 4 & 5 over

SUPPLEMENTAL TUNES

4 Bring to our world of strife
   Thy sov'reign word of peace,
   That war may haunt the earth no more
   And desolation cease.

5 O Day of God, draw nigh
   As at creation's birth,
   Let there be light again, and set
   Thy judgments on the earth. Amen.

R. B. Y. Scott, 1937, *alt.*

Harmony, copyright 1975 by The Church Pension Fund

784 B

Original Version
Melody in Tenor

785

Foundation

Early American Melody
harm. by Alastair Cassels-Brown, 1974

11. 11. 11. 11

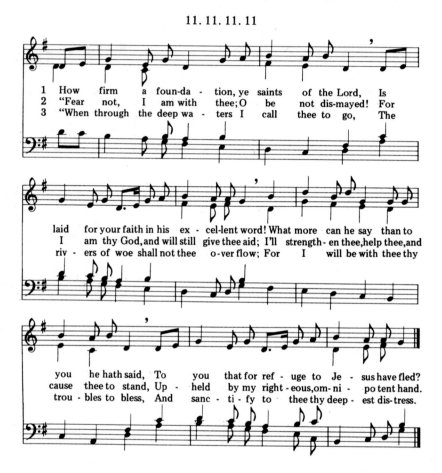

1 How firm a foun-da - tion, ye saints of the Lord, Is
2 "Fear not, I am with thee; O be not dis-mayed! For
3 "When through the deep wa - ters I call thee to go, The

laid for your faith in his ex - cel-lent word! What more can he say than to
I am thy God, and will still give thee aid; I'll strength- en thee, help thee, and
riv - ers of woe shall not thee o-ver flow; For I will be with thee thy

you he hath said, To you that for ref - uge to Je - sus have fled?
cause thee to stand, Up - held by my right - eous, om - ni - po tent hand.
trou - bles to bless, And sanc - ti - fy to thee thy deep - est dis- tress.

4 "When through fiery trials thy pathway shall lie,
My grace, all-sufficient, shall be thy supply;
The flame shall not hurt thee; I only design
Thy dross to consume, and thy gold to refine.

5 "The soul that to Jesus hath fled for repose,
I will not, I will not desert to his foes;
That soul, though all hell shall endeavor to shake,
I'll never, no, never, no, never forsake."

K *in* John Rippon's
Selection of Hymns, 1787 *alt.*

SUPPLEMENTAL TUNES

786

Vineyard Haven   Richard Dirksen, 1974

S. M., with Refrain

1 Re - joice, ye pure in heart! Re - joice, give thanks, and sing!
2 With all the an - gel choirs, With all the saints of earth,
3 Your clear ho - san - nas raise, And al - le - lu - ias loud;
4 Yes, on through life's long path, Still chant - ing as ye go,
5 Still lift your stand - ard high, Still march in firm ar - ray;

Your glo - rious ban - ner wave on high,
Pour out the strains of joy and bliss,
While an - swering ech - oes up - ward float,
From youth to age, by night and day,
As war - riors through the dark - ness toil,

The cross of Christ your King.
True rap - ture, no - blest mirth.
Like wreaths of in - cense cloud.   Ho - san - na,
In glad - ness and in woe.
Till dawns the gold - en day.

Ho - san - na

Ho - san - na

SUPPLEMENTAL TUNES

Ho - san - na

Ho - san - na, Re - joice, give thanks and sing.

6 At last the march shall end;
   The wearied ones shall rest;
   The pilgrims find their Father's house,
   Jerusalem the blest.
   REFRAIN

7 Then on, ye pure in heart!
   Rejoice, give thanks, and sing!
   Your glorious banner wave on high,
   The cross of Christ your King.
   REFRAIN

Edward Hayes Plumtre, 1865

787

ANGLICAN CHANTS

for general use unless otherwise noted

Antiphon   Richard Dirksen, 1974

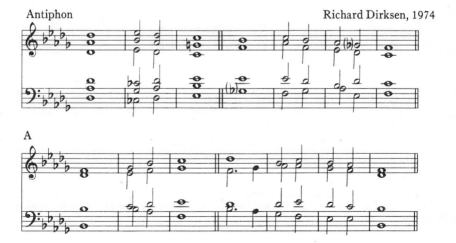

A

ANGLICAN CHANTS

788

Richard Dirksen, 1974

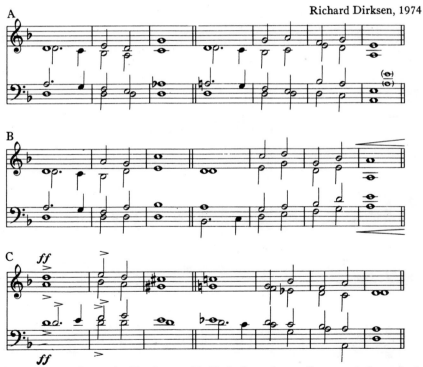

A and C maybe used as a double chant. If this is done the small notes at the end of A should be used as a splice. The triple chant is suggested for the first two sections of the Te Deum.

ANGLICAN CHANTS

789

John Fenstermaker, 1974

790

David Koehring, 1974

ANGLICAN CHANTS

791

Daniel Pinkham, 1974

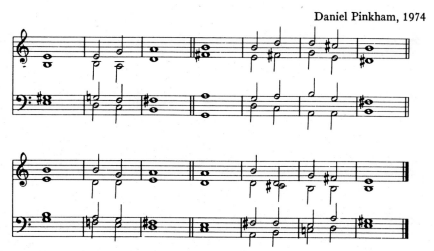

792

Daniel Pinkham, 1974

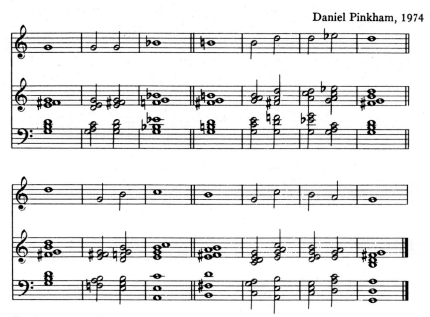

This chant is suggested for the Benedicite

ANGLICAN CHANTS

793

Ned Rorem, 1974

794

Ned Rorem, 1974

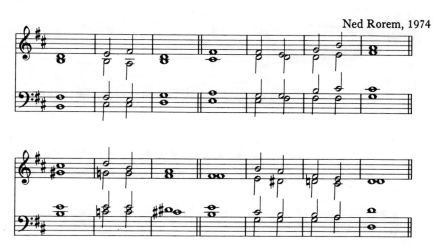

TE DEUM

795

Plainsong Tone VIII, 1

harm: Alastair Cassels-Brown
1974

Cantor

1 We práise thee O Gód; We ac-knówl-edge thée to be the Lórd.

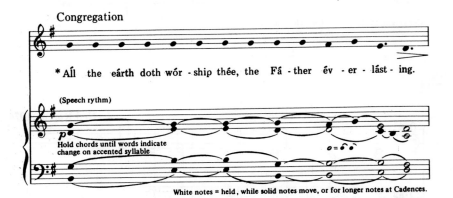

Congregation

* Aíl the eárth doth wór-ship thée, the Fá-ther év-er-lást-ing.

(Speech rythm)

p Hold chords until words indicate
change on accented syllable

o = ♪♪

White notes = held, while solid notes move, or for longer notes at Cadences.

2 To thée all Añ-gels crý a-lóud; the Héav'ns and aíl the Pówers there-in;

Dot indicates double length.

TE DEUM

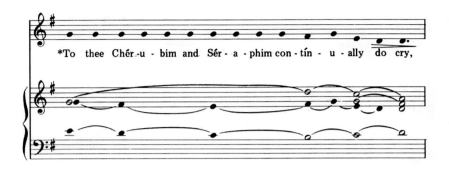

*To thee Chér-u - bim and Sér - a - phim con - tín - u - ally do cry,

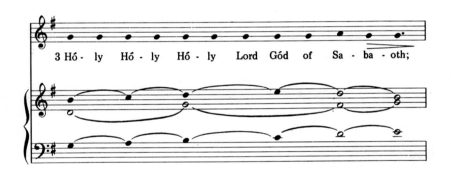

3 Hó - ly Hó - ly Hó - ly Lord Gód of Sa - ba - oth;

*Heav'n and eárth are fúll of the Má - jest - ty of thy gló - ry.

TE DEUM

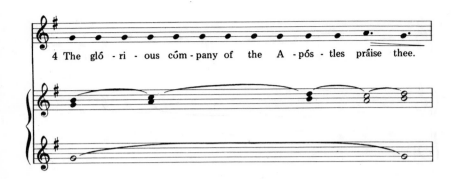

4 The gló - ri - ous cóm - pany of the A - pós - tles práise thee.

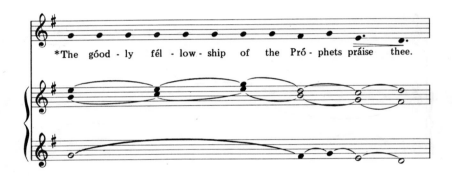

*The góod - ly fél - low - ship of the Pró - phets práise thee.

5 The nó - ble ár - my of Már - tyrs praise thee. *The hó - ly

TE DEUM

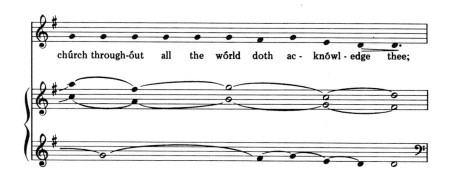

church through-óut all the wórld doth ac - knówl - edge thee;

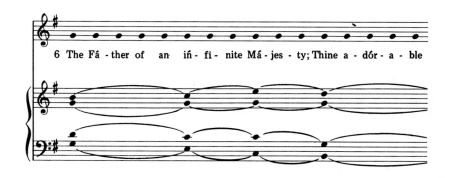

6 The Fá - ther of an iń - fi - nite Má - jes - ty; Thine a - dór - a - ble

trúe and ón - ly Son; *Aĺ - so the Hó - ly Ghóst the Cóm - fort - er.

TE DEUM

Tone VII, 3

7 Thóu art the Kíng of Gló - ry O Chríst. *Thou art the év - er -

lást - ing Són of the Fá - ther. 8 Whén thou tóok - est up - ón thee

to de - lív - er man, *thou didst húm - ble thy - sélf to be bórn

TE DEUM

of a Vír - gin. 9 Whén thou hadst ó - ver - cóme the shárp-ness of déath,

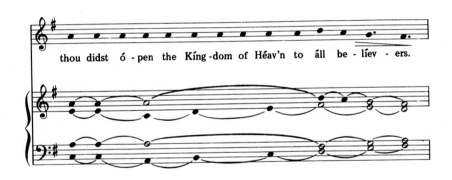

thou didst ó - pen the Kíng - dom of Héav'n to áll be - líev - ers.

10 Thou sít - test at the ríght hand of God, in the gló - ry of the

TE DEUM

Fá - ther. 11We be - lieve that thou shalt come to be our Judge* We thére-fore

práy thee hélp thy sér - vants, whómthou hast redéemed with thy précious blood.

12 Máke them to be núm-bered with thy sáints,*in gló - ry év - er - lást - ing.

FIRST COMMUNION SERVICE

796

SANCTUS

John Merbecke, 1549

HO - LY, HO - LY, HO - LY, Lord God of hosts,

Heav'n and earth are full of thy glo - ry: Glo - ry be to thee,

BENEDICTUS

O Lord Most High. Bless - ed is he that com - eth

in the Name of the Lord. Ho - san - na in the High - est.

SECOND COMMUNION SERVICE

SANCTUS

Healey Willan, 1928

Ho - ly, ho - ly, ho - ly,

Lord God of hosts, heav - en and earth are full ___ of ___ thy

glo - ry: Glo - ry be to thee, O Lord most High.

SECOND COMMUNION SERVICE

BENEDICTUS

Bless - ed ____ is he that com - eth ____ in ___ the name ___ of the Lord, Ho - san - na in the_high - est.

798

FOURTH COMMUNION SERVICE

SANCTUS

Plainsong, 14th century

HO - LY, HO - LY, Ho - LY,___

FOURTH COMMUNION SERVICE

Lord _____ God _____ of __ hosts,

Ped.

Heav- en __ and earth __ are full _____ of thy glo - ry:

Glo - ry __ be to __ thee, __ O __ Lord _____ Most __ High.

BENEDICTUS

Bless - ed is __ he that __ com - eth in the __

FOURTH COMMUNION SERVICE

Name of _____ the Lord. Ho

san - na in the _____ high est.

FIFTH COMMUNION SERVICE

799

SANCTUS

Leo Sowerby, 1957

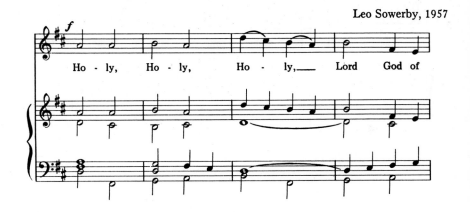

Ho - ly, Ho - ly, Ho - ly, _____ Lord God of

FIFTH COMMUNION SERVICE

hosts, Heav'n and earth are full__ of thy glo - ry:

Glo - ry be to__ thee, O Lord Most High.

BENEDICTUS

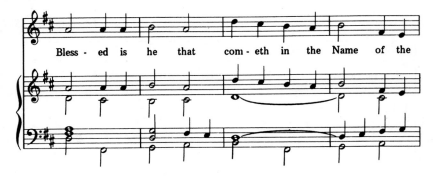

Bless - ed is he that com - eth in the Name of the

FIFTH COMMUNION SERVICE

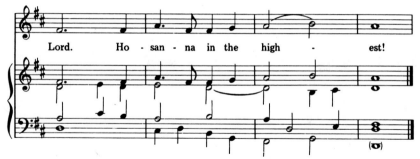

Lord.   Ho - san - na in the   high - est!

SIXTH COMMUNION SERVICE

800

SANCTUS

Willis Bodine, 1958

Priest — Ho - ly Ho - ly

prais - ing thee and say - ing

Ho - ly Lord God of hosts. Heav'n and earth are full of thy

SIXTH COMMUNION SERVICE

glo - ry: Glo - ry be to thee O Lord Most High

BENEDICTUS

Bless - ed is he that com - eth in the Name of the Lord. Ho - san - na in the high - est!

EIGHTH COMMUNION SERVICE

801

SANCTUS

Martin Shaw, 1918

(may be sung in unison and a semitone lower.)

♩ = about 69. (but quicker where suitable)

pp ... *mf*

Ho - ly, Ho - ly, Ho - ly, Lord God of Hosts; Heav - en and

f

earth are full of Thy glo - ry. Glo - ry be to Thee, O Lord most High.

BENEDICTUS

(may be sung in unison and a semitone lower.)

♩ = about 88

pp ... *a little quicker.*

Bless - ed is He that com - eth in the

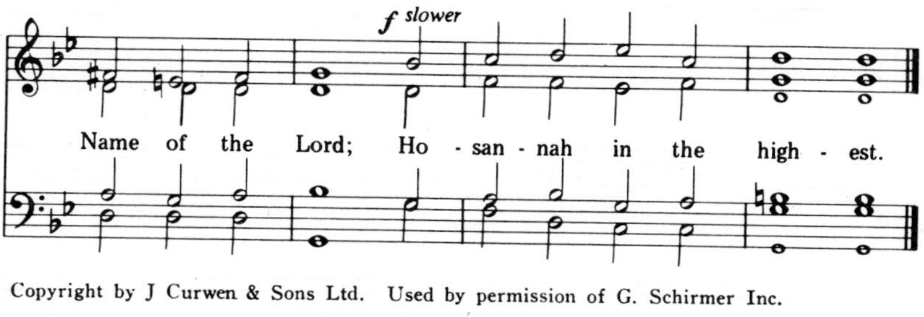

f slower

Name of the Lord; Ho - san - nah in the high - est.